The Rou

D

Guatemala

**ROUGH
GUIDES**

NEW YORK · LONDON · DELHI

www.roughguides.com

Contents

Indigenous costume
colour section
following p.184

Maya architecture
colour section
following p.344

◄◄ Antigua ◄ Woman wearing traditional costume, Ixil

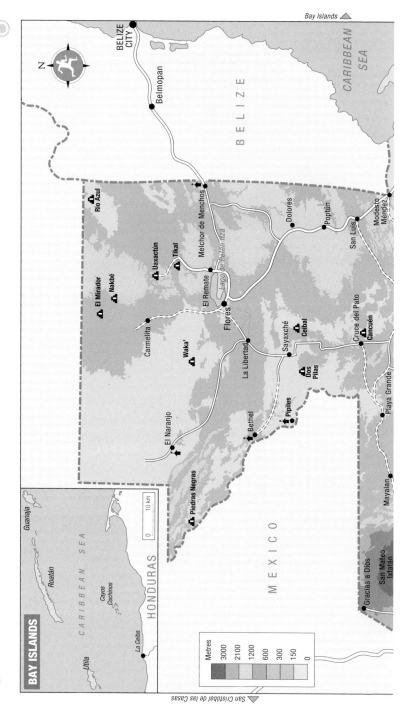

Bay Islands

N

CARIBBEAN SEA

BELIZE CITY

Belmopan

B E L I Z E

Río Azul

Dolores

Poptún

Modesto Méndez

San Luis

Uaxactún

Tikal

Melchor de Menchos

El Mirador

Nakbé

El Remate

Laguna de Petén Itzá

Carmelita

Flores

Sayaxché

Ceibal

Cruce del Pato

Cancuén

Waka'

La Libertad

Playa Grande

Dos Pilas

El Naranjo

Bethel

Pipiles

Mayalan

Piedras Negras

M E X I C O

Gracias a Dios

San Mateo Ixtatán

BAY ISLANDS

Guanaja

Roatán

C A R I B B E A N   S E A

Cayos Cochinos

HONDURAS

La Ceiba

Utila

0   10 km

Metres
3000
2100
1200
600
300
150
0

San Cristóbal de las Casas

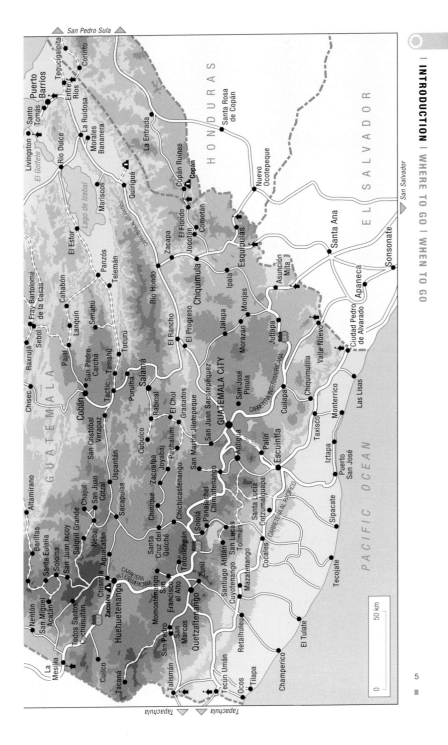

Introduction to

Guatemala

Spanning a mountainous slice of Central America immediately south of Mexico, Guatemala is loaded with incredible natural, historical and cultural appeal. As the birthplace and heartland of the ancient Maya, the country is in many ways defined by the legacy of this early civilization. Their rainforest cities were abandoned centuries ago, but Maya people continue to thrive in the Guatemalan highlands, where traditions and religious rituals, mingled with Catholic practices, endure to form perhaps the richest and most distinctive indigenous identity in the hemisphere.

Guatemala today is very much a synthesis of **Maya and colonial traditions**, fused with the omnipresent influences of twenty-first-century Latin and North American culture. Baroque churches dating back to the Spanish conquest coexist with pagan temples that have been sites of worship for millennia. Highland street markets prosper alongside vast glitzy shopping malls, and pre-Columbian festival dances are performed by teenage hip-hop fans.

Guatemala is still very much a developing nation, **a young democracy** with a turbulent and bloody history that's beset by deep-rooted inequalities. And yet, despite alarming levels of poverty and unemployment most Guatemalans are extraordinarily courteous and helpful to travellers, and only too eager to help you catch the right bus or practise your Spanish.

It's this genuine and profound hospitality combined with the country's **outstanding cultural legacy** and **astonishing natural beauty** that makes Guatemala such a compelling place for travellers.

Where to go

Guatemala offers a startling range of landscapes, defined by extremes. Most travellers first head for **Antigua**, the delightful former colonial capital, its refined atmosphere and café society

▶ Chichicastenango market

Fact file

• The republic of Guatemala is situated at the northern end of the Central American isthmus. Its 108,890 square kilometres include dozens of volcanoes (four are active), 328km of Pacific coastline and 74km of Caribbean coast.

• Guatemala's population was estimated at 14.6 million in 2008, with a growth rate of 2.4 percent per annum (the highest in the Western hemisphere). Over a million Guatemalans live in the USA and Canada.

• Ethnically, the population is almost equally divided between indigenous Maya and ladinos (who are mainly of mixed race), although there are tiny numbers of black Garífuna (about 8000 in all), ethnic Chinese and non-Maya Xinca. Though Spanish is the official language, 23 other languages are spoken, including K'iche', Mam, Kaqchikel and Q'eqchi'.

• Tourism is the nation's main income earner, followed by coffee, sugar, clothing exports and bananas.

• About 60 percent of Guatemalans are nominally Roman Catholic – the lowest figure in Latin America – though many highland Maya practise a unique mix of religions that's heavily dependent on ancient religious ritual. Most others worship at US-based evangelical Protestant churches.

• Guatemala's 36-year civil war ended in 1996. The nation is now a democratic republic, headed by a president who is head of both state and government.

▼ Nebaj

contrasting with the chaotic fume-filled streets of Guatemala City. Next on your list should be the Maya-dominated **western highlands**, a region of mesmerizing beauty, with volcanic cones soaring above pine-clad hills, traditional villages and shimmering lakes. The strength of the Maya culture here is evident with each village having its own textile weaving tradition and unique fiesta celebrations.

Lago de Atitlán, an astonishingly beautiful lake ringed by sentinel-like volcanoes, is unmissable. The shores of the lake are dotted with charming indigenous villages such as **Santa Cruz La Laguna**, where you'll find some fine places to stay and breathtaking shoreline hikes, and **San Pedro La Laguna**, with its bohemian scene and rock-bottom

An archeological hotbed

The remote jungles of Petén are one of the most exciting archeological zones in the world, the target of more than a dozen ongoing digs that have unearthed several revelatory findings. Major progress in the reading of Maya glyphs has meant that the history and the nature of Maya society is becoming increasingly clear. Ruling family lineages, dates of accessions and wars and the key political alliances are being steadily chronicled. Meanwhile, it's been established that blood-letting and human sacrifice were pivotal to Maya religious life. In the last few years discoveries have included a 2500-year-old ball court at Nakbé, some stupendous Preclassic murals at San Bartolo, thousands of ceramic pieces at La Blanca and even a complete "lost city" – Wakná, located near El Mirador, found using satellite imagery.

prices. High up above the lake, the traditional Maya town of **Sololá** has one of the country's best (and least-touristy) markets, a complete contrast to the vast twice-weekly affair at **Chichicastenango**, with its incredible selection of souvenirs, weavings and handicrafts. Further west, the proud provincial city of **Quetzaltenango** (Xela) is an important language school centre, and also makes an excellent base for exploring the forest-fringed crater lake of **Volcán Chicabal**, the sublime natural spa of **Fuentes Georginas** and some fascinating market towns. Guatemala's greatest mountain range, the **Cuchumatanes**, is a little further north. In these granite peaks you'll find superb scenery and some of the most isolated and traditional villages in the Maya world, with **Nebaj**, in the Ixil Triangle, and **Todos Santos Cuchumatán** both making good bases for some serious hiking and adventure.

The **Pacific coast** is generally hot, dull and disappointing to visit, with scrubby, desolate beaches backed by a smattering of mangrove swamps. One exception is the relaxed seaside village of **Monterrico**, which has some good accommodation and is part of a wildlife reserve where you can watch sea turtles come ashore to lay their eggs. There's even a bit of surf nearby at Iztapa.

Much of the **east** of the country is **tropical**, replete with banana and cardamom plantations and coconut palms. This region has some stunning lakes, including jungle-fringed **Laguna Lachúa** and **Lago de Izabal**, around whose shores are plenty of interesting spots, including an amazing hot spring waterfall and the Boquerón canyon. The lake drains into the

◄ Todos Santos Cuchumatán

Caribbean via the **Río Dulce**, which flows through a series of remarkable jungle-clad gorges. At the mouth of the river is the funky town of **Lívingston**, an outpost of Caribbean culture and home to Guatemala's only black community, the Garífuna.

Cloudforests cloak the fecund Verapaz hills of central Guatemala, harbouring the elusive quetzal, Guatemala's national symbol. **Cultural**

Volcanoes

Overshadowing the southern half of the country, a chain of volcanoes extends in an ominous arc from 4220m-high Tajumulco on the Mexican border to the frontier with Honduras. Depending on how you define a volcano – some vulcanologists do not classify lateral cones in the folds of a larger peak to be volcanoes for example – Guatemala has somewhere between 33 and 40. Three of these, Pacaya, Fuego and Santiaguito are highly active, regularly belching soaring plumes of smoke and ash. An ascent up Pacaya (see p.91) rarely fails to disappoint as it's usually possible to get very up close and personal with the orange lava flows, but there are myriad other incredible climbs.

Lago de Atitlán is actually the former caldera of a giant volcano that cataclysmically blew its top some 85,000 years ago. So much magma was expelled that most of the vast cone collapsed and centuries of rainwater filled the depression, creating today's lake.

Guatemala's volcanic, mineral-rich earth is highly fertile, and allows farmers to cultivate two crops a year. But with this fecundity comes instability and ruin – an eruption around 250AD devastated southern Guatemala and the ancient Maya city of Kaminaljuyú, while mud flows from Volcán de Agua destroyed the Spanish capital at Ciudad Vieja.

sites in the east are limited to the compact Maya site of **Quiriguá** in the Motagua valley and the first-class ruins of **Copán**, just over the border in Honduras. Further into Honduras are the idyllic **Bay Islands**, whose pristine coral reefs offer some of the finest scuba diving and snorkelling in the Caribbean.

The vast **rainforests** of Petén occupy most of the country's **north**. This unique lowland area, which makes up about a third of the country, is covered with dense tropical forest and savannah. Though loggers and ranchers have laid waste to large chunks of the terrain, nature reserves alive with wildlife remain, many dotted with outstanding Maya ruins. From the delightful town of **Flores**, superbly situated on an islet on Lago de Petén Itzá, or the low-key village of **El Remate**, it's easy to reach **Tikal**, the most impressive of all Maya sites, rivalling any ruin in Latin America. The region's

forest also envelopes numerous smaller sites, including the striking **Yaxhá**, **Aguateca** and **Uaxactún**. Adventurous travellers may also want to seek out Petén's more remote ruins, such as the dramatic, Preclassic sites of **El Mirador** (possibly even larger than Tikal) and **Nakbé**, which require days of tough travel to reach.

Traditional Marimba music

11

When to go

◀ Jaguar

Guatemala has one of the most pleasant climates on earth – the tourist board refers to it as the "**land of the eternal spring**" – with much of the country enjoying warm days and mild evenings year-round. The climate is largely determined by **altitude**. In those areas between 1300 and 1600m, which include Guatemala City, Antigua, Lago de Atitlán and Cobán, the air is almost always fresh and the nights mild and, despite the heat of the midday sun, humidity is never a problem. Parts of the departments of Quetzaltenango, Huehuetenango and El Quiché are above this height, and so have a cooler, damper climate with distinctly chilly nights between early December and late February. Low-lying Petén suffers from sticky, steamy conditions most of the year, as do the Pacific and Caribbean coasts, though here at least you can usually rely on the welcome relief of a sea breeze.

The **rainy season** runs roughly from May to October, with the worst of the rain falling in September and October. In Petén, however, the season

▲ Río Dulce

can extend into December. Even at the height of the wet season, though, the rain is usually confined to late afternoon downpours with most of the rest of the day being warm and pleasant. Visiting Petén's more remote ruins is best attempted between February and May, as the mud can be thigh deep during the height of the rains. The **Bay Islands' climate** is distinctly different, with clear skies between March and September, and rains starting in October and continuing until late February – Christmas and New Year are often very wet.

The **busiest times** for tourism are between December and March, and again in July and August. Language schools and hotels are fullest during these periods, and many of them hike their prices correspondingly.

Average daily temperatures (°C/°F)

	Jan	Feb	Mar	Apr	May	Jun	July	Aug	Sept	Oct	Nov	Dec
Guatemala City												
°C	23	25	27	28	29	27	26	26	26	24	23	22
°F	73	77	81	82	84	81	79	79	79	75	73	72
Huehuetenango												
°C	22	24	27	30	31	28	26	25	26	25	23	22
°F	72	75	81	86	88	82	79	77	79	77	73	72
Puerto Barrios												
°C	27	28	29	31	32	31	30	30	30	30	29	28
°F	81	82	84	88	90	88	86	86	86	86	84	82

things not to miss

It's not possible to see everything that Guatemala has to offer in one visit, and we don't suggest you try. What follows is a selective and subjective taste of the country's highlights, from wildlife-rich nature reserves to colonial cities and indigenous markets. They're arranged in five colour-coded categories, to help you find the best things to see, do, buy and experience. All highlights have a page reference to take you straight into the guide, where you can find out more.

01 Antigua Page **94** • The graceful former capital, with an incredible legacy of colonial architecture, is a UNESCO World Heritage site and one of the most elegant cities in the Americas.

03 **The Ixil region** Page **140** •
The Guatemalan highlands at their
most bewitching: the colour, costume and
scenery of this deeply traditional Maya region
are astonishing.

02 **Finca el Paraíso** Page **266** •
Soak away the chicken bus blues at
the blissful hot spring waterfall and natural
pools near Finca el Paraíso.

04 **Todos Santos Cuchumatán** Page **204** • A fascinating highland Maya town,
home to one of the finest textile traditions in Latin America, and hosts a legendary fiesta,
with a rip-roaring horse race.

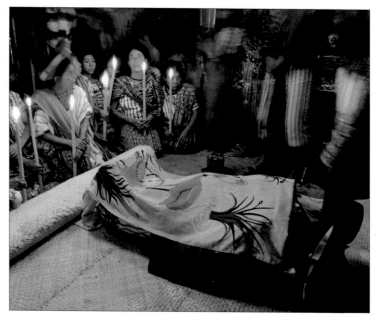

05 **Maximón** Pages **161** & **184** • Visit the pagan temple of this liquor-swilling, cigar-smoking evil saint.

06 **Tikal** Page **324** • This unmatched Maya site has it all: monumental temples and palaces set in a tropical forest alive with screaming howler monkeys and chattering parakeets.

07 Whale shark Page 380
• Snorkel with the world's largest fish, a year-round resident in the seas just north of Utila.

08 Studying Spanish Page 49
• Guatemala has dozens of excellent language schools that offer one-on-one tuition and home-stay packages at rock-bottom rates.

09 Copán ruins Page 363
• There's a plethora of exquisitely carved stelae and altars, a towering hieroglyphic stairway and an outstanding site museum at the magnificent Maya ruins of Copán.

10 Río Dulce Page 261
• Cruise up the jungle-cloaked gorges and estuaries of Guatemala's "sweet river" by boat, and marvel at the scenery and birdlife.

11 **Chichicastenango** Page **130** • For souvenir hunters, this twice-weekly highland market is unsurpassed.

12 **National Archeological Museum** Page **81** • Guatemala City's Museo Nacional de Arqueología y Etnología contains a wonderful collection of Maya artistry and breathtakingly carved monuments from many remote Petén sites.

13 **Volcán de Pacaya** Page **91** • Trek up for an unforgettable encounter with the lava-oozing cone of Pacaya, one of Central America's most active volcanoes.

14 Lívingston Page **255** • Tuck into *tapado* (coconut and fish soup) or grilled conch in the Garífuna village of Lívingston.

15 Laguna Lachúa Page **300** • In a remote region of northern Verapaz, this gorgeous near-circular crater lake is surrounded by pristine jungle inhabited by jaguar and tapir.

16 Quetzal Page **286** • Rare and elusive, Guatemala's national bird inhabits the cloudforests of the Verapaces.

17 Yaxhá Page **349** • This massive Maya site, superbly positioned on the banks of Lago de Yaxhá has dozens of large temples and is currently the subject of extensive archeological excavations.

18 Quiriguá Page **247** • Small but fascinating Maya site, with towering, beautifully carved stelae.

19 Fuentes Georginas Page **184** • A stunning natural spa, with steaming open-air pools fringed by a dense foliage of ferns, perched halfway up a volcano near Quetzaltenango.

20 **Lago de Atitlán** Page **149** • Encircled by three volcanoes, the awesome crater lake of Lago de Atitlán was famously described by Aldous Huxley as "the most beautiful lake in the world".

21 **Monterrico** Page **234** • A rich nature reserve and village on the Pacific coast, with a sweeping beach where three species of sea turtle nest, including the giant leatherback.

22 **Chicken buses** Page **70** • Garishly painted and outrageously uncomfortable, there's never a dull journey aboard Guatemala's iconic fume-belching *camionetas*.

23 Semana Santa Pages **101** & **161** • During Easter Week, head for either Antigua for its epic Catholic processions, or Santiago Atitlán to witness the symbolic confrontation between the pagan saint Maximón and Christ.

24 Highland hiking Page **206** • Explore the beguiling high trails that crisscross the granite mountains above the traditional Mam village of Todos Santos Cuchumatán.

25 **Scuba diving** Page **385** • Coral reef on the cheap: the Bay Islands have some of the world's least expensive dive schools and prolific sealife.

26 **Coffee** Page **288** • Sample some of the world's finest single estate roasts in Cobán, the easy-going capital of Alta Verapaz.

27 **Semuc Champey** Page **294** • Explore the exquisite turquoise pools and river system around Semuc Champey, a natural limestone bridge over the Río Cahabón.

28 **Jungle trekking** Page **337** • Tramp through the Reserva de la Biósfera Maya to the jungle-choked ruins of the Preclassic cities of El Mirador and Nakbé in Petén.

29 **San Francisco el Alto** Page **189** • A highland market par excellence – there's nothing much to buy, but plenty to experience.

30 **Eastern highlands** Page **268** • Ancient eroded volcanoes, cacti-spiked hills, Central America's largest pilgrimage centre and virtually no other tourists.

Basics

Basics

Getting there

Most people get to Guatemala by plane, arriving in the capital, Guatemala City. Flores airport, near Tikal, also has a few flights from Cancún and Belize City. Guatemalan land and sea entry-points are relatively hassle free, unless you're bringing your own transport, in which case you can expect plenty of red tape, dubious entry fees and delays.

Airfares always depend on the season, with the highest being from Christmas to February, around Easter, and in July and August.

If Guatemala is only one stop on a longer journey, you might want to consider buying an **airpass** that enables you to visit several other destinations in the region – though passes often exclude Cancún and Flores airports – consult a recommended travel agent.

Flights from the USA and Canada

Most flights to Guatemala are routed through a few US hub cities: Atlanta, Charlotte, Dallas, Fort Lauderdale, Houston, Los Angles, Miami, New York, New Orleans, San Francisco and Washington. You'll also find several non-direct options via San Salvador (with Taca) and Mexico City (Mexicana). Prices vary wildly, depending on the season and promotional fares, with return flights from Fort Lauderdale starting at US$90 with Spirit Airlines, while return fares from either Houston or New York are typically US$450–600.

From Canada, as there are no direct connections to Guatemala, your best bet is to fly via one of the US gateway cities. Return flights from Toronto typically cost C$600–925, from Vancouver C$675–950.

Flights from the UK and Ireland

There are no direct flights from the UK or Ireland to Guatemala; most itineraries travel via the US cities of Atlanta, Dallas, Houston or Miami. Other options include flying via Madrid on Iberia, via Panama with KLM/ Copa, or via Mexico with a number of airlines (including British Airways) and then on to Guatemala with a Mexican airline. Prices for

return flights to Guatemala City are around £540 low season/£680 high season, whichever airline and route you take. Note that although most flights priced from London airports, you can often travel from other UK airports for the same or only a slightly higher price.

The very cheapest way to get to Guatemala from the UK is to book a charter flight to Cancún (as low as £195 return, but tickets are very rarely valid for more than one month) and then travel overland through Belize or Chiapas, though these routes entail long overland journeys.

From Ireland, it's often cheapest to grab a low-cost airline ticket to one of the London airports and travel on from there, or there are numerous possibilities via gateway cities in the US. Expect to pay around €850 low season/€1050 high season.

Flights from Australia, New Zealand and South Africa

There are no direct flights from Australasia to Guatemala, so most travellers fly via the US. American Airlines offers some of the cheapest return fares to Guatemala from Australia and New Zealand, with tickets costing around A$2700–3000 (depending on the season) from Sydney via LA or NZ$2600–2900 from Auckland. American Airlines, United and Qantas/Air New Zealand usually have the best fares. If you want to visit Guatemala as part of a longer Latin American trip it often costs only a little more to book an open-jaw ticket flying into Guatemala City and returning from Panama.

From South Africa, the cheapest flights are forty-hour multi-stop marathons via London for around 14,000ZAR, but if you

Fly less – stay longer! Travel and climate change

Climate change is perhaps the single biggest issue facing our planet. It is caused by a build-up in the atmosphere of carbon dioxide and other greenhouse gases, which are emitted by many sources – including planes. Already, **flights** account for three to four percent of human-induced global warming: that figure may sound small, but it is rising year on year and threatens to counteract the progress made by reducing greenhouse emissions in other areas.

Rough Guides regard travel as a **global benefit**, and feel strongly that the advantages to developing economies are important, as are the opportunities for greater contact and awareness among peoples. But we also believe in travelling responsibly, which includes giving thought to how often we fly and what we can do to redress any harm our trips may create.

We can travel less or simply reduce the amount we travel by air (taking fewer trips and staying longer, or taking the train if there is one); we can avoid night flights (which are more damaging); and we can make the trips we do take "climate neutral" via a carbon offset scheme. **Offset schemes** run by climatecare.org, carbonneutral .com and others allow you to "neutralize" the greenhouse gases that you are responsible for releasing. Their websites have simple calculators that let you work out the impact of any flight – as does our own. Once that's done, you can pay to fund projects that will reduce future emissions by an equivalent amount. Please take the time to visit our website and make your trip climate neutral, or get a copy of the *Rough Guide to Climate Change* for more detail on the subject.

www.roughguides.com/climatechange

pay about 16,000ZAR your journey time is cut to around 31 hours using either South African Airways/Copa via São Paolo and Panama, or on United/American via New York and Miami.

Buses

From southern Mexico, six daily buses leave Tapachula for Guatemala City (see p.89). One daily minibus connects San Cristóbal de Las Casas with Antigua (see p.112), passing by drop-offs for Huehuetenango, Quetzaltenango and Panajachel. There's also a daily bus route linking Cancún with Flores, with one minibus taking you to the Belize–Mexico border and another connection travelling via Belize City and the Guatemalan border to Flores; see p.317 for more details.

Very regular buses connect San Salvador with Guatemala City (see p.89). From Honduras there are direct daily links between Copán and Guatemala City/Antigua, and also daily buses from both San Pedro Sula and Tegucigalpa to Guatemala City.

Finally there's a bus route run by King Quality between San José, Costa Rica, and Guatemala City via Managua, Tegucigalpa

and San Salvador, which involves a night in a hotel on the way; see p.89.

Boats

From Punta Gorda, Belize, there are two daily boats to Puerto Barrios, Guatemala (see p.253). There are also irregular links to Lívingston from Punta Gorda and Omoa in Honduras if there are enough passengers.

The once-popular boat journey between La Palma, Mexico, and El Naranjo no longer has scheduled connections, though occasional boats do still run (see p.348). Most travellers now use the route to the south, crossing the Usumacinta River into Guatemala at Frontera Corozal (see p.346).

Airlines, agents and operators

Booking your tickets online cuts out the costs of agents and middlemen. Good deals can often be found through discount or auction sites, though these tickets can be pretty inflexible as such sites usually offer non-refundable, non-changeable deals. Almost all airlines have their own websites, offering tickets that can sometimes be just as inexpensive – and often more flexible – as those found on discount sites.

Online booking

ⓦ www.expedia.co.uk (in UK), ⓦ www.expedia.com (in US), ⓦ www.expedia.ca (in Canada)
ⓦ www.lastminute.com (in UK)
ⓦ www.opodo.co.uk (in UK)
ⓦ www.orbitz.com (in US)
ⓦ www.travelocity.co.uk (in UK), ⓦ www.travelocity.com (in US), ⓦ www.travelocity.ca (in Canada)
ⓦ www.travelonline.co.za (in South Africa)
ⓦ www.zuji.com.au (in Australia), ⓦ www.zuji.co.nz (in New Zealand)

Airlines

Aer Lingus US & Canada ⓣ1-800/IRISH-AIR, UK ⓣ0870/876 5000, Republic of Ireland ⓣ0818/365 000, South Africa ⓣ1-272/2168-32838, New Zealand ⓣ1649/3083355; ⓦ www.aerlingus.com.
Air New Zealand ⓣ0800/737000, Australia ⓣ0800/132476, UK ⓣ0800/028 4149, US ⓣ1-800/262-1234, Canada ⓣ1-800/663-5494; ⓦ www.airnz.co.nz.
American Airlines US ⓣ1-800/433-7300, UK ⓣ0845/7789 789, Republic of Ireland ⓣ01/602 0550, Australia ⓣ1800/673486, New Zealand ⓣ0800/445442; ⓦ www.aa.com.
British Airways US & Canada ⓣ1-800/AIRWAYS, UK ⓣ0870/850 9850, Republic of Ireland ⓣ1890/626747, Australia ⓣ1300/767177, New Zealand ⓣ09/966 9777, South Africa ⓣ114/418600; ⓦ www.ba.com.
Continental Airlines US & Canada ⓣ1-800/523-3273, UK ⓣ0845/607 6760, Republic of Ireland ⓣ1890/925252, Australia ⓣ02/9244 2242, New Zealand ⓣ09/3083350, International ⓣ1-800/231-0856; ⓦ www.continental.com.
Copa Airlines US ⓣ1-800/FLY-COPA, ⓦ www.copaair.com.
Delta US & Canada ⓣ1-800/221-1212, UK ⓣ0845/600 0950, Republic of Ireland ⓣ1850/882031 or 01/407 3165, Australia ⓣ1300/302849, New Zealand ⓣ09/977 2232; ⓦ www.delta.com.
Iberia US ⓣ1-800/772-4642, UK ⓣ0870/609 0500, Republic of Ireland ⓣ0818/462000, South Africa ⓣ011/884 5909; ⓦ www.iberia.com.
KLM US & Canada ⓣ1-800/225-2525, UK ⓣ0870/507 4074, Republic of Ireland ⓣ1850/747400, Australia ⓣ1300/392192, New Zealand ⓣ09/921 6040, South Africa ⓣ11/961 6727; ⓦ www.klm.com.

Mexicana US ⓣ1-800/531-7921, Canada ⓣ1-866/281-3049, UK ⓣ020/8492 0000, Australia ⓣ03/9699 9355, New Zealand ⓣ09/9772213, South Africa ⓣ11/781 2111; ⓦ www.mexicana.com.
Qantas Airways US & Canada ⓣ1-800/227-4500, UK ⓣ0845/774 7767, Republic of Ireland ⓣ01/407 3278, Australia ⓣ13 13 13, New Zealand ⓣ0800/808767 or 09/357 8900, South Africa ⓣ11/441 8550; ⓦ www.qantas.com.
South African Airways ⓣ11/978 1111, US & Canada ⓣ1-800/722-9675, UK ⓣ0870/747 1111, Australia ⓣ1800/221699, New Zealand ⓣ09/977 2237; ⓦ www.flysaa.com.
Spirit Airlines US & Canada ⓣ1-800/772-7117, ⓦ www.spiritair.com.
Taca US ⓣ1-800/400-TACA, Canada ⓣ1-800/722-TACA, UK ⓣ0870/2410 340, Australia ⓣ02/8248 0020; ⓦ www.taca.com.
United Airlines US ⓣ1-800/UNITED-1, UK ⓣ0845/844 4777, Australia ⓣ13 17 77; ⓦ www.united.com.

Agents and operators

The tour prices below do not include airfares to the region, unless stated.
Adventure Life US ⓣ1-800/344-6118, ⓦ www.adventure-life.com. Small-group specialists with a choice of six excellent tours (US$825–1695) in

Guatemala, using experienced guides. Well-structured itineraries include many opportunities to visit community-run projects like women's weaving groups and coffee cooperatives.

Adventures Abroad US ☎1-800/665-3998, ⓦwww.adventures-abroad.com. Adventure specialists with a selection of comfortable small-group tours; their nine-day "Soul of the Earth" trip mainly concentrates on the Atitlán area.

Cayaya Birding Tours Guatemala ☎5308 5160, ⓦwww.cayaya-birding.com. Resident specialists with unmatched knowledge of birding hot-spots. Offer great tours and customized itineraries.

Ceiba Adventures US ☎1-800/217-1060, ⓦwww.ceibaadventures.com. Adventure trips, including rafting, kayaking, caving and archeological tours throughout the Maya region. The ten-day "River of Ruins" (US$2950) tour includes many of the Usumacinta sites, plus Tikal and Aguateca.

eXito US ☎1-800/655-4053, ⓦwww.exitotravel .com. North America's top specialist for travel to Latin America. Website has a particularly useful airfare finder, with a comparison of the merits of various airpasses.

Explore Worldwide UK ☎01252/760000, ⓦwww.exploreworldwide.com. Tours including La Ruta Maya (from £2052 including airfare from Europe), which covers all the main sites of Guatemala, Belize, Chiapas and Yucatán.

Far Horizons US ☎1-800/552-4575, ⓦwww .farhorizon.com. Superb small-group archeological trips, guided by Mayanists, including a "Capital Cities of the Maya" tour (US$6895 including airfare) that takes in the sites of Quiriguá and Copán.

Global Travel Club UK ☎01268/541732, ⓦwww.global-travel.co.uk. Small company with a tremendous selection of tours, mainly devoted to Belize. "Guatemala in Style" (US$1795) is a nine-day trip to Atitlán, Tikal, Antigua and parts of the highlands.

Guatemala Unlimited US ☎1-800/733-3350, ⓦwww.guatemalaunlimited.com. Experienced company with an eight-day tour of Guatemala, plus shorter trips to Tikal and Yaxhá.

Imaginative Traveller UK ☎0800/316 2717, ⓦwww.imaginative-traveller.com. Offers several tours that include Guatemala; the "Caribbean Sail-trek" (£825) includes a week in Guatemala and a week in coastal Belize.

Intrepid Travel UK ☎020/8960 6333, ⓦwww .intrepidtravel.com. Small-group trips with an emphasis on cross-cultural contact and low-impact tourism. Tours have different comfort-level options.

Journey Latin America UK ☎020/8747 3108 or 0161/832 1441, ⓦwww.journeylatinamerica.co.uk. UK-based experts for airfares, passes and all-round travel advice to Guatemala and the region. Also offers a few Central American tours.

Lost World Adventures US ☎1-800/999-0558, ⓦwww.lostworldadventures.com. A selection of tempting Guatemalan tours (US$764–2895) includes a cycling and hiking trip to the high *altiplano* and remote areas of Atitlán.

North South Travel UK ☎01245/608291, ⓦwww.northsouthtravel.co.uk. Friendly, competitive travel agency, offering discounted fares worldwide. Profits are used to support projects in the developing world, especially the promotion of sustainable tourism.

Scuba Safaris UK ☎01342/851196, ⓦwww .scuba-safaris.com. Dive specialists with well-planned scuba trips to Honduras's Bay Islands. Two liveaboard craft, and also resort-based diving at the *Fantasy Island Beach Resort* in Roatán (£475–590 per head per week).

South American Experience UK ☎020/7976 5511, ⓦwww.southamericanexperience.co.uk. Flights and tailor-made itinerary specialists, with competitive airfare prices on their website and high-quality tours to the Maya region.

STA Travel US ☎1-800/781-4040, UK ☎0871/2300 040, Australia ☎134 STA, New Zealand ☎0800/474 400, South Africa ☎0861/781 781; ⓦwww.statravel.com. Worldwide specialists in independent travel; also student IDs, travel insurance, car rental, rail passes, and more. Good discounts for students and under-26s.

Toucan Travel US ☎805/927-5885, ⓦwww .tucantravel.com. Latin America specialists with over a dozen inexpensive, sociable tours through the Maya region and Central America, some using public buses, others mainly camping. The 21-day "Tulum" trip from Cancún to Antigua costs US$2080.

Trailfinders UK ☎0845/058 5858, Republic of Ireland ☎01/677 7888, Australia ☎1300/780 212; ⓦwww.trailfinders.com. One of the best-informed and most efficient flight agencies for independent travellers, though currently offer no tours in Central America.

Trips UK ☎0117/311 4400, ⓦwww .tripsworldwide.co.uk. A superb operator offering bespoke trips to Guatemala for those who want as independent an experience as possible. Experts help you plan your trip, and all accommodation suggestions are very well chosen and non-corporate. Also offers a "Pure Guatemala" trip (from £2345, including airfares), which covers the highlands and Petén.

Tropical Travel US ☎1-800/451-8017, ⓦwww .tropicaltravel.com. Offers a selection of tours in Guatemala, to the highlands and beyond. Their "Guatemalan Markets" tour is very well priced at US$686.

Wilderness Travel US ☎1-800/368-2794, ⓦwww.wildernesstravel.com. Well-organized cultural and wildlife adventure trips. The nine-day

"Guatemala Private Journey" tour (US$2195) takes in all the main sites, as well as the Petexbatún lagoon. **Wildland Adventures** US ☎1-800/345-4453, ⊛www.wildland.com. Very well guided and thought-out tours, with "Guatemalan Highlands" (US$1695) and "Great Cities of the Maya" (US$2295) itineraries.

Wildlife Worldwide UK ☎020/8667 9158, ⊛www.wildlifeworldwide.com. Superb bird-watching trips by expert naturalists, visiting some remote protected areas and staying at biological stations and jungle lodges. From £1895 for an eight-day tour.

Getting around

With no passenger trains and few people able to afford a car, virtually everyone travels by "chicken bus" in Guatemala. These buses may be decrepit, uncomfortable, fume-filled and overcrowded, but they give you a unique opportunity to mix with ordinary Guatemalans. If you opt for sanitized tourist shuttles, you'll be missing out on one of the country's most essential experiences. More comfortable buses – some of them quite fast and luxurious – ply the main highways, but once you leave the central routes and head off on the byways, there's usually no alternative to a bumpy ride inside a chicken bus or a pick-up truck.

The country's road system has been substantially upgraded in the last few years, though it still suffers in comparison with neighbouring Mexico. Dirt roads are the norm in some rural areas, where the going can be painfully pedestrian. Fortunately, whatever the pace of your journey, you'll always have the spectacular Guatemalan countryside to wonder at.

By bus

Buses are cheap, convenient, and can be wildly entertaining. For the most part the service is extremely comprehensive, reaching even the smallest of villages, and drivers will usually stop to pick up passengers anywhere, regardless of how many people are already on board.

Guatemala has two classes of bus. **Second-class** or "chicken buses", known as *camionetas*, are the most common and easily distinguished by their trademark clouds of thick, black, noxious fumes and rasping exhausts. *Camionetas* are all old North American school buses, with limited legroom, and the seats and aisles are usually crammed with passengers. The driver always

seems to be a moustachioed ladino with an eye for the ladies and a fixation for speed and overtaking on blind corners, while his helper (*ayudante*) always seems to be overworked and under-age. It's the *ayundante*'s job to scramble up to the roof to retrieve your rucksack, collect the fares, and bellow out the destination to all. While travel by second-class bus may be uncomfortable, it is never dull, with chickens clucking, music assaulting your eardrums, and snack vendors touting for business.

Guatemala has hundreds of small bus companies, each determined to outdo the next in the garishness of their vehicles' paint jobs. Almost all chicken buses operate out of public bus terminals, often adjacent to the market; between towns you can hail buses and they'll almost always stop for you. **Tickets** are (nearly always) bought on the bus, and whilst they are always very cheap, gringos do sometimes get ripped off – try to observe what the locals are paying. Fares average out at US$1 an hour.

The so-called pullman, usually a Greyhound-style bus, is rated as first-class, and tickets can be bought in advance.

Air taxes

For international flights an **airport departure tax** of US$30 is charged (though it's included in the price of most tickets), while for domestic flights it's US$0.80. All passengers also have to pay a **security tax** of US$3 per journey. Taxes are payable in cash only, either in quetzals or dollars.

These "express" services are about 20–30 percent more expensive than the regular buses – around US$1.40 an hour, though there are some very luxurious, more pricey options. Services vary tremendously: some companies' buses are double-deckers, with reclining seats and ice-cold air-conditioning, while other operators use decrepit vehicles. Each passenger is allocated a seat and all pullmans are pretty punctual.

Pullmans usually leave from the private offices of the bus company and they only run the main routes, connecting the capital with Río Dulce and Flores/Santa Elena, Quetzaltenango, Huehuetenango, the Mexican border, Chiquimula and Esquipulas, Puerto Barrios, Cobán, Copán and the rest of Central America. Note that tickets are often collected by conductors at the end of the journey, so make sure you don't lose yours.

Providing fast, nonstop links between the main tourist centres, shuttle buses are now very popular in Guatemala. Conveniently, passengers are picked up from their hotels, so you won't have to lug any heavy bags around. Services are expanding rapidly and now cover virtually everywhere that tourists travel in any number, and it's usually easy to organize an "especial" service (for a price) if your destination is not on a regular route. At around US$4–5 an hour, shuttles are expensive, but drivers are almost always more cautious than regular bus drivers.

Non-tourist minibuses (*microbuses*) have also become very common in Guatemala, particularly on paved roads, where they have replaced chicken buses in many areas. They usually operate from the main bus station, or use a separate terminal close by. Travel on microbuses also costs about US$1 per hour. In remote parts of the country **pick-ups** (*picops*) supplement microbus services, and for sheer joy of travel, you can't beat the open-air views (unless it's raining!). Passengers are charged about the same (around US$1 per hr).

By plane

The only scheduled internal flight currently operating in Guatemala is from the capital to Flores. Flights cost US$210–250 return (one-way from US$123) and take fifty minutes (as opposed to some eight hours on the bus). Two airlines, Taca and TAG, offer a total of four daily flights; addresses and other details can be found in the Petén chapter (see p.317). Tickets can be bought from virtually any travel agent in the country.

A major programme of airport upgrades in Quetzaltenango, Puerto San José and Puerto Barrios may mean the commencement of internal flights in the near future. Meanwhile, it's also possible to fly to a number of other airstrips including Copán, Poptún, Playa Grande and Sayaxché by tiny charter airlines when there's sufficient demand; details are given in the relevant chapters.

Flying to Honduras from Guatemala is quite expensive, but internal flights in Honduras are affordable and can save a great deal of time; for details see p.371.

By car

Driving in Guatemala certainly offers unrivalled freedom, though traffic is incessantly heavy in the capital and always busy along the Inter-americana and the highway to Puerto Barrios. Be warned that local driving practices can be alarming, including overtaking on blind corners. All the main routes are paved, but beyond this many roads are often extremely rough. **Filling stations** (*gasolineras*) are common (unless you really venture off the beaten track). Fuel (*gasolina*) costs US$1 per litre (slightly over US$4 per gallon).

Parking and security are an issue, particularly in towns. Always leave your car in a guarded car-park and choose a hotel with protected parking space. Speed bumps (*tumulos*) are everywhere, even on main highways. Local **warning** signs are also worth getting to know. The most common is placing a branch, which indicates the presence of a broken-down car or a hazard ahead. *Derrumbes* means landslides, and *frene con motor* (brake with motor) indicates a steep descent.

Renting a car costs from US$40 a day for a tiny hatchback or around US$70 for a 4WD by the time you've added the extras. Always take full-cover insurance and be aware that many companies will make you sign a clause so you are responsible for the first US$1000 of damage in the event of an accident, damage or theft. Local rental companies are in the "Listings" sections of all the main towns.

Taking your own car into Guatemala entails a great deal of bureaucracy. You'll be issued a car permit (usually valid for 30 days) at the border, and there are hefty penalties if you overstay. An insurance policy for Central America (sold at the Guatemalan border) is necessary; Nelson Insurance (in US ℡1-800/638-9423, Ⓦwww.nelson internationalgroup.com) arranges insurance for Mexico and Central America and has a 24-hour emergency hotline. If you plan to continue further south into Central America, expect to pay for more entry permits (US$24–100) at the Honduran border.

US, Canadian, EU, Australian and New Zealand driving licences are valid in Mexico and throughout Central America.

By taxi and tuk-tuk

Taxis are available in all the main towns, and their rates are fairly low at around US$3 for a short ride (or US$5 in Guatemala City). Outside the capital, metered cabs are non-existent, so it's essential to fix a price before you set off. Local taxi drivers will almost always be prepared to negotiate a price for an excursion to nearby villages or sites (perhaps US$30 for a half-day or US$50 for a full day), and if time is short this can be a good way of seeing places where the bus service is awkwardly timed. If you can organize a group, this need not be an expensive option.

Three-wheeled Thai tuk-tuks have proliferated throughout Guatemala in the last few years, operating as taxis, buzzing around the streets, Bangkok-style. They are common in most towns, except in Guatemala City and Quetzaltenango. It's best to fix the fare in advance; a short ride usually costs US$0.75, more in Antigua.

By bike and motorbike

Bicycles are quite common in Guatemala, and cycling has to be one of the most popular sports. You'll be well received almost anywhere if you travel by bike, and if you've got the energy to make your way through the highlands, it's a great way to see the country. Most towns will have a repair shop where you can get hold of spare parts, although you still need to carry the basics for emergencies on the road. Mountain bikes make the going easier, as even the main roads include plenty of formidable potholes, and it's a rare ride that doesn't involve at least one steep climb. Chicken buses will carry bikes on the roof if you can't face the hills. In case you didn't bring your own bike, you can **rent** them in towns including Antigua, Panajachel and Quetzaltenango; mountain bikes can be rented by the day (about US$8) or week (US$25). In flat Utila it's easy to find a basic bike for about US$2 a day. For real two-wheel enthusiasts, Maya

Addresses

Almost all addresses are based on the grid system, with avenidas running in one direction (north to south) and calles east to west. All addresses specify the street first, then the block, and end with the zone. For example, the address "Av la Reforma 3–55, Zona 10" means that house is on Avenida la Reforma, between 3 and 4 calles, at no. 55, in Zona 10. Almost all towns have numbered streets, but in some places the old names are also used. In Antigua calles and avenidas are also divided according to their direction from the central plaza – north, south, east or west (norte, sur, oriente and poniente). Diagonales (diagonals) are what you'd expect – a street that runs in an oblique direction.

Mountain Bike Tours and Old Town Outfitters, both in Antigua (see p.109), offer a range of challenging bike trips.

Motorbikes are not that common in Guatemala, and locating parts and mechanical expertise can be tricky. There are rental outlets in Guatemala City, Panajachel, Antigua (see relevant "Listings") and Roatán, typically charging around US$40 a day for a 200cc machine.

By ferry and boat

Ferries operate between Puerto Barrios and Lívingston; between Puerto Barrios and Punta Gorda in Belize; and in Honduras between La Ceiba and the Bay Islands of Utila and Roatán, and connecting Trujillo and Guanaja.

In Petén, there are a number of possible boat routes and trips, including the journey across the Río Usumacinta from Bethel and La Técnica to Frontera Corozal, and on Lago de Petén Itzá. Several terrific boat trips start in the town of Sayaxché, including the trip to Lago de Petexbatún and Aguateca and along the Río de la Pasión to Ceibal. Precise details of schedules are given in the relevant chapters of the Guide.

Along the Pacific coast, the Chiquimulilla canal separates much of the shoreline from the mainland. If you're heading for a beach you'll find a regular shuttle of small boats to take you across the canal, including services from La Avellana to Monterrico.

Two of Guatemala's most unmissable **boat trips** are through the spectacular Río Dulce gorge, either starting in Lívingston or the town of Río Dulce, and across volcano-framed Lago de Atitlán.

You should be able to rent a boat somewhere on almost any of the country's other navigable waterways, though be prepared for hours of patient bargaining, as the boat owners ask serious money for any excursions.

Accommodation

Guatemalan hotels come in all shapes and sizes, and unless you're really off the beaten track there's usually a good range of accommodation to choose from. Inguat fixes a maximum price for every hotel room in the country, and there are bargains and bad deals at every level. Guatemala really is a budget-travellers' dream, and you should be able to find a clean double room for US$12 (or less) in any town in the country, except the capital. At the top end of the scale, you can stay in some magnificent colonial hotels decorated with real taste. In the mid-price bracket, you'll also find some brilliant places – you can still expect character and comfort, but perhaps without the service and facilities.

Accommodation options have a bewildering assortment of names: *hoteles*, pensiones, *posadas*, hospedajes and *casas de huespedes*. The names don't always mean a great deal; in theory a hospedaje is less formal than a hotel, but in practice the reverse is almost as common. There are no official youth hostels in Guatemala, but virtually all the main travellers' centres have backpacker-style **hostels** with dormitories and a sociable vibe.

On the whole you can expect hostels and the cheapest hospedajes to charge US$3–6 per head, and a reasonable but basic room with its own bathroom to cost US$12–20 (more in the capital and Antigua). Official prices are meant to be displayed in the room, but it's well worth trying to haggle a

Accommodation price codes

All accommodation listed in this guide has been graded according to the following price scale, which refers to the price in US dollars of the cheapest double room in high season. Dormitory beds are priced per head. Many places offer reductions at quieter times of the year, particularly those in the more popular tourist centres, where there is plenty of competition. It is always worth negotiating if you think the hotel is not very full.

❶ Under US$7
❷ US$8–12
❸ US$13–20
❹ US$21–30
❺ US$31–40
❻ US$41–60
❼ US$61–80
❽ US$81–100
❾ Over US$101

little, or asking if there are any cheaper rooms. If travelling in a group you can often save money by sharing a larger room, which almost all the cheaper hotels offer.

Prices are at their highest in Guatemala City, where the very cheapest rooms can be very grim. Costs are also higher than average in Antigua, Río Dulce and Flores, but extremely cheap in the western highlands. At fiesta and holiday times, particularly Holy Week and Christmas, rooms tend to be more expensive and harder to find, and the summer tourist season can also be crowded. At these times, particularly if you're going to arrive in Guatemala City at night, it's worth booking ahead. Wherever you are, you'll find that most mid- and top-range hotels charge solo travellers around 80 percent of the cost of a double. Always insist on seeing your room before any money changes hands, otherwise you may find their good rooms reserved for more discerning customers.

Most Guatemalan **hostels** tend to be owned and often run by expats, and are geared-up to budget travellers' needs, with excellent travel information, cheap grub and perhaps a bar. Hostel dormitories vary greatly, but the best places tend to have a maximum of eight beds per room. Many hostels offer single-sex dorms and also private rooms for couples.

The cheapest **hotels** (❶–❷) recommended in this book will be simple and sparse, usually with a shared bathroom at the end of the corridor. In the brackets above this (❸ & ❹), you can expect a private bathroom with hot water. Rooms in the ❺–❼ categories should

be very comfortable and attractive, while for US$80 and up (❽ & ❾), you can expect high standards of comfort and luxury, with facilities such as swimming pools, gyms and a good restaurant.

It's only in Petén, the eastern highlands, and on the Pacific and Caribbean coasts that you'll need a fan or air conditioning. In the highlands, even the luxury hotels rarely have air-conditioning – many have lovely logwood fires to keep out the winter chill instead. Mosquito nets are not that common, even in the lowland areas, so if you plan to spend some time in Petén or by the coast, it's well worth investing in one, and it's an essential purchase if you plan to so some jungle trekking.

Camping

Campsites are extremely few and far between. Unless you're working on an archeological dig it's really not worth bringing a tent as there are only a handful of places in the entire country that offer a designated, secure place to camp. If you do get stuck in a remote village, ask for the mayor (*alcade*) to see if you can stay in the town hall (*municipalidad*) or local school.

If you're planning to hike in the jungle or climb volcanoes, you'll need to hook up with an agency, and they'll sort you out with a tent (or hammock and mosquito net). For **renting camping gear** contact Old Town Outfitters in Antigua (see p.109), or Quetzaltrekkers inside the *Casa Argentina* hotel in Quetzaltenango (see p.182).

Food and drink

Guatemalan food is filling, good value, and can be very flavoursome. The cuisine has evolved from Mayan, Latin American and Western traditions though they usually overlap to a great extent now to form what Guatemalans call *comida típica*. Eateries in places popular with tourists tend to have varied menus and plenty of choice for vegetarians, and in Antigua and Lago de Atitlán you can feast on numerous different European cuisines, several Asian ones, and even sample Middle Eastern dishes.

In places orientated more to a Guatemalan clientele, you're likely to be offered a lot of simply prepared grilled or fried meat dishes and have much less choice. Off the beaten path in the highlands the diet can get pretty monotonous, with things revolving around the "three-card trick" of eggs, beans and tortillas for breakfast, lunch and dinner. You'll find that the concept of healthy eating has yet to really penetrate Central America, and a lot of local food tends to be full-fat by definition. For more on local food and speciality, see the boxed text "Guatemalan Cuisine", and for a menu reader see the "Language" section of Contexts at the back of this book.

Where to eat

Unless you're in a tourism-orientated place, your choice is usually between a restaurant and a comedor in most Guatemalan towns. The latter is like a traditional American diner or an old-school British café; in general, they are simple, often scruffy-looking local eateries serving big portions of food at inexpensive prices (a full meal for about US$2). In a comedor there is often no menu, and you simply ask what's on offer, or look into the bubbling pots. Restaurants, broadly speaking, are slightly more formal and expensive and only found in large towns.

Many locals will very rarely venture into either a comedor or a restaurant, preferring to eat from **street** food stalls, which sell the food of the poor at rock-bottom prices; they're usually clustered around the market-place. If your stomach can take it, you'll often find an interesting dish to try, though hygiene standards can be questionable.

You'll find fast-food joints in towns and on highways, modelled on (and including) the American originals. *Pollo Campero* is a *KFC*-style Guatemalan-owned fried-chicken chain that has expanded around the globe. While on the road, you'll also come across the local version of fast food: when buses pause they're besieged by vendors offering a huge selection of drinks, sweets, local specialities and even complete meals. Treat this kind of food with a degree of caution, bearing in mind the potential lack of hygiene.

In every main tourist centre you'll also find gringo-geared **café-restaurants**, often foreign-owned places with cosmopolitan menus featuring home-made sandwiches, curries, stir-fries and the like, and plenty of vegetarian options and salads. There's usually wine by the glass, cappuccinos and lattes, and fresh fruit shakes. Such indulgence does come at a price, but the eclectic nature of such places can be quite a relief if you've been up in the hills eating tortillas and beans for a week, and hygiene standards are likely to be high.

Breakfast

Traditionally, Guatemalans eat a substantial **breakfast** of tortillas, eggs and beans, sometimes with sour cream or fried plantains. Eggs can be served up a myriad of different ways (see p.464), using some superb, often spicy sauces. Pancakes (*panqueques*) are also common, but can be disappointing as they're often made from a ready mix rather than cooked with fresh eggs. Guatemalans do not usually consume fruit for breakfast, though cereals are popular.

Up in the highlands **breakfast** often includes a plate of *mosh*, which is made with milk and oats and tastes rather like porridge – it's the ideal antidote to the early morning chill.

In towns with large numbers of foreign visitors, things get a lot more eclectic, with all sorts of granola and muesli options available, which you can combine with fresh fruit, honey and yoghurt. The bread in these places is often freshly baked and there's usually a long list of juices and smoothies available.

Lunch

Lunch is the main meal of the day, and this is the best time to fill up as restaurants and comedores offer a *comida corrida*, or *menú ejecútivo*: a set two- or three-course meal that costs about US$2–3 and includes a drink. It's always filling and occasionally delicious; your set meal usually starts with a bowl of soup, followed by a main dish of grilled or fried meat served with rice or a salad.

Guatemalan cuisine does not vary that much regionally (except on the Caribbean coast, which is quite distinct) though some areas have famous local dishes including the *kak'ik* (a turkey broth) of the Cobán area. Most large towns have a place that special-izes in *ceviche* (raw fish marinated in lime juice) however, and on the coast it's customary to order fried fish or *camarones* (shrimps), and wash it down with Gallo beer.

Vegetarians are rarely catered for specifi-cally, except in tourist-geared restaurants. It is, however, fairly easy to get by eating plenty of beans and eggs (which are always on the menu) and often some guacamole.

In touristy towns, there's a wealth of choice with everything from panini and wraps with imported cheese to sushi and noodles on offer.

Snacks

Guatemalans are fond of their *refracciones* (snacks), which are served from street stalls or by vendors. Tostadas are one of the most popular, a crispy corn tortilla smeared with bean paste, topped with grated vegetables and sprinkled with a little salty cheese. Other common snacks are *tamales*, steamed cornmeal stuffed with chicken or another bit of meat, and *chuchitos*, which are smaller versions of the *tamal*, and tend to include a bit of tomato and a pinch of hot chilli.

For a quick snack, many locals head for a *shuco* (literally a "dirty", a food cart that sells Guatemalan-style hot dogs), which is a bread bun filled with a sausage (or *chorizo*) and guacamole for US$0.75. Taco stands (often priced at three for Q10 (US$1.30) are also very widespread.

Cakes and pastries are widely available, but tend to be pretty dull and dry.

Dinner

For Guatemalans, dinner (taken 7–9pm) is a lighter meal than lunch. Mexican-style dishes, including tacos and enchiladas are popular. In the tourist hot-spots, particularly Antigua, there's a tremendous choice of restaurants, serving cuisine from around the world, with Italian, Japanese, Indian, North American and of course Guatemalan and Mexican food available.

Drink

To start off the day most Guatemalans drink a cup of hot **coffee** or tea (both are usually taken with plenty of sugar). Espresso machines are becoming much more widespread in Guatemala and you'll be able to get a cappuccino in most towns. Out in the sticks it's usually instant coffee with powdered milk. Atol, a warm, sweet drink made with either maize, rice (or even plantain) and sugar is also very popular, especially in the highlands.

At other times of day, **soft drinks** are usually drunk with meals. Coca-Cola, Pepsi, Sprite and Fanta (all called *aguas*) are common, as are *refrescos*, thirst-quenching water-based drinks with a little fruit flavour added; *rosa de jamaica* and tamarindo are two of the more unusual variants. In many places, you can also get a *licuado*, a delicious, thick, fruit-based drink with either milk or water added (milk is safer).

Tap water in the main towns is purified, and you can usually taste the chlorine. However, this doesn't mean that it won't give you stomach trouble, and it's always safest to stick to bottled water (*agua pura*), which is almost always available.

Guatemalan cuisine

Most meals in Guatemala traditionally revolve around the basic staples of beans and maize, though diets are changing due to increased exposure to international cuisine. Beans (*frijoles*) are the black kidney-shaped variety and are usually served in two ways: *volteados*, which are boiled up, mashed, and then refried in a great dollop; or *parados*, which are boiled up whole, with a few slices of onion and garlic, and served in their own black juice.

Maize is the other essential, a food which for the Maya (and many other Native Americans) is almost as nourishing spiritually as it is physically – in Maya legend, humankind was originally formed from maize. It appears most commonly as a corn tortilla, which is similar to a wrap. Maize is traditionally ground by hand and shaped by clapping it between two hands, a method still in widespread use; the tortilla is then cooked on a *comal*, a flat pan of clay placed over the fire. Guatemalan tortillas should be eaten while warm, usually brought to the table wrapped in cloth. Fresh tortillas have a lovely pliable texture, with a delicate, slightly smoky taste. Maize is also used to make a number of traditional snacks (see below). Squash (*güisquil*) is the main Maya vegetable, often used in dishes along with meat, tomato and onion; you may also find *pacaya*, a rather stodgy local vegetable.

Chillies are another essential ingredient of the Guatemalan diet (especially for the Q'ek'chi Maya), usually served as a spicy sauce (*salsa picante*), or sometimes placed raw or pickled in the middle of the table.

The eastern coast of Guatemala has a different culinary tradition. Here Creole and **Garífuna** cooking (which incorporates the influences of the Caribbean with those of Africa) is easy to find in Puerto Barrios and Lívingston. Seafood dominates the scene, along with coconut and plantain. *Tapado* is probably the region's signature dish, a seafood soup that's a superb mix of fish (typically snapper), prawns, coconut milk, peppers, plantain and spices; though you'll also find plenty of grilled fish, lobster, conch fritters and *pan de coco*.

Dishes and specialities

If you're curious to try some Guatemalan dishes, markets and fiestas are particularly good grazing territory.

Nomenclature is confusing – **cornmeal** wrapped inside banana leaves or corn husks and steamed could take any number of names depending upon flavourings, and these change from region to region. Plain steamed cornmeal is a *tamal blanco*; stuff it with meat and tomato salsa, however, and it becomes either a *chuchito* or a *tamale*. If blended with potato, it's a *pache* – these are common in the Xela area. Near Rabinal, look out for *boxboles*, cornmeal flavoured with spices, almond and a pinch of chilli, and cooked inside a pumpkin leaf. Mixed with *frijoles*, a *tamal* is a *bollo*, *tayuyo* or *tamalito de frijol*. When sweet, it's a *camallito de cambray* (with

Gallo, a medium-strength lager, is the most popular **beer** in Guatemala, indeed many Guatemalan men consider it the national drink, and the brewer promotes it as "Nuestra Cerveza" (our beer). Unfortunately it's a pretty bland brew. The main competitor, Brahma, a Brazilian beer, is a little more interesting with a slightly spicy finish. Moza, a dark brew with a slight caramel flavour is worth trying but rarely available. Other hard-to-come-by brands (all lagers) include the premium beer Montecarlo, Dorada Draft and Cabro.

Imported brands are scarce. A 33cl bottle of beer costs about US$1.50–2.50 in a bar, but watch out for litre bottles (around US$3.50), which work out to be very good value.

As for spirits, **rum** (*ron*) and **aguardiente**, a clear and lethal sugarcane spirit, are very popular and cheap. Ron Botran Añejo is a half-decent rum (around US$4 a bottle), while the fabulously smooth Ron Zacapa Centenario (around US$30 a bottle) is one of the world's best; indeed, it regularly wins international prizes. Hard drinkers will soon anise) or an *elote*. Keep an eye out for a red lantern outside a house – this indicates the family has fresh *tamales* for sale.

The corn **tortilla** can also be prepared in a myriad of ways. Fried and topped (typically with guacamole and some salty cheese), it's a tostada, while rolled or folded around a filling – meat-and-cheese is always popular – it may be a taco, enchilada or *doblada*. Usually a salsa, based on a blend of ripe tomato and *miltomates* (green tomatoes), is served with these dishes. A *pupusa* (called a *baleada* in Honduras) is a fresh tortilla stuffed with anything, but usually including refried beans, *repollo* (pickled shredded cabbage leaves) and cheese.

Encasing food in an **egg batter** and frying it either *envueltos* ("wrapped") or *frituras* ("fritter style") is another popular cooking style. *Chiles rellenos*, chillies stuffed with vegetables and meat, are especially delicious. Simpler, often vegetarian variations abound using green bean or cauliflower, but look out for those made with *güisquíl* (squash), *flor de izote* (the slightly bitter petals of a palm) or *bledo*, a leaf similar in flavour to spinach.

Salads are often simple, though several variations are well worth trying, including *piloyada*, a hearty affair based on plump red beans with eggs, tomatoes and meat; *iguaxte*, cooked potato or vegetables flavoured with a distinct paste of pumpkin seeds, dried chillies and sometimes tomato; and *chojín*, which is radish-based and often made with cheese and either pork or pork crackling (*chicharrón*). *Fiambre*, a vast salad of pickled vegetables with cured sausage (mixed with beetroot in central Guatemala and often barley in the Quetzaltenango area) is perhaps the country's most celebrated dish; it's eaten on All Saints' Day around a family grave in the cemetery.

Many **traditional dishes** are chunky soups or subtly spiced tomato-based stews (*caldos*, *cocidos* or *sopas*). The spicy *pepián* sauce is made throughout the country and usually incorporates chicken and vegetables, but occasionally chocolate. The more lightly spiced *pulique* is flavoured with coriander and capsicum. *Suban-ik*, which hails from Chimaltenango, is a tasty dish with chicken and pork, while Cobán's *kak-ik* is a turkey broth with coriander and mint.

Sweets, snacks and desserts tend to be very sweet. *Rellenitos* – cooked, mashed plantain, stuffed with sweetened beans and fried – are widely available, as is *mole de plátano*, which is plantain served in a sweet, spiced cocoa-flavoured sauce. Vegetables – for example, sweet potato, pumpkin or *chayote* – may be simmered in sugar syrups until they are caramelized or stuffed with a sweet mixture. Cake making is generally a specialized business, but *pastel borracho* is one that is soaked in rum syrup before being iced, while *pastel de elote* is made with corn.

With help from Malia Dewse

get to know Quezalteca and Venado, two readily available *aguardientes* that fire up many a fiesta. If you're after a real bargain, then try locally brewed alcohol (*chicha*), which is practically given away. Its main ingredient can be anything: apple, cherry, sugarcane, peach, apricot and quince are just some of the more common varieties.

Chilean and Argentinean wines are now quite widely available anywhere where tourists gather. A glass of red or white house wine is usually around US$3 in most cafés or restaurants; bottles start at US$10 (or US$6 if purchased in a supermarket).

Health

Most visitors enjoy Guatemala without experiencing any health problems. However, it's always easier to become ill in a country with a different climate, food and germs – still more so in a poor country with lower standards of sanitation than you might be used to.

It's vital to get the best health advice you can before you set off. Consult the websites mentioned on p.42 for health precautions and disease prevention advice. Pay a visit to your doctor or a travel clinic as far in advance of travel as possible (at least eight weeks), and if you're pregnant or likely to become so, mention this at the outset. Many clinics also sell the latest travel health products, including mosquito nets, water filters, medical kits and so on. Finally you'll definitely need the security of health insurance (see "Insurance").

Once you're there, what you **eat and drink** is crucial. In addition to the hazards mentioned under "Intestinal troubles" below, contaminated food and water can transmit the hepatitis A virus, which can lay a victim low for several months with exhaustion, fever and diarrhoea, and can even cause liver damage.

Vaccinations, inoculations and malaria precautions

There are no obligatory inoculations for Guatemala (unless you're arriving from a "high-risk" area of yellow fever – northern South America and equatorial Africa). Nevertheless, there are several you should have anyway. Make sure you're up to date with tetanus and typhoid vaccinations and consider having hepatitis A and tuberculosis (TB) jabs. Long-term travellers or anyone spending time in rural areas should think about having the combined hepatitis A and B and the rabies vaccines (though see p.41 for a caveat on that).

Malaria is a danger in some parts of the country (particularly in the rural lowlands). It's not a problem in the big cities, or anywhere over 1500m – which includes Antigua, Guatemala City, Chichicastenango, Lago de Atitlán, Quetzaltenango and virtually all of the western highlands. However, if you plan to visit any lowland areas, including Petén, Alta Verapaz and the Pacific or Caribbean coasts, you should consider taking a course of tablets.

The recommended prophylactic is chloroquine (inexpensive, available without prescription, and safe in pregnancy); you'll need to begin taking the pills a week before you enter an area where there's a risk of malaria and continue for four weeks after you return. Malarone is an alternative drug, which you need start only two days before you go, though it's not suitable for pregnant women or babies.

Whichever anti-malarial you choose, you should still take **precautions** to avoid getting bitten by insects: always sleep in screened rooms or under nets in lowland areas; burn mosquito coils; cover up arms and legs, especially around dawn and dusk when mosquitoes are most active; and apply insect repellent (with 25–50 percent DEET; but not to children under two).

Also prevalent in some lowland areas (usually occurring in epidemic outbreaks in urban areas), dengue fever is a viral infection transmitted by mosquitoes, which are active during the day. Fever, aches and joint pain (its old name was "break-bone fever") are often followed by a rash. Though most people make a full recovery after a few days, children are particularly at risk. There is no vaccine or specific treatment, so you need to pay great attention to avoiding bites.

Intestinal troubles

Despite all the dire warnings given here, a bout of diarrhoea is the medical problem you're most likely to encounter. Even following all the usual precautions no one seems to avoid it altogether. Its main cause is simply the change of diet: the food in the region contains a whole new set of bacteria, and perhaps rather more of them than you're used to. If you're struck down, take it easy for a day or two, drink lots of bottled water and eat only the blandest of foods – papaya is good for soothing the stomach and is crammed with vitamins. Only if the symptoms last more than four or five days do you need to worry. Finally, if you're taking oral contraception or any other orally administered drugs, bear in mind that severe diarrhoea can reduce their efficacy.

Cholera is an acute bacterial infection, recognizable by watery diarrhoea and vomiting. However, risk of infection is extremely low in Guatemala (and symptoms are rapidly relieved by prompt medical attention and clean water). If you're spending any time in rural areas you also run the risk of picking up various parasitic infections: protozoa – amoeba and giardia – and intestinal worms; these are quite common around Lago de Atitlán. These sound hideous, but once detected they're easily treated with antibiotics. If you suspect you may have an infestation, take a stool sample to a good **pathology lab** and go to a doctor or pharmacist with the test results (see "Getting medical help").

More serious is amoebic dysentery, which is endemic in many parts of the region. The symptoms are similar to a bad dose of diarrhoea but include bleeding too. On the whole, a course of flagyl (metronidazole) will cure it.

Bites and stings

Taking steps to avoid getting bitten by **insects**, particularly mosquitoes, is always good practice. Sandflies, which are very common in the Bay Islands, are tiny, but their bites, usually on feet and ankles, itch like hell and last for days. Ticks, which you're likely to pick up if you're walking or riding in areas with domestic livestock (and sometimes in forests), need careful removal with tweezers. Head or body lice can be picked up from people or bedding, and are best treated with medicated shampoo; very occasionally, they may spread typhus,

characterized by fever, muscle aches, headaches and eventually a measles-like rash. If you think you have it, seek treatment from a doctor.

Scorpions are common; mostly nocturnal, they hide during the heat of the day – often in thatched roofs. If you're camping, or sleeping under a thatched roof, shake your shoes out before putting them on and try not to wander round barefoot. Their sting is painful (rarely fatal) and can become infected, so you should seek medical treatment if the pain seems significantly worse than a bee sting. You're less likely to be bitten by a spider, but seek medical treatment if the pain persists or increases.

You're unlikely to see a snake, and most are harmless in any case. Wearing boots and long pants will go a long way towards preventing a bite – tread heavily and they will usually slither away. If you do get bitten, remember what the snake looked like (kill it if you can), immobilize the bitten limb and seek medical help immediately; antivenins are available in most main hospitals.

Swimming and snorkelling might bring you into contact with potentially dangerous or venomous **sea creatures**. Jellyfish and some corals sting, especially fire coral. If you are stung by a jellyfish, clean the wound with vinegar or iodine. The spines of stingrays, stonefish and scorpion fish are all extremely poisonous, so be careful where you put your feet and hands.

Finally, rabies is present, but rare in Guatemala. The best advice is to give dogs a wide berth and not to play with animals at all. Treat any bite as suspect: wash any wound immediately with soap or detergent and apply alcohol or iodine if possible. Act immediately to get treatment – rabies can be fatal once symptoms appear. There is a vaccine, but it is expensive, serves only to shorten the course of treatment you need anyway and is effective for no more than three months.

Heat and altitude problems

Two other common causes of illness are **altitude** and the **sun**. The best advice in both cases is to take it easy; allow yourself time to acclimatize before you race up a volcano,

What about the water?

Contaminated water is a major cause of sickness in Guatemala and you should never even brush your teeth with tap water. Stick to bottled water (*agua pura*), which is available everywhere, either in bottles or small plastic bags.

You'll only need to consider treating your own water if you plan to travel to extremely remote areas. Although boiling water for ten minutes kills most microorganisms, it's not the most convenient method. Water filters remove visible impurities and larger pathogenic organisms (most bacteria and cysts). Chemical sterilization with either chlorine or iodine is effective (except in preventing amoebic dysentery or giardiasis), but the resulting liquid doesn't taste very pleasant. Iodine is unsafe for pregnant women, babies and people with thyroid complaints. Purification, involving both filtration and sterilization, gives the most complete treatment, and travel clinics and good outdoor-equipment shops will stock a wide range of portable water purifiers.

and build up exposure to the sun gradually. If going to altitudes above 2700 metres, you may develop symptoms of Acute Mountain Sickness (AMS), such as breathlessness, headaches, dizziness, nausea and appetite loss. More extreme cases might cause vomiting, disorientation, loss of balance and coughing up of pink frothy phlegm. The simple cure – a slow descent – almost always brings immediate recovery.

Tolerance to the sun, too, takes a while to build up. Use a strong sunscreen and, if you're walking during the day, wear a hat and try to keep in the shade. Avoid dehydration by drinking plenty of water or fruit juice. The most serious result of overheating is heatstroke, which can be potentially fatal. Lowering the body temperature (by taking a tepid shower, for example) is the first step in treatment.

Getting medical help

For minor medical problems, head for a *farmacia* – look for the green cross – there's one in every town and most villages. Pharmacists are knowledgeable and helpful, and many speak some English. They can also sell drugs over the counter that are only available on prescription at home. Every capital city has **doctors** and dentists, many trained in the US, who are experienced in treating visitors and speak good English. Your embassy will always have a list of recommended doctors, and we've included some in our "Listings" sections for the main towns.

Health insurance (see previous section) is essential and for anything serious you should

go to the best **private hospital** you can reach; again, these are located mainly in the provincial capitals. If you suspect something is amiss with your insides, it might be worth heading straight for the local **pathology lab** (all the main towns have them), before seeing a doctor. Many rural communities have a **health centre** (*centro de salud* or *puesto de salud*), where health care is free, although there may only be a nurse or health worker available and you can't rely on finding anyone who speaks English. Should you need an injection or transfusion, make sure that the equipment is sterile (it might be worth bringing a sterile kit from home) and ensure any blood you receive is screened.

US and Canada

CDC ☎1-877/394-8747, ⊛www.cdc.gov/travel. Official US government travel-health site.
International Society for Travel Medicine ☎1-770/736-7060, ⊛www.istm.org. Has a full list of travel-health clinics.
Canadian Society for International Health ⊛www.csih.org. Extensive list of travel-health centres.

Australia, New Zealand and South Africa

Travellers' Medical and Vaccination Centre ☎1300/658 844, ⊛www.tmvc.com.au. Lists travel clinics in Australia, New Zealand and South Africa.

UK and Ireland

British Airways Travel Clinics ☎0845/600 2236, ⊛www.britishairways.com/travel /healthclinintro/public/en_gb for nearest clinic.

Hospital for Tropical Diseases Travel Clinic
℡0845/155 5000 or 020/7387 4411,
ⓦwww.thehtd.org.
MASTA (Medical Advisory Service for
Travellers Abroad) ⓦwww.masta.org or
℡0870/606 2782 for the nearest clinic.

Travel Medicine Services ℡028/9031 5220.
Tropical Medical Bureau Republic of Ireland
℡1850/487 674, ⓦwww.tmb.ie.

The media

It's quite tough to find recent copies of foreign newspapers and magazines in Guatemala, but as the country is so well wired, it's easy to keep up to date with current affairs online by using cybercafés.

Newspapers and magazines

Guatemala has a number of daily newspapers with extensive national coverage and a more limited international perspective. The best of the dailies is the forthright *El Periódico* (ⓦwww.elperiodico.com.gt), which has some excellent columnists and investigative journalism, while the balanced, independent-minded *Siglo Veintiuno* (ⓦwww.sigloxxi.com) is also a good read. Guatemala's most popular paper is the *Prensa Libre* (ⓦwww.prensalibre.com), which features comprehensive national and quite reasonable international coverage. Picture-rich tabloids such as *Nuestro Diario* and *Al Día* concentrate on the shocking stories of the day. In the Quetzaltenango area, check out the local paper *Quetzalteco* (ⓦwww.elquetzalteco.com.gt). As for the **periodicals**, *La Crónica* is usually a decent read, concentrating on current Guatemalan political affairs and business news with a smattering of foreign coverage.

In theory, the nation's newspapers are not subject to restrictions, though pressures and threats are still exerted by criminal gangs, the military and those in authority. Being a campaigning journalist in Guatemala is a dangerous profession, and every year there's a contract killing or two.

English-language publications are thin on the ground, though a couple of interesting new magazines have emerged in recent years. *Revue* (ⓦwww.revuemag.com), a glossy colour magazine published in Antigua, has articles about Guatemalan culture and history plus hundreds of accommodation, restaurant and shopping advertisements. Also Antigua-based, *La Cuadra* adopts an irreverent, satirical tone, has some good photography and is loaded with articles about everything from politics to sex. In the Xela area, *Xela Who?* (ⓦwww.xelawho.com) concentrates on cultural life in the second city, with bar and restaurant reviews and a hilarious "Fashion Police" page; it also has a section dedicated to San Pedro La Laguna. For coverage of development issues and Guatemalan society pick up a copy of *Entremundos* (ⓦwww.entremundos.org), which is widely available in Quetzaltenango.

For really in-depth reporting and analysis, the *Central America Report* is superb, with coverage of all the main political issues, and investigations. It's published weekly by Inforpress Centroamericana and is available by subscription at ⓦwww.inforpressca.com.

As for **foreign publications**, *Newsweek* and *Time* are available in quality bookstores around the country and in some luxury hotel gift shops. Some American newspapers are also available: check in the *Camino Real Hotel* bookstore in Guatemala City and the bookshops in Antigua.

Honduran media

In Honduras, the most useful publications for travellers are *Honduras This Week* (ⓦ www.hondurasthisweek.com), an excellent weekly English-language newspaper with in-depth coverage of events in Honduras, plus tourist and business information, and Honduras Tips w ⓦ www.honduras.com/hondurastips), a free tourism magazine with plenty of valuable information and features, transport information, and hotel and restaurant listings. Both are widely available in Copán and the Bay Islands.

Radio and television

Guatemala has an abundance of **radio stations**, though variety is not their strong point. Most transmit a turgid stream of Latin pop and cheesy merengue, which you're sure to hear plenty of on the buses. Try Atmosfera (96.5FM) for rock, Radio Infinita (100.1FM) which is eclectic by nature and strong on indie and electronica, or La Marca on (94.1FM) for reggaeton. Radio Punto (90.5FM) has news and discussions. You'll also find a host of religious stations, too, broadcasting evangelical lectures, services, "miracles", and so on.

Television stations are also in plentiful supply. Viewers can choose from 26 stations, many of them beaming in Mexican and US shows (which are subtitled or dubbed into Spanish). Many hotel rooms have cable TV, which often includes (English-language) CNN and sometimes the National Geographic channel.

Sadly the BBC World Service is no longer broadcast in Central America. For Voice of America frequencies consult ⓦ www.voa.gov.

Festivals

Traditional fiestas are one of the great excitements of a trip to Guatemala, and every town and village, however small, devotes at least one day a year to celebration. The main day is normally prescribed by the local saint's day, though the celebrations often extend a week or two around that date. On almost every day of the year there's a fiesta in some corner of the country, and with a bit of planning you should be able to witness at least one – most of them are well worth going out of your way for. A list of all the regional fiestas appears at the end of each chapter in the Guide.

Fiestas come in two basic models (except on the Caribbean coast – see box, p.45). In towns with a largely **ladino** population, fairs are usually set up, and the days are filled with processions, beauty contests and perhaps the odd marching band; the nights are dominated by dancing to merengue, reggaeton and salsa. In the highlands, where the bulk of the population is **Maya**, you'll see traditional dances, costumes and musicians, and a blend of religious and secular celebration that incorporates pre-Columbian elements. What they all share is an astonishing energy and an unbounded enthusiasm for drink, dance and fireworks, all of which are virtually impossible to escape during the days of fiesta.

One thing you shouldn't expect is anything too dainty or organized: fiestas are above all chaotic, and the measured rhythms of traditional dance and music are usually obscured by the crush of the crowd and the huge volumes of alcohol consumed by participants. If you can join in the mood, there's no doubt that fiestas are wonderfully entertaining and that they offer a real insight into Guatemalan culture, ladino or indigenous.

Many of the **best fiestas** include some specifically local element, such as the giant kites at Santiago Sacatepéquez, the religious processions in Antigua, the horse race in Todos Santos Cuchumatán or the skull bearers of San José. The dates of most fiestas, along with their main features, are listed at the end of each chapter. At certain times virtually the whole country erupts simultaneously: Easter Week is perhaps the most important, particularly in Antigua, but All Saints' Day (Nov 1) and New Year's are also marked by partying across the land.

Fiesta dances

In Guatemala's Maya villages **traditional dances** – heavily imbued with history and symbolism – form a pivotal part in the fiesta celebrations. Most are rooted in pre-Columbian traditions. The drunken dancers may look out of control, but the process is taken very seriously and involves great expense on the part of the participants, who have to rent their ornate costumes. The most common dance is the **Baile de la Conquista**, which re-enacts the victory of the Spanish over the Maya, while at the same time managing to ridicule the conquistadors. Other popular dances are

the Baile del Venado, the dance of the deer; the Baile de la Culebra, the dance of the snake; and Moros y Cristianos, which dramatizes the Spanish victory over the Moors. One of the most impressive is the Palo Volador, in which men swing by ropes from a thirty-metre pole. Today this Maya-style bungy jump is only performed in Chichicastenango, Joyabaj and Cubulco.

Fiesta music

Guatemalan **music** combines many different influences, but yet again it can be broadly divided between ladino and Maya. For fiestas, bands are always shipped in, complete with a crackling PA system and a strutting lead singer.

Traditional Guatemalan music is dominated by the marimba, a type of wooden xylophone that originated in Africa. The oldest versions use gourds beneath the sounding board and can be played by a single musician, while modern models, using hollow tubes to generate the sound, can need as many as seven players. The marimba is at the heart of traditional music, and marimba orchestras play at every occasion, for both ladino and indigenous communities. In the remotest of villages you sometimes hear them practicing well into the night, particularly around market day. Other important instruments, especially in Maya bands, are the *tun*, a drum made from a hollow log; the *tambor*, another drum traditionally covered with the skin of a deer; *los chichines*, a type of maracas made from

---

Caribbean fiestas and music

Fiestas in Lívingston and the Honduran Bay Islands have different traditions from those in Guatemala and swing to other rhythms. In the Bay Islands, the Creole festivals are unabashedly hedonistic affairs, much more like a Caribbean carnival than a Latin fiesta, with floats, lashings of rum punch and plenty of heavy sexual innuendo and *perrero* (doggy-style dancing). Bass-lines boom from giant stacks of speakers and the streets and dancehalls are crammed with groovers grinding to Jamaican reggae and Latino reggaeton. In Lívingston, on Guatemala's Caribbean coast, some of the best dancing you'll ever see is to the hypnotic drum patterns of punta, the music of the Garífuna (see pp.258–259), which betrays a distinctive West African heritage. The Garífuna really know how to party, and if you get the chance to attend a fiesta, be prepared for some explosively athletic shimmying and provocative hip movements – nineteenth-century Methodists were so outraged they called it "devil dancing". **Garífuna day** (Nov 26) is the ideal time to see Lívingston really celebrate, though there seems to be a punta party going on most weekends.

hollow gourds; the *tzijolaj*, a kind of piccolo; and the *chirimia*, a flute.

Mainstream ladino music reflects modern Latin American sounds, much of it originating in Miami, Panama, the Dominican Republic and Puerto Rico. The sound on the street is currently reggaeton, which uses a dancehall reggae beat, fused with hip-hop vocals and techno. Merengue – fast moving, easy going and very rhythmic – is also very popular, as is salsa.

Sports and outdoor pursuits

Guatemalans have a furious appetite for spectator sports and the daily papers always devote four or five pages to the subject. Fútbol tops the bill, and if you get the chance to see a major game it's a thrilling experience, if only to watch the crowd. There's a great website, ⓦ www.guatefutbol.com (Spanish only), dedicated to the national sport. Otherwise, baseball, boxing and basketball are all popular.

Hiking

Hiking is perhaps the most popular sport among visitors, particularly volcano climbing, which is certainly hard work but almost always worth the effort – unless you end up wrapped in cloud, that is. Guatemala has 37 volcanic peaks; the tallest is Tajumulco in the far west, which at 4220m is a serious under-taking, and should only be tackled when you've been acclimatized to an altitude of over 2000m for a few days. Among the active peaks, Pacaya is a fairly easy climb and a dramatic sight, although not always actively spewing lava, as the tour companies' photographs would have you believe. Volcano-climbing trips are organized by a number of tour groups in Antigua and Quetzaltenango (see p.109 & p.182).

Sadly, there have been some occasional **attacks** (often armed, but usually non-violent) on hikers climbing volcanoes, though Pacaya is now much safer than it was, and around the shores of Lago de Atitlán. Incidents happen randomly, so take some precautions: it's much safer to walk in a group, and check the security situation before setting out.

Sport-fishing

As a participatory sport, fishing is also popular, with excellent ocean and freshwater fishing. On the Pacific side the coast offers exceptional **sport-fishing**, with some of the best waters in the world for sailfish, as well as dorado, mahi mahi and some blue marlin, jack crevalle, yellow and black tuna, snapper and bonito. Most companies operate out of Puerto Quetzal or Iztapa. The Caribbean side, including Lago de Izabal, also offers excellent opportunities for snook and tarpon. In Petén the rivers and lakes are packed with sport fish, including snook, tarpon and peacock bass, and lakes Petexbatún, Izabal and Yaxhá all offer superb fishing. Fishing trips are organized by local agencies including the highly recommended Guatemala-based Rods and Reels (☎5502 5353, ⓦwww.rodsandreelssportfishing .com). A five-night fishing package including an eight-metre boat, captain, meals, transport connections and accommodation in Iztapa and Antigua hotels costs from US$1550 per head, based on a group of four. If this is beyond your budget and you're looking for a more casual arrangement, talk to the local fishermen in Iztapa, Sayaxché or El Estor.

Whitewater rafting

Guatemala's dramatic highland landscape and tumbling rivers also provide some excellent opportunities for whitewater rafting.

Trips down the Río Cahabón and seven other rivers are organized by Maya Expeditions, 15 Calle A 14–07, Zona 10, Guatemala City (℡2363 4955, ⊛www.mayaexpeditions.com), giving you the chance to see some very remote areas and also visit some of the country's most inaccessible Maya sites. Children as young as six can raft some rivers.

Scuba diving

Scuba diving is another growing sport, although Guatemala has little to offer compared with the splendours of the neighbouring Belizean or Honduran coastal waters. Nevertheless, there are some diving possibilities here, including Lago de Atitlán and Lago de Izabal, as well as some reasonable Pacific and Caribbean dive sites. Highly recommended for freshwater, high-altitude dives and excellent instruction are ATI Divers, based in the *Iguana Perdida* hotel in Santa Cruz, Lago de Atitlán (see p.170).

Surfing

There is some **surfing** in Guatemala, but with a strong undertow along much of the Pacific coast, conditions are not ideal. Nevertheless there's a modest surf-camp near the village of Sipacate, and you'll find reliable breaks at Iztapa. Global Surf Guatemala, 4 Calle Poniente 16A (℡5588 6655, ⊛www.globalsurfguate.com), based in Antigua, run day-courses for beginners (US$90) on the south coast of Guatemala, and regular weekend surf trips (US$210) to El Salvador.

Culture and etiquette

Guatemalans have a deserved reputation as some of the most civil, polite people in Latin America. They're nowhere near as up-front as many Latinos and quite formal in social situations. Mastering an understanding of local social etiquette will greatly enhance your trip.

Greetings

Whether you're clambering aboard a packed public minibus in the country or attending a high-society dinner party in the capital, it's normal to introduce yourself with a polite greeting of "buenos días/tardes" (good morning/afternoon or evening). Up in the highlands, if you're walking a trail or passing through a small village, it's usual to say hello to everyone you meet. It's actually very common for locals, even senior officials, to say "a sus ordenes" (literally "at your orders") as they help you out. If you're introduced to someone, a gentle handshake and a "con mucho gusto" ("pleased to meet you") is appropriate.

Clothing

There's no special dress code for women to consider when visiting Guatemala, though you might want to avoid seriously short skirts or tight tops to avert potential hassle. Generally in indigenous areas, most local women wear a calf-length skirt, but it's fine for foreigners to wear trousers or knee-length short pants. By the coast or around a hotel pool, sunbathing in a swimsuit is perfectly acceptable, though it's best to keep your bikini top on.

Guatemalan men very rarely wear shorts, except on the beach, but foreigners can do as they please without offence – except perhaps to a formal engagement.

You should bear in mind that while most Maya are proud that foreigners find their textiles attractive, clothing has a profound significance, related to their identity and history – it's not wise for women travellers to wear men's shirts or trousers, or for men to wear *huipiles*. Whether you're male or female it's best to dress fairly conservatively when entering a church; knee-length shorts and T-shirts are suitable.

Women travellers

Guatemala is, on the whole, a perfectly safe country for female travellers, and it's an extremely popular destination for thousands of solo travellers, most of whom have an amazing experience. It's best to dress modestly (see above) and avoid getting yourself into situations where trouble might arise. In towns, particularly the capital, take a taxi home after dark. Trust your instincts. Guatemalan men do not adopt especially macho mannerisms compared with attitudes in some Latin countries, indeed most are softly spoken and quite deferential to foreign women. That said, if you do encounter hassle it's best to remain firm, assertive and disinterested. As most local men are very short in stature, it's possible to adopt an authoritative stance if you're tall. Some hustlers do hang around dance clubs and bars looking to pick up gringas, but most of these guys have a wife and kids at home.

Religion

Guatemala is the least Catholic Latin-American country. It's estimated that approaching 40 percent of the population now belong to one of several dozen US-based Protestant churches – for more about this evangelical movement, see Contexts at the end of this book. Many of Guatemala's Catholics also continue to practice ancient Maya religious customs in the indigenous villages of the highlands. There has been a resurgence of interest in Maya spiritualism among young, educated Guatemalans since the end of the civil war, and attending "shamanic colleges" has become fashionable. Guatemala City also has tiny Jewish and Muslim communities.

Tipping

In restaurants a 10 percent tip is appropriate, but in most places, especially the cheaper ones, tipping is the exception rather than the rule. Taxi drivers are not normally tipped.

Toilets

The most common names are *baños* or *servicios*, and the signs are *damas* (women) and *caballeros* (men). Toilets are nearly always Western-style (the squat bog is very rare), with a bucket for your used paper. Standards vary greatly, but in general the further you are from a city, often the worse the condition. Public toilets are rare; some are quite well looked after by an attendant who charges a fee to enter and sells toilet paper, others are filthy.

Shopping

Guatemalan crafts, locally known as *artesanías*, are very much a part of Maya culture, stemming from practices that in most cases predate the arrival of the Spanish. Many of these traditions are highly localized, with different regions and even different villages specializing in particular crafts. It makes sense to visit as many markets as possible, particularly in the highland villages, where the colour and spectacular settings are like nowhere else in Central America.

Artesanías

The best place to buy Guatemalan **crafts** is in their place of origin, where prices are reasonable and the craftsmen and -women get a greater share of the profit. If you haven't the time to travel to remote highland villages, the best places to head for are Chichicastenango on market days (Thurs and Sun) and the shops and street hawkers in Antigua and Panajachel.

The greatest craft in Guatemala has to be textile weaving. Each Maya village has its own traditional designs, woven in fantastic patterns and with superbly vivid colours. All the finest weaving is done on the backstrap loom, using complex weft float and wrapping techniques. Chemical dyes have been dominant in Guatemala for over a century now, but a few weavers are returning to use natural dyes in some areas, including Lago de Atitlán where San Juan La Laguna is something of a hot-spot.

One of the best places to start looking at textiles is in Antigua's Nim Po't (see p.110), a huge store with an excellent collection of styles and designs, and myriad other crafts too. Guatemala City's Museo Ixchel is another essential visit.

Alongside Guatemalan weaving most **other crafts** suffer by comparison. However,

if you hunt around, you'll find good ceramics, masks, basketry, blankets, mats, silver and jade. Antigua has the most comprehensive collection of shops, followed by Panajachel.

Markets

For shopping – or simply sightseeing – the markets of Guatemala are some of the finest anywhere in the world. The large markets of Chichicastenango, Sololá and San Francisco el Alto are all well worth a visit, but equally fascinating are the tiny weekly gatherings in remote villages like San Juan Atitán and Chajul, where the atmosphere is hushed and unhurried. In these isolated settlements market day is as much a social event as a commercial affair, providing the chance for villagers to catch up on local news, and perhaps enjoy a tipple or two, as well as sell some vegetables and buy a few provisions. Most towns and villages have at least one weekly event; for a comprehensive list, see p.125.

Study and work

Guatemala is one of the best – and most popular – places on the continent to study Spanish. The language-school industry is big business, with around sixty well-established schools and many less reliable setups. Thousands of foreigners from all over the world choose to study Spanish in Guatemala. Similarly there are myriad opportunities for voluntary workers, and dozens of excellent projects, though little in the way of paid work.

Studying Spanish

Most **language schools** offer a weekly deal that includes four or five hours one-on-one tuition a day, plus full board with a local family. This all-inclusive package works out at between US$100 and US$260 a week depending on the school and location – most are in the US$130–170 bracket. It's important to bear in mind that the success of the exercise is dependent both on your personal commitment to study and on the enthusiasm and aptitude of your teacher – if you are not happy with the teacher you've been allocated, ask for another. Insist on

knowing the number of other students that will be sharing your family house; some schools (mainly in Antigua) pack as many as ten foreigners in with one family. Virtually all schools have a student liaison officer, usually an English-speaking foreigner who acts as a go-between for students and teachers, so if you're a complete beginner there will usually be someone around with whom you can communicate.

The first decision to make is to choose where you want to study. The three most popular choices are Antigua, Quetzal-tenango and San Pedro la Laguna. Beautiful

Antigua is undoubtedly an excellent place to study Spanish, though the major drawback is that there are so many other students and tourists here that you'll probably end up spending your evenings speaking English. **Quetzaltenango** (Xela) has a different atmosphere, with a stronger "Guatemalan" character and far fewer tourists; here students tend to mix more with locals away from school. The third most popular location is now **San Pedro La Laguna** on Lago de Atitlán, which is becoming increasingly popular with young travellers. Though standards are not generally as high as the other two places there are several decent schools and very cheap prices (some offer a non-homestay package with accommodation and private tuition for as little as US$80 a week). Other towns with schools include Cobán, Flores, Guatemala City, Huehuetenango, Monterrico, Nebaj, Panajachel, San Marcos La Laguna, San Andrés and San José in Petén, Todos Santos Cuchumatán and, in Honduras, Copán, Utila and Roatán.

Many schools lay on **after-school activities** like salsa classes, cooking, visits to villages, films and cultural lectures, and even hiking trips. In Quetzaltenango most schools have a social ethos and fund development projects in the region; many offer volunteer opportunities on these projects.

Recommended language schools

Many of the schools below have academic accreditation agreements with North American and European universities; some also have US offices – consult the schools' websites for more information. The websites ⓦwww.guatemala365.com and ⓦwww.123teachme.com have feedback from students and some good tips about the relative advantages of different study centres.

Antigua

Academia de Español Antigüeña 1 C Poniente 10 ☎7832 7241, ⓦwww.spanishacademyantiguena.com.
APPE 6 C Poniente 40 ☎7882 4284, ⓦwww.appeschool.com. Also has a school in the nearby village of San Juan del Obispo.
Los Capitanes Generales 4 Av Sur 2 ☎7832 8769, ⓦwww.loscapitanes.com.

Centro Lingüístico Maya 5 C Poniente 20 ☎7832 0656, ⓦwww.clmmaya.com.
Christian Spanish Academy 6 Av Norte 15 ☎7832 3922, ⓦwww.learncsa.com.
Cooperación 7 Av Norte 15B ☎7832 0472, ⓦwww.spanishschoolcooperacion.com.
Probigua 6 Av Norte 41B ☎7832 2998, ⓦwww.probigua.org.
Projecto Lingüístico Francisco Marroquín 7 C Poniente 31 ☎7832 2886, ⓦwww.plfm-antigua.org. Also offers classes in Maya languages.
San José El Viejo 5 Av Sur 34 ☎7832 3028, ⓦwww.sanjoseelviejo.com.
Sevilla 1 Av Sur 17C ☎7832 5101, ⓦwww.sevillantigua.com.
Tecún Umán 6 C Poniente 34A ☎7832 2792, ⓦwww.tecunuman.centramerica.com. Also has a sister school in Lago de Atitlán.
La Unión 1 Av Sur 21 ☎7832 7337, ⓦwww.launion.edu.gt.

Quetzaltenango

Casa Latina Diagonal 12 6–58, Zona 1 ☎5613 7222, ⓔsol-latino-xela@hotmail.com.
Casa Xelajú Callejón 15, Diagonal 13–02, Zona 1, ☎7761 5954, ⓦwww.casaxelaju.com.
Celas Maya 6 C 14–55, Zona 1 ☎7761 4342, ⓦwww.celasmaya.com.
Centro Bilingüe Amerindia (CBA) 12 Av 10–27, Zona 1 ☎7761 8535, ⓦwww.xelapages.com/cba.
Educación para Todos Av Cenizal 0–58, Zona 5 ☎5935 3815, ⓦwww.spanishschools.biz.
Inepas 15A Av 4–59, Zona 1 ☎7765 1308, ⓦwww.inepas.org.
Juan Sisay 15 Av 8–38, Zona 1 ☎7765 1318, ⓦwww.juansisay.com.
Kie–Balam Diagonal 12 4–46, Zona 1 ☎7761 1636, ⓦwww.kiebalam.com.
La Democracia 9 C 15–05, Zona 3 ☎7763 6895, ⓦwww.lademocracia.net.
La Paz Diagonal 11 7–38, Zona 1 ☎7761 2159, ⓦwww.xelapages.com/lapaz.
Mesoamerican Academy 10 C 16–12, Zona 1 ☎7766 9531, ⓦwww.mesoamericaspanish.org. Also offers classes in Maya languages.
Miguel de Cervantes 12 Av 8–31, Zona 1 ☎7765 5554, ⓦwww.learn2speakspanish.com.
Pop Wuj 1 C 17–72, Zona 1 ☎7761 8286, ⓦwww.pop-wuj.org.
Proyecto Lingüístico Quetzalteco de Español 5 C 2–40, Zona 1 ☎7763 1061, ⓦwww.hermandad.com. Also has a sister school on the Pacific slope.
Sakribal 6 C 7–42, Zona 1 ☎7763 0717, ⓦwww.sakribal.com.

Lago de Atitlán

Casa Rosario on the trail between the docks, San Pedro La Laguna ☎5613 6401, ⓦwww .casarosario.com.
Cooperativa 200m up from the Santiago dock, San Pedro La Laguna ☎5398 6448, ⓦwww .cooperativeschoolsanpedro.com.
Corazón Maya south of Santiago dock, San Pedro La Laguna ☎7721 8160, ⓦwww.corazonmaya.com.
Flor del Maiz south of Santiago dock, San Pedro La Laguna ☎5384 9727, ⓦwww.flordmaiz.com.
Jabel Tinamit off c/Santander, Panajachel ☎5525 1282, ⓦwww.jabeltinamit.com.
Jardín de América C el Chali, Panajachel ☎7762 2637, ⓦwww.jardindeamerica.com.
San Pedro Spanish School lakeside, between the docks, San Pedro La Laguna ☎5715 4604, ⓦwww.sanpedrospanishschool.com. Also has a sister school in San Marcos la Laguna.

Huehuetenango

Xinabajul 4 Av 14–14, Zona 5, Colonia Los Encinos ☎7764 6631, ⓔacademyxinabajul@hotmail.com.

Cobán area

Eco Cabaña San Juan Chamelco ☎7951 5898, ⓔecocabana@yahoo.com.
Oxford Language Center 4 Av 2–16, Zona 3, Cobán ☎7951 2836, ⓦwww.olcenlgish.com.

Monterrico

Proyecto Lingüístico ☎5619 8200, ⓦwww .monterrico-guatemala.com/spanish-school.htm.

Todos Santos Cuchumatán

Hispano Maya opposite *Hotelito Todos Santos* ☎5163 9293, ⓦwww.hispanomaya.org.
Nuevo Amanacer ⓔescuela_linguistica@yahoo .com.

Nebaj

Nebaj Language School 3 C, El Descanco ☎5847 4747, ⓦwww.nebaj.org.

Petén

Dos Mundos C Fraternidad, Flores ☎5830 2060, ⓦwww.flores-spanish.com.
Eco-Escuela San Andrés, Lago de Petén Itzá ☎5940 1235, ⓦwww.ecoescuelaespanol.org.
Escuela Bio-Itzá San José, Lago de Petén Itzá ☎7928 8142, ⓦwww.ecobioitza.org.
Nueva Juventud San Andrés, Lago de Petén Itzá ☎5711 0040, ⓦwww.volunteerpeten.com.

Copán, Honduras

Guacamaya two blocks north of the parque ☎651 4360, ⓦwww.guacamaya.com.
Ixbalanque three blocks west of the parque ☎651 4432, ⓦwww.ixbalananque.com.

Bay Islands, Honduras

Central America Spanish School Main St, Utila ☎425 3788, ⓦwww.ca-spanish.com. Also has branches in Roatán and La Ceiba.

Volunteer and paid work

There are dozens of excellent organizations offering voluntary work placements in Guatemala. Medical and health specialists are always desperately needed, though there are always openings in other areas, from work helping to improve the lives of street children to environmental projects and wildlife conservation. Generally, the longer the length of time you can commit to, and the higher your level of Spanish, the more in demand you'll be. The best place to start a search is on the web (or in Guatemala itself).

Two excellent organizations provide links between volunteers and projects in Guatemala. Project Mosaic Guatemala, 3 Avenida Norte 3, Antigua (☎7832 0955, ⓦwww.promosaico.org), has links to over a hundred groups, while Quetzaltenango-based Entremundos at 6 Calle 7–31, Zona 1 (☎7761 2179, ⓦwww.entremundos.org), has contacts with dozens of development projects in the Xela area and a few further afield.

As for paid work, teaching English is your best bet, particularly if you have a recognized qualification like TEFL (Teaching English as a Foreign Language). Check the English schools in Guatemala City first (listed in the phone book). There are always a few vacancies for staff in the gringo bars of Antigua, and in backpackers' hostels through the country. The *Revue* and notice boards in the popular bars and restaurants in Antigua and Quetzaltenango also occasionally advertise vacancies. Finally, in the Bay Islands steady work is available in the dive centres for dive masters and instructors, and in the bars and restaurants, though pay is poor.

Project websites and email addresses

Ak'Tenamit ⓦ www.aktenamit.org. Health, education, business training and agriculture volunteer positions in a large, established project, working with Q'eqchi' Maya in the Río Dulce region.

Animal Aware ⓦ www.animalaware.org. Help out in an animal welfare centre for abandoned pets near Sumpango.

Arcas ⓦ www.arcasguatemala.com. Volunteers needed in Petén to help rehabilitate wild animals including monkeys for release back into forests, and opportunities to help out in a sea-turtle reserve at Hawaii on the Pacific coast.

Casa Alianza ⓦ www.casa-alianza.org. Charity helping street children in Guatemala and throughout Central America. The work is extremely demanding and volunteers need to give a long-term commitment.

Casa Guatemala ⓦ www.casa-guatemala.org. Skilled workers (particularly teachers and medical staff) and helpers needed to work with street children and orphans in the Río Dulce region. Short- and long-term positions available; the minimum age is 24.

Casa Xelajú ⓦ www.casaxelaju.com/volunteer. Language school with myriad opportunities and links to social projects in the Quetzaltenango region.

Escuela de la Calle ⓦ www.escueladelacalle .org. Help educate and mentor street kids in Quetzaltenango. Linked to hiking group Quetzaltrekkers (see p.182).

Habitat for Humanity ⓦ www.habitatguate.org. House-building projects; over 25,000 homes have been built in Guatemala since 1979 by this charity.

Hospital de la Familia ⓦ www .hospitaldelafamilia.com. Doctors, nurses and medical staff needed to help out at a remote hospital in the San Marcos region of the western highlands.

Idealist ⓦ www.idealist.org. A massive database of links to a wide range of projects in the region – from ecotourism to human-rights work, with both voluntary and paid work opportunities.

NISGUA ⓦ www.nisgua.org. Coordinates the Guatemalan Accompaniment Project, which monitors human-rights workers and campaigners deemed to be at risk in Guatemala; minimum commitment of one year.

Peace Corps ⓦ www.peacecorps.gov. US institution that recruits volunteers for two-year postings throughout Central America. Must be a US citizen.

Project Honduras ⓦ www.projecthonduras.com. Portal for voluntary opportunities (mainly medical staff, teachers, architects and builders) in Honduras.

Proyecto Eco-Quetzal ⓦ www.ecoquetzal.org. Opportunities in the Verapaces region for people with experience in ecotourism, environmental education or agriculture. A three-month commitment is necessary.

Remote Area Medical Corp ⓦ www.ramusa .org. Voluntary physicians, eye specialists, surgeons, dentists, nurses and veterinarians needed to work in poor areas of Central America.

Safe Passage ⓦ www.safepassage.org. Teachers, helpers, admin staff and cooks needed to direct, support and educate children who work on the Guatemala City rubbish dump.

Upavim ⓦ www.upavim.org. Community development on the outskirts of Guatemala City, with opportunities for nursery workers and kids' tutors.

Whale Shark & Oceanic Research Center ⓦ www.wsorc.com. Utila-based whale-shark centre that investigates whale shark behaviour and migration patterns. Volunteers are sought, there's no charge, and board and lodging is provided.

Travel essentials

Costs

Guatemala is one of the cheapest countries in the Americas for travellers, though there are plenty of opportunities for a modest (or serious) splurge if you feel like it. The extremely frugal may be able to get by on around US$140 a week in most parts of the country, or below US$120 in a budget travellers' hub like San Pedro La Laguna. However, if you're after a little more comfort (travelling by shuttle bus and staying in rooms with an en-suite bathroom) you can

Useful websites

US State Department ⓦwww.travel.state.gov. "Consular information sheets" detailing the dangers of travelling in most countries of the world. The information can be a little alarmist.

British Foreign and Commonwealth Office ⓦwww.fco.gov.uk. Constantly updated advice for travellers on circumstances affecting safety in more than 130 countries.

Australian Department of Foreign Affairs ⓦwww.dfat.gov.au. Advice and reports on unstable countries and regions.

expect to spend around US$200 per head per week, if you're travelling as a couple, while solo travellers should reckon on perhaps US$240 a week. For US$60–70 per day you can expect to live quite well. Things are more expensive in regions where the local economy is tourist driven (Antigua, Guanaja and Roatán in particular), though even in these places there are some inexpensive places to stay, and it's possible to keep to a reasonable budget if you can exercise some sense of thrift.

A sales tax (IVA) of 10 percent is usually included in the price you're quoted in most hotels, restaurants and shops but is often an extra cost to be factored in when staying at smart hotels. Similarly most budget and mid-range hotel rates include the 12 percent Inguat accommodation tax, but in luxury places it's usually extra.

Crime and personal safety

Personal safety is a serious issue in Guatemala. While the vast majority of the 1.7 million tourists who come every year experience no problems at all, general crime levels are high, and it's not unknown for criminals to target visitors, including tourist shuttle buses. There is little pattern to these attacks, but some areas can be considered much safer than others. Warnings have been posted in the Guide where incidents have occurred. It's wise to register with your embassy on arrival, try to keep informed of events, and avoid travelling at night. Officially, you should carry your **passport** (or a photocopy) at all times.

It's important to try to minimize the chance of becoming a victim. Petty theft and **pickpocketing** are likely to be your biggest worry. Theft is most common in Guatemala City's Zona 1 and its bus stations, but you should also take extra care when visiting markets popular with tourists (like Chichicastenango) and during fiestas. Avoid wearing flashy jewellery and keep your money well hidden. When travelling, there is actually little or no danger to your pack when it's on top of a bus as it's the conductor's responsibility alone to go up on the roof and collect luggage.

Muggings and **violent crime** are of particular concern in Guatemala City. There's little danger in the daylight hours but don't amble around at night, when you should use a taxi. There have also been a few cases of armed robbery in Antigua and on the trails around Lago de Atitlán. The Pacaya and San Pedro volcanoes are now well-guarded and considered safe, though there have been robberies on other volcanoes, including Agua.

If you are robbed, you'll have to report it to the police, and this can be a very long process; however, most insurance companies will only pay up if you can produce a police statement.

Drugs are readily available in Guatemala, and the country is a key link in the route between Colombia and the US. Marijuana and cocaine are both readily available. Be aware that **drug offences** can be dealt with severely. Even the possession of some weed could land you in jail – a sobering experience in Guatemala. If you do get into a problem with drugs, it may be worth enquiring with the first policeman if there is a "fine" (*multa*) to pay, to save expensive arbitration later. At the first possible opportunity, get in touch with your embassy and negotiate through them; they will understand the situation better than you. The addresses of embassies and consulates in Guatemala City are listed on p.87.

Guatemala's **police** force has a poor reputation. Corruption is rampant and inefficiency the norm, so don't expect that much help if you experience any trouble. That said, they don't have a reputation for intimidating tourists. If for any reason you do find yourself in trouble with the law, be as polite as possible. **Tourist police** forces have been set up in Antigua, Panajachel and Tikal, and English-speaking officers should be available to help you out in these places.

The sheer number of **armed security guards** on the streets and posted outside restaurants and stores is somewhat alarming at first, but after a few days you get used to their presence, even if it is disconcerting to see an eighteen-year-old with a gun outside *McDonald's*.

Electricity

Power (110–120 volts) and plug connections (two flat prongs) are the same as North America. Anything from Britain or Europe will need a transformer and a plug adapter. Cuts in the supply and fluctuations in the current are fairly common.

Entry requirements

Citizens from most Western countries (including the US, UK, Canada, Australia and New Zealand and most, but not all, EU states) need only a valid passport to enter Guatemala for up to 90 days. Your 90-day stamp is also valid for travel to El Salvador, Honduras and Nicaragua (collectively known as the CA–4 nations). Passport-holders from other countries (including some Eastern European nations) qualify for a Guatemalan visa, but have to get one from a Guatemalan embassy or consulate. Citizens from most developing world nations, including much of Asia and Africa, need to apply for a visa well in advance. If you're wondering whether you'll need a visa, phone an embassy for the latest entry requirements; Guatemala has embassies in all the region's capitals.

When you arrive at Guatemalan immigration you may be asked by the official how long you plan to stay, and offered 30, 60 or 90 days. If you want 90 days, make sure you get it. Although there's no charge to enter or leave the country, border officials at land

---

Useful numbers

Police ☎120
Tourism Police ☎110
Red Cross ambulance ☎125

---

crossings commonly ask for a small fee (typically US$2.50), which is destined straight for their back pockets. You might try avoiding such payments by asking for *un recibo* (a receipt); but prepare yourself for a delay at the border.

It's possible to **extend your visit** for a further 90 days, up to a maximum of 180 days. To do this, go to the **immigration office** (*migración*) in Guatemala City at 6 Avenida 3–11, Zona 4 (☎2411 2411; Mon–Fri 8am–2.30pm). You'll need to present your passport, photocopies of each page of your passport (there's a machine in the office), a photocopy of valid credit card (front and back), and pay the extension fee (US$17); your extension is usually issued the following day. After 180 days you have to leave the CA–4 region for 72 hours; Belize and Mexico are the nearest countries.

Your 90-day CA–4 stamp is also valid for travel **in Honduras**, but border officials usually ask for an entry/exit fee of a dollar or two, even to visit Copán. Nationalities that require a visa to travel in Honduras should contact an embassy in advance; there's a list at ⓦ www.sre.hn (in Spanish only).

Guatemalan embassies and consulates

For a full list of Guatemalan embassies consult ⓦ www.minex.gob.gt (Spanish only), and click on "directorios", and the link to embajadas.

Australia Contact Tokyo.
Austria Landstrasser Hauptstrasse 21, 1030 Vienna ☎714 3570, ⓔ embajada@embaguate.co.at.
Belgium Av Winston Churchill, Brussels ☎345.90.58, ⓔ embbelgica@minex.gob.gt.
Belize 8 A St, King's Park, Belize City ☎223 3150, ⓔ embbelice1@minex.gob.gt.
Canada 130 Albert St, Suite 1010, Ottawa ON K1P 5G4 ☎613/233-7237, ⓔ embcanada@minex .gob.gt.
Germany Joachim-Karnatz-Allee, 45–47 Ecke Paulstrasse, 10557 Berlin ☎030 2206 4363, ⓦ www.botschaft-guatemala.de.

Honduras Colonia Lomas del Guijaro, c/Alfonso XIII 3716, Tegucigalpa ☎232 5018, @embhonduras @minex.gob.gt. Consulate: 8 C 5–38, Barrio Guamilito, San Pedro Sula ☎533 3560.
Italy Vía dei Colii della Farnesina, 128, 00194 Roma, ☎3638 1143, @embitalia@minex.gob.gt.
Japan 38 Kowa Building, 9th floor, Room 905, 4-12-24, Nishi-Azabu, Tokyo 106–0031 ☎380-01830, @embjapon@minex.gob.gt.
Mexico Embassy: Av Explanada 1025, Lomas de Chapultepec 11000, Mexico D.F. ☎55/5540 7520, @mexico@minex.gob.gt. Consulates: Av Independencia 326, Chetumal, Q.R. ☎983 832 3045; 1 C Sur Poniente 26, Comitán, Chiapas ☎963 632 0491; 3 Av Norte 85, Tapachula, Chiapas ☎962 625 6380.
Netherlands Java Straat 44, 2585 AP The Hague ☎302 0253, @paisesbajos@minex.gob.gt.
New Zealand Contact Tokyo.
UK 13 Fawcett St, London SW10 9HN ☎020/7351 3042, @embgranbretana@minex.gob.gt.
US 2220 R St NW, Washington, DC 20008 ☎202/745-4952, @estadosunidos@minex.gob.gt. Consulates located in many cities, including Chicago, Houston, LA, Miami, New York, San Diego and San Francisco.

Gay and lesbian travellers

Homosexuality is legal for consenting adults aged 18 or over. However, though Guatemalan society is not as overtly macho as many Latin American countries, it's wise to be discreet and avoid too much affection in public. There's a small, almost entirely male scene in Guatemala City; see p.87.

Insurance

A comprehensive travel insurance policy is essential for visitors to Guatemala. Medical insurance (you want coverage of US$2,000,000) should include provision for repatriation by air ambulance, and your policy should also cover you for illness or injury, and against theft.

Contact a specialist travel insurance company, or consider the travel insurance deal we offer (see box below). A typical **travel insurance policy** usually provides cover for the loss of baggage, tickets and – up to a certain limit – cash or cheques, as well as cancellation or curtailment of your journey. Many of them exclude so-called dangerous sports (this can mean scuba diving, whitewater rafting, windsurfing and kayaking) unless an extra premium is paid. Try to ascertain if your medical coverage will be paid as treatment proceeds or only after return home, and whether there is a 24-hour medical emergency number.

When securing **baggage cover**, make sure that the per-article limit – typically under US$1000/£500 – will cover your most valuable possession. If you need to make a claim, you should keep receipts for medicines and medical treatment, and in the event you have anything stolen, you must obtain an official statement (*una afirmación*) from the police.

Internet

Web services are now very well established in Guatemala. You'll find cybercafés in virtually every town, and in many villages too. Connection speeds are generally quite swift in the main urban centres but can be painfully pedestrian in more remote areas. **Rates** vary, starting at US$0.80 per hour in Antigua, Quetzaltenango and Panajachel (which each

---

Rough Guides travel insurance

Rough Guides has teamed up with Columbus Direct to offer you **travel insurance** that can be tailored to suit your needs. Products include a low-cost **backpacker** option for long stays; a **short break** option for city getaways; a typical **holiday package** option; and others. There are also annual **multi-trip** policies for those who travel regularly. Different sports and activities (trekking, skiing, etc) can usually be covered if required.

See our website (@www.roughguides.com/website/shop) for eligibility and purchasing options. Alternatively, UK residents should call ☎0870/033 9988; Australians should call ☎1300/669 999 and New Zealanders should call ☎0800/55 9911. All other nationalities should call ☎+44 870/890 2843.

have over a dozen cybercafés) up to US$2–3 per hour in other towns. In the Bay Islands, where all calls are classified as long distance, surfing the web can work out to be much more pricey. Virtually all language schools are online, and many offer their students discount internet rates upon enrolment.

It's also becoming increasingly easy to **reserve hotels**, tours and services via email, though few budget places are yet online. Additionally many towns and regions now boast superb **community websites** (see p.59), replete with accommodation, restaurant, cultural and entertainment information.

Laundry

Almost every town has at least one laundry; most will wash and dry a load for you for about US$3–4. Self-service laundries are very rare. Many hotels and pensiones also offer laundry facilities; the budget places often have a *pila* (sink) where you can wash your own clothes.

Mail

Postal services are quite reliable, though many locals use courier companies to send important packages and documents overseas. The best way to ensure speedy delivery is to use the main **post office** (*correos*) in a provincial capital. Post boxes are rare. Generally, an airmail letter to the US takes about a week, to Europe from ten days to two weeks. **Receiving mail** is not generally a worry as long as you have a reliable address – many language schools and tour operators will hold mail for you. The Poste Restante (*Lista de Correos*) system is no longer operational. American Express in Guatemala City (see p.86) will also keep mail if you are a card holder or have Amex traveller's cheques.

Bear in mind it's very expensive to send anything heavy home. You may want to use a specialized shipping agency instead: see the Antigua and Panajachel "Listings" for recommended companies.

Courier companies (DHL, Federal Express, etc) are establishing more and more offices throughout the region; even small towns now have them.

Maps

Rough Guides publishes a *Guatemala and Belize* map (at a scale of 1:500,000), which also covers a sizeable part of western Honduras and most of northern El Salvador. International Travel Maps and Books (ITMB) also publishes a reasonable *Guatemala* map (1:470,000). Both are printed on waterproof, tear-resistant paper.

Locally produced alternatives include offerings by Intelimaps around (US$5) and Inguat (US$2), both using a scale of 1:1,000,000. Virtually all car rental outlets will provide you with a free map, though most are pretty ropey.

The Instituto Geográfico Militar produces the only **large-scale maps** of the country. At a scale of 1:50,000, these maps are accurately contoured, although many other aspects are now very out of date. You can consult and purchase them at the institute's offices, Avenida de las Américas 5–76, Zona 13, Guatemala City (Mon–Fri 9am–5pm; ☎2332 2611, ✆www.ign.gob.gt). Most can be bought for around US$6, and photocopies of these maps are usually available in hiking areas such as Todos Santos Cuchumatán and Nebaj.

Money

Guatemala's currency, the quetzal (Q), has been very stable for over a decade. But because fluctuations can and do take place, we have quoted all prices in US dollars. (At press time, the rate was Q7.5 to US$1, Q12.1 to £1 and Q9.76 to €1). The US dollar is by far the most widely accepted foreign currency in Guatemala; that said, it is not a semi-official one, and you can't get by with a fistful of greenbacks and no quetzals. Euros and other foreign currencies are tricky to cash; try foreign-owned hotels or stores.

Debit and **credit** cards are very useful for withdrawing currency from bank ATMs but are not widely accepted elsewhere, so don't count on paying with them except in upmarket hotels and restaurants. Beware expensive surcharges (10 percent is sometimes added) if you do want to pay by a card in many stores.

Cashpoints (ATMs) are very widespread, even in small towns. It's important to note that most Central American ATMs do not accept five-digit PIN numbers; contact your bank at home in advance if you have one. You'll probably never have to use them, but it's wise to have a back-up of a few traveller's cheques (American Express is by far the most widely accepted brand, and in US dollars) or US dollar bills in case the ATM network fails or your card gets gobbled by a machine.

The country's international airports have banks for currency exchange, while at the main land-border crossings there are usually banks and a swarm of moneychangers who generally give fair rates for cash. Even at the most remote borders, you'll usually find a wad-wielding local from whom you can get some local currency.

Opening hours and public holidays

Guatemalan opening hours are subject to considerable variation, but in general most offices, shops, post offices and museums are open between 8–9am and 4–6pm, though some take an hour or so break for lunch. Banking hours are extremely convenient, with many staying open until 7pm (and some as late as 8pm) from Monday to Friday, but closing at 1pm on Saturdays. You may not always be able to exchange money after 5.30pm in some places, however, even though the bank is open.

Archeological sites are open every day, usually from 8am to 5pm, though Tikal is open from 6am to 6pm. Principal public holidays, when almost all businesses close down, are listed below, but each village or town will also have its own fiestas or saints' days when many places will be shut.

Phones

There are no area codes in Guatemala. To call a number from abroad simply dial the international access code, followed by the country code (☎502) and the number (all are eight-digit).

Guatemala has a modern, efficient telephone network, and mobile coverage is very widespread. If you need to call home it's best to head to a private telephone office or a cybercafé where calling costs are far lower

Public holidays

January 1 New Year's Day
Semana Santa The four days of Holy Week leading up to Easter
May 1 Labour Day
June 30 Army Day, anniversary of the 1871 revolution
August 15 Guatemala City fiesta (Guatemala City only)
September 15 Independence Day
October 12 Discovery of America (only banks close)
October 20 Revolution Day
November 1 All Saints' Day
December 24 Christmas Eve (from noon)
December 25 Christmas
December 31 New Year's Eve (from noon)

than using Telgua (the former state telecom company). A call to the US typically costs around US$0.15–0.30 a minute, Europe about US$0.25–0.50 and to the rest of the world upwards of US$0.50. Often calls are routed via the internet, but line quality is usually clear.

With "pay-as-you-go" **cellular phones** costing as little as US$20 (and often loaded with hundreds of free minutes) many visitors now buy one, even for a short trip. There are three main networks: Claro, Movistar and Tigo (the latter has the most comprehensive coverage). Calls to Guatemalan numbers cost around US$0.15 per minute, or around US$0.25 to call the US, other countries are much more pricey (though texts to Europe are only a quetzal or two each). All the cellular companies have promotional days offering "doble" or "triple" minutes, so if you buy a Q50 card on a triple day you'll get Q150 credited; look out for the signs in stores or carried by street vendors.

Most (but not all) North American cellular phones work fine in Guatemala, but most UK and European phones do not. If your phone is unlocked it should be possible to insert a local SIM card and use your own handset. Alternatively you could purchase a local pre-paid **phone card** and use street telephones to make calls; Telgua has the best rates and plenty of card phones. Using a **telephone** charge card is another option for North Americans. AT&T, MCI, Sprint, Canada Direct and long-distance companies all enable their customers to make calls while overseas using toll-free numbers.

To make a collect call overseas (*llamar por cobrar*), dial ☎147120 from a Telgua phone, though the system does not always function well for non–North American numbers. You should be able to send (and receive) a fax from most telecom offices and many cybercafés.

Photography

In indigenous areas and the countryside you should avoid taking pictures of children unless you get permission from their parents. Sadly children are stolen from their families every year in Guatemala, and rumours persist that Westerners steal babies for adoption. There's less of an issue in urban areas, where the population is better educated, but even here be sensitive.

Otherwise Guatemala is an exceptionally rewarding destination for photographers with outstanding scenic and human interest. It's polite to ask before taking portraits, but if you're in a marketplace using a zoom it's easy to get shots of people without being too intrusive.

Memory cards for digital cameras are quite widely available (though Compact Flash cards are not common) and print film and video tapes can be bought in any town in the country. Slide film is very rare. Many cyber-cafés have card readers and will be able to burn your pictures to a CD for around US$2.

Time

Guatemala is on the equivalent of Central Standard Time in North America, six hours behind GMT. Daylight saving is not used. There is little seasonal change – it gets light around 6am, with sunset at around 5.30pm in December, or 6.30pm in June.

Tourist information

Information about Guatemala is easy to come by inside the country, but less available in Europe or North America. In the US, you can call Inguat, Guatemala's, tourist information authority, on the toll-free number ☎1-888/464-8281, while Guatemalan embassy staff in Europe and Canada can often help out too. The material produced by Inguat is colourful, though much of it is of limited practical use. Often specialist travel agents (see pp.30–31) are excellent sources of info.

Staff at Inguat, at 7 Avenida 1–17, Zona 4, Guatemala City (☎2331 1333, ⓦwww .visitguatemala.com), are always helpful and English-speakers are available. The organiza-tion has smaller branches in Antigua, Flores, Panajachel and Quetzaltenango, and at the airports in Flores and Guatemala City. All branches should have hotel listings, transport information and dozens of brochures and leaflets. The quality of information varies, but generally the main office and the Antigua outpost are the most reliable. Inguat also helps maintain a telephone assistance line for tourists in Guatemala, ☎1500.

Two highly useful resource centres are also located in London. The Guatemalan Maya Centre, 94A Wandsworth Bridge Rd, London SW6 2TF (☎&ⓕ020/7371 5291, ⓦwww.maya.org.uk; closed Christmas–New Year, Jan, Easter & Aug), is one of the finest Guatemalan resource centres in the world. Membership (£5 annually) gives you access to a library (reference only) stocked with over 2500 books on Guatemala, along with several hundred videos and all the main periodicals. The centre hosts monthly cultural events: lectures, films and exhibitions on all things Guatemalan. It also has an outstanding textile collection, and the centre's director, Krystyna Deuss, is the acknowledged British authority on historic and contemporary Maya dress and ritual.

The other resource centre, Canning House Library, 2 Belgrave Square, SW1X 8PJ (☎020/7235 2303, ⓦwww.canninghouse .com), has the UK's largest library (Mon–Fri 2–6pm; £3 per visit) of Latin American books, with numerous shelves devoted to Guatemala and Maya issues. You have to be a member to take books out and receive its twice-yearly *Bulletin*, a review of recently published books on Latin America.

Current political analysis and an interesting and informative overview of the society, economy and environment of Guatemala and other Central American countries is provided by the London-based Latin America Bureau (Ⓦwww.lab.org.uk), an independent, nonprofit research organization.

Useful websites

The Guatemala page on the Latin American Network Information Center's website, Ⓦwww.lanic.utexas.edu, is a fine place to begin a search; here you'll find a comprehensive set of links to websites for everything from nonprofits and language schools to magazines and museums, as well as various academic and tourism resources.

Ⓦ**www.aroundantigua.com** Dedicated to Guatemala's former colonial capital, with cultural events and listings.

Ⓦ**www.atitlan.com** Concentrates on the Atitlán region, with plenty of interesting features and photography, plus some hotel and restaurant listings.

Ⓦ**www.centramerica.com** Portal with a broad range of links.

Ⓦ**www.copanruinas.com** News, reviews and links to hotels, sights and restaurants in Copán.

Ⓦ**famsi.org** The web pages of the Foundation for the Advancement of Mesoamerican Studies include academic reports from Mayanists, maps, and articles about flora and fauna.

Ⓦ**www.fhrg.org** Website of the Foundation for Human Rights in Guatemala, offering comprehensive coverage of the current human-rights situation, plus news reports.

Ⓦ**www.frmt.org** Campaigning website of Nobel Peace Prize–winner Rigoberta Menchú's foundation, with links to many pressing issues in the human rights and justice arenas. Spanish only.

Ⓦ**www.ghrc-usa.org** Website of the Washington-based Guatemala Human Rights Commission/USA, which publishes regular reports plus urgent action notices.

Ⓦ**www.guatemala365.com** Good place to begin a search for a Spanish school, with a list of professional schools, student feedback and plenty of tips.

Ⓦ**www.guatemalaweb.com** Everything from ATM locations to Maya ceremonies, though much of the practical information is out of date.

Ⓦ**www.hondurasthisweek.com** The regularly updated site of *Honduras This Week*, an English-language newspaper that's the best information source about Guatemala's neighbour, publishes reliable news reports plus interesting content from regions including Copán and the Bay Islands.

Ⓦ**www.lanic.utexas.edu** The Latin American Network Information Center's website offers a wide range of links for Guatemala and other countries in the region.

Ⓦ**www.maya.org.uk** London-based Guatemalan Maya Centre's site has good articles and links, as well as news of forthcoming UK cultural events.

Ⓦ**www.mayadiscovery.com** Strong on art and history of the ancient Maya, plus some wide-ranging cultural essays.

Ⓦ**www.mayaparadise.com** Dedicated to the Río Dulce and Lago de Izabal area, with useful information for boaters and a busy message board.

Ⓦ**www.mesoweb.com** All the latest reports about the ancient Maya.

Ⓦ**www.mimundo-jamesrodriguez.blogspot .com** Superb photojournalism from an independent Guatemala-based reporter.

Ⓦ**www.mostlymaya.com** Useful practical travel information based on first-hand experience and good cultural content.

Ⓦ**www.promosaico.org** Website of Project Mosaic Guatemala, a nonprofit volunteer work organization, has dozens of opportunities and links to numerous local organizations.

Ⓦ**www.revuemag.com** Content from the popular Antigua-based tourism and travel magazine can be downloaded in PDF format.

Ⓦ**www.stetson.edu/~rsitler/TodosSantos** Cultural content and practical coverage of the Todos Santos Cuchumatán region.

Ⓦ**www.xelapages.com** Concentrates on the Quetzaltenango area, with comprehensive language-school and business listings, plus popular discussion boards.

Travellers with disabilities

Guatemalans are extremely helpful and eager to help disabled travellers. Nevertheless, visitors with disabilities are faced with many obstacles. Wheelchair users will have to negotiate their way over cobbled streets, cracked (or nonexistent) pavements and potholed roads in cities, towns and villages. Getting around Guatemala by public transport can be exhausting for anyone, but trying to clamber aboard a packed chicken bus with a wheelchair or walking sticks, even with a friend to help, presents a whole set of other challenges. Plenty of disabled travellers do successfully get their way around the country though. Most of the main sites are connected by tourist shuttle minibuses, which pick you up from your hotel, and have a driver whose job it is to assist passengers with their luggage. Many Guatemalan hotels are low rise (and larger, upmarket places often have lifts and ramps), so it shouldn't be too difficult to find an accessible room. You'll only find disabled toilets in the most expensive hotels.

Travelling with children

It can be exceptionally rewarding to travel with children in Guatemala. Most locals, particularly in indigenous areas, have much larger families than in the West so your kids will always have some company. By bringing your children along to Guatemala, you'll take a big step toward dismantling the culture barrier and families can expect an extra warm welcome. Hotels, well used to putting up big Guatemalan families, are usually extremely accommodating.

Obviously, you'll have to take a few extra precautions with your children's health, paying particular care to hygiene and religiously applying sunscreen. Dealing with the sticky tropical heat of Petén is likely to be one of the biggest difficulties, but elsewhere humidity is much less of a problem. As young children are rarely enthralled by either modern highland or ancient Maya culture, you may want to plan some **excursions**: the giant Xocomil water park and Parque Xetulul theme park (see p.227 in the Guide) and Auto Safari Chapín (also see p.240) make great days out for kids. The Museo de los Niños and Aurora zoo in Guatemala City (see p.81) are a lot of fun too. Take extra care if you head for the Pacific-coast beaches, as every year several children (and adults) drown in the strong undertow.

If you're planning to bring a **baby** to Guatemala, you'll find disposable baby milk and nappies (diapers) are widely available in supermarkets and pharmacies; but take an extra stock if you're visiting really remote areas. Every town in the country has at least a couple of pharmacies, and medication for children is available. Breast-feeding in public is fine.

Guide

Guide

Guatemala City, Antigua and around

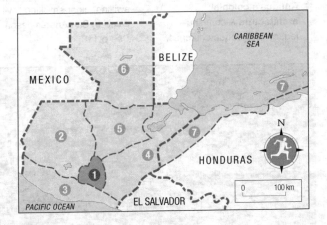

CHAPTER 1 # Highlights

✳ **Museo Nacional de Arqueología y Etnología** One of the world's most important collections of Maya sculptures and artefacts. See p.81

✳ **Volcán de Pacaya** Trek up one of Latin America's active volcanoes and explore its lava flows. See p.91

✳ **Semana Santa** Witness the sombre ceremony and processions of the continent's most fervent Easter-week celebrations. See p.101

✳ **Antigua's colonial architecture** A stunning legacy of Baroque churches, elegant mansions and graceful plazas has earned the Spanish colonial capital the designation of World Heritage Site. See pp.101–106

✳ **Gourmet dining** Antigua's restaurant scene is vibrant and eclectic, with everything from Zen Japanese to authentic Guatemalan. See pp.106–108

✳ **San Simón (Maximón)** Soak up the scene at the pagan temple of Guatemala's liquor-swilling, cigar-smoking "evil saint" in San Andrés Itzapa. See p.118

▲ Parque central, Antigua

Guatemala City, Antigua and around

S ituated just forty kilometres apart in Guatemala's highlands, the two cities of Guatemala City and Antigua could hardly be more different. The capital, Guatemala City, is a fume-filled maelstrom of industry and commerce with few attractions to detain the traveller, though a day or two spent visiting its museums and soaking up the (limited) cultural scene won't be wasted. Antigua is everything the capital is not: tranquil, urbane and resplendent with spectacular colonial buildings and myriad cosmopolitan cafés, restaurants and hotels. Not surprisingly, this is where most travellers choose to base themselves.

Guatemala City sprawls across a huge upland basin, surrounded on three sides by low hills and volcanic cones. The capital was moved here in 1776 after the seismic destruction of Antigua, but the site had been of importance long before the arrival of the Spanish. These days, its shapeless and swelling mass, ringed by shanty towns, ranks as the largest city in Central America, with a metropolitan area that's home to more than three million people; and it's the undisputed centre of politics, power and wealth.

The capital has an intensity and vibrancy that are both its fascination and its horror, and for many visitors dealing with the city is an exercise in damage limitation, as they struggle through a swirling mass of bus fumes and crowds. The centre of the city is run down and polluted, largely abandoned by the affluent middle classes and blue-chip businesses who long ago fled to the suburbs. But efforts are being made by a small group of conservationists to preserve what's left of the **centro histórico** in Zona 1, and a smattering of new cafés and bars have opened in restored buildings in the heart of the city. Some of the most exciting developments are taking place in the Cuatro Grados Norte area of Zona 4, where an expanding group of hip bars and restaurants represent the city's most interesting scene. These advances, however, have hardly transformed "Guate" into a hotbed of culture, and most travellers still choose to spend as little time as possible in the place. Nevertheless the city is the crossroads of the country, and you'll almost certainly end up here at some time, if only to hurry between bus terminals or catch a plane to Petén.

Antigua, on the other hand, is the most impressive colonial city in Central America, and its tremendous wealth of architectural riches has made it one of Guatemala's premier tourist attractions. With just 35,000 inhabitants and a small central zone, the city's graceful cobbled streets, elegant squares, churches and grand houses are ideal to explore on foot. Its renowned **language schools** also attract students from all over the world, and education and tourism are the city's prime sources of wealth.

The countryside around Antigua and Guatemala City – a delightful landscape of volcanoes, pine forests, meadows, *milpas* and coffee farms, punctuated with villages – also begs to be explored. Looming over the capital is the **Volcán de Pacaya**, one of the most active volcanoes in Latin America, which has been spewing sulphurous gas and molten rock regularly for years now. Close to Antigua the volcanoes of **Agua** and **Acatenango** are also well worth climbing, the latter offering a terrific perspective of the smoking cone of neighbouring Fuego.

There are countless interesting villages to visit in this area, including **San Andrés Itzapa**, where there is a pagan shrine to the "evil saint" San Simón; **Jocotenango**, which boasts a pair of museums dedicated to coffee and Maya music; and **San Juan del Obispo**, home to a huge colonial palace. The one

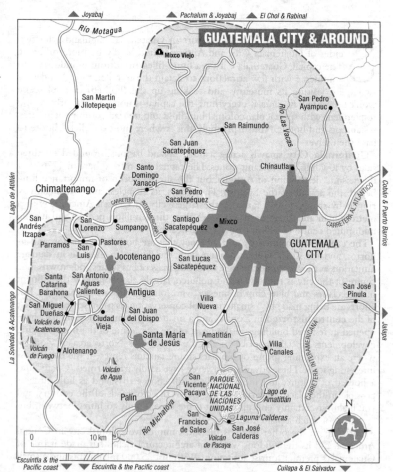

Maya ruin in the area that can compete with the lowland sites further north is **Mixco Viejo**, which is tricky to get to unless you have your own transport, but its splendidly isolated setting is tremendous. Little evidence remains of the ancient capital of **Kaminaljuyú**, today almost buried in the suburbs, but this was once one of the largest and most important cities of the Maya World.

Guatemala City and around

GUATEMALA CITY is not a place to visit for its beauty or architectural charm. If you arrive in the central area, your first impressions are grim, as a depressing vision of urban blight unfolds: potholed streets choked by fumes from rasping buses, thoroughfares blocked by street stalls and many of the city's fine buildings in a state of advanced decay. Understandably, few travellers take to *la capital*, and many avoid it completely.

But if you decide to spend a day or two in the city, it does offer some metropolitan pleasures that you won't find elsewhere in the country. There are two first-rate **museums** devoted to the ancient Maya and another to the country's terrific textile tradition. Culturally, a hip **artistic scene** is emerging in Cuatro Grados Norte, a vibrant barrio where you might catch an alternative rock band or find a DJ spinning progressive electronic mixes. It's also possible to find cinemas screening independent European and Latin American movies, as well as multi-screen theatres showing Hollywood blockbusters in vast North American-style shopping malls.

Guatemala City's **climate** is also benign: the city's altitude means that the heat here never gets too oppressive, and when you escape the pollution of the central area, the lush greenery of the outer suburbs lends a certain appeal. Its setting is certainly dramatic, positioned in a massive highland bowl split by plunging ravines.

That said, the disparities of life in the city are extreme, with glass skyscrapers towering over sprawling slums and shoeless widows peddling cigarettes to designer-clad nightclubbers. You should take a little extra care in the capital as **street crime** is a problem, mainly involving bag snatching – be particularly careful at transport terminals. Gang violence is a serious issue in the poor outer suburbs, though this rarely affects the central zones, and is highly unlikely to concern travellers.

Some history

The pre-conquest city of **Kaminaljuyú**, its ruins still scattered amongst the western suburbs, was well established here two thousand years ago. In Early Classic times (250–600 AD), the city was allied with the great northern power of Teotihuacán (near present-day Mexico City), and controlled key trade routes.

At the height of its prosperity, Kaminaljuyú was home to a population of some 50,000 and dominated the highlands. However, following the decline of Teotihuacán around 600 AD, it was surpassed by the great lowland centres, including Tikal, Calakmul and Yaxhá. By around 700 AD, Kaminaljuyú was abandoned.

Eight centuries later, in the early years of Spanish occupation, the only village in this area was La Ermita, founded in 1620. But in 1773, following months of devastating earthquakes, the Spanish were forced to flee Antigua and established a new capital at Guatemala City's present site. Early development was slow: the people of Antigua were reluctant to leave, and an 1863 census listed just 1206 residences. One of the factors retarding the city's growth was the existence of a major rival, Quetzaltenango, which competed with the capital in both size and importance, until 1902, when it was razed to the ground by a massive earthquake. After this, many wealthy families moved to the capital, finally establishing it as the country's primary city.

After recovering from more devastating seismic activity in 1917, Guatemala City has grown at an incredible rate, the flight from the fields escalating in the 1970s and 1980s as waves of internal refugees sought an escape from the civil war in the countryside. **Economic migrants** high on hope continue to flock to the capital, the resultant population explosion filling once-uninhabited deep ravines with precariously situated new barrios.

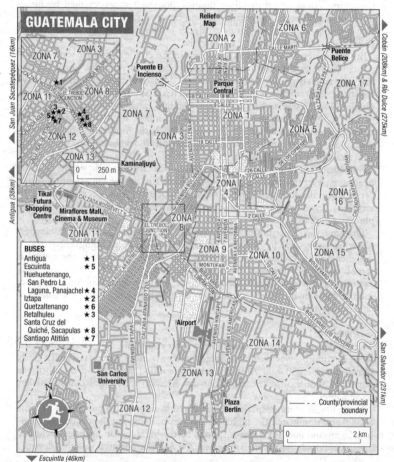

Addresses in Guatemala City

The system of **street numbering** in the capital is confusing at first, as the same numbers and street names are given to different streets in different zones. However, once learned, the system is pretty intuitive.

When it comes to finding an address, always check for the **zone** first and then the street. For example "4 Av 9–14, Zona 1" is in Zona 1, on 4 Avenida between 9 and 10 calles, house number 14. You may see street numbers written as 1a, 7a etc, rather than simply 1, 7. This is technically more correct, since the names of the streets are not One Avenue and Seven Street, but First (*primera*), Seventh (*séptima*) and so on. A capital "A" used as a suffix indicates a smaller street between two large ones: 1 Calle A is a short street between 1 and 2 calles.

A concerted effort to boost civic pride, improve transport, add greenery and address pollution has been made in the last few years as part of Mayor Arzú's "Guatemala 2020" plan to create a modern, functioning city. The mayor certainly has his work cut out: the overriding issue of security curtails investment and increases the perception of the capital as a threatening place. But at least some important groundwork has been done, and a vision of the future is apparent.

Orientation, arrival and information

Although the scale of Guatemala City, with its suburbs sprawled across some 25 **zones**, can seem overwhelming at first glance, the layout is straightforward and the central area is not that large. Like almost all Guatemalan towns, the capital is arranged on a strict grid pattern, with avenidas running north–south and calles east–west.

Broadly speaking, the city divides into two distinct halves. The northern section, centred on **Zona 1**, is the old part of town, containing the central plaza, or Parque Central, the main shopping streets (5 & 6 avs), fast-food restaurants, cinemas and many of the first-class bus company terminals.

To the south, **Zona 4** serves as a buffer between the two parts of town; here you'll find the **Centro Cívico**, home of the main administrative buildings, the tourist office, the trendy Cuatro Grados Norte area and the National Theatre.

Continuing south, the modern half of the city comprises wealthy **zonas 9 and 10**, which are separated by the main artery of Avenida La Reforma. Further south still, the neighbouring **zonas 13 and 14** hold wealthy, leafy suburbs, and are home to the airport, zoo, a cluster of guesthouses and more museums and cinemas.

Note that **security** is a concern in zonas 1, 2 and 4 after about 8pm, when it's best to get around by taxi.

Arrival

Arriving in Guatemala City is always a bit disconcerting. If you're laden with luggage, it's not a good idea to take on the bus system, and a taxi is well worth the extra cost (see p.71). For details on using the transport terminals to **move on** from the capital, see pp.88–89.

By air

Aurora airport (☎2334 7680) is in Zona 13, some way south of the centre, but close to Zona 10. The domestic terminal, though in the same complex, is separate, and entered by Avenida Hincapié. The airport is undergoing a huge renovation programme, which will create two very modern new terminals.

Several 24-hour ATMs that accept credit and debit cards are in the airport. The new international terminal will have a Banco del Quetzal where you can change US dollar cash and traveller's cheques (but don't count on exchanging euros or pounds) plus several **tourist information desks**, a Telgua phone office and a post office.

The easiest way to get to and from the airport is by **taxi**: you can pre-pay your fare from a taxi desk inside the arrivals hall, with a trip to zonas 9 or 10 costing about US$10, Zona 1 around US$12. Virtually all Guatemala City's four- and five-star hotels, as well as the guesthouses in Zona 13, offer free pick-ups from the airport, if you let them know when you're arriving. **Buses** also depart from directly outside the terminal; #83 heads through Zona 9 and Zona 4 to Zona 1 (though note the security warning below about bus travel in Guatemala City).

Regular shuttle buses run **to Antigua** from the airport (US$8–10) until about 10pm. They don't follow a fixed schedule, and only leave when they have at least four passengers, but you shouldn't have to wait long for a ride. Tickets are sold from a desk in the arrival hall. A taxi from the airport is US$30.

By bus

Travelling by **first-class** (pullman) **bus**, you'll arrive at the private terminal of the company you're using. Zona 1 has the majority of these terminals, including buses running to Petén, Mexico, Cobán and most routes to the western highlands. Note that many of these depots are located in an unsavoury part of the city; be on your guard for petty thieves and always take a taxi to your hotel. Other terminals are scattered around the southern half of the city in the safer areas of zonas 9, 10 and 15.

Second-class "chicken buses" now use two main transport terminals (both are located on the western side of the city near the Trébol junction and are just bus stops on the street with no other facilities). Routes from the western highlands, including buses from Quetzaltenango and Lago de Atitlán, use a series of bus stops on 41 Calle between 7 Avenida and 11 Avenida, Zona 7. All routes to and from southern Guatemala (including buses to the border with El Salvador, Escuintla, Retalhuleu and Mexican border) use another terminal at the junction of 8 Avenida and 4 Calle in Zona 12. Note that the old Zona 4 terminal is closed.

From Antigua it's far easier, quicker and safer to take a shuttle bus (US$5–7). Chicken buses terminate on the west side of Trébol at 1 Avenida and 3 Calle, Zona 7, from where you have to get another city bus.

For more information about the main bus companies and bus departure times, see "Moving on from Guatemala City" on pp.86–87.

Information and maps

The main Inguat **tourist office** (Mon–Fri 8am–4pm; ☎2331 1333, ℮info rmacion@inguat.gob.gt) is at 7 Avenida 1–17, Zona 4. The information desk on the ground floor has English-speaking staff and plenty of brochures; maps of Guatemala cost US$2.

City transport

Sadly robberies on the city's antiquated buses have increased in recent years, and though most of these incidents occur in the outer suburbs, many visitors (even hard-core backpackers) now opt to use taxis to get around the capital.

Useful bus routes

Heading north

83 Bolívar Airport–Zoo–Boulevard Liberación–Avenida Bolívar–5 Avenida–Zone 1

83 Terminal Airport–7 Avenida Zone 9–7 Avenida Zone 1

101 Avenida La Reforma–7 Avenida Zone 4–9 Avenida Zone 1

Heading south

101 10 Avenida & 10 Calle Zone 1–6 Avenida Zone 1–Avenida La Reforma–20 Calle Zone 10. This route passes many of the embassies, the Popol Vuh and Ixchel museums and the Los Próceres mall.

Heading west

Bolívar/Trébol Any bus marked "Bolívar" or "Trébol" will take you along the western side of the city, down Av Bolívar towards the Trébol junction, for connections to the western highlands.

If you do choose to use city buses, bear in mind that even locals are often baffled by Guate's anarchic web of **bus routes**. As most of Zona 1's streets are one-way, buses usually return along different roads. At least fares are cheap (US$0.15). After 9.30pm pick-ups and minibuses known as *ruteleros* effectively operate as buses, running along the main routes all night.

The big news is that a new network of modern buses with wheelchair access, called the **Transmetro**, using designated bus lanes and proper bus stops has been introduced. Municipal police officers patrol the green Volvo buses (known as "los verdes" by locals) for security. The first route inaugurated is of limited practical use to visitors, connecting the new Centra terminal in Zona 12 (in the far south of the city) with the civic centre in Zona 4, but the authorities plan to roll out more routes so that by 2020 the capital will have a network of efficient bus services. The next route planned will connect Zona 6 in the north of the city with Zona 4, passing through Zona 1. Tickets are US$0.15.

Taxis

Take a taxi to your hotel from the bus terminals and to get around at night. Although both metered and non-metered taxis ply the city's streets, it's best to stick to **metered cabs**: either the excellent Amarillo (℡2332 1515) cabs, which will pick you up from anywhere in the city, or Blanco y Azul (℡2360 0903), which are also reliable. The fare from Zona 1 to Zona 10 is about US$6. If you opt for a **non-metered taxi**, use your bargaining skills and fix the price beforehand.

Accommodation

Accommodation in Guatemala City suits all pockets, though you'll pay more here than in the rest of the country. Many budget and mid-range hotels are in **Zona 1**, which is not a particularly safe neighbourhood at night (or a great place for wandering around in search of a room). Many travellers are now choosing to stay close to the airport, in **Zona 13**, where there are some good options – virtually all of which offer free airport pick-ups and drop-offs, though be sure to book ahead. The disadvantage with this quiet, suburban location is that there are very few restaurants and cafés close by. Guatemala City's upmarket hotels are clustered in a relatively safe part of town, in **zonas 9 and 10**, within reach of the "Zona Viva", where there's a glut of restaurants and bars; there's one good budget Zona 10 option, too.

Zona 1

Hotel Colonial 7 Av 14–19 ☎2232 6722, ⓦwww.hotelcolonial.net. Attractive, good-value Spanish-style hotel with a pleasingly prim and proper air created by some classy wrought ironwork and tiling. The three classes of rooms (some without private bathroom) are well kept and have solid dark-wood furniture; most have cable TV. Parking available. ③–④

Hotel Fénix 7 Av 15–81 ☎2251 6625. Price-wise it's a winner, though this venerable place is showing its age. Offers clean, basic rooms (some with private bath) and has a quirky café downstairs. ②–③

Hotel PanAmerican 9 C 5–63 ☎2232 6807, ⓦwww.hotelpanamerican.com.gt. Historic hotel a block from the Parque Central, with a strong Guatemalan identity and a formal, civilized atmosphere. The 60 spacious rooms all have cable TV and private bathrooms, and the rate includes airport transfer. Try the restaurant for Sun breakfast, which is superb. ⑦

Hotel Posada Belén 13 C A 10–30 ☎2253 4530, ⓦwww.posadabelen.com. A great choice in the historic centre, this peaceful refuge is run by the hospitable and English-speaking Sanchinelli family. Occupies a beautiful old building, with a gorgeous garden patio and plenty of quiet areas for book reading. Excellent home-cooked meals are served in the stately dining room. Excursions, including walking tours of the city centre can be arranged. No children under 5. ⑥

Hotel Spring 8 Av 12–65 ☎2232 2858, ⓦwww.hotelspring.com. Long-established place, occupying a rambling structure in a safe location right in the heart of town. Rooms vary greatly, and some have private bathroom; the budget options are a little sparse. There's a pretty courtyard and a café. Popular, so book ahead. ③–④

Zonas 9 and 10

Camino Real 14 C 0–20 ☎2333 3000, ⓦwww.caminoreal.com.gt. Guatemala's first five-star hotel, in the heart of the Zona Viva, though the chintzy decor now looks rather dated. Good business facilities, the spa offers massages and treatments, and the sports facilities – including two pools, a spacious gym and floodlit tennis courts – are second to none. Ask for a corporate rate. Rooms from US$155. ⑨

Hotel Carillon 5 Av 11–25 Zona 9 ☎2332 4267, ⓔhcarillon@guate.net.gt. Slightly unusual but a decent-value place in a handy location. All the rooms in this small hotel have wood-panelled walls and carpeted floors, en-suite bathrooms and cable TV; some can be a little stuffy however. Breakfast is included. ⑥

Hotelito 12 C 4–51 ☎2339 1811, ⓦwww.hotelito.com. Squarely aimed at the hip hotel market, this small, modish hotel has fourteen stylish, updated rooms where the soothing cream furnishings are offset with parquet wood floors and tasteful photographs. There's a quality garden restaurant, (free) internet access and a great lounge bar. Call for a free ride from the airport. Double rooms US$120. ⑨

Hotel Real Inter-Continental 14 C 2–51 ☎2379 4444, ⓦwww.interconti.com. The city's most stylish luxury hotel. A monumental lobby featuring fine art and modern sculpture by leading Guatemalan artists sets the tone, and you'll find French, Japanese and international restaurants, plus a heated outdoor pool. The 239 wonderful rooms are supremely comfortable with great beds and Egyptian cotton sheets, CD players and preloaded iPods, and many have good city views. From US$150. ⑨

Xamanek Inn 13 C 3–57 ☎2360 8345, ⓦwww.mayaworld.net/xamanek. This is an excellent option for budget travellers, with three dorms (each with four or five beds; US$14 per head), private rooms (#5 is a good deal for couples), excellent showers, lockers, kitchen, laundry, internet and a library with DVDs, magazines and books; rates include breakfast. The Zona Viva location is as safe as it gets in the capital, and there's a multitude of bars and restaurants on your doorstep. Dorm beds US$14, rooms US$24–50. ④

Zona 13

El Aeropuerto Guest House 15 C A 7–32 ☎2385 8400, ⓦwww.hotelaeropuerto.centroamerica.com. Convenient for the airport this option has comfortable rooms, some a little musty, with or without private bathroom. There's a grassy garden area, a bar and free internet and continental breakfast. ⑥

Airport Inn 8 Av 17–74 ☎2261 2963, ⓦwww.theairportinn.com. Set on a quiet street this functional place has rock-bottom rates, free internet, a garden, and sitting room with TV. A complimentary breakfast is served from 5am. Call for a free lift from the airport. Dorm beds US$10, rooms ②–⑤

Casablanca 15 Calle C 7–35 ☎ 2261 3129, ⓦ www.casablancagt.com. A superb new guesthouse, in a tranquil location with very stylish accommodation. All rooms are light, airy and spacious, with private bathrooms (most en-suite) and good storage. There's a well-stocked bar and an attractive sitting room, parking, and meals can be prepared if ordered in advance. Breakfast and airport transfers are included. ⑥

Dos Lunas 21 C 10–92 ☎ 2261 4248, ⓦ www.xelapages.com/doslunas. The area's original guesthouse and still top of the pack, thanks to the indefatigable efforts of owner Lorena Artola, a fluent English-speaker. Comfortable rooms, with attractive bedspreads and reading lights are spread between two adjoining houses, or book the stylish new suite (with kitchenette) for more space. Lorena offers informed travel advice, and can arrange shuttle buses and taxis and almost anything else

you'll need. Free airport pick-up and drop-off, internet and wi-fi, and a filling breakfast. Very popular, so book well ahead. US$14 per bed, double with bath. ④

Hostal Los Volcanes 16 C 8–00 ☎ 2360 3232, ⓦ www.hostallosvolcanes.com. Decent B&B in a modern house close to the airport where all rooms have TV and some have private bath. There's a little garden in the back, two sitting rooms, and breakfast is included. Dorm US$18 per head; doubles ④–⑤

Hostal Villa Toscana 16 C 8–20 ☎ 2261 2854, ⓦ www.hostalvillatoscana.com. An immaculate new guesthouse with stylish, very well-presented rooms, with neutral colour schemes contrasting with vibrant Maya textiles; all have cable TV, #9 has a balcony and the suite has a private terrace. A big breakfast is included, there's ample parking and free internet. Keenly priced. ⑥

The City

Sights are slim on the ground in Guatemala City, but a handful of places are well worth your attention while you're here. The Ixchel, Popol Vuh and archeological **museums** are particularly good, while a few impressive renovated colonial-era buildings can be found in Zona 1. For nightlife head for the Zona Viva in Zona 10, while Zona 1 bustles with big-city streetlife.

▲ Guatemala City cathedral

Zonas 1 and 2: the old city

The hub of the old city is **Zona 1**, which is also the busiest part of town. Zona 1 is the run-down **centro histórico**, a world of low-slung, crumbling nineteenth-century town houses and faceless concrete blocks, broken pavements and car parks, noise and dirt. Tentative signs of regeneration are emerging, as a committed group of conservationists attempts to preserve the capital's heritage, and clusters of new bars and cafés are opening in historic buildings. But with the area beset by social problems, it's a process that will take decades to achieve and is dependent on the planned replacement of Guatemala's trademark thundering, fume-belching buses with the Trans-metro (see p.71). That said, the streets, thick with street vendors, harbour a certain brutal fascination and are undeniably the most exciting part of the capital.

The Parque Central and around

Zona 1's northern boundary runs just behind the Palacio Nacional, taking in the **Parque Central**, a square that forms the country's political and religious centre and the point from which all distances in Guatemala are measured. This plaza, with its giant Guatemalan flag, was originally the scene of a huge central market, which now operates from a covered site behind the cathedral (see p.76). The square is a strangely soulless place, patronized by bored taxi-drivers, *lustra-dores* (shoeshiners) and plenty of pigeons. It only really comes alive on Sundays and public holidays when a tide of Guatemalans descends on the square to stroll, chat and snack (or visit the excellent weekly *huipil* market).

Most of the imposing structures that face the parque today were put up after the 1917 earthquake, with the notable exception of the blue-tile-domed **cathedral** (daily 8am–noon & 3–7pm; free), which was completed in 1868. For years its grand facade, merging the Baroque and the Neoclassical, dominated the square, dwarfing all other structures. Its solid, squat form was designed to resist the force of earthquakes and, for the most part, it has succeeded. In 1917 the bell towers were brought down and the cupola fell, destroying the altar, but the central structure, though cracked and patched up over the years, remains intact. Inside there are three main aisles, all lined with arching pillars, austere colonial paintings and intricate altars supporting an array of saints. Some of this collection was brought here from the original cathedral in Antigua when the capital was moved in 1776. The cathedral's most poignant aspect is found outside: etched into the twelve pillars that support the entrance railings are the names of thousands of the **"disappeared"** victims of the civil war – children, parents and priests – including an astounding number from the department of El Quiché.

Presiding over the entire northern end of the square, the gargantuan stone-faced **Palacio Nacional** (entrance by tour only, in English or Spanish, daily 9am–4pm; free) faces south towards the neon maze of Zona 1. The palace was started in 1939 under the auspices of President Ubico – a characteristically grand gesture from the man who believed that he was a reincarnation of Napoleon – and completed a year before he was ousted in 1944. For decades the palace housed the executive branch of the government, and periodically its steps have been fought over by assorted coupsters. The interior of the palace is set around two attractive Moorish-style courtyards, with the most impressive rooms being the **Salas de Recepción**, at the front of the second floor. Along one wall is a row of flags and the country's coat of arms, topped with a stuffed quetzal, while the stained-glass windows represent key aspects of Guatemalan history. Back in the main body of the building the stairwells are decorated with

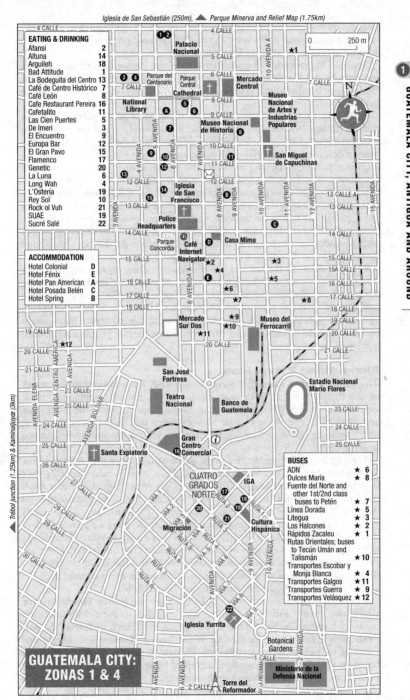

Iglesia de San Sebastián (250m), ▲ Parque Minerva and Relief Map (1.75km)

4 CALLE

EATING & DRINKING

Afansi	2
Altuna	14
Arguileh	18
Bad Attitude	1
La Bodeguita del Centro	13
Café de Centro Histórico	7
Café León	8
Cafe Restaurant Pereira	16
Cafetalito	11
Las Cien Puertes	5
De Imeri	3
El Encuentro	9
Europa Bar	12
El Gran Pavo	15
Flamenco	17
Genetic	20
La Luna	6
Long Wah	4
L'Ostería	19
Rey Sol	10
Rock ol Vuh	21
SUAE	19
Sucré Salé	22

ACCOMMODATION

Hotel Colonial	D
Hotel Fénix	E
Hotel Pan American	A
Hotel Posada Belén	C
Hotel Spring	B

Palacio Nacional

Parque del Centenario

Parque Central

Cathedral

Mercado Central

National Library

Museo Nacional de Artes y Industrias Populares

Museo Nacional de Historia

San Miguel de Capuchinas

Iglesia de San Francisco

Police Headquarters

Parque Concordia

Café Internet Navigator

Casa Mima

Mercado Sur Dos

Museo del Ferrocarril

San José Fortress

Teatro Nacional

Banco de Guatemala

Estadio Nacional Mario Flores

Gran Centro Comercial

Santa Expiatorio

CUATRO GRADOS NORTE

IGA

Migración

Cultura Hispánica

Iglesia Yurrita

Botanical Gardens

Ministerio de la Defensa Nacional

Torre del Reformador

Trébol junction (1.25km) & Kaminaljuyu (3km)

BUSES

ADN	★ 6
Dulces María	★ 8
Fuente del Norte and other 1st/2nd class buses to Petén	★ 7
Línea Dorada	★ 5
Litegua	★ 3
Los Halcones	★ 2
Rápidos Zacaleu	★ 1
Rutas Orientales; buses to Tecún Umán and Talismán	★ 10
Transportes Escobar y Monja Blanca	★ 4
Transportes Galgos	★ 11
Transportes Guerra	★ 9
Transportes Velásquez	★ 12

GUATEMALA CITY: ZONAS 1 & 4

0   250 m

GUATEMALA CITY, ANTIGUA AND AROUND

1

murals, again depicting historical scenes, mixed in with images of totally unrelated events: one wall shows a group of idealized pre-conquest Maya, and another includes a portrait of Don Quixote.

Opposite the cathedral, the western side of the Parque Central merges into the **Parque del Centenario**, an unremarkable concrete expanse with an ugly, shell-shaped bandstand that is occasionally used for live concerts and evangelical get-togethers.

Around the back of the cathedral is the hulking **Mercado Central** (Mon–Sat 6am–6pm, Sun 9am–noon), with a miserable mini-plaza and car park on its roof. Taking no chances, the architect of this building, which replaced an earlier version destroyed in the 1976 earthquake, apparently modelled the structure on a nuclear bunker, sacrificing any aesthetic concerns to the need for strength. Inside, you'll find textiles, leatherware and jewellery on the top floor; fruit, vegetables, snacks, flowers and plants in the middle; and **handicrafts**, mainly basketry and *típica*, in the basement. Unexpectedly, the market is a reasonably good spot to buy traditional weaving, with a comprehensive range of cloth from all over the country. It is only visited by a trickle of tourists so prices are fair and the traders are very willing to bargain. This was once the city's main food market but these days it's just one of many, and by no means the largest.

A block east of the market and one block south along 10 Avenida, you reach one of the city's less well known museums, **Museo Nacional de Historia**, 9 Calle 9–70, Zona 1 (Mon–Fri 9am–4.30pm; US$1.40), which features a selection of artefacts relating to Guatemalan history, including documents, clothes and paintings. Probably the most interesting displays are the photographs by Eadweard Muybridge, who, in 1875, was one of the first people to undertake a study of the country.

Along 6 and 7 avenidas

The garish heart of Zona 1 is formed by **6 and 7 avenidas**, running south of the Parque Central, thick with clothes shops, restaurants, cinemas, neon signs and bus fumes. What you can't buy in the shops is sold on the pavements, and *McDonald's* and *Pizza Hut* are all very much part of the scene. By 10pm or so, however, the streets are largely deserted, left to the cigarette sellers and street urchins.

Heading down 7 Avenida, the main **post office** (Mon–Fri 8.30am–5pm, Sat 8.30am–1pm), at the junction of 12 Calle, is a spectacular Moorish-style building with a marvellous arch that spans the road. From here it's a short walk to **Casa Mima**, at the corner of 14 Calle and 8 Avenida (Mon–Fri 9am–12.30pm & 2–5.30pm, Sat 9am–5pm; US$2.50), an immaculately restored late nineteenth-century town house. Inside, there's a terrific collection of original Moderne, Art Deco and French neo-Rococo furnishings, offering a fascinating glimpse of a wealthy middle-class household. There are excellent explanatory leaflets, and usually an English-speaking guide, plus a delightful little café, with good coffee and cookies, on the rear patio. Regular art exhibitions and book presentations are hosted here.

A block and a half west of here on 14 Calle are the **Police Headquarters**, which occupy an outlandish-looking mock castle complete with imitation medieval battlements. Next door, on 6 Avenida, the church of **Iglesia de San Francisco** is famous for its carving of the Sacred Heart, which, like several other of its paintings and statues, was brought here from Antigua. Building began in 1780, but was repeatedly interrupted by seismic activity – it's said that cane syrup, egg whites and cow's milk were mixed with the mortar to enhance its strength.

South along 6 Avenida, things go into a slow but steady decline as the commercial chaos starts to get out of control and the pavement is swamped by temporary stalls selling clothes and pirated CDs. On the left-hand side of 6 Avenida, beneath the trees, **18 Calle** becomes distinctly sleazy, the fried-food stalls mixed in with grimy nightclubs and "streap-tease" joints. By night, the streets are patrolled by prostitutes, and the local hourly-rate hotels are protected by prison-like grilles. Night or day it's best avoided.

On the east side of a square just off 9 Avenida the excellent **Museo del Ferro-carril** (Mon–Fri 9am–5pm, Sat & Sun 10am–5pm; free) is a museum dedicated to the history of Guatemalan railways. This splendidly renovated museum building was Guatemala City's main **train station** until it was mysteriously burnt down in 1996, with all its documents and records going up in smoke the night before auditors were due to start investigating the finances of the state railway company. Passenger trains are no longer running in Guatemala but you can get a great perspective of how the old network functioned here. There are several old steam engines and carriages to clamber over and examine, plus rooms stuffed with railway curiosities including staff uniforms and tickets as well as some fascinating monochrome photographs. Also on show are several lovingly polished classic cars, including a curvaceous chrome-bumpered Jaguar.

Back on 6 Avenida, just south of 18 Calle, is **Sur Dos**, the main food market (daily 6am–6pm), housed in a vast, multicoloured hangar. Traders who can afford it pay for a space inside, while those who can't spread themselves along the surrounding streets, which are littered with rubbish and rotten fruit. At the end of this extended block the character of the city is radically transformed as the aging and claustrophobic streets of Zona 1 give way to Zona 4 and the Centro Cívico.

North to Zona 2 and the Parque Minerva

North of the old city centre is Zona 2, bounded by a deep-cut ravine that prevents the sprawl from spreading any further in this direction. Three blocks north of the Parque Central, 6 Avenida passes a small residential square, the location where **Monsignor Juan José Geradi** (see Contexts, p.411) was bludgeoned to death on April 26, 1998, two days after publishing his REMHI report into the civil war atrocities. There's a modest stone and bronze monument to Geradi in the square, and flowers and candles are often laid at the garage door of his former residence where the murder was committed. Next to the house, on the east side of the square, the modern Iglesia de San Sebastián is another place of pilgrimage where services are held on the anniversary of his death.

Continuing north along 6 Avenida, it's a further 1.5km to the quirky attraction **Mapa en Relieve**, a **relief map of Guatemala** which covers 2500 square metres and has a couple of viewing towers. The map was finished in 1905 and designed to have running water flowing in the rivers, although the taps are usually shut off. Its vertical scale is out of proportion to the horizontal, making the mountains look incredibly steep. It does nevertheless give you a good idea of the general layout of the country, from the complexity of the highlands to the sheer enormity of Petén. Unsurprisingly, given the perpetual border squabbles between the two countries, Belize is included as Guatemalan territory.

The new city

South of Zona 1, the **new city** is far more spread out and the roads are much broader. The first zone you enter is Zona 4, from where, continuing south, the new city roughly divides into two, split down the middle by Avenida La Reforma. Zonas 10 and 14, on the east side of Avenida La Reforma, form the smartest part of town, with banks, hotels, restaurants, boutiques and walled residential compounds – the natural habitat of Guatemala's wealthy elite. The western half, zonas 9 and 13, incorporating several museums, the zoo and airport and more residential suburbs, is less exclusive, but still a nice part of town.

Zona 4, the Centro Cívico and around

At the southern end of the old city, the **Centro Cívico** spans the boundaries of zonas 1 and 4. A collection of concrete multistorey administrative buildings, mainly dating from the 1960s, the civic centre includes the **Banco de Guatemala** on 7 Avenida, which is bedecked with bold modern murals and stylized glyphs designed by Dagoberto Vásquez recounting Guatemala's history and the conflict between the Spanish and Maya.

Perched on a small hilltop a few blocks west is the landmark **Teatro Nacional**, also known as the Miguel Ángel Asturias cultural centre, one of the city's most prominent and unusual structures. It's well worth the climb to the top for the superb **views** across the city. Completed in 1978 and designed by Guatemalan architect (and artist) Efraín Recinos, its form evokes a huge ship, painted blue and white, with portholes as windows. The complex, which also includes an open-air theatre, was actually partly built over the foundations of the **San José Fortress**, a nineteenth-century castle that was all but destroyed during the 1944 revolution, though a few of original battlements survive.

Back on 7 Avenida, you'll find the main office of the country's tourist board, **Inguat** (see p.70 for details). Just off 7 Avenida is **Cuatro Grados Norte**, a hip, new and (largely) pedestrianized enclave centred around Vía 5 that's thick with warehouse-style restaurants and bars plus fashionable shops, as well as two **cultural centres**: the Instituto Guatemalteco Americano and the Centro Cultural de España (see p.87).

Continuing south on 7 Avenida, you pass the **Iglesia Yurrita**, an outlandish building designed in an exotic neo-Gothic style that belongs more to horror movies than to the streets of Guatemala City. It was finally completed in 1944, forty years after originally commissioned as a private chapel by the rich philanthropist Felipe Yurrite Casteñeda. His house, in the same style, stands alongside. The church, also known as Nuestra Señora de las Angustias, is usually open to the public (Tues–Sun 8am–noon & 3–6pm), and is well worth a look as the inside – which contains a fabulous carved wooden altar – is just as wild as the exterior.

A couple of blocks south of here is the illuminated **Torre del Reformador**, at the junction of 2 Calle. Guatemala's answer to the Eiffel Tower, this steel structure was built along the lines of the Parisian model, in honour of President Barrios, who transformed the country between 1871 and 1885; a bell in the top of the tower is rung every year on June 30 to commemorate the Liberal victory in the 1871 revolution.

About 300m southwest of the Centro Cívico on Avenida Bolívar, the **Santuario Expiatorio** (also known as the Iglesia Santa Cecilia de Don Bosco) is a superb modern church designed by a then-unqualified Salvadorean architect in the shape of a fish. It's part of a church-run complex that includes clinics and schools, and is well worth a browse, above all for the fantastic mural running down the side of the interior, which depicts the Crucifixion and Resurrection with vivid realism.

Zona 10: along Avenida La Reforma

Heading south of Zona 4 to Zona 10, the first place of note on Avenida La Reforma – the main artery in the south of the city – is the **Botanical Gardens** (Mon–Fri 8am–3pm, Sat 9am–noon; US$1.30) of San Carlos University. Inside, you'll find a beautiful, small garden with a selection of species, all neatly labelled in Spanish and Latin. In the grounds, there's also an anachronistic **natural history museum**, with a collection of mouldy stuffed birds, which includes a quetzal, and curios such as a llama skeleton, swordfish swords and some horrific pickled rodents. Continuing south along Reforma you pass the **Ministerio de la Defensa Nacional**, built in the style of a toy fort.

Far more interesting, however, are the two privately owned **museums** on the campus of the University Francisco Marroquín, reached by following 6 Calle Final off Avenida La Reforma, heading east. **Museo Ixchel** (Mon–Fri 9am–5pm, Sat 9am–12.50pm; US$3; Ⓦwww.museoixchel.org) is a striking, purpose-built edifice designed loosely along the lines of a Maya temple. The capital's best-organized museum, the Ixchel is dedicated to Maya culture, with particular emphasis on traditional weaving. It contains a stunning collection of hand-woven fabrics, including some very impressive examples of ceremonial costumes, with explanations in English. There's also information about the techniques, dyes, fibres and weaving tools used, and the way in which costumes have changed over the years. Although the collection is by no means comprehensive, and the costumes lose some of their impact and meaning when taken out of the villages where they're made, this is a fascinating exhibition. The building also houses a large library, and permanent exhibitions of paintings by Guatemalan artist Andrés Curruchich, who painted scenes of rural life around San Juan Comalapa, and Carmen Peterson, who depicted traditional costumes on canvas. Don't miss the very good miniature *huipil* collection in the basement, where there's also a café.

Next door, on the third floor of the *auditorio* building, is the excellent **Popol Vuh Archeological Museum** (Mon–Fri 9am–5pm, Sat 9am–1pm; US$3.50, students US$2; Ⓦwww.popolvuh.ufm.edu.gt). Standards here are just as high as at the Ixchel, but this time the subject is archeology, with an outstanding collection of artefacts from sites all over the country. The small museum is divided into Preclassic, Classic, Postclassic and Colonial rooms and all the exhibits are of top quality. The Preclassic room contains some stunning ceramics, stone masks and *hongo zoomorfo* (sculptures shaped like mushroom heads), while highlights of the Classic room include an altar from Naranjo, some lovely incense burners and a model of Tikal. In the Postclassic room is a replica of the Dresden Codex, one of only three extant pre-conquest Maya books, while the Colonial era is represented by assorted ecclesiastical relics and processional crosses.

A little south and east of here, centred around 10 Calle and 3 Avenida, is the swankiest commercial part of town, the **Zona Viva**, a tight bunch of expensive hotels, office blocks, restaurants, nightclubs and boutiques. This area, and the surrounding leafy streets (where the mansions' owners have numerous servants to keep the lawns clipped), has clearly escaped the Third World. If you've spent some time in the impoverished highland villages, the ostentation on show in this little enclave can come as quite a shock.

At the bottom of Avenida La Reforma is a giant roundabout known as **Parque Obelisco** – or Parque La Independencia – a regular destination for national celebrations; close by is the **Los Próceres** shopping mall. To get to Avenida La Reforma from Zona 1, take bus #82 from 10 Avenida, past the Iglesia Yurrita, and all the way along Avenida La Reforma. La Reforma is a two-way street, so you can return along the same route.

EATING & DRINKING

Café Barista	13
China Queen	9
Donde Mikel	4
El Establo	8
Kahlua	10
Olivadda	2
Piccadilly	3
Rattle & Hum	12
Schlotzsky's	7
Sopho's	5
Tacontento	6
Tamarindos	1
El Tapeo	11

ACCOMMODATION

Camino Real	F
Holiday Inn	D
Hotel Carillon	A
Hotelito	C
Hotel Real Inter-	
Continental	E
Xamenek Inn	B

GUATEMALA CITY: ZONAS 9 & 10

Zona 14 and around

Heading further south into Zona 14, Avenida La Reforma becomes **Avenida Las Américas**, where things become even more exclusive, with many of the large walled compounds belonging to embassies. At the southern end of the avenida, behind a statue of Pope John Paul II, is the **Plaza Berlín**, from where there are stunning views of the Pacaya volcano – it's a popular spot with picnicking families at weekends, and there are also several food and drink stalls here.

To the east, the main highway to the border with El Salvador runs out through zonas 10 and 15. As the road leaves the city, it climbs a steep hillside and passes through one of the most exclusive and expensive residential districts in the country, where every house has a superb view of the city below, and most are ringed by ferocious fortifications.

Zonas 9 and 13

The western side of Avenida La Reforma falls into **Zona 9**, a mixed suburb of middle-class housing, a restaurant and hotel or two and an eclectic array of businesses. Sights are slim on the ground, though **Plaza España**, at the junction of 7 Avenida and 12 Calle, is an attractive square that's marked by a fountain. This crossroads was once the site of a statue of King Carlos III of Spain, torn down when independence was declared, but some superb tiled benches dating from colonial times have survived.

To the southwest in **Zona 13**, the **Parque Aurora** houses the city's **zoo** (Tues–Sun 9am–5pm; US$2.50, children US$1; ⓦwww.aurorazoo.org.gt). One of the best in Central America, animals are divided into three main geographical zones. You'll find lions, hippos and giraffes in the African section; Bengal tigers, Indian elephants and the reticulated python (the world's longest snake) in the Asian area; tapirs, monkeys, and virtually all the continents' big cats, including some well-fed jaguars, in the Americas region. The zoo is also open on full moon nights, which are excellent for seeing nocturnal animals.

Just around the corner, the **Museo de los Niños** (Tues–Thurs 8am–noon & 1–5pm, Fri 8am–noon & 4–6 pm, Sat & Sun 10am–1.30pm & 2.30–6pm; US$4.50), the Museum for Children, is slightly more recreational than educational, with a huge ball-game room and trampolines as well as an operating theatre display, a hands-on music room and a giant jigsaw puzzle of Guatemala.

Just 250m to the east of the Museo de los Niños is a collection of state-run **museums** (all Tues–Fri 9am–4pm, Sat & Sun 9am–noon & 1.30–4pm). The best of these by far is the **Museo Nacional de Arqueología y Etnología** (US$4), which has a world-class selection of Maya artefacts, though the design and displays are very antiquated, and most labels are in Spanish only. The collection has sections on prehistoric archeology and ethnology and includes some wonderful stelae from Machaquilá and Dos Pilas, a re-creation of a royal tomb from Río Azul, spectacular jade masks from Takalik Abaj and a stunning replica of a wooden lintel from Tikal's temple IV. However, it's the exhibits collected from Piedras Negras, one of the most remote sites in Petén, that are most

▲ Altar at the Museo Nacional de Arqueología y Etnología

impressive. Stela 12, dating from 672 AD, brilliantly depicts a cowering captive king begging for mercy; also on display is a monumental carved stone throne (J–6) from the same site, richly engraved with superb glyphs and decorated with a twin-faced head.

Opposite the archeological museum, the **Museo Nacional de Arte Moderno** (US$1.50), which also suffers from poor presentation, boasts some imaginative geometric paintings by Dagoberto Vásquez, vibrant semi-abstract work by indigenous artist Rolando Ixquiac Xicará and a collection of startling exhibits of Efraín Recinos, including a colossal marimba–tank sculpture. The permanent collection also holds a selection of the bold Cubist art and massive murals by Carlos Mérida, Guatemala's most celebrated artist, which draws strongly on ancient Maya tradition. At the rear of the museum is a terrific **sculpture garden**, with contemporary work in white marble from international artists including Gé Pellini and Canadian Pascual Archambault.

Finally, the **Museo Nacional de Historia Natural** (US$1.50) is probably the most neglected of the trio of museums, featuring a range of mouldy-looking stuffed animals from Guatemala and elsewhere as well as a few mineral samples. About 200m east of here is a touristy handicraft market on 11 Avenida. To get to any of these museums take bus #83 from 10 Avenida in Zona 1, or from 6 Avenida in Zona 9.

The final point of interest in the southern half of the city is the **Ciudad Universitária**, the campus of San Carlos University, in Zona 12. A huge complex, it is heavily decorated with vivid political graffiti. The university, originally founded in Antigua by Dominican priests in 1676, is probably the best in Central America; it has an autonomous constitution and is entitled to five percent of the government's annual budget. The university also has a long history of radical dissent and anti-government protest, and hundreds of its students were victims of repression and political killings. Buses marked "Universitária" travel along 4 Avenida through Zona 1 to the campus.

Zona 7: the ruins of Kaminaljuyú

Way out on the western edge of the city, the modest ruins of **Kaminaljuyú** (daily 9am–4pm; parking free, temple access US$7) are all that's left of a city that once housed around fifty thousand people, three hundred mounds and thirteen ball courts. Unlike the massive temples of the lowlands, these structures were built of adobe, and most of them have been lost to erosion and urban sprawl. Today the archeological site, incorporating only a tiny fraction of the original city, is little more than a series of earth-covered mounds and a favourite spot for footballers and romantic couples. A couple of sections have been cut into by archeologists, and by peering through the fence you can get some idea of what lies beneath the grassy exterior, but it's virtually impossible to get any impression of Kaminaljuyú's former scale and splendour – for that you'll have to visit the new Miraflores museum (see p.83).

To get to the ruins, take bus #35 from 4 Avenida in Zona 1.

A history of Kaminaljuyú

First settled as far back as around 400 BC, Kaminaljuyú had grown to huge proportions by 100 AD with some two hundred flat-topped **pyramids**. Beneath each of these structures lay entombed a member of the nobility; a few have been unearthed to reveal the wealth and sophistication of the culture. The corpses were wrapped in finery, covered in cinnabar pigment and surrounded by an array of human sacrifices, pottery, jade, masks, stingray spines, obsidian and quartz crystals. But the power of the city faded throughout the second and third centuries, and the site may even have been abandoned.

Kaminaljuyú's renaissance took place shortly after 400 AD, when the Guatemalan highlands suffered a massive invasion from the north and fell under the domination of Teotihuacán in central Mexico. The invaders seized the city of Kaminaljuyú and established it as their regional capital, gaining control of obsidian mines and access to the coastal trade routes and the lowlands of Petén. With the political and economic backing of Teotihuacán, the city once again flourished, the new rulers constructing their own temples, tombs and ball courts. Kaminaljuyú's alliance with Tikal also enabled the latter to dominate Petén. But Kaminaljuyú was so bound up with the fortunes of its northern partner that the fall of Teotihuacán around 600 AD weakened the city, resulting in its eventual demise.

Kaminaljuyú has most recently been reclaimed as an important sacred site by Maya shamans and activists, and you may well stumble across a religious ceremony going on in the grassy plazas. This was also the setting chosen by the indigenous leader Rigoberta Menchú (see pp.439–440) to celebrate her 1992 Nobel Peace Prize, when thousands thronged to the old capital.

Museo Miraflores

To gain a greater insight into the ancient city, visit the excellent, compact and new **Museo Miraflores** (Tues–Sun 9am–7pm; US$5.50; ⓦ www.museomiraflores .org), a ten-minute walk south of the ruins, beside the very upmarket Miraflores shopping mall on Calzada Roosevelt (the main route to Antigua). The history of the city and its importance as a trading centre are explained in detail, and exhibits highlight striking stone sculptures and stelae pieces, ceramics, impressive jade jewellery and obsidian flints. The scale model of Kaminaljuyú allows you to grasp an idea of just how large the city once was, and the museum grounds also encompass several temple mounds.

Eating, drinking and entertainment

Despite being the capital, Guatemala City isn't a great place for socializing or indulging. Most of the population hurry home in the evening and, apart from a few streets in zonas 1, 4 and 10, there's little life after dark. As you would expect, **restaurants** can be found throughout the city, and they invariably reflect the type of neighbourhood they're in. Meanwhile, **nightclubs** and bars are concentrated in Zona 10. Movie watching is hugely popular, with a good selection of cinemas.

Restaurants and cafés

In Zona 1 you'll find a great selection of inexpensive places to eat. **Lunchtime** is a particularly good time for a filling feed, when plenty of good Guatemalan places offer excellent set-price, three-course menus for US$3–4 a head – try the area west of the Parque Central or around the post office. Zona 1 has a cluster of **Chinese** restaurants on 6 Calle, between 4 and 3 avenidas, plus vegetarian, Mexican and Italian places. In Cuatro Grados Norte, Zona 4, there's a lot of culinary variety, including Middle Eastern, sushi and Italian. You'll find the Zona Viva, in Zona 10 a terrific place for a splurge, with scores of upmarket cafés and stylish restaurants offering everything from Spanish tapas and Asian fusion cuisine to steak houses.

Zona 1

Altuna 5 Av 12–31, ⓦ www.restaurante altuna.com. Elegant, formal and expensive Spanish/Basque restaurant rich in ambience and the natural home of Guatemala's Eurocentric elite. Mains include seafood, paella, lobster and good *calamares* but also serves delicious meat dishes, pasta and imported Castilian treats like Manchego cheese, *bacalao* and *jamón ibérico*. Count on upwards of US$25 a head. There's a second branch in Zona 10 at 10 C 0–45.

Café de Centro Histórico 6 Av 9–50. Civilized café on the upper floor of a beautifully restored 1930s building, replete with original tiles, wood panelling and monochrome photographs of the capital. Serves breakfasts, inexpensive Guatemalan dishes (like *sopa de frijoles* and *tortillas con carne*), a daily set meal for US$2.50, pies and salads, plus great coffee. No smoking room.

Café León 8 Av 9–15. An absolute gem of a café, this long-running place is the downtown HQ for Guatemalan intellectuals, and the air is thick with political talk and tobacco smoke (though there is a nonsmoking section). It's all about the coffee here, with treacle-thick espresso and milky café con leche dispensed from gleaming machines, though they do sell cakes (*cubiletes*, empanadas) and a few sandwiches. Richly atmospheric, *Café León* is the antithesis of the corporate coffee-chain experience. Closes 1pm Sat and all day Sun.

Cafetalito 8 Av 10–68. Modern *Starbucks*-style café, with all the familiar coffee combinations, plus granitas and frapuccinos and a few local coffee blends (Huehuetenango, Atitlán and Cobán). Paninis and snacks are also served. Closed Sun.

De Imeri 6 C 3–34. Highly popular café-restaurant with a pleasant rear courtyard that's great for breakfasts, salads, snacks, soups and sandwiches. The set lunch (US$4) is a real deal.

Europa Bar 11 C 5–16. Classic expat hangout, set inauspiciously beneath a multi-storey car park where you can tuck into familiar dishes including decent burgers and sandwiches while watching North American sports. Closed Sun.

El Gran Pavo 13 C 4–41. Fairly authentic Mexican food at moderate prices. Things really kick off on weekends when mariachi bands prowl the tables – you'll have to put up with piped ranchero music at other times, though the long tequila list helps ease the pain. Other branches at 6 C 3–09, Zona 9, and 15 Av 16–72, Zona 10.

Long Wah 6 C 3–75. One of the better budget Chinese restaurants in this neighbourhood, consistently recommended by locals with a menu that includes *sopa mein*, *wontons* and *chow mein*. For food to go, dial ☎ 2232 6611.

Rey Sol 11 C 5–51. Vegetarian café-restaurant of the old-school persuasion, where the food – pasta, Mexican-style dishes, wholemeal bread sandwiches and *tamales* – can be a little stodgy at times, but it's all healthy enough. Also acts as a store, selling good bread, granola, soya milk, herb teas and veggie snacks.

Zona 4

Café Restaurant Pereira inside the Gran Centro Comercial mall, 6 Av and 24 C. Just a couple of blocks west of Inguat, this no-nonsense *comedor* is popular with office workers for its filling *comida típica* at fair prices.

Flamenco Vía 4 Cuatro Grados Norte. If you're hankering for Spanish food, this place fits the bill, though the tapas dishes (around US$6) are on the pricey side. Occupies a pleasant corner location with balcony seating.

L'Osteria Ruta 2 4–75, Cuatro Grados Norte. Very authentic, mid-priced Italian in Guatemala City's boho barrio with a huge outdoor terrace and an atmospheric interior with walls covered in art and cinematic posters. Excellent pizza and pasta, a decent wine list and staff that could not be more helpful; reckon on US$15 a head. Closed Mon.

Sucré Salé Ruta 6 8–52. Friendly, inexpensive little café located in the ground floor of Casa Yurrita, which adjoins the church of the same name (see p.78). All the dishes (including great soups, breakfasts, set lunches and desserts) are freshly prepared every day; there's also a shady garden. Daily 7am–3pm.

Zonas 9, 10 and 14

Café Barista 16 C & 5 Av, Zona 14. In an exclusive suburban neighbourhood, Guatemala's most upmarket café has big windows offering views of leafy avenues. It's a well-run, stylish place where you lounge on leather sofas, and has plenty of coffee choices, paninis and ice cream.

China Queen 6 Av 14–04, Zona 9. Excellent-value, good-quality Chinese restaurant that offers huge portions of tasty grub; the fried rice with shrimp is US$10 and enough for two.

Donde Mikel 13 C 5–19, Zona 10. Elegant, expensive Spanish restaurant whose authentic food has its regulars dreaming of the motherland, with delicious sizzling *camarones* (shrimp) and meats served *a la plancha* (grilled). Closed Sun.

Kacao 2 Av 13-44, Zona 10. Beautifully designed place set under a giant palapa thatch roof, and in the evening you enter past a bamboo forest to a dining room illuminated by dozens of candles. The menu is refined *comida guatemalteca*, with some regional dishes like tapado, though priced at Zona Viva rates.

Olivadda 12 C 4–51, Zona 10. Destination restaurant with a wonderful terrace garden where tables are bordered by giant ferns and bamboo. Fusion menu features salmon ginger, lomito porcini and sushi, with mains priced at US$7–16.

Piccadilly Plaza España, 7 Av 12–00, Zona 9. Clean, family-orientated restaurant with decent range of pasta and pizza and some Guatemalan dishes, all at moderate prices, served along with huge jugs of beer. There's another branch in Zona 1 on 6 Av and 11 C.

Schlotzsky's 14 C & 3 Av, Zona 10. This place offers generous sandwiches and wraps with plenty of greens; a combo meal including a drink is around US$4.

Sopho's Av La Reforma, Zona 10. A refined café-restaurant that adjoins one of the city's best bookshops. Sit on the covered terrace listening to classical music and enjoy a baguette, salad or a croissant with your wine, licuado or coffee.

Tacontento 2 Av & 14 C, Zona 10. One of the cheapest places for a serious feed in the Zona Viva, with generous portions of tasty tacos (from US$3) and other Mexican standards. Dine inside or on one of the pavement tables.

Tamarindos 11 C 2–19 A, Zona 10, ⓦ www.tamarindos.com.gt. Guatemala's most urbane restaurant, with seriously contemporary furnishings, a Japanese-style garden patio, electronica on the sound system and a fusion menu of innovative Asian and Mediterranean food. Expect to pay US$15–20 a head. Closed Sun.

El Tapeo 6 Av 16–01 Zona 10. Enjoyable, authentic Spanish restaurant, with gingham tablecloths, posters of Almería and excellent tapas and mains. Moderate prices.

Drinking and nightlife

Guatemala City quiets down very quickly in the evenings, though there are a few places where you can get your freak on. The three main areas – zonas 1, 4 and 10 – where people congregate each has its own distinct atmosphere. **Zona 1** has a grungy appeal and is popular with students; note that personal safety can be a concern here, so it's best to get around by taxi. For a night out in Zona 1, you could do a lot worse than heading to *Las Cien Puertas* or one of the bars on Pasaje Ayicinena for a few drinks and then on to *La Bodeguita* to see what's on.

In **Zona 4**, the vibrant enclave of Cuatro Grados Norte, which occupies a few pedestrianized streets around Vía 5, is a good bridge between zonas 1 and 10, with an arty, bohemian scene. It's best on weekend nights, when you can dart between the closely packed restaurants and bars (try *SUAE*) and then catch a band at *Rock ol Vuh*. Alternatively there's often an art-house film or exhibition worth catching at the Centro de la Cultural España, in the heart of the area on Vía 5.

Zona Viva in **Zona 10** is where the wealthy go to have fun. There's a surplus of American-style bars, upmarket restaurants, and clubs playing Latino and European dance music, pop hits and salsa.

Guatemala has a small but vibrant **electronic** party scene, though few reliable venues. The annual Rave de Castillo, a festival of electronic music held every year in a location close to the capital, is certainly worth a visit.

Bars and clubs

Arguileh Vía 5, Cuatro Grados Norte. Middle Eastern-style bar where you can lounge around on cushions and suck on a hubble-bubble pipe; some tables overlook the pedestrianized street below. Also serves decent Middle Eastern food. Closed Mon.

Bad Attitude 4 C 5–10, Zona 1, ⓦ www.myspace .com/badattitudebar. Love-it or hate-it music venue, dripping with death metal banners where you drink from skull-shaped goblets. Showcases heavy/death/metal/thrash/alternative rock bands on Thurs and Sat, while on Fri it's everything from reggae to trance. Free entrance some nights; maximum cover is US$5 (includes a drink) for popular groups.

El Establo 14 C 5–08, Zona 10. Large, classy European-owned bar that attracts a wealthy middle-aged crowd. Serves good food, and offers sounds ranging from jazz to bluesy rock music.

La Bodeguita del Centro 12 C 3–55, Zona 1, ☎ 2230 2976. Large, left-field venue with live music, comedy, poetry and all manner of arty events. Free entry in the week, around US$4 at weekends. Worth a visit for the Che Guevara memorabilia alone. Closed Sun, Mon.

La Luna Pasaje Aycinema, 9 C between 6 and 7 Av, Zona 1. Small, sociable little dive bar in a crumbling historic building that has live music most nights.

Las Cien Puertes Pasaje Aycinema, 9 C between 6 and 7 Av, Zona 1. Ever-bustling bohemian bar in a beautiful run-down colonial arcade popular with artists, students and political activists. Graffiti-splattered walls, good sounds and moderate prices.

Kahlua 1 Av 15–06, Zona 10. Huge upmarket club with four levels and a vast main dancefloor that draws a young party-minded crowd. Musically, it's usually mainstream Latin dance hits, and the atmosphere gets really revved up on weekend nights.

Rock ol Vuh Vía 5, Cuatro Grados Norte, Zona 4. Excellent, compact, new live-music venue with good acoustics. Some of Guatemala's best up-and-coming rock bands play here.

Rattle & Hum 4 Av & 16 C, Zona 10. Snug and stylish Australian-owned bar, popular with expats and locals alike, with lively atmosphere and Western music on the stereo.

Rec Lounge 9 Av 0–81, Zona 4. Bar-club showcasing underground electronica talent, with DJs spinning drum'n'bass, dubstep and breaks. Attracts a very young crowd, and not for the faint-hearted.

SUAE Vía 5, Cuatro Grados Norte, Zona 4. Lounge-cum-warehouse-style bar with arresting decor (including lime green plastic sofas) and artwork. Eclectic electronic tunes, cult movies on Sun, and there's a few racks of customized clothes for sale too. The bar staff here are well connected to the capital's underground dance scene.

Cinemas

The City has a good selection of cinemas, most showing Hollywood films in English with Spanish subtitles; check listings in the main national newspapers. In Zona 1, there are several cinemas on 6 Avenida between the Parque Central and the police HQ, and the Los Próceres mall in Zona 10 has a multi-screen. For quality picture and sound head to Cine Miraflores or the neighbouring Cine Tikal Futura, Calzada Roosevelt, Zona 11. **Art-house movies** (the *Revue* has listings) and the occasional classic are shown at La Cúpula, 7 Avenida 13–01, Zona 9, and the Centro de la Cultural España and IGA in Zona 4.

Listings

Airlines Airline offices are scattered throughout the city, with many along Avenida La Reforma. Note that AA and Continental passengers can check in a day early at the airlines' offices inside the *Marriott*, 7 Av 15–45, Zona 9, to pre-book seats and save queuing at the airport. American Airlines, *Marriott* (see note above) and *Hotel El Dorado*, Av La Reforma 15–45, Zona 9 ☎ 2337 1177, ⓦ www.aa .com; Continental, *Marriott* (see note above) and 18 C 5–56, Zona 10 ☎ 2366 9985, airport ☎ 2331 2051, ⓦ www.continental.com; Copa, 1 Av 10–1, Zona 10 ☎ 2385 5500, airport ☎ 2385 0658, ⓦ www.copaair.com; Cubana, 13 C 3–40, Zona 10 ☎ 2367 2288, ⓦ www.cubana.cu; Delta Air Lines, 15 C 3–20, Zona 10, Centro Ejecutivo building ☎ 2337 0642; Iberia, Av La Reforma 8–60, Zona 9 ☎ 2332 0911, airport ☎ 2332 5517; KLM, 6 Av 20–25, Zona 10, 5th floor of Edificio Plaza Marítima ☎ 2367 6179; Mexicana, 13 C 8–44, Zona 10,

Edificio Edyma Plaza ☎ 2366 4543, ⓦ www .mexicana.com; Spirit Airlines ⓦ www.spiritair.com; Taca, Av Hincapié 12–22, Zona 13 ☎ 2470 8222, ⓦ www.taca.com; TAG, Av Hincapié y 18 C, Zona 13, ☎ 2360-3038, ⓦ www.tag.com.gt; United Airlines, Av La Reforma 1–50, Zona 9, Edificio el Reformador ☎ 2336 9923, ⓦ www.united guatemala.com.

American Express Office inside Clark Tours, 7 Av 14–76, Zona 9 (Mon–Fri 8.30am–5pm; ☎ 2331 7422).

Baggage There's no central left-luggage facility, so you'll have to entrust any baggage to your hotel.

Banks and exchange At the airport there are several 24hr ATMs accepting MasterCard/Cirrus and Visa/Plus cards, and a branch of Banco del Quetzal should reopen when renovations are complete in 2009. You can exchange euros (at poor rates) at Banco Uno; there's a branch at 18 C 5–56,

Gay Guatemala City

Guatemala City's small **gay scene** is mostly underground and concentrated around a few (almost entirely male) venues; "in" places change quickly: consult ⓦwww .gayguatemala.com for the latest info. In **Zona 1**, *Afanasi*, 4 Calle 5–30, is a key club (Thurs–Sat) with a big dancefloor and dark room. Two cafés act as meeting points in the central area – *El Encuentro*, 5 Avenida 10–52, inside a mall, has frequent drinks specials, and *La Ermita*, 9 Avenida 13–19, Zona 1; both are closed on Sundays. In **Zona 4**, *Genetic*, Vía 3 & Ruta 3, ⓦwww.geneticguatemala.com, is the city's largest gay club with three floors and a VIP section, and plays throbbing Latin dance and house music to a young crowd (Fri and Sat only). Meanwhile, *Il Coliseum*, 17 Calle A 7–40, Zona 10, a gay sauna, hosts parties most nights of the week; entrance is US$10. There are no specifically **lesbian** clubs or bars in the city.

Zona 10. In Zona 1, Credomatic, 5 Av & 11 C, gives Visa and MasterCard cash advances (Mon–Fri 8.30am–7pm, Sat 9am–1pm) and will cash traveller's cheques. ATMs are thick on the ground in Zona 10, including several at Centro Gerencial Las Margaritas, at Diagonal 6 10–01, where you can also cash traveller's cheques. On Sun (9.30am–4pm) head to Banco Industrial, Centro Comercial Montúfar, 12 C 0–93, Zona 9.

Bookstores *Sopho's*, Av La Reforma 13–89, Zona 10, has a small selection of English-language non-fiction, glossy coffee-table books and litera-ture; it also has a coffee bar. Géminis, 3 Av 17–05, Zona 14, is worth a visit if you're in the south of the city. Antigua has far better bookstores.

Car rental About a dozen companies have desks at the airport. Two good local companies are Tabarini, 2 C A 7–30, Zona 10 ☎2331 6108, ⓦwww.tabarini.com, and Adaesa, Calzada Aguilar Batres 8–12, Zona 11 ☎2472 1122, ⓦwww .adaesa.com, International companies include Avis, 6 Av 7–64, Zona 9 ☎2339 3248, ⓦwww .avisenlinea.com and Thrifty, 6 Av 11–57, Zona 9 ☎2332 1456, ⓦwww.thrifty.com.

Dentist Central Dentist de Especialistas, 20 C 11–17, Zona 10 (☎2337 1773), is the best dental clinic in the country and superb in emergencies. Prices are reasonable.

Embassies Most of the embassies are in the south-eastern quarter of the city, along Avenida La Reforma and Avenida Las Américas, and they tend to be open weekday mornings only. Australia, contact the Canadian embassy; Austria, Edificio Plaza, 6 Av 20–25, Zona 10 ☎2364 3460; Belize, Av La Reforma 1–50, 8th floor, Suite 803, Edificio el Refor-mador, Zona 9 ☎2334 5531 or 2331 1137; Canada, 13 C 8–44, 6th floor, Edificio Edyma Plaza, Zona 10 ☎2333 6102; Cuba, Av Las Américas 20–72, Zona 13 ☎2332 4066; Germany, Edificio Plaza Marítima, 20 C 6–20, Zona 10 ☎2364 6700; Honduras, 19 Av A 20–19, Zona 10 ☎2366 5640; Italy, 12 C Av 6–49

Zona 14 ☎2366 9271; Mexico, 15 C 3–20, Zona 10 ☎2333 7254 or 2333 7255; Netherlands, 16 C 0–55, 13th floor, Torre Internacional, Zona 10 ☎2381 4300; Nicaragua, 10 Av 14–72, Zona 10 ☎2368 0785; South Africa (honorary), 11 Av 30–24, Zona 5 ☎2385 0482; Sweden, 8 Av 15–07, Zona 10 ☎2384 7300; Switzerland, Torre Internacional, 16 C 0–65, Zona 10 ☎2367 5520; United Kingdom, Torre Internacional 16 C 0–55, 11th floor, Zona 10 ☎2367 5425–9; United States, Av La Reforma 7–01, Zona 10 (Mon–Fri 8am–5pm; ☎2326 4000).

Immigration The main immigration office (*migración*) is at Zona 4 (Mon–Fri 8am–2.45pm; ☎2361 8476–9).

Internet Cybercafés in Zona 1 include Café Internet Navigator at 14 C & 6 Av. In Zona 10, head to the Géminis Diez mall at 12 C and 2 Av where there are two cybercafés. Rates are around US$1.50 per hour.

Laundry Lavandería Obelisco, Av La Reforma 16–30, charges around US$3 for a self-service wash and dry; there's also a self-service laundry at 4 Av 13–89, Zona 1.

Libraries The Guatemalan American Institute, or IGA, at Ruta 1 and Vía 4, Zona 4, has the best library for English books. Centro Cultural de España, Vía 5, Zona 4, has a small library collec-tion that includes a few books in English. There's also the National Library, Parque del Centenario, and specialist collections at the Ixchel and Popol Vuh museums.

Medical care Dr Manuel Cáceres Figueroa, 6 Av 8–92, Zona 9 (☎2332 1506), who speaks English and German, is highly recommended for consulta-tions; your embassy should also have a list of bilingual doctors. For emergency medical assist-ance, dial ☎125 for the Red Cross or head for the Centro Médico, a private hospital open 24hrs, at 6 Av 3–47, Zona 10 (☎2332 3555).

Pharmacies Farmacia Osco, 16 C and 4 Av, Zona 10. There are dozens in Zona 1.

Moving on from Guatemala City

For information about Guatemala City airport, see p.69. The **domestic terminal** cannot be accessed from the main building, but only via Avenida Hincapié to the east; you'll need to take a taxi. Note that all Taca domestic flights leave from the inter-national terminal. Airport taxes are dealt with on p.32.

If you're leaving by **first-class bus**, departures are from the bus company offices. Many are clustered around 18 Calle and 9 Avenida in **Zona 1**, with others spread around the southern half of the city.

Second-class buses leave from two main areas close to the Trébol junction southwest of the centre. All routes to the western highlands use a series of bus stops on 41 Calle between 7 Avenida and 11 Avenida, Zona 7. All buses to the coast and southern Guatemala (including Iztapa and the Mexican border crossing of Tecún Umán) use another terminal at the junction of 8 Avenida and 4 Calle in Zona 12.

International services to Tegucigalpa and Managua involve a night in a Tica Bus hotel in San Salvador; to San José, Costa Rica, involves two overnight stops.

Buses from Guatemala City

Websites are shown where available. The abbreviations we've used for the bus companies are as follows:

ADN	Autobuses del Norte ⓦ www.adnautobusesdelnorte.com
Blanca	ⓦ www.monjablanca.com
DM	Dulces María
FN	Fuente del Norte
HA	Hedman Alas ⓦ www.hedmanalas.com
KQ	King Quality ⓦ www.kingqualityca.com
L	Litegua ⓦ www.litegua.com
LD	Línea Dorada ⓦ www.tikalmayanworld.com
LH	Los Halcones
MI	Melva Internacional
P	Pullmantur ⓦ www.pullmantur.com
RO	Rutas Orientales ⓦ www.rutasorientales.com
RZ	Rápidos Zacaleu
TA	Transportes Álamo
TB	Ticabus ⓦ www.ticabus.com
TE	Transportes Escobar y Monja
TGG	Transportes Galgos ⓦ www.transgalgosinter.com.gt
TGR	Transportes Guerra
TV	Transportes Velásquez

To	Company	Terminal	Frequency	Duration
Antigua	2nd-class	1 Av & 3 C, Zona 7	15min	1hr
Chichicastenango	2nd-class	41 C & 10 Av, Zona 7	30min	3hr 15min
Chiquimula	RO (1st)	19 C 8–18, Zona 1	20 daily	3hr 30min
	TGR (1st)	19 C 8–39, Zona 1	20 daily	3hr 30min
Ciudad Pedro de Alvarado	2nd-class	8 Av & 4 C, Zona 12	30min	2hr 30min
Cobán	TE (1st)	8 Av 15–16, Zona 1	30min	4hr 30min
Copán	HA (1st)	2 Av 8–73, Zona 10	2 daily	5hr
Escuintla	2nd-class	8 Av & 4 C, Zona 12	20min	1hr 15min
Esquipulas	RO (1st)	19 C 8–18, Zona 1	30min	4hr

Flores	FD (1st)	17 C & 8 Av, Zona 1	19 daily	8–9hr
	LD (1st)	16 C 10–03, Zona 1	3 daily	8hr
	ADN (1st)	8 Av 16–41, Zona 1	3 daily	8hr
Huehuetenango	LD (1st)	16 C 10–03, Zona 1	2 daily	5hr 30min
	LH (1st)	7 Av 15–27, Zona 1	3 daily	5hr 30min
	TV (1st)	20 C 1–37, Zona 1	9 daily	5hr 30min
	RZ (1st)	5C 11–42, Zona 1	3 daily	5hr 30min
Iztapa	2nd-class	8 Av & 4 C, Zona 12	5 daily	3hr
La Mesilla	LD (1st)	16 C 10–03, Zona 1	2 daily	7hr
	TV (1st)	20 C 1–37, Zona 1	7 daily	7hr
Managua	KQ	18 Av 1–96, Zona 15	1 daily	18hr
	TB	Blvd Los Próceres 26–55, Zona 10	1 daily	28hr
Monterrico	travel via Iztapa			
Nebaj	2nd-class	41 C & 8 Av, Zona 7	4 daily	5hr 15min
Panajachel	2nd-class	41 C & 8 Av, Zona 7	8 daily	3hr
Puerto Barrios	L (1st)	15 C 10–40, Zona 1	14 daily	5hr 30min
Quetzaltenango	FN (1st)	17 C & 8 Av, Zona 1	8 daily	4hr
	LD (1st)	16 C 10–03, Zona 1	2 daily	4hr
	TA (1st)	12 Av A 0–65, Zona 7	7 daily	4hr
	TG (1st)	7 Av 19–44, Zona 1	2 daily	4hr
	2nd-class	41 C & 8 Av, Zona 7	hourly	4hr 15min
Rabinal	DM			
	1st & 2nd-class	17 C 11–32, Zona 1	every 30min	3hr 45min
Río Dulce	L (1st)	15 C 10–40, Zona 1	4 daily	5hr 15min
	Buses to Flores also stop at Río Dulce			
Salamá	DM			
	1st & 2nd-class	17 C & 11–32, Zona 1	every 30min	3hr 15min
San Pedro La Laguna	2nd-class	41 C & 8 Av, Zona 7	7 daily	3hr 30min
San Pedro Sula	RO (1st)	19 C 8–18, Zona 1	2 daily	12hr
	HA (1st)	2 Av 8–73, Zona 10	1 daily	8hr 30min
San Salvador	MI (1st)	3 Av 1–38, Zona 9	14 daily	5hr
	TB (1st)	Blvd Los Próceres 26–55, Zona 10	1 daily	5hr
	KQ (1st)	18 Av 1–96, Zona 15	2 daily	5hr
	P (1st)	*Holiday Inn*, Zona 10	2–3 daily	5hr
Santa Cruz del Quiché	2nd-class	41 C & 8 Av, Zona 7	hourly	4hr
Santiago Atitlán	2nd-class	8 Av & 4 C, Zona 12	6 daily	3hr
Tapachula	LD (1st)	16 C 10–03, Zona 1	1 daily	6hr 30min
	TB (1st)	Blvd Los Próceres 26–55, Zona 10	1 daily	5hr
	TG (1st)	7 Av 19–44, Zona 1	3 daily	6–7hr
Tegucigalpa	TB (1st)	Blvd Los Próceres 26–55, Zona 10	1 daily	28hr
Tikal	travel via Flores			

Photography The cybercafés recommended above can back up photos on a CD. Memory cards and print film are widely available, while slide and monochrome film can be found at the camera shops on 6 Av in Zona 1.
Police The main police station is on the corner of 6 Av and 14 C, Zona 1. In an emergency, dial ⓣ120.
Post office The main post office is at 7 Av and 12 C, Zona 1 (Mon–Fri 8.30am–5pm, Sat 8.30am–1pm).
Telephone Both cybercafés in Géminis Diez (see "Internet") have cheap international call rates. Cardphones can be found all over the city; the main Telgua office is one block east of the post office (daily 7am–midnight).
Tours *Hotel Posada Belén* (see p.72) offers excellent guided walking tours (in English or Spanish) of the historic centre of Guatemala City taking in Casa Mima, the Palacio Nacional, cathedral and other sites for US$40pp, and full-day museum tours for US$60pp. Clark Tours (see "Travel agents") also offer half-day city tours for US$27.
Travel agents Viajes Tivoli, 6 Av 8–41, Zona 9 (ⓣ2386 4200, ⓦwww.viajestivoli.com), is a good all-round agent with competitive rates for international flights. Flights to Petén can be booked at Servisa, Av La Reforma 8–33, Zona 10 (ⓣ2332 7526). Clark Tours, 7 Av 14–76 Zona 9 (ⓣ2412 4700. ⓦwww.clarktours.com.gt), organize trips to many parts of the country.
Work Hard to come by. The best bet is teaching at one of the English schools; check the classified sections of the *Revue*.

Around Guatemala City

In the event you're not dashing off straight away to Antigua, a couple of destinations are suited for day-trips from the city, while the rest of the surrounding hills are easily explored using other towns as a base.

To the south the main road runs to Escuintla and the Pacific coast, passing through a narrow valley overshadowed by the highly active **Volcán de Pacaya**, which often spouts smoke, gases, rocks and lava.

To the northwest of the capital, the villages of **San Juan Sacatepéquez** and **San Pedro Sacatepéquez** both have impressive markets, while further northwest lie the ruins of **Mixco Viejo**, the ancient capital of the Poqomam Maya.

▲ Volcán de Pacaya

South of the city

Heading out through the southern suburbs, the **Carretera al Pacífico** runs past the clover-leaf junction at El Trébol and leaves the city through its industrial outskirts. The route passes a swathe of new housing projects, and elaborate advertising posters on empty lots sing the merits of suburban life and mortgages. The highway also runs past many of Guatemala's giant *maquila* (clothing assembly) factories, and the town of **Villa Nueva**, which has now been virtually swallowed up by the capital's sprawl. Eventually the valley starts to narrow, overshadowed by the volcanic cones of Agua and Pacaya.

A few kilometres east of the highway, **Lago de Amatitlán** nestles at the base of the Pacaya volcano, encircled by forested hills. It's a superb setting, but one that's been sadly undermined by the abuses the lake has suffered at the hands of property speculators (bungalows and industry have proliferated around the shoreline, and the waters are polluted).

The Pacaya volcano

Heading further down the valley towards the Pacific coast, a branch road leaves the main highway to the left (east) and heads into the hills to the trailhead for the highly active **Volcán de Pacaya**. Rising to a height of 2250m, the volcano regularly spits out clouds of rock and ash in the country's most dramatic sound-and-light extravaganza. The current period of eruption began in 1965, and colonial records show that it was also active between 1565 and 1775. Today it certainly ranks as one of the most accessible and exciting volcanoes in Central America, and a trip to the cone is an unforgettable experience (although sulphurous fumes and very high winds can make this ascent impossible some days). The best time to watch the eruptions is at night, when the volcano often spouts plumes of brilliant orange lava.

Though it is possible to climb the cone independently, virtually everyone chooses to join a group as part of a tour, escorted by a guide. Antigua is the best place to organize a climb; Gran Jaguar Tours, 4 Calle Poniente 30 (℡7832 2712), handles most tours (US$5–7 per head) and there are many adventure-sports specialists (see p.109) in town all of which run more comfortable and expensive (around US$40) trips that include food and drink. Most cheap tours leave Antigua around 2pm and return by about 9pm. **Safety** on Pacaya (once the site of regular attacks by bandits) is now much less of a concern since park guards, who accompany groups, were posted on the volcano's slopes.

Tour minibuses drop you off in the village of **San Francisco de Sales**, where you'll be surrounded by dozens of young boys urging you to buy a walking "steek", rent a torch (flashlight) or a horse (US$16 return). Once you've paid your US$3.50 entrance fee to the protected Pacaya area you'll be assigned a local guide to accompany your group up the trail. It's a steep but steady hour's climb up a good path through *milpas* and thickish forest until you suddenly emerge on the lip of an exposed ridge from where you can see the cone in all its brutal beauty. In front of you is a massive bowl of cooled lava, its fossilized currents flowing away to the right; opposite is the cone itself, a jet-black triangular peak that occasionally spouts rock and ash. It's possible to descend, and pick your way carefully across the lava fields until you reach a section that's oozing molten lava. If you've brought a marshmallow along, toast yourself a snack.

Many standard tours don't allow enough time, but it's a further 45 minutes to the summit of the cone itself. The route passes between charred stumps of trees, and then up the slippery ashen sides of the cone itself, a terrifying but thrilling ascent, eventually bringing you face to face with bubbling patches of molten magma and minor eruptions (if conditions permit). A noxious brew of sulphurous fumes (that choke the throat) swirls around the lip of the crater and you'll feel the heat of the ash and lava beneath your feet. The ascent certainly shouldn't be attempted when Pacaya is highly active – check with your tour agency about the state of the eruptions before setting out.

Parque Natural Canopy Calderas

Nestling in the northern slopes of Pacaya below the village of San Francisco de Sales is the **Parque Natural Canopy Calderas** (daily 8am–6pm; ☎5538 5531, Ⓦwww.parquenaturalcalderas.com), a protected zone that encompasses a delightful highland lake and a dense patch of rainforest, close to the *aldea* of San José Calderas. The parque is a privately owned nature reserve where you can camp (US$7 per head) beside the clean lake, go horseriding (US$8 per hr) or swing through the jungle from professionally built wooden platforms along a 700m network of cable (US$20) which slices through the forest. If you go privately, stop in the village of San José and ask the mayor for the canopy tour, and well-trained guides will accompany you and show you how to use the cable canopy ropes correctly.

Northwest of the city

To the northwest of the capital lies a hilly area that, despite its proximity, is little tainted by the influence of the city. Here the hills are still covered by pine forests, and heading out this way you'll find a couple of interesting villages with markets well worth visiting. Further afield are the **Mixco Viejo** ruins, impeccably restored and enjoying the most dramatic setting of any archeological site in Guatemala.

San Pedro Sacatepéquez and San Juan Sacatepéquez

Leaving the city to the northwest you travel through the suburb of **Florida**, then the road starts to climb into the hills through an area that's oddly uninhabited – save for the occasional mansion, hidden in the forest.

The first of the two villages you come to is **SAN PEDRO SACATEPÉQUEZ**, which had to be almost completely rebuilt after the 1976 earthquake. The Friday market here, though not very large, is still worth a browse. Another 6km takes you over a ridge, past a profusion of makeshift greenhouses and into the village of **SAN JUAN SACATEPÉQUEZ**, famous for its flower cultivation industry. By far the best time to visit is for the Friday market, when the whole place springs into action and the village is packed. Keep an eye out for the *huipiles* worn in San Juan, which are unusual and impressive, with bold geometric designs of yellow, purple and green.

Buses to both villages run every fifteen minutes or so from 41 Calle and 8 Avendia, Zona 7, in Guatemala City.

Mixco Viejo

Beyond San Juan the road divides, one branch heading north to El Chol and Rabinal along a rough dirt route, the other going northwest towards **Mixco Viejo** along a smooth paved road. Taking the western route, the scenery changes dramatically, leaving behind the pine forests and entering a huge, dry valley. Small farms are scattered here and there, and the Politécnica, Guatemala's military academy, is also out this way. About thirty minutes beyond San Juan, in a massive valley, are the ruins of Mixco Viejo.

The ruins

MIXCO VIEJO (8am–5pm; US$7) was the capital of the Poqomam Maya, one of the main pre-conquest tribes. The original Poqomam language has all but died out – it's now spoken only in a few isolated areas and in the villages of Mixco and Chinautla – and the bulk of their original territory is swamped by Kaqchikel speakers. The site itself is thought to date from the thirteenth century, and its construction, designed to withstand siege, bears all the hallmarks of the troubled times before the arrival of the Spanish. Protected on all sides by deep ravines, it can be entered only along a single-file causeway. At the time the Spanish arrived, in 1525, this was one of the largest highland centres, with nine temples, two ball courts, and a population of around nine thousand.

Spanish historian Fuentes y Guzmán actually witnessed the conquest of the city, so for once there's a detailed account. At first Alvarado sent only a small force; after this group failed, the Spanish leader launched an attack himself, using his Mexican allies, two hundred Tlaxcala warriors. With a characteristic lack of subtlety he opted for a frontal assault, but his armies were attacked from behind by a force of Poqomam fighters who arrived from Chinautla. The battle was fought on an open plain in front of the city, and by sunset the Spanish cavalry had won the day, killing some two hundred Poqomam men, although the city remained impenetrable. According to Fuentes y Guzmán, the Poqomam survivors then pointed out a secret entrance to the city, allowing the Spanish to enter virtually unopposed and to unleash a massacre of its inhabitants. The survivors were resettled at a site on the edge of the city, in the suburb of Mixco.

Today the site has been impressively restored, with its plazas and temples laid out across several flat-topped ridges. Like all the highland sites the structures are fairly low – the largest temple reaches only about 10m in height – and are devoid of decoration. It is, however, an interesting site in a spectacular setting, and during the week you'll probably have the ruins to yourself, which gives the place all the more atmosphere. Buses (4 daily) to Pachalum from 41 Calle and 8 Avenida, Zona 7, in Guatemala City pass Mixco Viejo. There are cold drinks for sale at the site, and some attractive shelters where you can **camp** overlooking the ruins.

From Guatemala City to Sumpango

Heading out to the west from Guatemala City along the Carretera Interamericana the first place you pass through is **Mixco**, once a Poqomam Maya town, but now a suburb of the capital. The highway then roars past several large villages devoted to market gardening before reaching **San Lucas Sacatepéquez**, just before the turning for Antigua. The village dates back to before the Conquest but these days it serves the weekend needs of city dwellers, with cheap comedores and family restaurants lining the road.

Beyond this is **SANTIAGO SACATEPÉQUEZ**, just a kilometre or so north of the highway. The best time to visit Santiago is on November 1, for a local fiesta to honour the **Day of the Dead**, when massive paper kites are flown in the cemetery to release the souls of the dead from their agony. The festival is immensely popular, and hundreds of Guatemalans and tourists come every year to watch the spectacle. The colourful kites, made from paper and bamboo, are massive circular structures, measuring up to 6–7m in diameter. Teams of young men struggle to get them aloft while the crowd looks on with bated breath, rushing for cover if a kite comes crashing to the ground.

At other times of the year, there are **markets** in Santiago on Tuesday and Sunday and the town has a small **museum** (Mon–Fri 9am–4pm, Sat & Sun 9am–noon & 2–4pm), just below the plaza, which is crammed with tiny Maya artefacts found locally, and some traditional costumes.

The neighbouring village of **SUMPANGO**, 6km west along the Interamericana, has an identical Day of the Dead tradition – so every few years, when there's not enough wind and the kites at Santiago fail to rise to the occasion, everyone heads there in the hope of better weather.

You'll have no problem reaching either Santiago Sacatepéquez or Sumpango on fiesta day, when travel agencies and language schools send fleets of minibuses up to the villages from Antigua; to get there by public transport take any bus as far as San Lucas Sacatepéquez on the Interamericana and catch a connection there.

Antigua and around

Superbly situated in a sweeping highland valley, suspended between the cones of Agua, Acatenango and Fuego volcanoes, is one of the Americas' most enchanting colonial cities: **ANTIGUA**. In its day this was one of the great cities of the Spanish empire, ranking alongside Lima and Mexico City and serving as the administrative centre for all of Central America and Mexican Chiapas.

These days Antigua is a haven of tranquillity, and it has become Guatemala's foremost tourist destination, a favoured hangout for travellers looking to recharge. The beauty of the city itself is the main attraction, particularly its neat cobbled streets and grand Baroque-style colonial buildings. You'll find the ambience unhurried and enjoyable, with a sociable bar scene and superb choice of restaurants adding to the city's appeal. Antigua's **language schools**, some of the best in all Latin America, are another big draw, pulling in students from around the globe, and forming a vital part of the local economy. Expats contribute to the town's cosmopolitan air, mingling with local villagers selling their wares in the streets and the middle-class Guatemalans who come here at weekends to eat, drink and enjoy themselves. The downside is that though it's a great place to wind down and eat well for a few days after you've been travelling hard, eventually this civilized, isolated world can perhaps seem a little too smug and comfortable. After a few days of sipping cappuccinos and munching croissants, you could almost forget that you're in Central America at all.

Some history

Antigua was actually the third capital of Guatemala. The Spanish settled first at the site of **Iximché** in July 1524, so that they could keep a close eye on their Kaqchikel Maya allies. In November 1527, when the Kaqchikel rose up in defiance of their new rulers, the capital was moved into the Almolonga valley, to the site of **Ciudad Vieja**, a few kilometres from Antigua. In 1541, however, shortly after the death of Alvarado, the entire town was lost beneath a massive mud slide. Only then did the capital come to rest in Antigua. Here, despite the continued seismic threats – the first earthquake came after just twenty years – the capital grew to achieve astounding prosperity.

One by one the religious orders established themselves in Antigua, competing in the construction of schools, churches, monasteries and hospitals. Bishops built grand palaces that were soon rivalled by the homes of local merchants and corrupt government officials.

The city reached its peak in the middle of the eighteenth century, after the 1717 earthquake prompted an unprecedented building boom, and the population rose to around fifty thousand. By this stage Antigua was a genuinely impressive place, with a university, a printing press, a newspaper, and streets that were seething with commercial and political rivalries. But as is so often the case in Guatemala, earthquakes brought all of this to an abrupt end, and in 1773 Antigua suffered two devastating shocks. The damage was so bad that the decision was made to abandon the city in favour of the modern capital: fortunately, despite endless official decrees, there were many who refused to leave and Antigua was never completely deserted.

Since then the city has been gradually repopulated, particularly in the last hundred years or so. As Guatemala City has become increasingly congested, some of its middle classes have relocated to Antigua. They've been joined by a large number of resident and visiting foreigners attracted by the city's relaxed and sophisticated atmosphere, lively cultural life, benign climate and lack of traffic congestion.

The fate of Antigua's ancient architecture has become a growing concern in recent years. Of the city's tremendous colonial legacy, many buildings still lie in atmospheric ruin, others are steadily decaying, and many others have been transformed into hotels or restaurants. Efforts are being made to preserve this unique legacy, especially after Antigua was listed as a UNESCO World Heritage Site in 1979. Local **conservation** laws are very strict (extensions to houses are virtually impossible and businesses are pressured to paint their premises in officially sanctioned colours) and at times verge on the absurd. More commendably, the construction of a new ring-road around the west of Antigua and the exclusion of trucks from the city streets have helped reduce noise and environmental pollution considerably.

Arrival

Antigua is laid out on the traditional grid system, with avenidas running north–south, and calles east–west. Each street is numbered and has two halves, either a north and south (*norte/sur*) or an east and west (*oriente/poniente*), with the plaza, **Parque Central**, regarded as the centre. Despite this apparent simplicity, poor street lighting, the use of old street names and a local law banning overhanging signs ensure that most people get lost at some stage. But Antigua is small and if you get confused, remember that the Agua volcano, the one that hangs most immediately over the town, is to the south.

Arriving by public bus you'll end up in the main bus terminal, a large open space beside the market, three long blocks to the west of the plaza. The noise, fumes and bustle of this part of town are similar to any other in Guatemala, and you may well be greeted by a hustler or two trying to push a hotel or language school. To get to the centre of town walk straight up 4 Calle Poniente, which leads directly to the plaza.

Information

The **tourist office** (Mon–Fri 8am–1pm & 2–5pm, Sat & Sun 9am–1pm & 2–5pm; ☎7832 0763, ✉info-antigua@inguat.gob.gt) is currently at 5 Calle Poniente 9, though it will return to its usual location on the south side of the plaza sometime in 2009. Staff are reliably informative, English is spoken and you can pick up a free city map and get advice about monuments and city walks. The **tourist police** are somewhat inconveniently located at the back of the market (☎7832 7290), but they will try to help you with any difficulties (though few officers speak English). They escort visitors up to the Cerro de la Cruz – which offers a panoramic view of Antigua and the surrounding volcanoes – and also to the city cemetery on request.

The most comprehensive **guidebooks** devoted to Antigua are *Antigua Guatemala: The City and Its Heritage* by Elizabeth Bell and *Antigua for You*, by Barbara Balchin De Koose. Both are available from bookshops in town (see p.109). Although **guides** of the human variety are often to be found in the plaza hustling for business, it's better to take a city tour (see p.109).

Notice boards in various popular tourist venues advertise everything from salsa classes to apartments and private language tuition. Check those in popular hostels like the *Black Cat* and *El Hostel*, and those at *Doña Luisa's* restaurant, 4 Calle Oriente 12, and the *Rainbow Reading Room*, 7 Avenida Sur 8.

Accommodation

Antigua has an excellent selection of hotels and hostels, and whether you're after a room in a colonial mansion or a bed in a dorm, you shouldn't have a problem (except around Holy Week, see p.101, when the place is packed and prices soar). Rates are often slashed in mid-range and luxury hotels at quiet times of year.

Touts often greet arriving bus passengers with hotel offers; be aware, though, that they get paid a commission if you take a room, so if you arrive at the hotel with one in tow your bargaining powers have already been affected – only at very busy times is it worth taking up one of these guides. Many of the budget hotels are situated in the streets opposite the market and bus terminal, and can be noisy; hotels located in all other parts of the city are much more tranquil.

Another excellent option is a delightful rural guesthouse 7km outside of Antigua, the *Earth Lodge* (see p.117), which is beautifully set in the hills north of the town.

Budget options

Black Cat Hostal 6 Av Norte 1A ☏7832 1229, ⓦwww.blackcatantigua.com. Party central for young backpackers, this place has a handy location just a block from the parque and a street-facing bar that is packed from lunch till late. There's no kitchen and the dorms have eight beds, but there's a comfy TV/DVD room, breakfasts are generous and staff helpful. Dorm US$7, rooms ❸

El Hostal 1 Av Sur 8 ☏7832 0442, Ⓔelhostal.antigua@gmail.com. Antigua's most comfortable hostel, this well-run, spotless place offers colonial ambience on the cheap, with a delightful central courtyard for relaxed daytime chilling. Dorms (with six beds and lockers) and private rooms are very spacious; the bathrooms (male and female) have steaming hot showers and there are laundry facilities. Breakfasts here are legendary – à la carte from a full menu. Dorm beds US$8–10. ❹

International Mochilero Guest House 1 C Poniente 33 ☏7832 0520, ⓦwww.inter nacionalmochilero.com. Inexpensive if basic singles, doubles (some with bathroom) and a dorm (US$7.50); those at the rear have better natural light. There's a lovely garden and a kitchen for guests. ❷

Jungle Party Hostal 6 Av Norte 20 ☏7832 0463, ⓦwww.junglepartyhostal.com. Sociable, popular hostel with capacity for 30 guests that attracts a young backpacking crowd. Offers three- and five-bed dorms (US$7), all with solid-wood bunk beds and private lockers, though bathroom facilities could be improved. There's also a chill-out area with hammocks, and a bar/café with an inexpensive menu. Breakfast is included. ❸

Posada Doña Angelina 4 C Poniente 33 ☏7832 5173. Old-school travellers' place where many of the 42 small rooms are a bit gloomy, but there's usually space available. Has a secure store room where you can leave your baggage. ❷

Posada Juma Ocag Av Alameda Santa Lucía Norte 13 ☏7832 3109. An excellent choice at the upper end of the budget category, this is a very well-run little hotel owned by a hospitable family. Eight spotless, comfortable, if smallish, rooms are decorated with local fabrics; all have good beds, a wardrobe or clothes rack, private bathroom, and reading lights. There's a small upper patio for relaxing, free drinking water, and a laundry room. Book well ahead. ❸

Yellow House 1 C Poniente 24 ☏7832 6646. This popular hostel offers inexpensive dorms, clean bathrooms, a rooftop garden terrace and a guests' kitchen. There's free internet access and a large, healthy breakfast is included. Dorm US$8, rooms ❸

Moderate

Albergue Andinista 6 Av Norte 34 ☏7832 3343, Ⓔdrrios@intel.net.gt. Secure, good-value apart-ments, most with kitchens, set around a peaceful garden bursting with flowers, with discounts for stays of a week or more. Daniel Rios, the English-speaking owner, is a good host and also provides luggage storage. ❺

Alcazár del Toboso Callejón del Hermano Pedro 12 ☏7832 3600, ⓦwww.hotel alcazardetoboso.com. An outstanding place to stay, in spacious grounds, for those who don't mind being a 10min walk from the parque. The gorgeous, large and artistically-decorated rooms, some with little balconies, are light and airy with solid-wood furniture, and are set on two levels around two grassy courtyards. Very tranquil and there's ample parking and wi-fi. ❹

Casa Cristina Callejón Campo Seco 3A ☏7832 0623, ⓦwww.casa-cristina.com. This spotless small hotel is superb value for money, with ten very clean and attractive rooms, all with private hot-water bathrooms and bedside reading lights, and some with fridges. There's a rooftop sun terrace, free coffee, drinking water, wi-fi and internet. It's set on a quiet street a 10min walk north of the plaza. ❹

La Casa de Santa Lucía 2 Av Alameda Santa Lucía Norte 21 ☏7832 6189. Popular, good-value hotel with secure and spacious, if a little plain, rooms, all with decent beds and private hot-water baths. Has a roof terrace and parking, but don't expect too much in the way of service. There are two other nearly identical branches: *No. 1*, Alameda Santa Lucía Sur 9 (☏7832 3302), and *No. 3*, at 6 Av Norte 43A (☏7831 1386). ❹

Hostal El Montañes 6 C Poniente & 5 Av Sur ☏7832 8804, ⓦwww.hostalelmontanesantigua .com. A charming B&B with spotless rooms (most with private bathroom) run by friendly locals. There's a lovely sitting room, with a high vaulted ceiling, piano and TV/DVD player. They'll cook up whatever you like for breakfast, and there's internet access in the lobby. ❻

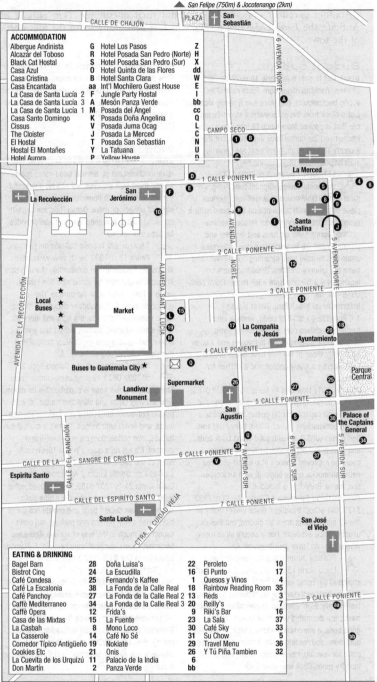

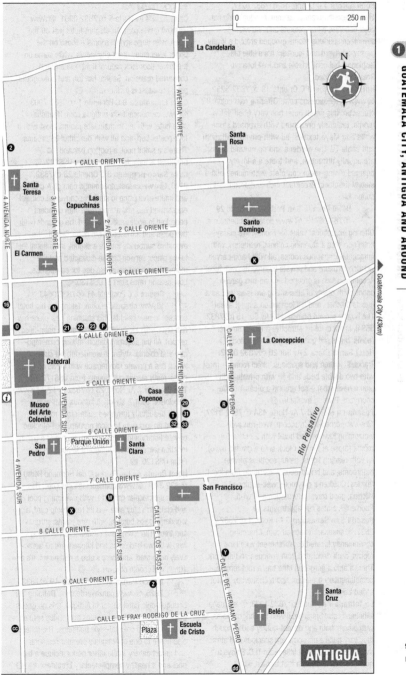

0 — 250 m

N

La Candelaria

1 AVENIDA NORTE

Santa Rosa

4 AVENIDA NORTE

❷

1 CALLE ORIENTE

Santa Teresa

3 AVENIDA NORTE

Las Capuchinas

2 AVENIDA NORTE

2 CALLE ORIENTE

Santo Domingo

⓫

El Carmen

3 CALLE ORIENTE

Ⓚ

⓰

Ⓝ

⓮

Ⓞ

㉑ ㉒ ㉓ Ⓟ

4 CALLE ORIENTE

㉔

La Concepción

CALLE DEL HERMANO PEDRO

Catedral

1 AVENIDA SUR

5 CALLE ORIENTE

ⓘ

Museo del Arte Colonial

Casa Popenoe

㉙

3 AVENIDA SUR

㉛

Ⓣ

Ⓡ

6 CALLE ORIENTE

㉜

㉝

San Pedro

Parque Unión

Santa Clara

Río Pensativo

4 AVENIDA SUR

7 CALLE ORIENTE

San Francisco

Ⓦ

CALLE DE LOS PASOS

Ⓧ

2 AVENIDA SUR

8 CALLE ORIENTE

CALLE DEL HERMANO PEDRO

Ⓨ

9 CALLE ORIENTE

Ⓩ

Santa Cruz

ⒸⒸ

CALLE DE FRAY RODRIGO DE LA CRUZ

Belén

Plaza

Escuela de Cristo

ANTIGUA

ⒹⒹ

▶ Guatemala City (43km)

San Juan del Obispo (5km) & Santa María de Jesús (11km) ▼

Hotel Aurora 4 C Oriente 16 ☏ 7832 0217, Ⓦ www.hotelauroraantigua.com. Antigua's original hotel occupies a fine colonial building with seventeen spacious rooms grouped around a lovely grassy courtyard and fountain. It's a little old-fashioned, but comfortable and well located. Breakfast included. ⓐ

Hotel Los Pasos 9 C Oriente 19 ☏ 7832 5252, Ⓦ www.hotellospasos.com. Offering real colonial character, this small hotel has very good-value rooms, tastefully presented with exposed stone walls and cable TV. The gardens and communal areas are equally attractive, and there's a lovely beamed dining-room complete with niches and a stately fireplace. Breakfast included. Rooms ⓖ, suites ⓐ

Hotel Posada San Pedro 7 Av Norte 29 ☏ 7832 0718, Ⓦ www.posadasanpedro.net. Offering exceptional value for money, this classy hotel occupies a stunning colonial residence, with immaculate, spacious rooms, all with hand-carved wooden furniture and private bathrooms (with tubs). Accommodation is grouped around two garden patios, with plenty of little sitting areas as well as a guests' kitchen, and it's located on a quiet street. The hotel's second branch, at 3 Av Sur 15 (☏ 7832 3594), is not quite as attractive and has smaller rooms, but is still good value. Both locations ⓖ

Hotel Santa Clara 2 Av Sur 20 ☏ 7832 0342. Tranquil location and spacious, clean rooms – most with two double beds and all with private bath (some have tubs) – set around a pleasant little courtyard. Parking available. ⓓ

Posada La Merced 7 Av Norte 43A ☏ 7832 3197, Ⓦ www.merced-landivar.com. Well-run and welcoming Kiwi-owned hotel with 23 cheerful rooms (those at the rear look onto a garden patio), all with reading lights, safes, spotless private bathrooms, and bright bedcovers made from local textiles. Children's playroom, well-equipped kitchen, good travel information and wi-fi. Rooms ⓖ, suites ⓑ, apartments ⓐ

Posada San Sebastián 3 Av Norte 4 ☏ 7832 2621, Ⓔ snsebast@hotmail.com. Charming, conveniently located establishment with nine rooms, each decorated with antiques and artwork. There's also a gorgeous little bar, a roof terrace, complimentary breakfast and a chatterbox parrot called Lorenzo. ⓖ

La Tatuana 7 Av Sur 3 ☏ 7832 1223, Ⓔ latatuana@hotmail.com. Small hotel with five bright rooms, all with private bath and decent-quality beds, though they vary quite a bit: some are spacious and attractive, others could use a little more TLC. Enjoys a quiet location and has a roof terrace. ⓔ

Expensive

Casa Azul 4 Av Norte 5 ☏ 7832 0961, Ⓦ www.casazul.guate.com. An elegant hotel just off the plaza, with huge stylish rooms – those on the upper level enjoy great city views, while some on the lower floor lack natural light – in a grand converted mansion. Sauna, hot tub and a delightful pool; breakfast is included. ⓑ–ⓐ

Casa Encantada 9 C Poniente 1 ☏ 7832 7903, Ⓦ www.casaencantada-antigua.com. Boutique-style hotel with ten immaculate rooms, most with a four-poster bed, and all with delightful bathrooms. There's a small pool, a rooftop bar and full breakfast is included. Rooms from US$122. ⓐ

Casa Santo Domingo 3 C Oriente 28 ☏ 7832 0140, Ⓦ www.casasantodomingo.com.gt. A dramatic and impressive place to stay, this converted colonial-era convent has real atmosphere with corridors bedecked in ecclesiastical art and the grounds (with two pools and a museum) are huge. Despite the evocative surrounds there's a slightly impersonal feel to the place; service can be distracted and the rooms, though spacious, are due for an upgrade. Low-season rates start at US$130. ⓐ

Cissus 6 C Poniente 41 ☏ 7832 0643, Ⓦ www.cissushotel.com. Taking the hip hotel concept to new heights, this stunning new place has real style, with lovely sitting areas and a palm-filled garden. All the accommodation, mixing contemporary and colonial styles, is wonderful, but suite #2, which has a private roof terrace with views on three sides, really stands out. Rooms from US$172. ⓐ

The Cloister 5 Av Norte 23 ☏ 7832 0712, Ⓦ www.thecloister.com. A stylish, luxurious B&B with seven beautifully furnished suite-sized rooms around an exquisite tropical garden. Well-stocked private library and reading room, wi-fi and a handy location (almost under Antigua's famous arch). From US$120. ⓐ

Hotel Quinta de las Flores C del Hermano Pedro 6 ☏ 832 3721, Ⓦ www.quintadelasflores.com. This hotel's spectacular garden – with swimming pool and children's play area – is its real trump card, a wonderful oasis bursting with rare plants, shrubs and trees. The rooms and *casitas* (each sleeping five, with two bedrooms and kitchen) are all attractively decorated, and there's also a restaurant. It's a 10min walk south of town. ⓐ–ⓐ

Mesón Panza Verde 5 Av Sur 19 ☏ 7832 2925, Ⓦ www.panzaverde.com. Defining the boutique-chic hotel sector in Antigua, this gorgeous place has commodious doubles and suites spread throughout two colonial-style buildings. The hotel is also home to one of Antigua's premier restaurants and an art gallery, while other perks include a lap pool and a healthy complimentary breakfast. ⓑ–ⓐ

The City

In accordance with its position as the seat of colonial authority in Central America, Antigua was once a centre of secular and religious power, trade and, above all, wealth. Here the great institutions competed with the government to build the country's most impressive buildings. Churches, monasteries, schools, hospitals and grand family homes were constructed throughout the city, all with tremendously thick walls to resist earthquakes. Today Antigua has an incredible number of ruined and restored **colonial buildings** that provide an idea of its former status. Mentioned below are only some of the highlights; armed with a map from the tourist office you could spend days exploring the ruins. The sheer volume of sights can seem overwhelming; if you'd rather just visit the gems, make La Merced, Las Capuchinas, the Casa Popenoe and San Francisco your targets.

The Parque Central

Antigua's focal point has always been its commanding central plaza, the **Parque Central**. In colonial times the plaza held a bustling market, which was cleared periodically for bullfights, military parades, floggings and public hangings. The calm of today's shady plaza, largely isolated from the city's traffic and replete with well-tended flowering scrubs, is relatively recent. Don't miss the risqué central fountain, its water jets gushing from the nipples of breast-squeezing mermaids.

The Cathedral of San José

The most imposing of the plaza's surrounding structures is the **Cathedral of San José**, on the eastern side, its intricate facade evocatively illuminated

---

Semana Santa in Antigua

Antigua's **Semana Santa (Holy Week) celebrations** are perhaps the most extravagant and impressive in all Latin America – a week of vigils, processions and pageants commemorating the most solemn week of the Christian year. The celebrations start with a procession on Palm Sunday, representing Christ's entry into Jerusalem, and continue through the week, climaxing on Good Friday. On Thursday night the streets are carpeted with meticulously drawn patterns of coloured sawdust, and on Friday morning a series of processions re-enacts the progress of Christ to the Cross. Setting out from the churches of La Merced and Escuela de Cristo and the village of San Felipe at around 8am, groups of penitents, clad in purple or white and wearing peaked hoods, carry images of Christ and the Cross on massive platforms, accompanied by solemn dirges played by local brass bands and clouds of incense. After 3pm, the hour of the Crucifixion, the penitents change into black.

It is a great honour to be involved in the procession but no easy task – the great cedar block carried from La Merced weighs some 3.5 tonnes and needs eighty men to lift it. Some of the images displayed date from the seventeenth century, and the procession itself is thought to have been introduced by Alvarado in the early years of the Conquest.

Check the exact details of events with the tourist office, which should be able to provide you with a map detailing the routes of the processions. During Holy Week virtually every hotel in Antigua is full, and the entire town is packed. But even if you have to make the trip from Guatemala City or Lago de Atitlán, it's well worth it, especially on Friday.

at night. The first cathedral on this site was begun in 1545, using some of the vast fortune left by Alvarado's death. The construction was so poor, however, that the structure was in a constant state of disrepair, and an earthquake in 1583 brought down much of the roof. In 1670 work started on a new cathedral worthy of the town's role as a capital city. For eleven years the town watched as conscripted Maya laboured and the most spectacular colonial building in Central America took shape. The scale of the new cathedral was astounding: a vast dome, five naves, eighteen chapels, and a central chamber measuring 90m by 20m. Its altar was inlaid with mother-of-pearl, ivory and silver, and carvings of saints and paintings by the most revered of European and colonial artists covered the walls.

The new cathedral withstood earthquakes in 1689 and 1717, but its walls were weakened and the 1773 earthquake brought them crashing to the ground. Today, two of the chapels have been restored as the **Church of San José**, which opens off the Parque Central; inside is a figure of Christ by the colonial sculptor Quirio Cataño, who also carved the famous Black Christ of Esquipulas (see p.272). Behind the church, entered from 5 Calle Oriente, are the **ruins** (US$0.40) of the rest of the structure, a mass of fallen masonry, broken arches and hefty pillars, cracked and moss-covered, the great original cupola now just a window to the sky. Buried beneath the floor are said to be some of the great names of the Conquest, including Alvarado; his wife, Beatriz de la Cueva; Bishop Marroquín; and the historian Bernal Díaz del Castillo. At the very rear of the original nave, steps lead down to a burial vault, blackened by candle smoke, that's regularly used for Maya religious ceremonies, an example of the coexistence of pagan and Catholic beliefs that's so characteristic of Guatemala.

▲ Palace of the Captains General

The Palace of the Captains General

Along the entire south side of the Parque Central runs the squat two-storey facade of the **Palace of the Captains General**, with a row of 27 arches along each floor. It was originally built in 1558, but as usual the first version was destroyed by earthquakes. It was rebuilt in 1761, only to be damaged again in 1773 and finally restored along the lines of the present structure. The palace was home to the colonial rulers and also housed the barracks of the dragoons, the stables, the royal mint, law courts, tax offices, great ballrooms, a large bureaucracy, and a lot more besides. It's normally the home of the Sacatepéquez police department and the tourist office, but currently the subject of a restoration project.

The Ayuntamiento

Directly opposite, on the north side of the plaza, is the **Ayuntamiento**, the city hall also known as the *Casa del Cabildo*, or town house. Dating from 1740, its metre-thick walls balance the solid style of the Palace of the Captains General. Unlike most others, this building survived earlier rumblings and wasn't damaged until the 1976 earthquake, although it has since been repaired. The city hall was abandoned in 1779 when the capital moved to Guatemala City, but it was later reclaimed for use by the city's administration. If you climb to the upper level of the building, there's a wonderful vista of the three volcanoes that ring the city, especially fine at sunset.

The Ayuntamiento also holds a couple of minor museums. The first of these, the **Museo de Santiago** (Tues–Sun 9am–4pm; US$1.40, Sun by donation), houses a collection of colonial artefacts, including bits of pottery, a sword said to have been used by Alvarado, some traditional Maya weapons, portraits of stern-faced colonial figures, and some paintings of warfare between the Spanish and the Maya. At the back of the museum is the old city jail, beside which there used to be a small chapel where condemned prisoners passed their last moments before being hauled off to the gallows in the plaza. Also under the arches of the city hall, the **Museo del Libro Antiguo** (same hours and fees as above) is located in the rooms that held the first printing press in Central America. The press arrived here in 1660 from Puebla de los Ángeles in Mexico, and churned out its first book three years later. A replica of the press is on display alongside some copies of the works produced on it.

South and east of the Parque Central

Across the street from the ruined cathedral, in 5 Calle Oriente (Calle de La Universidad), is the **Museo de Arte Colonial** (Tues–Fri 9am–4pm, Sat & Sun 9am–noon & 2–4pm; US$3), housed in the former site of the University of San Carlos Borromeo. The founding of a university was first proposed by Bishop Marroquín in 1559, but it wasn't until 1676 that the plan was authorized, using money left by the bishop. Classes began in 1681 with seventy students applying themselves to everything from law to the Kaqchikel language. At first only pure-blooded Castilians could study here, but later a broader spectrum of the population was admitted. The Moorish-style courtyard, deep-set windows and beautifully ornate cloisters make it one of the finest architectural survivors in Antigua. The museum contains a good collection of brooding religious art, sculpture, furniture, murals depicting life on the colonial campus and a seventeenth-century map of Antigua by the historian Antonio de Fuentes y Guzmán.

Further west up 5 Calle Oriente, on the corner of 1 Avenida Sur, the superbly restored colonial mansion **Casa Popenoe** (Mon–Sat 2–4pm; US$1.40) offers a welcome break from church ruins as well as a window into domestic life in colonial times. The house, originally built in 1634 was in ruins when, in 1932, Dr Wilson Popenoe, a United Fruit Company scientist, began its comprehensive restoration. Sifting through the rubble piece by piece, the doctor and his wife restored the building to its former glory, filling it with an incredible collection of colonial furniture and art. Among the paintings are portraits of Bishop Marroquín and the menacing-looking Alvarado himself. Every last detail has been authentically restored, down to the original leather lampshades painted with religious musical scores and the great wooden beds, decorated with a mass of accomplished carving. The kitchen and servants' quarters have also been carefully renovated, and you can see the bread ovens, herb garden and pigeon loft, which would have provided the original occupants with their mail service. A narrow staircase leads up from the pigeon loft to the roof, from where there are spectacular views over the city and volcanoes. Dr Popenoe died in 1972, but two of his daughters still live in the house.

Around Parque Unión

A block south and a block west of the parque, on 6 Calle Oriente, two churches face each other at opposite ends of the slim, palm-tree-lined plaza of **Parque Unión**. At the western end is the **San Pedro church** and hospital. Originally built in 1680, and periodically crammed full of earthquake victims, the church was finally evacuated in 1976 when one of the aftershocks threatened to bring down the roof. Reconstruction was completed in 1991 and the facade now has a polished perfection that's strangely incongruous in Antigua. At the other end of the plaza is the convent and church of **Santa Clara**, founded in 1699 by nuns from Puebla in Mexico. In colonial times this became a popular place for well-to-do young ladies to take the veil, as the hardships were none too hard, and the nuns earned a reputation for their cooking by selling bread to the aristocracy. The original convent was totally destroyed in 1717, as was the second in 1773, but the current building was spared in 1976 and its ornate facade (floodlit at night) remains intact. In front of Santa Clara are the huge arches of an open-air *pila*, a wash house where local women gather to scrub, rinse and gossip.

Just southwest on 1 Avenida Sur, the imposing **church of San Francisco** (daily 8am–6pm) is one of the oldest churches in Antigua. Dating from 1579, it grew into a vast religious and cultural centre that included a school, a hospital, music rooms, a printing press and a monastery. The church originally boasted highly decorative mouldings and sculpture along its nave, but these were ruined by earthquakes and were left off during restoration in 1960. Inside the church is the tomb of **Hermano Pedro de Betancourt**, a Franciscan from the Canary Islands who founded the Hospital of Belén in Antigua and is credited with powers of miraculous intervention by the faithful – hundreds of little plaques give thanks for his services, while Pope John Paul II made him Central America's first saint in 2002. The **ruins** (same hours; US$0.40) of the monastery are among the most impressive in Antigua, and you're welcome to picnic next to the colossal fallen arches and pillars on the pleasant grassy verges.

North of the Parque Central

Setting out northwards from the Parque Central, you'll find the remains of the hermitage of **El Carmen** on 3 Avenida Norte. This was originally one of the city's great churches, first built in 1638 and rebuilt many times since; the top half of the facade finally collapsed in 1976, but the remains hint at its former glory.

Just northeast of here, at the junction of 2 Calle Oriente and 2 Avenida Norte, is the site of **Las Capuchinas** (9am–5pm; US$4), the largest of the city's convents, whose ruins are some of the best preserved but least understood in Antigua. The Capuchin nuns, who came from Madrid, were rather late on the scene, founding the city's fourth convent in 1726. They were only granted permission by the colonial authorities on the condition that the convent would exact no fees from its novices. The Capuchin order was the most rigorous in Antigua. Numbers were restricted to 25, with nuns sleeping on wooden beds with straw pillows. Once they had entered the convent it's thought the women were not allowed any visual contact with the outside world; food was passed to them by means of a turntable and they could only speak to visitors through a grille.

The ruins are the most beautiful in Antigua, with fountains, courtyards and massive earthquake-proof pillars. The tower or "retreat" is the most unusual feature, with eighteen tiny cells set into the walls of its top floor, each having its own independent sewage system. Two of the cells have been returned to their original condition to demonstrate the extreme austerity of the nuns' lives. The lower floor is dominated by a massive pillar that supports the structure above and incorporates seventeen small recesses, some with rings set in the walls. Theories about the purpose of this still abound – as a warehouse, a laundry room, a communal bath or even a torture chamber – though most scholars now agree that it probably functioned as a storage room, and the rings were meat hooks. The exterior of this architectural curiosity is also interesting, ringed with small stone recesses that represent the Stations of the Cross.

Heading northwest, the church and convent of **Santa Teresa**, located where 4 Avenida Norte meets 1 Calle, was originally founded by a Peruvian philanthropist for a group of Carmelite nuns from Lima; these days, however, it serves as the city jail.

A block further west along 1 Calle is the church of **La Merced**, which boasts one of the most intricate and impressive facades in the entire city. It has been beautifully restored, painted mustard yellow and white, and crammed with plaster moulding of interlaced patterns. Look closely and you'll see the outline of a corn cob, a design not normally seen on Catholic churches and probably added by the original Maya labourers. The church is still in use, but the cloisters and gardens (US$0.80) lie ruined, exposed to the sky. In the centre of one of the courtyards is a monumental tiered fountain with four pools that's known as the *Fuente de Pescados*; the pools were used by the Mercedarian brothers for breeding fish. The colonial fountain in front of the church is also worth a look for its superbly preserved, carved decoration.

From La Merced it's a few steps to 5 Avenida Norte, spanned by the **arch of Santa Catalina**, one of Antigua's most emblematic structures and all that remains of the original convent founded here in 1609. By 1697 it reached maximum capacity with 110 nuns and six novices, and the arch was built in order that they could walk between the two halves of the establishment without being exposed to the pollution of the outside world. Somehow it managed to defy the constant onslaught of earthquakes and was restored in the middle of the nineteenth century; it is now a favoured, if clichéd, spot for photographers as the view to the Volcán de Agua is unobstructed from here.

Further out to the northeast along 1 Avenida Norte, the badly damaged ruins of the churches of **Santa Rosa**, **Candelaria** and **Nuestra Señora de los Dolores del Cerro** are of interest to ruined-church buffs only.

West of the Parque Central

The last of the major ruins lie west of the plaza, near the bus station. At the junction of 4 Calle Poniente and 6 Avenida Norte stands **La Compañia de Jesús**, an educational establishment and church that was operated by the Jesuits until King Carlos III of Spain, feeling threatened by their tremendous and growing power, expelled them from the colonies in 1767. Renovated recently by Spanish experts, the building now hosts cultural exhibitions and events.

Turning to the right in front of the bus station, walk to the end of tree-lined Avenida Alameda Santa Lucía, and you reach the spectacular remains of **San Jerónimo** (daily 9am–5pm; US$4), a school built in 1739. The site, with its well-kept gardens woven between the huge blocks of fallen masonry and crumbling walls, is regularly used as a spectacular site for classical music concerts. Behind San Jerónimo, a cobbled road leads to the even larger, and more chaotic, ruin of **La Recolección** (daily 9am–5pm; US$4), where the middle of the church is piled high with the remains of the roof and walls. Friars first arrived here and asked for permission to build in 1685, but it wasn't until 1701 that they started the church, and a further fourteen years before it was finished. Only months after its completion, the church was brought to the ground by a huge earthquake. This second version was destroyed in 1773 and has been steadily decaying ever since.

On the southern side of the bus station, along Avenida Alameda Santa Lucía, is an imposing monument to **Rafael Landívar** (1731–93), a Jesuit composer who is generally considered the finest poet of the colonial era. Along with the other members of his order, he was banished from the Americas in 1767. Walking back to the plaza along 5 Calle Poniente, you'll pass the **Iglesia de San Agustín**, the remains of a vast convent complex that once occupied about half the block but has stood derelict since the earthquake of 1773, after which the Augustinians followed the government in the exodus to Guatemala City.

Eating

Antigua boasts a terrific array of **cafés** and **restaurants**, with most types of global cuisine represented. It's possible to snack well for a few bucks or dine in style for around US$15–20 a head, and round it off with a perfect espresso or latte. The only thing hard to come by is authentic Guatemalan *comida típica* – which will be a relief if you've been subsisting on eggs and beans in the mountains.

Volcano tours from Antigua

Volcán de Pacaya (see p.91) near Guatemala City is a spectacular and very active volcano that regularly spews towering plumes of smoke and brilliant orange sludge – though such fire'n'brimstone shows only happen sporadically. Gran Jaguar Tours, 4 C Poniente 30 (℡7832 2712, ℗www.granjaguartours.com), offers basic trips for US$5–7 per head, while adventure-tour specialists (see p.109) charge around US$40 per head for a day-hike or US$75 for overnight camping trips on the volcano, using comfortable minibuses and including meals. Entrance to the Pacaya National Park is an additional US$3.50.

Other cones to climb include **volcanoes Agua** (see p.115) and **Acatenango** (see pp.112–113), the toughest climb in this region, which gives a great view of the highly active neighbouring cone of **Fuego**.

The best **deli** is *Epicure*, 6 Avenida Norte 35A, where you'll find lots of gourmet treats produced in Guatemala, including salami and sausages, and some fine cheeses, as well as wine and culinary treats from Europe, North America and Asia. They'll also make you up a sandwich here.

Cafés

Bagel Barn 5 C Poniente 2. Ideal for an early breakfast (it opens at 6am) or a tasty, if a little pricey, filled bagel. They also show movies.

Café Condesa west side of Parque Central – go through the Casa del Conde bookshop. Classy place that's highly popular with both moneyed Guatemalans and tourists, where the cobbled patio and a gurgling fountain add to the colonial charm. Excellent (if expensive) breakfasts and lunches, cakes and snacks.

Café La Escalonia 5 Av Sur 36 C. About 800m south of the parque, this café (located inside a plant nursery) is a really peaceful retreat and much of the food is organic. Tuck into healthy breakfasts, *pan de hierbas* sandwiches, pies and salads.

Caffè Opera 6 Av Norte 17. Swanky, expensive café with lavish wall-to-wall operatic parapher-nalia, comfortable seating and a tiled floor. Good for coffee and a panini (though the licuado prices are stratospheric); they also offer daily specials that sometimes include *gnocchi*. Closed Wed.

Cookies Etc 3 Av Norte 7. Offers a near-endless list of yummy cookies, as well as breakfasts sandwiches, muffins and free coffee refills. Takeouts available.

Doña Luisa's 4 C Oriente 12. Ever-popular café-restaurant set in a historic colonial mansion. A straightforward menu of sandwiches, burgers and salads, but the in-house bakery really is the best in town. Bread and pastries can be purchased from an adjoining shop.

Fernando's Kaffee 7 Av Norte 43. Arabica-bean aficionados should look no further, this place serves up unquestionably the finest coffee – roasted, ground and blended on the premises – in Antigua. Owner Fernando is a friendly, English-speaking Guatemalan and his partner Belinda bakes the absolutely delicious pastries and cakes. There's a nice courtyard at the back.

La Fuente 4 C Oriente 14. Attractive, moderately priced courtyard restaurant/café where you can eat a decent plate of pasta, a sandwich or soup and sip good coffee. On Sat indigenous women set up a *huipil* market around the central fountain.

Peroleto Alameda Santa Lucía Norte 36. One half of this place is a hole-in-the-wall juice bar that serves breakfasts, the other a comedor. Both are inexpensive and very Guatemalan.

Rainbow Reading Room 7 Av Sur 8. One of Antigua's most enjoyable places to while away an hour or two, this café-restaurant has tables grouped around a central patio and a menu of imaginative salads, vegetarian and international choices, shakes and Chilean wine by the glass (US$3). There are cultural lectures, live music (around a campfire when weather permits), wi-fi, and it's also home to one of Antigua's best secondhand bookstores and travel agents.

Y Tú Piña Tambien 1 Av Sur & 6 C Oriente. The perfect place for a healthy kick-start to the day this hip little café has an amazing selection of juices (try "gamma" with mango, carrot, apple and ginger) as well as pancakes, omelettes, cakes and baguettes. Wi-fi and magazines to browse, too.

Restaurants

Bistrot Cinq 4 C Oriente 7 ⊛ www .bistrotcinq.com. Ticking all the right boxes, this exciting new French place has a short, uncom-plicated menu (sourced from premium imported ingredients), an open kitchen and stylish modern decor. Classic dishes like steak *frites* or magret of duck are superbly executed, and there are always a couple of good fish options. Opens at noon for brunch (around US$10); dinner upwards of US$25 a head.

Café Panchoy 6 Av Norte 1B. Dependable cooking with a Guatemalan flavour, with tables set around an open kitchen. Plenty of grilled meats, plus tacos and local dishes like *chiles rellenos*. Famous for its *horchata* and they serve good margaritas too. Closed Tues.

Caffè Mediterraneo 6 C Poniente 6A. Real Italian cooking, with fresh pasta, *bruschette* and always a daily special. Very civilized and popular with Antigua's resident foodies. Closed Tues.

Casa de las Mixtas 1 Callejón, off 3 C Poniente. For comedor cooking this bright little place is inexpensive and hard to beat. Very extensive breakfast options.

La Casserole Callejón de la Concepción 7. Elegant, expensive restaurant in a pretty garden patio shaded by a lime tree, with a deserved rep for delivering quality French cuisine – leave some room for the epic desserts. Closed Mon.

Comedor Típico Antigüeño Alameda Santa Lucía Sur 5. Set inauspiciously opposite the bus terminal and market, this humble place offers unbeatable

US$2 set lunches (such as *pollo a la carbon* and *pepián*), which all include a soup starter.

La Cuevita de los Urquizú 2 C Oriente 9. A good place to try some typical Guatemalan dishes – choose from the bubbling pots at the restaurant entrance. Around US$6 per head, including a drink and sweet. Open daily 9am–7pm.

Don Martín 4 Av Norte 27. Smallish place that serves up creative, appetizing Guatemalan food-with-a-twist (plus an Italian dish or two). The classically trained chef's moderately priced menu includes *pepián* (spicy meat stew), *lomito* and pasta. Closed Mon.

La Escudilla 4 Av Norte 4. Given the gorgeous colonial surrounds, the prices at this courtyard restaurant are a steal. The breakfast special (until 10.30am) is just US$1.40, while the set lunch (US$3) changes on a daily basis. Eat à la carte and you'll find an excellent choice of European dishes (US$5–8), salads (try the *jardinera*), vegetarian options and Mexican staples like nachos and fajitas. Always busy, but you can have a drink, if you have to wait, in *Riki's Bar*, which is on the same premises.

La Fonda de la Calle Real three branches: upstairs at 5 Av Norte 5; 5 Av Norte 12; and a third (the nicest location) at 3 C Poniente 7, ⓦwww.lafondadelacallereal.com. For really delicious, authentic Guatemalan food, this long-running, moderately pricey restaurant has a terrific reputation. Specialities are *caldo real* (chicken soup with rice, spices and lemon), *pepián* and charcoal-grilled meats including wonderful local sausages. The coffee even comes from the foothills around Antigua. Closed Wed.

Frida's 5 Av Norte 29. All your usual Mexican favourites and a lively atmosphere, especially at weekends. The dining rooms are intimate and festooned with 1950s Americana.

Nokiate 1 Av Sur 7 ⓦwww.nokiate.com. Very hip and stylish restaurant that presents itself as an Asian–Latino restaurant, a combination that might ring alarm bells, but all the dishes are well thought out and executed beautifully. Sushi and *ceviche* are the best in town, and there are always daily specials like Vietnamese-style chicken wings. Staff are very well trained, and they serve both wine and sake. Also operates as a lounge bar; look out for the Martini specials. Closed Mon.

Palacio de la India 4 Av Norte 42. Casual, intimate place serving authentic Indian food, with several choices for vegetarians. All dishes are delicately spiced and reasonably priced.

Panza Verde 5 Av Sur 19. Highly rated, stylish and consistently good European restaurant, whose Swiss chef has created a well-chosen menu of fish and meat mains and desserts to die for. The setting is elegant, too, with tables grouped around a delightful courtyard garden. Expensive.

El Punto 7 Av Norte 8A. Looks humble, but serves the most authentic Italian food in town at moderate prices. Meat, pasta and *gnocchi* as well as some interesting wines. Closed Mon.

Quesos y Vinos 1 C Pon 1. This Italian restaurant has shifted location several times, but now resides in an exceptionally graceful spot, with a lovely garden terrace and elegant colonial-style interior. Feast on delicious crostini, salads, meat dishes, pasta or pizza (from a wood-fired brick oven).

Su Chow 5 Av Norte 38. Good, inexpensive Chinese food, cooked and served by a charming Belizean family. Closed Tues.

Travel Menu 6 C Poniente 14. This small Dutch-owned place serves up large portions of very tasty Latin American and Western food, with an atmospheric candlelit setting.

Drinking, nightlife and entertainment

Antigua's main *zona viva* (lively zone) is centred around the arch on 5 Avenida Norte, though there are bars spread around the town. The club scene here is small but lively, though the nationwide 1am curfew often draws the action to a premature end. "After hours" parties are held most weekends in private houses, publicized by flyers and word-of-mouth.

If you want to learn to dance **salsa**, the teacher Gloria Villata is highly recommended; contact her at ☏5857 0344 or Ⓔgvillata@yahoo.com.

A number of small video **cinemas** show a range of Western films on a daily basis; weekly listings are posted on notice boards all over town. Two places are the *Bagel Barn*, 5 Calle Poniente 2, and *Café 2000*, 6 Avenida Norte. The Proyecto Cultural El Sitio, at 5 Calle Poniente 15, has a fairly good choice of Latin American and art-house movies.

Bars and clubs

Café No Sé 1 Av Norte 11C. For conversation and atmosphere this scruffy-looking bar, well west of the centre, is the best bet in Antigua as there are always local and visiting characters around. There's a tiny front bar, a hidden tequila/mescal bar (stocked with over a dozen artisan liquors including the house *Ilegal* brand) and a dining area for inexpensive, filling grub. Live music most nights at 9pm, though at times the artists churn out too many sentimental cover songs.

Café Sky 1 Av Sur. Offers terrific views from the upper deck of a three-storey building (there's a restaurant below). With a full cocktail list, this is the perfect place for sunset.

La Casbah 5 Av Norte 30 ⓦ www.lacasbah antigua.com. Nightclub that attracts a well-heeled crowd, with a spectacular venue overlooking the floodlit ruins of a Baroque church. Latin dance and house music rule the dancefloor at weekends, but electronic DJs mix up underground sounds on Thurs, and Wed is salsa night. There's a roof terrace; drinks are expensive. Tues–Thurs US$3, Fri & Sat around US$6.

Mono Loco 2 Av Norte 6B. Huge, clichéd gringo sports bar-style place, with mediocre mainstream music and dreary food. For some reason, however, it's one of the most popular places in town.

Onis 7 Av Norte & 6 C Poniente. Boho-looking two-storey bar which serves some snacks and has stunning views over the ruined church of San Agustín. Only gets busy at weekends.

Reds 1 C Pon 3. Large British-owned bar with good beer selection, pool tables, and a full menu that takes in local, Mexican, Thai and English comfort food. The perfect location for a big football game.

Reilly's 5 Av Norte 31. Antigua's Irish bar is always popular and offers comfort food (including roast beef some days), and hosts a great quiz (trivia) on Sun evenings.

Riki's Bar 4 Av Norte 4. Small, stylish place that's packed most nights due to its excellent location inside *La Escudilla* and extended happy hour (7–9pm). Musically things are often quite interesting with funk, jazz and lounge on the system.

La Sala 6 C Poniente 9. Enjoyable, fairly upmarket bar that has live music (Latin/funk/rock) on weekend nights and a good drinks list.

Listings

Adventure sports Old Town Outfitters, 5 Av Sur 12 (ⓣ 5399 0440, ⓦ www.bikeguatemala.com), runs volcano hikes including Acatenango (US$60), mountain-bike excursions (half-day US$39), rock-climbing trips for all levels, sea kayaking (2 days US$150) and offers tent, sleeping bag, pack and bike rental. Maya Mountain Bike Tours, 1 Av Sur 15 (ⓣ 7832 3383, ⓦ www.guatemalaventures.com), also has an excellent range of trips (a 6-day bike adventure is US$659), plus bike rental. Ox Expeditions, 1 Av Sur 4B (ⓣ 7832 0074, ⓦ www .guatemalavolcano.com), is very well set up for volcano hiking (Agua costs US$29).

Banks and exchange Banco Industrial, 5 Av Sur 4, just south of the plaza, has a 24hr ATM for Visa cardholders. Banco del Quetzal, on north side of the plaza, has a MasterCard ATM and changes travel-ler's cheques. There are several more ATMs in town.

Bike rental Maya Mountain Bike Tours and Old Town Outfitters (see Adventure sports above) both rent quality mountain-bikes for US$20 a day.

Bookstores Casa del Conde and Un Poco de Todo are both on the west side of the plaza for new books, including *Rough Guides*. The best places for secondhand titles are the *Rainbow Reading Room*, 7 Av Sur 8, and Dyslexia Books at 1 Av Sur 11.

Car and motorbike rental Avis, 5 Av Norte 22 (ⓣ 7832 2692, ⓦ www.avis.com.gt), and Tabarini, 6 Av Sur 22 (ⓣ 7832 8107, ⓦ www.tabarini.com), both have cars from around US$35 a day and 4WD from US$60. CA Tours, 6 C Oriente 14 (ⓣ 7832 9638, ⓦ www.catours.co.uk), rent scooters for US$36 per day or trail bikes from US$50; contact them about motorbike tours around Guatemala.

City tours Excellent walking tours (US$20) are led by historian Elizabeth Bell, *Hotel Casa Santo Domingo* (ⓣ 7832 5821, ⓦ www.antiguatours.net).

Gym La Fábrica, C Del Hermano Pedro 16 (ⓣ 7832 0486), has excellent facilities, including running machines, weights, fitness and martial arts classes.

Horseriding Ravenscroft Stables, 2 Av Sur 3 (ⓣ 7832 6229) in the village of San Juan del Obispo; see p.113.

Internet There are dozens of cybercafés; rates are about US$1 an hour. Conexión, in the *La Fuente* courtyard at 4 C Oriente 14 (daily 8.30am–7pm), is probably the best setup, with flat screens and fast connections. Funky Monkey, 5 Av Sur 6 (next to *Mono Loco*), is another good place. Both can burn digital photos to CDs.

Laundry Rainbow Laundry, 6 Av Sur 15 (Mon–Sat 7am–7pm).

Studying Spanish in Antigua

Antigua's **language schools** are a key local employer, with a couple dozen or so established schools, and many more or less reliable setups, some operating in the front room of someone's house. Whether you're just stopping for a week or two to learn the basics, or settling in for several months in pursuit of total fluency, there can be no doubt that this is one of the best places in Latin America to learn Spanish: it's a beautiful, relaxed town, lessons are inexpensive (though tend to cost more than in other areas of Guatemala) and there are several superb schools.

Choosing a school

The following schools are well established, recommended and towards the top end of the price scale, charging between US$140 and US$240 per week for daily four-hour-long one-on-one sessions and full family-based lodging and meals.

Academia de Español Antigüeña 1 C Poniente 10 ☎7832 7241, ⓦwww.spanish academyantiguena.com

APPE 6 C Poniente 40 ☎7882 4284, ⓦwww.appeschool.com. Also has a school in the nearby village of San Juan del Obispo.

Los Capitanes Generales 4 Av Sur 2, ☎7832 8769, ⓦwww.loscapitanes.com.

Centro Lingüístico Maya 5 C Poniente 20 ☎7832 0656, ⓦwww.clmmaya.com.

Christian Spanish Academy 6 Av Norte 15 ☎7832 3922, ⓦwww.learncsa.com.

Cooperación 7 Av Norte 15B ☎7832 0472, ⓦwww.spanishschoolcooperacion.com.

Probigua 6 Av Norte 41B ☎7832 2998, ⓦwww.probigua.org.

Projecto Lingüístico Francisco Marroquín 7 C Poniente 31 ☎7832 2886, ⓦwww.plfm-antigua.org. Also offers classes in Maya languages.

San José El Viejo 5 Av Sur 34 ☎7832 3028, ⓦwww.sanjoseelviejo.com.

Sevilla 1 Av Sur 17C ☎7832 5101, ⓦwww.sevillantigua.com.

Tecún Umán 6 C Poniente 34 A ☎7832 2792, ⓦwww.tecunuman.centramerica.com.

La Unión 1 Av Sur 21 ☎7832 7337, ⓦwww.launion.edu.gt.

Libraries and cultural institutes El Sitio, 5 C Poniente 15 (☎7832 3037, ⓦwww.elsitio cultural.org), has an active theatre, library and art gallery, and regularly hosts exhibitions and concerts; see their website or *Revue* for listings.

Medical care There's 24hr emergency service at the Santa Lucía Hospital, Calzada Santa Lucía Sur 7 (☎7832 3122). Dr Aceituno, who speaks good English, has an office at 2 C Poniente 7 (☎7832 0512).

Pharmacies Farmacia Santa María, west side of the plaza (daily 8am–10pm).

Police The police HQ is on the south side of the plaza (☎7832 0251). The tourist police are behind the marketplace (☎7832 7290).

Pool hall 3 C Poniente 4–5A. Very much a male-dominated institution, although tourists of either sex are welcome, providing they can handle the smell.

Post Main post office is on Av Alameda Santa Lucía, opposite the bus terminal (Mon–Fri 8am–4.30pm). Federal Express, 2 C Poniente 3.

Shopping Nim Po't, 5 Av Norte 29 (ⓦwww .nimpot.com), sells some of the finest textiles in the country at fair prices. The warehouse-like store is something of a museum of contemporary Maya weaving, with a stunning array of complete costumes, plus other artesanías including wooden masks and some souvenirs. For original gifts check out the superb store Doña Gavi, 3 Av 2, which has natural soaps and lotions, herbal remedies and white linen clothes all created by the owner. The Fuente centre, at 4 C Oriente 14, has a number of upmarket clothing and handicraft stores while Al Pie del Volcán, on 4 Av Norte 7, also sells quality handicrafts. Chocolandia, inside Deliciosa, 3 C Poniente 2, is great for truffles and handmade chocolate, all made by a professional chocolatier.

Supermarket La Bodegona, at 4 C Poniente and Alameda Santa Lucía.

Swimming pool *Villa Antigua*, 9 C, just south of town on the road to Ciudad Vieja, has two (non-heated) pools that non-guests can use for US$15 per day, which also includes a lunch and gives you access to a small gym and sauna. Or you could just try and sneak in.

Taxis On the east side of the plaza, near the market or call ℡7832 0479. For a female cab driver, call Chiqui on ℡5715 5720.

Telephones Australis, 4 C Poniente 15, is a professional outfit with soundproofed cabins. Calls cost US$0.15 to North America and around US$0.30 to the rest of the world. The cybercafés (see "Internet") also offer cheap internet calls.

Travel agents Of the dozens of travel agents in Antigua, some of the most professional are: Rainbow, 7 Av Sur 8 (℡7832 4202,

ⓦwww.rainbowtravelcenter.com), for flights and tours; Atitrans, 6 Av Sur 8 (℡7832 3371, ⓦwww.atitransguate.com), and Adrenalina Tours, 5 Av Norte 31 (℡7832 1108, ⓦwww.adrenalinatours.com), are both excellent for shuttle buses; Viajes Tivoli, 4 C Oriente 10 (℡7832 4274, Ⓔantigua@tivoli.com.gt), is a recommended all-rounder. Adventure Travel Center Viareal, 5 Av Norte 25B (℡7832 0162, Ⓔviareal@guate.net), has some good adventure trips.

Around Antigua: villages and volcanoes

The countryside surrounding Antigua is superbly fertile and breathtakingly beautiful. The valley is dotted with small villages, ranging from the traditional indigenous settlement of Santa María de Jesús to genteel San Juan del Obispo, which is dominated by a huge colonial palace. You'll also find two excellent museums in Jocotenango, just north of Antigua. No place is more than thirty minutes away and all make interesting day-trips. For the more adventurous, the **volcanic peaks** of Agua and Acatenango offer strenuous but superb hiking.

Southwest of Antigua

Heading out of Antigua on the highway to Escuintla and the coast, the Panchoy valley is a broad sweep of farmland, overshadowed by three volcanic cones and peppered with olive-green coffee bushes.

The first settlement of interest is **CIUDAD VIEJA**, just east of the highway, a scruffy and unhurried place with a distinguished past: it was near here that the Spanish established their second capital in Guatemala, Santiago de los Caballeros, in 1527. Today, however, there's no trace of the original city, and all that remains from that time is a solitary tree, in a corner of the plaza, which bears a plaque commemorating the site of the first mass ever held in the country. The plaza also boasts an eighteenth-century colonial church that has recently been restored.

Three kilometres west of Cuidad Vieja, on the other side of the highway is **SAN ANTONIO AGUAS CALIENTES**, an indigenous village set on one side of a steep-sided bowl beneath the peak of Acatenango. San Antonio is famous for weaving, characterized by its complex floral and geometric patterns, and there's an indoor textile market next to the plaza where you can find a complete range of the local output. This is also a good place to learn the traditional craft of back-strap weaving; if you're interested, the best way to find out about possible lessons is simply by asking the women in the market.

There's a steady stream of **buses** leaving the Antigua terminal for Ciudad Vieja and San Antonio; the last ones return around 7pm.

Some three kilometres beyond San Antonio is **SAN MIGUEL DUEÑAS**, a dried-out, scrappy-looking sort of place where the roads are lined with bamboo fences and surrounded by coffee fincas. There's little to delay you in San Miguel itself, but a kilometre before the village the **Valhalla Experimental Station** (daily 8am–5pm; ⓦwww.exvalhalla.net) is well worth investigating. Owned by an eccentric American, Lorenzo Gottschamer, with a passion for the environment, the farm has nearly 60,000 macadamia nut trees, using non-grafted stock

Moving on from Antigua

Because of its small size, and its position off the Interamericana, few **bus routes** originate in Antigua. If you're heading to anywhere in the east of the country, take the first bus to Guatemala City and change there or, for convenience, consider a shuttle minibus service. If you're heading into the western highlands it's best to catch the first bus to Chimaltenango and transfer there. The following buses all leave from the main terminal (except the Panajachel bus).

Guatemala City 1hr. A constant flow of buses leaves for the capital (Mon–Sat 4am–8pm, Sun 6am–8pm).

Ciudad Vieja every 20min; 20min

Chimaltenango, via Parramos every 20min; 40min

Escuintla, via El Rodeo hourly; 1hr

Panajachel A bus leaves at 7am from 4 Calle Poniente 34.

San Antonio Aguas Calientes every 30min; 20min

San Juan Del Obispo every 30min; 15min

Santa María de Jesús every 30min; 30min

Yepocapa and **Acatenango** 9 daily; both 40min

Shuttles

Minibus **shuttle services** run from Antigua to many parts of the country and can be booked through most travel agents, including Atitrans and Adrenalina Tours (see "Listings"). Shuttles cost typically triple the price of public buses, but they are much more comfortable and a bit quicker. Very frequent shuttles run between the airport and Guatemala City (US$6–8) depending on the time of day; several daily to Panajachel (US$8–12); at least one daily shuttle to Monterrico (US$10). Chichicastenango (US$8–12) is very well served on market days (Thurs & Sun). There are also shuttles to Copán, Honduras (US$15–20), or you can travel with Hedman Alas, by 4am minibus from *Hotel Posada de Don Rodrigo*, 5 Av Norte 17, to Guatemala City and then on a luxury bus for US$35.

When there's enough demand, shuttles also run to Río Dulce (around US$22), Quetzaltenango (US$20), Huehuetenango (US$30) and San Cristóbal de las Casas, Mexico (US$50).

(which bear bigger crops and are more disease resistant). Visitors are very welcome, and a short tour will reveal all the secrets of nut harvesting and roasting, while later there's a chance to sample delicious macadamia pancakes in the café or buy cosmetics and chocolates.

San Miguel Dueñas is also the best starting-point for climbing the Acatenango and Fuego volcanoes. **Buses** head out to San Miguel every half-hour or so from Antigua.

Climbing Acatenango

Several travel agencies in Antigua run hiking trips (see p.109) up **Acatenango**, but it's also possible to do it yourself.

The trail starts as you enter **LA SOLEDAD**, an impoverished village perched on an exposed ridge high above the valley. It's best to take a taxi or tuk-tuk here from Antigua and to get an early start. Alternatively, sporadic pick-ups run from San Miguel Dueñas.

Locals will help you establish the trailhead, which is close to a cluster of bamboo huts, with a soccer field to the right and a small tienda to the left. A short way beyond the tienda, a track leads up to the left, heading above the village and towards the wooded lower slopes of Acatenango. It crosses another largish trail and then starts to wind up into the pine trees. Just after you enter the trees, you have to turn onto a smaller path that leads away to the right; 100m or so further on, take another small path that climbs to the left. This brings you onto a low ridge, where you meet a thin trail that leads to the left, away up the volcano – this path eventually finds its way to the top, somewhere between six and seven hours away. At times it's a little vague, but most of the way it's fairly easy to follow.

After ninety minutes you pass a beautiful grassy clearing, an ideal **campsite** – the path cuts straight across, so don't be tempted by the larger track heading off to the right. Another ninety minutes up, a wooden shelter clings to a patch of level ground among the pine trees; you're now about halfway to the top.

The trail itself is a pretty exhausting climb, a thin line of slippery volcanic ash that rises with unrelenting steepness through thick forest. Only for the last 50m or so does it emerge above the tree line, before reaching the top of the lower cone. To the south, another hour's gruelling ascent, is the main cone, accessed via a great grey bowl that rises to a height of 3975m. From here there's a magnificent view out across the valley below. On the opposite side is the Agua volcano and, to the right, the fire-scarred cone of Fuego. Looking west you can see the three cones that surround Lake Atitlán and beyond them the Santa María volcano, high above Quetzaltenango.

When it comes to getting down again, the direct route towards Alotenango may look invitingly simple but is in fact very hard to follow. It's easiest to go back the same way you came up.

Southeast of Antigua

The smooth paved road to Santa María de Jesús runs out along a narrow valley, sharing the shade with acres of coffee bushes. Before it starts to climb, the road passes the small village of **SAN JUAN DEL OBISPO**, invisible from the road but marked by what must rank as the country's finest bus shelter, beautifully carved in local stone. The village itself is an attractive, quiet little place of

The unlucky one

After abandoning their short-lived first settlement near the Kaqchikel capital of Iximché, the Spanish founded **Santiago de los Caballeros** on St Celia's Day in 1527. Set amid perfect pastures in the shadow of the Acatenango and Agua volcanoes, the new city quickly flourished, and within twenty years things had really started to take shape, with a school, a cathedral, monasteries, and farms stocked with imported cattle. But while the bulk of the Spaniards were still settling in, their leader, the rapacious **Alvarado**, was off in search of action, wealth and conquest. In 1541 he set out for the Spice Islands, travelling via Jalisco, where he met his end, crushed to death beneath a rolling horse.

When news of Alvarado's death reached his wife, **Doña Beatriz**, she plunged the capital into an extended period of mourning, staining the entire palace with black clay, inside and out. She appointed herself as her husband's replacement, and on September 9, 1541, she became the first woman to govern in the Americas, signing the declaration as *La Sin Ventura* (the unlucky one) – a fateful premonition.

On the night of Beatriz's inauguration, an earthquake shook Volcán de Agua's crater, releasing a great wave of mud that swept away the capital, killing the new ruler and most of her courtiers. Today the exact site of the original city is still the subject of some debate, but the general consensus puts it about 2km to the east of Ciudad Vieja.

cobbled streets with fine views of the great domes of Antigua. Its one outstanding sight is the **Palacio de Francisco Marroquín**, who was the first bishop of Guatemala. The place is currently home to a dozen or so nuns, and if you knock on the great wooden double doors one of them will give you a tour in Spanish (daily 9am–noon & 2–4pm; by donation). Marroquín arrived in Guatemala with Alvarado and is credited with having introduced Christianity

▲ Volcán de Agua

to the Maya, as well as reminding the Spaniards about it from time to time. On the death of Alvarado's wife he assumed temporary responsibility for the government, and was instrumental in the construction of Antigua. He died in 1563, having spent his last days in the vast palace he'd built for himself here in San Juan. The palace interior, arranged around two courtyards, is spectacularly beautiful and several rooms still contain their original furniture, as well as a portrait of Marroquín himself. Excellent information panels (in Spanish and English) detail the life of the bishop, who many Guatemalans see as the first father of the nation and credit for introducing the concept of multiculturalism. Attached to the palace is a fantastic church and chapel with ornate wood carvings, plaster mouldings and austere religious paintings.

San Juan is also renowned for its **chocolate** production, which is something of a local cottage industry. Cacao beans are brought here from the coast, and turned into bars in several homes, including Doña Josefa's, 200m northeast of the palace – just look out for the "chocolate" sign. You're welcome to drop by and watch the process (mornings only) or buy a bar or two (from US$1.60) anytime; flavours include cinnamon and almond, though beware that local tastes are very sweet. The excellent, English-owned Ravenscroft Stables is also located in the village, a block from the *palacio* (see Antigua "Listings" for more information).

Hourly **buses** to San Juan leave from the market in Antigua (7am–6.30pm; 20min) or you can catch any bus heading for Santa María de Jesús, and it's a five-minute walk from the main road.

Santa María de Jesús

Up above San Juan the road arrives in **SANTA MARÍA DE JESÚS**, starting point for the ascent of the Agua volcano. Perched high on the shoulder of the volcano, the village is some 500m above Antigua, with magnificent views of the Panchoy valley and east towards the smoking cone of Pacaya. It was founded at the end of the sixteenth century for Maya transported from Quetzaltenango: they were given the task of providing firewood for Antigua and the village earned the name "Aserradero", lumber yard. Since then it has developed into a farming community where the women wear beautiful purple *huipiles*. The village has a certain scruffy charm, with the only place **to stay** being the hospedaje *El Oasis* (☎7832 0130; ❶), just off the plaza on the road into town; it's a friendly, clean institution that serves meals that are as simple as the rooms. The owner, Aurelio, can organize guides for the hike up Agua as well as horseriding trips.

Buses run from Antigua to Santa María every thirty minutes or so from 6am to 7pm; the trip takes thirty minutes.

Volcán de Agua

Agua is the easiest and by far the most popular of Guatemala's big cones to climb, and on Saturday nights dozens of people spend the night at the summit. It's an exciting ascent with a fantastic view to reward you at the top. The trail starts in Santa María de Jesús – to reach it, head straight across the plaza, between the two aging pillars, and up the street opposite the church doors. Take a right turn just before the end, and then continue past the cemetery and out of the village. From here on it's a fairly simple climb on a clear (often garbage-strewn) path, cutting across the road that goes some of the way up. The climb takes five to six hours, and the peak, at 3766m, is always cold at night. There is shelter (though not always room) in a small chapel at the summit, and the views certainly make it worth the struggle.

Sadly, there have been (very occasional) robberies of hikers reported on the outskirts of Santa María in recent years, so before starting an ascent it's safest to check out the situation first at Inguat in Antigua or consider going with a group tour (see p.109).

North of Antigua

The route to Chimaltenango passes through a succession of sprawling villages, presenting a scruffy introduction to the western highlands, though there are some interesting attractions on the way. The nearest of these places, **SAN FELIPE DE JESÚS**, is so close that you can walk there from Antigua; it's just a kilometre to the north up 6 Avenida Norte. San Felipe has a small, Gothic-style church housing a famous image of Christ, Jesús Sepultado, said to have miraculous powers. Severely damaged in the 1976 earthquake, the church has been well restored since, and there's a fiesta here on August 30 to celebrate the anniversary of the arrival of the image in 1670. The village's other attraction is a **silver workshop**, where silver mined in the highlands of Alta Verapaz is worked and sold. To find the workshop, follow the sign to the Platería Típica La Antigüeña.

Merging into San Felipe to the west, the grimy suburb of **JOCOTENANGO**, "place of bitter fruit", is set around a huge, dusty plaza where there's a magnificent, but weathered, dusty-pink Baroque church. In colonial times, Jocotenango was the gateway to Antigua, where official visitors would be met to be escorted into the city. Long notorious for its seedy bars, the town's main industries are coffee production and wood carving. There's an excellent selection of bowls and fruits in the family-owned Artesanías Cardenas Barrios workshop on Calle San Felipe, where they have been working at the trade for five generations.

Joco's principal attraction is 500m west of the plaza in the shape of the **Centro La Azotea** cultural centre (Mon–Fri 8.30am–4pm, Sat 10am–1pm; US$3.50, including tour in English or Spanish; ⓦwww.centroazotea.com). **Casa K'ojom**, which forms one half of the compound, is a purpose-built museum dedicated to Maya culture, especially music. The history of indigenous musical traditions is clearly presented from its pre-Columbian origins, through sixteenth-century Spanish and African influences – which brought the marimba, bugles and drums – to the present day, with audiovisual documentaries of fiestas and ceremonies. Other rooms are dedicated to the village weavings of the Sacatepéquez department and the cult of Maximón (see box below). Next door, the **Museo de Café** is an extensive plantation dating from 1883,

---

The wicked saint of San Andrés Itzapa

San Andrés shares with many other western-highland villages (including Zunil and Santiago Atitlán) the honour of revering **San Simón**, or Maximón, the wicked saint, whose image is housed in a pagan chapel in the village. His abode is home to drunken men, cigar-smoking women and hundreds of burning candles, each symbolizing a request. Curiously this San Simón attracts a largely ladino congregation and is particularly popular with prostitutes. Inside the dimly lit shrine, the walls are adorned with hundreds of plaques from all over Guatemala and Central America, thanking San Simón for his help. For a small fee, you may be offered a *limpia*, or soul cleansing, which involves one of the resident women workers beating you with a bushel of herbs, while you share a bottle of local firewater, *aguardiente*, with San Simón (it dribbles down his front) and the attendant will periodically spray you with alcohol from her mouth. If you are in the region, try to get to San Andrés on October 28 when San Simón is removed from his sanctuary and paraded through the town in a pagan celebration featuring much alcohol and dancing.

Fiestas

Although the region around Guatemala City and Antigua is not prime fiesta territory, a few villages, listed below, have some firmly established traditions and dramatic celebrations. Also listed here are some events in villages not covered in the text that may be worth visiting around fiesta time, if you're in the area.

January
1–4 Fraijanes
1–5 Santa María de Jesús, main day 1st
Varies San Pedro Ayampuc

February
First Friday in Lent Antigua; San Felipe de Jesús has a huge pilgrimage.

March
6–14 Villa Canales, main day 14th
6–20 San Pedro Pinula, main day 19th
18–20 San José del Golfo, main day 19th

Holy Week
Celebrated with fervour in Antigua (see box, p.101)

April
26–30 Palencia, main day 30th

May
1 Guatemala City; Labour Day is marked by marches and protests.
1–7 Amatitlán, main day 3rd

June
24 San Juan del Obispo and Comalapa have large fiestas.
22–27 San Juan Sacatepéquez, main day 24th
27–30 Yepocapa, main day 29th

July
25 Antigua, in honour of Santiago
24–30 Palín, climaxes on final day

August
4 Mixco
15 Jocotenango
15 Guatemala City

September
29 San Miguel Dueñas; dances include Los Toritos

October
18 San Lucas Sacatepéquez; dances include Moors and Christians
28 San Andrés Itzapa; all-nighter with San Simón paraded through the town

November
1 Sumpango and Santiago Sacatepéquez, massive paper kites flown in village cemeteries
20–28 San Catarina Pinula, main day 25th
27–Dec 1 San Andrés Itzapa, main day 30th

December
4–9 Chinautla, main day 6th
6–11 Villa Nueva, main day 11th

and offers the chance to look around a working organic coffee farm. All the technicalities of husking, sieving and roasting are clearly explained, and an interpretive trail leads through the bushes of the finca. If you're here in February or March when the coffee plants flower, there's a wonderfully fragrant scent in the air, a little like jasmine. Special minibuses (US$0.75 return) leave from Antigua's 4 Calle Oriente (just east of the plaza) hourly to the Centro La Azotea.

For a rustic place to stay in these parts, consider the ⚑ **Earth Lodge** (☎5664 0713 or 5613 6934, ⓦwww.earthlodgeguatemala.com; ❶–❸), a spectacular rural retreat high in the hills above Jocotenango. It's about 7km northeast of Antigua, with stunning views of the Panchoy valley and its volcanoes, and run by a hospitable Canadian–American couple who have been in Guatemala for years. Accommodation options include solid, comfortable A-frame cabañas, a wood-cabin dorm (US$4 per bed), and two tree houses – the deluxe has the best vistas.

Wholesome meals are served, with a communal dinner in the evenings. You'll also find a *chuj* (Maya sauna), good walking trails and plenty of space for frisbee throwing or football. Volunteers qualify for half-price meals and beds. Book ahead at weekends and busy times; pick-ups from Antigua are offered.

Another 4km past Joco is **SAN LORENZO EL TEJAR**, which has some superb hot springs; they're a couple of kilometres from the main road. If you want to bathe in the sulphurous waters, you can either use the cheaper communal pool or, for a couple of dollars, rent one of your own – a little private room with a huge tiled tub set in the floor. The baths are open daily from 7am to 5.30pm, except Tuesday and Friday afternoons, when they are closed for cleaning; Sundays can get very busy with local families.

Continuing north you can either take the broad Antigua bypass highway (that connects Chimaltenango with Santa Catarina Barahona) or follow a single-lane road that passes through **Parramos**, a dusty, overgrown farming village. A couple of kilometres beyond Parramos, a side road branches to **SAN ANDRÉS ITZAPA**, one of the many villages badly hit by the 1976 earthquake. Today, however, San Andrés' main claim to fame is as home to the cult of San Simón, or Maximón (see box, p.116). To pay the so-called wicked saint a visit, head for the central plaza from the branch road into the village, turn right when you reach the church, walk two blocks, then up a little hill and you should spot street vendors selling charms, incense and candles. If you get lost, ask for the Casa de San Simón. The other point of interest in the village is the particularly intricate weaving of the women's *huipiles*. The patterns are delicate and bold, similar in many ways to those around Chimaltenango. San Andrés' Tuesday market is also worth a visit. Hourly buses run between San Andrés Itzapa and Antigua.

Travel details

Guatemala City is at the transport heart of the country, with literally thousands of buses travelling in and out of the city each day connecting it with provincial capitals and tiny villages alike. Most of these routes are covered in the "Travel details" sections of other chapters; for the main **bus services** from Guatemala City, however, see the "Moving on" box on pp.88–89; for buses from Antigua, see p.112.

International **flights** depart from Guatemala City's Aurora airport, and domestic flights connect the capital with Flores in Petén, the site of the only other international airport in the country. Most Flores-bound departures are in the early morning, at around 7am; tickets for the 50min trip can be bought from virtually any travel agent in the capital (see p.90) or Antigua (see p.111) and cost from US$200 return.

2

The western highlands

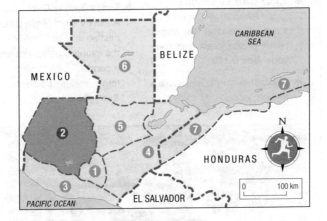

CHAPTER 2 # Highlights

* **Chichicastenango** Hunt for textiles and souvenirs at this scenic town's legendary market. See p.130

* **The Ixil Triangle** Hike the hillside trails of this remote, intensely traditional indigenous region. See p.140

* **Lago de Atitlán** An awesome steep-sided crater lake ringed by volcanoes and diminutive indigenous villages, with a plethora of great places to chill. See p.149

* **Santa Cruz La Laguna** Idyllic lakeside village with a uniquely relaxed vibe and plenty of spa treatments and yoga. See p.169

* **Quetzaltenango** Guatemala's refined second city enjoys a great highland setting and makes an excellent base for studying Spanish. See p.173

* **Fuentes Georginas** The perfect place to kill an afternoon, these sublime hot spring–fed pools are situated halfway up a volcano. See p.184

* **San Francisco el Alto** Its weekly market is a maelstrom of highland humanity, animals, fruit and vegetables. See p.189

* **Todos Santos Cuchumatán** A sleepy Mam Maya village nestled in a high valley in the mighty Cuchumatanes mountain range, with a famous textile tradition. See p.204

▲ Church in San Mateo Ixtatán

The western highlands

Guatemala's western highlands, stretching from the outskirts of Antigua to the Mexican border, are perhaps the most beautiful and captivating part of the entire country. Two main features delineate the area: a chain of awesome volcanoes that lines its southern side, and the high Cuchumatanes mountain range that dominates the north of the region. Strung between these two natural barriers is a series of spectacular forested ridges, lakes, gushing streams and plunging, verdant valleys.

The highland landscape is defined by many factors, but above all **altitude**. At lower levels the vegetation is almost tropical, supporting dense forests and crops of **coffee**, **cotton**, **bananas** and **cacao**. Higher up in the hills, **pine**, **cedar** and **oak** forests are interspersed with patchwork fields of **maize** and potatoes. In the highest terrain, known as the *altiplano*, the land is largely treeless and often wrapped in cloud, suited only to hardy herds of sheep and goats. The seasons also play their part: in the rainy season, from May to October, the land is superbly green with life from emerging young crops, while during the dry winter months the hillsides gradually turn a dusty yellow.

The western highlands are the heartland of the **Maya**, who have lived here continuously for the past two thousand years, and whose society, languages and traditions remain largely unchanged.

Some history

A peripheral area during the Classic Maya civilization (300–900 AD), the western highlands were colonized towards the end of the twelfth century by **Toltecs** from central Mexico. With the Toltecs established as overlords, local tribes (each speaking a separate language and based around a ceremonial centre) bitterly contested regional hegemony. These traditional tribal demarcations (see map, p.430) still endure today.

The K'iche' language, centred on the town of Santa Cruz del Quiché and reaching west into the Quetzaltenango valley, is the most widely spoken language. Mam-speakers inhabit the highlands around Huehuetenango, while the Tz'utujil occupy the southern shores of Lago de Atitlán, and the Kaqchikel are to the east. Smaller tribal groups, such as the Ixil and the Chuj, also occupy clearly defined areas in the Cuchumatán mountains, with distinct languages and costumes.

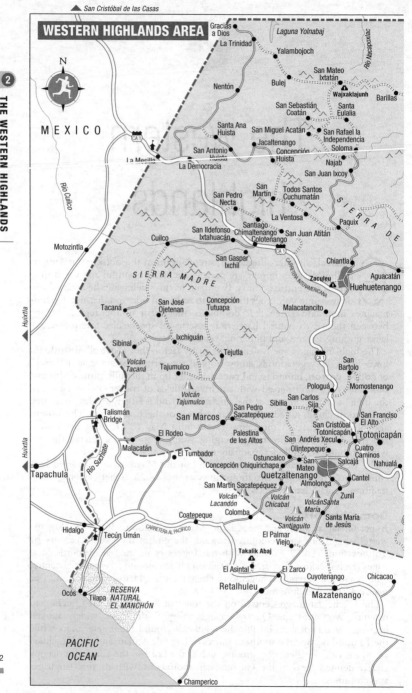

WESTERN HIGHLANDS AREA

▲ San Cristóbal de las Casas

N

MEXICO

Gracias a Dios
La Trinidad
Laguna Yolnabaj
Río Macapoxlac
Yalambojoch
Nentón
Bulej
San Mateo Ixtatán
Wajxaklajunh
Santa Eulalia
Barillas
San Sebastián Coatán
CA 1
Santa Ana Huista
San Miguel Acatán
San Rafael la Independencia
Soloma
La Mesilla
San Antonio Huista
Jacaltenango
Concepción Huista
Najab
La Democracia
San Juan Ixcoy
Río Cuilco
San Pedro Necta
San Martín
Todos Santos Cuchumatán
SIERRA DE
Motozintla
Cuilco
Santiago Chimaltenango
La Ventosa
Paquix
San Ildefonso Ixtahuacán
Colotenango
San Juan Atitán
San Gaspar Ixchil
CARRETERA INTERAMERICANA
Chiantla
SIERRA MADRE
Zaculeu
Aguacatán
Huehuetenango
Tacaná
San José Ojetenan
Concepción Tutuapa
Malacatancito
Sibinal
Ixchiguán
Volcán Tacaná
Tejutla
CA 1
Tajumulco
San Bartolo
Pologuá
Momostenango
Volcán Tajumulco
San Carlos Sija
Talismán Bridge
San Pedro Sacatepéquez
San Marcos
Sibilia
San Francisco El Alto
El Rodeo
Palestina de los Altos
San Cristóbal Totonicapán
Totonicapán
Malacatán
San Andrés Xecul
Río Suchiate
El Tumbador
Olintepeque
Cuatro Caminos
Tapachula
Ostuncalco
San Mateo
Salcajá
Nahualá
Concepción Chiquirichapa
Quetzaltenango
Cantel
San Martín Sacatepéquez
Almolonga
Zunil
Volcán Lacandón
Volcán Chicabal
Volcán Santa María
Coatepeque
Colomba
Santa María de Jesús
CARRETERA AL PACÍFICO
Volcán Santiaguito
Hidalgo
Tecún Umán
El Palmar Viejo
Takalik Abaj
El Zarco
Cuyotenango
Chicacao
El Asintal
Retalhuleu
Mazatenango
Ocós
Tilapa
RESERVA NATURAL EL MANCHÓN
PACIFIC OCEAN

◄ Huixtla

◄ Huixtla

Champerico

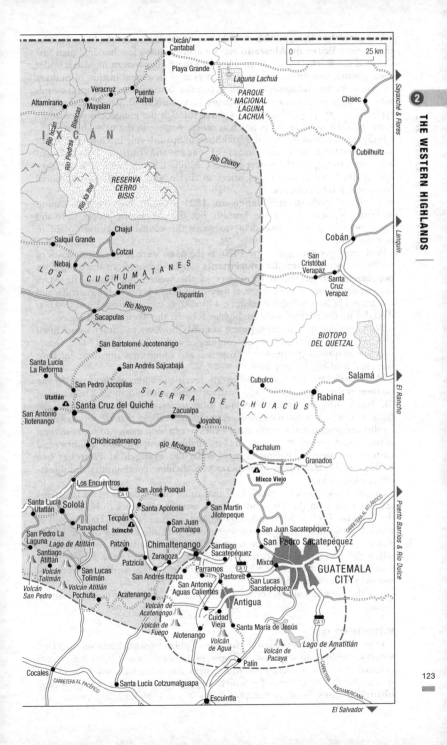

The **arrival of the Spanish** in 1523 was a total disaster for the Maya population. Leader **Pedro de Alvarado** and his army of just a few hundred men first defeated the K'iche' tribe, and by 1527 had the entire western highlands under their control, overrunning capital after capital, with a combination of military discipline, stealth and strategic alliances. But the damage done by Spanish swords was nothing compared to the **diseases** they introduced. Waves of smallpox, typhus, bubonic plague and measles swept through the indigenous population, reducing their numbers by as much as ninety percent in the worst-hit areas.

Indigenous labour became the backbone of Spanish rule in Guatemala, with income coming from plantations of **cacao** and **indigo**. The colonists attempted to impose the power of the Catholic Church, but a lack of clergy had enabled village-based allegiances to thrive, and allowed the traditional Maya religion to continue.

At village level, **independence in 1821** brought little change. Ladino authority replaced that of the Spanish, but the indigenous people were still press-ganged (or lured into debt) to work the coastal plantations, often in horrific conditions.

Fresh pressures emerged in the 1970s as the Maya were caught up in waves of political violence. **Guerrilla movements** sought support from the indigenous population and established themselves in the western highlands. The Maya became the victims in this process, as they were caught between the guerrillas and the army. Thousands fled the country, 440 villages were destroyed, and 200,000 died during the conflict, with the highlands by far the worst-affected region.

With the signing of the 1996 **peace accords**, however, political tensions lifted and there is evidence of a new self-confidence within the highland Maya. Grass-roots development groups have prospered, and indigenous organizations have launched land-rights campaigns.

Many challenges remain, with poverty levels still some of the worst in the hemisphere, exacerbated by high birth rates and unemployment. The allure of "El Norte" (the US) entices more and more jobless young men away from the highlands. It's often the most remote, traditional villages that are most affected by this emigration, and though many exiles return with money to invest in their communities, social structures are inevitably disrupted and centuries-old customs threatened. The influence of American **evangelical churches** (see p.432) can also undermine local hierarchies, dividing communities and threatening Maya culture.

Despite these pressures, you'll find that more than a dozen Maya languages are still spoken in the highlands, native costume continues to be worn, and the 260-day Tzolkin Maya calendar is used in some villages. Trade is still as much a social function as an economic one, with life focused on the village and its unique civil and religious hierarchy. Visit on **market** and **fiesta** days when the villages fill to bursting, and you'll clearly sense the values of the Maya World in the subdued bustle and gossip of the market or from the intense joy of celebration.

It is this unique culture, above all else, that is Guatemala's most fascinating feature.

Where to go

You're spoilt for choice in the western highlands, with beautiful highland scenery yielding atmospheric **villages** of cobbled lanes and whitewashed colonial churches at every turn. Along with the colourful market towns and spectacular mountainscapes for which the region is famed, a few fascinating **historical sites**, such as the pre-conquest cities of Iximché, Utatlán and

Market days

Throughout the western highlands **weekly markets** are the main focus of economic and social activity, drawing people from the area around the town or village where they're held. Make an effort to catch as many market days as possible – they're second only to local fiestas in offering a glimpse of a way of life unchanged for centuries.

Monday
Chimaltenango; San Juan Atitán; Santa Bárbara; Zunil.

Tuesday
Chajul; Comalapa; Olintepeque; Patzún; Salcajá; San Andrés Semetabaj; San Antonio Ilotenango; San Marcos; San Pedro Jocopilas; Sololá; Totonicapán; Yepocapa.

Wednesday
Almolonga; Chimaltenango; Colotenango; Cotzal; Huehuetenango; Momostenango; Palestina de los Altos; Patzicía; Sacapulas; San Sebastián.

Thursday
Aguacatán; Chichicastenango; Chimaltenango; Jacaltenango; La Libertad; Nebaj; Panajachel; Patulul; Patzite; Patzún; Sacapulas; San Juan Atitán; San Lucas Tolimán; San Luis Jilotepeque; San Mateo Ixtatán; San Miguel Ixtahuacán; San Pedro Necta; San Pedro Pinula; San Rafael La Independencia; Santa Bárbara; Santa Cruz del Quiché; San Pedro Sacatepéquez; Soloma; Tajumulco; Tecpán; Totonicapán; Uspantán; Zacualpa.

Friday
Chajul; Chimaltenango; San Andrés Itzapa; San Francisco el Alto; San Martín; Santiago Atitlán; Sololá; Tacaná.

Saturday
Almolonga; Colotenango; Cotzal; Ixchiguan; Malacatán; Nentón; Palestina de los Altos; Patzicía; Santa Clara La Laguna; Santa Cruz del Quiché; Todos Santos Cuchumatán; Totonicapán; Yepocapa.

Sunday
Aguacatán; Cantel; Chichicastenango; Chimaltenango; Cuilco; Huehuetenango; Jacaltenango; Joyabaj; La Libertad; Malacatancito; Momostenango; Nahualá; Nebaj; Nentón; Ostuncalco; Panajachel; Patzite; Patzún; Sacapulas; San Bartolo; San Carlos Sija; San Cristóbal Totonicapán; San Juan Comalapa; San Lucas Tolimán; San Luis Jilotepeque; San Martín Jilotepeque; San Mateo Ixtatán; San Miguel Acatán; San Miguel Ixtahuacán; San Pedro Necta; San Pedro Sacatepéquez; Santa Bárbara; Santa Cruz del Quiché; Santa Eulalia; Sibilia; Soloma; Tacaná; Tecpán; Tejar; Uspantán; Yepocapa; Zacualpa.

Zaculeu, are also worthy of your attention – although they don't bear comparison to Tikal and the lowland sites.

Travelling west from Guatemala City, the Carretera Interamericana sweeps through a densely populated region around the scruffy town of Chimaltenango before climbing steadily into the highlands. Just north of the highway in the department of **El Quiché** is the renowned market town of **Chichicastenango** and the ruins of **Utatlán**. South of here, **Lago de Atitlán** is the jewel of the western highlands, ringed by volcanoes and some of the country's most fascinating villages – it's reached via the colourful town of **Sololá**. To the north are the wildly beautiful peaks of the **Cuchumatanes**, beneath which nestle the remote and intensely traditional communities of the **Ixil Triangle**.

Heading on to the west is Guatemala's second city, **Quetzaltenango** (Xela), an ideal base for visiting local villages or climbing the nearly perfectly proportioned volcanic cone of **Santa María**. Beyond this, the border with Mexico is marked by the departments of **San Marcos** and **Huehuetenango**, both of which offer superb mountain scenery, dotted with isolated villages, including the beautifully situated **Todos Santos Cuchumatán**.

Buses flow continuously along the Carretera Interamericana, and tourist shuttle buses serve all the main centres. Many minor roads have been paved in recent years, and transport connections have improved greatly. Often the most practical plan of action is to base yourself in one of the larger places and then make a series of day-trips to village markets and fiestas, although even the smallest places will usually offer some kind of accommodation.

Into the highlands: the Carretera Interamericana

The serpentine **Carretera Interamericana** forms the main artery of transport in the highlands, and this highway and its junctions will inevitably become very familiar. Most of the route between Guatemala City and the turn-off for Quetzaltenango is now a smooth four-lane highway, though traffic is always heavy. The first of three major junctions you'll get to know is **Chimaltenango**, from where you can make connections to Antigua. Continuing west, **Los Encuentros** is the next main junction, where one road heads off to the north for Chichicastenango and another branches south to Panajachel and Lago de Atitlán. Beyond this, the highway climbs high over a mountainous ridge before dropping to **Cuatro Caminos**, from where side roads lead to Quetzaltenango, Totonicapán and San Francisco el Alto. The Carretera Interamericana continues on to Huehuetenango before it reaches the Mexican border at La Mesilla. Virtually every bus travelling along the highway will stop at all of these junctions, and you'll be able to buy fruit, drink and fast food from an army of vendors, some of whom will storm the bus looking for business, with others content to dangle their wares at your window from the street.

Chimaltenango and around

Grimy **CHIMALTENANGO**'s main focal point is the Carretera Interamericana, which cuts through the southern side of the town, bringing with it an endless flow of trucks and buses. The town extracts what little business it can from this stream of traffic, and the roadside is crowded with cheap comedores, workshops and sleazy bars. There's absolutely no reason to hang around here – especially with Antigua so near – and you should take care with your bags if you are changing buses as pickpockets have been known to target disorientated travellers.

Chimal suffered terribly from the 1976 earthquake, which flattened much of the surrounding area, but the town's **plaza**, two blocks north of the highway, is more attractive and sedate. An impressive colonial fountain is positioned exactly on the continental divide – half the water drains to the Caribbean, the other half to the Pacific – and there's also a striking peace monument that depicts a Maya woman bearing a broken rifle over her head.

Buses passing through Chimaltenango run to all points along the Carretera Interamericana, and those headed for Antigua leave every twenty minutes between 5am and 7.30pm from the market in town – though you can also wait at the turn-off on the highway.

San Martín Jilotepeque

To the north of Chimaltenango, it's 19km past plunging ravines and pine forests to the village of **SAN MARTÍN JILOTEPEQUE**. San Martín had to be rebuilt following the 1976 disaster, but the sprawling Sunday market is well worth a visit. The local weaving, women's *huipiles* especially, is some of the finest you'll see, with intricate and ornate patterning, predominantly in reds and purples.

Buses to San Martín leave the market in Chimaltenango every thirty minutes from 5am to 6pm for the half-hour trip, with six continuing on north to **Joyabaj**.

San Juan Comalapa, Patzicía and Patzún

Heading west from Chimaltenango, a series of turnings lead off the Carretera Interamericana to interesting but seldom-visited villages. The first of these, 16km to the north of the road on the far side of a deep-cut ravine, is **SAN JUAN COMALAPA**. The village was founded by the Spanish, who brought together the populations of several Kaqchikel centres. A collection of eroded pre-Columbian sculptures is displayed in the plaza, where there's a monument to Rafael Alvarez Ovalle, a local man who composed the Guatemalan national anthem. Looking out over the plaza is a fine, recently restored Baroque church that dates from colonial times.

In the past few decades, the villagers of Comalapa have developed something of a reputation as **folk artists**. The tradition began with **Andrés Curuchich** (1891–1969), who painted simple scenes documenting village life and exhibited his work as far afield as New York; there's a permanent exhibition devoted to his paintings at the Museo Ixchel in Guatemala City. Several dozen painters continue Curuchich's tradition, and their work can be bought in galleries in the town. A new museum, the Museo de Arte Maya, is also planned.

As ever, the best time to visit is for the **market**, on Sunday, which brings people out in force. **Buses** to Comalapa run hourly from Chimaltenango (45min), though microbuses also wait at the highway turn-off.

Patzicía and Patzún: a route to the lake

Further to the west another branch road runs down towards Lago de Atitlán, connecting the Carretera Interamericana with several small villages. First is **PATZICÍA**, its bedraggled-looking appearance belying its history of independent defiance, as in 1944 it was the scene of a Maya uprising that left some three hundred dead. Believing that a nationwide rebellion against ladino rule had begun, villagers charged through the town killing any non-indigenous inhabitants they could set hands on. Armed ladinos, arriving from the capital, managed to put down the uprising, killing the majority of the rebels. Coincidentally, the Declaration of Patzicía was signed here in 1871, setting out the objectives of the liberal revolution.

PATZÚN, 11km from the main highway heading towards Lago de Atitlán, is a sprawling, scruffy-looking Maya town where traditional costume of brilliant red is still worn. It's best visited for its colourful Sunday market. Beyond Patzún the road continues to **Godínez**, high above the northern shore of Lago de Atitlán. Some tourist shuttles travel along this short cut to the lake, which traverses a thickly forested ravine. If you're driving, you should consider that vehicles have been occasionally targeted by armed bandits, though incidents have decreased in recent years.

Tecpán and Iximché

The small town of **TECPÁN** is just a few hundred metres south of the Carretera Interamericana, ninety minutes or so from Guatemala City. This may well have been the site chosen by Alvarado as the first Spanish capital, to which the Spanish forces retreated in August 1524 after they'd been driven out of Iximché. Today it's a modest little town with a fine sixteenth-century Baroque **church**, complete with a magnificent original beamed ceiling and silver altars.

There are several **restaurants** around the plaza, but for a real treat head to *El Granero*, 4km south of town on the road to the ruins, which is owned by the deli *Epicure* in Antigua and has superb locally sourced meats and regional dishes.

Iximché, the pre-conquest capital of the Kaqchikel, is 5km south of Tecpán on a beautiful exposed hillside site, isolated on three sides by plunging ravines and surrounded by pine forests. From the early days of the Conquest, the Kaqchikel allied themselves with the Spanish, so the structures here suffered less than most. Since then, however, time and weather have taken their toll, and the majority of the buildings, originally built of adobe, have disappeared, leaving only a few stone-built pyramids, clearly defined plazas and a couple of ball courts. Nevertheless the site, which housed a population of about ten thousand, is very atmospheric, and its grassy plazas are marvellously peaceful, especially during the week, when you may well have the place to yourself.

The Kaqchikel Maya established their capital here in about 1470 after a long conflict with the neighbouring K'iche' and, when the Spanish arrived, joined forces with Alvarado in order to defeat their tribal enemies. Grateful for the

▲ The ruins of Iximché

assistance, the Spanish established their first headquarters near here on May 7, 1524 – probably where Tecpán stands today. The Kaqchikel referred to Alvarado as *Tonatiuh*, the son of the sun, and as a mark of respect he was given the daughter of a Kaqchikel king as a gift.

But within months the Kaqchikel rebelled, outraged by Alvarado's demands for tribute. The conquistador retaliated by burning Iximché and then moved operations to the greater safety of Ciudad Vieja, a short distance from Antigua.

More than four hundred years later in 1980, the Campesino Unity Committee, a predominantly Maya group, met here and issued the **Declaration of Iximché**. Provoked by the massacre of their leaders during an occupation of the Spanish embassy in Guatemala City that year, the declaration identified this atrocity as the latest episode in more than four centuries of state-sponsored genocide against the Maya race.

George W. Bush stopped by Iximché in 2007 and was treated to a marimba display and a demonstration of the Maya ball game. Not everyone was pleased with his appearance, and Maya elders later held a ceremony to spiritually cleanse the site and the residual "bad energy".

The site

The **ruins of Iximché** (daily 8am–5pm; US$6.50) are made up of four main plazas, a couple of ball courts and several small pyramids. In most cases only the foundations and lower parts of the original structures were built of stone, while the upper walls were of adobe, with thatched roofs supported by wooden beams. You can make out the ground plan of many of the buildings, but it's only the most important all-stone structures that still stand. The most significant buildings were those clustered around courts A and C, which were probably the scene of rituals. On the sides of **Temple 2** you can make out some badly eroded murals, the style of which is very similar to that used in the codices.

It's thought that the site itself, like most of the highland centres, was a ceremonial centre used for religious rituals, and Maya worship still takes place here down a small trail through the pine trees behind the final plaza. Archeological digs have unearthed a number of interesting finds, including the decapitated heads of sacrifice victims, burial sites, grinding stones, obsidian knives, a flute made from a child's femur and large numbers of incense burners.

Iximché's shady location is perfect for a picnic or barbeque, and you can buy *aguas* at the site. **To get there**, hop off any bus travelling along the Carretera Interamericana at the turn-off for Tecpán. The centre of town is about 500m from the road, from where microbuses leave for the ruins (every 30min; 10min). Be back on the Carretera Interamericana by 5.30pm to be sure of a bus onwards.

El Quiché

At the heart of the western highlands, sandwiched between the Verapaces and Huehuetenango, is the department of **El Quiché**. Encompassing the full range of Guatemalan scenery, the south is fertile and heavily populated while to the north the landscape becomes increasingly dramatic, rising to the massive, rain-soaked peaks of the **Cuchumatanes**, beyond which the land drops away into the plains and lowland forests of the **Ixcán**.

The department takes its name from the greatest of the pre-conquest tribal groups, the **K'iche'**, who overran much of the highlands by 1450 from their capital at Utatlán. Although their empire was in decline by the time the Spanish arrived, they put up a substantial fight against the conquistadors. With little in the way of plunder, this remote, mountainous terrain remained an unimportant backwater for the Spanish. The region became a centre of guerrilla activity in the late 1970s and was the scene of unrivalled repression in Guatemala, as tens of thousands of villagers were wiped out by the military. Catholic priests, who were often connected with the cooperative movement, were also singled out and murdered; indeed, the Church withdrew all its priests from the department in 1981. Today these highlands remain a stronghold of Maya culture, and El Quiché, dotted with small villages and mountain towns, is the scene of some superb fiestas and markets.

For the traveller, El Quiché has a lot to offer, in both the accessible south and the wilder north. **Chichicastenango** is the scene of a vast, twice-weekly market and still a pivotal centre of Maya religion. Beyond this, at the heart of the central valley, is the departmental capital of **Santa Cruz del Quiché**, stopping-off point for the ruins of **Utatlán**. Further to the north, the mountains really begin and the extraordinary scale of the scenery is exhilarating. Isolated villages, set in superb highland bowls, sustain a wealth of indigenous culture and occupy a misty, mysterious world of their own. Passing over the Sierra de Chuacús, and down to the Río Negro, you reach **Sacapulas** at the base of the **Cuchumatanes**. From here you can travel across the foothills to Cobán in the east or Huehuetenango to the west, or, for real adventure, up into the mountains to the three towns of the **Ixil Triangle** – Nebaj, Chajul and Cotzal.

The road for Chichicastenango and the department of El Quiché leaves the Carretera Interamericana at Km127.3, the **Los Encuentros** junction.

Chichicastenango

Heading north from Los Encuentros, you soon drop down through dense, aromatic pine forests into a deep ravine housing a tributary of the Río Motagua. The road then begins a tortuous ascent from the valley floor around a seemingly endless series of switchbacks until it reaches **CHICHICASTE-NANGO**, 17km from the junction. Dubbed Guatemala's "Mecca del Turismo" by Inguat, it is a compact and traditional town of cobbled streets, though the charming old adobe houses are now outnumbered by modern concrete structures. Twice a week the town's highland calm is shattered by the Sunday and Thursday **markets**, which attract a myriad of day-tripping tourists and commercial traders, as well as Maya weavers from throughout the central highlands. On these days you'll probably find yourself embroiled in one of provincial Guatemala's rare traffic jams, as traders, tourists and locals struggle to reach the town centre.

Chichicastenango was founded by the Spanish to house K'iche' refugees from nearby Utatlán, which they conquered and destroyed in 1524. The town's name is a Nahuatl word meaning "the place of the nettles".

The market is by no means all that sets Chichicastenango apart, however, and for the local population it's an important centre of culture and religion. Over the years,

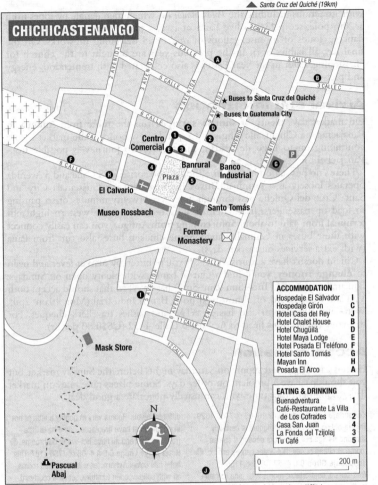

CHICHICASTENANGO

Santa Cruz del Quiché (19km)

★ Buses to Santa Cruz del Quiché
★ Buses to Guatemala City

Centro Comercial

Banrural

Banco Industrial

Plaza

El Calvario

Museo Rossbach

Santo Tomás

Former Monastery

Mask Store

N

Pascual Abaj

ACCOMMODATION

Hospedaje El Salvador	I
Hospedaje Girón	C
Hotel Casa del Rey	J
Hotel Chalet House	B
Hotel Chugüilá	D
Hotel Maya Lodge	E
Hotel Posada El Teléfono	F
Hotel Santo Tomás	G
Mayan Inn	H
Posada El Arco	A

EATING & DRINKING

Buenadventura	1
Café-Restaurante La Villa de Los Cofrades	2
Casa San Juan	4
La Fonda del Tzijolaj	3
Tu Café	5

0   200 m

Los Encuentros ▼ & Carretera Interamericana (18km)

Maya traditions and folk Catholicism have been treated with a rare degree of respect in Chichicastenango, although inevitably this blessing has been mixed with waves of arbitrary persecution and exploitation. Today the town has an important collection of Maya artefacts, parallel indigenous and ladino governments, and two churches that make no effort to disguise their acceptance of unconventional pagan worship. Locals adhere to the ways of traditional weaving, the women wearing superb *huipiles* with flower motifs. The men's costume of short trousers and jackets of black wool embroidered with silk is highly distinguished, although it's very expensive to make and these days almost all men opt for Western dress. For Sundays and fiestas, however, a handful of *cofrades* (elders of the religious hierarchy) still wear the traditional clothing and parade through the streets bearing spectacular silver processional crosses and antique incense-burners.

Chichicastenango's appetite for religious fervour is especially evident during the **fiesta** of Santo Tomás, from December 14 to 21. It's a spectacular occasion, with attractions including the *Palo Volador* (in which men dangle by ropes from a 20m pole; see p.434), a live band or two, a massive procession, traditional dances, clouds of incense, gallons of *chicha* and deafening fireworks. On the final day, all babies born in the previous year are brought to the church for christening. Later in the year Easter is also celebrated with tremendous energy and piety.

Arrival and information

On market days plenty of **shuttle services** run the route from Antigua to Panajachel via Chichi, allowing you to spend a few hours at the market before continuing on to Lago de Atitlán; and the reverse journey is possible from Panajachel too.

There's no bus station in Chichi, although the corner of 5 Calle and 5 Avenida operates loosely as a terminal. **Buses** heading between Guatemala City and Santa Cruz del Quiché pass through here every twenty minutes or so, pausing to load up passengers. In Guatemala City buses leave the western highlands terminal from 4am to about 5pm; coming from Antigua, you can easily connect with these buses in Chimaltenango. Some chicken buses also run from Pana (with extra services on market days).

Chichi doesn't have a tourist office. If you're bitten by market fever and need to **change money**, you'll find a glut of banks, with plenty open on Sundays: Banrural on 6 Calle (Tues–Sun 9am–5pm) has an ATM that should accept both Visa and MasterCard, or, almost next door, Banco Industrial (Mon 10am–2pm, Wed–Sun 10am–5pm) also has an ATM and cashes traveller's cheques. For **internet** connections head to Acses at 6 Calle 4–52 (US$0.80 per hr).

Accommodation

Hotels can be in short supply on Saturday nights before the Sunday market, but you shouldn't have a problem on other days. Some places raise rates on market days, though at other times you can usually negotiate a good deal.

Hospedaje El Salvador 5 Av 10–09 ☏7756 1329. This rambling travellers' stronghold is certainly showing its age but still offers decent, if sparse rooms at cheap prices. Hot water can be erratic. ❷

Hospedaje Girón 6 C 4–52 ☏7756 1156. Well-priced, comfortable rooms with pine furnishings – most with private bath – plus parking. Good value for single travellers. ❸

Hotel Casa del Rey 1km south of centre ☏7756 1053, Ⓦwww.hotelcasadelrey.com This large hotel has fine views, but the accommodation is unattractive in motel-style blocks. Pool and restaurant on site. ❻–❼

Hotel Chalet House 3 C 7–44 ☏7756 1360, Ⓦwww.chalethotelguatemala.com. Enjoys a quiet location a 5min walk north of the market action. Fourteen attractive, if smallish, double rooms, all with en-suite bathrooms (some have a tub) and comfortable beds with highland blankets. Breakfast is available, there's free internet and a roof terrace. ❹

Hotel Chugüilá 5 Av 5–24 ☏7756 1134. A long-running place with plenty of spacious rooms, all on different levels. Rooms vary in quality a little (if not in price), most have fireplaces, some have little front porches and all have hot-water bathrooms. ❺

Hotel Maya Lodge 6 C A 4–08 ☏7756 1167. This hotel has colonial character, with large tiled rooms, all with solid wooden furniture, set off a courtyard. It's a little overpriced, so try asking for a discount. ❺

Hotel Posada El Teléfono 8 C 1–64 ☏7756 1197. Humble but friendly little place with an array of small, clean, bare-bones rooms up and down steep staircases. There's a guests' kitchen and the communal bathroom is kept tidy. ❷

Hotel Santo Tomás 7 Av 5–32 ☏7756 1061. Large hotel with spacious, modern rooms, all well appointed with pleasant bathrooms boasting tubs, and set around two colonial-style courtyards and a (heated) swimming pool. The sheer size of the place and fact that it's block-booked by tour groups can make it a little impersonal. Has a restaurant and a pleasant lounge/bar. ❽

Mayan Inn 8 C & 3 Av ☏7756 1176, Ⓦwww.mayaninn.com.gt. Something of a colonial-era timewarp, this venerable hotel offers classy rooms with period furniture and fireplaces. Guests are assigned a member of the staff, who all wear mock-traditional dress; one will guard your door (there are no locks) and light your fire at night. Not everyone will relish the master/servant setup. US$104. ❾

🏃 **Posada El Arco** 4 C 4–36 ⓣ 7756 1255.
Excellent guesthouse, run by friendly

English-speaking brothers, who really look after their visitors well (try their home-made jams and peanut butter). Seven large, attractive rooms with good wooden beds and reading lights; rooms 6 & 7 have access to a pleasant terrace. There's also a beautiful garden with stunning views of the highlands and secure parking. ❹

The Town

Though most visitors come here to see the market, Chichicastenango also offers an unusual insight into traditional religious practices in the highlands. At the main **Santo Tomás church** in the southeast corner of the plaza, the local K'iche' Maya (called *Maxeños*) have been left to adopt their own style of worship, blending pre-Columbian and Catholic rituals. The church was built in 1540 on the site of a Maya altar and rebuilt in the eighteenth century. It's said that indigenous locals became interested in worshipping here after Francisco Ximénez, the priest from 1701 to 1703, started reading their holy book, the **Popol Vuh** (see p.134). Seeing that he held considerable respect for their religion, they moved their altars from the hills and set them up inside the church. Today this ancient, unique hybrid of Maya and Catholic worship still takes place in the church.

Before entering the building, it is customary to make offerings in a fire in front of the church or burn *copal* and *estoraque* incense in perforated cans, a practice that leaves a cloud of thin, sweet smoke hanging over the steps. Inside is an astonishing scene of avid worship. A soft hum of constant murmuring fills the air as the faithful kneel to place candles on low-level stone platforms for their ancestors and the saints. For these people, the entire building is alive with the souls of the dead, each located in a specific part of the church. The place of the "first-people", the ancient ancestors, is beneath the altar railing; former officials

Chichicastenango's market

There's been a **market** at Chichicastenango for hundreds, if not thousands, of years. Despite the tourist-geared stalls hawking bric-a-brac, local people continue to come two times a week to trade their wares. On Sundays and Thursdays, Chichicastenango's streets are lined with stalls and packed with buyers, and the choice is overwhelming, ranging from superb-quality Ixil *huipiles* to wooden dance-masks and everything in between, including pottery, gourds, belts and blankets, plus a gaudy selection of fabrics. You can still pick up some authentic weaving, but you need to be prepared to wade through a lot of very average material – and haggle hard. Your chances of getting a good deal are better before 10am, when the tourist buses arrive, or in the late afternoon once things have started to quiet down. The best of the stuff from the local villages is generally found in the centre of the plaza. Prices are pretty competitive, but for a real bargain you need to head further into the highlands – though Panajachel is a better bet for *típica* clothes.

For a brilliant **vantage point** over the vegetable market, head for the indoor balcony on the upper floor of the Centro Comercial building on the north side of the plaza. You'll be able to gawk at the villagers below (as well as take photographs without fear of being intrusive) as they haggle and chat over bunches of vegetables. It's possible to pick out costumes from all over the highlands, including *huipiles* from the Atitlán villages, and even from as far away as Chajul; the funky "space cowboy" shirts and pants are worn by men from the neighbouring Sololá area.

are around the middle of the aisle; ordinary folk to the west in the nave; and deceased native priests beside the door. Equally important are the Catholic saints, who receive the same respect and are continuously appealed to with offerings of candles and alcohol. Last, but by no means least, certain areas within the church, and particular patterns of candles, rose petals and *chicha*, are used to invoke specific types of blessings, such as those for children, travel, marriage, harvest or illness. Don't enter the building by the front door, which is reserved for *cofrades* and senior church officials, but through the **side door**. It's highly offensive to take **photographs** inside the building – don't even contemplate it.

Next to the church is a former **monastery**, now used by church administrators. This is where Spanish priest Francisco Ximénez discovered the Popol Vuh (see box below), a masterpiece of indigenous literature, buried amongst the parish archives in the early eighteenth century.

On the south side of the plaza, often hidden by stalls on market day, **Museo Rossbach** (Tues, Wed, Fri & Sat 8am–noon & 2–4pm, Thurs 8am–4pm & Sun 8am–2pm; US$0.80) houses a wide-ranging collection of pre-Columbian artefacts, mostly small pieces of ceramics (including some demonic-looking incense burners), jade necklaces and earrings, and stone carvings (some 2000 years old). A few interesting old photographs of Chichi as well as local weavings and masks are also on display.

On the west side of the plaza, the whitewashed **El Calvario** chapel is like a miniature version of Chichi's main church. Inside, the atmosphere is equally reverential as prayers are recited around the smoke-blackened wooden altar, and women offer flowers and stoop to kiss a supine image of Christ, entombed inside a glass cabinet, which is paraded through the street during Holy Week. The steps are the scene of incense-burning rituals, and the chapel is considered good for general confessions and pardons.

The shrine of Pascual Abaj

Churches are certainly not the only scenes of Maya religious activity, and the hills that surround the town, like so many throughout the highlands, are

---

The Popol Vuh

Written in Utatlán shortly after the arrival of the Spanish, the more than nine thousand lines of the **Popol Vuh** detail the cosmology, mythology and traditional history of the K'iche'. The first of the two parts of this sacred poem is an account of the K'iche's **creation** by their god, who is known as Heart of Sky. According to the Popol Vuh, at first there was only water and sky; the creator then formed earth and mountains, plants and trees. Heart of Sky turned his attention to animals, and created creatures of the forest including deer, birds and jaguars. Unsatisfied with these animals – which could only howl, roar or squawk – the creator fashioned humans from corn paste after twice failing to make man from mud and wood. The Popol Vuh then recounts the adventures of the ancestors of mankind, the hero (or wizard) twins Hunahpú and Xbalanqué, which culminate in an epic struggle with the death lords of Xibalbá, the Maya underworld. The twins ultimately triumph, and the cycle of creation is born.

The Popol Vuh's second half describes the wanderings of the K'iche' ancestors as they migrate south from the Toltec area of Mexico and settle in the highlands of Guatemala. Evidence gathered by archeologists and epigraphers strongly supports the accuracy of this part of the epic. The book concludes with a history of K'iche' royalty, and suggests a shared lineage with these kings and their gods. Dennis Tedlock's translation of the Popol Vuh (see "Books", p.453) is regarded as the definitive text.

Moving on from Chichicastenango

Direct buses head to Guatemala City every twenty minutes or so (3hr), the last one leaving at around 6pm, and seven buses daily head westwards to Quetzaltenango between 6am and 3pm (2hr 30min). For Antigua, catch a Guatemala City–bound bus and change at Chimaltenango, except on market days when you can get a direct shuttle. If you're heading north, it's often quickest to take the first bus to Santa Cruz del Quiché (every 20min; 30min), from where buses go to Nebaj or Uspantán. If you need a **shuttle bus** from Chichicastenango, head to Chichi Turkaj Tours, 5 Avenida 5–24 (☏7756 1579).

topped with shrines. The closest of these, less than a kilometre from the plaza, is known as **Pascual Abaj**. Although the site is regularly visited by tourists, it's important to remember that the **Maya ceremonies** held here are deeply religious and you should keep your distance and be sensitive about taking any photographs. The shrine is laid out in a typical pattern with several small altars facing a stern-looking pre-Columbian sculpture. Ceremonies, usually overseen by a shaman, always incorporate clouds of incense, liquor swilling and incantations, along with offerings of flowers and maybe a sacrificed chicken. In 1957, during a bout of religious rivalry, Pascual Abaj's altars were smashed by reforming Catholics, but the traditionalists gathered the scattered remains and patched them together.

To get to Pascual Abaj, walk south downhill along 5 Avenida from the Santo Tomás church, take the first right, 9 Calle, and follow it as it winds its way out of town. You'll soon cross a stream, after which a well-signposted route takes you through the courtyard of a workshop making wooden masks. If a ceremony is in progress, you may be able to pick out Pascual Abaj by a thin plume of smoke. Continue to follow the path uphill for ten minutes through a dense pine forest to the shrine.

Eating

Chichi is a good place to indulge in hearty, good-value Guatemalan comedor food. For smarter surrounds, head to either the *Hotel Santo Tomás* or the *Mayan Inn*. The plaza on **market days** is the place to come for authentic highland eating: try one of the makeshift food stalls, where you'll find cauldrons of stews and broths.

Buenadventura upper floor, inside the Centro Comercial. Above the vegetable market and ideal for no-nonsense *comida típica* – the breakfasts are some of the cheapest in town.

Café-Restaurant La Villa de Los Cofrades 6 C & 5 Av, first floor. A good choice for breakfast (try the porridge) and good-value set meals – soup, a main dish and salad, fries and bread is around US$4. The house coffee has a kick, and wine is available too.

Casa San Juan beside El Calvario church. The most stylish place in town, this enjoyable little bar-restaurant makes a real effort with plenty of artwork on display and an enjoyable menu: tasty sandwiches and western snacks as well as Guatemalan and Mexican dishes.

La Fonda del Tzijolaj upper floor of the Centro Comercial. Head here for a terrific perspective of the market and church of Santo Tomás from the balcony tables. Moderately priced, filling dishes, including pizza and pasta, or try the house special *chiles rellenos*.

Tu Café east side of plaza. Owned by a friendly Guatemalan who worked as a cab driver in New York for many years. There are plenty of breakfast options, snacks like nachos with guacamole and sandwiches, and all lunchtime mains come with rice, salad and soup.

Santa Cruz del Quiché and around

The capital of the department of El Quiché, **SANTA CRUZ DEL QUICHÉ**, lies half an hour north of Chichicastenango. A good paved road connects the two towns, running through pine forests and ravines, and past the **Laguna Lemoa**, a lake which, according to local legend, was originally filled with tears wept by the wives of K'iche' kings after their husbands had been slaughtered by the Spanish. Quiché, as it is usually called, is a large featureless town, but serves as the jumping-off point for the nearby ruins of Utatlán. It's also a transport hub for the Ixil Triangle.

The Town

Dominating the central **plaza** of Santa Cruz del Quiché is a large colonial church and clock tower built with stone from the ruins of Utatlán. In the middle of the plaza, a defiant statue of the K'iche' hero Tecún Umán stands prepared for battle, but his position is undermined somewhat by an ugly urban tangle of shabby stores and streets that surround the square. **Market** days are the same as in Chichicastenango – Thursday and Sunday – with stalls sprawling south and east of the plaza down to the bus station. Palm weaving is a local speciality, and Maya people can sometimes be seen threading a band or two as they walk through town.

Practicalities

The **bus terminal**, a large, grubby open-aired affair, is about four blocks south and a couple east of the central plaza. Connections are generally good from Quiché. Second-class buses to Guatemala City leave every thirty minutes until 5pm (3hr 30min), all via Chichicastenango (30min) and Los Encuentros (1hr). Regular services run to Nebaj (5 daily; 2hr 15min), Joyabaj (hourly; 1hr 45min), Uspantán (6 daily; 2hr 45min) and Quetzaltenango (10 daily; 3hr). Microbuses provide even more frequent connections to Uspantán (every ninety minutes until 6pm), Nebaj (roughly hourly until 7pm) and Joyabaj. The road to Totonicapán is being upgraded and regular bus services should commence in 2009.

Banrural at the northwest corner of the plaza has an ATM and changes traveller's cheques.

There's a limited range of **hotels** in Quiché and nothing luxurious. The best budget place is the *Hotel San Pascual*, at 7 Calle 0–43, Zona 1 (℡7755 1107; ❷), with clean rooms on two floors around a patio while *Hotel Maya Quiché*, a block west of the plaza at 3 Avenida 4–19, Zona 1 (℡7755 1464; ❸), is a step up in quality with spacious rooms, some with bathroom. Most **places to eat** are close to the plaza. *El Torito Steakhouse*, 7 Calle 1–73, just southwest of the plaza, with kitsch cowboy decor and a meat-based menu that includes huge steaks is as posh as it gets in Quiché, or for typical comedor food head to *Las Rosas*, 1 Avenida 1–28.

The ruins of Utatlán (K'umarkaaj)

Early in the fifteenth century, riding on a wave of successful conquest, the K'iche' king Gucumatz (Feathered Serpent) founded a new capital, K'umarkaaj. A hundred years later the Spanish arrived, renamed the city **Utatlán**, and then destroyed it. Today the **ruins** (daily 8am–5pm; US$6.50) can be visited, about 4km to the west of Santa Cruz del Quiché.

According to the Popol Vuh, Gucumatz was a lord of great genius, assisted by powerful spirits. And there's no doubt that this was once a great city, with several separate citadels spread across neighbouring hilltops. It housed the nine dynasties of the tribal elite, including the four main K'iche' lords, and contained a total of 23 palaces. The splendour of the city embodied the strength of the K'iche' empire, which at its height boasted a population of around a million.

By the time of the Conquest, however, the K'iche' had been severely weakened and their empire fractured. They first made contact with the Spanish on the Pacific coast, suffering a heavy defeat at the hands of Alvarado's forces near Quetzaltenango, including the loss of their leader Tecún Umán. The K'iche' then invited the Spanish to their capital, a move that made Alvarado distinctly suspicious. On seeing the fortified city, the conquistador feared a trap and captured K'iche' leaders Oxib-Queh and Beleheb-Tzy. His next step was characteristically straightforward: "As I knew them to have such a bad disposition to service of his Majesty, and to ensure the good and peace of this land, I burnt them, and sent [soldiers] to burn the town and destroy it."

The site

Utatlán is nowhere near as grand as the large ruins of Petén, but its dramatic setting, surrounded by deep ravines and pine forests, is impressive, and its historical significance intriguing. Little restoration has taken place since the Spanish destroyed the city, and only a few of the main structures are recognizable, most buried beneath grassy mounds and shaded by pine trees. The small **museum** has a scale model of what the original city may once have looked like.

The central plaza is almost certainly where Alvarado burned the two K'iche' leaders alive in 1524. Nowadays it's where you'll find the three remaining **temple buildings**, the great monuments of Tohil, Auilix and Hacauaitz, which were simple pyramids topped by thatched shelters. The Temple of the Sovereign Plumed Serpent once stood in the middle of the plaza, but these days just the foundations of this circular tower can be made out. The only other feature that's still vaguely recognizable is the **ball court**, which lies beneath grassy banks to the south of the plaza.

Perhaps the most interesting thing about the site today is that *costumbristas* (Maya religious practitioners) still come here to perform sacred rituals that predate the arrival of the Spanish by thousands of years. The entire area is covered in small burnt circles – the ashes of incense – and chickens are regularly sacrificed in and around the plaza.

Beneath the plaza, a long constructed **tunnel** runs underground for about 100m. Follow the sign for *la cueva*; the entrance is usually littered with empty incense wrappings and *aguardiente* liquor bottles. Inside are nine shrines, the same number as there are levels of the Maya underworld, Xibalbá. Devotees pray at each shrine, but it is the ninth one, housed inside a chamber, that is most actively used for sacrifice, incense and alcohol offerings. Why the tunnel was constructed remains uncertain, but local legends suggest that it was dug by the K'iche' to hide their women and children from the advancing Spanish, whom they planned to ambush at Utatlán. Others believe it represents the caves of Tula mentioned in the Popol Vuh (see p.134). Whatever the truth, today the tunnel is the focus for Maya rituals and a favourite spot for sacrifice; the floor is carpeted with chicken feathers and candles burning in the alcoves at the end. Tread carefully inside the tunnel, as some of the side passages end abruptly with precipitous drops. If a ceremony is taking place, you'll hear the mumbling of prayers and smell incense smoke as you enter, in which case it's wise not to disturb the proceedings by approaching too closely.

To **get to** Utatlán from Santa Cruz del Quiché, you can either catch a bus heading to Totonicapán, walk, or take a taxi (around US$12 return trip, with an hour at the ruins). It's a pleasant forty-minute stroll, heading south from the plaza along 2 Avenida, then turning right down 10 Calle, which will take you all the way out to the site.

The road continues west from the ruins to San Antonio Ilotenango and on to Totonicapán. A lot more traffic will pass along this back route when improvements are completed in 2009, including a regular bus service between Quiché and Toto.

East to Joyabaj

A paved road runs east from Santa Cruz del Quiché, beneath the impressive peaks of the **Sierra de Chuacús**, through a series of villages set in beautiful rolling farmland. The first of these, **Chiché**, is a sister village to Chichicastenango, with which it shares costumes and traditions, though the market here is on Wednesday. Next is **Chinique**, followed by larger **Zacualpa**, which has Thursday and Sunday markets in its beautiful broad plaza. The latter village's name means "where they make fine walls", and in the hills to the north are the remains of a pre-conquest settlement.

The small town of **JOYABAJ**, the last place out this way, also has a small archeological site to its north. During the colonial period, Joyabaj was an important staging post on the royal route to Mexico, but all evidence of its former splendour was lost when the 1976 earthquake almost totally flattened the town, killing hundreds of people. The crumbling facade of the colonial church that stands in front of the new prefabricated version is one of the few physical remains. In recent years the town has bounced back, however, and it is once again a prosperous traditional centre. The Sunday **market**, which in fact starts up on Saturday afternoon, is a huge affair well worth visiting, as is the **fiesta** in the second week of August – five days of unrelenting celebration that includes some fantastic traditional dancing and the spectacular *Palo Volador*, in which "flying" men or *ángeles* spin to the ground from a huge wooden pole. Though the fiesta is in many ways a hybrid of Maya and Christian traditions, the *ángeles* symbolize none other than the wizard twins of the Popol Vuh, who descended into the underworld to do battle with the Lords of Death.

It's possible to **hike** from Joyabaj, over the Sierra de Chuacús, to Cubulco in Baja Verapaz. It's a superb but exhausting hike, taking at least a day, though it's perhaps better done in reverse.

Practicalities

Buses run between Guatemala City's western highlands terminal and Joyabaj, passing through Santa Cruz del Quiché about every hour (8am–3.30pm from the capital and 3am–3pm from Joyabaj); there are frequent microbus services from Quiché too. Joyabaj has a few basic **pensiones** (among which the *Hospedaje Mejia* (❶), on the plaza, is one of the best), plenty of **comedores** and two **banks**; the Banrural has an ATM.

It's also possible to do a loop back towards Guatemala City via a rough, seldom-travelled route that passes through **Pachalum** and the ruins of **Mixco Viejo**. One daily bus (leaving at 2.30am) operates this route, though pick-ups run at other times.

To the Cuchumatanes: San Andrés Sajcabajá, Sacapulas and Uspantán

The land to the north of Santa Cruz del Quiché is sparsely inhabited and dauntingly hilly. About 17km northeast of town, only accessed by a rough dirt track, the *Posada San Rafael* (T 5570 3336, W www.posada-sr.com; ❹–❺) is a wonderful rural hotel, set in the grounds of an old finca near the village of **San Andrés Sajcabajá**, deep in the Quiché hills. The French–Guatemalan owners offer horseriding to the minor Maya ruins of Chijoj (with an impressive ball court), indigenous villages, hot springs and waterfalls, and serve up delicious organic food. If you call first, there's a good chance that someone will pick you up from Santa Cruz del Quiché, as few buses run up this way; alternatively, ask around at the bus station to see if there's a pick-up leaving for San Andrés. The journey takes an hour.

Heading out of Santa Cruz, the road passes through **San Pedro Jocopilas** before skirting the western end of the Sierra de Chuacús and eventually dropping to the isolated town of **SACAPULAS**, an hour and a half from Quiché. Set in a spectacular position on the Río Negro beneath the dusty foothills of the Cuchumatanes, Sacapulas has a small colonial church, with some finely carved wooden images of saints, and a good market every Thursday and Sunday, held beneath the two huge ceiba trees in the plaza. Some of the women still wear impressive *huipiles* and tie their hair with elaborate pom-poms, similar to those of Aguacatán.

Since long before the arrival of the Spanish, **salt** has been produced here in beds beside the Río Negro, a valuable commodity that earned the town a degree of importance. The town's original name was Tajul, meaning "hot springs", but the Spanish changed it to Sacapulas, "the grassy place", as they valued the straw baskets made locally. Along the riverbank, downstream from the bridge, there are several little pools where warm water bubbles to the surface, used by local people for washing. On the opposite bank trucks and buses break for lunch at some ramshackle comedores and fruit stalls.

Getting to Sacapulas is straightforward – catch any bus or microbus from Santa Cruz del Quiché heading to Uspantán (hourly; 1hr 45min) or Nebaj (hourly; 1hr 15min). The last bus to Quiché is at 7.30pm, to Nebaj at 5pm. Microbuses also run to Aguacatán (7 daily; 1hr 30min) where there are excellent connections to Huehuetenango. If you do get stuck in Sacapulas you'll find rooms with river views at *Comedor y Hospedaje Tujaal* (❷), and very basic beds at the *Hospedaje y Restaurant Río Negro* (T 5410 8168; ❶). For a meal, the *Tujaal* is the best bet; try the local *mojarra* fish and *papas fritas*. Look out too for stalls selling the (very) sweet local snack called *melcocha*, sold all over the country. There's a **bank** on the north side of the plaza, Banrural, where you can cash traveller's cheques and dollars.

East to Uspantán, and on to Cobán

East of Sacapulas, a dirt road rises steeply, clinging to the mountainside and quickly leaving the Río Negro far below. As it climbs, the views are superb, with tiny Sacapulas dwarfed by the sheer enormity of the landscape. The road eventually reaches a high valley and arrives in **USPANTÁN**, a small town lodged in a chilly gap in the mountains and often soaked in steady drizzle. Rigoberta Menchú, the K'iche' Maya woman who won the 1992 Nobel Peace Prize, is from Chimel, a tiny village in this region. Few people hang around long here, but there are some decent hotels, including the excellent *Hotel Posada Doña Leona* at 6 Calle 4–09, Zona 1 (T 7951 8045, ❷–❸), with very clean rooms, all with TV and bathrooms. For a bite to eat, the small *Cafetería María Luisa*, 6 Avenida and 7 Calle, Zona 2, has inexpensive breakfasts, snacks and set lunches for US$2. **Microbuses** leave for Cobán (hourly until 5pm; 3hr) and Santa Cruz del Quiché (every 90min until 6pm; 2hr 30min); regular chicken buses also serve these routes.

The Ixil Triangle: Nebaj, Chajul and Cotzal

High up on the spine of the Cuchumatanes, in a landscape of steep hills, bowl-shaped valleys and gushing rivers, is the **Ixil Triangle**. Here Nebaj, Chajul and Cotzal, three remote and extremely traditional towns, share a language spoken nowhere else in the country. This triangle of towns forms the hub of the **Ixil-speaking region**, a massive highland area that drops away towards the Mexican border and contains at least 130,000 inhabitants. These lush and rain-drenched hills are hard to reach and have proved notoriously difficult to control, and today's relaxed atmosphere of highland Maya colour and customs conceals a bitter history of protracted conflict.

The beauty of the landscape and the strength of indigenous culture in the Ixil are both overwhelming. When church leaders moved into the area in the 1970s, they found very strong communities in which the people were reluctant to accept new authority for fear that it would disrupt traditional structures, and where women were included in the process of communal decision-making. Counterbalancing these strengths are the horrors of the human–rights abuses that took place here during the civil war, which must rate as some of the worst anywhere in Central America.

Before the arrival of the Spanish, Nebaj was a sizeable centre, producing large quantities of jade and possibly allied with the Mam capital, Zaculeu. The Conquest was particularly brutal in these parts, however. After several setbacks, the Spaniards finally managed to take Nebaj in 1530, by which time they were so enraged that the town was burnt to the ground and the survivors enslaved as punishment for their resistance. In the years that followed, the land was repeatedly invaded by the Lacandón Maya from the north and swept by devastating epidemics. Things didn't improve with the coming of independence: the Ixil were regarded as a source of cheap labour and forced to work on the coastal plantations. Many never returned, and even today large numbers of local people still migrate to the coast, Guatemala City and even the US in search of work.

In the late 1970s and 1980s, the area was hit by waves of horrific violence as it became the main theatre of operation for the Guerrilla Army of the Poor (the EGP). Caught up in the conflict, the people suffered enormous losses, with the majority of the smaller villages destroyed by the army and their inhabitants herded into "protected" camps. Since the 1996 peace accords, normality steadily returned to the area, as villagers have returned to their ancestral settlements and rebuilt their homes.

Despite this terrible legacy, the fresh green hills are some of the most beautiful in the country, and the towns are friendly and accommodating, with a relaxed and distinctive atmosphere in a misty world of their own.

Nebaj

NEBAJ is the centre of Ixil country and the largest of the three settlements. Until a few years ago, virtually all structures in the town were single-storey dwellings of adobe walls, but concrete buildings now dominate the centre. Nevertheless, the town remains highly atmospheric and attractive, if a little scruffy around its edges, and pulls in a trickle of adventure-minded travellers, drawn by the superb highland hiking, a language school and the opportunity to get off Guatemala's main gringo trail.

The **textiles** woven here are unusual and intricate, especially the women's *huipiles*, which are a mass of complex geometrical designs. Until very recently, greens, yellows, reds and oranges were omnipresent, worn with brilliant red

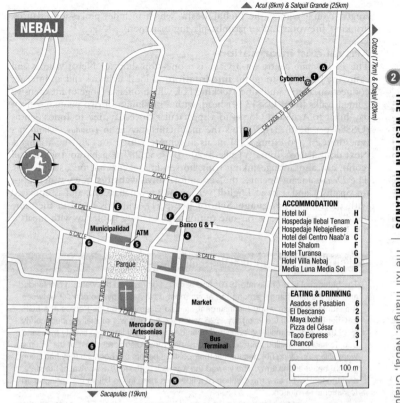

▲ Acul (8km) & Salquil Grande (25km)

NEBAJ

Cotzal (17km) & Chajul (20km)

Cybernet

N

I CALLE

2 CALLE

3 CALLE

4 CALLE

5 CALLE

Municipalidad   ATM

Banco G & T

Parque

5 CALLE

Market

Mercado de
Artesenías

8 CALLE

Bus
Terminal

ACCOMMODATION	
Hotel Ixil	H
Hospedaje Ilebal Tenam	A
Hospedaje Nebajeñese	E
Hotel del Centro Naab'a	C
Hotel Shalom	F
Hotel Turansa	G
Hotel Villa Nebaj	D
Media Luna Media Sol	B

EATING & DRINKING	
Asados el Pasabien	6
El Descanso	2
Maya Ixchil	5
Pizza del César	4
Taco Express	3
Chancol	1

0   100 m

▼ Sacapulas (19km)

cortes (skirts), though clothes of other hues are now worn. The most spectacular part of Nebaj *traje* is the dramatic women's headcloth, a length of hand-loomed fabric that's decorated with "pom-pom" tassles that they pile up above their heads. Almost no men now wear traditional dress, preferring to buy secondhand North American clothes from the market. The scarlet male ceremonial jackets are dusted down for fiestas, however; formal looking and ornately decorated, they're modelled on those worn by Spanish officers.

Nebaj's pretty, recently remodelled **plaza** is the focal point for the community and houses the main municipal buildings and the large whitewashed Catholic church – inside its door on the left are dozens of crosses, forming a memorial to those killed in the civil war. There's not that much to do in Nebaj itself, though the small **market**, a block east of the church, is worth investigation. It's fairly quiet most days, but presents the best photographic opportunities, as you can capture Nebajeños going about their daily business without too much disturbance. On Thursdays and Sundays, the numbers swell and traders visit from out of town selling secondhand clothing and chickens, eggs, fruit and vegetables from the highlands.

Women and girls will approach you as you walk around town, keen to sell you their clothing, but you'll also find an excellent selection at the smart new **Mercado de Artesenías** just south of the main market area on 2 Avenida. There's a pool hall on 7 Avenida. If you're in town for the second week in

August, you'll witness the **Nebaj fiesta**, which includes processions, dances, drinking, fireworks and a marimba-playing marathon.

Arrival and information

The *El Descanso* centre on 3 Calle is a one-stop shop for Nebaj visitors and easily the best place to go for **information** on local activities and an internet connection. Here you'll find Trekking Ixil, which offers a range of inexpensive guided walks (from US$13 per head, with a minimum of two people) – from day-hikes to Acul and Cocop to a spectacular three-day trek to Todos Santos (US$80 per head). Trips across the mountains staying in *posadas comunitarias* (guesthouses) and eating local meals in remote villages can also be arranged. Next door, Pablo's Tours, 3 Calle 3–20 (T 7755 8287, @pablostours@hotmail .com), can also arrange hiking trips, horseriding excursions or a shuttle bus. The *Descanso* team operates the very informative **websites**, W www.nebaj.org (in Spanish) and a basic English version W www.nebaj.com, and is affiliated with the **Nebaj Language School** (see p.51), which is based in the same building; a week of one-on-one tuition and a family homestay with meals is just US$120.

Guerrilla warfare in the Ixil Triangle

The bitter **civil war** of the late 1970s and early 1980s ravaged the western highlands, and left the Ixil Triangle among the areas most devastated by the conflict between the Guatemalan army and the insurgent Ejército Guerrillero de los Pobres (the EGP, or Guerrilla Army of the Poor). By 1996, when the guerrilla war officially ended, nearly all of the region's smaller villages had been destroyed and fifteen to twenty thousand people had been killed, with tens of thousands more displaced. Most of the victims were villagers, dying not because of their political beliefs but because they had been caught between the army, who viewed the war as a battle for the survival of the state, and the EGP, who saw the creation of a liberated zone in the Ixil as the springboard to national revolution.

The severity of the violence is a measure of the success of the EGP, who fought the army in northern Quiché for more than two decades. The EGP first entered the area in 1972, when a small group of guerrilla fighters (some of whom had been involved in the 1960s guerrilla campaign) crossed the Mexican border and began building links with locals. With little military presence in the area at the time, they were able to work swiftly, impressing the Ixil Maya with their bold plans for political and social revolution. The guerrillas opened their military campaign in 1975 with the assassination of Luis Arenas, the owner of Finca La Perla, to the north of Chajul, where hundreds of labourers were kept in a system of debt bondage. The EGP shot Arenas in front of hundreds of his employees as he was counting the payroll. According to the group, "Shouts of joy burst from throats accustomed for centuries only to silence and lament, and with something like an ancestral cry, with one voice they chanted with us our slogan, 'Long live the poor, death to the rich.'" But other accounts describe how people walked for days to pay their last respects to Arenas.

Such early actions prompted a huge response from the armed forces, who began killing, kidnapping and torturing suspected guerrillas and sympathizers. The organization was already well entrenched, however, and the army's brutality only served to persuade more and more people to seek protection with the guerrillas. By late 1978, the EGP were regularly occupying villages, holding open meetings and tearing down debtors' jails. In January 1979 they killed another local landowner, Enrique Brol, of Finca San Francisco near Cotzal. On the same day, the EGP also briefly took control of Nebaj itself, summoning the whole of the town's population, including Western travellers, to the central plaza, where they denounced the barbaric inequalities of life in the Ixil.

For your **banking** needs, Banrural, on the north side of the plaza, has an ATM, and Banco G&T on Calzada 15 de Septiembre exchanges cash and traveller's cheques.

The **bus terminal** is two blocks southeast of the plaza. Getting to Nebaj is straightforward, with hourly microbuses from Santa Cruz del Quiché (2hr 15min) until 7pm. As the roads to Chajul and Cotzal are now paved, **getting around** the Ixil Triangle is much easier than it used to be, with regular microbuses, pick-ups and the odd chicken-bus. Schedules are not set in stone, but there are microbuses roughly every hour for Chajul and Cotzal and more frequently to Acul.

Moving on from Nebaj, microbuses and buses leave hourly for Quiché until 5.30pm, and there's one direct chicken-bus to Guatemala City at 12.30am. There should be a 6am daily service to Cobán, but if you miss it take a Quiché-bound microbus as far as the junction for Uspantán and catch an onward connection there. If you're heading to Huehuetenango, change in Sacapulas. For shuttle buses to destinations around the country, such as Antigua, Quetzaltenango and Cobán, contact Pablo's Tours – though these can be pricey unless you have a group.

The army responded with a wave of horrific attacks on the civilian population. Army units swept through the area, committing atrocities, burning villages and massacring thousands, including women and children. Nevertheless, the strength of the guerrillas continued to grow, and in 1981 they again launched an attack on Nebaj, by then a garrison town. Shortly afterwards the army chief of staff, Benedicto Lucas García (the president's brother), flew into Nebaj and, in a simple speech before the townspeople, he warned them that if they didn't "clean up their act" he'd bring five thousand men "and finish off the entire population".

After the ouster of President Lucas García in the military coup of early 1982, the army changed its tactics. The new president, **General Ríos Montt**, used anti-Communist propaganda and conscripted civilian patrols (PACs), which were placed on the conflict's front lines, to ensure the loyalty of the people. Villagers were given ancient M1 rifles and told to protect their communities from the guerrillas. Meanwhile, the army began aggressive sweeps through the highlands, razed 50 Ixil villages to the ground and brought the displaced people back into Nebaj to be fed and eventually settled in new "model" villages. With the EGP retreating to more remote terrain, Ixil communities began to adapt to the army's newfound dominance, and many opted to reject contact with the guerrillas.

Hit hard, the EGP responded with desperate acts. On June 6, 1982, guerrillas stopped a bus near Cotzal and executed thirteen civil-patrol leaders and their wives; eleven days later a guerrilla column entered the village of Chacalté, where the civil patrol had been particularly active, and killed a hundred people, wounding thirty-five.

The army's offer of amnesty, twinned with a continuous crackdown on the guerrillas, soon drew refugees out of the mountains: between 1982 and 1984 some 42,000 people turned themselves in, fleeing a harsh existence under guerrilla protection. Others returned after years spent living like nomads, hunting animals in the jungles of the Ixcán to the north. By 1985 the guerrillas had been driven back into a handful of mountain strongholds in Xeputul, Sumal and Amachel, all to the north and west of Chajul and Cotzal. Skirmishes continued until the mid-1990s, but ceased with the signing of peace accords. Since then, ex-guerrillas and former civil-patrol members have resettled the old village sites and begun the task of rebuilding communities.

Accommodation

Nebaj has plenty of good budget places, many with inimitable highland charm, though nothing luxurious. Except for *Media Luna*, all the places below have secure parking.

Hospedaje Ilebal Tenam Calzada 15 de Septiembre, ☎7755 8039. An immaculate, well-run hospedaje with 35 rooms, ranging from the small and functional to attractive and comfortable, with TV and private bathroom, in the new block at the rear. Towels and tissue paper are provided, and the hot water is reliable. It's a bit of a hike from the centre, about 400m north of the plaza, and has a small garden. ❶–❸

Hospedaje Nebajeñese 5 Av & 4 C ☎7755 8071. Bare-bones rooms and communal bathrooms only at this place, which is above a store. However, the Xed family who own it could not be more friendly, and there's a kitchen for guests' use. ❶

Hotel del Centro Naab'a 3 C 3–18, Zona 1 ☎7755 8101. Offering a good deal, this place has very clean rooms, slightly spartan but comfortable, all with bathrooms, TV and good beds. It's run by friendly people. ❸

Hotel Ixil 2 Av 9–15, Zona 5 ☎7756 0036. Agreeable, secure place with twelve clean and decent-sized rooms, with tiled floors, TVs and private bathrooms, all set around a lovely, large garden courtyard. ❷

Hotel Shalom Calzada 15 de Septiembre & 4 C ☎7755 8028. Large rooms, some with wood-panelled walls and all with desks and TV, plus a sitting area upstairs. ❸

Hotel Turansa 5 C & 6 Av ☎7755 8219. Two-storey hotel with smallish but neat rooms featuring pine furnishings, comfortable beds, cable TV and private bathrooms; those upstairs enjoy more natural light. ❸

Hotel Villa Nebaj Calzada 15 de Septiembre 2–37 ☎7755 8115, ⓦwww .villanebaj.com. This garish four-storey construction is something of a blot on the landscape, but the accommodation is extremely comfortable – all the very clean, attractive rooms have quality beds, bedside lights, TVs and phones, and the Ixil fabrics add a splash of colour. Those without private bathroom are very competitively priced. ❸–❹

Media Luna Media Sol 3 Calle 6–15 ☎5311 9100. Hostel-style place with clean dormitory facilities and a private room. There's a TV lounge, ping pong and very basic cooking facilities; it's right next to a (loud) evangelical church. ❷

Eating and drinking

This is an isolated highland town so choices are quite limited and only one place has an atmosphere that's vaguely cosmopolitan. For superb local cheese, made in the valley of Acul (see below), head to the store Chancol on Calzada 15 de Septiembre.

Asados el Pasabien 5 Av & 9 C. Dark place that looks a bit uninviting, but it has excellent grilled meats including *churrascos* and *pollo a la plancha*.

El Descanso 3 Calle. Popular with travellers and development workers, and has breakfasts (including granola), filling burritos and specials that include *boxboles* (an Ixil dish of steamed corn dough served with lemon and either tomato or peanut sauce) on Thurs. They also serve cold beer, Cuba Libres and wine, and

you'll find magazines to browse and sofas to lounge on.

Maya Ixchil on the north side of the plaza. Has good breakfasts, some pasta and barbecued meat dishes and offers a set lunch for US$2.50.

Pizza del César 2 Av. Reasonable pizzas, also available by the slice.

Taco Express 3 C 3–18. Tiny, clean little place ideal for inexpensive Mexican snacks: tacos (US$1.50), *gringas* (tortillas and chopped salad) and burritos.

Around Nebaj

With a temperate climate and gorgeous scenery, Nebaj is wonderful **hiking** country, though some places can also be reached by microbus if you're not feeling so energetic.

To Acul

One of the most interesting walks takes you to the village of **Acul**, an hour and a half away up a steep track. Starting from the church in Nebaj, head east downhill along 5 Calle past the *Hotel Turansa*. At the bottom of the dip, as the road divides, take the right-hand fork and head out of town.

Just after you pass the last houses, it's just possible to make out some pre-Columbian burial mounds on your right. These are still used for religious ceremonies, and if you take a close look you'll find burnt patches marking the site of offerings.

Beyond this, the wide track carries on, switchbacking up a steep hillside, and heads over a narrow pass into the next valley, where it drops down into the village. **ACUL** was one of the original so-called "model villages" into which people were herded after their homes were destroyed by the army. It's steadily developing its identity thanks to efforts by the United Nations and other organizations; the municipality now has a population of around five hundred

▲ Children wearing traditional costumes in Nebaj

Ixil and K'iche' Maya families. Sights are few, but it's fascinating to see how well the place has come on in the past few years; every home has a little plot of land for growing maize and vegetables, and there's a lovely Baroque-style white-washed church. You can **stay** in the village at the excellent *Posada Doña Magdelena* (T5782 0891; ❷), with rooms fronting a pretty flowering garden. It's run by a friendly Ixil lady who also serves tasty meals. **Minibuses** (roughly every 30min) connect Acul with Nebaj until 5pm, so if your feet are aching you won't have to wait long for a ride.

Heading out of the village on the road back to Nebaj you'll soon arrive at two superb **country hotels**, both run by the Italian–Guatemalan Azzari family, who have been farming here for generations. The setting is simply breathtaking, with views over a paradisal valley of rich pastureland and pine trees to a mighty fold in the Cuchumatanes mountains. *Hacienda Mil Amores* (T5704 4817, Wwww .haciendamilamores.com; ❺) has four very well-built stone cottages, each with fireplaces, comfortable rooms and verandas with views. Just across the fields is *Finca San Antonio* (T5599 3352; ❹), the original family home, where the stylish, simply furnished rooms have lovely rustic furniture and private bathrooms. Home-cooked meals at both places cost about US$6 per head, horseriding costs US$18 for a four-hour trip, including a guide. Two varieties of Guatemala's best **cheese** are made at the finca, and non-guests are welcome to drop in and buy some produce.

To Cocop

A half-day circular walk climbs up the steep eastern edge of the natural bowl that surrounds Nebaj to the village of **COCOP** and back to the main Nebaj–Cotzal road. Starting in the centre of town, walk along 2 Avenida through the market area, then past *Hotel Ixil* until the end of the road, bear right, and then take the first left downhill to the bridge. Cross the bridge and continue walking until you reach the pueblo of **Xemamatzé** on the edge of Nebaj. This village used to be home to a huge internment camp where Ixil villagers who had surrendered to the army were subject to lengthy "repatriation" treatment before being allowed to return to their native villages. In Xemamatzé, take the well-trodden trail uphill just after the *Pepsi tienda* sign, and after five minutes there's a green signpost to **COCOP** – this trail climbs steadily for about an hour to 2300m. Back across the valley there are spectacular views towards Nebaj. When the trail eventually begins to level out, directly facing a maize field, the path then turns a sharp left and continues round the mountain. The path grips the side of the slope and twists and turns, then gradually starts to descend as the small village of Cocop comes into view below. The village has recently been rebuilt on old foundations; during the civil war it was razed to the ground and 98 villagers were massacred by the army. Today, however, it's a pretty little settlement in a delightful setting beside a gurgling river, with a few stores where you can buy a warm, fizzy drink. If you want to **stay**, ask for Gaspar Brito (the village's tourism coordinator), who will organize a bed and may show you Cocop's *cusha* liquor distillery. To head back, walk straight ahead from the crossroads in the centre of the village, past the Emmanuel church for a lovely hour's stroll along the V-shaped valley through sheep-filled meadows. At the end of the trail is the village of **Río Azul** on the main Cotzal–Nebaj road, from where you can wait for a microbus or pick-up, or hike back to Nebaj in an hour and a half.

La Casada waterfall

A short walk to a beautiful little **waterfall**, La Cascada de Plata, is so strewn with trash that it's not worth the effort unless a clean-up has been undertaken (check in *El Descanso*). Take the road to Chajul and turn left just before it crosses the bridge, a kilometre or two outside Nebaj. Don't be fooled by the smaller version you'll come to shortly before the main set of falls.

San Juan Cotzal and around

Regular minibuses also run from Nebaj to the Ixil Triangle's two other main towns, San Juan Cotzal and Chajul, though it's probably best to coincide your visit with market days when there's more going on. (Cotzal holds its market on Wed & Sat, while Chajul does so on Tues & Fri.) All roads between the three towns are now paved.

SAN JUAN COTZAL is slightly closer to Nebaj, beautifully set in a gentle dip in the valley, sheltered beneath the Cuchumatanes and often wrapped in a damp blanket of mist. In the 1920s and 1930s, this was the largest and busiest of the three Ixil towns, as it was from here that the fertile lands to the north were colonized. Cotzal is a quiet, friendly little place with a very attractive little plaza and an excellent new **community tourism** project called Tejidos Cotzal (☎5428 8218, ⓦwww.tejidoscotzal.org), based just behind the market place. The project aids thirty local weavers, who use natural dyes and backstrap looms; you can buy their work at the office. A two-day guided tour (US$13 per head, minimum two people) is offered, taking in visits to the weavers' homes and to see other craftspeople at work, as well as learning about and sampling local cuisine like *boxboles*. The next day you can hike to a Maya hilltop altar to watch a religious ceremony and visit local waterfalls.

There's one simple **place to stay**, *El Maguey* (☎7765 6199; ❷), two blocks north of the plaza, where all the clean, basic rooms have TV; bathrooms are shared. The hotel's comedor is also the best in town with large set meals for US$2.25.

Santa Avelina

Continuing west, a dirt road passes through a beautiful broad valley to the small coffee-growing village of **Santa Avelina**, 10km from Cotzal. Close to this village is a huge waterfall known as Xej Sibelá, which drops 30m or so to pools which are good for swimming. As it's located in private land, you'll have to pick up the access key first from *Tienda Lux*, just below the church, and cough up US$0.80 per head; the path to the waterfall is behind this shop, which is a fifteen-minute walk away. You could also drop by the village Café Cooperativa, which exports organic, fair-trade, shade-grown coffee to North America, most of it to the Ethical Bean company; a pound costs US$3.

Chajul

Last but by no means least of the Ixil settlements is **CHAJUL**, replete with a good stock of old adobe houses, their wooden beams and red-tiled roofs blackened by the smoke of cooking fires. It is also the most traditional and least bilingual of the Ixil towns. The streets are usually bustling with activity: you'll be met by an army of small children, and the local women gather to wash clothes at the stream that cuts through the middle of the village. Here boys still use blowpipes to hunt small birds, a skill that dates from the earliest of times but is now little used elsewhere. The women of Chajul are terrific weavers, their *huipiles* richly embroidered with animals and symbols, filling the streets with colour. Until the past few years, all the textiles created here used to be woven in red, though nowadays blue is almost as common. Look out, too, for the women's earrings, which are made of old coins strung up on lengths of wool. The traditional red jackets of the men are an extremely rare sight these days. Make sure you visit the shop run by the local weaving cooperative, Va'l Vaq Quyol, between the church and the market, where you'll find some of the best-quality handmade textiles in the country at very decent prices.

The colonial church on the plaza is fascinating: you enter through a colossal wooden door carved with animal motifs, and the huge old structure is full of gold leaf and topped by a timber ceiling of massive beams. It's home to the **Christ of Golgotha** and the target of a large pilgrimage on the second Friday of Lent – a particularly exciting time to visit.

Chajul's cobbled plaza in front of the church is pretty filthy, but between the dirt are some interesting painted figures including two quetzals. This is the place where Rigoberta Menchú, in her autobiography, describes the public execution of her brother at the hands of the army. According to Menchú, her brother and several suspected communists and labour organizers were brought before the town's population by the army, all showing signs of hideous torture. She describes the commander delivering an anti-communist lecture, then ordering the prisoners to be burnt alive. Although there is no doubt that atrocities took place, painstaking investigation by author David Stoll and evidence by EGP member Mario Payeras contradicts Menchú's version of events – eyewitnesses testify that the prisoners were machine-gunned, and the date of the killings is in dispute, as is the fact that Menchú was there at all. Though the show-trial execution was horrific enough under any circumstances, the reliability of Menchú's account has undoubtedly come into question.

If you want to **stay**, by far the best place is the charming *Posada Vetz K'aol* (☎7765 6114; ❸) about 300 metres south of the plaza and signposted from the highway. It's a gorgeous old historic building, formerly a clinic, which has wood-panelled walls and is kept very clean. The big rooms, with good wooden bunk-beds and blankets, are set up for groups but anyone is welcome. There's a lovely sitting room with fireplace and TV and the guardian Eduardo Molina cooks tasty, inexpensive food, and serves a mean espresso. The only other pensiones in town are very run down. You'll find a few comedores just off the plaza, including *Las Gemelitas*, two blocks downhill from the church. Local families also rent out beds in their houses to the steady trickle of travellers now coming to Chajul; you won't have to look for them, they will find you. The Banrural on the plaza will change cash dollars.

Beyond the triangle: the Ixcán

The thinly populated area north of the Ixil Triangle known as the **Ixcán**, which drops down towards the Mexican border to merge with the Lacandón rainforests, has long been one of Guatemala's great, untamed frontiers. Like the Ixil Triangle, this region, a former EGP stronghold, was heavily fought over until the mid-1990s. In the 1960s and 1970s, land-hungry migrants from Quiché and Huehuetenango began moving here, carving out new communities from the forest. However, the EGP moved into the Ixcán in the early 1970s, and a decade later bitter fighting between the insurgents and the army devastated the area, with virtually every village burned to the ground and thousands fleeing to Mexico.

Now many refugees and ex-guerrillas have returned to northern Ixcán, and a number of new villages have been established. The backroad route across the very northern part of Ixcán from Playa Grande to Barillas is covered on p.302, though currently only very rough tracks (and no public transport) link this area with the Ixil.

Lago de Atitlán

Lake Como, it seems to me, touches the limit of the permissibly picturesque; but Atitlán is Como with the additional embellishments of several immense volcanoes. It is really too much of a good thing. After a few days of this impossible landscape one finds oneself thinking nostalgically of the English Home Counties.

Aldous Huxley, *Beyond the Mexique Bay* (1934)

Whether or not you share Huxley's refined sensibilities, there's no doubt that **LAGO DE ATITLÁN** is astonishingly beautiful, and most people find themselves captivated by the lake's scenic excesses. The effect is so intoxicating that a handful of gringo devotees have been rooted to its shores since the 1960s, and today Atitlán rates as the country's number-one tourist attraction.

Hemmed in on all sides by volcanoes and steep hills, it's at least 320m deep and has no visible outlet, draining through an underground passage to the Pacific coast. The lake measures 18km by 12km at its widest point and shifts through an astonishing range of blues, steely greys and greens as the sun moves across the sky. In the morning the surface of the lake is normally calm and clear, but by early afternoon the *xocomil*, "the wind that carries away sin", blows from the coast, churning the surface and making travel by boat quite a rock'n'roll experience. A north wind, say the Maya, indicates that the spirit of the lake is discarding a drowned body, having claimed its soul.

Another remarkable aspect of the Atitlán area is the strength of Maya culture evident in its lakeside villages. Despite the holiday homes and the thousands of tourists who venture here each year, many of the pueblos remain intensely traditional – **San Antonio Palopó**, **Santiago Atitlán** and **Sololá**, in the hills above the lake, are some of the very few places in the entire country where Maya men still wear *traje*. Around the southwestern shores, from Santiago to San Pablo La Laguna, the indigenous people are **Tz'utujil** speakers, and are the remnants of one of the smaller pre-conquest tribes, whose capital was on the slopes of the San Pedro volcano. On the other side of the water, from San Marcos La Laguna to Cerro de Oro, **Kaqchikel** is spoken, marking the western boundary of this tribe.

Thirteen villages grace the shores of the lake – from cosmopolitan **Panajachel** to tiny, isolated **Tzununá** – with many more in the hills behind. The villages are mostly subsistence farming communities, and it's easy to hike and boat around the lake staying in a different one each night. The lakeside area has been heavily populated since the earliest of times, but only relatively recently has it attracted large numbers of tourists. For years few people stayed outside Panajachel, but hotels, guesthouses and tourism facilities have recently spread to most villages.

Atitlán's beauty remains overwhelming, although recent pressures are decidedly threatening. Despite its status as a national park, large swathes of the coastline are now owned by foreigners and wealthy investors from Guatemala City. A population boom in the Maya villages has also had a damaging impact as the desperate need to cultivate more land leads to deforestation and soil erosion. A third of indigenous children who live in the lake environs suffer from malnutrition. Meanwhile, the fishing industry, once thriving on the abundance of small fish and crabs, has been crippled by the introduction of **black bass**, which eat the smaller fish and water birds, and are, moreover, much harder to catch.

Where to go

Most people reach the lake via Panajachel, a small town on the northern shore that is dominated by tourism and has an abundance of hotels and restaurants. To

---

Tourist crime around Lago de Atitlán

The robbery of hikers is rare but not unknown in the Atitlán area, and a couple of rapes have been reported in recent years. Statistically, the chance of you becoming a victim is extremely small, and hundreds of hikers enjoy trouble-free walks around the lakeshore every month. Nevertheless, if you plan to hike any of the volcanoes or the trails between San Pedro and Santa Cruz, check out the security situation first. Guesthouse staff in Santa Cruz are usually well informed, and some language-school teachers in San Pedro can advise you about the situation, as can the tourist office in Panajachel.

get a sense of a more typical Atitlán village, however, travel by boat to Santiago Atitlán or San Antonio Palopó, while for an established travellers' scene and a surplus of cheap hotels, try **San Pedro**. The north coast between San Marcos and **Santa Cruz** is the place to head for if you're looking for real peace and quiet and some good hikes.

The **website** Ⓦ www.atitlan.com has some good historical and cultural information and up-market accommodation options.

Sololá and around

Some 12km south of the Los Encuentros junction on the Carretera Interamericana is **SOLOLÁ**, the departmental capital and gateway to the lake. Perched on a natural balcony some 600m above the water, the town itself isn't much to look at, with a huge central plaza (that's good for people watching) with a clock tower on one side and a modern church on the other. However, its **Friday market** (there's also a smaller one on Tues) is one of Central America's finest, a mesmeric display of colour and commerce which Aldous Huxley described as "a walking museum of fancy dress". Traders are drawn from all over the highlands, as well as thousands of Sololá Maya, the women covered in striped red cloth and the men in their outlandish "space cowboy" shirts, woollen aprons and wildly embroidered trousers.

Sololá is one of the only places in the country that has parallel indigenous and ladino governments, and is one of Guatemala's largest Maya towns. Tradition dominates daily life, and the town is said to be divided into sections, each administered by a Maya clan, just as it was before the Conquest. The town's symbol, still seen on the back of the men's jackets, is an abstraction of a bat, referring to the royal house of Xahil, who were the rulers of the Kaqchikel at the time of the Spanish invasion.

Another interesting time to visit Sololá is on Sunday, when the **cofradías**, the elders of the indigenous religious hierarchy, parade through the streets in ceremonial costume to attend late-morning Mass. They're easily recognizable, carrying silver-tipped canes and wearing broad-brimmed hats and particularly elaborate jackets. Inside the church the sexes are segregated, and the women wear shawls to cover their heads.

Virtually no one stays in Sololá, but the *Hotel y Restaurante Posada del Viajero*, on the east side of the plaza, offers basic **rooms** (❷) and good *comida típica*. Popular *Comedor Las Rosas*, on the north side of the plaza, is another good dining option. **Buses** run to both Panajachel and Los Encuentros every twenty minutes until 7.30pm.

Nearby villages

Several other villages can be reached from Sololá, most of them within walking distance. About 8km to the east is tiny **Santa María Concepción**, an exceptionally quiet farming village with a spectacularly restored, whitewashed colonial church whose altar has some wonderful gilded cherubs. The walk out here, along a dirt track skirting the hills above Panajachel, offers superb views across the lake. The odd minibus and pick-up ply this route.

Clinging to a hillside below Sololá, **San Jorge La Laguna** is a small hamlet built of cinder block and adobe with sweeping lake vistas. Villagers have suffered a long history of disasters: the settlement was founded by refugees from the 1773 earthquake in Antigua, and its original lakeside incarnation was swept into the water by a landslide, persuading the people to move up the hill. But in the last few years a group of land-hungry San Jorge residents have returned to the lakeshore and established a tiny new community of shiny-roofed homes called Bahía La Laguna, despite its location in a flood plain.

Panajachel

Ten kilometres beyond Sololá, separated by a precipitous descent, is **PANAJACHEL**. Over the years what was once a small Maya village has become something of a resort, with a sizeable population of long-term foreign residents, whose numbers are swollen in the winter by an influx of North American seasonal migrants and a flood of tourists. Back in the 1960s and 1970s, Panajachel was the premier Central-American hippie hangout, though it's now fully integrated into the tourism mainstream and is as popular with Guatemalans (and Mexicans and Salvadoreans) as Westerners. The lotus-eaters and crystal-gazers have not all deserted the town, though – many have simply reinvented themselves as capitalists, owning restaurants and exporting handicrafts. There is much talk about Atitlán being one of the world's few vortex energy fields, along with the Egyptian pyramids and Machu Picchu. Though you are unlikely to see fish swimming backwards or buses rolling uphill to Sololá, the lake does have an undeniable draw and Panajachel attracts a polyglot population of healers, therapists and masseurs. In many ways it's this **gringo** crowd that gives the town its modern character and identity – vortex energy centre or not.

Not so long ago (although it seems an entirely different age) Panajachel was a quiet little village of **Kaqchikel** Maya, whose ancestors were settled here after the Spanish crushed a force of Tz'utujil warriors on the site. In the early days of the Conquest, the Franciscans established a church and monastery in the village, using it as the base for their regional conversion campaign. The old village has been enveloped by a construction boom, and though most of the new buildings are pretty nondescript, its lakeside setting is superb. Most of the Maya continue to farm in the river delta behind the town, and the Sunday market, bustling with people from all around the lake, remains oblivious to the tourist invasion.

Arrival and information

Most buses from Sololá stop beside Calle del Embarcadero and then again at the end of the main drag, Calle Santander, which runs down to the lakeshore. Pana has two piers, where you'll find boats to towns around the lake (see box, p.154). The Inguat **tourist office**, just off Calle Santander (daily 9am–5pm; ☎7762 1106, ✉info-panajachel@inguat.gob.gt), has helpful English-speaking staff and hotel information and boat schedules. **Tuk-tuks** (US$0.80 per head) are everywhere in Pana, while taxis wait by the Santiago dock, or you can call one on ☎7762 1571. There are about a dozen or so inexpensive **internet** cafés around town, with rates around US$1 per hour. Among the best are Mayanet, midway along Calle Santander, and ICC further south on the same road.

Pana also has two language schools where you can **study Spanish** (see p.51).

Accommodation

The streets of Panajachel are overflowing with inexpensive **hotels**, and there are plenty of "**rooms**". Campers should head to the shady *Campaña* (☎7762 2479; US$3 per head), on the corner of the road to Santa Catarina and Calle del

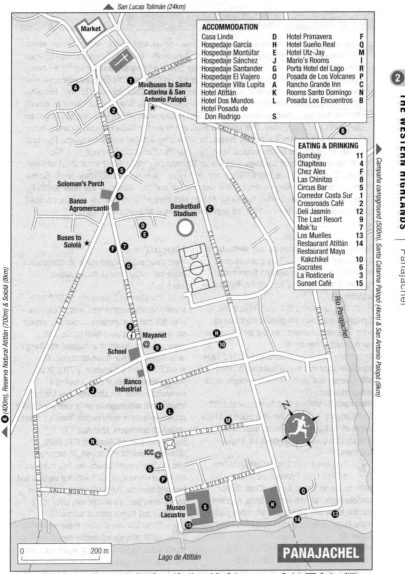

ACCOMMODATION

Casa Linda	D	Hotel Primavera	F
Hospedaje García	H	Hotel Sueño Real	Q
Hospedaje Montúfar	E	Hotel Utz-Jay	M
Hospedaje Sánchez	J	Mario's Rooms	I
Hospedaje Santander	G	Porta Hotel del Lago	R
Hospedaje El Viajero	O	Posada de Los Volcanes	P
Hospedaje Villa Lupita	L	Rancho Grande Inn	C
Hotel Atitlán	K	Rooms Santo Domingo	N
Hotel Dos Mundos	L	Posada Los Encuentros	B
Hotel Posada de			
Don Rodrigo	S		

EATING & DRINKING

Bombay	11
Chapiteau	4
Chez Alex	F
Las Chinitas	8
Circus Bar	5
Comedor Costa Sur	1
Crossroads Café	2
Deli Jasmín	12
The Last Resort	9
Mak'tu	7
Los Muelles	13
Restaurant Atitlán	14
Restaurant Maya Kakchikel	10
Socrates	6
La Rosticería	3
Sunset Café	15

San Lucas Tolimán (24km)

Market

Minibuses to Santa Catarina & San Antonio Palopó

Soloman's Porch

Banco Agromercantil

Buses to Sololá

Basketball Stadium

Mayanet

School

Banco Industrial

ICC

Museo Lacustre

PANAJACHEL

Campaña campground (500m), Santa Catarina Palopó (4km) & San Antonio Palopó (9km)

Río Panajachel

(400m), Reserva Natural Atitlán (700m) & Sololá (8km)

Boats to north coast villages including Santa Cruz and San Marcos & San Pedro — Boats to Santiago Atitlán

Lago de Atitlán

0 — 200 m

Cementerio, over the river bridge. There's a kitchen, hook-up facilities, sleeping bags and tents for rent, and a few little, clean cabañas (③) too.

Budget

Casa Linda down an alley off the top of C Santander ☏7762 0386. A secure, well-run and friendly place, with a gorgeous central garden. All the rooms are spotless and some have private bath. ③

Hospedaje García C El Chali ☏7762 2187. Plenty of very clean, very plain tiled rooms, some with private bathrooms; those at the back share a large open balcony. Checkout is 10am. ②–③

Boats

Most lakeside villages are served by **lanchas** – small, fast boats, which depart when the owner has enough passengers to cover fuel costs. You usually won't have to wait long, but at quiet times of the day you may have to hang around for up to an hour. Panajachel has two piers. The **main pier**, at the end of Calle del Embarcadero, serves the villages on the northern side of the lake: Santa Cruz (about 15min), Jaibalito (25min), Tzununá (30min) and San Marcos (40min). This pier is also home to direct (15min) and non-direct (50min) boats to San Pedro, from where you can easily get to San Juan and San Pablo. The **second pier**, at the end of Calle Rancho Grande, is for Santiago Atitlán (1hr by hourly boats, or 20min by *lancha*) and lake tours. The last boats on all routes leave around 6pm, but there's often a final service at 7.30pm.

A semi-official **fare system** is in place: tourists pay US$1.50–2 for a short trip like Pana–Santa Cruz, or US$2.50–3 for a longer journey. Locals pay less. Some *lancheros* try to charge more for the last boat of the day. **Tours of the lake** (US$10), usually visiting San Pedro, Santiago Atitlán and San Antonio Palopó, can be booked in travel agencies (see p.157); all leave around 9am and return by 4pm.

Hospedaje Montúfar down an alley off the top of C Santander ☎7762 0406. Very clean, secure accommodation on three separate floors and a quiet location make this a good choice. Triples also available. ❷

Hospedaje Sánchez C El Chali ☎7762 2224. If price is a real issue this place is worth considering. The rooms are very bare, but the indigenous management is friendly. ❶

Hospedaje Santander C Santander ☎7762 1304. Agreeable place with a leafy courtyard bursting with greenery and clean, inexpensive rooms, some with private bath. ❷

Hospedaje El Viajero C off Santander ☎7762 0128. Down a little alley, this little place has nine rooms all with private hot-water bath, facing a pretty little garden. Good deals for single travellers. ❷–❸

🏃 **Hospedaje Villa Lupita** Callejón El Tino ☎7762 1201. Excellent-value family-run place on a quiet lane in the old village. Sixteen spotless rooms, all with bedside lights, rugs and mirrors; those with private bath are only a fraction more. Huge sun-terrace and free purified water and coffee. ❷

Mario's Rooms C Santander ☎7762 1313. Popular place, in the thick of things, with appealing, clean, if smallish rooms, some airy and light with private bath, others more basic. Showers are hot. ❷–❸

Rooms Santo Domingo down a path off C Monterrey ☎7762 0236. Age-old travellers' stronghold, set nicely away from the bustle and hustle of C Santander, with a lovely garden ideal for chilling. A few old wooden shacks remain, but most rooms here are now tidy and modernish, some with en-suite bathrooms. ❷–❸

Moderate

There's also excellent mid-range accommodation inside the nearby Reserva Natural Atitlán (see p.157).

Hotel Dos Mundos C Santander ☎7762 2078, 🖳www.hoteldosmundos.com. Just off the main drag, this hotel has spacious comfortable *casitas* set to one side of a palm-filled garden with a swimming pool. Breakfast is included, and there's an authentic in-house Italian restaurant. ❻

Hotel Primavera C Santander ☎7762 2052, 🖳www.primaveraatitlan.com. Adopting a minimalist mantra, this attractive hotel has ten smart rooms with magnolia walls, pale wood and a notable absence of *típica* textiles. There's a smart restaurant downstairs, *Chez Alex*. ❻

Hotel Sueño Real C Ramós ☎7762 0608, Ⓔhotelsuenoreal@hotmail.com. An extremely well run, family-owned place, this little hotel has ten immaculate rooms, each with ikat curtains and highland blankets. The small sitting-terrace has partial lake views, it's located very close to the lakeshore and there's internet access. ❺

🏃 **Hotel Utz-Jay** C 15 de Febrero ☎7762 0217, 🖳www.hotelutzjay.com. There's so much space here that it's easy to just relax and enjoy the lovely garden, with lemon trees, hot tub and *tuj* sauna. Stylish rooms and adobe-and-stone *casitas* all have hand-carved furniture, rugs and private bath. The neighbouring annexe has another four fine rooms with fireplaces. Ample parking. ❺

Posada Los Encuentros Callejón Chotzar 0–41 ☎7762 2093, 🖳www.atitlan.com/losencuentros. A 15min walk from the centre, this American-owned B&B has large rooms and an apartment, a leafy garden, sauna, thermal pool and gym. ❻–❼

Posada de los Volcanes C Santander ☎7762 0244, ⊛www.posadadelosvolcanes.com. Bright, clean rooms, all with good beds, private bath and cable TV. Slightly overpriced, however, so try asking the helpful management for a discount at quiet times of year. ❻

Rancho Grande Inn C Rancho Grande ☎7762 2255, ⊛www.ranchograndeinn.com. Pana's original B&B offers bungalows and rooms bedecked with local fabrics and period furnishings; however, some are a little dark and starting to show their age. The huge grassy gardens are wonderful, and there's a small pool. A filling breakfast with German-style pancakes is included. ❺–❻

Luxury

Hotel Atitlán 1km west of the centre ☎7762 1441 or 7762 1416, ⊛www.hotelatitlan.com. Panajachel's premier hotel enjoys an unrivalled lakeside location, with stunning gardens stretching down to the shore, an "infinity" hot tub and swimming pool. Rooms have all mod-cons, updated bathrooms and volcano views. From US$138. ❾

Hotel Posada de Don Rodrigo C Santander ☎7762 2326, ⊛www.posadadedonrodrigo.com. Colonial-style hotel with large outdoor pool, sauna and squash court. Most of the accommodation, if comfortable enough, lacks a lake view, so go for a room in the new wing (nos. 301–311), which offers better value, vistas and much more space for a few dollars more. Rooms from US$122. ❾

Porta Hotel del Lago right on the lakeshore ☎7762 1555, ⊛www.portahotels.com. Big, corporate all-inclusive hotel with plenty of high-end facilities but little in the way of character. Rooms from US$178. ❾

The town

Panajachel is one of those inevitable destinations for travellers, and although no one ever owns up to actually liking it, most people seem to drop by for a day or two. The **old village** – a handful of narrow lanes grouped around a sombre, stone-faced Catholic church that dates from 1567 – is not particularly picturesque, though its narrow lanes are worth a little exploration. The **market** has recently been revamped, but is still resolutely geared to local needs rather than tourist tastes; it's a block to the north of the church.

There's far more hustle and bustle in evidence along Pana's main drag, **Calle Santander**, which cuts a colourful path through the modern heart of the town. This kilometre-long street boasts dozens of stores and stalls, loaded up with a kaleidoscopic collection of weaving and handicrafts from all over Guatemala, as well as an amazing selection of places to eat, drink and surf the net. Street hawkers, weighed down with armfuls of *típica* textile shirts and gaudy trinkets, ply their goods with daunting persistence, and buzzing tuk-tuks weave their way along the lane touting for business.

At the southern end of Calle Santander, Pana's **beach** is a scruffy stretch of sand that's not an attractive place for swimming and sunbathing, even if water quality has recently improved – there are certainly much nicer spots for a swim. You can rent out kayaks from Pana beach (note that the lake is usually calmer in the morning), or even scuba dive with ATI Divers (see "Listings").

Cultural sights are hardly abundant in Pana, though there is the stylish **Museo Lacustre** (daily 8am–6pm; US$4.75, students US$3) dedicated to the Atitlán region. Located in the grounds of the *Hotel Posada de Don Rodrigo* on Calle Santander, it has well-presented displays in Spanish and English, outlining the turbulent geological history that led to the creation of the lake. There's also an interesting collection of Maya artefacts, including Preclassic- and Classic-era ceramics and some wonderfully grotesque ceremonial incense-burners.

Eating, drinking and entertainment

Panajachel has an abundance of cafés and **restaurants**, though standards are pretty mediocre. There's certainly plenty of variety, with Italian, Mexican, Asian and, yes, even some Central American places. Cheap comedores can be found on and just off the beach promenade and close to the market.

Bombay halfway along C Santander. An eclectic vegetarian place which, despite the name, has little Indian food, instead featuring offerings such as Indonesian *gado-gado*, Mexican dishes, pita bread sandwiches and organic coffee.

Chez Alex halfway along C Santander. High-end dining with a European menu of classics like Swiss fondue, and dishes like *robalo* with mussels and shrimp. It's expensive, with starched tablecloths and fancy cutlery.

Las Chinitas northern end of C Santander. Can be a bit hit-and-miss but worth a try if you're hankering for Asian food: Nonyan (Malay–Chinese) dishes, curries, stir-fries and *sate*. Closed Mon.

🏃 **Circus Bar** C de los Árboles. The best pizza in Pana, this atmospheric place is divided into little sections with walls covered in circus posters. There's a full bar, good coffee, and live music most evenings.

Comedor Costa Sur just off C Principal, in the old village. Pana's best comedor: clean and inexpensive and great for breakfast or lunch, with a bargain daily US$2 set menu.

🏃 **Crossroads Café** C del Campanario, in the old village. There's no competition in the Atitlán area, and probably the entire country, for this little place that serves up Pana's very finest coffee. Beans are selected, blended and roasted by an American perfectionist who even imports coffee from Ethiopia to mix with local varieties to get the right house blend. Also offers herbal teas, rich hot chocolate and fresh pastries. Closed Sun and Mon and for siesta 1–3pm.

🏃 **Deli Jasmín** C Santander. The best café in town, this lovely little place has a healthy menu of breakfasts, sandwiches, salads (try the tabouli), Mexican dishes and tempeh; most dishes are priced between US$3–5. It enjoys a great tropical garden setting with a delightful rear patio area. Closed Tues. There's a second branch, with the same menu, halfway up C Santander. Closed Wed.

Guajimbos halfway down C Santander. Ideal for a South American–style feast, all the meat – including kebabs, *chorizo* and giant steaks – is barbecued on a giant *parrilla*. Well-priced breakfasts too. Closed Thurs.

The Last Resort C El Chali. Looks vaguely like an English pub, but does great American breakfasts. Also serves pasta, rib-eye steak (US$4.50) and vegetarian dishes.

Los Muelles lakeside, by the Santiago Pier. Right above the water, this simple place is inexpensive for its location. Plenty of set-lunch meals available for US$3, or eat from the menu, which includes fish, *pollo a la plancha* and sandwiches.

Restaurante Atitlán lakeside, by the Santiago Pier. A huge palapa-roofed place with fine lake views and a reliable menu offering big portions of Guatemalan favourites: try *camarones especial Atitlán*.

Restaurant Maya Kakchikel C El Chali 2–25. Run by a friendly indigenous family; come here for good set breakfasts, huge *caldos* and *comida típica*.

La Rosticería C de los Árboles. Specializes in delicious spit-roasted chicken (a half-portion is US$3.50), though they also have good set-breakfast options, burgers and sandwiches. Closed Sun.

Nightlife and entertainment

Panajachel buzzes at weekends and during holidays, when many young Guatemalans head to the lake to drink and flirt. Things are quieter at other times, however. You could start with a cold one at the appropriately named *Sunset Bar* by the lake and then head up to the *Mak'tu* bar on Calle Santander, which has a big garden and **live bands** most nights. Other bars and clubs are located around the southern end of Calle de los Árboles, where you'll find the *Circus Bar* for live music plus the *Chapiteau* **nightclub**. Close by on Calle Principal, *Socrates* is a mainstream disco–club where a young, mainly Guatemalan crowd dances to Latin tunes.

Movies are also shown at the Turquoise Buffalo video cinema on Calle de los Árboles. Check out *unital Soloman's Porch* for fascinating social and environmental **lectures**, including talks by former gang members and Maya activists.

Listings

Banks and exchange Banco Agromercantil has an ATM and exchanges traveller's cheques, or head to Banco Industrial, C Santander, which also has an ATM.

Bicycle and motorbike rental Emanuel, C 14 de Febrero (☎7762 2790), has mountain bikes (US$7 a day) and trail bikes (US$30).

Bookstores Vrisa, C Principal 0–99, opposite north end of C Santander, stocks a great selection of secondhand books, or try The Gallery, C de los Árboles, for used titles. Librería Libros del Lago, C Santander 9, has a decent choice of books on Maya culture, maps and guidebooks.

Laundry Lavandería Automático, C de los Árboles 0–15 (Mon–Sat 7.30am–6.30pm). US$3.50 for a full load washed, dried and folded.

Medical care Dr Edgar Barreno speaks good English; his office is down the first street that branches to the right off C de los Árboles (☎7762 1008).

Pharmacy Farmacia La Unión, C Santander.

Police On the plaza in the old village (☎7762 1120).

Post office C Santander and C 15 de Febrero, or try Get Guated Out on C de los Árboles (☎7762 0595) for bigger shipments.

Telephone Many of the businesses and cybercafés on C Santander offer good rates to call long-distance, including ICC, where it's US$0.25 per minute to North America and US$0.40 to Europe.

Travel agents Unión Travel, C Santander (☎7762 2426, ⓦwww.igoguate.com).

Water sports Canoes, kayaks and windsurfers can be rented on the main beach. Scuba-divers can dive the lake with ATI Divers based in Santa Cruz, but they have an office in Pana at Plaza Los Patios, C Santander (☎7762 2621, Ⓔatidivers@gmail .com); one fun dive is US$30, while a PADI Open Water course is US$210.

Around Panajachel

About a kilometre west of central Panajachel, the **Reserva Natural Atitlán** (8am–5pm; US$5; ⓦwww.atitlanreserva.com) is a privately run forest reserve on the steep slopes of the lake. There are several walking trails (20–75min) through dense foliage, and viewing platforms from where spider monkeys and small mammals like possum and kinkajou are often spotted. Inside the reserve there's a **butterfly park** with dozens of species, including golden orange monarch and blue morpho, plus a breeding laboratory; there are also orchid gardens and aviaries. Eight zip lines (US$18.50), ranging between 90 and 320 metres, are well managed by helpful staff and offer an unparalleled perspective of the forest and lake. There are also a few very stylish stone-and-timber

▲ Lago de Atitlán

rooms (**❻**–**❼**) with huge balconies, a campground and a restaurant. To **get to** the reserve head for the *Hotel Atitlán* (see p.155), from where sign-posted trails lead to the adjacent reserve.

Around the lake

The villages that surround the lake are all easily accessible. For an afternoon's outing, head along the shore southeast of Panajachel to **San Antonio** and **Santa Catarina Palopó**. If you want to spend a day or two exploring the area, then it's well worth crossing the lake to **Santiago Atitlán** and **San Pedro La Laguna**. It's perfectly feasible to walk round the whole lake in four to five days; alternatively, you could cut out a section or two by catching a boat between villages. Perhaps the finest **walking** is on the northwestern side, between San Pedro and Santa Cruz, which is around a six-hour hike.

The eastern shore

There are two roads around the lake's eastern shore from Panajachel: one clings to the shoreline, and the other runs parallel up along the ridge of hills towards Godínez. Next to the lake, backed up against the slopes, are a couple of villages, the first of which, **SANTA CATARINA PALOPÓ**, is just 4km from Panajachel. The people of Santa Catarina used to live almost entirely by fishing and trapping crabs, but these days the black bass have put an end to all that and they've turned to farming and migratory work, with many of the women travelling to Panajachel and Antigua to peddle their weaving. The women's *huipiles* here are unusual in that they have dazzling zigzags in vibrant shades of turquoise or purple, though the traditional design was predominantly red with tiny geometric designs of people and animals. The changes are partly due to a North American who visited the village in the 1970s and commissioned a *huipil* to be made in purple, blue and green as opposed to the traditional colours. These new shades became very popular in the village and are now worn almost universally.

Much of the shoreline around here has been bought and developed, and great villas, ringed by impenetrable walls, and a burgeoning array of **luxury hotels** have come to dominate the environment. *Hotel Villa Santa Catarina* (☎7762 1291, ⓦwww.villasdeguatemala.com; **❼**–**❽**) enjoys a prime lakeside plot, with 36 very comfortable, but not huge, **rooms** in an attractive colonial-style building with a large pool. Continuing south, next up is the *Tzam Poc* (☎7762 2680, ⓦwww.atitlan.com/tzampoc; rooms from US$148; **❾**), owned by a welcoming Italian, where the spacious accommodation has some stylish touches, and there's an infinity pool, though all this comes at a price. A kilometre beyond Santa Catarina, high above the lakeshore, is the best hotel on this sybaritic strip, the sumptuous and very tasteful ⚒ *Casa Palopó* (☎7762 2270, ⓦwww.casapalopo.com; doubles from US$140, suites US$165; **❾**), which offers stunning rooms with wood-beam ceilings – and each suite has a private sun-terrace – and Aveda-stocked luxury bathrooms. The restaurant is also excellent (meals cost upwards of US$25) and has a great lake-facing view. If you're looking for a **luxury villa** *Casa B'alam* (☎7832 1745, ⓦwww.panzaverde.com/en/atitlan.htm) has two gorgeous self-catering houses, both with uninterrupted lake views.

Continuing along the lakeside road, just as the steep profile of San Antonio comes into view, the road dips and passes a beautiful, secluded little beach, almost hidden among the reeds.

SAN ANTONIO PALOPÓ is a larger and more traditional village, squeezed in beneath a steep hillside. The village is also on the tour-group itinerary, which has encouraged some persistent sales techniques on the part of the inhabitants. The hillsides above San Antonio are well irrigated and terraced, reminiscent of rice paddies, and most men wear the village *traje* of red shirts with vertical stripes and short woollen kilts. Women wear almost identical shirts, made of the same fabric but with subtle variations to the collar design. The whitewashed central church is worth a look; just to the left of the entrance are two ancient bells, while inside is a model of the birth of Jesus, San Antonio–style, with Joseph wearing the village costume.

Minibuses (6am–7pm, every 20min) run along the lakeshore to both villages from Calle El Amate, Panajachel; or you could walk to San Antonio from above the lake (see below). San Antonio has a couple of **places to stay**: the good-value *Hotel Terrazas del Lago* (T7762 0037, Wwww.hotelterrazasdellago.com; ❺), by the water, which has comfortable rooms with stone walls and beautiful views, or the very simple but clean pensión (❶) owned by Juan López Sánchez, near the entrance to the village. Try the comedor below the church for a cheap **meal**.

The higher road to San Lucas Tolimán

The higher of the two roads around the lake's eastern shore heads back into the rich river delta behind Panajachel, before climbing up above the lake to **San Andrés Semetabaj**, where there's a fantastic ruined colonial church. A path opposite the church's main entrance leads back to Panajachel, winding down through fields and coffee bushes – a nice walk of an hour or so. Beyond San Andrés the road curves around the edge of the ridge, offering a sweeping view of the lake below and the irregular cone of the Tolimán volcano opposite, arriving eventually in Godínez. A short way before is a *mirador*, from where paths lead down to the lakeside village of San Antonio Palopó.

At **Godínez**, a ramshackle and wind-blown village, the road divides, one way running out to the Carretera Interamericana (through Patzicía and Patzún – though if you're driving, you should bear in mind there have been occasional attacks and robberies on this road), and the other on around the lake to **SAN LUCAS TOLIMÁN**. Set apart from the other lakeside settlements in many ways, this largely ladino town is probably the least attractive of the lot. The surrounding land is almost all planted with coffee, which dominates the flavour of the place. The setting, however, is special: at the back of a small inlet of reed beds, with the Tolimán volcano rising above. Both the Tolimán and Atitlán **volcanoes** can be climbed from here, though taking a guide is essential as the trails are difficult to find – ask in one of the hotels or use a tour operator based in San Pedro or Panajachel. The main **market** days are Thursday and Sunday.

If you need somewhere to **stay**, head for the rustic *Hotel Don Pedro*, at the end of Calle Principal (T7722 0023; ❸) with lake views, safe parking and a restaurant; or consider the tranquil *Hotel Tolimán* (T7722 0033, Wwww.atitlan /toliman.htm; ❻–❼), which has lovely grassy lakefront grounds, with a pool, comfortable rooms and complimentary breakfast. South of San Lucas at Km164 on the road to Cocales is *Los Tarrales* (T5136 3410, Wwww.tarrales.com; ❻–❼), a coffee finca, nature reserve and rural lodge. Specialist birding tours (US$10 per head for a half-day guided hike or US$30 for a cloud forest walk) are offered; over 300 species have been recorded in the reserve. The guides here really know their stuff and the lodge has an engaging old-world charm.

Very regular **buses** run from San Lucas to Santiago Atitlán and there are hourly buses to Guatemala City via Cocales. There are also five daily buses to Panajachel (1hr) plus occasional boat connections.

Santiago Atitlán

In the southwest corner of the lake, set to one side of a sheltered horseshoe inlet, **SANTIAGO ATITLÁN** is overshadowed by the cones of the San Pedro, Atitlán and Tolimán volcanoes. It's the largest and most important of the lakeside villages, and also one of the most traditional, being the main centre of the Tz'utujil-speaking Maya. At the time of the Conquest, the Tz'utujil had their fortified capital, **Chuitinamit-Atitlán**, on the slopes of San Pedro, while the bulk of the population lived spread out around the site of today's village. Alvarado and his crew, needless to say, destroyed the capital and massacred its inhabitants, assisted this time by a force of Kaqchikel Maya, who arrived at the scene in some three hundred canoes.

Today Santiago is an industrious sort of place in a superb setting. During the day the town becomes fairly commercial, its **main street** (which runs up from the dock) lined with weaving shops and art galleries. Expect to be hustled by persistent hawkers, particularly if you visit during the huge Friday-morning **market**.

There's not that much to see in Santiago, but you could drop into the new weaving museum, **Museo Cojolya** (Mon–Fri 9am–4pm, Sat 9am–1pm; free), about 100m up the main drag from the dock, on the left. Here you'll find excellent displays (in English and Spanish) about the tradition of backstrap weaving in Santiago, and you can see some of the weavers in action at 11am and 1pm daily. They sell a range of very good quality shirts, bags and souvenirs too.

Otherwise the fabulous old colonial Catholic **church** is well worth a look for its fascinating Maya religious detail. Its huge central altarpiece, carved when the church was under *cofradía* control, culminates in the shape of a mountain peak and a cross, symbolizing the Maya world tree. Dozens of statues of saints (all bedecked in indigenous attire) line the walls. On the right as you enter, a stone memorial commemorates **Father Stanley Rother**, an American priest who served in the parish from 1968 to 1981. Father Rother was a committed defender of his parishioners in an era when, in his own words, "Shaking hands with an Indian has become a political act". Branded a communist by President García, he was assassinated by a paramilitary death squad like hundreds of his countrymen before and after him. His body was returned to his native Oklahoma for burial, but not before his heart was removed and buried in the church. There's an informative article about the church on ⓦ www.mesoweb.com.

As is the case in many other parts of the Guatemalan highlands, the Catholic Church in Santiago is locked in bitter rivalry with several evangelical sects, who are building churches here at an astonishing rate. Folk Catholicism also plays an important role in the life of Santiago, and the town is one of the main places where Maya pay homage to **Maximón**, the "evil" saint. It costs a few quetzales to enter his abode, and you'll have to pay extra to take his picture. Local children will lead you to his current residence (Maximón moves every year) for a small tip.

The traditional costume of Santiago, still worn a fair amount by the older men, is both striking and unusual. The men wear long shorts, which, like the women's *huipiles*, are white- and purple-striped, intricately embroidered with birds and flowers. Some women also wear a *xk'ap*, a band of red cloth approximately 10m long, wrapped around their heads, which has the honour of being depicted on the 25 centavo coin. Sadly, this headcloth has almost gone out of use, though you may still see it at fiestas and on market days, when it's worn by canny girls eager to attract the eye of tourists (and charge for a photo).

Holy smoke

Easter celebrations are particularly special in Santiago, and as Holy Week draws closer the town comes alive with expectation and excitement. **Maximón** maintains an important role in the proceedings. On Monday of Holy Week his effigy is taken to the lakeshore where it is washed, on Tuesday he's dressed, and on Wednesday the idol is housed in a small chapel close to the plaza. Here he waits until Good Friday, when the town is the scene of a huge and austere religious procession, the plaza packed with everyone dressed in their finest traditional costume. Christ's statue is paraded solemnly through the streets, arriving at the church around noon, where it's tied to a cross and raised above the altar. At around 3pm the *cofradres* arrive to cut him down from the cross, and Christ is lowered into a coffin. Then pandemonium erupts as dozens of the faithful spray his image with perfume, and the air becomes thick with fragrance and aerosol fumes. Penitents bear Christ out of the church on a vast cedar platform, inching forward and back, taking around two hours to exit the church, before there's a symbolic confrontation in the plaza with Maximón, who is carried out of an adjoining chapel by his bearers.

The presence of Maximón, decked out in a felt hat and Western clothes, with a cigar in his mouth, is scorned by reforming Catholics and revered by the traditionalists. The precise origin of the saint is unknown, but he's also referred to as San Simón, Judas Iscariot and Pedro de Alvarado, and always seen as an enemy of the Church. Some say that he represents a Franciscan friar who chased after young indigenous girls, and that his legs are removed to prevent any further indulgence. "Max" in the Mam dialect means tobacco, and Maximón is always associated with ladino vices such as smoking and drinking; more locally he's known as *Rij Laj* or *Rilej Mam*, the powerful man with a white beard. Throughout the year he's looked after by a *cofradía*; if you feel like dropping in to pay your respects to him, ask for *La Casa de Maximón* and someone will show you the way. Take along a packet of cigarettes and a bottle of Quezalteca for the ever-thirsty saint and his minders, who will ask you to make a contribution to fiesta funds. For details on visiting San Simón in Zunil and for a warning about the gravity of the process, see p.185. For more on indigenous religion, see the Contexts section of this book.

Around Santiago: volcanoes and the nature reserve

The land around Santiago is mostly volcanic, with only the odd patch of fertile soil mixed in with the acidic ash. Farming, fishing and the traditional industry, the manufacture of *cayucos* (canoes), are no longer enough to provide for the population, and a lot of people travel to the coast and beyond, or work on the coffee plantations that surround the volcano. The Tolimán and Atitlán **volcanoes** can both be climbed from here, but it's always best to take a guide to smooth the way as there have been robberies – ask at *Hotel Chi-Nim-Ya* (see below).

If you're here for the day, then you can walk out of town along the track to San Lucas Tolimán, or rent a **canoe** and paddle out into the lake – just ask around at the dock. To the north of Santiago is a small island, which has been designated a **nature reserve**, originally for the protection of the *poc*, or Atitlán grebe, a flightless water bird. The *poc* used to thrive in the waters of the lake but two factors drove it into extinction: the overcutting of reeds where it nested and the introduction of the predatory black bass, which ate all the young birds. Despite the disappearance of the *poc*, the island is still a beautiful place to spend an hour or two and is a fine destination if you're paddling around in a canoe.

Santiago Atitlán practicalities

Lanchas connect Santiago with both San Pedro (15min) and Panajachel (20min); they leave when full. Larger boats also make the **crossings**; there are timetables at the dock.

The town is well connected by bus to Cocales and Guatemala City (7 daily between 3am and 4pm), and microbuses leave for San Lucas Tolimán. Pick-ups and buses leave for San Pedro from a stop by the Hotel Chi-Nim-Ya.

As for **accommodation**, two backpacker favourites are the basic, clean and friendly *Hotel Chi-Nim-Ya* (T 7721 7131; ❷–❸), on the left uphill from the dock, where some rooms have private bath; and the good-value *Hotel Lago de Atitlán*, in the centre of town (T 7721 7174; ❷). For something special, there are a couple of good options that can be reached by road or water-taxi from the dock. The excellent ⚐ *Posada de Santiago*, 1km south of town (T 7721 7366, Ⓦ www.posadadesantiago.com; ❹–❽), is a wonderful lakeside B&B, with a wide range of accommodation: rooms, volcanic-stone cottages and suites. Guests have free access to mountain bikes, canoes, wi-fi, a hot tub and sauna, and there's a fine restaurant (with a good wine list) and pool. About a ten-minute walk north of the dock, *Hotel Bambú* (T 7721 7332, Ⓦ www.ecobambu.com; ❻–❼) is another good choice with beautiful thatched-roofed stone bungalows and rooms set around a large plot of land, all with lake views, plus an excellent restaurant with Spanish specialities and fine wines.

Of the **restaurants** in town, there are two good places about 400 metres up from the dock: *Wach'alal* has great *comida típica* and lake fish, while *El Horno* is

The expulsion of the army from Santiago Atitlán

Santiago Atitlán's recent history, like that of so many Guatemalan villages, is marked by trouble and violence. The village assumed a unique role, however, when it became the first in the country to successfully expel the armed forces. Relations between the army and the village had been strained since the early 1980s, when the army, wary of the presence of ORPA guerrillas in the area, established a permanent base in Santiago. The army accused the villagers of supporting the insurgents and attempted to terrorize the population into subservience. Throughout the 1980s, villagers were abducted, tortured and murdered – around three hundred were killed over an eleven-year period.

Under civilian rule after 1986, the guerrilla threat dropped off considerably, and the people of Santiago grew increasingly confident and resentful of the unnecessary army presence. Matters came to a head on the night of December 1, 1990, when two drunken soldiers shot a villager. The men fled to the army base on the outskirts of the village, but they were soon followed by an unarmed crowd that eventually numbered around two thousand. Believing that they were about to be overwhelmed, the six hundred soldiers inside the garrison opened fire on the crowd, killing thirteen people, including three children, and wounding a further twenty. Following the incident some twenty thousand villagers signed a petition calling for the army's expulsion from Santiago. After intense international pressure, the army finally withdrew, shutting down the base.

Difficulties then arose with the police, when on December 6 the local civil patrol discovered a group of policemen on a suspicious nightime mission. A mob soon surrounded the police station, and the police were also forced to leave. When replacements arrived from Guatemala City, Santiago's residents refused to sell the new recruits any food for two weeks – and it was a month before they agreed to allow them use of the public toilet.

In June 1991, Santiago's example was followed by neighbouring San Lucas Tolimán, where the killing of a community leader by a soldier led to the army's expulsion there too. Other villages in sensitive areas, including Joyabaj and Chajul, subsequently took steps to shut down army bases. The 1996 peace accords went some way toward curtailing military interference in civilian affairs, and in 2004 President Berger slashed military numbers considerably. Increasing societal instability, however, has seen troops once again return to the streets in some areas and resume highway patrols as well.

a fine bakery with fresh baguette sandwiches, cakes (including macadamia nut pie) and good coffee. There's an ATM on the north side of the plaza.

San Pedro La Laguna

Around the other side of the San Pedro volcano is the town of **SAN PEDRO LA LAGUNA**, which has now usurped Panajachel to become *the* place for young travellers to hang out and party. More than anywhere else in Guatemala, San Pedro has a distinctively bohemian feel, and there's plenty of bongo-bashing and bong-smoking counterculture in evidence. Despite the obvious culture clash between locals (most of whom are evangelical Christians) and foreigners, everyone seems to get on reasonably well.

San Pedro is actually a lot more than just a party-hard place, and has established itself as an important **language school** centre in recent years – the beautiful location and inexpensive schools drawing increasing numbers of students. Standards are improving but prices are still extremely cheap, ranging from US$90 to US$150 per week for four hours' one-on-one tuition and full board with a local family (see p.51 for a list of recommended institutions).

The setting is simply spectacular. The town sits on the lower slopes of the San Pedro volcano, while to the northwest the steep ridged edge of the Atitlán caldera rises to an irregular peak known as Indian Nose. You'll find plenty of places for swimming and sunbathing, with a little beach area just west of the Panajachel dock and grassy lakeside verges off the main trail.

Tradition isn't as powerful here and only a few elderly people, mostly men, wear the old costume, although there is a sense of permanence in the narrow cobbled streets and old stone houses. Pedreños are famed for their *cayucos* (canoes), made from the great cedar trees that grow on the slopes of the San Pedro volcano. They also have a reputation for driving a hard bargain when trading their coffee and avocados, and have managed to buy up a lot of land from neighbouring San Juan, with whom there's endless rivalry.

The **San Pedro volcano**, which towers above the village to a height of some 3020m, is largely covered with tropical forest; get an early start to maximize your chances of a clear view and to avoid the worst of the heat. It can be climbed in around four hours, and takes between two and three hours to descend. The hike is now very well organized and secure, with a "base camp" (☏5593 8302, @www.volcansanpedro.org) 2km south of town. Official guides (US$13 per head) escort hikers up the volcano along a well-maintained trail with a stop at a *mirador* deck, which has superb lake views. The peak itself is ringed by forest, which blocks the view over San Pedro, although an opening on the south side gives excellent views of Santiago. Excursion Big Foot (see below) also offers guided hikes (about US$11pp) up Indian Nose, which arguably provides even better vistas of the lake and its three volcanoes. This summit is regularly used for Maya religious ceremonies – if you do happen to come across a ritual during your hike, it's best not to take photographs.

Excursion Big Foot (☏7721 8203), just left of the Panajachel dock, offers horse-riding for US$2.50 an hour (guide included), bicycles for US$8 a day and canoes for US$1.30 per hour. **Atitlán Adventures**, on the main trail (☏4130 5025) has snorkelling gear and spear-fishing tours, plus mountain bikes and kayaks for rent. To unwind, head to the **thermal pools**, between the two docks, for some serious relaxation.

Arrival and information

There are two docks in San Pedro. All **boats** from Panajachel and villages on the north side of the lake, including Santa Cruz and San Marcos, arrive and

SAN PEDRO LA LAGUNA

ACCOMMODATION

Casa Elena	C
Hospedaje Casa María	F
Hotelito El Amanecer Sakcari	I
Hotel Gran Sueño	E
Hotel Mansión del Lago	G
Hotel Maria Elena	B
Hotel Mikaso	J
Hotel Nahual Maya	D
Hotel San Francisco	K
Hotel Valle Azul	H
Posada Casa Domingo	A

EATING & DRINKING

Alegre Pub	3
El Barrio	10
Buddha	7
Café La Puerta	9
D'Noz	2
Freedom	5
Jardín	8
Matahari	11
Nick's Place	1
Shanti Shanti	6
Zoola	4

depart from the Panajachel dock on the north side of town. Boats from Santiago Atitlán use a separate dock to the southeast, a ten-minute walk away. The path between the docks is known as **the trail**; along here you'll find a myriad of colourful bars, restaurants and hotels; this is the main gringo part of town.

Buses connect San Pedro with Quetzaltenango (7 daily, the last at 11am; 2hr 30min) and Guatemala City (9 daily, last at 2pm; 3hr 15min); all leave from the plaza. Pick-ups (about every 15min) connect the town with San Juan, San Pablo and San Marcos, or you can hire a tuk-tuk, which are everywhere in San Pedro. Speak to Excursion Big Foot about **shuttle buses**, which can be arranged to Quetzaltenango (US$8), Antigua (US$8) and San Cristóbal de las Casas, Mexico (US$40). In the centre of town, you'll find the market (busiest on Thurs and Sun), post office and a Banrural **bank**, which has an ATM and changes traveller's cheques. Of several internet places, *D'Noz* is the best setup; here you can also burn photos to disk or buy MP3 CDs. Zuvuya Books, between the docks, has a small but interesting selection of used titles.

Accommodation

San Pedro has some of the cheapest accommodation in all Latin America, with some basic, clean **guesthouses** that charge less than US$3 a person per night. There's not much in the mid-range sector as yet, but new places are opening up every year. Street names are just starting to be used in San Pedro, but to locate a hotel you can let one of the local children guide you; a tip of a quetzal or two is appropriate.

Casa Elena left from the Pana dock ⓣ5310 9243. A three-storey place with plain, clean, functional rooms, you pay a little more for a private bath. There's a dock at the rear for swimming. ❷–❸

Hospedaje Casa María between the docks ⓣ4145 0307. Relaxed, friendly little hospedaje owned by a charming Israeli–Guatemalan couple. Rooms, all with double beds and private bathroom, are well kept, and there's a guest kitchen. ❷

Hotel Gran Sueño left from the Pana dock ⓣ7721 8110. A neat and well-managed place, owned by the welcoming González family. All eight clean little rooms have private bathrooms and TV, some have nice touches like wall maps; the two on the upper level have lake views. ❷

Hotel Mansión del Lago up from Pana dock ⓣ7721 8041, ⓦwww.hotelmansiondellago.com. A well-built hotel with light, clean rooms all with nice pine beds, private bath and balcony areas with lake views. Also has a rooftop hot tub and internet café. Book ahead at weekends. ❸

Hotel Maria Elena left from Pana dock ⓣ5098 1256. New hotel where the two-storey block has eleven spacious rooms, all with private bathroom. The communal balconies have hammocks at the front for quality swinging time. ❸

Hotel Mikaso close to Santiago dock ⓣ5973 3129, ⓦwww.mikasohotel.com. San Pedro's best hotel is very Spanish in style, an attractive building with lovely tilework. Rooms are elegant and comfortable, there's a comfy dorm (with en-suite bathroom) and a great roof-terrace restaurant (see review). Dorm US$8–10, rooms ❺

Hotel Nahual Maya left from the Pana dock ⓣ7721 8158. A smart, whitewashed colonial-style place with two floors of very well-kept, attractive rooms; all have plenty of natural light and private bathrooms. There's a little garden at the front, ample parking and friendly management. ❸

Hotel San Francisco 5 Av 2–32, Zona 3 ⓣ7721 8016. Cheap and cheerful with clean little rooms, some with bathrooms, many with lake-view balconies. Guest kitchen available. ❷

Hotel Valle Azul turn right from the Pana dock ⓣ5011 6564. Vaguely Soviet-style concrete monster of a hotel, but there are plenty of clean, bare rooms (some with private bath) and those on the upper deck have great views. ❷

Hotelito El Amanecer Sakcari 7 Av 2–12, Zona 2 ⓣ7721 8096, ⓦwww.hotelsakcari.com. Offers a selection of well-kept, if plain rooms with private bathrooms, in separate, brightly painted accommodation blocks. Most enjoy communal balconies that face the lake. ❹

Posada Casa Domingo between the docks. Six attractive, clean rooms, all with tiled floors, private bath and good mattresses, facing Volcán San Pedro. Ultra-basic, cell-like accommodation in a separate block also available. ❶–❸

Eating

San Pedro's **cafés** and **restaurants** have a decidedly international flavour, and most are also excellent value for money. Vegetarians are well catered for, and there are also a few typical Guatemalan comedores in the centre of the village and by the Santiago dock.

Café La Puerta between the docks. With a huge grassy lakeshore plot, you could spend all day here taking in the scenery and munching on the sandwiches, tacos and quesadillas. Wash it all down with a cold beer or great, fresh juices.

D'Noz above *Nick's Place*, Pana dock. Very popular bar-restaurant with a long menu that includes baguettes, bagels, curries and Chinese food. If you've been out of touch for a while, they have a weekly newssheet, and also an excellent clippings file about Guatemala. Open until 1am.

La Crêperie turn left from the Pana dock. Pretty authentic, flavourful crêpes and snacks.

Matahari turn right from the Santiago dock. The best comedor in San Pedro, this clean place has good Guatemalan grub and amazingly tasty fries.

Mikaso close to Santiago dock. A special place to eat, this hotel restaurant occupies a roof terrace with wonderful elevated lake views. Pasta, fish, huge salads or paella can be prepared if you order in advance. Quite expensive.

Munchies between the docks. Veggie stronghold where you can tuck into a healthy soup or salad in a pleasant patio setting.

Nick's Place by the Pana dock. Popular, locally owned restaurant with a superb-value menu of international and Guatemalan food (most meals cost around US$3) and a fine lakefront location.

Pinocchio between the docks. Decent Italian, where you can feast on lake fish, pizza or pasta in a pretty garden.

Zoola between the docks. Gorgeous garden restaurant with Israeli and international food.

Drinking, nightlife and entertainment

For a **drink**, there's a cluster of places close to the Pana dock. If you'd rather just catch a film, *D'Noz* shows a **movie** every night at 8.30pm, while the Zuvuya bookstore screens documentaries in the afternoons.

Alegre Pub just up from the Pana dock. This intimate bar has Premiership football, plus nightly drinks and food specials (like fish'n'chips).

El Barrio between the docks. There's plenty of bar action during its extended (5–8pm) happy hour. Stocks hundreds of liquors, though music can be a bit mainstream.

Buddha between the docks. A triple-deck place that once was vaguely stylish in a boho way but is now looking a tad run-down and shabby. Nevertheless it's a good bet for live music, including regular performances by the house blues band.

Freedom turn right from the Pana dock. Funky bar with plenty of little alcoves and low-cushioned seating facing the lake. In the later hours, trance and house DJs fire up the dancefloor, which is powered by a big sound system. Also has an inexpensive menu.

Shanti Shanti Spilling down the hillside, this relaxed place with bamboo walls is good for a bite or a drink. Also has a full menu and is renowned for its falafel.

The northern shore

The **northern side** of the lake harbours a string of isolated, traditional villages. From San Pedro, a rough road runs as far as Tzununá and from there a spectacular path continues all the way to Sololá. Non-direct *lanchas* to Panajachel will call in at any village en route, but the best way to see this string of isolated settlements is **on foot**: it makes a fantastic day's walk (though see warning, p.150). A narrow strip of level land is wedged between the water and the steep hills most of the way, and where this disappears the path is cut into the slope, yielding dizzying views of the lake below. It takes between five and six hours to walk from San Pedro to Santa Cruz. You can get drinks, snacks and meals at several of the villages along the way, and all of the villages now have accommodation.

From San Pedro it's just 2km to the tidy, tranquil little town of **SAN JUAN LA LAGUNA**, at the back of a sweeping bay surrounded by shallow beaches. The town has developed an excellent **community tourism** project (☎5964 0040, ⓦwww.sanjuanlalaguna.com) that allows visitors to visit natural dye-weaving co-ops, local forests for birdwatching, and coffee plantations, and to learn about local crafts (mats called *petates* are made from lake reeds), culture, and folklore. Or you can just drop by one of the many good artist galleries or weaving co-ops – Las Artesanías de San Juan is signposted on the left from the dock and the Asociación de Mujeres de Color is on the right – all have plenty of goods for sale.

San Juan has two **hotels**, the simple *Hospedaje Estrella del Lago* (☎7759 9126; ②) just up from the dock has secure simple rooms, none with private bath, and a guests' kitchen. Otherside *Uxlabil Eco-Lodge* (☎2366 9555, ⓦwww.uxlabil .com; ⑥–⑦) is a large stone hotel with fine views and a good restaurant. In the centre of the village is a good little comedor, *Restaurant Chi'nimaya*, and almost next door, a shrine to **Maximón** (see p.185). Inside you'll find the evil saint dressed in local garb – as this shrine attracts fewer visitors than those elsewhere, you may want to bring him some liquor or a cigar. Pick-ups and minibuses run between San Pedro and San Juan about every twenty minutes.

Leaving San Juan, you'll pass below the Tz'utujil settlement of **SAN PABLO LA LAGUNA**, perched high above the lake a fifteen-minute walk away. The village's traditional speciality is the manufacture of rope from the fibres of the maguey plant; you can sometimes see great lengths being stretched and twisted in the streets.

A precipitous but paved road continues from San Pablo up to **Santa Clara La Laguna**, a sprawling town situated in a plateau high above the western shore of the lake, renowned for its basketry. Women use *cañvera*, which is similar to bamboo, to make fine fruit bowls and other household goods, you can check out a good selection at the Copikaj weavers co-op at 4 Avenida 2–71. Nine kilometres north of here is the spectacular **Parque Chuiraxamoló** (☎7927 1859), a forest reserve and adventure centre with some of Central America's longest zip lines (US$10), hiking and bike trails, and picnic and camping areas. It's professionally run and a great day out. From the parque it's just 6km further north to the Carretera Interamericana. All buses running between Xela and San Pedro pass through Santa Clara and the entrance to the reserve.

San Marcos La Laguna

Guatemala's premier New Age centre, the small village of **SAN MARCOS LA LAGUNA**, is about a two-hour walk from San Pedro, or a twenty-minute ride in one of the regular pick-ups that bump along the road between the villages. The land close to the lakeshore – densely wooded with banana, mango, jocote and avocado trees – is where San Marcos's bohemian hotels and guesthouses have been sensitively established, while the Maya village is centred on higher ground away from the shore. Relationships between the two communities remain a little distant. Apart from a huge new stone **church**, built to replace a colonial original destroyed in the 1976 earthquake, there are no real sights in the Maya village. If you continue uphill from the village following the river bed it's a short walk to Cambalacha, an arts project that teaches dance, music and theatre to local children; volunteers are always welcome and shows are also performed.

San Marcos has a decidedly tranquil appeal – there's little in the way of partying and no bar scene at all. One of the main draws is the *Las Pirámides* yoga and meditation retreat, and there's a surplus of yoga teachers and masseurs, plus the requisite organic bakery and a healing centre (San Marcos Holistic Center and the Jazmin Flower House), which offers acupuncture, reflexology, massages, crystal therapy and natural remedies. You can also study here at the San Marcos Spanish School, in the grounds of *Il Guardino* restaurant; contact its sister school, San Pedro Spanish School (see p.51), for information.

The village has a mesmerizing view of Atitlán's three volcanoes, including a perspective of the double-coned summit of Tolimán, plus glimpses of the grey 3975m peak of Acatenango, more than 50km to the east. There's excellent swimming from a number of wooden jetties by the lakeshore, kayaks can be rented from a cabin close to *Aaculaax*, and paragliding can be organized for US$65 a flight: contact Guy (☎5854 5365) at the *Sol y Tul* (see below).

For **internet**, Rapinet (US$1.75 per hr) is 300 metres inland from *Posada Schumann*.

Accommodation

Most of San Marcos's hotels and guesthouses are best reached from the westernmost of San Marcos's two docks by *Posada Schumann*; all accommodation is signposted from there. Avoid the *Hotel Jivana*.

Aaculaax ☎5803 7243, ⊛www.aaculaax .com. An astonishing labour of love, this fantasy ecohotel was built by an (eccentric) German visionary craftsman from thousands of recycled bottles and wood, with stained-glass detailing and giant glass butterflies doubling as lampshades. Most rooms have hand-painted murals and bathrooms, while the 'Mirador' also has a kitchen. There's an excellent café-restaurant here too. ❸–❹

Hospedaje Panabaj ☎5483 1225. A simple, locally-owned place in the village (behind the Instituto Vascó) with six clean basic rooms that are good value. ❷

Hotel La Paz ☎5702 9168. Chilled place with comfortable, rustic rooms, a bungalow (with three beds) and excellent dorms (US$7) set in spacious grounds, which also feature a sauna/massage room. Home cooking is often available; Benjamin, the Guatemalan owner, once ran a restaurant in Liverpool. ❸

Hotel Silam lakeshore on extreme eastern side ☎2425 8088, ✉silanihotel@yahoo.com. Enjoys a prime plot with direct lake views, a small beach and private dock. The Guatemalan photographer-owner plans to build several new wood-and-stone bungalows to add to those (some with private bath) already constructed. A café is planned, and there's live music some nights. ❸–❹

El Paco Real ☎4084 5974, ⊛www.paco-real .com. Very well built stone, timber and thatch bungalows, some sleeping up to four, in a shady garden. No private bathrooms, but the communal facilities are kept absolutely spotless. ❸

Las Pirámides ☎5205 7151, ⊛www .laspiramidesdelka.com. It's not exactly a hotel, but a life experience. This meditation retreat centre is set in leafy grounds and has monthly courses, which begin the day after the full moon (though you can also enrol on a daily or weekly basis). These include hatha yoga, metaphysics, meditation techniques and an esoteric learning week, followed by a final week of fasting and complete silence. All accommodation is in comfortable pyramid cabañas; there's also delicious vegetarian food. The cost is US$15/420 per head (per day/month), which includes courses but not food. ❹

Posada Schumann ☎5202 2216. Attractive solar-powered lakeside rooms and stone bungalows (nos. 8 & 10 have stupendous volcano views). There's a great, grassy lakeside garden with hammocks, a jetty for sunbathing and swimming, restaurant and a Maya-style sauna. Unfortunately everything is priced in dollars. ❺–❼

Eating

There's a good range of cuisines in San Marcos, where vegetarians are particularly very well catered for; prices don't change that much in the gringo places (around US$3–5 for a meal). For cheap comedor cooking head to the village.

Aaculaax Some of the best food in town is served at this hotel's terrace café where they have great breakfasts, sandwiches and crêpes. In the evenings it's run by a different team and offers tapas and global specials.

Los Abrazos behind the church. A small Maya-owned place that's good for inexpensive *comida típca*; has a wood-fired pizza oven. The sculptured seating (made from mud, clay and sand) styled with condor heads is amazing.

Il Giardino This vegetarian restaurant has a lovely garden setting and serves mainly Italian food, plus a few Latin American dishes.

Moonfish at western edge of village. Lakeside café with salads, falafel, hummus with panini and sandwiches. Service can be slow.

El Paco Real Good for Mexican food and cocktails, including piña coladas, margaritas and mojitos. Closed Mon.

Las Pirámides Offers excellent veggie food (including delicious sandwiches and salads).

Tul y Sol The best place for meat, this lakeside restaurant has good views and serves fairly expensive French food like pork steak with peppercorn sauce, as well as smaller dishes including burritos and sandwiches.

Tzununá to Jaibalito

Beyond San Marcos, the villages have a greater feeling of isolation, and you'll find the people surprised to see you and often eager for a glimpse of passing gringos. The first one you come to is **TZUNUNÁ**, a scruffy looking place strung up a steep hillside. Originally it sat at the lakeside, but after it was badly damaged by a flood in 1950, the people rebuilt their homes on higher ground. As ever the local costume is striking, the women wearing vivid red *huipiles* striped with blue and yellow on the back.

Tzununá is perhaps Lago de Atitlan's most isolated and poorest settlement, and until the last few years received little or no income from tourism. However with the construction of a fine new hotel, the solar-powered *Lomas de Tzununá* (☎5201 8272, ⊛www.lomasdetzununa.com; ❼), a ten-minute walk east of the dock, things have started to change. It's a magnificently sited place, owned by a hospitable couple from Uruguay and Belgium, perched high above the lake with stupendous views. An excellent value, with ten very well-built cottages, all with huge, sliding glass doors that make the most of the unsurpassed lake vistas. There's a small pool, a good restaurant with a healthy menu and home-made ice cream. The hotel is a very steep climb up from the lakeshore, but if you call in advance, they'll pick you up in a car from the village dock.

You'll find the road indisputably ends at *Lomas*, giving way to a narrow path cut out of the steep hillside. The next village, **JAIBALITO**, nestling between soaring *milpa*-clad slopes, is another place that was extremely isolated until recent years. It still remains resolutely Kaqchikel – little Spanish is spoken, and few women have ever journeyed much beyond Lago de Atitlán – though the opening of four tourist-geared businesses means that outside influence is growing. There's more community information at Ⓦwww.jaibalito.com.

Just off the main pathway, the very welcoming Norwegian-owned ⚑ *Vulcano Lodge* (Ⓣ5410 2237, Ⓦwww.vulcanolodge.com; ❺) has an amazing garden bursting with exotic scrubs and cacti. Although it lacks lake views, there's loads of space to enjoy with sun loungers and hammocks scattered around the grounds. All the rooms and cottages are absolutely spotless and very comfortable and there's gourmet European and Guatemalan food in the restaurant; dinner (US$13) is a multi-course communal affair. In the centre of the village the new backpacker-geared *Posada Jaibalito* (Ⓣ5598 1957, Ⓦwww.posada-jaibalito.com; ❷–❸) is one of the cheapest places to stay on this side of the lake with good dorms (US$4 per head) and a couple of rooms in a large shady plot; the food menu has nothing above US$3. At the lakeshore the swanky new *Ven Acá* (Ⓦwww.clubvenaca.com) is an upmarket bar-restaurant geared towards the wealthy, with a hot tub and pool, a fusion menu and excellent cocktails.

Heading west, it's a steep five-minute walk from the village along the cliff path to the spectacularly sited and highly popular ⚑ *La Casa del Mundo* (Ⓣ5218 5332, Ⓦwww.lacasadelmundo.com; ❸–❺). It's an astounding place with sixteen accommodation options that cling to a cliff side, including a budget room, doubles (room nos. 1 & 3 have the best views), detached stone cabins and a suite. There's also a great restaurant (dinner is US$9 per head), but some of the facilities involve extra charges: kayaks cost US$3–7 per hour and the lakeside tub is US$35 for up to 10 people). From the hotel it's about thirty minutes to Santa Cruz along a glorious, easy-to-follow path that parallels the steep hillside.

Santa Cruz La Laguna

Gorgeous **SANTA CRUZ LA LAGUNA**, stretching for about two kilometres in a verdant ribbon along the lakeshore, is a supremely tranquil and beautiful village. With some terrific accommodation, spa facilities, yoga and excellent hiking, it's not surprising that its star is on the rise, as more and more people discover the settlement's unspoilt appeal. Above all, it's the (almost) complete lack of roads that really makes this place – just one little lane snakes up to the Maya village high above the lakeshore, and the only access is by boat. With no traffic to contend with, the lake really comes into its own, and it's very easy to be seduced by the mellow pace of life, strolling the lakeshore paths, and watching hummingbirds buzz between exotic flowers or Maya boatmen fish for crabs. You really can get back to nature here.

The lakeshore itself has been mainly bought up by foreigners and wealthy Guatemalans, while the Maya village is on a shelf 150m or so above the water. The contrast between the two worlds is sharp, with the indigenous population of around six thousand living in rudimentary conditions while by the shore things are very different. Nevertheless, the two communities coexist well, with many villagers employed in foreign businesses, and the charity Amigos de Santa Cruz (ⓦ www.amigosdesantacruz.org) does sterling work improving opportunities for the local Maya by funding environmental, educational and health programmes; volunteers are always welcome.

There isn't much to actually see in Santa Cruz, though you could take a look around the Maya village where there's a sixteenth-century church. Most people spend their time chilling out with a book or **swimming**. The lake water is cleaner away from the centre, towards the bay of Paxanax, one kilometre to the east. Alternatively, you can scuba dive in the lake with ATI Divers (see below), or there's some excellent **hiking**, including a walk to a waterfall above the village football pitch, and another to Sololá along a spectacular path. Staff at the *Iguana Perdida* will be able to get you on the right track for these walks.

Accommodation and restaurants

Santa Cruz has some great places, all strung out along the lakeshore. The village dock is at the centre of things, beside the *Iguana Perdida* and *Arca de Noé*, but boatmen will drop you off at any of the following places; all have private docks.

Casa Erik ☎ 5410 2237. On the eastern side of the village, a 5min walk from the shore, these two lovely studio apartments and *casita* (which sleeps six) all enjoy stunning lake views and have kitchens and luxury bathrooms. They're located in a gorgeous garden and managed by the *Vulcano Lodge* in Jaibalito. Studios from US$275 per week, *casita* from US$500.

Hotel Arca de Noé ☎ 7848 1407, ⓦ www .arcasantacruz.com. A choice of rustic but comfortable stone cottages and rooms spread around an expansive, very beautiful, terraced lakeside garden; there's so much space to enjoy here. Good home-cooking, with large breakfasts for US$4 and the communal set dinner is US$9. Also has a small gym and a water's-edge "beer garden". Owned by an Austrian couple who manage the place for half the year. ❸–❺

🏃 **Iguana Perdida** ☎ 5706 4117, ⓦ www .laiguanaperdida.com. This long-running budget travellers' hangout offers a myriad of cheap, very simple accommodation – simple wooden shacks, tree houses, dorm beds (US$3–4.50) and single/double rooms – but has also expanded into the plot next door where good-quality, very spacious mid-range rooms, some with lake views, are steadily being added. Though a little intimacy has been lost, the vibe remains sociable and friendly, with guests eating together in the evenings, yoga sessions, and the infamous Sat-night BBQ and cross-dressing party. There are kayaks for rent, internet and wi-fi, a movie room, and this is also the home of ATI Divers, a professional scuba school. Budget rooms ❷–❸, mid-range rooms ❺

🏃 **Isla Verde** A 10min walk west of the dock ☎ 5760 2648, ⓦ www.islaverde atitlan.com. Run by a well-travelled Spaniard, this hotel has chic, simply furnished A-frame bungalows built in tiers up a steep slope. There's a really relaxed vibe about the whole place, with a lovely lakeside garden, and books and mags to read. The gorgeous lakeside restaurant serves some of the best food in Guatemala with creative, delicious global cuisine, including many dishes from the Mediterranean; a meal is about US$4–7, with the set dinner US$10. ❹

Jacaranda Lakeshore, 5min east of dock. A superb English-run café, with a stunning view overlooking the lake and a healthy menu of breakfasts (from 7am), sandwiches and daily specials. Sunbathers can use their private dock.

Casa Rosa ☎ 5803 2531, ⓦ www.atitlanlacasarosa .com. Offers beautiful, peaceful gardens, spacious bungalows and smallish rooms, plus a restaurant with home cooking. The management here can be inflexible at times however. ❹–❻

🏃 **Villa Sumaya** in Paxanax bay, a 10min walk west of the dock ☎ 5617 1209, ⓦ www.villasumaya.com. This American-owned, luxury guesthouse has a prime lakefront location and sixteen rooms – those in the *torre* are larger – but each has a stupendous lake view, plush beds and stylish decor. Also boasts a great restaurant, library, hot tub and sauna; a pool is planned. Spa treatments and massages are available, and there are daily yoga/meditation/pilates sessions in a stunning rooftop space. ❼–❾

Along the Carretera Interamericana: Los Encuentros to Cuatro Caminos

Heading west from the Los Encuentros junction to Cuatro Caminos and the Quetzaltenango valley, the Carretera Interamericana runs through some fantastic high-mountain scenery. The views alone are superb, and if you have a Sunday morning to spare then it's well worth dropping into Nahualá for the market.

Nahualá

West of Los Encuentros the Carretera Interamericana runs through some spectacular and sparsely inhabited countryside. The only place of any size before Cuatro Caminos is **NAHUALÁ** ("place of sorcerers"), a small and intensely traditional town a kilometre or so to the north of the highway, at the base of a huge, steep-sided and intensely farmed bowl. The unique atmosphere of isolation from and indifference to the outside world makes Nahualá one of the most impressive and unusual K'iche' towns.

The town itself is not much to look at, a sprawl of old cobbled streets and adobe houses mixed with newer concrete structures, but the inhabitants of Nahualá have a reputation for fiercely preserving their independence and have held out against ladino incursions with exceptional tenacity. At the end of the nineteenth century the government confiscated much of their land, as they did throughout the country, and sold it to coffee planters. In protest, the entire male population of Nahualá walked the 150km to Guatemala City and demanded to see President Barrios in person, refusing his offers to admit a spokesman and insisting that they all stood as one. Eventually, they were allowed into the huge reception room where they knelt with their foreheads pressed to the floor, refusing to leave until they were either given assurances of their land rights or allowed to buy the land back, which they had done twice before. The action managed to save their land that time, but since then much of it has gradually been consumed by coffee bushes all the same.

On another occasion, during the 1930s under President Ubico, ladinos were sent to the town as nurses, telegraph operators and soldiers. Once again the Nahualáns appealed directly to the president, insisting that their own people should be trained to do these jobs, and once again their request was granted. Ubico also wanted to set up a government-run drink store, but the villagers chose instead to ban alcohol, and Nahualeños who got drunk elsewhere were expected to confess their guilt and face twenty lashes in the town's plaza.

These days the ban's been lifted, and if you're here for the fiesta on November 25 you'll see that the people are keen to make up for all those dry years. However, only a handful of ladinos live in the town, and the indigenous Maya still have a reputation for hostility, with rumours circulating about the black deeds done by the local shamen. You don't have much to worry about if you drop in for the **Sunday market**, though, as this is one time that the town is full to bursting and the people seem genuinely pleased to welcome visitors. There is also a smaller market on Thursdays.

The town is also a major centre of artisan craft. The **weaving** is outstanding: the *huipiles*, designed in intricate geometrical patterns of orange on white, particularly impressed the Spanish because they featured a double-headed eagle, the emblem of the Habsburgs who ruled Spain at the time of the

Conquest. The men wear bright yellow and pink shirts with beautifully embroidered collars; short woollen "skirts" called *rodilleras*, which are worn with white trousers underneath; and huge hats and leather sandals similar to those of the ancient Maya. Woollen garments, including *capixay* cloaks and jackets, are also woven locally. The town is also famous for its woodwork, and Nahualá carpenters churn out a good proportion of the country's hand-carved pine- and cedar-wood bedsteads and wardrobes.

To get to Nahualá, take any bus along the Carretera Interamericana between Los Encuentros and Cuatro Caminos, and get off at the Puente Nahualá, from where minibuses run the kilometre or so uphill to the town centre. There are a few basic pensiones, but it's best to visit the town as a day-trip from the lake or Quetzaltenango.

Santa Catarina and the Alaskan heights

Beyond Nahualá the highway climbs westwards up a mountainous ridge and passes the entrance road to **SANTA CATARINA IXTAHUACÁN**, a sister and bitter rival of Nahualá, just north of the highway. Santa Catarina used to be located on notoriously unstable land on the south side of the Carretera Interamericana, only moving to its present position in December 2000 after huge sink holes destroyed several houses. The costumes and traditions of Santa Catarina and Nahualá, which are together known as the **Pueblos Chancatales**, are fairly similar, and they're both famous as producers of *metates*, the stones used for grinding corn. These days much corn-grinding is done by machine, and they've turned to making smaller toy versions and rustic wooden furniture – both of which you'll see peddled by the roadside.

Just west of Santa Catarina, the highway bottoms out on a flat plateau high up in the hills – one of the most impressive sections of the Carretera Interamericana. Known as **Alaska**, this 3000-metre-high exposed tract of land is prime sheep-grazing country, and shines white with frost in the early mornings.

Further on, the road drops to reveal the Quetzaltenango plain on the left and the cone of the Santa María volcano. **Cuatro Caminos** crossroads is the key junction in these parts, from where side roads lead to the city of Quetzaltenango and Totonicapán; it's straight on for Huehuetenango and the Mexican border.

Quetzaltenango and around

The **Quetzaltenango basin**, a sweeping expanse of fertile farmland, forms the natural hub of the western highlands. Originally part of the Mam kingdom, the K'iche' Maya overran this area sometime between 1400 and 1475, and founded a walled city named Xelajú. Today, the western side of the region is Mam-speaking and the east K'iche'. It was here that conquistador Pedro de Alvarado first struggled up into the highlands, and fought the K'iche' in a decisive battle, massacring the Maya warriors – legend has it that Alvarado himself killed the king, Tecún Umán, in hand-to-hand combat. The victorious Spanish subsequently founded a new town, Quetzaltenango, "the place of the quetzals", the name probably chosen because of the brilliant green quetzal feathers worn by the K'iche' nobles and warriors, including, no doubt, Tecún Umán himself.

Where to go

The city of **Quetzaltenango** can't claim to be a tourist attraction in its own right, but its ordinariness is in many ways its strength – a resolutely Guatemalan highland centre, off the main gringo trail but with a hospitality and friendliness that belies its size. It certainly makes an excellent base for exploring this part of the country, making day-trips to markets and fiestas, basking in hot springs like Fuentes Georginas, or hiking in the mountains.

The Xela plain and surrounding hills feature numerous smaller towns and villages, mostly indigenous agricultural communities and weaving centres. On **market and fiesta days** these villages explode into life; you should certainly try to get to San Francisco el Alto or Almolonga, both of which offer a terrific assault on the senses, their streets packed with colour. The pick of the region's **hiking** is the wonderful excursion up to Volcán Chicabal's crater lake, while if you really yearn to get off the beaten path, the remote high-country landscapes in the neighbouring department of San Marcos are wildly impressive.

Quetzaltenango (Xela)

Completely unlike the capital, and only a fraction of its size, Guatemala's second city, **QUETZALTENANGO (XELA)**, has the slightly subdued provincial atmosphere you might expect in the capital of the highlands. Bizarre though it may seem, Quetzaltenango's character and appearance is vaguely reminiscent of an industrial town in northern England – grey and cool with friendly, down-to-earth inhabitants. Ringed by high mountains, and bitterly cold in the early mornings, the city wakes up slowly, getting going only once the warmth of the sun has made its mark. The main plaza, heavily indebted to Neoclassicism, is a monument to stability, with great slabs of grey stone belying a history of turbulence and struggle. The heart of town has the calm order of a regional administrative centre, though things deteriorate as you head away from the plaza, with thick traffic and fumes blighting the highland air, particularly around the main bus terminal. Locally, the city is usually referred to as Xela (pronounced "shey-la"). Meaning "under the ten", the name probably a reference to the surrounding peaks.

A brief history

Under colonial rule Quetzaltenango flourished as a commercial centre, benefiting from the fertility of the surrounding farmland and good connections to the port at Champerico. When the prospect of independence eventually arose, the city was set on deciding its own destiny. After the Central American Federation broke with Mexico in 1820, Quetzaltenango declared itself the capital of the independent state of **Los Altos**, which incorporated the modern departments of Huehuetenango, Sololá, San Marcos and Totonicapán. But the separatist movement was soon brought to heel by President Carrera in 1840, and a later attempt at secession, in 1848, was put down by force. Despite having to accept provincial status, the town remained an important centre of commerce and culture, consistently rivalling Guatemala City. The coffee boom at the end of the last century was particularly significant, as Quetzaltenango controlled some of the richest coffee land in the country. Its wealth and population grew

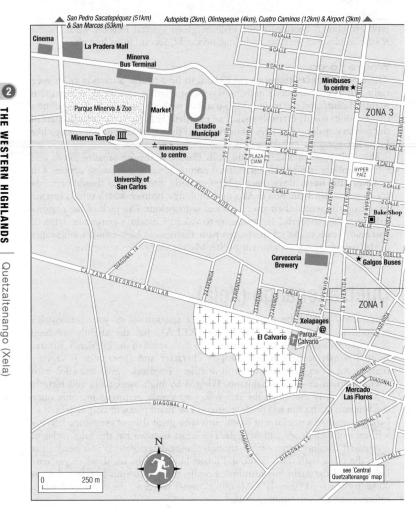

see 'Central Quetzaltenango' map

rapidly, incorporating a large influx of German immigrants, and by the end of the nineteenth century Quetzaltenango was firmly established as an equal to Guatemala City.

All this, however, came to an abrupt end when the city was almost totally destroyed by the massive **1902 earthquake**. Rebuilding took place in a mood of high hopes; all the grand Neoclassical architecture dates from this period. A new rail line was built to connect the city with the coast, but this was washed out in the early 1930s, and the town steadily fell further and further behind the capital, unable to regain its former glory.

Today, nevertheless, Quetzaltenango has all the trappings of wealth and self-importance: the grand imperial architecture, the great banks, and a list of famous sons. But it's oddly devoid of the rampant energy you'd expect in a city with a population of around 140,000. At times, it seems strangely suspended in the late nineteenth century, with a calm, dignified air, perhaps

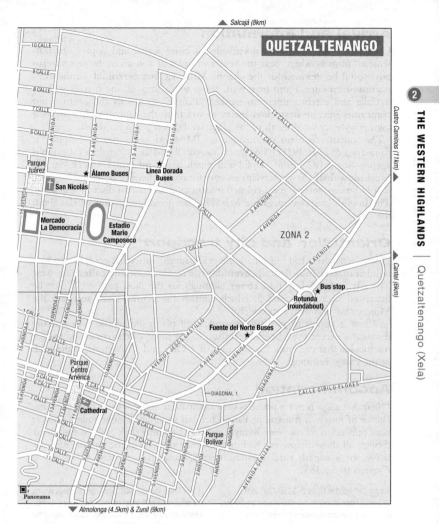

10 CALLE
9 CALLE
8 CALLE
7 CALLE
6 CALLE

15 AVENIDA
14 AVENIDA
13 AVENIDA
12 AVENIDA

13 CALLE
11 CALLE
10 CALLE

Cuatro Caminos (11km) ▶

Parque
Juárez
★ **Álamo Buses**   ★ **Línea Dorada
Buses**
† **San Nicolás**

3 AVENIDA
4 AVENIDA

5 CALLE

**Mercado
La Democracia**   **Estadio
Mario
Camposeco**

16 AVENIDA

ZONA 2

6 AVENIDA

7 CALLE

Cantel (6km) ▶

★ **Bus stop**
**Rotunda
(roundabout)**

1 CALLE
2 CALLE
3 CALLE

14 AVENIDA
13 AVENIDA

4 AVENIDA
1 AVENIDA

5 CALLE

Fuente del Norte Buses
★

6 AVENIDA
7 AVENIDA

**Parque
Centro
América**

AVENIDA JESÚS CASTILLO

DIAGONAL 2

15 AVENIDA
3 AVENIDA

5 CALLE
7 CALLE

11 CALLE
12 CALLE
13 CALLE

DIAGONAL 1   CALLE CIRILO FLORES

Cathedral

6 CALLE
7 CALLE
8 CALLE
9 CALLE
10 CALLE
11 CALLE

12 AVENIDA
7 AVENIDA
6 AVENIDA
5 AVENIDA

**Parque
Bolívar**

3 AVENIDA
4 AVENIDA
1 AVENIDA

DIAGONAL 1

AVENIDA CENTRAL

▣
Panorama

▼ Almolonga (4.5km) & Zunil (9km)

in part because of the character of the Quetzaltecos themselves, who have a reputation for formality and politeness, and pride themselves on their restraint.

The city arguably now matches the capital as an **educational centre**, with universities and private colleges, which attract high-school students from all over the country, and from as far away as El Salvador. Since the early 1990s Quetzaltenango has also established itself as one of Latin America's principal **language-school** hubs, and can now boast dozens of good Spanish schools (see p.180). More and more **development** projects are also basing themselves here, and this growing influx of international students, travellers and volunteers is steadily adding a cosmopolitan influence to the city's bars, restaurants and cultural life. Many of these overseas visitors settle easily into the relatively easy-going pace of the city, making firm local friendships, and end up staying a lot longer than they'd planned.

Arrival and information

Unhelpfully for the traveller, virtually all buses arrive and depart Quetzaltenango from nowhere near the centre of town. If you arrive by second-class bus, you'll be destined for the chaotic **Minerva bus terminal** on the city's northwestern edge. From here walk 300m south through the market stalls to 4 Calle and catch a microbus marked "Parque" to get to the centre. Four companies operate **first-class buses** to and from the capital, each with their own private terminal north of the plaza; see box on p.178 for details.

The tourist office on the main plaza (Mon–Fri 8am–1pm & 2–5pm, Sat 8am–1pm; ☎7761 4931) is not much use; you'll find the Adrenalina Tours travel agency (see p.182) more helpful and much better informed. Check out the excellent **website** Ⓦ www.xelapages.com for comprehensive hotel and language school listings, lots of good cultural information and useful discussion forums. The English language magazine *Xela Who?* has good listings and articles about the city.

Orientation and city transport

Quetzaltenango is laid out on a loose grid pattern, somewhat complicated by a number of steep hills. Basically, **avenidas** run north–south, and **calles** east–west. The city is divided up into **zones**, although for the most part you'll only be interested in zonas 1 and 3, which contain the central plaza area and the Minerva bus terminal respectively.

When it comes to **getting around**, most places are within easy walking distance – except the Minerva terminal. To get there, catch one of the regular microbuses that run from the junction of 4 Calle and 13 Avenida, at the back of the Pasaje Enríquez.

Accommodation

Quetzaltenango is not a prime tourist destination, and does not have the same choice of hotels as Antigua or Panajachel, but some good new budget choices have opened in recent years. Many hotels can be a little dark and old-fashioned, though all those below are within a ten-minute walk of the parque. Alternatively, for a superb rural location near Quetzaltenango, head to *Hotel Las Cumbres* (see p.185).

Black Cat Hostel 13 Av 3–33 ☎7761 2091, Ⓦ www.blackcathostels.net. Welcoming hostel that occupies a historic building with many nice features including a very hip lounge bar and central patio. The six-bed dorm (US$7 a bed) is comfortable and there are private rooms with futon-style beds; the one with a private bathroom is overpriced. Rates include breakfast. ❸

Casa Argentina 12 Diagonal 8–37 ☎7761 2470. First choice for young travellers for over a decade, but now faces increasing competition. Run by the friendly Morales family, with dozens of smallish, good-value rooms (most with TV and a few with bathroom), a huge dorm (US$3 a bed), kitchen, sun terrace and a café. It's a 10min walk from the plaza, and also the home of Quetzaltrekkers (see p.182). ❷

Casa Mañen 9 Av 4–11 ☎7765 0786, Ⓦ www.comeseeit.com. Xela's best upmarket place to stay is this Texan-owned B&B. Spacious, spotless rooms are decorated with local textiles, numbers 8 and 9 have fireplaces, and the two huge suites offer sofas and fridges. There's also a wonderful rooftop terrace and a large complimentary breakfast. Rooms ❻–❼, suites ❾

Hotel Casa Florencia 12 Av 3–61 ☎7761 2811, Ⓦ www.hotelcasaflorencia.com. Has a very central location just off the plaza, with nine fairly comfortable if old-fashioned rooms with flowery bedspreads and fitted carpets – but no outside windows. ❹

Hostal Don Diego 6 C 15–12 ☎5482 4294, Ⓔ hostaldondiego@gmail.com. A secure, well-run budget place with plenty of simple, clean rooms (though few with private bathroom) and two five-bed dorms (US$6pp). There's a kitchen and a nice outdoor patio. Offers discounted weekly and monthly rates. ❸

Hotel Modelo 14 Av A 2–31 ℡7761 2529, 🖃hotelmodelo1892@yahoo.es. A classy, historic hotel with a wonderful dining room, stately reception area, wi-fi and plenty of character. The rooms are spacious if a little creaky, all have private bathrooms and TV, many face a small garden courtyard (note that streetside rooms can be noisy on weekend nights). The annexe is a slightly cheaper, similar alternative. Breakfast included. ④–⑤

Hotel Villa Real Plaza 4 C 12–22 ℡7761 4045, 🖃villareal@xelaenlinea.com. Comfortable-enough hotel with 54 rooms, located across the plaza from the *Bonifaz*, to which it is a modern(ish) rival – the decor and ambience are a little soulless, however. ⑥

Hotel Virginia 11 Av 8–11 ℡7761 7355. Good-value hotel with twenty carpeted rooms with nice wooden beds and decent mattresses, desks and cable TV. There's a roof terrace with tables, chairs

and parasols. The design of the building – it's above a basement car park – is very weird. ⑤

Pensión Altense 9 C 8–48 ℡7761 2811. Old-fashioned place with fairly spacious, clean (if not "Swiss clean") rooms, most of which have a TV and private shower. Safe parking. ②–③

Pensión Andina 8 Av 6–07 ℡7761 4012. Excellent value, this hotel has neat, smallish but well-scrubbed rooms, all with private bathroom, set around a covered courtyard. ②

Pensión Bonifaz northeast corner of the plaza ℡7761 2182, 🖃bonifaz@intel.net.gt. Landmark hotel, founded in 1935 with an impressive facade and lobby area, but in some aspects the rooms (particularly the bathrooms) are a bit dated. Still retains an air of faded upper-class pomposity, however, and has a smart restaurant and small pool. ⑦

The City

Quetzaltenango does not have an excess of sights, but if you have a day to spare then it's well worth wandering through the streets, soaking up the atmosphere and visiting a museum. The hub of the place is the **central plaza**, officially known as the Parque Centro América. Here you'll find the requisite stone benches and well-tended flowers and shrubs as well as a monument to former President Barrios – all overshadowed by a mass of Greek columns. With an atmosphere of dignified calm, the plaza is the best place to appreciate the sense of self-importance that accompanied the city's rebuilding after the 1902 earthquake. The buildings have a look of defiant authority, although there's none of the buzz of business you'd expect – except on the first Sunday of the month when it plays host to a good artesanías market, with blankets, basketry and piles of *típica* weavings for sale.

The Greek columns were probably intended to symbolize the city's cultural importance and its role at the heart of the liberal revolution, but today many of them do nothing more than support street lights. The northern end of the plaza is dominated by the grand Banco de Occidente, complete with sculptured flaming torches. On the west side is Bancafé, and the impressive **Pasaje Enríquez**, which was planned as a sparkling arcade of upmarket shops, spent many years derelict, and is now slowly on the up again. Inside you'll find one of Xela's best bars, the *Salón Tecún*, the *Dos Tejanos* Tex-Mex restaurant and a travel agency.

At the bottom end of the plaza, next to the tourist office, the **Casa de la Cultura** (Mon–Fri 8am–noon & 2–6pm, Sat 9am–1pm; US$0.75) is the city's most blatant impersonation of a Greek temple, with a bold grey frontage. The main part of the building is given over to an odd mixture of local exhibits. On the ground floor, to the left-hand side, you'll find a display of assorted documents, photographs and pistols from the liberal revolution and the State of Los Altos (see p.173), sports trophies, and a room dedicated to the marimba. Upstairs there are some modest Maya artefacts, historic photographs and a bizarre natural-history room where, amongst the dusty displays of stuffed bats and pickled snakes, you can see the macabre remains of assorted freaks of nature, including a four-horned goat.

Along the eastern side of the plaza is the **cathedral**, with a new cement version set behind the spectacular crumbling front of the original. There's another unashamed piece of Greek grandeur, the **municipalidad**, or town hall, a little further up. Take a look inside at the courtyard, which has a neat little garden set out around a single palm tree. Between the cathedral and the Casa de la Cultura, the old **mercadito** still functions, although

Quetzaltenango transport connections

As the focus of the western highlands, Quetzaltenango is served by literally hundreds of buses. **Getting to Quetzaltenango** is fairly straightforward: there are direct pullmans from Guatemala City, and at any point along the Carretera Interamericana you can flag down a bus for Xela (they pass about every 30min) or take the first bus as far as the Cuatro Caminos junction and change there. Coming from the coast you can catch a bus from the El Zarco junction, Coatepeque or Retalhuleu. **Leaving the city** there are pullman services to Guatemala City, but otherwise all are second class and leave from the Minerva terminal.

Shuttle buses are offered by travel agents such as Adrenalina Tours (see p.182), which operates a comprehensive service to destinations including Panajachel (US$13), Antigua ($25), Guatemala City (US$32) and San Cristobal de las Casas in Mexico (US$25). Adrenalina Tours also offers a very useful backroads, hop-on hop-off shuttle that runs daily between Quetzaltenango and Cobán (US$37) via Huehuetenango (US$17) and Nebaj (US$27).

Pullman buses

All first-class buses run to Guatemala City only; on Sundays, it's essential to book ahead. If you're heading for Antigua and want to travel comfortably, consider travelling by pullman as far as Chimaltenango, and catch a connecting bus there – this works out a lot cheaper than using a shuttle.

Fuente del Norte 7 Avenida 3–33, Zona 2 ☎7761 4587, 5 daily.
Línea Dorada 12 Avenida & 5 Calle, Zona 1 ☎7767 5198, 2 daily.
Transportes Álamo 14 Avenida 5–15, Zona 3 ☎7761 7117, 5 daily.
Transportes Galgos 21 Calle 0–14, Zona 1 ☎7761 2248, 3 daily.

Second-class ("chicken") buses

The main routes from Xela are listed below; all of these buses leave from the **Minerva terminal**. Transport details to villages in the Quetzaltenango area are given in the relevant accounts.

To	Frequency	Journey time
Chichicastenango	10 daily	2hr 30min
Coatepeque	every 30min	1hr 45min
Guatemala City	20 daily	4hr
Huehuetenango	22 daily	2hr
La Mesilla	6 daily	3hr 30min
Momostenango	every 45min	1hr 15min
Panajachel	6 daily	2hr 30min
Retalhuleu	every 30min	1hr 15min
San Francisco el Alto	every 30min	45min
San Marcos	every 45min	1hr 30min
San Pedro La Laguna	5 daily	2hr 15min
Tecún Umán	hourly	3hr
Totonicapán	every 30min	1hr
Zunil	every 30min	30min

Increasingly **minibuses** are supplementing buses on popular local routes like Totonicapán and Momostenango; they also leave from the Minerva terminal and cost the same.

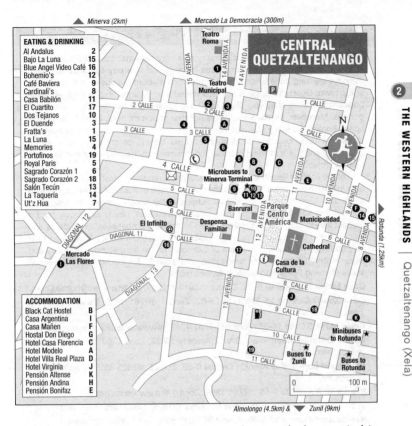

Minerva (2km) ▲   **Mercado La Democracia (300m)** ▲

CENTRAL QUETZALTENANGO

EATING & DRINKING

Al Andalus	2
Bajo La Luna	15
Blue Angel Video Café	16
Bohemio's	12
Café Baviera	9
Cardinali's	8
Casa Babilón	11
El Cuartito	17
Dos Tejanos	10
El Duende	3
Fratta's	1
La Luna	15
Memories	4
Portofinos	19
Royal Paris	5
Sagrado Corazón 1	6
Sagrado Corazón 2	18
Salón Tecún	13
La Taquería	14
Ut'z Hua	7

ACCOMMODATION

Black Cat Hostel	B
Casa Argentina	I
Casa Mañen	F
Hostal Don Diego	G
Hotel Casa Florencia	C
Hotel Modelo	A
Hotel Villa Real Plaza	D
Hotel Virginia	J
Pensión Altense	K
Pensión Andina	H
Pensión Bonifaz	E

Almolonga (4.5km) & ▼ Zunil (9km)

nowadays it's eclipsed by the much larger market near the bus terminal in Zona 3.

Beyond the plaza

Away from the plaza the city spreads out, a mixture of the old and new. The commercial heart is 14 Avenida, complete with pizza restaurants and neon signs. At the top of 14 Avenida, at its junction with 1 Calle, stands the restored **Teatro Municipal**, another spectacular Neoclassical edifice. The plaza in front of the theatre is dotted with busts of local artists, including Osmundo Arriola (1886–1958), Guatemala's first poet laureate, and Jesús Castillo, "the re-creator of Maya music" – another bid to assert Quetzaltenango's cultural superiority. On clear days, there's a spectacular perspective of the Volcán Santa María from the steps of the plaza.

Further afield, the city's role as a regional centre of trade is more evident. Out in Zona 3 is the **Mercado La Democracia**, a vast, covered market complex with stalls spilling out onto the streets. A couple of blocks north of the market, next to the Parque Juárez, stands the modern **Iglesia de San Nicolás**, a bizarre and ill-proportioned neo-Gothic building, sprouting sharp arches.

On the western edge of town, there's another Greek-style monument: the **Minerva Temple**. Just behind the temple is a little **zoo** (Tues–Sun 9am–5pm; free), doubling as a kids' playground. The cages are small but all the animals – including birds, monkeys and pizotes – are well cared for. Below

179

Studying Spanish in Quetzaltenango

With dozens of language schools, many of a very high standard, Quetzaltenango is now one of the most popular places in the world to **study Spanish**. Although the days are long gone when schools could boast about the absence of foreigners in the town, Quetzaltenango is still less visited than Antigua and its relatively large population means that you shouldn't have to share a family home with other gringos. Moreover, because tourism is not that important here, fewer local people speak English, so many students find that the city is an excellent place to progress quickly in their language studies. An added benefit of choosing to study in Quetzaltenango is that most schools fund community development and environmental projects.

All of the schools listed here are well established, employ professional teachers and offer intensive Spanish classes plus the chance to live with a local family (usually with full board). Most run trips to local attractions or the beach, some hold lectures on political and social issues and others offer salsa classes. Nearly all schools have a student liaison officer who speaks English to act as a go-between for students and teachers. You can expect to pay from US$130 to US$180 a week (often rates rise in July and Aug) for four or five hours of individual tuition from Monday to Friday and seven nights' full-board accommodation with a family. For background information about studying Spanish in Guatemala, see p.51.

Casa Latina Diagonal 12 6–58, Zona 1 ☎5613 7222, ✉sol-latino-xela@hotmail.com.

Casa Xelajú Callejón 15, Diagonal 13–02, Zona 1 ☎7761 5954, ⊛www.casaxelaju.com.

Celas Maya 6 Calle 14–55, Zona 1 ☎7761 4342, ⊛www.celasmaya.com.

Centro Bilingüe Amerindía (CBA) 12 Avenida 10–27, Zona 1 ☎7761 8535, ⊛www.xelapages.com/cba.

Educación para Todos Avenida Cenizal 0–58, Zona 5 ☎5935 3815, ⊛www.spanishschools.biz.

Inepas 15 A Avenida 4–59 ☎7765 1308, Zona 1 ⊛www.inepas.org.

Juan Sisay 15 Avenida 8–38, Zona 1 ☎7765 1318, ⊛www.juansisay.com.

Kie–Balam Diagonal 12 4–46, Zona 1 ☎7761 1636, ⊛www.kiebalam.com.

La Democracia 9 Calle 15–05, Zona 3 ☎7763 6895, ⊛www.lademocracia.net.

Mesoamerican Academy 10 Calle 16–12 Zona 1 ☎7766 9531, ⊛www.mesoamericaspanish.org. Also offers classes in Maya languages.

Miguel de Cervantes 12 Avenida 8–31 Zona 1 ☎776.5 5554, ⊛www.learn2speakspanish.com.

La Paz Diagonal 11 7–38, Zona 1 ☎7761 2159, ⊛www.xelapages.com/lapaz.

Pop Wuj 1 Calle 17–72, Zona 1 ☎7761 8286, ⊛www.pop-wuj.org.

Proyecto Lingüístico Quetzalteco de Español 5 Calle 2–40, Zona 1 ☎7763 1061, ⊛www.hermandad.com. Also has a sister school on the Pacific slope.

Sakribal 6 Calle 7–42, Zona 1 ☎7763 0717, ⊛www.sakribal.com.

the temple are the sprawling, dusty **market** and **bus terminal**. It's here that you can really sense the city's role as the centre of the western highlands, with indigenous traders from all over the area doing business, and buses heading to or from every imaginable village and town. Just behind the market, the spanking new shopping mall **La Pradera** boasts over a hundred stores, and there's a neighbouring multiplex cinema. To get to this side of the city, take a microbus from the corner of 13 Avenida and 4 Calle in Zona 1, at the rear of the Pasaje Enríquez.

Eating

Quetzaltenango has a moderate, but improving restaurant scene, suiting its character as a modest, unpretentious city. Almost nowhere opens before 8am, so forget early breakfasts.

Al Andalus 2 C 14 Av A–30. Spanish place with authentic tapas, mains including paella, sangría and wine, and you dine in a pleasant courtyard setting. Some evenings there's live jazz, bossa or soul music.

Bake Shop 18 Av and 1 C, Zona 3. Mennonite-run bakery famous for its wholewheat bread, cakes, glazed donuts and pastries. Open 9am–6pm Tues & Fri only.

Café Baviera 5 C 12–50, a block from the plaza. Old-school coffeehouse, with plenty of period photos of Xela's local notables on the walls. There's also a selection of teas, as well as cakes, sandwiches and soups, plus a no-smoking area and wi-fi.

Cardinali's 14 Av 3–41. Long-running Italian place with gingham tablecloths and Chianti flasks on the walls. Good for pizza or pasta with huge portions at (fairly) moderate prices. For delivery, call ☎ 7761 0924.

Casa Babilón 13 Av and 5 C. There's far too much on the menu at this café, with everything from sushi to Thai to Middle Eastern food. Best to stick to what they do best: filling sandwiches and salads. Closed Sun.

El Cuartito 13 Av 7–09. Xela's hippest little café has a shabby-chic appeal with lighting made from old beer bottles, live chillout DJs and acoustic music. Offers a simple menu of falafel, cheeses and snacks plus good espresso and wine by the carafe. Wi-fi; closed Tues.

Dos Tejanos 4 C 12–33. The "two Texans" is an elegant restaurant with delicious Tex-Mex dishes like garlic grilled fish, barbecued ribs and *lomito a la diablo*. Mains cost US$8–16. Open for breakfast; located inside the Pasaje Enríquez.

La Luna 8 Av 4–11. Crammed with curios and antiques, *La Luna* has seven different varieties of drinking chocolate, though the food is mediocre. Mon–Fri 9.30am–9pm, weekends 4–9pm only.

Memories 15 Av & 3 C. Part civilized café, part toy museum, this quirky café is good for sandwiches, cakes (try the *pay de queso*), and fine coffee, which is roasted out front. All the collectible model planes, helicopters and dolls are showcased in cabinets.

Panorama south of 11 C. A 20min walk south of the plaza, this villa restaurant overlooks the city from a lofty position. It's Swiss owned, and the menu is European based. Open Wed–Fri 5–10pm, weekends 1–10pm.

Portofinos 12 Av 10–21. Friendly, family-run place where the chef, Daniel, cooks up fine pasta and gnocchi. Also doubles as a low-key bar and has two pool tables.

Royal Paris 14 Av A 3–06. Large upper-storey restaurant with authentic French and some Italian food at moderate-to-high prices. A nice atmosphere on Wed, Fri and Sat nights when there's live jazz, rumba or accordion music.

Sagrado Corazón 1 14 Av 3–08. Run by a formidable *señora*, this small, informal place is a great spot to try Guatemalan specialities like *pepián* or *jocón* (meat cooked with peppers and tomatillos).

Sagrado Corazón 2 9 C 9–00. Modest, inexpensive little comedor with good-value breakfasts, a huge US$2.75 set lunch and friendly service.

La Taquería 8 Av & 5 C. Tasty Mexican food, moderately priced and fairly authentic.

Ut'z Hua 12 Av & 3 C. Diners sit under a palapa roof at this intimate, busy place specializing in Guatemalan cuisine. There's an excellent choice of mains, costing about US$3–4, including *jocón*, *quichóm*, local sausages, *mojarra* fish and seven kinds of soup.

Drinking, nightlife and entertainment

After dark, things are generally quiet in the week, but a number of lively **bars** and **clubs** fill up at the weekend. In Zona 1 there's an expanding scene around the parque, centred on Pasaje Enríquez where *Salón Tecún* is a highly popular, historic bar and *Bohemio's* is an atmospheric alternative with hip-hop and reggae music. Close by, the funky *El Cuartito* has a chilled lounge-bar vibe while over at the **Zona Viva** on 14 Avenida A you'll find many more places, some with dancing: *El Duende*, *La Bodega Duende* and *El Zaguán*. Salsa freaks gravitate to the clubs *La Parranda* at 6 Calle and 14 Avenida (with free classes on Wed) and *Kokoloko's*, 15 Avenida and 4 Calle (free salsa lessons on Fri). For a quieter drink, try the intimate *Bajo La Luna*, on the corner of 4 Calle and 8 Avenida, where you can choose from a great selection of bottled wines and tuck into platters of cheese and ham.

Quetzaltenango is a good place to catch a **movie**. In the centre of town, Blue Angel, 7 Calle 15–79, shows films every night, while a multi-screen theatre is located by La Pradera mall, near the Minerva terminal. To find **what's on** in town, pick up a copy of *Xela Who?* (ⓦ www.xelawho.com).

Listings

Banks and exchange Several banks on the main plaza will change traveller's cheques, including Banrural, which has an ATM that accepts all cards, and Banco Industrial with a Visa/Plus ATM.

Bike rental Vrisa bookstore (see below) has bikes for US$6 per day, US$13 per week and US$26 per month.

Bookstores Vrisa, 15 Av 3–64, has thousands of used titles, and buys and trades as well. North & South, 8 C & 15 Av, stocks cultural and political titles and guidebooks, and there's a good café in the same building.

Car rental Tabarini, 9 C 9–21 (☏ 7763 0418), has cars from US$33 per day.

Consulates Mexican Consulate, 9 Av 6–19, Zona 1 (Mon–Fri 9am–noon & 2–3pm). Most nationalities do not need a visa or tourist card.

Internet There are dozens of places in Xela; most charge around US$1 per hour. Xelapages, 4 C 19–48, has quick connections, or try El Infinito, 7 C 15–18.

Laundry Lavanedía El Centro, 15 Av 3–51; US$3 for a full-load wash and dry.

Medical care Hospital San Rafael, 9 C 10–41, Zona 1 (☏ 7761 4414).

Post office 15 Av and 4 C.

Telephone Both Xelapages and El Infinito (see "Internet" above) have the best rates: web calls on clear lines are US$0.15 per minute to the US and Canada, US$0.25 to Europe.

Tours and travel agencies Adrenalina Tours, inside Pasaje Enríquez, Plaza Central (☏ 7761 4509, ⓦ www.adrenalinatours.com), is highly recommended for shuttle buses, tours of the Xela region, including trips to Takalik Abaj and Olintepeque, hikes and volcano climbs (Volcán Santa María costs from US$20 per head). Maya Explorer, 1 Av A 6–75 (☏ 7761 5057, ⓦ www .mayaexplor.com), is an experienced agency that organizes excursions to most of the volcanoes and sights in Guatemala. Quetzaltrekkers, inside *Casa Argentina* (see "Accommodation", p.176; ☏ 7761 4520, ⓦ www.quetzalventures.com), offers cultural tours and hiking trips to volcanoes (a two-day Santiaguito hike is US$54), with all profits going to a charity for street children.

Around Quetzaltenango

The Xela area offers some of the country's most evocative highland scenery, with volcanic cones soaring above forested ridges, and a number of fascinating indigenous villages to explore. Straddling the coast road south of the city are **Almolonga** and **Zunil**, where you'll find superb hot springs, including **Fuentes Georginas**, a wonderful natural spa. Just west of here, the **Santa María volcano**, towering above Quetzaltenango, is a terrific, if exhausting, excursion. The most accessible climb in the area lies southwest of the city, up **Volcán Chicabal** to an exquisite crater lake set in the extinct volcano's cone.

Heading northwards, the traditional Maya town of **Olintepeque** is renowned for its shrine devoted to the pagan saint of San Pascual. A little further distant are **Totonicapán**, a departmental capital, and the famous market town of **San Francisco el Alto**, perched on a rocky outcrop. Beyond here, in the midst of a pine forest, lies **Momostenango**, the country's principal wool-producing centre. Maya culture remains strong throughout this network of simple rural towns and villages, whose lifeblood is a series of weekly markets.

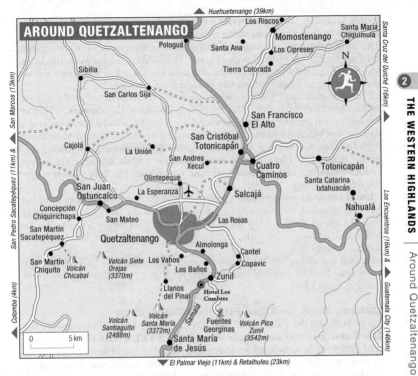

South to Almolonga and Zunil

The most direct route from Quetzaltenango to the coast takes you through a narrow gash in the mountains to the village of **ALMOLONGA**, sprawled around the sides of a steep-sided, flat-bottomed valley just 5km from Quetzaltenango. Almolonga is K'iche' for "the place where water springs", and streams gush from the hillside, channelled to the waiting crops. This is the region's market garden: the flat land, far too valuable for houses, is parcelled up into neat, irrigated fields.

In markets throughout the western highlands, the women of Almolonga corner the vegetable trade; it's easy to recognize them, dressed in their bold, orange zigzag *huipiles* and wearing beautifully woven headbands. The village itself has **markets** on Wednesday and Saturday mornings – the latter being the larger one – when the town is crammed with people, while piles of scrubbed radishes and gleaming carrots are swiftly traded. The Almolonga market may not be Guatemala's largest, but it has to be one of the most frenetic, and is well worth a visit. While you're here, it's also worth dropping by the village **church**, an arresting banana-yellow-and-white affair that backs onto the plaza. Inside, beneath the cupola, there's a wonderfully gaudy gilded altar complete with a silver statue of a crusading San Pedro, complete with bible, set behind protective bars. Pay the caretaker a quetzal and the whole altar lights up in a riot of technicolour fluorescent tubes, including a halo for the saint.

A couple of kilometres beyond the village lie **Los Baños**, where about ten different operations offer a soak in waters heated naturally by the volcano; Fuentes Saludable and El Recreo (daily 5am–10pm) are good options. For a couple of dollars you get a private room, a sunken concrete tub, and enough hot water to drown an elephant. In a country of lukewarm showers, it's paradise. The baths echo with the sound of indigenous families, some of whom queue barefoot for the pleasure of a good scrub. Below the road, between the baths and the village, there's a warm swimming pool known as Los Chorros – follow the sign to Agua Tibia – which you can use for a small fee.

If, on the other hand, you'd prefer to immerse yourself in steam, you're in luck as this also emerges naturally from the hillside. To hike to the **vapores**, as they're known, get off the bus halfway between Quetzaltenango and Almolonga at the sign for Los Vahos, and head off up the track. Take the right turn after about forty minutes, and follow this track for another thirty minutes, and you'll come to the steam baths. Here you can sweat it out for a while in one of the rooms and then step out into the cool mountain air, or have a bracing shower to get the full sauna effect.

Buses run to Almolonga from Quetzaltenango every fifteen minutes from the Minerva terminal, stopping to pick up passengers at the junction of 9 Avenida and 10 Calle in Zona 1. They pause in Almolonga itself before going on to the baths, and, although the baths stay open until 10pm, the last bus back is at around 7.30pm.

Beyond Los Baños the road heads through another narrow gully to join the main coast road in Zunil. If you're bound for Zunil, buses pass this way every thirty minutes or so.

Cantel, Zunil and the Fuentes Georginas

Many buses to the coast avoid Almolonga, leaving Quetzaltenango via the **Las Rosas** junction and passing through **CANTEL FÁBRICA**, an industrial village built up around an enormous textile factory. The factory's looms produce a range of cloths, using indigenous labourers, German dyes, English machinery, and a mixture of American and Guatemalan cotton.

A kilometre beyond Cantel on the road to Zunil is the **Copavic glass factory** (ⓦwww.copavic.com), one of Guatemala's most successful cooperatives. Copavic uses one hundred percent recycled glass and exports the finished product all over the world. Visitors are welcome to see the glass-blowers in action (Mon–Fri 8am–1pm), or visit the factory shop (Mon–Fri 8am–5pm & Sat 8am–noon), which sells a fine selection of glasses, vases, jugs and other assorted goods.

Further down the valley is **ZUNIL**, another centre for vegetable growing. As at Almolonga, the village is split in two by the need to preserve the best land. The plaza is dominated by a beautiful white colonial church with twin belfries and a magnificent Baroque facade – complete with a Buddha-like figure, a quetzal and vines. Inside an intricate silver altar is protected behind bars. The women of Zunil wear vivid purple *huipiles* and carry incredibly bright shawls, and during the Monday market the plaza is awash with colour. Just below the plaza is a **textile cooperative** (Mon–Sat 8.30am–5pm, Sun 2–5pm), where hundreds of women market their beautiful weavings; lessons are also offered here. Zunil is also renowned for its adherence to the cult of **San Simón** (or Maximón), the evil saint. In the face of disapproval from the Catholic Church, the Maya are reluctant to display their Judas, who also goes by the name Alvarado, but his image is usually paraded through the streets during Holy Week, dressed in Western clothes and smoking a cigar. At other times of year, you can meet the man himself (see box, p.185).

In the hills above Zunil is **Fuentes Georginas**, a spa natural spring spa on the evergreen slopes of Volcán Pico Zunil. The pools (US$2.50) here are

Indigenous costume

There are few more astonishing sights in the Americas than a visit to a highland market in Guatemala, which are always a riot of colour because of the superbly vivid textiles worn by the villagers. Every region has its own textile-weaving heritage, and traditional costume is still worn in most Maya settlements. Weaving is not a relic of the past but a living skill, responding to new ideas and impulses, and a key source of indigenous identity and pride.

Spinning cotton ▲

Weaver in Todos Santos ▼

Weaving processes

Weaving is one of the oldest of Maya crafts and was practised for centuries before the arrival of the Spanish. The Maya goddess Ix Chel, "she of the rainbow", is often depicted at her loom. The nobility wore elaborately embroidered cotton tunics, skirts and headdresses, dyed with indigo and cochineal, though most ordinary Maya wore much simpler garments.

Cotton is still the most important fibre today; most is factory-spun and dyed, but some weavers in remote regions still use a hand spindle and untreated yarn. Some wool is also used to make the short, kiltlike skirts worn by men in the central highlands, while embroidery is frequently made with artificial fibres like acrylic and rayon. Synthetic dyes are ubiquitous, though a tiny amount of indigo is still used, and in villages where weavers are making products for the export market (such as San Juan La Laguna) natural dyes have been reintroduced.

Back-strap (or hip-strap) **looms** – very similar to those used by the Postclassic Maya – are still employed today. These are small portable devices used by women (mainly for *huipil* production), with two sticks to support the warp. One stick is secured to a post while the other is attached to a strap that goes around the lower half of the weaver's back. Foot looms are far more bulky and used by both sexes for making skirts and lengths of fabric.

All sorts of weaving **techniques** are performed, including warp-faced (the most common process used by back-strap weavers), *ikat* (similar to tie-dying), tapestry (a weft-faced design used to make the ribbons of Santiago Atitlán), brocading and embroidery.

Women's clothing

The most eye-catching and important part of a Maya woman's costume is her *huipil*: a loose-fitting, intricately decorated blouse made from thick cotton. *Huipil* designs, usually in dazzling colours, are specific to each village but frequently include dizzying geometric patterns. Longer ceremonial *huipils*, reserved for fiestas, are usually more extravagant, and often hang low to the knee. Particularly noteworthy *huipils* include those with the spectacular star motifs unique to San Mateo Ixtatán and the incredibly intricate *huipils* of the Ixil region.

Under the *huipil* a skirt (*corte*) is worn. This is most commonly formed from a simple piece of cloth, up to five metres long, sewn together to form a tube. Maya women step into this fabric, before wrapping the material around their bodies and securing it with an elaborate sash. Gathered skirts, traditional to the Quetzaltenango and Verapaz regions, are now worn by indigenous women all over the country. Some skirt colours are associated with particular regions: in the mountains of northern Huehuetenango it's indigo blue; the Ixil is known for its brilliant reds; while yellow skirts predominate in San Pedro and San Marcos.

Perhaps the most outlandish part of women's costume is the **headdress**. The halo-style *xk'ap* of Santiago Atitlán – a twelve-metre strip of cloth – is the most famous of these, while the turbans of Nebaj and Aguacatán are some of the finest. *Tzutes*, used to carry babies or food, and shawls that ward off the highland chill are also woven.

Fashions are constantly changing as weavers travel further from their villages and gain influences from other regions.

▲ Traditional dress in Nebaj

▼ Chichicastenango market

▼ Headdress

Menswear, cowboy-style ▲

Designs from Nebaj ▼

Motifs from Santa Catarina Palopo ▼

Men's clothing

Men's traditional costume is worn in just twenty or so villages as most male Maya favour Western-style clothes today. Nevertheless there are some spectacular male designs; among them the cowboy-style woven shirts of Todos Santos and Sololá (see p.151), and the superbly embroidered knee-length shorts of Santiago Atitlán and Santa Catarina Palopó. Other unusual features are *rodilleras* (or *delanteras*) – short woollen skirts worn in Nahualá and San Antonio Palopó.

Traditional jackets are only worn rarely now by a few elderly men – those from Nebaj are said to be modelled on those worn by Spanish officers, while the ornate Sololá jackets look like tuxedos. In the Cuchumatanes some men wear *capixays*, a type of poncho-style garment, those from San Juan Atitán (see p.206) are particularly striking and hang to the knee.

Designs

The **designs** used in the traditional costume of both men and women are as diverse as the costumes themselves – an amazing collection of sophisticated patterns using superb combinations of colour and shape. Figures used include a range of animals, birds, plants, trees and people, as well as an array of abstract and geometric designs, words and names. Zig-zag designs are said to symbolize Chaac, the god of lightning and rain. Many motifs probably date from long before the Conquest: we know that the double-headed eagle, or *k'ot*, was emblematic in San Juan Cotzal and that the sun, moon and snake were commonly used in classic Maya design. Monkeys are associated with disaster while the **quetzal** was seen as the spiritual protector of K'iche' kings.

surrounded by fresh green ferns, thick moss and lush forest, and to top it all there's a restaurant (meals US$3–8) with a well-stocked bar. Unfortunately the eco-vibe is spoiled sometimes by cheesy piped music, but otherwise the steaming pools are heavenly, and just large enough for a few swimming strokes. Facilities are being upgraded, and a new changing room is under construction to add to the barbecue and picnic areas. Stone **bungalows** are also available (℡7765 4442; ❹), complete with bathtub, two double beds and fireplace (wood is provided); they're a little musty but have a certain rustic charm.

The journey to the pools – up a road which switchbacks through magnificent volcanic scenery – is also exhilarating. The easiest way to **get here** is to hop on the chicken bus operated by Adrenalina Tours (US$6 return), which travels between their office in Xela and the pools twice daily, except Mondays. Otherwise pick-ups also leave the plaza in Zunil and cost US$7 per trip, no matter how many passengers there are; it's another US$7 for the return ride.

Buses to Cantel and Zunil run from Quetzaltenango's Minerva bus terminal every thirty minutes or so, though you can also catch a bus from the centre of town beside the Shell gas station at 10 Calle and 9 Avenida in Zona 1. The last bus back from Zunil leaves at 6pm. All buses to the coastal town of Retalhuleu also pass through this way.

Just a kilometre beyond Zunil is one of Guatemala's most enjoyable **places to stay**, the spa hotel *Las Cumbres* (℡7767 1746; ❺–❻), perched on the side of a steep slope with tremendous views across the valley to the forested foothills of the Volcán Pico Zunil. It's a tremendously well run hotel, with a dozen or so spotlessly clean rooms, all with chunky wooden beds and fireplaces, and most complete with huge bathtubs fed by hot spring water and private saunas (room nos. 6–9 enjoy the best views). There's also a great restaurant with tasty *comida típica* (US$5–9 a meal), a small gym and squash court. No alcohol is served and smoking is not permitted. If you just want a steam and a soak, seven great sauna rooms (US$4 per hour) can be used by visitors.

Visiting San Simón in Zunil

Zunil's reputation for the worship of San Simón is well founded, and as in Santiago Atitlán, you can pay a visit to the man himself with a minimum of effort. Every year on November 1, at the end of the annual fiesta, San Simón (also known as Maximón) is moved to a new house. His effigy sits in a darkened room, dressed in Western clothes, and guarded by several attendants, including one whose job it is to remove the ash from his lighted cigarettes – this is later sold off and used to cure insomnia, while the butts are thought to provide protection from thieves. San Simón is visited by a steady stream of villagers, who come to ask his assistance, using candles to indicate their requests: white for the health of a child, yellow for a good harvest, red for love and black to wish ill on an enemy. The petitioners touch and embrace the saint, and just to make sure that he has heard their pleas they also offer cigarettes, money and rum. The latter is administered with the help of one of the attendants, who tips back San Simón's head and pours the liquid down his throat, presumably saving a little for himself. Meanwhile, outside the house a small fire burns continuously and more offerings are given over to the flames, including whole eggs – if they crack it signifies that San Simón will grant a wish.

If you visit San Simón, you will be expected to contribute to his upkeep (US$0.75 or so), and pay to take photographs. While the entire process may seem chaotic and entertaining, it is in fact deeply serious and outsiders have been beaten up for making fun of San Simón – so proceed with respect.

David Dickinson

Volcán Santa María

Due south of Quetzaltenango, the perfect cone of the **Volcán Santa María** rises to a height of 3772m. From town, only the peak is visible, but seen from the rest of the valley the entire cone seems to tower over everything around. The view from the top is, as you might expect, spectacular, and if you're prepared to sweat out the climb, you certainly won't regret it. It's possible to climb the volcano as a day-trip, but to really see it at its best you need to be on top at dawn, either sleeping on the freezing peak, or camping at a site part of the way up and climbing the final section in the dark by torchlight. Either way you need to bring enough food, water and stamina for the entire trip, and you should be acclimatized to the altitude before attempting it.

For more **information** on climbing Santa María, or any of the volcanoes in the region, contact the tour operators in Xela (see p.182). Sadly, you should also check the current security situation with either of these tour operators or on the forum of Ⓦwww.xelapages.com, as robberies have been reported.

Climbing the cone

To get to the start of the climb, you need to take a pick-up (approximately hourly between 7am & 5pm) to the village of **Llanos del Pinal**; pick-ups leave from the El Calvario church, beside Quetzaltenango's main cemetery on the south side of the Calzada Sinforoso Aguilar road. The village is set on a high plateau beneath the cone, and drivers will drop you off at the right spot. From here, the road heads uphill, soon becoming a trail. Painted arrows mark the way along this first section. As you push on, the path soon arrives at a flat football-pitch-sized grassy area, about ninety minutes to two hours from the start – an ideal place to **camp**. The path cuts off to the right from here, heading more or less straight up the side of the cone, a muddy and backbreaking climb of two or three hours.

At the top the cone is a mixture of grass and volcanic cinder, usually frozen solid in the early morning. The highest point is marked by an altar where the Maya burn copal and sacrifice animals, and on a clear day the **view** will take your breath away – as will the cold if you get here in time to watch the sun rise. In the early mornings the Quetzaltenango valley is blanketed in a layer of cloud, and while it's still dark the lights of the city create a patch of orange glow; as the sun rises, its first rays eat into the cloud, revealing the land beneath.

Below, to the south, is the angry, lava-scarred cone of **Santiaguito**, which has been in constant eruption since 1902. Every now and then it spouts a great grey cloud of rock and dust hundreds of metres into the air. To the west, across a chaos of twisting hills, are the cones of Tajumulco and Tacaná, marking the Mexican border. But most impressive is the view to the east. Wrapped in the early morning haze, four more volcanic cones can be seen, two above Lago de Atitlán and two more above Antigua. The right-hand cone in this second pair is Fuego, which sometimes emits a stream of smoke in the early morning.

West to San Juan Ostuncalco and Laguna Chicabal

Heading west from Quetzaltenango, a good paved road runs 15km along the valley floor to the prosperous village of **SAN JUAN OSTUNCALCO**, the commercial centre for the west side of the Xela plain. The large Sunday market draws people from all the surrounding villages; here you can see the furniture made locally from wood and rope, painted in garish primary colours. The village's other famous feature is the Catholic church's Virgen de

Rosario, who is reputed to have miraculous powers. Almost merging into Ostuncalco, its centre just 2km or so to the south, is the quiet, traditional village of **CONCEPCIÓN CHIQUIRICHAPA**, which hosts a very local market on Thursday, attended by only a few outsiders and conducted in hushed tones. **Buses** and microbuses run every thirty minutes between Quetzaltenango and Ostuncalco.

Beyond Chiquirichapa the road to the coast climbs into the hills and through a gusty pass before winding down to the farming centre of **SAN MARTÍN SACATEPÉQUEZ**, also known as San Martín Chile Verde, an isolated Mam-speaking village set in the base of a natural bowl and hemmed in by steep, wooded hills. The men here wear a particularly unusual costume made up of a long white tunic with thin red stripes, ornately embroidered around the cuffs and tied around the middle with a red sash; the women wear beautiful red *huipiles* and blue *cortes*.

A two-hour hike from San Martín brings you to **Laguna Chicabal**, a spectacular lake set in the cone of the Chicabal volcano that is the site of Maya religious rituals. To get there, get the bus to drop you off the stop for "la laguna", head down to a small bridge, then uphill to the Arca de Noe yellow-and-red church, where you bear left. The dirt track climbs steeply uphill for forty minutes before levelling out near the entrance to the Chicabal reserve (US$2.50 entrance) where there's a football field and some palapas, each with four bunk beds (US$3 per head).

A signposted route then ascends again through a forest, winding around the cone to the rim, from where there are two routes to the lake: either to the left via a *mirador* (from where there are stunning views of the emerald lagoon, and the volcanoes of Santa María and Santiaguito, Tajamulco and Tacaná), or alternatively via precipitous steps straight down to the shore. At the water's edge, you come into a different world, eerily still, disturbed only by the soft buzz of a hummingbird's wings or the screech of parakeets. Small sandy bays bear charred crosses and bunches of fresh-cut flowers mark the site of ritual sacrifice. On May 3 every year *costumbristas* gather here for ceremonies to mark the fiesta of the Holy Cross; at any time, but around this date especially, you should take care not to disturb any rituals that might be taking place. You are welcome to camp at the shore, though you'll have to bring all your own supplies.

Buses run between the Minerva terminal in Quetzaltenango and Coatepeque (for the coast) passing San Martín every thirty minutes or so. The journey time is forty minutes; the last returns from San Martín about 7pm.

Olintepeque and around

To the north of Quetzaltenango, perched on the edge of the flat plain, is the small textile-weaving town of **OLINTEPEQUE**. According to some accounts this was the site of the huge and decisive battle between the Spanish and K'iche' warriors, but these days it's better known as a peaceful little place with a fascinating pagan shrine and a great Tuesday **animal market**. This gets going soon after daylight, winding down by midday, by which time hundreds of pigs-on-leads, chickens, goats and cattle have been prodded and poked over, bought and sold.

Olintepeque's other curious attraction, the **Capilla de Rey San Pascual**, lies right in the centre of town, behind the huge mustard-coloured Catholic church. This pagan temple is dedicated to an idol, believed by devotees to have supernatural powers: numerous plaques on the walls of his shrine commissioned by believers give thanks to San Pascual for his ability to heal the sick (and bring misfortune to enemies). San Pascual is certainly a curious sight:

a foot-high effigy with an exposed skull bedecked in gaudy robes, surrounded by hundreds of candles and offerings of flowers. A flight of steps leads up to an exposed platform known as the *quemadero* ("bonfire") where the faithful whisper incantations through clouds of pungent copal (pine incense) smoke. **Buses** for Olintepeque (20min) leave from the Minerva terminal in Quetzaltenango every thirty minutes.

Northeast to Cuatro Caminos

Between the Cuatro Caminos junction and Quetzaltenango, heavy traffic cuts right through the unappealing ladino town of **SALCAJÁ**, one of Guatemala's main commercial weaving centres. Lengths of fabric, much of it woven for the *cortes* worn by Maya women, are often stretched out by the roadside, either to be prepared for dyeing or laid out to dry.

Salcajá's other claim to fame is that (according to some historians at least) it was the site of the first Spanish settlement in the country. Its modest-looking Iglesia de San Jacinto, with a simple facade embellished with plasterwork pineapples and bananas, is therefore regarded as the first Catholic foundation in Guatemala. The ideal time to visit Salcajá is for its Tuesday market, after which you might want to sample a drop of the local *caldo de fruitas* (fruit-based) or *rompopo* (egg and *aguardiente*) liquor; many places can sell you a dram.

A couple of kilometres beyond Salcajá, a left turn runs to the edge of the valley and the village of **SAN ANDRÉS XECUL**. Bypassed by almost everything, and enclosed by steep, dry hills to the rear, the breezeblock grey suburban outskirts present an unfavourable first impression that doesn't do the village justice. Facing the central plaza, San Andrés' canary-yellow Catholic **church** is quite astonishing, with a facade that's a riot of vines dripping with plump, purple fruit, and podgy little angels scrambling across the surface. The twin jaguars at the top are said to represent the hero twins of the Maya holy book, the Popul Vuh. Inside there are some fabulously chintzy chandeliers made of glass stones, coins and rosary beads.

The village's other religious activities are less orthodox. In the 1970s the artist Carmen Peterson even claimed to have discovered that a "university" for *brujos* was operating in the village, attracting young students of shamanism from K'iche' villages throughout the country. Her observations remain unsubstantiated, but there's no doubt that San Andrés is an important Maya religious centre. Uphill on 1 Calle at **La Casa de Maximón**, Guatemala's pagan saint (see p.185) holds court and a wooden case contains some rare Maya ceramics. Continuing up 1 Calle, you'll reach the yellow-and-green Calvario church, next to which is a Maya altar that's actively used for ceremonies and often shrouded in thick copal smoke. There are said to be dozens more in the hills around the town. Hourly **buses** leave the Minerva terminal in Quetzaltenango for San Andrés; the last returns at around 5pm.

At **Cuatro Caminos**, the most important junction in the western highlands, the main roads from Quetzaltenango and Totonicapán intersect with the Carretera Interamericana. One kilometre to the west, the ladino town of **SAN CRISTÓBAL TOTONICAPÁN** is built at the junction of the Sija and Salamá rivers. It's generally a quiet place that holds a position of importance as a source of **fiesta costumes**, which can be rented from various outfitters. If you'd like to see one of these, drop in at 5 Calle 3–20, where they rent costumes for around US$50 a fortnight, depending on age and quality. The colossal Baroque **colonial church**, on the other side of the river, is the main landmark in town, with a magnificent wood-beamed roof and some fantastic frescoes. Look out, too, for the extravagant side-altars with images of saints made from ornate silverwork – St Michael is particularly striking. Easter week is an impressive time to visit San Cristóbal, when there are huge processions to the church, or you could drop by for the Sunday market. **Buses** going to San Francisco el Alto pass by the village – they leave from the Minerva terminal.

San Francisco el Alto and Momostenango

From a magnificent hillside setting, the small market town of **SAN FRANCISCO EL ALTO** overlooks the Quetzaltenango valley. It's worth a visit for the view alone, with the great plateau stretching out below and the cone of the Santa María volcano marking the opposite side of the valley. At times a layer of early morning cloud fills the valley, and the volcanic cone, rising out of it, is the only visible feature.

The **Friday market** – the largest weekly market in the country – is an equally good reason for visiting the village. Traders from every corner of Guatemala make the trip, many arriving the night before, and some starting to sell as early as 4am by candlelight. Throughout the morning a steady stream of buses and trucks fills the town to bursting; by noon the market is at its height, buzzing with activity.

The town is set into the hillside, with steep cobbled streets connecting the different levels. Two areas in particular are monopolized by specific trades. At the very top is an open field used as an **animal market**, where everything from pigs to parrots changes hands. The teeth and tongues of animals are inspected by the buyers, and at times the scene degenerates into a chaotic wrestling match, with pigs and men rolling in the dirt. Below is the town's plaza, dominated by **textiles** and clothing. Most of the stalls deal in imported *ropa americana* and denim, but under the arches and in the covered area opposite the church you'll find a decent selection of traditional cloth. (For a really good view of the market and the surrounding countryside, pay the church caretaker a quetzal and climb up to the church roof.) Below, the streets are filled with vegetables, fruit, pottery, furniture, cheap comedores and plenty more. By early afternoon the numbers start to thin out, and by sunset it's all over – until the following Friday.

Plenty of **buses** connect Quetzaltenango with San Francisco, leaving every twenty minutes from 6am or so from the Minerva terminal; some also stop at the rotunda on the east side of town. San Francisco's best place to stay is the *Hotel Galaxia*, 2 Calle 1–81 (T7738 4007; ❷), which has plain rooms with private bathrooms. For a bite there are some simple comedores but little else.

Momostenango

Above San Francisco a smooth paved road continues over the ridge, then drops down through pine forests to **MOMOSTENANGO**, less than an hour away. This small, isolated town is the centre of **wool** production in the highlands, and Momostecos travel throughout the country peddling their blankets, scarves and rugs. Years of experience have made them experts in the hard sell and given them a sharp eye for tourists. The wool is also used in a range of traditional costumes, including the short skirts worn by the men of Nahualá and San Antonio Palopó as well as the jackets of Sololá. The ideal place to buy Momostenango blankets is in the **Sunday market**, which fills the town's two plazas, or the smaller Wednesday occasion.

A visit at this time will also give you a glimpse of Momostenango's other feature: its rigid adherence to Maya tradition. Opposite the entrance to the church, you may see people making offerings of incense and alcohol on a small fire, muttering their appeals to the gods. Momostenango's religious **calendar**, like that of only one or two other villages, is still based on the 260-day *Tzolkin* year – made up of thirteen twenty-day months – which has been in use since ancient times. The most celebrated ceremony is *Guaxaquib Batz*, "Eight Monkey", which marks the beginning of a new year. Originally, this was a purely pagan ceremony, starting at dawn on the first day of the year, but the Church has muscled in on the action and it now begins with a Catholic service the night before. The next morning the people make for Chuitmesabal (Little Broom), a small hill about 2km to the west of the town. Here offerings of broken pottery are made before age-old altars. (Momostenango means "the place of the altars".) The entire process is overseen by shamen responsible for communicating with the gods. At dusk the ceremony moves to Nim Mesabal (Big Broom), another hilltop, where the *costumbristas* pray and burn incense throughout the night.

As a visitor, however, even if you could plan to be in town at the right time, you'd be unlikely to see any of this, and it's best to visit Momostenango for the market, or for the fiesta on August 1. If you decide to stay for a day or two, you can take a walk to *los riscos*, a set of bizarre sandstone pillars on the northern edge of town, or beyond to the **hot springs** of Pala Chiquito about 2km further on. Throughout the day weavers work at the springs washing and shrinking their blankets – it's always best to go early, before most people arrive and the water is discoloured by soap.

Practicalities

Hospedaje Paglóm (❷) on 1 Calle has cleanish, basic rooms, and serves good grub. You'll find more comedores on the main plaza. Banrural **bank**, 1 Calle and 1 Avenida, has an ATM and changes cash and traveller's cheques.

Buses run here from the Minerva terminal in Quetzaltenango, passing through Cuatro Caminos and San Francisco el Alto on the way, every 45 minutes from 7am (1hr 15min). The last bus returns at around 5pm. On Sunday, special early-morning buses leave Quetzaltenango every thirty minutes from 6am, some stopping at the rotunda.

Totonicapán

TOTONICAPÁN, capital of one of the smaller departments, is a pleasant, if unremarkable, provincial town reached down a direct road leading east from Cuatro Caminos. Entering the village you pass one of the country's finest *pilas* (communal washing places), ringed with Gothic columns. Surrounded by rolling hills and pine forests, the town stands at the heart of a heavily populated and intensely farmed region. The Toto valley has always held out against outside influence, isolated in a world of its own, and in 1820 was the scene of one of the most famous **Maya rebellions**, sparked by demands for tax. The indigenous people expelled all of the town's ladinos and crowned their leader, Antanasio Tzul, the "king and fiscal king". His reign lasted only 29 days, ending when state troops from the capital violently quashed the rebellion – a stone memorial commemorates the event in the town's southern plaza.

Tensions in the town boiled over again in August 2001, after a VAT increase provoked widespread rioting; buildings including a bank and the mayor's house were burned down. The disturbances were only quelled when a state of emergency was declared and army tanks were sent in to restore order.

Periodic rebellions aside, Totonicapán is normally a quiet place whose faded glory is ruffled only by the Tuesday and Saturday markets, which fill the two plazas to bursting. Until fairly recently a highly ornate traditional costume was worn here but now the town has instead become one of the chief centres of commercial weaving, producing much of the *jasped* cloth worn as skirts by indigenous women throughout the country. To take a closer look at the work of local artisans, head for the **visitor centre**, the Casa de la Cultura, 8 Avenide 2–17 (☎7766 1575, ⓦwww.larutamayaonline.com/aventura.html). It organizes guided walks around the fringes of town (US$7–10per head, for 2–6 people) that take in sacred Maya sites, mask and fiesta costume-making workshops and weavers' houses (lunch included); the funds raised help benefit the community.

Alternatively there's a forest reserve called **El Abrisco** (8am–6pm; US$7 including guide), 7km north of town on the road to Santa Cruz del Quiché. Trails lead around the protected area (which was once a US special forces base) and your guide will explain (in Spanish only) the trees and their significance to the local Maya culture. Large owls the locals call *buho* are common here, and you'll find rustic cabañas (US$9), a campground and kids' play area.

Totonicapán is pretty quiet after dark; if you do want to stay, however, the best **hotel** is the *Hotel Totonicapán*, at 8 Calle and 8 Avenida (☎7766 4458, ⓦwww .hoteltotonicapan.com; ❺), which has large, modern, comfortable rooms, a restaurant and parking. Otherwise *Hospedaje San Miguel*, a block from the plaza at 8 Avenida and 3 Calle (☎7766 1452; ❷–❸), is acceptable for a night. For inexpensive **eats**, try one of the comedores scattered around the town's two plazas, while *Dino's* upstairs at 6 Calle and 8 Avenida, Zona 4, has pizza, steak, sandwiches and salads and is the most upmarket place in town. **Buses** and minibuses for Totonicapán leave Quetzaltenango's Minerva terminal between 6am and 5pm every thirty minutes, passing through Cuatros Caminos; the last minibus returns from Toto at 7.30pm.

The Department of San Marcos

Leaving Quetzaltenango you can head west to the rather neglected, little-visited department of **San Marcos** – a potential **route to Mexico** by the coastal crossing, and the home of the country's highest volcano, **Tajumulco**. Set in some of the finest highland scenery in Guatemala, the area offers excellent **hiking**.

West of Quetzaltenango the main road heads out of the valley through San Mateo and Ostuncalco and climbs a massive range of hills, dropping down on the other side to the village of Palestina de los Altos. Beyond this it weaves through a U-shaped valley to the twin towns of **San Marcos** and **San Pedro Sacatepéquez**. These towns form the core of the country's westernmost department that once served as a major trade route. There's little to detain you in either place, but they make useful bases for a trip into the mountainous countryside to the north.

San Pedro Sacatepéquez and San Marcos

SAN PEDRO SACATEPÉQUEZ is the larger and busier of the two towns, a bustling and unattractive commercial centre with a huge plaza that's the scene of a market on Thursday and Sunday. In days gone by this was a Maya settlement, famed for its brilliant yellow weaving, in which silk was used. Over the years San Pedro has been singled out for some highly questionable praise: in 1876 it was honoured by President Rufino Barrios, who with a stroke of his pen raised the status of the people from Indians to ladinos.

A dual carriageway road connects San Pedro with its sister town of **SAN MARCOS**, 2km west. Along the way, a long-running dispute about the precise boundary between the two towns has been solved by the construction of the departmental headquarters at **La Unión**, halfway between the two. The building, known as the **Palacio Maya**, is an outlandish and bizarre piece of architecture that goes some way to compensate for the otherwise unrelenting blandness of the two towns. The structure itself is relatively sober, but its facade is covered in imitation Maya carvings. Elaborate decorative friezes run around the sides, two great roaring jaguars guard the entrance, and above the main doors is a fantastic clock with Maya numerals and snake hands. A few kilometres away there's a recreation area with spring-fed **swimming pools**; the complex includes a mini-pool for kids, some dive platforms and a comedor. To get there walk from the plaza in San Pedro down 5 Calle in the direction of San Marcos, and turn left in front of the Templo de Candelero along 2 Avenida. Follow this road through one valley and down into a second, where you take the left turn to the bottom. The pool – marked simply *Agua Tibia* – is open from 6am to 4pm; a small entrance fee is charged.

Practicalities

The best **places to stay** are in San Marcos. *Hotel Fairmont*, 10 Calle 8–74 (T7760 4893; ❷), has clean, plain rooms; while *Hotel Pérez*, 9 Calle 2–25 (T7760 1007; ❸), is a dignified and long-standing establishment with en-suite rooms and a restaurant.

Both towns have their fair share of cheap **comedores**, but San Pedro boasts real Italian food, too, at *La Cueva de los Faraones* at 5 Calle 1–11, while San Marcos has the excellent *Antigua Café*, just off the main road, which serves fresh local food like *tablita antigüena* (a large plate of grilled meat) and there's live music most Saturday nights. Both towns have branches of Banrural with ATMs.

Shared **taxis** (US$0.30 per head) connect the two towns. Second-class **buses** run every thirty minutes from Quetzaltenango to San Marcos via San Pedro (1hr 30min) from 5am until 5pm. Marquensita pullmans go direct from San Marcos to Guatemala City, passing through the plaza in San Pedro eight times daily from 2.30am until 4pm.

To Tacaná and the high country

Some magnificent high country lies northwest of San Pedro, strung up between the Tajumulco and Tacaná volcanoes and forming an extension of the Mexican Sierra Madre. A rough dirt road runs through these mountains, connecting a series of isolated villages that lie exposed in the frosty heights.

Leaving San Pedro to the north, the road climbs steeply, winding up through thick pine forests and emerging onto a high, grassy plateau. Here it crosses a great boggy expanse to skirt around the edge of **Volcán Tajumulco**, whose 4220m peak is the highest in Central America. It's best climbed from the roadside hamlet of **Tuichán** (the exact drop-off point is called Llana de la Guardia) from where it's about five hours to the summit. It's not a particularly hard climb as long as you're **acclimatized** – the risk of altitude sickness is a serious concern at this height. Quetzaltrekkers and Adrenalina Tours, both in Quetzaltenango, conduct guided trips up Tajumulco. Skies are clearest between October and March.

Up here the land is sparsely inhabited, dotted with adobe houses and flocks of sheep and goats. The rocky ridges are barren and the trees twisted by the cold. The air is thin and what little breath you have left is regularly taken away by the astonishing views that – except when consumed in the frequent mist and cloud – open up at every turn. After Tuichán the village of **Ixchiguán**, on an exposed hillside at 3050m, is the first place of any size, surrounded by bleak rounded hills

▲ View from Volcán Tajumulco

and in the shadow of the two towering volcanic cones. Buses generally stop in Ixchiguán for lunch, giving you a chance to stretch your legs and thaw out with a steaming bowl of *caldo*.

Moving on, the road climbs to the **Cumbre de Cotzil**, a spectacular pass that reaches some 3400m and marks one of the highest points on any road in Central America. From here on it's downhill all the way to the scruffy village of **TACANÁ**, a flourishing trading centre that signals the end of the road – 73km from San Marcos and less than 10km from the Mexican border. Up above the village, spanning the border, is **Volcán Tacaná** (4064m), which can be climbed from the village of Sibinal. It's technically active, but last erupted in 1855, so it should be safe enough. Four **buses** a day leave the terminal in San Pedro for Tacaná, mainly in the late morning; some pick-ups also make the four-hour trip. There's also a bus service to Sibinal and Concepción Tutuapa – at similar times. In Tacaná, the *Hotel Pérez* (❶) is clean and very cheap, and the town has a couple of comedores.

Heading on from Tacaná, pick-ups provide links with Cuilco (from where there are regular buses to Huehuetenango) and to a remote crossing-point on the Mexican border called Niquimiul (foreigners are not permitted to leave Guatemala here, though).

Towards the Mexican border

The main road through San Pedro continues west, through San Marcos and out of the valley. Here it starts the descent towards the Pacific plain, dropping steeply around endless hairpin bends and past acre after acre of coffee bushes. Along the way, the views towards the ocean are superb. Eventually, you reach the sweltering lowlands, passing through San Rafael and El Rodeo with their squalid shacks for plantation workers. About an hour and a half out of San Pedro, you arrive in **MALACATÁN**, a relatively sedate place by coastal standards. If you get stuck here on your way to or from the border, try the basic *Pensión Lucía*, on the plaza

(☎7776 9415; ❷), or *Hotel Don Arturo*, 5 Calle & 7 Avenida (☎7776 9169; ❹), for more comfort. There are several banks with ATMs in town.

Buses between Malacatán and San Marcos run about every 45 minutes from 5am to 5pm. Minibuses leave Malacatán for the border at Talismán every thirty minutes, and regular buses pass through on their way between the border and the capital. (See Chapter 3 for more details on this border crossing.)

Huehuetenango and the Cuchumatanes

The **department of Huehuetenango**, slotted into the northwest corner of the highlands, is a wildly beautiful part of the country that's bypassed by the majority of visitors. The area is dominated by the mountains of the **Cuchumatanes** but also includes a limestone plateau in the west and a strip of dense forest to the north. With adequate time and a sense of adventure, this can be one of the most rewarding and spectacular parts of the country to explore.

Travelling along the Carretera Interamericana, which runs to the Mexican border, you can only get a peripheral sense of the isolated nature of this massive landscape. With more time and energy to spare, a trip into the mountains to **Todos Santos Cuchumatán**, or even all the way out to **San Mateo Ixtatán**, reveals an exceptional wealth of Maya culture. It's a world of jagged peaks and deep-cut valleys, where Spanish is definitely the second language, and where women rigidly adhere to traditional costume. Heavily populated before the Conquest, the area has pre-Columbian ruins scattered throughout the hills, with the largest at **Zaculeu**, immediately outside **Huehuetenango**, a surprisingly lively town with good budget hotels and some decent restaurants, cafés and bars.

Despite the initial devastation, the arrival of the Spanish had surprisingly little impact in these highlands, with some of the communities remaining amongst the most traditional in Guatemala. A visit to these mountain villages, either for a market or fiesta (and there are plenty of both), offers an ideal opportunity to see Maya life at close quarters.

Heading on from Huehuetenango you can be at the **Mexican border** in an hour and a half, reach Guatemala City in five or six hours, or use the back roads to travel across the highlands through **Aguacatán** towards Sacapulas, Nebaj or Cobán.

Huehuetenango

Five kilometres from the highway, at the foot of the mighty Cuchumatanes, the town of **HUEHUETENANGO** is a departmental capital and the focus of trade and transport for a vast area of northwest Guatemala. Its atmosphere is

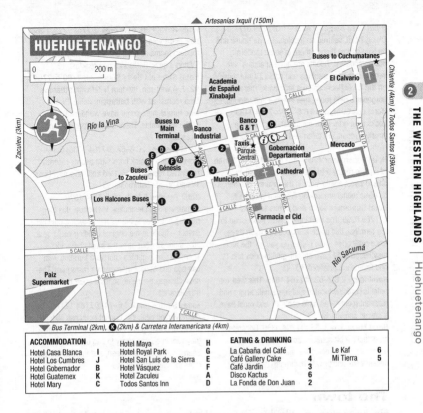

▲ Artesanías Ixquil (150m)

HUEHUETENANGO

0   200 m

Buses to Cuchumatanes

El Calvario

Academia
de Español
Xinabajul

Río la Viña

Buses to
Main
Terminal

Banco
Industrial

Banco
G & T

Taxis
Parque
Central

Gobernación
Departamental

Mercado

Buses
to Zaculeu

Génesis

Municipalidad

Cathedral

Los Halcones Buses

Farmacia el Cid

Paiz
Supermarket

Río Sacumá

Zaculeu (3km)

Chiantla (4km) & Todos Santos (39km)

▼ Bus Terminal (2km), Ⓚ (2km) & Carretera Interamericana (4km)

ACCOMMODATION				EATING & DRINKING			
Hotel Casa Blanca	I	Hotel Maya	H	La Cabaña del Café	1	Le Kaf	6
Hotel Los Cumbres	J	Hotel Royal Park	G	Café Gallery Cake	4	Mi Tierra	5
Hotel Gobernador	B	Hotel San Luis de la Sierra	E	Café Jardín	3		
Hotel Guatemex	K	Hotel Vásquez	F	Disco Kactus	6		
Hotel Mary	C	Hotel Zaculeu	A	La Fonda de Don Juan	2		
		Todos Santos Inn	D				

provincial and pretty relaxed, though heavy traffic, much of which thunders through the town centre, reduces this appeal somewhat. The name is a Nahuatl word meaning "the place of the old people", and before the arrival of the Spanish it was the site of one of the residential suburbs that surrounded the Mam capital of Zaculeu. Under colonial rule it was a small regional centre with little to offer beyond a steady trickle of silver and a stretch or two of grazing land. The supply of silver dried up long ago, but other minerals are still mined, and coffee has been added to the area's produce.

Arrival and information

Huehuetenango, known simply as Huehue, is fairly small with most places grouped around the Parque Central. A helpful **information office** sits at 2 Calle, just off the plaza (Mon–Fri 8am–1pm & 2–5pm; ☎5539 1984).

All buses stop at the chaotic **bus terminal**, halfway between the Carretera Interamericana and town (Los Halcones pullmans continue on to their offices in town). Microbuses make continuous trips between the town centre and the bus terminal.

Accommodation

Huehuetenango has a pretty good range of **hotels**, but no luxury options. If you don't care to venture into town, you'll find a few mid-priced options located near the bus terminal.

195

Hotel Casa Blanca 7 Av 3–41 ☎7769 0777. Classy hotel, centred on a colonial-style house and its twin patios, though there is some modern accommodation. Rooms are quite spacious with very attractive furnishings and cable TV, but those on the lower floor can be a little dark. There's a gorgeous dining room, free internet and parking. ❺

Hotel Los Cumbres 4 C 6–83 ☎7764 1189. Looks a bit grim from the street, but the plain, smallish rooms are clean and acceptable for a night. ❷

Hotel Gobernador 4 Av 1–45 ☎7764 1197. Warren of a place run by a friendly family, though they should invest a little more in the fixtures and fittings as some rooms are looking tired and weary. ❷

Hotel Guatemex south side of bus terminal ☎7769 0398. The best inexpensive hotel close to the terminal, this place has good rooms in three price categories – the higher up you go, the nicer they become. All have decent-quality beds and TV, and towels are provided. ❸–❹

Hotel Mary 2 C 3–52 ☎7764 1618. This well-run hotel is centrally located and has small, bright and pleasant rooms – all have cable TV and most have a private shower. ❷

Hotel Maya 3 Av 3–55 ☎7764 0369. Concrete hotel that's a bit soulless, but does represent decent value. All rooms are quite spacious, with decent beds and private bathroom. Parking. ❹

Hotel Royal Park 6 Av 2–34 ☎7762 7774. Flashy new place with a gaudy colour-scheme, but the modern rooms all have excellent mattresses, huge TV and a desk. Rates include breakfast. ❻

Hotel San Luis de la Sierra 2 C 7–00 ☎7764 9217. A well-run, modern hotel with attractive tiled rooms, all with bathroom, cable TV and pine furnishings; some have wonderful views of the mountains. There's ample parking and a restaurant. ❹

Hotel Vásquez 2C 6–67 ☎7764 1338. Garish-looking, salmon-pink rooms: all are tiled and have new beds, TV and private bathrooms. ❸

Hotel Zaculeu 5 Av 1–14 ☎7764 1086. Something of an institution in Huehue, this long-running hotel has spacious rooms with a colonial flavour – those in the original building could be a little more airy, but have the most character. There's a lovely garden courtyard bursting with bamboo and bougainvillea, and a restaurant. The hotel charges per head, so it's a great deal for solo travellers. ❺

Todos Santos Inn 2 C 6–74 ☎7764 1241. A pretty good deal, this budget hotel has sixteen smallish, bright rooms (some with private bath); they vary in quality, so try to bag one upstairs. Shared bathrooms are clean, and there are cheap rates for singletons. ❷–❸

The town

Huehuetenango is a likeable if unremarkable provincial town, its character best expressed in the unhurried atmosphere of the attractive **plaza**, where shaded walkways are surrounded by grand administrative offices. Overlooking this square, perched above the pavements, are a shell-shaped bandstand, a clock tower and a grandiose Neoclassical church, a solid whitewashed structure with a facade crammed with Doric pillars and Grecian urns. In the middle of the plaza, there's a **relief map** of the department with flags marking the villages. The details are vague and the scale a bit warped, but it gives you an idea of the mass of rock that dominates the region, and the deep river valleys that slice into it.

If that all seems a bit sedate, wander over a few blocks to the **market** area, where the streets are crowded with traders from Mexico and campesinos from every corner of the department. Centred on 1 Avenida, this part of town is always alive with activity, its streets packed with people and littered with rotten vegetables.

Eating and drinking

Most of the better **restaurants** are either in the central area around the plaza, or a short walk to the southwest around 6 Calle (which also acts as a focal point for nightlife in Huehue). *Mi Tierra*, on 4 Calle, is a good bet for a quiet drink. *Disco Kactus* on 6 Calle is a popular **club**, with Latin hits, including the latest reggaeton tunes.

▲ Hotel Las Cumbres, next Quetzaltenango

La Cabaña del Café 2 C 6–50. A logwood cabin lookalike, this café offers an excellent range of coffees, including espresso (US$0.80), sandwiches and baguettes, tostadas, nachos and plenty of great cakes. Also has *National Geographic* magazines to browse.

Café Gallery Cake 3 C 6–69. Popular café with flavoured coffee, breakfasts, cakes and pancakes as well as a set lunch. Closed Sun.

Café Jardín 3 C and 6 Av. Good for filling *comida típica*, this friendly place serves a US$2.75 set lunch, snacks and breakfasts.

Hotel Casa Blanca 7 Av 3–41. This elegant hotel dining room, with tables looking over a pretty patio garden, makes a memorable setting for a meal. Great for breakfast, or the menu includes sandwiches (US$2), omelettes and delicious mains including the house special, roast pork.

La Fonda de Don Juan 2 C 5–35. Large, vaguely Mediterranean-looking restaurant with gingham tablecloths, though the pizza, pasta and burgers are a bit overpriced, and portions could be bigger. A set lunch costs US$3.

Le Kaf 6 C. Large, modern place popular with a young crowd. Fairly pricey pizza and pasta, and they offer some cocktails too. Call ☎7764 3202 for a delivery.

Mi Tierra 4 C 6–46. Brightly painted, civilized little café-restaurant set in a covered patio with a welcoming atmosphere. Offers a set menu for US$3, hot dogs, pasta, plus Guatemalan and Mexican food including *dobladitas*. Also serves good-quality coffee, and it's mostly no-smoking.

Listings

Banks Banco G&T Continental on the plaza and Banco Industrial on 6 Av both have ATMs.

Immigration Inside the Farmacia el Cid on the plaza's south side.

Internet Génesis on 2 C charges US$0.75 an hr.

Language schools Huehuetenango is a good place to learn Spanish as you don't rub shoulders with many other gringos. Academia de Español Xinabajul,

6 Av 0–69 (☎&℻7764 1518, ✉academiaxinabajul @hotmail.com), receives positive reports from students. Abesaida Guevara de López gives positive private lessons: call ☎7764 2917.

Laundry Turismundo Commercial Centre, 3 Av 0–15.

Mexican consulate Inside the Farmacia el Cid on the plaza's south side (☎7764 1366).

Moving on from Huehuetenango

Virtually all transport leaves from the main **bus terminal** on the edge of town. Microbuses connect the town centre with the terminal, leaving from 6 Avenida, between 2 and 3 Calle. The terminal is an outdoor affair, dusty and scruffy but pretty well laid out. Each bus company has its own office, at which you should ask for the latest schedule as the timetables painted on the walls are often wrong. Also note that it is standard practice, even for second-class buses, to buy your ticket in advance from the relevant office. Generally, buses for all destinations leave more frequently in the mornings.

Buses to the **Mexican border** (1hr 45min) leave every half-hour from 5am onwards, with the last departure at 6pm. Buses also depart every thirty minutes from 4am to 6pm to **Quetzaltenango** (2hr). Four companies operate pullman buses to **Guatemala City** (6hr): Los Halcones, 7 Avenida 3–62 (☎7764 2251), have buses at 2am, 4.30am, 7am and 2pm on weekdays (three services on Sundays) departing from their own terminal; Transportes Velásquez and Rápidos Zaculeu together have twelve departures from the main terminal. Línea Dorada run the most comfortable buses, leaving at 2.30pm and 11pm daily from the *Hotel California*, opposite the terminal. Second-class buses to Guatemala City also leave from the main bus terminal every thirty minutes. If you want to go to **Antigua**, take a capital-bound bus and change at Chimaltenango; for **Lake Atitlán** or Chichicastenango change at Los Encuentros.

Heading north into the Cuchumatanes mountains, some buses to Todos Santos (10 daily; 2hr 15min) continue on to San Martín and Jacaltenango. Several companies offer buses for Barillas (7 daily; 6hr), all via Soloma and San Mateo Ixtatán; four daily buses also run to San Miguel Acatán and San Rafael La Independencia. Nentón (3hr) and Gracias a Dios (4hr) are served by five daily buses, Yalambojoch by two daily buses (4hr). Microbuses connect many towns on these routes too.

To the west, five daily buses head for isolated Cuilco (2hr). Heading **east** half-hourly buses and microbuses run to Aguacatán (40min), from where very regular microbuses run to Sacapulas, where there are good connections to **Nebaj and Uspantán**.

Adrenalina Tours (see p.182) operates a hop-on hop-off **shuttle bus** between Quetzaltenango and Cobán that passes though Huehue at 9.30am returning for Quetzaltenango at 1.15pm, and a daily service to La Mesilla and San Cristóbal de las Casas in Mexico at 10am.

Finally, pick-ups to **San Juan Atitán** leave from outside the *Cafetería Tucaná*, 2 Calle 2–15, the last at about 4pm; and buses to **Zaculeu ruins** from the corner of 2 Calle and 7 Avenida.

Post office 2 C 3–54 (Mon–Fri 8am–4.30pm).
Shopping Superb textiles can be bought at Artesanías Ixquil – located at 1 C 1–115, a 15min walk north of the plaza up 6 Av to the top of a hill, then on the right – where both the prices and quality are high.
Supermarket Paiz, southwest of the town centre at 6 C and 10 Av.
Telephone Telgua, next to the post office at 2 C 3–54 (daily 7am–10pm), though it's much cheaper to call abroad (and nationally) from the phone stalls on the plaza's west side.
Tours Mario Martínez (☎5762 1903), who used to work for Adrenalina Tours in Quetzaltenango is a reliable and informative local guide/driver. Trips throughout the Huehue department, including remote Laguna Yolnabaj and Todos Santos, can be set up.

Zaculeu

A few kilometres to the west of Huehuetenango are the ruins of **ZACULEU**, capital of the **Mam**, who were one of the principal pre-conquest highland tribes. The site (daily 8am–6pm; US$6.50) includes several large temples, plazas and a ball court, but unfortunately it was restored pretty unsubtly by a latter-day colonial power, the United Fruit Company, in 1946 and 1947. The walls and surfaces were levelled off with a layer of thick white plaster, leaving them stark and undecorated. There are no roof-combs, carvings or stucco mouldings, and only in a few places does the original stonework show through. Even so, the site has a peculiar atmosphere of its own and is worth a look; surrounded by trees and neatly mown grass, with fantastic views of the mountains, it's also an excellent spot for a picnic.

Not all that much is known about the early history of Zaculeu as no Mam records survived the Conquest. The site is thought to have been a religious and administrative centre housing the elite, with the bulk of the population living in small surrounding settlements or scattered in the hills. Zaculeu was the hub of a large area of Mam-speakers, its boundaries reaching into the mountains as far as Todos Santos and along the Selegua and Cuilco valleys, an area throughout which Mam remains the dominant language.

To put together a history of the site means relying on the records of the K'iche', a more powerful neighbouring tribe. According to their mythology, the K'iche' conquered most of the other highland tribes, including the Mam, some time between 1400 and 1475: the Popol Vuh tells that "our grandfathers and fathers cast them out when they inserted themselves among the Mam of Zakiulew". The K'iche' maintained their authority under the rule of the leader Quicab, but following his death in 1475 the subjugated tribes began to break away from the fold. As a part of this trend, the Mam managed to reassert their independence, but no sooner had they escaped the clutches of one expansionist empire, than the **Spanish** arrived with a yet more brutal alternative.

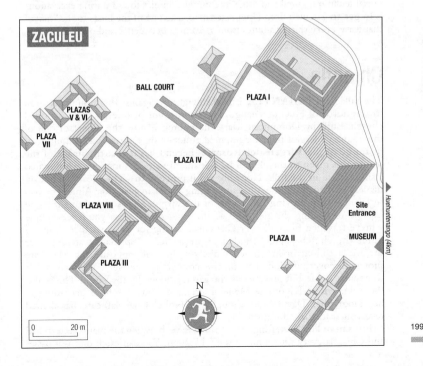

At first the Spaniards devoted themselves to conquering the K'iche', still the dominant force in the highlands. They then turned their attention to the Mam, especially after being told by Sequechul, leader of the K'iche', that a plan to burn the Spanish army in Utatlán had been suggested to his father by **Caibal Balam**, king of the Mam. In response, Spanish leader Pedro de Alvarado dispatched an army under the command of his brother Gonzalo to mete out punishment. The Spanish were met by about five thousand Mam warriors near the present-day village of Malacatancito, and promptly set about a massacre. Seeing that his troops were no match for the Spanish, Caibal Balam withdrew them to the safety of Zaculeu, where they were protected on three sides by deep ravines and on the other by a series of walls and ditches. The Spanish army settled outside the city, preparing themselves for a lengthy siege, while Gonzalo offered the Maya a simple choice – become Christians "peacefully" or face "death and destruction".

Attracted by neither option they struggled to hold out against the invading force. At one stage a relief army of eight thousand arrived from the mountains, but again they were unable to ruffle Gonzalo's well-disciplined ranks. Finally, after about six weeks under siege, his army starving to death, Caibal Balam surrendered to the Spanish. With the bitterest of ironies a bastardized version of his name has been adopted by one of Guatemala's crack army regiments – the "Kaibiles", who were responsible for numerous massacres during the 1970s and early 1980s.

Excavations at the site have unearthed hundreds of burials carried out in an unusual variety of ways; bodies were crammed into great urns, interred in vaults and even cremated. These burials, along with artefacts found at the site, including pyrite plaques and carved jade, have suggested links with Nebaj. There's a small **museum** on site (daily 8am–noon & 2–6pm) with examples of some of the burial techniques used and some interesting ceramics found during excavation.

To **get to** Zaculeu from Huehuetenango, take one of the buses to the "*ruinas*" that leave every thirty minutes from 7 Avenida between 2 and 3 calles.

Chiantla

The village of **CHIANTLA** is backed right up against the mountains, 5km to the north of Huehuetenango. The main point of interest is the colonial church. Built by Dominican friars, the church is now the object of one of the country's largest pilgrimages, held annually on February 2 in honour of its image of the **Virgen del Rosario**. Legend has it that the image of the Virgin was given to the church by a Spaniard named Almengor, who owned a silver mine in the hills. Not only did it proceed to yield a fortune, but on his last visit to the mine, the entire thing caved in just after Almengor had surfaced – thus proving the power of the Virgin. She is also thought to be capable of healing the sick, and at any time of the year you'll see people who've travelled from all over Guatemala asking for her assistance. A mural inside the church depicts a rather ill-proportioned Spaniard watching over the Maya toiling in his mines, while on the wall opposite the Maya are shown discovering God. The precise connection between the two is left somewhat vague, but presumably the gap is bridged by the Virgin. This is also the town where Rigoberta Menchú attended convent school, according to her biographer David Stoll, though the Nobel Prize laureate has denied receiving a formal education.

Buses from Huehuetenango to Chiantla travel between the main bus terminal and Chiantla every fifteen minutes until 7.30pm. You can catch one as it passes the plaza in the town centre, or wait at the Calvario (by the junction of 1 Av and 1 C), instead of heading out to the terminal.

East to Aguacatán

To the east of Huehuetenango, a paved road turns off at Chiantla to weave along the base of the Cuchumatanes, through dusty foothills, to **AGUACATÁN**. This small agricultural town is strung out along one main street, shaped entirely by the dip in which it's built. The village was created by Dominican friars, who in the early years of the Conquest merged several smaller settlements inhabited by two distinct peoples. The remains of one of the pre-conquest settlements can still be seen a couple of kilometres to the north, and minute differences of dress and dialect linger – indeed, the village remains loosely divided along pre-Columbian lines, with the Chalchitek to the east of the market and the Awakatek to the west. It used to be said that both people spoke Awakateko, but recently it's been decided locally that the 18,000 or so people in this valley speak separate languages.

During the colonial period gold and silver were mined in the nearby hills, and the Maya are said to have made bricks of solid gold for the king of Spain, to persuade him to let them keep their lands. Today the town is steeped in tradition and the people survive by growing vegetables, including huge quantities of garlic, much of it for export.

Aguacatán's vast Sunday **market** gets under way on Saturday afternoon, when traders arrive early to claim the best sites. On Sunday morning a steady stream of people pours down the main street, cramming into the market and plaza, and soon spilling out into the surrounding area. Around noon the tide turns as the crowds start to drift back to their villages, with donkeys leading their drunken drivers. Despite the scale of the market, its atmosphere is subdued and the pace unhurried: for many it's as much a social event as a commercial one.

The traditional costume worn by the women of Aguacatán is unusually simple: their skirts are made of dark blue cotton and the *huipiles*, which hang loose, are decorated with bands of coloured ribbon on a plain white background. This plainness, though, is set off by the local speciality – the *cinta*, or headdress, an intricately embroidered piece of cloth combining blues, reds, yellows and greens, in which the women wrap their hair.

Aguacatán's other attraction is the source of the **Río San Juan**, which emerges from beneath a nearby hill, fresh and cool, a kilometre east of the centre. The source itself, bubbling up beneath a small bush and then channelled by concrete walls, looks a bit disappointing to the uninitiated (though as far as cavers and geologists are concerned, it's a big one), but if you have an hour or two to kill it's a good place for a chilly swim or a picnic – there's a small entrance charge to the area.

Minibuses and **buses** run from Huehuetenango to Aguacatán every thirty minutes until about 7pm (40min). A good **place to stay** is the *Hotel y Restaurant Ray* (☎7766 0877; ❸) on 1 Avenida, Zona 1, which has very clean, well-kept tiled rooms with bathroom and good food. Or the new *Hotel 3 Oros*, 3 Calle 4–03 (☎7766 0656; ❸), a decent second choice with comfy beds, cable TV and towels provided. There's a branch of Banrural on the main street that will change traveller's cheques.

Beyond Aguacatán a paved road runs out along a ridge, with fantastic views stretching out below, eventually dropping down to the Chixoy valley and the riverside town of **Sacapulas** an hour and a half to the east. Minibuses run this route every thirty minutes until about 5.30pm.

The Cuchumatanes

The **Cuchumatanes**, rising to a frosty 3837m just to the north of Huehuetenango, are the largest non-volcanic peaks in Central America. The mountain chain rises from a limestone plateau close to the Mexican border, reaches its full height above Huehuetenango, and falls away gradually to the east, continuing through northern Quiché to form part of the highlands of Alta

▲ Men in Todos Santos

Verapaz. Appropriately enough, the name translates as "that which was brought together by great force", from the Mam words *cucuj*, to unite, and *matan*, superior force.

The mountain scenery is magnificent, ranging from wild, exposed craggy outcrops to lush, tranquil river valleys. The upper parts of the slopes are barren, scattered with boulders and shrivelled cypress trees, while the lower levels, by contrast, are richly fertile, cultivated with corn, coffee and some sugar. Between the peaks, in the deep-cut valleys, are hundreds of tiny villages, isolated by the enormity of the landscape. This area had little to entice the Spanish, and they could only be bothered to exercise vague control, occasionally disrupting things with bouts of religious persecution or disease, but rarely maintaining a sustained presence. The people were, for the most part, left to revert to their old ways, and their traditions are still very much evident in the fiestas, costumes and folk Catholicism.

More recently, the mountains were the site of bitter fighting between the army and guerrilla forces. In the late 1970s and early 1980s, a wave of violence and terror swept across the area, sending thousands fleeing across the border to Mexico. Most families returned from exile in the 1990s, settling back to life in their old communities, but the cycle of emigration has repeated itself again in recent years, as thousands of young villagers have sought work in the USA.

Travel here is slow, and hotels and restaurants are pretty basic, but if you can summon the energy it's an immensely rewarding area, offering a rare glimpse of Maya life and some of the country's finest fiestas and markets. The mountains are also ideal for hiking, particularly if you've had enough of struggling up volcanoes.

Where to go

The region offers a good chunk of Guatemala's most spectacular scenery and most absorbing villages. The most accessible of these, and the only one yet to receive a steady trickle of tourists, is **Todos Santos Cuchumatán**, which is also one of the most interesting. At any time of year, the town's Saturday market is well worth visiting, and its horse-race fiesta on November 1 has to be the most outrageous in Guatemala. From Todos Santos, you can walk over the hills to **San Juan Atitán**, or head on down the valley to **Jacaltenango**. Further into the mountains is the traditional village of **San Rafael La Independencia** from where you can explore more terrific mountain scenery and isolated Maya shrines. North of here, the village of **San Mateo Ixtatán**, which has markets on Thursday and Sunday, is another fascinating place with strong Maya cultural traditions. Beyond San Mateo is **Barillas**, a ladino town from where the jungle lowlands beyond are being colonized. One of the roughest roads in the country swings east from here to Playa Grande in Alta Verapaz.

From Huehuetenango to Paquix

Heading north out of Huehuetenango, the road to the Cuchumatanes – smoothly paved until Soloma – passes through Chiantla before beginning the long climb up the vertiginous south face of the mountain chain. Buses sway around endless switchbacks as they struggle up the arid hillside, but the views back across the valley are superb. If you're driving, you can stop at a *mirador* almost at the top of the 1000-metre ascent for a spectacular vista of the chain of volcanoes away to the south, including the near-flawless coned peak of the Volcán Santa María.

At the top of the slope, 1km after the *mirador*, a signposted dirt track heads off to the right to the *Unicórnio Azul* (☏ 5205 9328, ⓦ www.unicornioazul.com; ⓐ),

6km from the paved road, a wonderful French–Guatemalan-owned ranch that organizes superb **horseriding** excursions (a 1hr ride is included in the room rate). Accommodation is in attractive adobe-walled rooms and the food (breakfast is complimentary, dinner is US$8) is farm fresh and very filling. The same turn-off from the highway also heads east across the hills, via San Nicolás to Salquil Grande – this rough road can be impassable during heavy rains, but if you're in search of an unpredictable adventure it makes a spectacular trip.

Back on the paved road north, you enter into the *región andina* or *altiplano*, a desolate, grassy 3000-metre-high plateau suspended between the peaks that's strewn with boulders and usually wrapped in cloud in the late afternoon. At this altitude the air is cool, thin and fresh, the ground sometimes hard with frost and occasionally dusted with snow. About 10km beyond the *mirador* is the **Paquix junction**, where you'll find a couple of comedores, a gas station and the turn-off for Todos Santos.

Todos Santos Cuchumatán

Taking the western turn at the Paquix junction, a beautifully scenic road heads across the *altiplano* towards the tiny village of **La Ventosa**, perched between peaks at an altitude of around 3400m. From here a trail leads north to **La Torre** (at 3837m the highest non-volcanic mountain in Guatemala). It's around an hour and a half to the top, a stunning hike that passes one-room adobe farmsteads and then weaves through a pine- and cedar-tree forest before arriving at the summit, which is topped with antennae. On clear days (mornings are best) a jagged profile of distant volcanoes, from Tacaná to Tolimán, pierces the horizon to the south.

Continuing along the road west of La Ventosa, you'll soon start to see villagers wearing the traditional costume of Todos Santos, the men in their red-and-white-striped trousers, black woollen breeches and brilliantly embroidered shirt collars; the women in dark blue *cortes* and superbly intricate purple *huipiles*. Further down, at the bottom of the steep-sided, deep-cut river valley, is **TODOS SANTOS CUCHUMATÁN** itself – strung out along an elongated main street that's plotted with tiendas and some venerable old wooden houses. There's an excellent community **website** – Ⓦ www.stetson.edu/~rsitler/Todos Santos – dedicated to the Todos Santos region.

Todos Santos was originally put on the map by the writer Maud Oakes (whose *The Two Crosses of Todos Santos* was published in 1951) and photographer Hans Namuth, who has been recording the faces of the villagers for more than forty years. It's the endurance of tradition and the isolation that have made the village so attractive to visitors, and photographers in particular, though you should be wary of taking pictures of people – particularly of children. Rumours persist locally that some foreigners steal babies and are involved with Satanism, and a tragic misunderstanding led to the death of a Japanese tourist here in 2000.

As usual, most of the people the village serves don't actually live here. The immediate population is around 2500, but there are perhaps ten times that many people in the surrounding hills who depend on Todos Santos for trade, supplies and social life. This population is more than the land can support, and many travel to the coast, the capital and the US in search of work. One annual event brings them all home, however – the famous November 1 **fiesta** for All Saints (*todos santos*). For three days the village is taken over by unrestrained drinking, dance and marimba music. The event opens with an all-day **horse race**, which starts out as a massive stampede. The riders tear up the course, thrashing their horses, capes flowing out behind them. At either end of the run they take a drink before burning back again. As the day wears on some riders retire, collapse, or tie themselves on, leaving only the toughest to ride it out. On the second day, "The Day of the Dead", the action moves to the cemetery, with marimba bands and drink stalls setting up amongst the graves for a day of intense ritual that combines grief and celebration. By the end of the fiesta, the streets are littered with collapsed villagers and the jail packed with brawlers.

If you can't make it for the fiesta, the Saturday **market** also fills the village – although it's not as riotous – and is well worth checking out. During the week the village is fairly quiet, making it a pleasant and peaceful place to spend some time and the surrounding scenery is unbelievably beautiful. You could drop by the little **museum** (9am–5pm; US$0.75) a couple of blocks from the plaza, which has some festival costumes, a marimba or two and some wonderful old photos. The **language schools** also organize evening events, showing films and documentaries and cultural lectures.

Todos Santos is one of the few places where people are still said to use the 260-day *Tzolkin* calendar, which dates back to Maya times. Above the village – follow the track that goes up behind the *Comedor Katy* – is the small Maya site of **Tojcunanchén**, where you'll find a couple of grass-covered mounds sprouting pine trees. The site is occasionally used by *costumbristas* for the burning of incense and the ritual sacrifice of animals.

Practicalities

Ten daily **buses** leave Huehuetenango for Todos Santos (2hr 15min), the last at 4.30pm – get there early to mark your seat and buy a ticket. A few buses carry on down the valley to Jacaltenango. Check the latest schedule at the Hispano Maya.

Of the places **to stay**, *Hospedaje Casa Familiar* (☏7783 0656; ❷), just uphill from the plaza, has large sparse rooms with wood-plank walls and a very popular terrace café. *Hotelito Todos Santos* (☏7783 0603; ❸) – turn left just before you reach the *Casa Familiar* – is another good choice with small clean rooms, a few with bathroom, friendly staff and a comedor. Just uphill from the end of this street, *El Viajero* (☏7783 0705; ❷) is a two-storey concrete structure with humble, fairly clean rooms, and shared bathrooms.

For a **meal**, cheap and cheerful *comida típica* is served at the *Comedor Katy*, just behind the church; a veggie meal goes for just over US$1. *Casa Familiar*'s café

Learning Spanish or Mam in Todos Santos

Todos Santos is home to two **language schools**. The well-regarded Hispano Maya (⊛www.hispanomaya.org), opposite the *Hotelito Todos Santos*, offers Spanish instruction (plus cooking classes and escorted hikes) while Nuevo Amanacer (🅔escuela _linguistica@yahoo.com), another good institution that's located about 150m along the main street, teaches Spanish and Mam (it also offers weaving classes).

As Spanish is the second language here (after Mam), students only get a limited chance to practise it with their Mam-speaking host families. However, if you're looking for **cultural exchange**, you'll find the courses highly rewarding – especially if you don't mind pretty basic living conditions. Some students can be placed with ladino, Spanish-speaking families, though these houses are in short supply. Courses – which consist of four to five hours' instruction a day – plus accommodation and meals with a local family cost between US$110 and US$140 a week. A percentage of the profits from both schools goes to local development projects, and after-school activities are also arranged.

enjoys a great setting, and has granola and porridge on the breakfast menu, but the prices are a little steep at around US$3–4 a meal. Some 250m east of the plaza, the *Restaurant Chuchumajlaán* styles itself as the fanciest place in town, with steaks and pizza, and though the food is pretty average there's a book exchange and it's not a bad place for a cold Gallo.

The Banrural **bank** on the plaza changes traveller's cheques. Textile shoppers will find two excellent co-ops selling quality **weavings**: one is located next to the *Casa Familiar* and the other (named Cooperativa Estrella de Occidente) is just east of the plaza on the main street – there's a slow, pricey **internet** place above the latter. Most of the fun of Todos Santos is simply hanging out, but it would be a shame not to indulge in a traditional **smoke sauna** (*chuc*) while you're here. Most of the guesthouses will prepare one for you.

Hikes from Todos Santos

The scenery around Todos Santos is some of the most spectacular in all Guatemala, and there's no better place to leave the roads and set off on foot. In a day you can walk across to **San Juan Atitán**, and from there continue to the Carretera Inter-americana or head on to **Santiago Chimaltenango**. From the highway you'll be able to catch a bus back to Huehuetenango for the night, and if you make it to Santiago you shouldn't have any problem finding somewhere to stay. Thursday is the best day to do this hike – if you set out early in the morning (around 6.30am) you can arrive in San Juan before the market there has finished.

Alternatively, you can walk down the valley from Todos Santos to **San Martín** and on to **Jacaltenango**, a route that offers superb views.

Walking to San Juan Atitán

The village of **SAN JUAN ATITÁN** is around five hours from Todos Santos, across a beautiful, isolated valley. The walk follows the path up past the *Casa Familiar*, and climbs steeply above the village through endless muddy switch-backs, bearing gradually across to the right. You reach the top of the ridge after about an hour and, if the skies are clear, you'll be rewarded by an awesome view of the Tajumulco and Tacaná volcanoes. Here the path divides: to the right are the scattered remains of an ancient cloudforest and a lovely grassy valley, while straight ahead is the path to San Juan, dropping down past some huts, through beautiful forest. The route takes you up and down endless exhausting ridges, through lush trees, and over a total of five gushing streams, only the first and third of which are bridged.

Between the fourth and fifth streams – about three hours on from Todos Santos – you'll find an ideal place for a **picnic** overlooking the valley. Soon after here the path swings up to the left, over another pass, and the village of San Juan, strung out along the steep hillside, comes into view in the distance (though it is still more than an hour's walk away). Bear left here.

San Juan is an intensely traditional place: all the men wear dark-brown woolen *capixayes* (a kind of knee-length poncho) over a scarlet shirt, held in place by a sash, and plain white trousers. The high-backed sandals worn here are a style depicted in ancient Maya carving – they are also worn in some of the villages around San Cristóbal de las Casas in Chiapas, Mexico.

Like most of these mountain villages, San Juan is a pretty quiet place, active only on market days, Monday and Thursday. The central square has a giant palm tree and a pretty garden, and from the marketplace, below the health centre, there are spectacular views across the valley.

There are a couple of basic hospedajes in San Juan; the *San Diego* (❶) is the better of the two and has a small comedor beneath it (watch out for the fearsome *picante* sauce). Pick-ups to Huehuetenango leave every hour or so from 6am (1hr). From Huehuetenango, the pick-ups for San Juan leave from outside the *Cafetería Tucaná*, 2 Calle 2–15, the last at about 4pm. Get there early for a space. In this direction the journey can take a little longer.

On to Santiago Chimaltenango

SANTIAGO CHIMALTENANGO, which everyone in the region simply calls "Chimbal", makes a good alternative destination. If you want to go straight here from Todos Santos, turn right when you reach the top of the pass overlooking San Juan, head along the side of the hill and over another pass into a huge bowl-like valley. The village lies on the far side. Although it's not as attractive as some of the other villages of the region, Chimbal does retain some character, with narrow cobbled streets and adobe houses juxtaposed with modern concrete structures. The women wear terrific red *huipiles*, crisscrossed with white thread, and pile up their hair up into buns with slender lengths of scarlet cloth.

Pick-ups run down the valley through coffee plantations to the village of San Pedro Necta, and beyond to the Carretera Interamericana, or you can walk to the highway in two or three hours. *Mini Tienda La Benedición* (❶), below the market, has very basic **rooms** here.

From Todos Santos to San Martín and Jacaltenango

Heading down the valley from Todos Santos, the road arrives at the one-street village of **SAN MARTÍN**, a three-hour walk away. It is inhabited almost entirely by ladinos, but has a Friday market that attracts indigenous people from the land all around, including many from Todos Santos. A little beyond the village the road down the valley divides, with a right fork that leads 11km around the steep western edge of the Cuchumatanes. On a clear day there are spectacular views, reaching well into Mexico. At the end of the old road, on a rocky outcrop, is the poor and ragged village of **Concepción Huista** from where a road plunges to Jacaltenango, the final destination of two of the Todos Santos buses.

Perched on a plateau overlooking the limestone plain that stretches out across the Mexican border, **JACALTENANGO** is the heart of an area that was once very traditional, inhabited by a small tribe of Akateko-speakers. Several notable books about Maya customs were researched here in the early twentieth century, including the classic *The Year Bearer's People* by Douglas Byers (for more on Maya religion and prayersayers, see box, p.209). More recently, the village's most famous resident, Víctor Montejo, documented his experiences during the dark days of the civil war, when he worked here as a teacher, in his book *Testimony: Death of a Guatemalan Village* (for more about this and other tomes about Guatemala, see the Contexts section of this book).

Things have calmed down considerably since then, however, and in recent years the surrounding land has been planted with coffee, and waves of ladinos have swelled the population of the town. Today the place has a calm and fairly prosperous feel to it. The pick of several simple pensiones is the *Hospedaje Buen Samaritario* (❶); you'll find plenty of comedores along the side of the market, which is at its busiest on Sunday. Banrural **bank** here, with an ATM, is at 2 Calle 2–11, Zona 2.

The town is actually more easily reached by a paved branch route that leaves the Carretera Interamericana close to the Mexican border. Five daily **buses** run from Huehuetenango to Jacaltenango, and microbuses also run to and from the highway.

The high road to Barillas

North of the Paquix junction (see p.204), a single road, paved until Soloma, runs across the mass of the Cuchumatanes, crossing the exposed central plateau and snaking across vast valleys before finally dropping into the more temperate coffee country around Barillas. This magnificent highland area, one of the most isolated parts of Guatemala, encompasses a network of deeply traditional indigenous villages and three separate **linguistic zones**: between San Juan Ixcoy and Santa Eulalia, Q'anjob'al is spoken; around San Miguel Acatán, it's Acateko; and in the San Mateo Ixtatán region the language is Chuj.

The road to Barillas was something of a one-way street until the past few years, but new bridges across the mighty rivers of the Ixcán and road improvements have opened up an enticing, if very challenging, route east into Alta Verapaz, as the odd pick-up now connects Barillas with Playa Grande.

To San Juan Ixcoy

Beyond Paquix the road runs through a couple of magical valleys, where great grey boulders lie scattered among ancient-looking oak and cypress trees, their trunks gnarled by the bitter winds. A few families manage to survive the rigours of the altitude, collecting firewood and tending flocks of sheep. Sheep have been grazed here since they were introduced by the Spanish, who prized this wilderness as the best pasture in Central America, though lamb is very rare on the menus up here, or anywhere in Guatemala.

Continuing north the road gradually winds down off the plateau, emerging on the other side at the top of an incredibly steep valley. This northern side of the Cuchumatanes contains some of the most dramatic scenery in the entire country, and the road is certainly the most spine-chilling. Here the road clings to the hillside, cut out of the sheer rock-face that drops hundreds of metres to the valley floor. On your right, as the road plunges in altitude, are the two huge incisor-shaped rocky outcrops, known locally as the **Piedras de Captzín**, which are sacred to the Q'anjob'al Maya of these parts.

The first village reached by the road is **SAN JUAN IXCOY**, an apple-growing centre drawn out along the valley floor. There's no particular reason for breaking the journey here, but if you do the basic *Hotel Captzín de Tomas* (☎7780 6152; ❷) has invigoratingly hot showers, and the *Comedor El Viajero* two doors down serves up cheap meals. In season, around the end of August, passing buses are besieged by an army of fruit sellers. This innocent-looking village has a past marked by violence. On the night of July 17, 1898, following a dispute about pay, the Maya of San Juan murdered the local labour contractor, and in a desperate bid to keep the crime secret they slaughtered all but one of the village's ladino population. The authorities responded mercilessly, killing about ten Maya for the life of every ladino. In local mythology the revolt is known as *la degollación*, the beheading.

There are fourteen daily **buses** between Huehuetenango and San Juan Ixcoy (2hr 45min).

Soloma

Over another range of hills, and down in the next valley, is the town of **SOLOMA**, the largest, busiest and richest of the settlements in the northern Cuchumatanes. Its flat valley floor was once the bed of a lake, and the steep hillsides still come sliding down at every earthquake or cloudburst. Soloma translates (from Q'anjob'al, the dominant language on this side of the mountains) as "without security", and its history is blackened by disaster: it was destroyed by earthquakes in 1773 and 1902, half burnt down in 1884, and

The Maya priests of the Cuchumatanes

The high peaks and rugged terrain of the Cuchumatanes guard one of the country's most traditional Maya cultures. Ethnographer Krystyna Deuss, author of Shamans, Witches, and Maya Priests: Native Religion and Ritual in Highland Guatemala, has been studying rituals in these remote communities for more than twenty years, focusing her attention on the prayersayers, who occupy a position parallel to that of local priests. Here she explains their role and some of the key rituals surrounding their office.

Some of the purest **Maya rituals** today can be found among the Q'anjob'al of the northwestern Cuchumatanes. The office of **alcalde resador** (chief prayersayer) still exists here and the 365-day *Haab* calendar is used in conjunction with the 260-day *Tzolkin*. The former ends with the five days of *Oyeb' ku'*, when adult souls leave the body; the return of the souls on the fifth day brings in the new year. As this always falls on a day of *Watan*, *Lambat*, *Ben* or *Chinax*, these four-day lords are known as the "Year Bearers" or "Chiefs". Depending on the community, the *Haab* year begins either at the end of February or the beginning of March, coinciding with the corn-planting season.

The duty of the *alcalde resador* is to protect his village from evil and ensure a good harvest by praying for rain at planting time and for protection against wind, pests and disease while the corn is maturing. His year of office – during which he and his wife must remain celibate – begins on January 1, the day all the voluntary municipal officials change; in the towns of Santa Eulalia, Soloma and San Miguel Acatán where traditions are particularly strong, he lives in a house which has been specially built for him. Traditionalists regularly visit to ask for prayers and leave gifts of corn, beans, candles and money. On the altar of the house stands the **ordenanza**, a chest that not only contains religious icons but also ancient village documents, a throwback to the time when religious and civil authorities worked as one. The chest now serves both as a symbol of authority and as a sacred object, and it can only be opened by the *alcalde resador*, in private, once a year. The *resador's* whole day is spent in prayer: at his home altar before the *ordenanza*, in church and at sacred village sites marked by crosses. Prayers for rain are often accompanied by the ritual sacrifice of turkeys whose blood is poured over the candles and incense destined to be burned at the sacred places the following day. These ceremonies are not open to the general public.

Festivals more in the public domain happen on January 1 when the incumbent *alcalde resador* hands over his responsibilities to his successor. In **Soloma** after an all-night vigil the *ordenanza* is carried in procession to the middle of the market square and put on a makeshift altar under a pine arch. When the incoming group arrives there are prayers and ritual drinking, and they receive their wooden staffs of office; after this, the outgoing *alcalde resador* (usually a man in his sixties or seventies) is free to leave for his own home. The new prayersayer's group stays in the marketplace, collecting alms and drinking until 3pm, when they carry the *ordenanza* back to the official residence in a somewhat erratic procession. Notwithstanding a further night of vigil and ceremonial drinking, at 7am the following morning the *alcalde resador* sets out on his first prayer-round to the sacred mountains overlooking the town.

In **San Juan Ixcoy** the year-end ceremonies differ in that the new *resador* is not appointed in advance. Here the outgoing group carries the *ordenanza* to a small chapel outside the church on the night of the 31st and leaves it in the care of a committee of traditionalists. The usual all-night vigil with prayers, ritual drinking and collecting alms continues throughout the following day while everyone waits anxiously for a candidate to turn up. As the office of *resador* is not only arduous, and with dwindling support from the community, but also expensive, the post is not always filled on January 1. The *ordenanza* sometimes stays locked in the chapel for several days before a volunteer (usually an ex-prayersayer) takes on the office again rather than let the *ordenanza* and the tradition be abandoned.

– Krystyna Deuss, the Guatemalan Maya Centre, London

decimated by smallpox in 1885. The long white *huipiles* worn by the women of Soloma are similar to those of San Mateo Ixtatán and the Lacandones, and are probably as close as any in the country to the style worn before the Conquest. These days only a few elderly ladies don them for **market** days (Thurs & Sun), by far the best time to visit.

About three hours from Huehuetenango, Soloma makes a good spot to break the trip and has several **places to stay**. The well-run, clean and friendly *Hotel Estrella del Norte*, Diagonal 1 6–10 (☎5715 7636; ❸), is a good choice where all rooms have TV and most a bathroom. Otherwise, the towering *Hotel Don Chico* (☎7780 6087; ❸), north of the plaza, is the smartest place in town, with modern rooms, a restaurant and underground parking. For **food**, try *Restaurante California* on the south side of the plaza. Several places offer internet in the streets around the plaza, while Banrural at 6 Calle 7–03 has an ATM and will change traveller's cheques. **Buses** from Huehuetenango pass through Soloma about every hour on their way to Barillas and other villages to the north; the last bus leaves Huehue at 5pm.

Santa Eulalia

Leaving Soloma the paved road soon ends, and you continue over another range of hills to the large village of **SANTA EULALIA**, where highland religious ritual is adhered to very strongly. The church here is fascinating: a large, dusty pink-coloured building where the faithful assemble on their knees to recite prayers, and the air is thick with the smoke from hundreds of candles. Many then stop to burn incense at a separate Maya altar, wrapped in smoke, in front of the church. The clean and very cheap *Hotel y Restaurante Eulalense* (☎7765 9634; ❶), just below the church, has hot water and neat little rooms, while next door the *Cafetería Margol* serves up tasty *comida típica*.

Beyond Santa Eulalia is the Cruce Pett junction after which the Barillas road pushes on north through pastureland, skirting patches of pine forest, with exhilarating views west into Mexico. The sense of isolation is immense up on this beautiful 3000-metre-high plateau, and you'll barely see a soul except for shepherd boys and their goats.

San Rafael La Independencia, San Miguel Acatán and around

At the **Cruce Pett** junction, 5km north of Santa Eulalia, there are three comedores and a branch road that cuts off to the west, curving around the peaks of the Cuchumatanes to the village of **SAN RAFAEL LA INDEPENDENCIA**, 11km to the southwest. Perched on a west-facing outcrop with magnificent views down towards the Mexican border, this peaceful Akateko-speaking settlement amounts to not much more than a scattering of old timber houses and utilitarian concrete structures. Nevertheless, it makes an enjoyable place to spend a day or two, at the heart of a very traditional region where Maya customs remain very strongly observed. The Centro Cultural Maya Akateko (☎7779 7239), above the *municipalidad*, has a fascinating collection of old artefacts, including polychrome ceramics, obsidian flints, a two-metre blowpipe and some interesting photographs. The staff can put you in touch with guides (Pedro Juan Méndez Martinez is recommended) who can lead you to the Maya ruins of **Tenam**, the Chimbam chapel, Xeyatak ceremonial centre, and the numerous sacred caves and altars that dot the hills around. A new **hotel** is due to open on the way in from Cruce Pett, or you can stay in basic rooms above the *Tienda San Andrés* (❶), a block downhill from the plaza, though there's no hot water here.

From San Rafael it's just 4km to the larger, much less attractive village of **SAN MIGUEL ACATÁN**, where you'll find a couple of hospedajes (❶), plenty of comedores, a Sunday market and a branch of Banrural that will change traveller's cheques. **Buses** leave Huehuetenango for San Miguel, via San Rafael, four times daily (4hr 30min). If you want to return via a different route, a narrow but reasonable dirt road heads southeast from San Miguel through a series of remote, steep-sided valleys and the tiny village of **Najab**, to join up with the Huehue–Barillas road just north of Soloma. You'll have to hitch a ride in a pick-up if you want to take this route, as there are no buses.

From San Miguel Acatán, a spectacular day-long **hike** takes you along the edge of the mountains to Jacaltenango. Setting out from San Miguel, cross the river and follow the trail that bears to the right as it climbs the hill opposite. At the fork, halfway up, take the higher path that crosses the ridge beside a small shelter. On the other side it drops down into the head of the next valley. Here you want to follow the path down the valley on the near side of the river, and through the narrow gorge to an ancient wooden bridge. Cross the river and climb up the other side of the valley, heading down towards the end of it as you go. The path that heads straight out of the valley runs to Nentón, and the other path, up and over the ridge to the left, heads towards **Jacaltenango**. Along the way there are stunning views of the rugged peaks of the southern Cuchumatanes and the great flat expanse that stretches into Mexico – on a clear day you can see the Lagunas de Montebello, a good 50km away, over the border. On the far side of the ridge, the path eventually drops down to Jacaltenango through the neighbouring village of San Marcos Huista: some eight or nine tough but worthwhile hours in all from San Miguel.

San Mateo Ixtatán

Back on the high road to Barillas, it's a further 24km from Cruce Pett to **SAN MATEO IXTATÁN**, the most traditional, and quite possibly the most interesting, of this string of villages. Its name derives from the Nahuatl for "abundance of salt", which is still a major industry in the communally owned mines around the village. Little more than a thin sprawl of wooden-tiled houses, the village tumbles down a steep east-facing hillside, occupying the ground between two plunging river valleys. The people here speak **Chuj** and form part of a Maya group who occupy the extreme northwest corner of the highlands and some of the forest beyond; their territory borders that of the Lacandón, a jungle tribe never subjugated by the Spanish, who constantly harassed these villages in colonial times. The best time to visit, other than for the fiesta (Sept 17–21), is on a market day, Thursday or Sunday – during the rest of the week the village is virtually deserted.

Traditional dress is becoming less common, but the older women here still wear unusual and striking *huipiles*, long white gowns embroidered in brilliant reds, yellows and blues, radiating out from a star-like centre. You may also see men wearing short woollen poncho-like tunics called *capixayes*, often embroidered with flowers around the collar and quetzals on the back.

San Mateo's cream-coloured **church**, its wonky facade embellished with niches and the images of saints, is one of the most interesting in Guatemala, with a pagan character that barely offers a passing reference to conventional Catholicism. Smoke from a Maya altar attended by *costumbristas* drifts across the courtyard in front of the church, while inside devotees kneel on the bare earth of the nave clutching candles, the stone walls reverberating with the constant murmur of solemn incantations.

Just below the village are the quite substantial unrestored Maya ruins of **Wajxaklajunh**, which enjoy a magical position overlooking the San Mateo valley and down to ridge after ridge of hills on the horizon to the east. Here you'll find several temples, including the pyramid-shaped structure known as Yolk'u, meaning "inside the warm place", a ball court and a couple of weathered stelae shaded by cypress trees.

The best of the very simple places to **stay** is *Hotel Ixtateco* (℡7756 6586; ❶), which has hot water. *Restaurante Wajxaklajunh*, above the police station, is clean and cheap and there's a little cybercafé where you can surf the **internet**. The website ⓦ www.ixtatan.org, run by development project the Ixtatán Foundation, is a great source of information, you may run into their staff in town. Eight daily **buses** leave Huehuetenango for San Mateo (5hr 15min). It's also possible to travel by pick-up from San Mateo northwest to the village of Yalambojoch in around two and a half hours (see p.217).

Barillas and around

Beyond San Mateo the road drops steadily east to **BARILLAS**, an unlovely ladino frontier town 28km away in the relative warmth of the lowlands and devoted to coffee production. At least *Hotel el Quetzal* (❷), bordering the plaza, is clean and friendly, and *Hotel Sol* (℡7870 2618; ❷) next to the bus station is also good; and there are several comedores in town. Banrural has a **bank** at 3 Avenida 2–28, Zona 1, which has an ATM. There are eight daily buses to Barillas (6hr 30min) from Huehuetenango, passing through all the villages en route. There's also an airstrip, and you may be able to hitch a ride on one of the missionary flights (three weekly; around US$55) in a five-seater plane to Guatemala City.

About 18km to the north of the village (take the dirt road towards the village of Yolhuitz) is the beautiful hourglass-shaped **Laguna Maxbal**, which is ringed by forest – locals say it's possible to see a quetzal bird here some mornings. Heading west from Barillas, a very rough road penetrates a landscape of pastureland and patches of thick, uninhabited jungle known as the **Ixcán** – this terrain slopes down into the Usumacinta river basin. The odd pick-up pushes through this near-forgotten corner of the country, covering the route from Barillas to Playa Grande in five hours or more, depending on the state of the road.

West to the Mexican border

From Huehuetenango the Carretera Interamericana runs for 79km through the narrow Selegua valley to the Mexican border at **La Mesilla**. Travelling direct, this takes less than two hours on one of the buses that thunder out of Huehuetenango every thirty minutes or so between 5am and 6pm. Along the way, just off the main road, are some interesting traditional villages, largely oblivious to the international highway that carves through their land. Most are best reached as day-trips out of Huehuetenango.

The first of these, 22km from Huehue, is **San Sebastián Huehuetenango**, a quiet little place barely 200m north of the highway. The village was the site of a pre-conquest centre, and of a settlement known as Toj'jol, which was swept away by the Río Selegua in 1891. Further on the road runs through a particularly narrow part of the valley known as **El Tapón**, "the cork", and past a turning for San Juan Atitán (12km) and another for San Rafael Petzal, 2km from the main road. Beyond this it passes roads that lead to Colotenango, Nentón and Jacaltenango.

You pass one last roadside village, La Democracia, before reaching the border at **LA MESILLA** where there's a bank (with ATM) and plenty of moneychangers. If you get stuck here, there's **accommodation** at the *Hotel Maricruz* (❷), which is clean, with private bathrooms and a restaurant, or at the slightly cheaper *Hospedaje Marisol* (❷). The two sets of customs and immigration are 3km apart; collective taxis (US$0.50) run between the immigration points, and on the Mexican side you can pick up buses from the border settlement of **Ciudad Cuauhtemoc** to **Comitán**, or even direct to **San Cristóbal de las Casas**. Heading into Guatemala, buses to Huehuetenango leave the border every thirty minutes (1hr 45min) until roughly 7pm. Wherever you're aiming for in Guatemala, it's best to take the first bus to Huehue and change there.

Colotenango, San Ildefonso Ixtahuacán and Cuilco

The most important of the villages reached from the highway is **COLOTENANGO**, perched on a hillside 1km or so south from the main road. The municipality of Colotenango used to include San Rafael Petzal and San Ildefonso, until 1890 when they became villages in their own right. Ties are still strong, however, and the red *cortes* worn by the women of all three villages are almost identical. Colotenango remains the focal point for the smaller settlements, and its Saturday market is the largest in the Selegua valley. From early Saturday morning the plaza is packed, and the paths that lead into the village are filled with a steady stream of traders, indigenous families, cattle, chickens, reluctant pigs and the inevitable drunks. Here you'll see people from all of the surrounding villages, most of them wearing traditional costume. The village is also worth visiting during Holy Week, when elaborate and violent re-enactments of Christ's Passion take place (the bravest of villagers takes the role of Judas, and is shown no mercy by the rest), and for its fiesta from August 12 to 15.

To get to Colotenango from Huehuetenango, take any **bus** heading towards the Mexican border and ask the driver to drop you at the access road to the village; the journey takes around 45 minutes.

On to San Ildefonso and Cuilco

Behind Colotenango a paved road goes up over the hills and through a pass into the valley of the Río Cuilco. Here it runs high above the river along the top of a ridge, with beautiful views up the valley: below you can make out the tiny village of San Gaspar Ixchil, which consists of little more than a church and a graveyard.

Another few kilometres brings you to the larger village and mining centre of **SAN ILDEFONSO IXTAHUACÁN**. Similar in many ways to Colotenango, it has a large and traditional Maya population and a history of defiance. In 1977 miners who were refused permission to form a union walked 260km to Guatemala City to put their case to the authorities, an action which captured the imagination of the entire nation and 100,000 people turned out to welcome them. Controversy returned again in 2005 when Canadian company Glamis Gold (later Goldcorp) started developing an open-pit gold mine 15km south of here with a US$45 million loan from the World Bank, despite widespread local opposition. Protesters set up barricades

Fiestas

The western highlands are the home of the traditional Guatemalan fiesta. Every village and town, however small, has its own saint's day, around which a fiesta is based that can last anything from a day to two weeks. All of these fiestas involve traditional dances that mix pre-Columbian moves with more modern Spanish styles, and each has its own signature event, whether it's a horse race or a fireworks spectacular.

January

3–6 San Gaspar Ixchil, a tiny village on the road to Cuilco
3–8 El Tumbador, department of San Marcos
9–15 Sibilia, main day 13th
10–16 Santa María Chiquimula, in honour of the Black Christ of Esquipulas
12–15 Chinique, a very traditional fiesta
12–16 La Libertad
12–16 Colomba
13–16 Nentón
15–17 San Antonio Ilotenango
18–20 San Sebastián Coatán
19–21 Santa Lucía La Reforma
19–24 Ixtahuacán
22–26 San Pablo La Laguna, main day 25th
23–27 San Pablo, department of San Marcos

February

Jan 28–Feb 2 Chiantla, main day 2nd
Jan 28–Feb 2 Jacaltenango
1–4 Cunén, main day 2nd
6–10 Patzité, El Quiché, main day 8th
8 San Juan Ostuncalco
8–13 Santa Eulalia, main day 8th
Varies Palestina de los Altos, department of San Marcos, celebrating the first Friday in Lent

March

14–20 San José el Rodeo, main day 19th
19 San José Poaquil, near Chimaltenango
Varies Chajul and La Democracia, the second Friday in Lent marked by huge pilgrimages

Holy Week

Santiago Atitlán, Maximón paraded through the streets, usually on the Wednesday; San Cristóbal Tonicapán, the biggest processions in the Xela area

April

22–28 San Marcos, main day 25th
24 San Jorge La Laguna
25 San Marcos La Laguna
29–May 4 Barillas
30–May 4 La Esperanza
Varies Zacualpa and Aguacatán, fiestas to mark forty days from Holy Week

May

1–3 Cajola
6–10 Uspantán, main day 8th

8–10 Santa Cruz La Laguna
8–10 Santa Cruz Balanya, department of Chimaltenango
20 Patzún

June

12–14 San Antonio Palopó, Lago de Atitlán, main day 13th
12–14 San Antonio Huista
21–25 San Juan Ixcoy, north of Huehuetenango
21–25 Olintepeque, just north of Quetzaltenango
22–25 San Juan Cotzal, main day 24th
22–26 San Juan Atitán, main day 24th
23–26 San Juan La Laguna, main day 24th
24 Comalapa
24–30 San Pedro Sacatepéquez
26–30 Soloma, main day 29th
27–30 San Pedro Jocopilas
27–30 San Pedro La Laguna, main day 29th
28–30 Almolonga, main day 29th
Varies Corpus Christi celebrations, held throughout Guatemala in June, are particularly spectacular in Patzún

July

1–4 Santa María Visitación, near Sololá, main day 2nd
12–17 Huehuetenango
21–Aug 4 Momostenango, the 25th is a very important day in the Maya religious calendar, and the 1st is the main fiesta day
22–27 Tejutla, main day 25th
22–27 San Cristóbal Totonicapán, main day 25th
22–27 Chimaltenango, main day 26th
22–27 Patzicía, main day 27th
23–26 Malacatancito
23–27 Santiago Atitlán, main day 25th
25–27 Santa Ana Huista, main day 26th
29–31 Ixchiguan, main day 31st

August

1–4 Sacapulas, main day 4th
9–15 Joyabaj, main day 15th. Superb fiesta; traditional dances here include the *Palo Volador*
10–13 Santa Clara La Laguna, main day 12th
11–17 Sololá, main day 15th
12–15 Nebaj, main day 15th
12–15 Colotenango, main day 15th
12–15 Tacaná, main day 15th
12–18 Cantel, near Quetzaltenango, main day 15th
14–19 Santa Cruz del Quiché, main day 18th
18–25 San Bartolo, main day 24th
21–27 Pologuá
22–25 Sipacapa
22–28 Salcajá, main day 25th
27–30 Sibinal, main day 29th

(cont...2)

September
12–18 Quetzaltenango, main day 15th
17–21 San Mateo Ixtatán, main day 21st
21 San Mateo, west of Quetzaltenango
24–30 Totonicapán, main day 29th
25–30 San Miguel Acatán, main day 29th
26–Oct 5 Tecpán

October
1–6 San Francisco el Alto, main day 4th
2–6 Panajachel, main day 4th
15–20 San Lucas Tolimán, Lago de Atitlán, main day 18th
21–Nov 2 Todos Santos Cuchumatán, a long warm-up to the big day

November
1–2 Todos Santos Cuchumatán, a wild, alcohol-infused horse race on the 1st, with
   everyone heading to the cemetery on the 2nd for All Souls' Day
7–12 San Martín Jilotepeque, main day 11th
14–18 Malacatancito, main day 18th
22–26 Zunil, main day 25th
23–26 Nahualá, main day 25th
24–26 Santa Catarina Ixtahuacán, main day 25th
25 Santa Catarina Palopó, Lago de Atitlán
27–Dec 1 Cuilco, main day 28th
27–Dec 1 San Andrés Semetabaj, main day 30th
27–Dec 1 San Andrés Xecul, main day 30th

December
1–4 Santa Bárbara
5–8 Huehuetenango, main day 8th
5–8 Concepción Huista, main day 8th
7 The Burning of the Devil is celebrated in most highland towns with bonfires and
   men running around dressed as devils
7–9 Concepción
9–14 Malacatán
11–15 Santa Lucía Utatlán, main day 13th
14–21 Chichicastenango, very impressive fiesta, main day 21st
25–28 Chiché, main day 28th

on the Carretera Interamericana and a demonstrator was shot dead, but mining started in 2007.

Beyond San Ildefonso the road slopes down towards the bottom of the valley and crosses the river before arriving at **CUILCO**, a sizeable ladino town 36km from the Carretera Interamericana that marks the end of the road. The Mexican border is just 15km away, and the town maintains cross-border trade links both inside and outside the law. Beyond today's village are the ruins of an earlier settlement known as **Cuilco Viejo**. Cuilco has also earned itself something of a reputation for producing heroin, but anti-drug campaigns have stamped out a lot of the poppy cultivation in recent years.

Buses run between Huehuetenango and Cuilco every two hours between 5am and 3pm. There are a few basic places to stay in Cuilco including the *Hospedaje Osorio* (❶) while the large *Hotel Perla Escondida*, Calle la Paz (☎7861 2889; ❹–❺), has air-conditioned rooms. If the roads are in reasonable condition, trucks and pick-ups run south from Cuilco to the mountain village of Tacaná, from where there is a regular bus service to San Pedro.

North to Nentón and Yalambojoch

A short distance before the border, from the roadside village of **Camoja Grande**, a paved road leads off to the north, running parallel to the border. A new **language school** has been set up in the village of Río Azul in these parts, which should make a fascinating place to learn Spanish; see ⓦwww .xelapages.com/rioazul for more information. The road continues across a dusty white limestone plateau to the village of **Nentón**, then continues up into the extreme northwest corner of the country, where there are a couple of wonderful natural attractions. The first of these is the startling **El Cimarrón** *cenote* (a sink hole in the limestone crust), a near-perfect cylindrical depression measuring about 500m wide and around 300m deep. Locals attest all sorts of legends to the *cenote*, and say that the bottom (which harbours a lake and dense forest) is unexplored. El Cimarrón is about 4km from the tiny village of **La Trinidad**, which is 35km north of Nentón.

East of La Trinidad, it's 9km along a dirt track to the larger village of **YALAM-BOJOCH**, something of a transport hub for these parts, with two daily **buses** (both leaving in the early morning) for Huehue and pick-ups for San Mateo Ixtatán. It's also the jumping-off point for the spectacular cobalt-blue waters of **Laguna Yolnabaj**, a large lake 5km to the north, that's also known as Laguna Brava. Locals, many of whom are *repatriados* (returned refugees from Mexico), have launched a reforestation programme around the lake, and successfully fought off American real-estate speculators (so far). The tour guide Mario Martínez (see p.198), based in Huehuetenango, runs trips here.

The recent history of Yalambojoch is bound up with that of **Finca San Francisco**, a smaller village a further 3km to the east. In 1982 the army massacred around three hundred people here and the entire population of the surrounding area fled for their lives, crossing the border into Mexico. After more than a decade, people started to return, and today life in the region seems to have returned to normal. Finca San Francisco has a small Maya temple, and also a plaque commemorating those who died in the massacre.

Finally, there is a remote **border crossing** into Mexico at Gracias a Dios (5km northwest of La Trinidad). Guatemalans and Mexicans regularly cross the frontier here, but foreigners are recommended to get your exit stamp first from immigration in Huehue. Just over the border, the village of Carmixán has transport for Comitán where you can get your Mexican entry stamp.

Travel details

Buses

An almost constant stream of buses plies the Carretera Interamericana – between roughly 8am and 6pm you should never have to wait more than twenty minutes for one – and the major towns of the western highlands are generally just off the highway. The main routes from these hubs are covered below, while other, more local schedules are provided in the relevant accounts throughout the chapter.

Chichicastenango to: Guatemala City (every 20min; 3hr); Quetzaltenango (7 daily; 2hr 30min); Santa Cruz del Quiché (every 20min; 30min).

Chimaltenango (the junction for Antigua) to: Antigua (every 20min; 40min); Guatemala City (every 20min; 1hr); Quetzaltenango (every 30min; 3hr).

Huehuetenango to: Aguacatán (every 30min; 40min); Guatemala City (17 daily pullmans, plus half-hourly chicken buses; 6hr); La Mesilla (26 daily; 1hr 45min); Quetzaltenango (22 daily; 2hr); Todos Santos Cuchumatán (10 daily; 2hr 15min).

Panajachel to: Antigua (1 daily at 10.45am; 3hr); Chichicastenango (5 daily Thurs & Sun, 1–2 daily other days; 1hr 30min); Cocales (8 daily; 2hr); Guatemala City (10 daily; 3hr 30min); Quetzaltenango (6 daily; 2hr 30min).

Quetzaltenango to: Chichicastenango (10 daily; 2hr 30min); Guatemala City (15 pullmans, plus half-hourly chicken buses; 4hr); Huehuetenango (22 daily; 2hr); Momostenango (every 45min; 1hr 15min); Panajachel (6 daily; 2hr 30min); San Francisco el Alto (every 30min; 45min); San Pedro La Laguna (5 daily; 2hr 15min); Totonicapán (every 30min; 1hr); Santa Cruz del Quiché (10 daily; 3hr); Zunil (every 30min; 30min).

San Marcos to: Guatemala City (8 daily; 5hr 30min); Malacatán (hourly; 1hr 30min); Quetzaltenango (hourly; 1hr 30min).

Santa Cruz del Quiché to: Guatemala City, via Chichicastenango (every 20min; 3hr 30min); Joyabaj (hourly; 1hr 45min); Nebaj (5 daily; 2hr 15min); Quetzaltenango (10 daily; 3hr); Uspantán (11 daily; 2hr 30min).

The Pacific coast

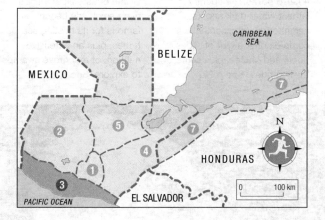

CHAPTER 3 Highlights

* **Tilapa** and **Tilapita** Palm trees line these fine, dark-sand beaches whose gently shelving profile makes this one of the coast's best spots for a swim. See p.224

* **Takalik Abaj** This small but rewarding archeological site features well-executed Olmec and Maya carvings. See p.226

* **Xocomil** and **Xetulul** leisure parks The country's largest water-park and its neighbouring amusement complex offer a glut of slides, pools and chutes, plus some thrilling rides. See p.227

* **La Democracia** A startling collection of pot-bellied carved-stone sculptures, or "fat boys", inhabit this village's main plaza. See p.231

* **Sport-fishing** World-class conditions are offshore Guatemala's Pacific coast: the two main centres are Puerto Quetzal and Iztapa. See p.233

* **Monterrico** This oceanside village boasts Guatemala's most enjoyable beach, famous for its nesting sea turtles, plus an extensive network of mangrove swamps to explore. See p.234

▲ White pelican, Monterrico

The Pacific coast

A chain of volcanoes divides the cool air of the mountains from a sweltering strip of low-lying, tropical, ladino-populated land, some 300km long and 50km wide. Usually known simply as **La Costa**, this fairly featureless yet supremely fertile coastal plain – once swamp, forest and savannah – is now a land of vast fincas, dull commerce-driven towns and ramshackle seaside resorts scattered along an unrelentingly straight, black-sand shoreline.

Several ancient Mesoamerican cultures once flourished in the region, leaving some important archeological remains. Today it's large-scale agriculture – sugarcane, palm oil, cotton and rubber plantations – that dominates and accounts for a substantial proportion of the country's exports. Only in some isolated sections, particularly in the extensive mangrove swamps, can you still get a sense of the maze of tropical vegetation that once covered this area. One such place is the **Monterrico Reserve**, where the unique coastal environment is protected, offering a refuge to sea turtles, iguanas, crocodiles and an abundance of bird life.

Little of the region's archeological heritage remains, though you can glimpse the fine art of the Pipil around the town of Santa Lucía Cotzumalguapa. The one site in the area that comes close to ranking with those elsewhere in the country is **Takalik Abaj**, outside Retalhuleu, which displays both Maya and Olmec heritage.

The main attraction of the region should be the **coastline**, though sadly much of it is dotted with scruffy villages and plagued by a dangerous undertow. Generally **surf** conditions are much better in El Salvador and Mexico, but there are a few breaks in Iztapa and **Sipacate**, where a surf camp has been set up. In the last few years **sport-fishing** has taken off in Guatemala-offshore waters have stupendous numbers of sailfish, tarpon, tuna and marlin; Iztapa and Puerto Quetzal are the main bases for excursions.

It's certainly not a resort, but the little seaside settlement of **Monterrico** has a certain unspoilt charm and is worth a visit. Here you'll find one of the country's finest beaches, with a superb stretch of clear, clean sand and a coastal nature reserve to explore.

The main transport link in this region is the coastal highway, the **Carretera al Pacífico** (CA-2), the country's fastest road. This is the usual route for pullman buses speeding between Guatemala City and the Mexican border, so travel is normally swift and comfortable.

Some history

The earliest history of the Pacific coast remains something of a mystery. It's generally held that the sophisticated **Olmec** influence – in what is now Mexico – spread along the coast, shaping both the emerging **Ocós** and **Iztapa** cultures,

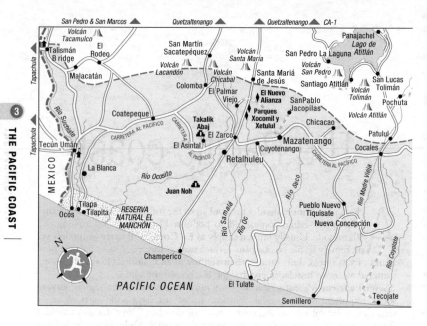

which thrived here after 1500 BC. These were small, village-based societies that developed considerable skills in the working of stone and pottery.

Between 400 and 900 AD, parts of the coastal plain were overrun by the **Pipil**, who migrated south from Mexico, possibly after the fall of Teotihuacán. These migrants brought with them their architectural styles and artistic skills, and the remains of their civilization show that they used a foreign calendar and worshipped the gods familiar in Mexico. The Pipil built half a dozen sites, all compact ceremonial centres with rubble-filled pyramids, and traded cacao. But by the time of the Conquest the tribes of the highlands had started to encroach upon the coastal plain and claim a slice of the action.

The first **Spaniards** to set foot in Guatemala did so on the Pacific coast, where Pedro de Alvarado first confronted K'iche' warriors. Once they'd established themselves, the Spanish dispatched a handful of Franciscans to convert the coastal population and were faced with a long, hard fight from the Pipil. In **colonial times** the land was mostly used for the production of indigo and cacao and for cattle ranching, but the inhospitable climate and accompanying disease soon took their toll, and for much of that era the coast remained a miserable backwater. It was only after **independence** that commercial agriculture – coffee, bananas and sugarcane – began to dominate. By the early twentieth century, the area was important enough to justify the construction of two railways to the coast and a line to the Mexican border.

Today the coastal strip is the country's most intensely farmed region, with entire villages being effectively owned by vast fincas. Much of the nation's income is generated here and the main towns are alive with commercial activity, ringed by the ostentatious homes of the wealthy and dominated by the assertive machismo of ladino culture. Typically, most towns here are unrelentingly featureless, though **Retalhuleu** is a little more attractive. If you plan to spend any time on the coast, **Monterrico** is your best bet, but if you just want to head for the beach, then **Tilapa** is within easy reach of Quetzaltenango.

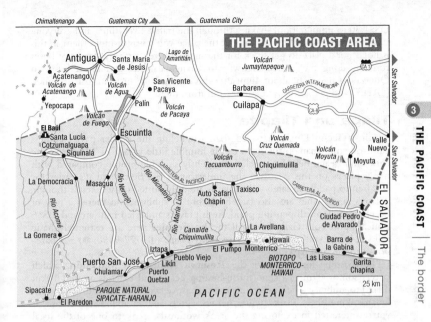

The border

Most travellers forgo the limited appeal of Guatemala's Pacific coast and head straight from the border to Quetzaltenango or Guatemala City. Three companies – Galgos, Ticabus and Línea Dorada (see pp.88–89) – run **direct buses** between Tapachula, Mexico, and Guatemala City (via Escuintla, from where there are good connections to Antigua).

Few nationalities need a visa for Guatemala (for more on this, see the Basics section of this book), but there's a consulate in Tapachula if you don't qualify for a waiver. The same is true for Mexico, though there are Mexican consulates in Retalhuleu, Quetzaltenango, Huehuetenango and Guatemala City for those who do need a visa.

The Talismán Bridge and Tecún Umán

The coastal border with Mexico is the busiest of Guatemala's frontiers, with two crossing points, Talismán and Tecún Umán; both are open 24 hours. Minibuses run every twenty minutes or so from posts to Tapachula (30min away) until 9pm.

The northernmost crossing is the **Talismán Bridge**, also referred to as El Carmen, which is the more relaxed of the two. Bus connections are not good as Tecún Umán further south, but there's a regular flow to **Malacatán**, where you'll find hotels and buses heading along on a slow, mountainous route for San Marcos and Quetzaltenango.

The **Tecún Umán** crossing, on the edge of the dusty, bustling border-town of Ciudad Tecún Umán, is favoured by most Guatemalans and all commercial traffic. The town has an authentic frontier flavour with all-night bars, lost souls, contraband and moneychangers, and its streets are almost permanently choked by a chaos of articulated lorries and buses, with cycle rickshaws (charging

US$1.30 to immigration) snaking through the traffic. Everything and everyone is on the move, and after one look at the place you'll want to join them, as this is not a good place to get stuck for the night. There's a steady stream of buses running along the coastal highway to Guatemala City and direct buses to Quetzaltenango until about 4pm; after this time get the first bus to Retalhuleu ("Reu") and get an onward connection from there.

Tilapa and Tilapita

South of Tecún Umán, a paved road paralleling the border passes endless palm-oil and banana plantations to the humble little village of **TILAPA**. The dark-sand beach here has a relatively gently shelving profile compared with many places on this coast, so the undertow is less fierce and it's easier for children to paddle in safely – lifeguards are only posted on weekends though. Tilapa's sandy lanes are also largely devoid of rubbish, and there's a row of beach comedores dispensing good, fresh prawns and fried fish (around US$6 a meal), plus cold Gallo beer. All the **hospedajes** here are extremely basic indeed, but if you're very desperate *Hotel Tilapa* (☎4777 9190; ❶) has bare-bones rooms and parking.

The coastline forms part of the **Reserva Natural El Manchón**, which covers some 30km of prime turtle-nesting beach and extends around 10km inland to embrace a belt of swamp and mangrove, which is home to crocodiles, iguanas, kingfishers, storks, white herons, egrets and an abundance of fish. If you're interested in exploring the area's **wetlands**, speak to one of the local boatmen about taking a tour of the canals and lagoons.

On the other side of an estuary is the even tinier, and more agreeable beach settlement of **TILAPITA**. Here there's a real opportunity to get away from it all and enjoy a superb stretch of clean, dark sand and the ocean (with not too much undertow). There's a good **hotel**, *El Pacífico* (☎5940 1524; ❸), owned by charming local couple Siria and Alex Mata, with eighteen functional, large

▲ Tilapita beach on the Pacific coast

> ### Undertow
>
> Most of Guatemala's Pacific coastline is affected by a strong undertow, which occurs when big waves break on a shore with a steep profile. Because there's nowhere for the water to escape, it retreats backwards under the next breaking wave, creating a downward force close to the shore. Unless you're very confident in the ocean, it's best not to mess around if the surf is big. By not getting out of your depth, you can use your feet to jump up into the oncoming waves and let their force push you toward the shore. If you do get caught in an undertow, don't panic, as the downward force only lasts a second or two and you'll soon surface. Catch a breath, duck under the next breaker, and then work your way steadily back to shore.

rooms, all with decent mattresses, fans and showers – though you might want to bring your own mosquito net. The 18m swimming pool is filled at weekends. Good food, including fresh fish, is served and cold beers are just US$1.25 a pop.

Just next to the hotel is a small **turtle hatchery**, with protected enclosures where eggs are buried until they hatch, and some information boards (the Olive Ridley turtle is the main visitor here).

It's easiest to **get to Tilapa** by one of the shuttle-bus packages offered by Adrenalina Tours in Xela (see p.182), though these are very pricey at US$75 per head return. Doing it under your own steam isn't so hard though, with regular buses connecting Coatepeque and Tilapa (every 30min, last bus returns at 6pm; 2hr 30min). If you're travelling along the Carretera al Pacífico, just wait at the Tilapa junction on the highway for a connection. Boatmen buzz you up the canal for the ten-minute ride from Tilapa **to Tilapita** for US$1.25 per head; it is possible to wade over at low tide.

The coastal highway: Coatepeque and Retalhuleu

East from the Mexican border, **COATEPEQUE** is the first place of any importance on the main road, a furiously busy, purely commercial town where most of the locally produced coffee is processed. As this shabby town is infamous for its street gangs, and the climate is oven hot and perpetually sticky, it's best to avoid hanging around. From the **bus terminal** buses run every twenty minutes to the two Mexican border crossings and Quetzaltenango (via both Colomba and Zunil) until about 7pm, and hourly to Guatemala City until 6pm. If you do get stuck, *Villa Real*, 6 Calle 6–57 (T 7775 1308; ❹), is a modern hotel with a restaurant and secure parking or the family-run *Hotel Baechli*, 6 Calle 5–35 (T 7775 1483; ❷), is a cheaper option.

Retalhuleu and around

Beyond Coatepeque lies the most densely populated section of the Pacific coast, centred on **RETALHULEU**, which is usually referred to as **Reu** (pronounced "Ray-oo"). Set 6km kilometres south of the Carretera al Pacífico and surrounded by the walled homes of the wealthy, Reu has managed to avoid the worst excesses of the coast, protected to some extent by a combination of wealth and tradition.

Reu is a relatively civilized place compared with the chaos evident elsewhere on the coast. Grand-looking palm trees line the entrance road to the town, while the **plaza** retains a degree of faded authority – you'll find the towering Greek columns that define the *municipalidad* (the subject of a huge renovation project) and a large, attractive colonial church. The mood is relaxed and easy-going, and in the warmth of the evening, young couples canoodle on the park benches. The small **Museo de Arqueología y Etnología** in the *municipalidad* was closed at the time of research, but should reopen in 2010 with a collection of Maya anthropomorphic figurines that show a strong Mexican influence and some evocative old photographs of the region.

Retalhuleu practicalities

Budget **accommodation** is in short supply in Retalhuleu. One decent inexpensive place is *Hotel América*, 8 Avenida 9–32 (T7771 1154; ❸), which has clean rooms with fan and private bath. A step up in quality, ﹖ *Hotel Casa Santa María*, 4 Calle 4–23 (T5202 8180; ❹–❺), is an excellent colonial-style place with a small pool and eight lovely rooms, some with air-conditioned. The owners, who run the Reuxtreme tour agency (see below), provide excellent information about the region and offer tasty meals (weekdays only) in the café here. Otherwise the modern *Hotel Posada de Don José*, 5 Calle 3–67 (T771 0180, Edonjose@terra .com.gt; ❻), has comfortable, air-conditioned rooms, a decent restaurant and a pool; there's a cheaper annexe (❹) too.

Around the **plaza** are several **banks**, including the Banco Agromercantil, with an ATM. Plenty of **restaurants** are also close by including *Cafetería la Luna* for inexpensive Guatemalan meals, and the café-bar *Lo de Chaz*, 5 Calle 4–83, just west of the plaza, which is the best bet for a beer.

Adventure trips around the Reu region, including mountain-bike trips to Takalik Abaj and kayaking through mangrove lagoons are organized by Reuxtreme (T7771 0443, Wwww.reuxtreme.com) based in *Hotel Casa Santa María*. Most **buses** running along the coastal highway pull in to the Retalhuleu terminal on 7 Avenida and 10 Calle, a ten-minute walk from the plaza. There's a half-hourly service to and from Guatemala City, the Mexican border and Quetzaltenango; very regular buses also depart for Champerico and El Tulate. Retalhuleu's **Mexican consulate** is at the *Posada de Don José* (Mon–Fri 4–6pm).

Takalik Abaj

The archeological site of **Takalik Abaj** (daily 7am–5pm; US$6.50, guide US$6.50), some 15km west of Retalhuleu, has cast fresh light on the development of early Maya civilization, particularly the influence of **Olmec** culture. The city presided over trade routes along the Pacific littoral, controlling the movement of jade, cacao and obsidian. An unlooted Maya royal grave was uncovered in 2002, and excavations are ongoing. You can only access the Olmec's urban centre, while the city's outskirts are spread over five coffee plantations. First settled around 1800 BC, early ceremonial buildings and monuments were executed in Olmec style between 800 and 400 BC, including the characteristic pot-bellied humans with swollen eyelids. But by the late Preclassic period, Maya-style carvings of standing rulers were beginning to replace Olmec art. Later in the Classic era some of the Maya World's most exquisite jade masks were created here – they now reside in Guatemala City's Museo Nacional de Arqueología y Etnología (see p.81).

The first substantial structure you encounter is **Terraza 3**, a low, rectangular stepped temple with three stone Olmec-head statues facing a ceremonial Maya altar. Some of the finest carved stelae are in front of **Temple 12**, which is the site's largest with a 56-metre-wide base; Monument 67 depicts a jaguar head; Monument 68 is toad-like; Monument 9, a rare representation of an owl; and, most impressive of all, the grouping of **Altar 8** and **Monument 5** (which has a date of 126 AD and shows twin kings presiding over bound captives). Facing Temple 12 is **Temple 11**, resembling a grassy mound, which is mid- to late Classic Maya and has seven more stelae in front of it. More good carvings lie round the back of Temple 12 including Olmec-style Monument 99, which shows a baboon-like creature with a protruding jaw.

Behind Temple 12 is a small building that serves as a **museum**, containing a model of Takalik Abaj along with assorted carvings and ceramics. There are also several fairly miserable animal enclosures that contain pizotes, spider monkeys and porcupines, among other creatures. You should be able to get a warm fizzy *agua* near the entrance, but there's no food available.

To **get to Takalik Abaj**, take a local bus from Reu to **El Asintal**, a small village 15km to the west, from where you can either hire a pick-up or walk the 4km to the site through coffee and cacao plantations. If you're driving, take the Astinal turn-off from the coastal highway.

There are two **places to stay** in rural locations nearby, both a couple of kilometres further north along the same minor road from El Astinal. The fine eco-resort, *Takalik Maya Lodge* (℡2337 0037, ⓦwww.takalik.com; ⑨), is one of the best hotels along the Pacific slope, with stylish and attractive accommodation in two separate buildings, horseriding and birdwatching trips, guides for the ruins and a pool. It's managed with the local community as a kind of "fair trade" partnership. Close by, the *San Isidro Piedra Parada* also offers bed and breakfast (⑥) in an elegant main house. A tour of the finca, which employs eighty workers, is included; packages here can be arranged by Adrenalina Tours in Quetzaltenango (see p.182).

Retalhuleu towards Quetzaltenango

North of Retalhuleu on the Carretera al Pacífico, the **El Zarco** junction marks the start of one of the country's most scenic roads, which heads up into the highlands passing two impressive leisure parks, the abandoned village of El Palmar Viejo and an organic coffee finca. It then skirts the plunging lower slopes of the Santa María and Zunil volcanoes before emerging in the valley of Quetzaltenango.

Xocomil and Xetulul theme parks

Some 6km north of the Zarco junction is a superb theme-park complex landscaped into the foothills of the highlands owned by Irtra (ⓦwww.irtra.org .gt). The **Parque Acuático Xocomil** (Thurs–Sun 9am–5pm; US$11.50, children US$7.50) is a vast complex containing 1.2km of water slides, wave pools and artificial rivers amidst grounds replete with Maya temples and copious greenery. The neighbouring **Parque Xetulul** (Thurs–Sun 10am–6pm; US$28, children aged 5–12 US$14, ride package US$6.50 extra) is divided into different zones, with the Plaza Chapina having re-creations of famous Guatemalan buildings, the Plaza España showcasing a galleon, and Plaza Francia boasting replicas of Parisian structures such as the Gare de France. The park has some terrific rides, including the thrilling La Avalancha rollercoaster and, like its sister complex, is clean, well run and extremely popular with Guatemalan families. Four excellent, family-friendly **hotels** – including colonial- and ranch-style places – are located here too, though these are pricey for foreigners, with basic double rooms starting at US$45 and many costing US$100 or more. **Buses** between Retalhuleu and Quetzaltenango pass the water park every thirty minutes in daylight hours.

El Palmar Viejo

Beyond these parks it's about 14km to the left-hand turn-off that leads to the absorbing remains of the village of **El Palmar Viejo**. After torrential rains in 1998, the Río Nimá burst its banks and mud-flows swept through the centre of this farming community, cutting the village church in two and leaving its western facade hanging over a ravine. Villagers were evacuated to the other side of the highway – and while the remains of El Palmar Viejo hardly amount to a Guatemalan Pompeii, the overgrown ghost town makes an intriguing sight and represents a haunting reminder of the destructive powers of Hurricane Mitch, which killed hundreds in Guatemala and thousands in Honduras and Nicaragua.

Fizzy-drink vendors and pick-ups congregate near the ravine, where there's a rickety bridge. If you cross this bridge and follow a path that winds past mud-flows and a second bridge, there's a pretty hourglass-shaped **laguna** that's a good spot for a picnic; it's a fifteen-minute walk from the ravine.

To get to El Palmar Viejo, you can take any bus heading between Retalhuleu and Quetzaltenango and get off at the El Palmar Viejo turn-off, from where you can walk or wait for a pick-up to cover the 3.5km route. There are also tours from Quetzaltenango (see p.182).

El Nuevo Alianza

On the other side of the highway from El Palmar, **Nuevo Alianza** (℡5539 6898, Ⓦwww.comunidadnuevaalianza.org) is an organic, fair-trade coffee and macadamia farm run as a cooperative. You can tour the finca's handsome colonial-style mansion and its extensive grounds that lead to a waterfall and learn about coffee cultivation and processing. Dorm beds (US$8 per head), private rooms (US$10 per head) and meals (US$3) are available, and volunteers are welcome. Many Spanish schools and tour operators in Quetzaltenango run trips here.

Champerico

South from Retalhuleu, a good paved road heads to the beach at **CHAMPERICO**, which, though it certainly doesn't feel like it, is the country's fourth port. Founded in 1872, it was originally connected to Quetzaltenango by rail and enjoyed a brief period of prosperity based on the export of coffee. In 1934 Aldous Huxley passed through but was distinctly unimpressed, pleased to escape "the unspeakable boredom of life at Champerico". Little has improved here except that the rusty old pier has been fixed up a little. Champerico spends most of its time waiting for the weekend, when hordes of weary city-dwellers descend on the coast to gorge on greasy fried fish and cratefuls of cold Gallo. Although the sheer scale of the dark-sand **beach** is impressive, it's essential to watch out for the dangerous **undertow**, even when lifeguards are present. There's very little to distinguish the palapa-roofed beach **restaurants**, but paella is served at the *Hotel Miramar*, 2 Calle and Avenida Coatepeque (℡7773 7231; ❷), which also has a fantastic wooden bar – the best place in town to tackle your thirst – and dark, windowless rooms.

Buses run between Champerico and Retalhuleu every ten minutes or so from 7am to noon; the last bus leaves Champerico around 8pm. If you're heading anywhere else, catch a bus from Champerico to Retalhuleu (from where there are buses to Quetzaltenango every 30min).

Cuyotenango to Cocales

Beyond Retalhuleu the highway runs east through **Cuyotenango**, a featureless town blighted by the thunder of the highway. Another branch road turns off from here to the isolated, palm-lined black-sand beach **EL TULATE**. Here the village and the ocean are separated from the access road by a narrow expanse of mangrove swamp; boats ferry passengers across for US$0.50. As it's a small place, you're virtually guaranteed a quiet place to chill once you're away from the strip of shore-side seafood comedores. The beach has a gentle shelving profile, so it's much better for paddling and swimming than most places along the Pacific coast. There are a few simple **places to stay** in the village, and the beachside *Playa Paraíso* (☏5985 0300; ⑥), 1km east of the centre, has comfortable bungalows with verandas, two pools and a restaurant. **Buses** (every 30min; 1hr 30min) struggle down here every hour or so from both Retalhuleu and Mazatenango.

Back on the highway, the next stop is **MAZATENANGO**, another seething commercial town, though away from the highway around the plaza things are calmer, with long, shaded streets. There's no reason to linger, but budget **accommodation** options include *Hotel La Cabaña*, 2 Calle 2–10, Zona 2 (☏7872 1635; ⑨), which offers good-value rooms with private bath and parking. For more comfort, head for *Hotel Alba*, on the main highway (☏7872 0264; ④–⑤), which has secure parking and a restaurant. Plenty of restaurants and banks are around the plaza.

Continuing east from Mazatenango, there's a turn-off after 48km for **COCALES**, a crossroads town from where **buses** run north to Santiago Atitlán, Panajachel and San Lucas Tolimán. If you're Atitlán bound, the best option is to take the first bus to San Lucas and catch a boat or bus from there to other points around the lake. The last bus to San Lucas leaves Cocales at around 6pm.

Santa Lucía Cotzumalguapa and around

Another 23km along the Carretera al Pacífico brings you to **SANTA LUCÍA COTZUMALGUAPA**, an uninspiring Pacific town a short distance north of the highway. The only reason to visit the area is to take in the Pipil and Maya **archeological** sites and carvings around Santa Lucía, the colossal Olmec carved figures at nearby La Democracia or the **surf** at Sipacate to the south.

Santa Lucía Cotzumalguapa

This largely featureless place is rightly bypassed by most travellers, but if you have an hour or two to kill in the area, a group of unusual carvings and archeo-logical remains, scattered in the surrounding cane fields, are worth a look. Bear in mind, though, that getting to them is not easy unless you rent a taxi. As usual, the **plaza** is the main centre of interest, a shady square that's disgraced by one of the ugliest buildings in the country, a horrific concrete municipal structure. Several cheap, scruffy **hotels** can be found close to the plaza, but the nearest half-decent place is *Hotel Internacional* (☏7882 5504; ⑨–⑤) just south of the Carretera al Pacífico, which has clean rooms with either fan or air-conditioning. For **food** try the popular *Taquería Palankiny* at 4 Calle 3–60, or the *Cevichería La Española* on 4 Avenida for fresh seafood and a beer. There are several **banks**; Banco Agromercantil on 3 Avenida has an ATM.

Pullman buses passing along the highway will drop you at the entrance road to town, a ten-minute walk from the centre. Second-class "directo" buses (every 30min; 1hr 45min) from the capital go straight into the terminal, a few blocks from the plaza.

Sites around Santa Lucía Cotzumalguapa

A tour of the **sites** around Santa Lucía Cotzumalguapa can be an exhausting and frustrating process, taking you through a sweltering maze of cane fields. Doing the whole thing on foot is certainly the cheapest way, but also by far the hardest and riskiest – visitors have been robbed occasionally. You're far better off taking a round trip by taxi instead – you'll find plenty in the plaza in varying degrees of decrepitude – and, if you bargain, US$15 should cover all the sites.

Bilbao

In 1880 more than thirty Late Classic stone monuments were removed from the Pipil site of **Bilbao**, and nine of the very best were shipped to Germany. Four sets of stones are still visible in situ, however, and two of them perfectly illustrate the magnificent precision of the carving, beautifully preserved in slabs of black volcanic rock. To **get to** the site, walk uphill from the plaza, along 4 Avenida, until you reach the Convento Las Hermanas where you bear left following a dirt track along the side of a cane field. About 200m further on is a fairly wide path leading left into the cane for about 20m. This brings you to two large stones carved with bird-like patterns, with strange circular glyphs arranged in groups of three: the majority of the glyphs are recognizable as the names for days once used by the people of southern Mexico. In the same cane field, further along the same path, is another badly eroded stone, and a final set with a superbly preserved set of figures and interwoven motifs.

▲ Dios Mundo at Finca El Baúl

Finca El Baúl

The second site is about 5km further afield in the grounds of the **Finca El Baúl**, reached by following 3 Avenida north out of town. The hilltop site has two stones, one a standing figure wearing a skirt and a spectacular headdress, the other a massive half-buried stone head (known as Dios Mundo) with wrinkled brow and patterned headdress – this is possibly Huhuetéotl, the fire god of the Mexicans. In front of the stones is a set of small altars on which local people make animal sacrifices, burn incense and leave offerings of flowers. Excavations have revealed a network of buried causeways – one stretches to the north to a site called **Gloria**, where some giant carved stones have been unearthed – you can view these in the Popul Vuh museum in Guatemala City. El Baúl also makes an ideal shaded spot for a **picnic** lunch, with fine vistas towards the twin peaks of volcanoes Agua and Fuego to the north.

The next stones of interest are at the **finca** (Mon–Fri 7am–5pm, Sat 8am–noon; free) itself, a few kilometres further away from town. The carvings include some superb heads, a stone skull, a massive jaguar and an extremely well-preserved stela of a ball-court player (Monument 27) dating from the Late Classic period. Alongside all this antiquity is the finca's old steam engine, a miniature machine that used to haul the cane along a system of private tracks, and a vintage German steam tractor.

Finca Las Ilusiones

On the other side of town, the third site is at **Finca Las Ilusiones**, where another collection of artefacts and some stone carvings has been assembled in the **Museo Cultura Cotzumalguapa** (Mon–Fri 8am–4pm, Sat 8am–noon; US$1.40). Two of the most striking figures are an Olmec-style pot-bellied statue (Monument 58), probably from the middle Preclassic era, and a copy of Monument 21 which bears three figures, the central one depicting a ball player. There are several other carved pieces, including a fantastic stela, plus some more replicas and thousands of small stone carvings and pottery fragments. The museum is located 1km east along the highway and 400m up a signposted side road on the left.

La Democracia and Sipacate

Heading east from Santa Lucía Cotzumalguapa the highway arrives at **Siquinalá**, a run-down sort of place from where another branch road heads to the coast. Along the way, 9km to the south, **LA DEMOCRACIA** is an orderly little town that's of particular interest as the home of another collection of archeological relics. To the east of town lies the archeological site of **Monte Alto**; many of the best pieces found there are now spread around the town plaza under a vast ceiba tree. These "fat boys" are massive stone heads with simple, almost childlike faces, grinning with bizarre, Buddha-like contentment. Some are attached to smaller rounded bodies and rolled over on their backs, clutching their swollen stomachs. . The figures are strikingly similar to ancient Olmec sculptures found near Villahermosa in the Gulf of Mexico, and they probably date from the mid-Preclassic period around 500 BC. Also on the plaza, the town **museum** (Tues–Sun 8am–4pm; US$4) houses carvings, ceremonial yokes worn by ball-game players, pottery, grinding stones, a wonderful jade mask and a few more carved heads.

The road continues 21km further south to **La Gomera**, a mid-sized agricultural centre where buses usually wait for a while, and beyond to the coast at the low-key village of **SIPACATE**, located inside the Parque Natural

Sipacate-Naranjo, a mangrove coastal reserve that's also home to Guatemala's best **surf**. The beach is separated from the village by the black waters of the **Canal de Chiquimulilla** (which parallels Guatemala's southern coast from here to Las Lisas, 100km to the east) across which boats ferry a steady stream of passengers. Beachside there's a nascent surf scene. Waves average six feet and are most consistent between December and April (for more details see *El Paredón*'s website, listed below). **Accommodation** includes *Rancho Carillo* (☎5517 1069, ⊛www.marmaya.com; ❼), a comfortable place with rooms and cabañas, a pool and a restaurant; they also run fishing trips and offer surfing lessons on weekends. About 6km east of here is the rustic *El Paredón Surf Camp* (☎4593 2490, ⊛www.surf-guatemala.com; ❷), set up by Guatemalan enthusiasts; **surf lessons** are US$10 per hour. This place has two dorms, both with four bunk beds (US$5), space for hammock slingers and campers, and there's a beachfront dining area for breakfast, fresh fish, beer and juices. It's possible – but tricky and lengthy – to reach *El Paredón* by public transport; it involves changing buses several times and a final pick-up from Sipacate. If you get in touch with the camp management ahead of time, owner Adolfo Cruz (who speaks good English) will arrange lifts from Antigua and help take care of local transport details.

Regular **buses** to La Democracia (every 30min; 15min) and Sipacate (8 daily; 2hr) leave Siquinalá on the highway.

East from Escuintla towards El Salvador

The eastern section of the Pacific coast is dominated by **Escuintla**, the region's largest town, and **Puerto San José**, formerly its most important port – though neither place is at all attractive. Further to the east is **Monterrico**, an impressive beach where you'll find the coast's most important wildlife reserve, a protected area of mangrove swamps that's home to some superb birdlife. Beyond that the coastal highway runs to the border with El Salvador, with branch roads heading off to a couple of small seashore villages.

Escuintla

Located at the junction of the two principal coastal roads from the capital, bustling **ESCUINTLA** ranks as Guatemala's third largest city with a population of 130,000. Despite its size there's nothing to see here, but you do get a good sense of life on the coast – its heat, pace and energy, as well as the frenetic industrial and agricultural commerce that drives it. Below the plaza a huge, chaotic **market** sprawls across several blocks, spilling out into 4 Avenida, the main commercial thoroughfare, which is also notable for a mock castle that functions as the town's police station.

There are plenty of cheap **hotels** near 4 Avenida, most of them sharing a general air of dilapidation; for air-conditioning and secure parking head for the fair-value *Hotel Costa Sur*, 12 C 4–13 (☎7888 1819; ❸–❹). The best area for **food** is the row of *cevicherias* on 1 Calle near the Plaza Palmeras mall; ☆ *Blanqui*, 1 Calle 3–55, Zona 2, is a large, efficient place that specializes in fresh seafood, *ceviche* and fried fish – a mixed plate is US$10. Mariachis prowl the tables, and there's a great atmosphere at lunchtime and during the early afternoon, while things wind down by the evening.

Buses to Escuintla leave Guatemala City from Treból every twenty minutes until 7pm, returning from 8 Calle and 2 Avenida in Escuintla. For other destinations, there are two terminals: for places en route to the Mexican border, buses run through the north of town and stop by the Esso station opposite the Banco Uno (take a local bus up 3 Av); buses east towards El Salvador leave from the main terminal on the south side of town, at the bottom of 4 Avenida (local bus down 4 Av). Buses leave every twenty minutes for Puerto San José and the eastern border, and hourly to Antigua until 5pm.

To the coast: Puerto San José

South from Escuintla the coast road heads through acres of cattle pasture to **PUERTO SAN JOSÉ**, the capital's nearest and most popular, if ramshackle, resort. Opened as a port in 1853, San José was once Guatemala's main shipping terminal, funnelling goods to and from the capital. Now, however, the port has been made virtually redundant by the modern facilities at Puerto Quetzal, a few kilometres to the east, and both town and port are somewhat run-down. Everything is geared to extracting as many quetzales as possible from the rowdy day-trippers who fill the beaches at weekends.

The shoreline is separated from the mainland by the Canal de Chiquimulilla, which divides the black-sand beach from the main resort area. This is where you'll find all the **bars** and **restaurants**, most of them crowded at weekends with big ladino groups feasting on seafood and playing the jukebox until the small hours. The **hotels** are poor value and not at all enjoyable, catering as they do to a largely drunken clientele. If you want to spend a few days on the coast, head to Iztapa or Monterrico instead.

Buses between the plaza in San José and Guatemala City run every twenty minutes or so all day, with many services continuing on to Iztapa.

Puerto Quetzal and Likín

Leaving San José and following the coast in either direction brings you to the beach resorts of Guatemala's wealthy elite, who have established their own enclaves, with holiday homes built in a pale imitation of Miami Beach.

Just east of San José, there's a container port and new **marina** at **PUERTO QUETZAL** with good facilities for yachts. It's also one of the main bases for sport-fishing excursions (see p.46) in Guatemala, though there are no hotels, just a restaurant and dozens of berths. Next up is **Likín**, a wealthy residential complex based around a neat grid of canals and streets, but there's nothing to detain you here unless you want to drop by to watch the rich at play.

Iztapa and around

East of Puerto San José, it's 13km to **IZTAPA**, a venerable little port that's both a small domestic resort and an important base for **sport-fishing**. Of all the country's redundant ports, Iztapa is the oldest, as it was here that the conquistadors chose to harbour their fleets – Spanish leader Pedro de Alvarado built boats here that took him to Peru and back.

There's little sense of this historical past in Iztapa today, but the sleepy little town does have a certain low-key charm and a nice setting on the bank of the Canal de Chiquimulilla. The sweeping black-sand beach is on the other side at a separate village called **Pueblo Viejo** – a new bridge (US$2 per car) spans the canal. There's pretty reliable **surf**, with right-handers and an occasional hollow, though you'll find no facilities. That said, there are also no crowds either, with only a couple of local surfers.

Hotels in Iztapa are either pretty basic, salt-bitten places that attract domestic tourists or luxury lodges orientated squarely at sports fishermen. Of the former, the best is the family-run *Sol y Playa Tropical* (℡7881 4365; ❹) with rooms (all with private bath, and some with a/c) set around a decent-sized pool that's surrounded by palms and banana trees. The three following upmarket places work with sport-fishing tour companies, and include accommodation as part of inclusive fishing packages; all have air-conditioning and restaurants. The *Sailfish Bay Lodge* (℡2426 3909, ⓦwww.sailfishbay.com; ❾) has eight double rooms right on the beach, with a waveside pool and hot tub. *Buena Vista Resort* (℡7880 4203, ⓦwww.buenavistasportfishing.com; ❾) has a spacious canalside plot with a pool and good facilities; a marina and condos are planned here. Finally the *Pacific Fins Resort* (℡7881 4767, ⓦwww.pacificfins.com; ❾) has four attractive two-bedroom villas, a couple of private rooms and a pool in attractive landscaped grounds.

For a **meal**, *Rancho San Rafael*, right by the bridge in Iztapa, offers good seafood including *ceviche* and garlic shrimp. **Buses** run from Iztapa to both Guatemala City and Monterrico every hour (5am–5pm), and minibuses run every half-hour to Puerto San José.

Beyond Iztapa a paved road traces the 25km coastline from Pueblo Viejo to Monterrico through a littoral landscape punctuated with loofa farms. Patches of this coastline are being developed but there are still vast empty stretches of clean, dark sand to enjoy if you pull down one of the side tracks. About 6km before Monterrico in the pueblo of El Pumpo, *Utz Tzaba* (℡5318 9452, ⓦwww.utz-tzaba.com; ❼–❾) is a smart Dutch-owned place with ten immaculate rooms and four bungalows (each with living room and two bedrooms) on a spacious seafront plot where the lawns are kept well clipped; there's a large pool and a bar area.

Monterrico and around

The setting of **MONTERRICO** is one of the finest on the Pacific coast, with the scenery reduced to its basic elements: a strip of dead-straight sand, a line of powerful surf, a huge empty ocean and an enormous curving horizon. The village is a bit scruffy but steadily being tidied up, and several excellent new accommodation options have opened in recent years. It's a friendly and relaxed place fringed by the waters of the Canal de Chiquimulilla, which weaves through a fantastic network of **mangrove swamps**. The atmosphere changes a little on weekends when party-geared visitors from the capital fill up the hotels.

Monterrico sits at the heart of the **Biotopo Monterrico–Hawaii**, a nature reserve that embraces a twenty-kilometre-long beach-blessed slice of the Pacific coast and includes a vital turtle-nesting ground, abundant wetlands and the small villages of Monterrico and Hawaii. Sadly, however, the reserve's officially protected status does not prevent the widespread poaching of turtle eggs. It's well worth making your way to Monterrico, if only for the fantastically beautiful ocean setting, though if you intend to swim, be aware of the vicious **undertow**. Lifeguards are posted here at weekends, but swimmers regularly get into trouble and drownings occur.

Arrival and information

Because of the hassles involved in travelling by pubic transport to Monterrico, most people now use the fast direct **shuttle bus** services (2hr 15min; US$7–10; see box, p.110) that leave Antigua daily.

By **public transport**, you have two options. From Guatemala City's south-coast terminal at 8 Avenida & 4 Calle, Zona 12, take a bus bound for Iztapa (five daily), then a minibus to Monterrico (every 30min; 40min); or travel via Puerto

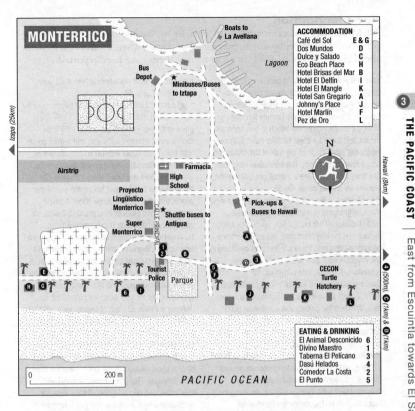

MONTERRICO

Boats to
La Avellana

Lagoon

Bus
Depot

★ Minibuses/Buses
to Iztapa

Iztapa (25km)

Airstrip

Farmacia
High
School

Proyecto
Lingüístico
Monterrico

★ Shuttle buses to
Antigua

★ Pick-ups &
Buses to Hawaii

Super
Monterrico

Tourist
Police

Parque

CECON
Turtle
Hatchery

Hawaii (8km)

N

Ⓐ (500m), Ⓒ (1km) & Ⓓ (1km)

0   200 m

PACIFIC OCEAN

ACCOMMODATION
Café del Sol   E & G
Dos Mundos   D
Dulce y Salado   C
Eco Beach Place   H
Hotel Brisas del Mar B
Hotel El Delfín   I
Hotel El Mangle   K
Hotel San Gregario A
Johnny's Place   J
Hotel Marlín   F
Pez de Oro   L

EATING & DRINKING
El Animal Desconicido   6
Divino Maestro   1
Taberna El Pelícano   3
Dasú Helados   4
Comedor La Costa   2
El Punto   5

San José and get connections from there to Iztapa, and then Monterrico. The other route is complicated and longer, perhaps taking four hours or so. Start by jumping aboard a bus bound for the El Salvador border at Ciudad Pedro de Alvarado (leaving every 30min from the same Guatemala City Zona 12 terminal), jump off at Taxisco, from where buses trundle down to La Avellana. **Boats** shuttle passengers (8 daily; 40min; US$0.60) and cars (US$13) from here back and forth to Monterrico on the opposite side of the mangrove swamp. The last buses leave Taxisco for Guatemala City around 6pm.

From the dock in Monterrico, Calle Principal passes through the coconut palms past tiendas, a football pitch, and plenty of pigs, chickens and dogs. Continue along until you come to a paved, palm-lined lane lined with open-air restaurants and you'll soon hear the pounding of the Pacific and see what all the fuss is about: Baule beach.

It's possible to **study Spanish** in Monterrico at the good Proyecto Lingüístico Monterrico (☎5619 8200, ⦿www.monterrico-guatemala.com/spanish-school) where a study package costs US$125 for twenty hours of teaching and a family homestay with all meals. Check out the community **website**, ⦿www.monterrico-guatemala.com, for up-to-date hotel and transport information.

Dial-up internet access is available beside *El Pelícano*. There's one **ATM** inside the Super Monterrico store on Calle Principal, but no **banks** in Monterrico. Otherwise, Puerto San José has several banks and ATMs. The **tourist police** (☎5551 4075) have an office on Calle Principal.

Accommodation

All Monterrico's **accommodation** is right on or just off the beach. Many places increase prices by 20–30 percent at weekends, when it's also best to book ahead. Avoid the *Hotel Baule Beach* as regular thefts have been reported.

Café del Sol turn right at the beach, walk for 250m ☎5810 0821, ⓦwww.cafe-del-sol.com. Swiss–Guatemalan-owned place with large attractively presented rooms with bright, homely furnishings. Most are set back from the beach in two separate blocks, and there's a great mirador room with sea views, but avoid those at the rear of the restaurant, which have zero privacy. The beachside restaurant has tasty food, and there's a small pool. Check the website for special deals. **❹–❺**

Dos Mundos 1.5km east of centre. Luxurious new place, with stunning minimalist-style, palapa-roofed, detached a/c bungalows, each with a huge terrace and swanky bathroom, set in immaculate beachfront gardens. There's a fine pool overlooking the rollers, a kids' pool and a good, if pricey, restaurant. Rates include breakfast. **❽**

Dulce y Salado 2km east of village centre ☎5817 9046. Enjoys a great beachside location and has nice, thatched bungalows that come with good wooden beds, mosquito nets and private bathrooms. There's also a decent-sized pool, plus fine Italian and Latin American food. **❺**

Eco Beach Place turn right at the beach, walk for 250m ☎5611 6637, ⓔecobeachplace@hotmail .com. A very hospitable guesthouse run by charming Luis (who lived in England for two years) and son Juanito. The rooms are comfortable enough, all are large and some sleep up to four; all but one have private bath. Twelve new rooms are planned on the plot next door, all with en-suite bathrooms and five with sea views. There's good grub and a nice bar area with stunning Pacific vistas from the veranda. **❺**

Hotel Brisas del Mar in the village ☎5517 1142. A bit bland but a pretty good deal, with 26 plain, tiled rooms, most with private bath, and some with a/c. There are a couple of half-clean pools here. **❸**

Hotel El Delfín at the end of C Principal, on the right ☎5702 6701. Plenty of dark, pokey rooms with fan, but head elsewhere unless it's a very busy time of year. **❷**

Hotel El Mangle turn left at beach, walk for 300m ☎5514 6517 or 5490 1336. Great place with plenty of very attractive, cosy little rooms, most with fan, bathroom and a front porch with hammock. Other a/c options are overpriced. Friendly Guatemalan management, leafy garden area, small pool and beachside restaurant. **❹**

Hotel Marlín turn left just before the end of the beach, walk for 120m ☎5208 9350. A single-storey thatched block of nine smallish rooms, all with fan and bathroom. Run by party animal DJ Roberto, so standards can slip alarmingly from time to time. Weekday rate is US$8 per head. **❹**

Hotel San Gregario behind *Johnny's Place* (in Guatemala City ☎2238 4690). Large modern block with a swimming pool and motel-style rooms. It was open, but for sale when we passed by. **❺**

Johnny's Place turn left at beach, walk for 150m ☎5812 0409. Popular with backpackers, this place has functional dorms (US$6 per head), bungalows divided into reasonable rooms (some a/c), and suites. All accommodation shares little plunge pools (though these are not always filled on weekdays). This place could be great with a little more love and attention. Things improve beachside where there's a row of hammocks, a good café-restaurant with a full bar, and a beach volleyball court. **❸–❺**

Pez de Oro turn left at beach and walk for 350m ☎7920 9785 or 2368 3684, ⓦwww.pezdeoro.com. A very well run and attractive place to stay, with lovely, spotless, thatched cottages, all with mosquito nets, wooden furniture, and bedcovers made from Guatemalan textiles (book no. 13 for a sea view). The hotel's shady plot has two small pools, and the beach-facing restaurant serves Italian and international food. **❻**

Monterrico's beach, mangrove swamp and turtle hatchery

Monterrico's impressive **beach**, a prime turtle-nesting ground (see box, pp.238–239), is a fifty-metre-wide strip of dark grey sand that's continuously pummelled by the Pacific. Its steep profile means there's usually a strong **undertow** – take particular care when the waves are big. You'll find the beach is near deserted away from the village centre, with just the odd holiday-home or fisherman's palapa between the shoreside palms. Squadrons of pelicans – flying in formation and nicknamed the "Monterrico air force" by locals – skim over the ocean, angling their wings to clip the crest of the wave as they glide along the coastline.

Behind the beach and village, the extensive **mangrove swamp** is an unusually rich environment, formed as rivers draining from the highlands find their path blocked by the black sands of the beach and spill out into this enormous watery expanse before finally finding their way to the sea through estuaries. These dark, nutrient-rich waters are superbly fertile, and four distinct types of mangrove form a dense mat of branches, interspersed with narrow canals, open lagoons, bull rushes and water lilies. The tangle of roots acts as a kind of marine nursery, offering small fish protection from their natural predators, while above the surface the dense vegetation and ready food supply provide an ideal home for hundreds of species of bird and a handful of reptiles and mammals, including racoon, iguana, alligator and opossum.

A trip into the swamp is an adventure, taking you through a complex network of channels and best done with a **guide**. Conservation group CECON, which administers the Monterrico reserve and is part of the University of San Carlos, has trained local guides – look for them on the beachfront outside the group's visitor centre (they should be sporting an ID badge). Otherwise most of the hotels can recommend a local boatman, or you could even rent a small *cayuco* (US$1.30 per hr) and paddle around yourself from the ferry dock. Note that if you rent a larger boat with an engine you won't see as much because the noise of the engine will frighten off the wildlife. You shouldn't expect to encounter anteaters and racoons, but you probably will see a good range of bird life, including kingfisher, white heron and several species of duck. The Palmilla lagoon is a particularly good spot. Failing all else, the trip is worthwhile just to watch the local fishermen casting their nets.

Be sure to drop by the headquarters of CECON, which also runs the renowned local **turtle hatchery**. The visitor centre (daily 8am–noon & 2–5pm; US$1.30) occupies a large beachside area with a shaded section of

▲ Monterrico mangroves

sand where **turtle eggs** are reburied after they have been laid. A short trail runs from the headquarters along the edge of the reserve, past enclosures of freshwater turtles, alligators and green iguanas, which are also bred for release into the wild. There are information boards, some in English. The organization seeks Spanish-speaking volunteers, as well as contacts with overseas universities. If you're interested in helping out, write to CECON USAC, Reserva Natural Monterrico, 06024 Taxisco, Santa Rosa.

Eating and drinking

Eating in Monterrico basically comes down to either dining in one of the village **comedores** on Calle Principal, or at a beachside **restaurant**. All the comedores have near-identical menus and prices, with large portions of fried fish and shrimp costing about US$6, or pasta about US$3; two good places are *Divino Maestro* and *Comedor La Costa*.

The turtles of Monterrico

The huge, sparsely populated expanses of beach around Monterrico are prime nesting sites for three types of **sea turtle**, including the largest of them all, the giant leatherback. The reserve was originally established to protect the turtles from the soup pot and curb the collection of their eggs, which are considered an aphrodisiac in Guatemala. Further dangers to the turtles include being hunted for their shells, drowned inside fishing nets and poisoned by pollution, especially plastic bags that resemble jellyfish, a favourite food. Turtles almost always nest in the dark, and on a moonless night during egg-laying season, you have a good chance of seeing one in Monterrico.

Leatherback The gargantuan leatherback is by far the largest of the world's turtles, growing to more than 2m in length and weighing up to 900kg. Called *baule* in Spanish, the leatherback gives the beach at Monterrico its name. It feeds almost exclusively on jellyfish, diving as deep as 1200m below the surface in search of its prey. As its name suggests, it's the only turtle not to have a hard exterior shell; instead it has a layer of black, soft, rubbery skin. The leatherback frequents tropical and temperate waters from Malaysia to Scotland and makes one of the longest migrations of any creature on earth – one turtle was tracked journeying 20,000km from Indonesia to the US. The species, which has been around for one hundred million years, is in severe danger of extinction as a result of long-line fishing and gill netting. It nests at Monterrico between mid-October and late December.

Olive Ridley Spread throughout the tropical waters of the Pacific, Atlantic and Indian oceans, the Olive Ridley is the most numerous of the world's eight species of marine turtle and also one of the smallest, typically around 80cm long and weighing around 35kg. Olive Ridleys gather in huge numbers off favoured beaches to mate, after which the females return en masse to nest. They are omnivores, feeding on fish and shrimp as well as sea grass and algae. They are common visitors at Monterrico (where they are known as *parlamas*) during their nesting season between July and December.

Green turtle Until very recently it was thought that a dark subspecies of the green turtle, called the East Pacific Black Turtle, nested in Monterrico. However, research published in 2007 seems to indicate that this black turtle was a misclassified green turtle. Green turtles reach more than a metre in length, typically weigh 200kg and have a characteristic dark heart-shaped shell. They are found throughout the tropics and are mainly herbivores, eating sea grasses. Historically, green turtles have been killed for their fat in many parts of the world. It's this fat, which is green in colour – their shells are usually muddy brown or grey – that gives the turtle its name. The green turtle nesting season in Monterrico is also from July to December.

On the beach, *Johnny's* is one of the more inexpensive places, with fish, spaghetti and burgers, though service can be slow. The *Eco Beach Place* specializes in top-quality **grilled meats**, including parrillas, while *Pez de Oro* has a nice dining area with checked tablecloths and Italian food, omelettes (US$3.50) and sandwiches ($4). *Dos Mundos* also serves great, if pricey Italian food, plus specials like paella, and *caldo de mariscos*. *Café del Sol* is a relaxed place for a snack or meal with a fine view of the waves from its terrace. Probably the finest cuisine in town is just inland from *Johnny's* at the attractive palapa-roofed, Swiss-owned *Taberna El Pelícano* (℡7848 1645; closed Tues) which has a European-style menu, including pasta and risotto and daily specials. Meals here cost around US$10–15 a head; reserve a table for Saturday night. Finally there's a superb Sicilian-owned **ice-cream** shack called *Dasú Helados*, between *Pez de Oro* and *Dos Mundos*; they also sell handicrafts here.

Eggs and hueveros

All the species of turtle use similar **nesting** techniques, hauling themselves up the beach, laboriously digging a hole about 50cm deep with their flippers, and then with great effort depositing a clutch of a hundred or so soft, golfball-sized eggs. The turtles then bury the eggs and head back into the ocean. The eggs of the two smaller turtles take about fifty days to hatch, those of the leatherback require 72. When their time comes, the tiny turtles, no larger than the palm of your hand, use their flippers to dig their way out and make a mad dash for the water, desperately trying to avoid the waiting seabirds. Once they are in the water, their existence is still very hazardous for the first few years of life; only one in a hundred makes it to maturity.

Watching a turtle lay her eggs at Monterrico should be a memorable experience, but the presence of the local *hueveros* (egg collectors) may ensure that it's not. In season, Baule beach is patrolled by sentries, torches in hand, scanning the waves for turtles. After a turtle comes ashore and lays its eggs, these poachers delve straight into the nest. Most foreign witnesses are content to take a photo and touch one of the bewildered creatures before it claws its way back to the ocean (note that you shouldn't use flash photography as it can upset and disorient the turtles), although some braver souls have challenged the *hueveros* and been threatened with machetes.

Officially, the taking of eggs is outlawed, but an informal deal has been struck so that out of every clutch of eggs collected, a dozen are donated to the reserve's turtle hatchery, from where thousands of baby turtles are released each year. This agreement is designed to ease relations between the local community, who sell the eggs for US$2.50 a dozen, and the conservationists. The ethics may be debatable, but some visitors buy entire clutches from *hueveros* (most of whom are extremely poor) and donate these eggs to the CECON hatchery.

During nesting season, visitors can donate to the project by backing a turtle hatchling in the Saturday "**turtle race**" on the beach. The sponsor of the winning baby turtle gets a dinner for two at a shore-side restaurant. However, most experts are now uneasy about encouraging such races (as well as close contact or "petting" of turtles), as the races involve grouping baby hatchlings together in buckets for days, a practice that exhausts and disorients the turtles and interferes with the natal homing instinct by which they return to their beach of birth.

There are a few **bars** in Monterrico that tend to be quiet during the week and get rowdy at weekends when the Guatemala City kids cruise into town. One of the liveliest is the beachfront *El Animal Desconicido*, which has a booming sound system and plenty of drink specials. In a prime spot at the end of Calle Principal, the new Dutch-owned bar *Sed* promises to be a great location for a cocktail or beer, with stylish lounge-bar decor. Inland from the beach, the bar-club *El Punto* is owned by electronic DJ/music producer Roberto so expect a serious rave-up to driving techno and drum'n'bass; there's a pool table here too.

East to Hawaii

About 7km east along the beach from Monterrico, isolated **HAWAII** is a tiny, relaxed little fishing village. There's a large **turtle project** (daily 9am–6pm; donation expected) a kilometre before the village, run by the group ARCAS, which releases around 30,000 turtles each year into the Pacific. There's plenty for the visitor to see, with a couple of trails, egg-count charts and lots of information about turtles and the myths and beliefs associated with them throughout the world. **Volunteers** are always needed (at any time of year, though June to Nov is the main nesting season), and though they prefer you to get in touch first, you can always just show up. The work is primarily nocturnal, with volunteers walking the beach collecting sea-turtle eggs and assisting in the management of the hatcheries. You can also assist in environmental education, mangrove reforestation, construction, and caiman and iguana captive-breeding. Dorm accommodation costs US$60 a week (meals not included). Contact ARCAS (T5849 8988, Wwww.arcasguatemala.com). The two upmarket **hotels** in Hawaii are poor value and not that attractive; a couple of stores offer simple meals. Four daily **buses** connect Hawaii with Monterrico.

From Escuintla to El Salvador

Heading east from Escuintla the coastal highway brings you to **TAXISCO**, a quiet farming centre, famous for its cheese, which is set to the north of the main road. From here a branch road runs to La Avellana, from where you can catch a boat to Monterrico.

Shortly before it reaches Taxisco the highway passes one of Guatemala's most unusual tourist sights, the **Auto Safari Chapín** (Wwww.autosafarichapin.org; Tues–Sun 9.30am–5pm; US$8), Central America's only safari park. The park, a kilometre south of the highway (at Km87.5), has animals including giraffes, hippos, a pair of black rhinos, tapir and big cats including African lions, pumas and jaguar. There's a superbly comprehensive collection of Central American animals, snakes and birds. The park is clean and well organized with viewing platforms and wildlife trails, and the animals are well cared for. Every species, except for the black rhino, has been successfully bred here in captivity.

The entrance fee entitles you to a trip through the park in a minibus, although you can drive yourself if you have a car, and there are swimming pools, a restaurant and picnic areas.

Chiquimulilla and Las Lisas

Beyond Taxisco is **CHIQUIMULILLA**, from where another branch road heads up into the eastern highlands, through acres of lush coffee plantations, to the town of Cuilapa. Chiquimulilla is in the heart of ladino cowboy country, and superb **leather goods**, including machete cases and saddles, are handcrafted in the market. It also has several banks with ATMs including Banrural, at 1 Calle and

Fiestas

Ladino culture dominates on the Pacific coast – despite the presence of a massive migrant labour force – so fiestas here tend to be more along the lines of fairs, with parades, amusement rides, fireworks, sporting events and heavy drinking. You'll see very little in the way of traditional costume or pre-Columbian dances, although marimba bands are popular and many of the fiestas are still held on local saints' days. There's no doubt that the people of the coast like to have a good time and know how to enjoy themselves. Allegiances tend to be less local than those of the Maya population, and national holidays are celebrated as much as local ones.

January
11–18 Cuyotenango, main day 15th, events include some traditional dancing
12–15 Taxisco, events include bullfighting
12–16 Colomba, events include bullfighting

February
Varies Tecún Umán

March
11–19 Coatepeque, main day 15th
16–22 Puerto San José, main day 19th
Varies Ocós

April
30–May 4 Chiquimulilla, main day 3rd

July
25 Coatepeque, in honour of Santiago Apóstol

August
4–8 Champerico, main day 6th

October
20–26 Iztapa, main day 24th

November
23–26 Siquinalá

December
6–12 Retalhuleu, main day 8th
6–15 Escuintla, main day 8th
18–21 Chicacao, includes traditional dancing
31 La Democracia

1 Avenida, Zona 3. If you need a bed, try the good-value *Turicentro Baru* (☎7885 0374; ❹), on the main highway at Km114.5, which has motel-style rooms, most with air-conditioning and TV, and a pool. Buses run every thirty minutes to both the border and Guatemala City via Taxisco, and hourly to Cuilapa.

Heading on towards the border, the highway is raised slightly above the rest of the coastal plain, allowing great views to the sea. A few kilometres south of the road, archeological digs at a long-forgotten Maya site called **La Nueva** have recently yielded some fascinating stelae and evidence that more than five thousand people lived here between the years 250 and 900 AD.

A short distance before the border a side road runs off to the seashore village of **LAS LISAS**, another good spot for spending time by the sea – especially if you plan to stay at the fine hotel *Isleta de Gaia* (☎7885 0044, ⓦwww.isleta-de-gaia .com; ❽–❾). This idyllic place, located on a sandy offshore islet, has twelve gorgeous bamboo-and-thatch bungalows with either ocean or lagoon views, a big pool, restaurant food prepared by a French chef and a lovely clean beach – though again watch out for the undertow. You'll have to hire a boat (around US$15) to get to the hotel from the village of Las Lisas.

Hourly **buses** run between Las Lisas and Chiquimulilla 8am to 5pm (1hr 30min).

The border with El Salvador

The coastal highway finally reaches the border with El Salvador at the small settlement of **CIUDAD PEDRO DE ALVARADO**. Most of the commercial traffic and all of the pullman buses use the highland route to El Salvador, and consequently things are fairly quiet and easy-going here; the border is open 24 hours. The few places to stay on the Guatemalan side are run-down. Second-class buses run to and from Guatemala City every thirty minutes or so until about 7pm, though minibuses run later to Chiquimulilla.

Travel details

Buses

Buses are the best way to get around on the Pacific coast, and the main highway, from Guatemala City to the Mexican border, is served by a constant flow of pullmans. Fewer pullmans head in the other direction, to the border with El Salvador, though there is a regular stream of second-class buses. On either of these main routes you can hop between buses and expect one to come along every thirty minutes or so, but if you plan to leave the highways, then it's best to travel to the nearest large town and find a local bus from there.

The coastal highway

Buses travelling from Guatemala City to the **Mexican border** (5hr) call every thirty minutes or so at all the main towns along the coastal highway. The bulk of these leave from the terminal at 19 Calle and 9 Avenida in Zona 1. The main companies plying the route to the Talismán and Tecún Umán border crossings are Fortaleza del Sur (hourly, midnight–7pm; ☎2230 3390) and Chinita (16 daily, 1am–6pm; ☎2251 9144); both outfits have offices on 19 Calle between 8 and 9 avenidas in Zona 1. If you're heading direct into Mexico, three companies offer buses to **Tapachula** (see p.89 for details).

Heading in the other direction, buses leave every thirty minutes for **Taxisco** (3hr) and **Chiquimulilla** (3hr 30min) from the Zona 12 Trébol terminal in Guatemala City. Many buses continue on to the border with El Salvador at **Cuidad Pedro de Alvarado** (1hr from Chiquimulilla).

Coatepeque to: Retalhuleu (50min); Tecún Umán (40min).

Cocales to: Escuintla (30min).

Escuintla to: Antigua (1hr 15min); Guatemala City (1hr).

Retalhuleu to: Cocales (50min); Mazatenango (30min).

Branching off the coastal highway

To Champerico: From Retalhuleu (every 30min; 1hr 20min).

To Iztapa: From Guatemala City (five daily; 2hr 30min).

To Las Lisas: From Chiquimulilla (hourly; 1hr 30min).

To Monterrico: From Iztapa (hourly; 40min).

To Puerto San José: From Guatemala City (every 30min; 2hr); hourly buses continue on to Iztapa (30min from San José).

To Tilapa: From Coatepeque (every 30min; 2hr 30min).

East to the Caribbean

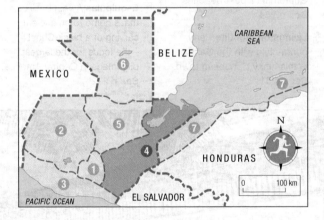

CHAPTER 4　Highlights

* **Quiriguá's carvings** Miniature Maya site with colossal stelae stones and some astonishing carved altars. See p.247

* **Hotel del Norte** Enjoy the faded Caribbean class of Puerto Barrios' oldest hotel. See p.252

* **Punta de Manabique** A Caribbean-coast nature reserve, rich in wildlife and boasting some of Guatemala's best beaches. See p.254

* **Lívingston nightlife** Party punta-style with the Garífuna in this funky Caribbean town. See p.261

* **Río Dulce** The boat journey through this soaring, jungle-clad gorge is a hair-in-the-air, exhilarating trip. See p.261

* **Hot spring waterfall** Soak away an afternoon or two at the exquisite hot spring–fed waterfall at the *Finca el Paraíso*. See p.265

* **Volcán de Ipala** This remote volcano's summit has a stunning crater lake. See p.270

* **Esquipulas** A vast basilica that's home to an ancient carving of a black Christ – the focus for the largest pilgrimage in Central America. See p.272

▲ Hotel del Norte, Puerto Barrios

East to the Caribbean

The main highway northeast from the capital, the Carretera al Atlántico, at first descends through a particularly arid, virtually unpopulated region before meeting up with the Río Motagua at the El Rancho junction, where the road is surrounded by desert. From here on the highway runs through the **Motagua valley**, a broad corridor of low-lying land that separates the Sierra del Espíritu Santo, marking the border with Honduras, from the Sierra de las Minas. This valley soon opens out into a massive flood plain with parallel ridges rising on either side. The land is fantastically fertile and lush with vegetation at all times of the year, and the air is thick with humidity.

Dampened by tropical heat and repeated cloudbursts, the eastern section of the valley was densely populated in Maya times, when it served as an important trade route connecting the highlands with the Caribbean coast, and also was one of the main sources of jade. Following the decline of the Maya civilization, the area lay virtually abandoned until the end of the nineteenth century when the **United Fruit Company** cleared and colonized the land, planting thousands of acres with bananas and reaping massive profits. At the height of its fortunes, the company was powerful enough to bring down the government and effectively monopolized the country's trade and transport. Today bananas are still the main crop, though cattle are becoming increasingly important.

For the traveller, the Motagua valley is the main route to and from Petén, and most people get no more than a fleeting glimpse of it through a bus window on the Carretera al Atlántico. But two fascinating Maya sites are in this area: **Quiriguá**, just 4km from the main road, and the great ruins of **Copán**, just across the border in Honduras (a side-trip of a day or two) and covered in depth in Chapter Seven.

The region to the north of the Motagua valley is dominated by the subtropical **Río Dulce** and **Lago de Izabal**, a vast expanse of freshwater ringed by isolated villages, swamps and hot springs. From Lago de Izabal, you can sail to the Caribbean past a manatee nature-reserve and through the spectacular gorges of the **Río Dulce** to the coast at **Lívingston**, a laid-back town that's home to Guatemala's black Garífuna people. Boats connect Lívingston with the largely forgettable port of **Puerto Barrios**, jumping-off point for the coastal route into Honduras or boats to Belize.

The **eastern highlands**, a seldom-visited region east of the capital, offer few sights for the traveller. The towns are hot and dusty, but the scenery is magnificent in places, with the beautiful isolation of the **Ipala volcano** and its stunning crater lake a highlight. **Esquipulas**, home of the famous Black Christ and the scene of Central America's largest annual pilgrimage, is another curiosity.

The Motagua valley

Leaving Guatemala City, the Carretera al Atlántico also forms the main route to Cobán, until the road divides at the **El Rancho junction**, besides the decaying carcass of a huge abandoned paper mill. Here a branch road climbs into the highlands of the Verapaces, while the main highway continues down the Motagua valley through a dry and distinctly inhospitable landscape. The first place of any note is the **Río Hondo junction** where the road divides, with one arm heading south to Esquipulas and the three-way **border** with Honduras and El Salvador, and the main branch continuing on to the coast. At the junction, you'll find an army of food sellers swarming around every bus that stops and a line of comedores, as well as a number of motels scattered around. About 22km east of Río Hondo is the impressive, well-organized **Valle Dorado** water park (Tues–Sun 9am–5pm; adults US$7.50, children US$5.50 per day), where a plethora of slides and pools set in shady grounds makes for a popular weekend retreat for Guatemalans. If you stay at the *Valle Dorado* motel, at Km149 (℡7933 1111, Ⓦwww.hotelvalledorado.com; ⑥), you get free entry to the park. Otherwise there are other options around Km126 including the *Hotel Nuevo Pasabién* (℡7933 0606; Ⓦwww.hotelpasabien.com; ⑥), with spacious air-conditioned bungalows and a pool.

On down the valley the landscape starts to undergo a radical transformation; the flood plain opens out and the cacti are gradually overwhelmed by a

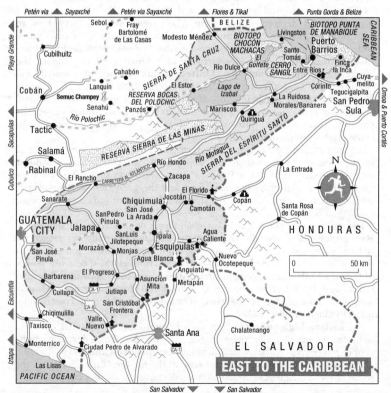

profusion of tropical growth. It was this supremely rich flood-plain that was chosen by both the Maya and the United Fruit Company, to the great benefit of both.

The ruins of Quiriguá

Of one thing there is no doubt; a large city once stood there; its name is lost, its history unknown; and no account of its existence has ever before been published. For centuries it has lain as completely buried as if covered with the lava of Vesuvius. Every traveller from Yzabal to Guatimala [sic] has passed within three hours of it; we ourselves had done the same; and yet there it lay, like the rock-built city of Edom, unvisited, unsought, and utterly unknown.

John Lloyd Stephens (1841)

In 1841 John Stephens was so impressed with the ruins at **Quiriguá** that he planned to take them home, using the Río Motagua to float the stones to the Caribbean so that "the city might be transported bodily and set up in New York". Fortunately the asking price was beyond his means and the ruins remained buried in the rainforest until 1909, when the land was bought by the United Fruit Company.

Today things are somewhat different: the ruins themselves are partially restored and reconstructed, and banana plantations stretch to the horizon in all directions. Few travellers visit Quiriguá, which is a shame because it has some of the finest of all Maya carving. Only nearby Copán can match the magnificent stelae, altars and zoomorphs that are covered in well-preserved and superbly intricate glyphs and portraits.

A dense patch of lush rainforest surrounds the ruins, and weather conditions are decidedly **tropical**. Indeed, cloudbursts are the rule and the buzz of mosquitoes is almost uninterrupted – bring repellent.

A brief history of Quiriguá

The **early history** of Quiriguá is still fairly vague, and all that is certain is that towards the end of the Late Preclassic period (400 BC–250 AD) migrants from the north, possibly Putun Maya from the Yucatán peninsula, established themselves as the rulers here. Thereafter, in the Early Classic period (250–600 AD), the centre was dominated by Copán and doubtless valued for its position on the banks of the Río Motagua, an important trade route, and as a source of jade, which is found throughout the valley. At this stage the rulers themselves may well have come from Copán, just 50km away. There certainly seems to have been close ties between the two sites: the architecture, and in particular the carving that adorns it, makes this very clear.

In the Late Classic period (600–800 AD) Quiriguá really started to come into its own. The site's own name glyph is first used in 731 AD, just six years after its greatest leader, **Cauac Sky**, ascended to the throne. As a member of the long-standing Sky dynasty, Cauac Sky took control of a city that had already embarked upon a campaign of aggressive expansion and was in the process of asserting its independence from Copán. In 738 AD matters came to a head when he captured and executed Eighteen Rabbit, Copán's ruler, thus making the final break (see p.365). For the rest of his 56-year reign the city experienced an unprecedented building boom: the bulk of the great stelae date from this period and are decorated with Cauac Sky's portrait. For a century Quiriguá dominated the lower Motagua valley and its highly prized resources. Cauac Sky

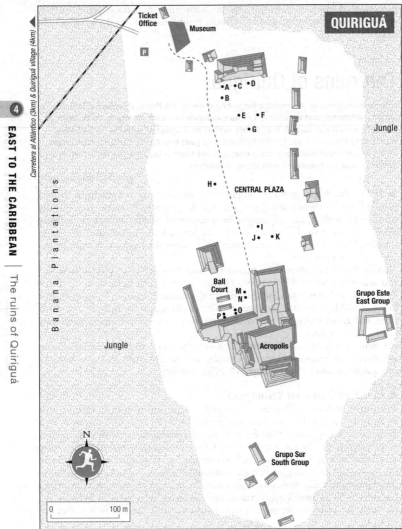

Carretera al Atlántico (3km) & Quiriguá village (4km)

QUIRIGUÁ

Ticket Office

Museum

P

Jungle

CENTRAL PLAZA

Ball Court

Grupo Este East Group

Acropolis

Jungle

Banana Plantations

N

Grupo Sur South Group

0   100 m

died in 771 and was succeeded by his son, Sky Xul, who ruled for nineteen years until being usurped by Jade Sky, who took the throne in 790 AD. Under Jade Sky, Quiriguá reached its peak, with fifty years of extensive building, including a radical reconstruction of the acropolis. But from the end of Jade Sky's rule, in the middle of the ninth century, the historical record fades out, as does the period of prosperity and power.

The ruins

Entering the site beneath the ever-dripping trees, you emerge at the northern end of the **Great Plaza**. To the left-hand side of the path from the ticket office is a badly ruined pyramid; directly in front of this are the **stelae** for which Quiriguá is justly famous. The nine stelae in the plaza are the tallest in the Maya World and their carving is some of the best. The style, similar in many ways to that of Copán, always follows a basic pattern, with portraits on the main faces and glyphs covering the sides. As for the figures, they represent the city's rulers, with Cauac Sky depicted on no fewer than seven (A, C, D, E, F, H and J). Two unusual features are particularly clear: the vast headdresses, which dwarf the faces, and the beards, a fashion that caught on in Quiriguá thirty years after it became popular in Copán. Many of the figures are shown clutching a ceremonial bar, the symbol of office, which has at one end a long-nosed god – possibly Chaac, the rain god – and at the other the head of a snake. The glyphs, crammed into the remaining space, record dates and events during the reign of the relevant ruler.

Largest of the stelae is E, which rises to a height of 8m and weighs 65 tonnes. All the stelae are carved out of an ideal fine-grained sandstone, from a quarry about 5km from the site. The stones were probably rolled to the site on skids, set up, and then worked by sculptors standing on scaffolding. Fortunately for them the stone was soft once it had been cut, and fortunately for us it hardened with age.

Another feature that has helped Quiriguá earn its fame is the bizarre, altar-like **zoomorphs**: six blocks of stone carved with interlacing animal and human figures. Some, like the turtle, frog and jaguar, can be recognized with relative ease, while others are either too faded or too elaborate to be easily made out. The best of the lot is P, which shows a figure seated in Buddha-like pose, interwoven with a maze of others.

Around the plaza are several other interesting features. Along the eastern side are some unrestored structures that may have had something to do with Quiriguá's role as a river **port** – since the city's heyday the river has moved at least 1km from its original course. At the southern end of the plaza near the main zoomorphs, you can just make out the shape of a **ball court** hemmed in on three sides by viewing stands. The **acropolis** itself, the only structure of any real size that still stands, is bare of decoration. Trenches dug beneath it have shown that it was built on top of several previous versions, the earliest ones constructed out of rough river stones. Apart from these central structures, there are a few smaller unrestored complexes scattered in the surrounding forest, but nothing of particular interest.

Quiriguá practicalities

The **ruins** (daily 7.30am–5pm; US$10.50) are situated 66km beyond the junction at Río Hondo, and 4km from the main road, reached down a side road that serves the banana industry. All buses running between Puerto Barrios and Guatemala City pass by. From the access road minibuses, motorbikes and pickups shuttle passengers back and forth to the entrance to the ruins, where there are a couple of mini-tiendas and a coconut vendor or two. A small site **museum** has informative displays about the site's historical significance and its geopolitical role in Maya times as well as a diorama showing the extent of the ruins that remain unexcavated.

To get back to the highway, wait until a bus or tuk-tuk turns up. If you want to walk back to Quiriguá village, you can take a short cut by heading towards the highway for 2km along the access road, then turning left (west) and following the (disused) train track – it's a further kilometre to the village.

The **village** – also known as Quiriguá – is just off the highway, about 2km back towards Guatemala City. It's a run-down sort of place, strung out along the railway track, but in the past it was famous for its hospital specializing in the treatment of tropical diseases, run by the United Fruit Company. This imposing building, which still stands on the hill above the track, is now a state-run workers' medical centre; there's a statue of Scots doctor Neil Macphail (who ran the hospital here for forty years) in front of the structure. The two basic **places to stay** in the village are not great, but the *Hotel y Restaurante Royal* (T7947 3639; ❷–❸), with old rooms downstairs (some are windowless) and better rooms on the upper floor, will do for a night or a meal.

To the coast: Puerto Barrios

Heading on towards the Caribbean, an additional 15km brings you to **La Trinchera**, junction for the branch road to Mariscos on the shores of Lago de Izabal. Further down the Motagua valley, the road pushes on through an evergreen landscape of cattle ranches and fruit trees, splitting again at the junction for the twin towns of **MORALES** and **BANANERA**, a ramshackle collection of railway tracks that was the headquarters of the United Fruit Company (see p.403) for much of the twentieth century. Today these squalid towns represent nothing but an inconvenient delay for the traveller, as many second-class buses pull in here for a stop of thirty minutes or so.

A short distance beyond the turn for Morales/Bananera, you pass the **Ruidosa junction**, from where the highway heads northwest, across the Río Dulce. A further 47km to the northeast and you reach the Caribbean, with the road dividing for the last time, right to the old port of Puerto Barrios and left to Puerto Santo Tomás de Castillo, the modern town and dock.

Puerto Barrios and around

At the final junction on the highway, unless you happen to be driving a banana truck, the turn for **PUERTO BARRIOS** is the one to take. Hot and sprawling, the town is a pretty forlorn place, its wide, poorly lit streets badly potholed. Barrios' once fine legacy of old wooden Caribbean-style buildings is disappearing fast, only to be replaced by faceless concrete hotels and stores and an excess of hard-drinking bars. The only reason most travellers come here is to get somewhere else: to Lívingston or Belize by boat or south to Honduras via Corinto.

The town was founded in the 1880s by President Rufino Barrios, but its port soon fell into the hands of the United Fruit Company, who used their control of the railways to ensure that the bulk of trade passed this way. Puerto Barrios was Guatemala's main port for most of the twentieth century, and although the fruit company was exempt from almost all tax, the users of its port were obliged to pay heavy duties. In the 1930s it cost as much to ship coffee to New Orleans from Brazil as it did from Guatemala. In the late years of the last century a decline set in, however, as exporters used modern docks elsewhere.

In recent years Barrios has seen something of an upturn in its fortunes as key infrastructure – including the container port and airstrip – have been modernized. A new cruise-ship terminal has also been constructed offshore, but tourists are quickly whisked away from the town itself to more attractive destinations such as Quiriguá and Río Dulce.

Arrival and information

Puerto Barrios lacks a purpose-built bus station. Litegua **buses**, which serve all destinations along the Carretera al Atlántico, have their own terminal in the

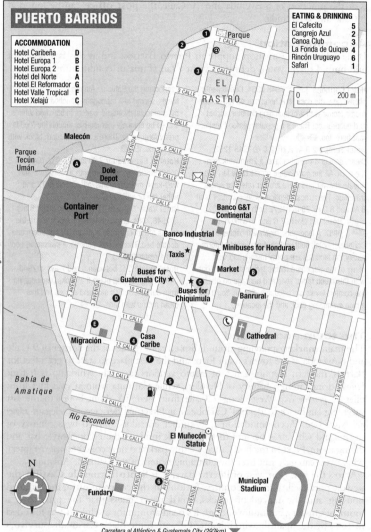

PUERTO BARRIOS

ACCOMMODATION
Hotel Caribeña	D
Hotel Europa 1	B
Hotel Europa 2	E
Hotel del Norte	A
Hotel El Reformador	G
Hotel Valle Tropical	F
Hotel Xelajú	C

EATING & DRINKING
El Cafecito	5
Cangrejo Azul	2
Canoa Club	3
La Fonda de Quique	4
Rincón Uruguayo	6
Safari	1

Parque

1 CALLE

2 CALLE

EL RASTRO

3 CALLE

4 CALLE

0   200 m

Malecón

Parque Tecún Umán

5 CALLE

6 CALLE

Dole Depot

3 AVENIDA · 4 AVENIDA · 5 AVENIDA · 6 AVENIDA · 7 AVENIDA · 8 AVENIDA · 9 AVENIDA

Container Port

7 CALLE

Banco G&T Continental

8 CALLE

Banco Industrial

9 CALLE

Taxis ★   ★ Minibuses for Honduras

Market

Buses for Guatemala City ★   ★ Banrural
Buses for Chiquimula ★ C

Boats to Livingston & Punta Gorda

2 AVENIDA · 3 AVENIDA

D

10 CALLE

E

11 CALLE

Casa Caribe

Cathedral

Migración

F

12 CALLE

5

13 CALLE

Bahía de Amatique

14 CALLE

Río Escondido

15 CALLE

El Muñecón Statue

N

16 CALLE

G

6

Municipal Stadium

Fundary

17 CALLE

18 CALLE

Carretera al Atlántico & Guatemala City (293km) ▼

centre of town on 6 Avenida, between 9 and 10 calles. Second-class buses to Chiquimula and Esquipulas arrive and depart from a stop opposite Litegua's depot, beside the railway tracks. **Taxis** (called *carreras* here) are everywhere in Barrios – drivers toot for customers as they ply the streets.

There's no Inguat tourist office in town. Check at the Litegua terminal for bus schedules and at the **dock** at the end of 12 Calle for boat departures to Living-ston and to Punta Gorda in Belize (see "Travel connections"). For **internet**, head to Café Internet on 5 Avenida. There are plenty of **banks** in Puerto Barrios, including Banrural at 8 Avenida and 9 Calle, and Banco Industrial at 7 Avenida and 7 Calle; both have ATMs. The **Telgua** office (daily 7am–midnight) is at the junction of 8 Avenida and 10 Calle; the **post office** can be found at 6 Calle and 6 Avenida.

Accommodation

Budget **hotels** are in short supply in Puerto Barrios, and as this is a very hot and humid town, you'll definitely want a fan, if not air conditioning.

Hotel Caribeña 4 Av ☎7948 0384. Conveniently placed near the dock, this hotel has 43 reasonable rooms (some with a/c) including doubles, triples and quadruples. There's a popular seafood restaurant here, too. ❸–❹

Hotel Europa 2 3 Av and 12 C ☎7948 1292. Clean, safe and friendly place, a 2min walk from the dock. All the good-value rooms have fan and private shower and there are fair rates for single travellers. The almost identical *Hotel Europa 1* is at 8 Av and 8 C (☎7948 0127). Both ❸

🏃 **Hotel del Norte** 7 C and 1 Av ☎7948 0087. A landmark, highly atmospheric Caribbean hotel, built entirely from wood. Unfortunately the facilities are pretty historic too, and many of the clapboard rooms lack bathrooms, but with this much faded style and heritage on offer the comfort levels are adequate enough. You'll find a nice swimming pool, and the location,

overlooking the Bahía de Amatique, is magnificent. Meals, served in a mahogany-panelled restaurant by immaculately attired waiters in starched whites, should be uniquely memorable, though the food is pretty forgettable. There's also a modern block with a/c rooms. ❹–❺

Hotel El Reformador 7 Av and 16 C ☎7948 0533. Efficiently run place with a restaurant and well-kept, modern rooms, all with cable TV and either fan or a/c. ❸–❹

Hotel Valle Tropical 12 C, between 5 and 6 avs ☎7948 7084. Large motel-style block where the rooms are all equipped with a/c, TV, bathroom and double bed. There's safe parking, a swimming pool and a restaurant. ❻

Hotel Xelajú 9 C, between 6 and 7 avs ☎7948 0482. Long-running place that looks unappetizing from outside, but it's safe and secure and has clean rooms with fans. ❷–❸

The town and around

The main **market**, sprawling around disused railway lines at the corner of 9 Calle and 6 Avenida, is the town's main focus and the best place to start to get a feel for Barrios' modern identity. Lines of ladino vendors furiously whisk up lush fruit *licuado* drinks from a battery of blenders, while Garífuna women swat flies from piles of *pan de coco*. West along 7 Calle from here, it's about 800m to the last surviving landmark to Barrios' Caribbean architectural heritage, the elegant *Hotel del Norte* (see "Accommodation"), its timber corridors warped by a century of storms and salty air – be sure to take a look inside at the colonial-style bar and dining room. Next to the hotel, there's a tiny park and new concrete *malecón* (pier), where you can gaze out over the glistening waters of the Bahía de Amatique.

Across the bay, 7km west of Puerto Barrios, is **Santo Tomás de Castillo**, the newest port facility in the country. To look at the concrete plaza, the planned housing and the fenced-off docks, you'd never guess that the place had a moment's history, but oddly enough it's been around for a while. It was founded in 1604 by the Spanish, who inhabited it with some Black Caribs, the survivors of an expedition against pirates on Roatán Island. The pirates in turn sacked Santo Tomás, but it was revived in 1843, when a Belgian colony was established here. Today it's connected by a regular shuttle of local buses to Puerto Barrios, though other than the docks themselves there's nothing much to see.

Eating

Puerto Barrios really excels at **fish and seafood**, and you should certainly try some *tapado* (seafood soup with coconut, plantain and spices) while you're here, though it's not a cheap dish to prepare. **Comedores** are around the market – look out for *pan de coco* (coconut bread) and local speciality *tortillas de harina* (wheat tortillas stuffed with meat and beans).

El Cafecito 13 C, between 6 & 7 avs. A cheery little café with an espresso machine, plenty of sweet and savoury snacks, plus some Portuguese dishes.

Cangrejo Azul end of 4 Av. Huge, barn-like seafood restaurant with a good local reputation that also has a dining table or two set on stilts out in the bay. Try the *camarones a la plancha* or *sopa pescado*.

Rincón Uruguayo 7 Av and 16 C. Meat-eaters won't do better than this (relatively) moderately priced place, which excels at *parrilladas* (South American-style meat barbecues). A few veggie dishes like barbecued spring onions and *papas asados* are also on the menu. Closed Mon.

Safari northern end of 5 Av. North of the centre in the Rastro barrio, this large restaurant is renowned for its seafood (around US$8–10), particularly *tapado*. It is, however, a bit overrated.

Drinking, clubs and cultural activities

Puerto Barrios has its share of striptease **bars** – a lot of the action is centred near 6 and 7 avenidas and 6 and 7 calles. Reggaeton and punta rock are the sounds on the street in Barrios, and you'll catch a fair selection at weekends in the *Canoa Club*, on 5 Avenida and 2 Calle. For more cerebral pursuits, Casa Caribe, on the corner of 11 Calle and 5 Avenida, is a small **culture centre** that features art and photographic exhibitions.

Overland to Honduras

Puerto Barrios is the jumping-off point to the north coast of Honduras and the Bay Islands, a fairly straightforward, if slow, journey via San Pedro Sula, Honduras's second city. To **get to Honduras** from Barrios, minibuses depart from the marketplace (every 30min, 6.30am–4.30pm; 1hr) and pass through the town of Entre Ríos (for *migración*) before continuing on to the border. You may be asked for unofficial border taxes of a dollar or two as you pass through. Note that travellers with their **own vehicles** have reported lengthy delays and hassles entering Honduras here, including the need to pay a fee of about US$30 for a "custodian" to accompany you to the main immigration office in Puerto Cortés where vehicle permits (typically US$40 per motorbike and around US$125 per car, but some have negotiated discounts) are issued. The El Florido border (see p.358) is much less hassle.

On the Honduran side, pick-ups and microbuses leave the border to the village of **Corinto**, 3km away, from where buses depart for Puerto Cortés

---

Puerto Barrios: travel connections

Litegua **pullmans** – which are some of the country's best – ply the Carretera al Atlántico to Guatemala City 22 times daily from 1am to 4pm (5hr–5hr 30min) from their private terminal just southeast of the market on 6 Avenida. Seven of these travel via a detour to Morales, which adds thirty minutes to the journey; the other *directos* (some double-deckers) travel direct to the capital. Tickets can be bought in advance, although it's not necessary except perhaps on a Sunday afternoon. **Second-class buses** go from Puerto Barrios to Chiquimula, all via Morales, every hour from 6am to 5pm (4hr 30min). Hourly minibuses leave from the marketplace for Río Dulce, or take any bus heading west as far as La Ruidosa junction and get a connection there. If you're heading for Copán in a hurry it's quickest to get a *directo* as far as Río Hondo and an onward connection from there.

Lanchas leave for Lívingston from the **dock** at the end of 12 Calle when full (about every 40min; 6.30am–6pm; US$3.50; 30min); a much slower daily ferry departs at 10am and 5pm (US$2; 1hr 30min). To Punta Gorda in Belize, a *lancha* leaves at 10am (US$20; 1hr 15min). If you're heading to Belize, remember to clear **migración** (7am–7pm) first and pay your US$10 exit tax; the office is on 12 Calle, a block inland from the dock.

(hourly; 2hr) via Omoa. If you set out early from Puerto Barrios, you should get to San Pedro Sula by lunchtime, and it's certainly possible to catch an afternoon flight to one of the Bay Islands (see Chapter 7), arriving in time for a sunset cocktail at one of the beach bars. San Pedro Sula is well connected with Puerto Cortés by Citul and other buses (every 30min, 5am–8pm; 1hr 15min); the Citul terminal is located just across the plaza from the *migración*.

Punta de Manabique

North of Puerto Barrios, the hooked peninsula that juts into the Bahía de Amatique, the **Punta de Manabique**, contains most of Guatemala's best Caribbean beaches and offers superb ecotourism opportunities. Most of the area has been designated a nature reserve, the Biotopo Punta de Manabique, which is managed by the conservation group **Fundary**. It's one of the richest wetland habitats in Central America, and the swamps, mangroves and patches of flooded rainforest are home to caimen, iguana, spider and howler monkeys, peccary, plus a few manatee, some jaguar, tapir and bountiful birdlife, including the extremely rare yellow-headed parrot (*Amazona oratrix*). The reserve also includes the adjacent coastal water and the only coral-reef outcrops in Guatemalan waters.

About one thousand people, mainly immigrants from western Guatemala, eke out a living in Manabique, surviving by subsistence fishing (mainly for sardines, which are then salted) and hunting (particularly iguana) and cultivating small rice paddies. Their livelihood is increasingly under threat from cattle ranchers who are starting to encroach into the drier lands in the south of the reserve. Most locals are very poor, and Fundary have been busy establishing basic health care measures, setting up schools and providing teachers, and raising environmental awareness. They've also been working to develop **ecotourism** in the area, an initiative that's included the establishment of a rustic lodge, *El Saraguate* (reservations through Fundary; US$9 per bed), which offers four clean rooms, each with three or four beds, and a restaurant that serves tasty meals: lobster, grilled fish and chicken dishes. From the lodge there's a purpose-built wooden walkway over nearby swampland, jungle paths and coastal walks along stunning palm-fringed white-sand beaches, as well as excellent swimming. Boat trips also can be arranged along the **Canal Inglés** ("English Channel") – named after British loggers who dug a ten-kilometre trench between Laguna Santa Isabel and the Río Piteros – which offers superb birdwatching. Local guides can be hired at the hotel, while sport-fishing in the Bahía la Graciosa or open sea can be organized, too. It's also possible to stay at the reserve's solar-powered scientific **research station**, a kilometre east of the Punta de Manabique in Cabo Tres Puntos (details coordinated through Fundary). Here there are rooms with mosquito nets, and space for campers, and you'll find a white-sand beach on your doorstep.

Trips to Manabique are best organized with Fundary, 17 Calle between 5 and 6 avenidas (T7948 0435), or in Guatemala City, Diagonal 6 17–19, Zona 10 (T7333 4957, Wwww.guate.net/fundarymanabique). This environmental group can arrange transport and accommodation packages (from US$125 per head) for two nights in the reserve including meals, and has good contacts with local guides. The other alternative is to travel to Manabique on a day-trip (around US$40, minimum of six people) from Lívingston; speak to Exotic Travel (see p.256).

Lívingston, Río Dulce and Lago de Izabal

Guatemala is at its most sultry and tropical in the fascinating region fringing the nation's slither of Caribbean coastline. This area's distinctive identity – more reminiscent of neighbouring Belize than the bulk of the country – is most apparent in **Lívingston**, which draws travellers eager to experience the intoxicating music and culture of the Garífuna people. Inland from Lívingston it's easy to spend several days exploring the plunging gorges of the **Río Dulce** and the shoreline of the huge, freshwater **Lago de Izabal**, with its hot springs, jungle-fringed creeks and lakeside hotels. The western fringes of the lake, best explored from the sleepy town of **El Estor**, are protected as part of the **Reserva Bocas del Polochic**, which harbours a tremendous variety of wildlife (including alligators, iguanas and turtles, as well as large numbers of migratory birds and resident parrots and toucans).

Lívingston

Enjoying a superb setting overlooking the Bahía de Amatique, **LÍVINGSTON** offers a unique fusion of Guatemalan and Caribbean culture where marimba mixes with Marley. The town acts as a hub for both the displaced **Garífuna** (or Black Caribs) who are strung out along the Caribbean coast between southern Belize and northern Nicaragua, and also for the Q'eqchi' Maya of the Río Dulce region.

Lívingston is undoubtedly one of the most fascinating places in Guatemala, but travellers' opinions about it tend to be sharply divided: many enjoy the languid rhythm of life and Lívingston's slightly ramshackle appeal while others just find the town shabby. Whatever your take, Lívingston certainly offers a welcome break from mainstream Latino culture: Carib **food** is generally excellent and varied, and Garífuna punta rock and reggae make a pleasant change from the regular merengue beat.

The general atmosphere is pretty chilled, but not unaffected by the pressures of daily life in Central America. Whilst Lívingston is not a threatening place, and there are no particular security concerns, the town does have its share of small-time hustlers eager to sell weed to travellers or scrounge a beer.

Arrival and information

The only way you can get to Lívingston is **by boat**, either from Puerto Barrios, the Río Dulce, Belize or, very occasionally, from Honduras. Wherever you come from, you'll arrive at the main dock on the south side of town.

Lívingston is a small place with only a handful of streets, and you can see most of what there is to see in an hour or two. Straight ahead up the hill is Calle Principal, the main drag with most of the restaurants, bars and shops, and the **immigration office** (daily 6am–7pm), where you can get an exit stamp, if you're heading for Belize, or an entrance stamp, if you've just arrived.

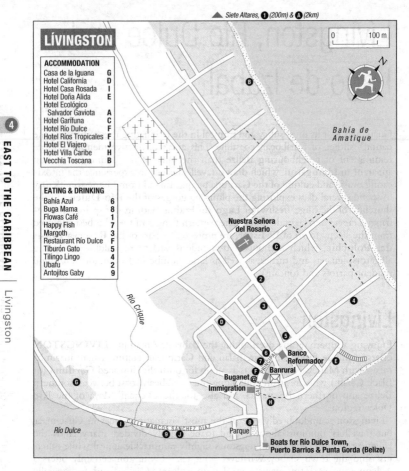

Siete Altares, ① (200m) & Ⓐ (2km)

LÍVINGSTON

0   100 m

ACCOMMODATION

Casa de la Iguana	G
Hotel California	D
Hotel Casa Rosada	I
Hotel Doña Alida	E
Hotel Ecológico	
Salvador Gaviota	A
Hotel Garífuna	C
Hotel Río Dulce	F
Hotel Ríos Tropicales	F
Hotel El Viajero	J
Hotel Villa Caribe	H
Vecchia Toscana	B

EATING & DRINKING

Bahía Azul	6
Buga Mama	8
Flowas Café	1
Happy Fish	7
Margoth	3
Restaurant Río Dulce	F
Tiburón Gato	5
Tilingo Lingo	4
Ubafu	2
Antojitos Gaby	9

Bahía de Amatique

Nuestra Señora del Rosario

Banco Reformador

Banrural

Buganet @

Immigration

Río Crique

Río Dulce

CALLE MARCOS SÁNCHEZ DÍAZ

Parque

Boats for Río Dulce Town, Puerto Barrios & Punta Gorda (Belize)

To **change money**, try either Banco Reformador (with Visa ATM), or Banrural on the main drag. The **Telgua** office (daily 7am–midnight) is on the right, up the main street from the docks, next door to the **post office**. Several places offer **internet** access including Buganet.

Exotic Travel (℡7947 0133, Ⓦwww.bluecaribbeanbay.com), in the same building as the *Bahía Azul* restaurant, is the best **travel agent** in town. The helpful owners can arrange **trips** (minimum six people) around the area, including visits to the fine white-sand beach of Playa Blanca (US$14), the Sapodilla Cayes off Belize for **snorkelling** (US$45, plus exit/entry taxes) and a jungle/culture trek that takes in a Garífuna village and the Siete Altars waterfalls (US$10). There's an excellent **notice board** here, too.

Tickets (US$13 per head) for the **river trip up the Río Dulce** can be booked by any travel agent in Lívingston. Most *lanchas* leave at 9am. The trip takes around 2hr 30min, depending on how many stops the skipper makes – most stop at the Castillo de San Felipe but are otherwise eager to get to Río Dulce Town quickly. If you want a more leisurely cruise so that you can take in the attractions along the way, and perhaps stop for a swim, you're looking at

4 EAST TO THE CARIBBEAN | Lívingston

chartering a boat; speak to agents or try bargaining hard with the *lancheros* based at the dock.

Scheduled **ferry boats** leave for Puerto Barrios daily at 5am and 2pm (1hr 30min; US$1.75), supplemented by **lanchas**, which leave when full (roughly every 40min 6.30am–5.30pm; 30min; US$3.50). Boats also run to Punta Gorda in **Belize** on Tuesdays and Fridays at 7am (1hr; US$22) and to Omoa in **Honduras** when there are sufficient numbers (US$300 per boat; 2hr 30min). Combined boat/shuttle-bus tickets are sold by Exotic Travel to Antigua, Copán (both US$37), San Pedro Sula (US$45) and La Ceiba (US$55).

Accommodation

Lívingston has some decent budget places, though little choice in the mid-range and luxury brackets. Those right on the beach are quite a hike from town. Book ahead on holidays, but at other times you should easily be able to find a bed.

Casa de la Iguana C Marcos Sánchez Díaz ☎7947 0064. Sociable travellers' place, run by a hedonistic gringo crew who've been kicking up a storm in Guatemala for years. All accommodation – a couple of dorms with six and four beds (US$4.50 per head) and attractive private cabañas – is in well-constructed wooden buildings set in a large grassy plot; there's also overflow hammock space and camping. You'll find a very lively bar-resto and excellent travel information. ②–③

Flowas ☎7947 0376, ⓦwww.flowascafe.com. Run by a bohemian Spanish couple, this beachside place has good two-storey bungalows with bathrooms downstairs and a restaurant with great food. Boasts a very relaxing setting, about a 30min walk from the centre. ③

Hotel California C Minerva ☎7937 0178. The concrete exterior is a bit foreboding but this functional hotel has sparse, clean rooms, all with fan and most with private bath. ②

Hotel Casa Rosada C Marcos Sánchez Díaz ☎7947 0303, ⓦwww.hotel casarosada.com. A superb waterfront hotel run by a very hospitable couple from Guatemala and Belgium. The small, cheery wooden cabins are kept immaculately clean and have twin beds, nets and nice hand-painted detailing. Bathrooms are all shared. It's a great retreat from the streets, with a huge, lush garden to enjoy and a private dock for sunbathing. Excellent, wholesome meals are served; see "Eating". ④

Hotel Doña Alida ☎7947 0027. Welcoming owners and a selection of spacious modern rooms in a quiet cliffside location, with a little beach below. Rooms 10 & 11 both have excellent sea (and sunset) views. ③–④

Hotel Ecológico Salvador Gaviota Playa Quehueche ☎7947 0874, ⓦwww.hotelecologico salvadorgaviota.com. Right on a slim, clean beach, with good rooms (with or without private

bathroom) and large thatched bungalows in grassy grounds. Tasty, inexpensive local food including fresh fish is available. It's about a 40min walk west of the town centre; take a taxi from the main dock. ③–⑦

Hotel Garífuna ☎7948 1091. Well-managed and secure, locally owned guesthouse with neat, clean and good-value rooms, all with fan and private shower. ③

Hotel Río Dulce C Principal ☎7947 0764. Renovations were nearing completion at this gorgeous, old wooden Caribbean-style property at time of research. Clean, light and airy rooms with fans either above the restaurant or more expensive options at the rear. ③–④

Hotel Ríos Tropicales C Principal ☎7947 0158, ⓦwww.mctropic.com. Attractive, welcoming hotel with ten well-presented rooms, some very spacious, with chunky wooden beds and fans; five have en-suite bathrooms. There's a sunny patio at the rear and a little espresso bar at the front. ③–④

Hotel El Viajero C Marcos Sánchez Díaz ☎5718 9544. Pretty rough, with concrete rooms that have little light but will just about do for a night. ③

Vecchia Toscana ☎7947 0883, €vecchia toscanan@yahoo.it. Offering the most stylish accommodation in town, this Italian-owned beachside place has immaculate modern rooms, though many are on the small side for the price. There's a large pool and a restaurant with fine cuisine and an extensive wine list. Rarely busy. ⑥–⑨

Villa Caribe just off C Principal ☎7947 0072, ⓦwww.villasdeguatemala.com. Luxury hotel, with spacious, attractive modern rooms boasting balconies with views to the bay. Pleasant bar, swimming pool and gardens stretching to the shore. Service can be erratic at times though. Rooms from US$115. ⑨

4

Garífuna history and culture

The Garífuna trace their history back to the island of **St Vincent**, one of the Windward Islands in the eastern Caribbean. At the time of Columbus's landing in the Americas, the islands of the Lesser Antilles had recently been settled by people from the South American mainland who had subdued the previous inhabitants, the Arawaks. These new people called themselves *Kalipuna*, or *Kwaib*, from which the names *Garífuna*, meaning "cassava-eating people", and *Carib* probably derived; St Vincent was then known as Yurimein. The natives the Europeans encountered were descendants of Carib men and Arawak women. A few thousand descendants of the original Caribs still live in Dominica and St Vincent.

In the early seventeenth century, Britain, France and the Netherlands vied for control of the islands, fighting each other and the Caribs. The admixture of African blood came in 1635 when two Spanish ships, carrying slaves from Nigeria to their colonies in America, wrecked off St Vincent and the survivors took refuge on the island. At first there was conflict between the Caribs and the Africans. The Caribs had been weakened by wars and disease, however, and eventually the predominant race was black, with some Carib blood. These people became known by the English as the **Black Caribs**. In their own language, they were *Garinagu*, or *Garífuna*. For most of the seventeenth and eighteenth centuries, St Vincent was nominally under British control but in practice belonged to the Garífuna, and in 1660 with the Treaty of Basse Terre the islands of Dominica and St Vincent were granted "perpetual possession" to the Caribs.

A century later, however, Britain attempted to gain full control of St Vincent, but was driven off by the Caribs, with French assistance. Another attempt twenty years later was more successful, and in 1783 the British imposed a treaty on the Garífuna, allowing them more than half of the island. The treaty was never accepted, however, and the Garífuna continued to defy British rule, resulting in frequent battles in which the French consistently lent the Garífuna support. The last serious attempt by the Garífuna to establish their independence took place in 1795, when both sides suffered horrendous casualties. The Garífuna lost their leader, Chief Joseph Chatoyer, and on June 10, 1796, after a year of bitter fighting, the French and the Garífuna surrendered to the British.

The colonial authorities could not allow a free black society to survive among slave-owning European settlers, so it was decided to deport the Garífuna population. They were hunted down, their homes (and in the process some of their culture) destroyed, and hundreds died of starvation and disease. The survivors, 4300 Black Caribs and 100 Yellow Caribs, as they were designated by the British, were transported to the nearby island of Balliceaux; within six months more than half of them had died, many of yellow fever. In March 1797, the remaining survivors were loaded aboard ships and sent to **Roatán**, one of the Bay Islands, off the coast of Honduras (see Chapter 7). One of the ships was captured by the Spanish and taken to Trujillo, on the mainland. Barely 2000 Garífuna lived to make the landing on Roatán, where the British abandoned them.

Perhaps in response to pleas for help from the Garífuna, who continued to die on Roatán, the Spanish commandante of Trujillo arrived and took possession of the

The town and around

There's not much to do in Lívingston itself, other than relax in local style. Traffic is very light (there are no roads to the outside world), so the horn-honking and clouds of black exhaust smoke that characterize life in urban Guatemala are mercifully (almost) absent. The local palm-fringed **beaches** are slim and, though not of the Caribbean-dream variety, do offer decent swimming once you're away from the centre; you'll find that the sand slopes into the sea very gradually here. If you drop by the modest little **Museo Multicultural de** island, shipping survivors to Trujillo where they were in demand as labourers. The Spanish had never made a success of agriculture here and the arrival of the Garífuna, who were proficient at growing crops, benefited the colony considerably. The boys were conscripted, and the Garífuna men gained a reputation as soldiers and mercenaries. Soon they began to move to other areas along the coast, and in 1802, 150 of them were brought as wood-cutting labourers to southern Belize, from where they moved along the Caribbean coast and settled in Lívingston in 1806.

By the start of the twentieth century, the Garífuna were well established in the Lívingston area, with the women employed in bagging and stacking *cohune* nuts and the men working as fishermen. As in the previous century, the Garífuna continued to travel widely in search of work, and in World War II Garífuna men supplied crews for both British and US merchant ships. Since the 1970s, many have left Central America for the US, where there's now a 50,000-strong population in New York, plus smaller Garífuna communities in New Orleans, Los Angeles and other cities. There's even a small community in London. Today most Garífuna live in villages along the Caribbean coast of Honduras (where they number more than 100,000) with smaller populations in Belize (around 18,000) and Nicaragua.

Most Garífuna speak Spanish (and some English) plus the unique Garífuna **language** that blends Arawak, French, Yuroba, Banti and Swahili words. Though virtually all worship at either Catholic or evangelical churches, their Afro-Carib **dugu** (religion) – centred on ancestor worship and comparable in some respects to Haitian voodoo – continues to be actively practised. *Dugu* is immersed in ritual, and death is seen as the freeing of a spirit, a celebration that involves dancing, drinking and music. Garífuna music, or **punta**, is furiously rhythmic, characterized by mesmeric drum patterns and ritual chanting, and it's very easy to hear its West African origins.

For many Guatemalans, the Garífuna remain something of a national curiosity, a mysterious and somewhat mistrusted phenomenon. They are not only subjected to the same discrimination that plagues the Maya population, but also viewed with a strange awe that gives rise to a range of fanciful myths. Uninformed commentators have argued that their society is matriarchal, polygamous and directed by a secret royal family. Accusations of voodoo and cannibalism are commonplace too. The prejudices, and the isolated nature of the community – numbering only around 6000 in Guatemala – mean many young Garífuna are more drawn to African-American (hip-hop) and Jamaican (rastafari) influences than to Latin culture.

Internationally, the late **Andy Palacio**, a widely respected award-winning Belizean cultural activist, is the most renowned Garífuna musician. His 2007 album *Wátina*, recorded with the Garífuna Collective (artists from all corners of the Garífuna world) is considered his masterpiece. Critically acclaimed *Umalali: The Garífuna Women's Project* is another superb compilation of Garífuna music.

For more on the Garífuna, consult ⓦ www.garifuna.com, the portal ⓦ www.garinet .com or the September 2001 feature in the *National Geographic* magazine.

Lívingston (daily 9am–5pm; US$0.75) just up from the dock, there are informative displays about the multiethnic make-up of the region, including the Garífuna and Q'eqchi' Maya communities.

The most popular side-trip is to the **Siete Altares**, an imposing series of waterfalls, much more impressive in the rainy season. Robberies have occurred here occasionally, and though no incidents have been reported for some time, it's best to hire a local guide or visit as part of a **tour**. The falls are about 5km west of town, accessed by following the main beach past *Flowas Café* and, just before the beach eventually peters out, taking a path to the left. Follow this inland and you'll soon reach the first of the falls. All of the falls are idyllic places to swim, but the highest one is the best of all.

Eating

Lívingston is a great place to eat out. For local food, you must try the *tapado* (coconut-based fish soup): *Tiburón Gato, Tilingo Lingo, Buga Mama* or *Margoth* are good places to hit; reckon on paying about US$8–10 for a huge bowl.

▲ Lívingston

Otherwise seafood is a speciality, with plenty of fresh lobster and shrimp available. Restaurant prices are quite high for Guatemala (but cheap if you've just arrived from Belize).

Antojitos Gaby C Marcos Sánchez Díaz. A cheap, clean little comedor with a few streetside tables and a menu that includes the usual Guatemalan staples plus great *sopa caracol*, omelettes and fried fish.

Bahía Azul C Principal. A very popular café-restaurant in a fine old Caribbean building, with an inexpensive menu (try the *coco burguesa*) and an excellent terrace for watching the world go by.

Buga Mama just left of the jetty. Stylish little wood-framed restaurant with balcony tables that catch the breeze. Good shrimp, *tapado*, pasta and strong coffee. Profits aid the Ak'Tenemit project (see p.262).

🏃 **Hotel Casa Rosada** ☎ 7947 0303. Dinner at this lovely hotel restaurant is a communal, three-course affair, served from 6.30pm

and costing US$13. Mains include filet mignon, lobster, sea bass and *tapado*, and there's always a vegetarian option. Book ahead.

Tilingo Lingo C Principal Run by María, a well-travelled Mexican lady, this place has an international menu that includes Latino and Indian food, plus great cocktails.

Vecchia Toscana on the beach ☎ 7947 0883. This hotel restaurant offers authentic, if expensive Italian cuisine, with a wood-fired oven for pizza, fresh pasta, fish and meat dishes including *milanesas*; reckon on spending US$18 a head. There's a superb Italian wine list too. It's very rarely busy so you might want to call ahead to place your order.

Drinking

For evening entertainment, Lívingston has lots of groovy hangouts, including *Ubafu*, usually the liveliest bar, which is the best place to hear live music, especially Garífuna punta. The beach bars at the end of Calle Principal have dancefloors and play reggae, punta, r'n'b and Latin sounds. It may not have a local flavour, but the bar scene at the *Casa de la Iguana* (happy hour 6–8pm) has a lively vibe and can be a riot, with anything from drinking games to mud-wrestling going on if the owners are in the mood; there's a big screen for sports here too. The best **coffee** in town is served in the tiny espresso bar at the entrance to *Hotel Ríos Tropicales*.

The Río Dulce

In a few moments we entered the Río Dulce. On each side, rising perpendicularly from three to four hundred feet, was a wall of living green. Trees grew from the water's edge, with dense unbroken foliage, to the top; not a spot of barrenness was to be seen; and on both sides, from the tops of the highest trees, long tendrils descended to the water, as if to drink and carry life to the trunks that bore them. It was, as its name imports, a Río Dulce, a fairy scene of Titan land, combining exqui-site beauty with colossal grandeur. As we advanced the passage turned, and in a few minutes we lost sight of the sea, and were enclosed on all sides by a forest wall; but the river, although showing us no passage, still invited us onward.

John Lloyd Stephens (1841)

Another excellent reason to come to Lívingston is the spectacular trip up the **Río Dulce**, a roughly thirty-kilometre journey that eventually brings you to Río Dulce Town. From Lívingston, the river passes through a system of gorges with sheer, 100-metre-high rock faces draped in tropical vegetation and cascading vines. Here and there you might see some white herons or flocks of squawking parakeets as you cruise upriver taking in the stunning tropical scenery.

Around 7km from Lívingston there are a couple of delightful river tributaries, on either side of the Río Dulce, both with **eco-hotels**. Boats travelling between

Río Dulce and Lívingston will drop you off at either place. On the southern side, just up the Río Lámpara, ✈ *Hotelito Perdido* (☎5725 1576, ⓦwww.hotelito perdido.com; ❸–❹) is a superb new lodge owned by a welcoming English–Polish couple, set in a verdant tropical garden of water apple, lychee, cashew and banana trees. It's an intimate place with three split-level wooden cabañas, plus dorm beds (US$6) above the restaurant. There's very tasty home-made grub (dinner is US$8), a really relaxed vibe and kayaks available to explore the wonderful wetlands.

On the north bank is the **Río Tatín**, which most boatmen venture up into briefly, where the *Finca Tatín* (☎5902 0831, ⓦwww.fincatatin.centroamerica .com; ❸–❹) offers rustic dorms (US$6 per bed) and private rooms, some with bathroom; all accommodation has mosquito nets. It's set in dense jungle and the rainforest habitat means that you will encounter plenty of bugs. However there's excellent, healthy food (communal dinner US$5.50), kayaks for hire, table tennis, walking trails and Spanish classes available. Q'eqchi' Maya guides also can be arranged to accompany you to local villages and caves, as well as Ak'Tenamit.

A further kilometre west along the Río Dulce is **Ak'Tenamit** (ⓦwww .aktenamit.org), a health and development centre that caters to the needs of 124 Q'eqchi' Maya villages. Until the project was started in 1992 the people had neither schools, medical care, nor much else. Now there is a 24-hour clinic, primary and secondary schools and a floating dental clinic. Self-help programmes, a women's craft-making cooperative, an ecotourism centre and Maya cultural initiatives have also been launched. Volunteer doctors, nurses and dentists who can commit themselves for at least three months are needed, and visitors are invited to take a look around.

Travel another kilometre or so upriver and you'll find a spot where warm sulphurous waters emerge from the base of a cliff – a good place for a dip. Just beyond, the gorge opens into a small lake, **El Golfete**, on whose northern shore is the **Biotopo Chocón Machacas** (daily 7am–4pm; US$3), a nature reserve designed to protect the habitat of the **manatee**, or sea cow, a threatened species that's seen around here from time to time. The manatee is a massive seal–shaped mammal that lives in both sea- and freshwater and, according to some, gave rise to the myth of the mermaid. Female manatees breastfeed their young, clutching them in their flippers, though – tipping the scales at as much as a ton – they're hardly as dainty as fairytale mermaids. The reserve was also set up to protect the area's rich wetlands and lowland rainforests (home to jaguar and tapir and wonderful birdlife) but recent encroachment by campesinos has lead to a bitter battle over land use. In 2008 a group of Belgian tourists were detained for a day here by protesting farmers, and tensions remain high, so enquire about the current state of affairs if you want to explore this reserve.

At the western end of the Golfete is another **charity operation**, this one an orphanage for 250 children. Casa Guatemala is an astonishing success story, and has grown (despite a huge earthquake in 1999 that demolished most of the buildings) to include a hostel, *Hotel Backpackers* (see p.265), where some of the older children work, a farm, fish pond, greenhouses and a meat store in Río Dulce Town. Volunteers with the right background, who can stay a few months (preferably six), are always desperately needed. The work is hard, and conditions are pretty basic but it's time very well spent. For contact information, see "Work and study" in the Basics section of this book.

Lago de Izabal and around

Heading on upstream, across the Golfete, the river closes in again and passes the marina and bridge at the squalid settlement of **RÍO DULCE TOWN** (sometimes also known as Fronteras), on the northern side of the river.

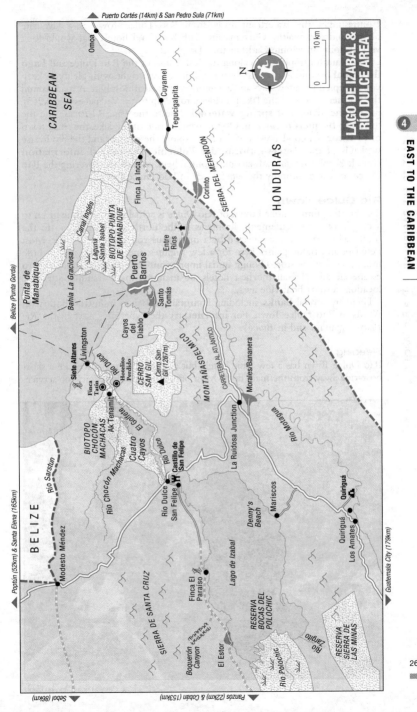

0   10 km

N

CARIBBEAN
SEA

▲ Puerto Cortés (14km) & San Pedro Sula (71km)

Omoa

Cuyamel

Tegucigalpita

Corinto

SIERRA DEL MERENDÓN

HONDURAS

Finca La Inca

BIOTOPO PUNTA
DE MANABIQUE

Entre Ríos

Punta de
Manabique

Canal Inglés

Laguna
Santa Isabel

Bahía La Graciosa

Puerto Barrios

Santo Tomás

▲ Belize (Punta Gorda)

Cayos
del Diablo

Livingston

Siete Altares

Finca Tatín

Hotelito
Perdido

Río Dulce

CERRO SAN GIL

Cerro San Gil (1267m)
▲

MONTAÑAS DEL MICO

CARRETERA AL ATLÁNTICO

Morales/Bananera

Río Motagua

▲ Poptún (52km) & Santa Elena (165km)

BIOTOPO CHOCÓN
MACHACAS

Ak'Tenamit

El Golfete

Cuatro Cayos

Río Chocón Machacas

Río Dulce

Castillo de
San Felipe

Río Dulce
San Felipe

La Ruidosa Junction

Río Sarstún

BELIZE

Modesto Méndez

SIERRA DE SANTA CRUZ

Boquerón
Canyon

Finca El
Paraíso

El Estor

Lago de Izabal

RESERVA
BOCAS DEL
POLOCHIC

RESERVA
SIERRA DE
LAS MINAS

Denny's Beach

Mariscos

Quiriguá

Quiriguá

Los Amates

Río Tanijó

Río Polochic

▲ Panzós (22km) & Cobán (153km)

▲ Sebol (86km)

▲ Guatemala City (179km)

Contrastingly, the waterfront away from Río Dulce Town is a favourite playground for wealthy Guatemalans, with boats and hotels that would look very at home in Monte Carlo or the Hamptons.

The beautiful tropical area along the lush banks of the Río Dulce and **Lago de Izabal** beyond is a tourist destination in its own right, with plenty to keep you occupied for a few days and a genuinely relaxed atmosphere. A road around the northern shore of the lake provides a route up to the Verapaces (see p.265), passing the idyllic **hot spring waterfall** close to the *Finca El Paraíso* and the towering **Boquerón canyon**. On the western side of the lake, the small town of **El Estor** is a good alternative base to explore these sights and the biodiverse wetlands of the **Reserva Bocas del Polochic**. For **tourist information** consult ⓦwww.mayaparadise.com, a comprehensive **website** covering the Río Dulce region, or drop by the *Sundog* café in Río Dulce Town.

Río Dulce Town

The bustling fume-choked town of Río Dulce is actually a new name given to a couple of older settlements, Fronteras to the north and El Relleno to the south, which are now connected by a monstrous concrete road-bridge. Most Petén-bound traffic pauses here for a few minutes, and the town itself is little more than a truck stop. Though initial impressions are terrible it's very easy to escape all this, and all the best hotels are in much more tranquil, attractive locations a short boat-ride away.

There are several **banks**, including Banrural and Banco Industrial, both with ATMs in Río Dulce Town. For **internet**, try the cybercafés next to the *Río Bravo* restaurant and in *Bruno's*.

Sleeping

Río Dulce Town has a few basic hotels, but all the following places are a short boat-ride away from the main dock. Most offer a free, or cheap, pick-up service.

▲ Canyon near Lago de Izabal

Casa Perico 2km northeast of the bridge ☎5930 5666. Up a small lakeside inlet, this rustic Swiss-owned jungle hideaway has a relaxed, sociable atmosphere and is the most popular spot for budget travellers. All the buildings are wooden, built on stilts and connected by walkways. Accommodation includes dorm beds (from US$6), and rooms (US$7 per head) with porches and hammocks; the owners plan to add cabañas with private bathrooms. Meals cost around US$4, dinner is US$7 and there's a popular Sun barbecue. ❷–❹

Hacienda Tijax just across from the dock ☎7930 5505, ⓦwww.tijax.com. Nicely located on the lakefront, and has a pool. Accommodation is either in basic rooms (❸), A-frame cabins with or without bathrooms (❸–❹) or bungalows (❻), and the restaurant is tasty, if a little overpriced. Also offers a canopy jungle walk, hiking trails and horseriding (US$20 for 2hr 30min).

Hotel Backpackers underneath the south side of the bridge ☎7930 5169, ⓦwww.hotel backpackers.com. Unfortunately this place has become pretty unappealing due to a lack of maintenance and care, which is a shame, as the hotel benefits the Casa Guatemala children's home, and many of the young staff here are former residents. Dorms (beds are US$4) are huge but sheets are not provided, while the private double rooms are sparsely furnished. Best to drop by for a drink on the long deck facing the river, or for the Sat-night disco. ❷–❹

Hotel Catamaran ☎7930 5494, ⓦwww .catarmaranisland.com. Occupies a fine position on a tiny private island, a 5min *lancha* ride from Río Dulce Town and has pleasant grounds with a smallish pool, restaurant, bar and tennis courts. Most cabañas back onto the river and are comfortable enough, but not great value for money, with small bathrooms and fairly basic facilities. ❼

Tortugal 4min by water taxi from Río Dulce Town ☎5334 1946, ⓦwww.tortugal.com. This very well run place has a great selection of very good quality accommodation, all attractively presented and well finished. The two dorms (US$7–10 per bed) have quality mattresses, mossie nets and lockers and little windows that catch the breeze, there are lovely spacious rooms and wood-and-thatch bungalows (both ❹) and a stunning luxury *casita* (❾). Above the river-facing restaurant (meals are in the US$6–10 range) there's a chill-out area with free internet, pool table and library. Free kayaks for guests. ❸–❾

Eating

For meals, all the hotels listed have restaurants, but there are several alternatives in Río Dulce Town too. The nicest little café is the very friendly and relaxed Dutch-owned 🏃 *Sundog*, just up from the dock, where there are baguettes, sandwiches, espresso coffee and wine by the glass; the kitchen closes at 8pm. Next door *Río Bravo* is known for its pizza and pasta, while just to the south *Bruno's* serves international food and offers North American sports coverage – it's very popular with the sailing fraternity. For cheap grub, you'll find a strip of undistinguished comedores on the main drag but the best place is undoubtedly *Benedición a Dios*, down a little side-road, which is renowned for its huge wheat tortillas, topped with cabbage and marinated beef (though there are veggie options) and fine, fruit-packed licuados.

Castillo de San Felipe

Looking like a miniature medieval castle and marking the entrance to Lago de Izabal, the *castillo* (8am–5pm; US$3) is a tribute to the audacity of British pirates, who used to sail up the Río Dulce to raid supplies and harass mule trains. The Spanish were so infuriated by this that they built the fortress here in 1652 to seal off the entrance to the lake, and a chain was strung across the river. Inside there are a maze of tiny rooms and staircases, plus plenty of canons and panoramic views of the lake.

The hot spring waterfall and Boquerón canyon

Beyond the *castillo*, the broad sweep of Lago de Izabal opens before you, with great views of the fertile highlands beyond the distant shores. Some 25km from Río Dulce, a **hot spring waterfall** (daily 8am–6pm; US$1.30) in land owned by the

Río Dulce travel connections

Buses leave every thirty minutes or so to both Guatemala City (5–6hr) and Flores (3hr–3hr 30min) until 6pm; Litegua (☏7930 5251) is one good company that has an office on the highway. Minibuses depart for both Poptún (every 30min; 1hr 45min) and Puerto Barrios (hourly; 2hr) until 6pm. Hourly minibuses (until 6pm) run around the lakeshore for El Estor (1hr 45min), passing *Finca el Paraíso*. Speak to Atitrans (☏5218 5950) on the highway about **shuttle buses** to Antigua (about US$40), Copán (US$32) or other destinations. The *Sundog* café also offers **tours** to Quiriguá and a banana plantation (US$22).

If you're heading **for Lívingston** via the Río Dulce gorge, *lancha* captains will ambush you as soon as you step off a bus; *colectivo* boats (US$13 per head) leave Río Dulce Town from a designated dock under the north side of the bridge. If you book through your hotel on either the 9.30am or 1.30pm departures a pick-up can usually be arranged. Downstream, the trip takes around two hours, depending on how many stops are made. The boatmen usually cruise up to the Castillo de San Felipe for photographs (but do not stop there) and then slow down at a couple of islets to look at nesting cormorants and pelicans. Most boats then stop at a place for fifteen minutes where hot springs bubble into the river and there are some caves (you'll find toilets and refreshments here), and at another spot where water lilies are profuse. To explore the lake and river at a more leisurely pace, you're looking at hooking up with a private yacht (ask around in *Bruno's* or at your hotel) or chartering a boat with captain. César Catalan (☏5819 7436) is recommended; a full day-trip costs US$100 for up to seven people.

Finca el Paraíso, 300m north of the road, is one of Guatemala's most remarkable natural phenomena. Bathtub-temperature spring water cascades into pools cooled by a separate chilly flow of fresh river water, creating a sublime, steamy spa-like environment where it's easy to soak away an afternoon. Above the waterfall is a series of caves whose interiors are crowded both with bats and extraordinary shapes and colours – made even more memorable by the fact that you have to swim by torchlight to see them (bring your own flashlight). Two kilometres south of the waterfall, the *Finca el Paraíso* **hotel** (☏7949 7122; ❺) sits on the waterfront, with two rows of large, comfortable, but rarely occupied cabañas, each with front porch and hammock, and a good, if pricey, restaurant. The hotel enjoys a delightfully peaceful location, there's good swimming from the black-sand beach and campers are welcome to pitch here for a small fee. Buses between Río Dulce and El Estor pass the hot springs and hotel hourly in both directions until 6pm.

Continuing west along the lakeshore, it's a further 7km to the **Boquerón canyon**, completely hidden yet just 500m from the road. Near-vertical cliffs soar to more than 250m above the Río Sauce, which flows through the bottom of the startling jungle-clad gorge, the river bed plotted with colossal boulders. To see the canyon, you'll have to employ one of the local boatmen who wait at the end of the signposted track from the main road. They'll paddle you upstream in logwood canoes for a small fee. The return trip takes thirty minutes or so, though it's possible to get your boatman to drop you off and return to pick you up later in the day. If you want to explore Boquerón further, the canyon extends for an additional 5km; make sure you have sturdy footwear and enjoy a scramble.

El Estor

Heading west beyond Boquerón, it's just 6km to the sleepy lakeside town of **EL ESTOR**, allegedly named by English pirates who came up the Río Dulce to buy supplies at "The Store". It's an easy-going, friendly place but located close to high-grade nickel deposits, the presence of which has provoked bitter disputes between mining companies and indigenous locals. In 2008 preparations for a resumption of **strip mining** (after a lapse of 27 years) were suspended due to market credit conditions. If mining does resume, its environmental impact – the nickel is just below the topsoil – would undoubtedly seriously impact the vast ecotourism potential of the region.

There are no sights in El Estor itself, though you'll find a pool in the plaza that harbours fish, turtles and alligators. Keep an eye out, too, for huge green iguanas in the trees around town; locals shoot at them with slingshots. You could easily spend a few days exploring the surrounding area – including the hot spring waterfall, the Boquerón canyon and Bocas del Polochic – much of which remains undisturbed. For local **information** the best contacts are Hugo at *Hugo's Restaurant*, or Óscar Paz, who runs the *Hotel Vista del Lago* and is an enthusiastic promoter of the area. He will arrange a boat and guide to explore any of the region's attractions. Banrural, on 3 Calle and 6 Avenida, changes traveller's cheques and has an ATM, while there are several **internet** places in town, including *El Portal* on the plaza.

Accommodation and eating

The town has a decent choice of good-quality budget **places to stay**, though nothing much in other price categories. For tasty *comida típica* head to *Hugo's Restaurant* or *Café El Portal*, both on the main plaza, or *Chaabil* has good seafood and grilled meat – a large portion is around US$7–10.

Chaabil lakeshore on 3 C ☎7949 7272. This place is a good choice where the cabaña-style rooms have chunky wooden beds and private bathrooms. ❸
Hotel Central 5 Av & 2 C ☎7949 7244. Offering very good value, these clean, well-presented, modern rooms each have private bath and fan. ❸
Hotel Ecológico Cabañas del Lago ☎7949 7245. Set in a tranquil lakeside plot a kilometre east of the centre, the wooden bungalows are comfortable, spacious and attractive. There's a private sandy beach too. Hugo, the owner, will

take you there if you drop by his restaurant in the plaza. ❹
Hotel Villela 6 Av 2–06 ☎7949 7214. A venerable place with basic, slightly musty rooms, some with private shower, surrounding a pretty garden. ❷
Hotel Vista del Lago lakeside ☎7949 7205. Offering a really classy setting, this beautiful old wooden building by the lakeshore is claimed to be the original "store" that gave the town its name. Small, clean rooms with private bath; those on the second floor boast superb views of the lake. ❸

Reserva Bocas del Polochic

Encompassing a substantial slice of lowland jungle on the west side of the lake, the **Bocas del Polochic** nature reserve is one of the richest wetland habitats in Guatemala. The green maze of swamp, marsh and forest harbours at least 224 different species of bird, including golden-fronted woodpecker, Aztec parakeet and keel-billed toucan. It's also rich in mammals, including howler monkeys, which you're virtually guaranteed to see (and hear), plus rarely encountered manatees and tapirs. There's good accommodation next to the tiny Q'eqchi' village of **SELEMPÍM** just outside the reserve – the large mosquito-screened wooden house with bunk beds (US$15 per head per day, including three substantial meals) provides villagers with employment. Locals also lead guided walks up into the foothills of the Sierra de las Minas and conduct kayak tours of the river delta.

The major drawback for visitors wanting to get to the reserve is that it's only accessible by infrequent public *lanchas* or expensive chartered boats. If you do want to go, drop by Defensores de la Naturaleza, at 5 Avenida and 2 Calle in El Estor (☎7949 7427 or 5815 1736, ⓦ www.defensores.org.gt), who manage the reserve and can help with information. Three weekly public *lanchas* run to and from Selempím on Monday, Wednesday and Saturday, leaving Selempím at 7am and returning from El Estor at 11am (US$9; 1hr 15min) – check times at Defensores' office. Day-trips to the fringes of the reserve cost around US$50; ask Hugo or Oscar to recommend a local boatman. A special charter to Selempím costs around US$120 (return).

Mariscos and Denny's Beach

MARISCOS, the main town on the south side of Lago de Izabal, sees very few visitors now that the road around the northern shore of the lake is complete. But if you're craving a good swim, the Canadian-run **Denny's Beach** (T 5398 0908, W www.dennysbeach.com) is a fine resort in a blissfully quiet spot on the lake 4km to the east. It's an ideal place to get away from it all, with detached cabañas (❹–❻) and a dorm (US$10 per bed) above the sandy beach. There's an open-air restaurant here with good cooking (meals are US$4–12). Kayak use is gratis, while horseriding (US$25) and trips around the lake can be arranged. They'll pick up and drop off guests for free from Mariscos.

The eastern highlands

The eastern highlands, often just called El Oriente, connect Guatemala City with El Salvador and Honduras and must rank as the least-visited part of the entire country. Virtually the entire population is ladino, speaking Spanish and wearing Western clothes, although many are by blood pure Maya. Only a very few elderly people, in a couple of isolated areas, still speak Poqomam Maya, the region's indigenous language. The ladinos of the east have a reputation for behaving like cowboys, and demonstrations of macho pride are common.

The landscape lacks the immediate appeal of the western highlands. Not only are its peaks lower, but its features are generally less clearly defined. The volcanoes, unlike the neatly symmetrical cones of the west, are heavily eroded, merging with the lower-lying hills. Close to the border with El Salvador the hills are incredibly fertile and the broad valleys lush with vegetation, but in the north of the area, around the key town of **Chiquimula**, the landscape is very different, with dry rounded peaks and dusty fields. From here it's a short hop to the ruins of Copán in Honduras, while **Esquipulas**, with its famous basilica, and the magical volcanic crater lake of **Ipala** are also close by.

From Guatemala City to El Salvador

Although several routes run between the capital and the El Salvadorean border, it's the fast highland route via the town of **CUILAPA**, passing through lush valleys, that draws the most traffic. The town itself harbours no appeal, but if you want to break your trip the pleasant *Turicentro Los Esclavos* (T 7886 5139; ❺) on the highway 4km beyond Cuilapa is a good choice, with a small pool, good café-restaurant and spotless rooms. South of Cuilapa, a branch road heads through stunning scenery, between the peaks of Volcán Tecuamburro and Volcán Cruz Quemada to the town of **Chiquimulilla** (buses every hour; see p.240).

Eleven kilometres beyond Cuilapa the highway splits at the **El Molino junction**. The southern fork, highway CA-8, is the most direct route to the border, heading straight for the crossing at **VALLE NUEVO**, less than 50km away. This road is straight, fast and scenic, but the border crossing is little more than a customs post and there's nowhere to stay when you get there, or on the way.

The Carretera Interamericana

Heading west from El Molino, the Carretera Interamericana turns towards the mountains, running through an isolated valley, then climbing to a high plateau and then on to **JUTIAPA**. The centre of trade and transport for the entire eastern region, this is a busy and not particularly attractive place, but it has serviceable hotels and banks if you pull in.

Heading on from Jutiapa towards El Salvador, the Carretera Interamericana runs through **El Progreso** and then **Asunción Mita** (from where there's a constant stream of buses and minibuses to the border). The actual crossing-point is at the small town of **SAN CRISTÓBAL**, where you'll find a couple of basic pensiones (❶–❷) and an Inguat desk. The last **bus** for Guatemala City leaves the border at around 7pm, and the last minibus for Asunción Mita leaves at around 8pm.

Jalapa to Ipala

Any trip through the eastern highlands should include the road **between Jalapa and Ipala**, which takes you through some truly breathtaking scenery. From Jutiapa very regular buses run to Jalapa, passing over the shoulder of the Volcán Tahual and through a huge bowl-shaped valley, thick with fields of sugarcane, tobacco and maize. The main towns along the way are **Monjas** and **Morazán**, two busy agricultural centres.

JALAPA itself is a prosperous but isolated town, resting on a high plateau surrounded by low peaks and cattle pasture. There are plenty of places **to stay**: *Hotel Casa del Viajero*, at 1 Avenida 0–70 (☎7922 4086; ❷–❸), is a friendly place with a good comedor and rooms, some with private bathroom, while the *Posada Don Antonio*, Avenida Chipilapa A 0–64 (☎7922 5751; ❹), is more comfortable; all rooms have an en-suite shower room here. The town has several **banks**, including Banco G&T at 1 Avenida 1–66, with an ATM. Try the excellent *Restaurante Casa Real* on 1 Calle for huge salads, soups and grilled meats or *Antojitos Acuarios* opposite for a snack. Jalapa's busy bus terminal has half-hourly buses to Guatemala City (3hr) via both Jutiapa and Sanarate; hourly buses also run to Chiquimula (3hr) via Ipala.

San Luís Jilotepéque and Ipala

Heading on from Jalapa towards Chiquimula and Esquipulas the road climbs into the hills for the most beautiful section of the entire trip to Ipala, leading up onto a high ridge with superb views, and then dropping down to the isolated villages of San Pedro Pinula and **SAN LUÍS JILOTEPÉQUE**, two outposts of Maya culture. The plaza of San Luís is particularly impressive, with two massive ceiba trees, a colonial church, and a couple of replica stelae from Copán – and on Sundays, it's the scene of a vast Maya market.

Fourteen kilometres beyond San Luís, this back road joins the main road from Jutiapa at the small town of **IPALA**, an important crossroads. The village itself is a pretty forlorn place, with a few shops and a couple of **hotels**. The best place to stay is the clean *Hopsedaje Pinal* (**②**), where some rooms have private bath; failing that, head for *Hotel Ipala Real* (**☎**7923 7107; **②**), where the rooms have cable TV and (very) en-suite showers and toilets.

Ipala inhabits an open plain at the base of **Volcán de Ipala** (1650m), which looks like a rounded hill. The cone is filled by a beautiful little **crater lake** ringed by trees, and has a patch of virgin cloudforest on its north side. A unique species of the *mojarra* fish, which apparently has six prominent spines on its back, inhabits the lake, and there's a dock for sunbathing. You can amble around the lake in a little over an hour, and it makes a wonderful place to **camp**, though you'll have to bring all your own supplies.

The easiest route to the top is via a trail (built by EarthCorps volunteers) from the village of **El Chagüitón**, south of Ipala heading towards the small town of Agua Blanca. It's two hours to the top via a visitor centre where you pay a US$1.30 entrance fee. Buses and pick-ups run from Ipala towards the village of Agua Blanca hourly; get off at **El Sauce** at Km26.5, from where it's an hour and a half to the summit via El Chagüitón.

The north: Zacapa, Chiquimula and Esquipulas

In the northern part of the region, the machismo of the Oriente is at its most potent – the majority of the population are ladinos, and furiously proud of it, with a reputation for quick tempers, warm hearts and violent responses. **Chiquimula** and **Esquipulas** are the most important towns, offering access to two interesting sites: the Maya ruins at **Copán** (see p.357) over the border in Honduras, and the shrine of the **Black Christ** in Esquipulas.

The direct road branches off the Carretera al Atlántico at the Río Hondo junction, running through dry, dusty hills to Zacapa, and on through Chiquimula and Esquipulas to the three-way border with Honduras and El Salvador. Before Zacapa there's a turn-off to the remote town of **ESTANZUELA**, which, oddly enough, has its own museum of paleontology, **El Museo de Paleontología Bryan Patterson** (daily 8am–5pm; free), with curious exhibits including the fossil of a blue whale, manatee bones and the entire skeleton of a mastodon said to be some fifty thousand years old. More recent pieces include a small Maya tomb and some stelae. The town centre is just a kilometre off the highway.

Zacapa

Just 13km from the Río Hondo junction, **ZACAPA** is one of the hottest towns in the country, with maximum temperatures regularly peaking close to 40°C. This fairly featureless place gives its name to what is perhaps the world's finest rum – Ron Centenario Zacapa – though it's not actually made here. Around the plaza you'll find several Chinese **restaurants**, including *Po Wing* where the portions are huge, Banco G&T with an ATM, and several hotels, though there's no reason to linger.

Chiquimula

Set to one side of the highway the large town of **CHIQUIMULA** is an ugly, hot, bustling town with a population of around 45,000. Its huge plaza area,

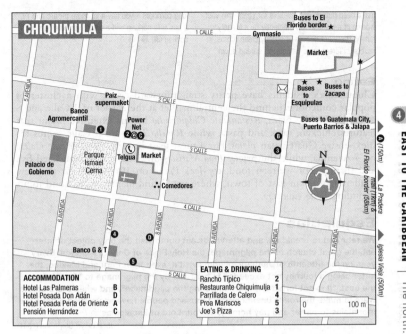

shaded by ceiba trees, and downtown streets are permanently congested by traffic and sights are slim on the ground. You could take a wander around the **market** just east of the plaza, which has a kitsch selection of cowboy gear and leatherware or visit the massive ruined colonial **church**, the Iglesia Vieja, on the eastern side of town. Damaged in the 1765 earthquake and left behind as the town has shifted over the years, it retains an impressive, if fractured, Baroque facade.

There are plenty of **banks** in the central area with ATMs, and you'll find Powernet for **internet** connections on the plaza. The **bus terminal**, a ten-minute walk northeast of here, has hourly buses to Guatemala City (3hr 30min) and Puerto Barrios (5hr) until 6pm, microbuses to Esquipulas (every 20min; 1hr), Ipala (hourly; 1hr; many continuing on to Jalapa, 3hr) and Anguiatú (every 30min; 1hr). Heading for Copán, microbuses leave for the border at El Florido (every 30min; 1hr 30min) until 6pm, making a stop in Jocotán on the way.

Accommodation

This is a very hot place, so shell out for air-conditioning or make sure you have a good fan in your room.

Hotel Las Palmeras 10 Av 2–00 ☏ 7942 4647. A basic place to crash for the night, where some of the rooms have a/c and private bathroom. ❷–❸

Hotel Posada Don Adán 8 Av 4–30 ☏ 7942 0549. A genteel, old-fashioned family-run hotel where the eighteen large rooms all have a/c, cable TV and hot-water bathrooms. Parking. ❹

Hotel Posada Perla de Oriente 2 C & 12 Av ☏ 7942 0014. Lush tropical gardens, a large swimming pool and restaurant, and the rooms (with or without a/c) are spacious and clean, if a bit garishly decorated. Fan-only single rooms are well priced. ❹–❻

Pensión Hernández 3 C 7–41 ☏ 7942 0708, ⓔ chapin54@yahoo.com. Long-standing favourite that's been putting up travellers for years, this vast warren of a place is run efficiently by a friendly family. There are dozens of orderly clean rooms, in several different price categories, spread down long corridors – you pay a lot more for a/c and TV. It has safe parking and a small concrete pool for cooling off. ❷–❹

Eating

Chiquimula's residents have pretty straightforward tastes, with a cluster of popular comedores behind the central market at the corner of 4 Calle and 8 Avenida. On the plaza, *Restaurante Chiquimulja* has an extensive menu that features chicken, steak and pasta, while *Rancho Típico* on 3 Calle scores for inexpensive Guatemalan *platos*. For a meat feast head to *Parrillada de Calero* on 7 Avenida, while the pricey *Proa Mariscos* on 5 Calle has good fried fish and shrimp. For western food, try *Joe's Pizza* on 10 Avenida or the new Pradera mall, 1km east of town, where you'll find plenty of fast-food joints including *Pollo Campero*.

Esquipulas

We returned to breakfast, and afterwards set out to visit the only object of interest, the great church of the pilgrimage, the Holy Place of Central America. Every year, on the fifteenth of January, pilgrims visit it, even from Peru and Mexico; the latter being a journey not exceeded in hardship by the pilgrimage to Mecca. As in the east, "it is not forbidden to trade during the pilgrimage", and when there are no wars to make the roads unsafe eighty thousand people have assembled among the mountains to barter and pay homage to "our Lord of Esquipulas".

John Lloyd Stephens (1841)

The Esquipulas pilgrimage

The history of the **Esquipulas pilgrimage** probably dates back to pre-Conquest times, when the valley was controlled by Chief Esquipulas. Even then the area was the site of an important religious shrine, perhaps connected with the nearby Maya site of Copán. When the Spanish arrived, the chief was keen to avoid the usual bloodshed and chose to surrender without a fight; the grateful Spaniards named the city they founded at the site in his honour. The famed colonial sculptor Quirio Cataño was then commissioned to carve an image of Christ for the church constructed in the middle of the new town, and in order to make it more likely to appeal to the local people he chose to carve it from balsam, a dark wood. Another version has it that Cataño was hired by the Maya after one of their number had seen a vision of a dark Christ on this spot. In any event, the image was installed in the church in 1595 and soon became accredited with miraculous powers. After the bishop of Guatemala, Pardo de Figueroa, was cured of a chronic ailment on a trip to Esquipulas in 1737 things really took off. The bishop ordered the construction of a new church, which was completed in 1758, and had his body buried beneath the altar.

Although all this might seem fairly straightforward, it doesn't explain why this figure has become the most revered in a country full of miracle-working saints. One possible explanation is that it offers the Maya, who until recently dominated the pilgrimage, a chance to blend pre-Columbian and Catholic worship. It's known that the Maya pantheon included several Black deities such as Ek Ahau, the black lord, who was served by seven retainers, and Ek'Chuach, the tall black god, who protected travellers. When Aldous Huxley visited the shrine in 1934 his thoughts were along these lines: "So what draws the worshippers is probably less the saintliness of the historic Jesus than the magical sootiness of his image ... numinosity is in inverse ratio to luminosity."

▲ Pilgrims at Esquipulas basilica

The final town on this eastern highway is **ESQUIPULAS**, which, now as in Stephens' day, has a single point of interest; it is almost certainly the most important Catholic shrine in Central America, famous above all for its dark-hued statue of Christ. Arriving from Chiquimula, buses wind through the hills, beneath craggy outcrops and forested peaks, and emerge suddenly at the lip of a huge bowl-shaped valley centring on a great open plateau. On one side of this, just below the road, is Esquipulas itself. The place is entirely dominated by the four perfectly white domes of the church, brilliantly floodlit at night. Below, the rest of the town is a messy sprawl of cheap hotels, souvenir stalls and overpriced restaurants. The pilgrimage, which continues all year, has generated numerous sidelines, creating a booming resort where people from all over Central America come to worship, eat, drink and relax, in a bizarre combination of holy devotion and indulgence.

The principal day of **pilgrimage**, when the religious significance of the shrine is at its most potent, is January 15. Even the smallest villages will save enough money to send a representative or two on this occasion, their send-off and return invariably marked by religious services. These plus the thousands who can afford to come in their own right ensure that the numbers attending are still as high as in Stephens' day, filling the town to bursting and beyond. Buses chartered from all over Guatemala choke the streets, while the most devoted pilgrims arrive on foot (some dropping to their knees for the last few kilometres). There's a smaller pilgrimage annually on March 9, and faithful crowds visit year-round. The town has also played an important role in modern-day politics: it was here that the first **peace accord** initiatives to end the civil wars in El Salvador, Nicaragua and Guatemala were signed in 1987.

January
12–15 El Progreso (near Jutiapa), main day 15th
15 Esquipulas, the biggest pilgrimage in Central America
19–21 Cabañas (near Zacapa), main day 19th
20–26 Ipala, main day 23rd (includes bullfighting)

February
1–4 San Pedro Pinula, a fine traditional fiesta, main day 4th
5–10 Monjas, main day 7th
24–28 Río Hondo, main day 26th
Varies Both Pasaco (in the department of Jutiapa) and Huite (near Zacapa) have fiestas around carnival time

March
3–5 Jeréz (in the department of Jutiapa), main day 5th
9 Esquipulas, a smaller day of pilgrimage to the Black Christ
12–15 Moyuta (near Jutiapa) and Olapa (near Chiquimula)
15–21 Morales, main day 19th
Varies Jocotán

April
22–25 La Unión (near Zacapa), main day 25th

May
2–5 Jalapa, main day 3rd
5–9 Gualán (near Zacapa)

June
23–26 Usumatlán

July
16–22 Puerto Barrios, the (riotous) main day is the 19th
22–26 Jocotán (near Chiquimula)
23–27 Esquipulas, a fiesta in honour of Santiago Apóstol, main day 25th

August
11–18 Chiquimula, main day 15th (includes bullfighting)
12–15 Asunción Mita
25 San Luís Jilotepéque

September
22–25 Sansare (between Jalapa and Sanarate), main day 24th

November
7–14 Sanarate
10–16 Jutiapa, main day 13th
26 Lívingston, Garífuna day here is a huge celebration
26–30 Quesada (near Jutiapa)

December
4–9 Zacapa, main day 8th
13–16 San Luís Jilotepéque
22–27 Cuilapa
24–31 Lívingston, a Caribbean-style carnival

Inside the **church** there's a constant scurry of hushed devotion amid clouds of smoke and incense. In the nave pilgrims approach the image on their knees, while others light candles, mouth supplications or simply stand in silent crowds. The image itself is most closely approached by a separate side entrance, where you can join the queue to shuffle past beneath it and pause briefly in front before being shoved on by the crowds behind. Back outside you'll find yourself among swarms of souvenir- and relic-hawkers, and pilgrims who, duty done, are ready to head off to eat and drink away the rest of their stay. Many pilgrims also visit a set of nearby **caves**, Las Cuevas de las Minas (US$1.75), a ten-minute walk south of the basilica, said to have miraculous powers; and there are some **hot baths** – ideal for ritual ablution.

Practicalities

Hotels in Esquipulas fill up quickly on weekends, when prices (which are always negotiable) also increase. The bulk of the budget places are grubby and bare, with tiny monk-like cells – not designed in a spirit of religiosity, but simply to up the number of guests.

Cheap places are clustered just north of the main road, 11 Calle. The good-value *Hotel Posada Santiago* (☎7943 2023; ❸) and family-run *Hotel Villa Edelmira* (☎7943 1431; ❷–❸), both on 2 Avenida, are two good choices at the lower end of the scale; both have rooms with private bathrooms. For more comfort *Hotel Portal de la Fe* (☎7943 4124; ❺) on 11 Calle has clean, attractive rooms with wrought-iron bed frames and nice decorative touches. Just west of the church on the south side of 2 Avenida are several mid-range places including *Hotel Los Ángeles* (☎7943 1254; ❺) with large, comfortable accommodation, and *Hotel Payaquí* (☎7943 2025; ❻), which has a pool, restaurant, spa treatments and spacious, well-equipped air-conditioned rooms.

There are also dozens of **restaurants** and **bars** to choose from. Breakfast is a bargain in Esquipulas, and you shouldn't have to pay more than US$2 for a good feed. Many places advertise lunch specials though dinner can be expensive. The *Hacienda Steak House*, a block from the plaza at 2 Avenida and 10 Calle, is one of the smartest places in town, while many of the cheaper places are on 11 Calle and the surrounding streets – *Taquería Andalé* at 2 Avenida and 10 Calle has tasty tacos. You'll find plenty of **banks** with ATMs in town including Banco Industrial at 9 Calle and 3 Avenida.

Rutas Orientales runs a superb half-hourly **bus** service between Guatemala City and Esquipulas; its office is at the junction of the main street and 1 Avenida. There are also half-hourly microbuses from 11 Calle to the borders with **El Salvador** (1hr) and **Honduras** at Agua Caliente (30min) until 6pm. If you want to get to the ruins of Copán, you'll need to catch a microbus towards Chiquimula (every 20min) and change buses at the junction on the highway that leads to Jocotán and the El Florido border post (see p.358).

On to the borders: El Salvador and Honduras

The **Honduran** border crossing at **Agua Caliente**, open 24 hours, is just 10km from Esquipulas. There's a **Honduran consulate** (Mon–Fri 8am–1pm & 3–6pm) in the *Hotel Payaquí*, beside the church in Esquipulas, though most nationalities do not need a visa.

The border with **El Salvador** at Anguiatú (also open 24 hr) is 33km from Esquipulas; most nationalities do not need a visa to enter this country either.

Travel details

Buses

Bus travel is convenient and pretty rapid in this region, and the main highways are all paved and in good condition. Details of services from Guatemala City can be found on pp.88–89, Puerto Barrios on p.253, Río Dulce on p.266.

Chiquimula to: El Florido (every 30min; 1hr 30min); Guatemala City (hourly; 3hr 30min); Ipala (hourly; 1hr).

Esquipulas to: Agua Caliente (every 30min; 30min); Anguiatú (every 30min; 1hr); Guatemala City (every 30min; 4hr 15min).

Boats

Lívingston to: Omoa, Honduras (charters only; 2hr 30min); Puerto Barrios, by ferry (2 daily; 1hr 30min) or *lancha* (about every 40min; 30min); Punta Gorda, Belize (2 weekly; 1hr); Río Dulce Town (regular services; about 2hr 30min).

Puerto Barrios to: Lívingston, by ferry (2 daily; 1hr 30min) or *lancha* (about every 40min; 30min); Punta Gorda, Belize (2 daily; 1hr 15min).

Río Dulce Town to: Lívingston (regular services until 4pm; about 2hr).

Cobán and the
Verapaces

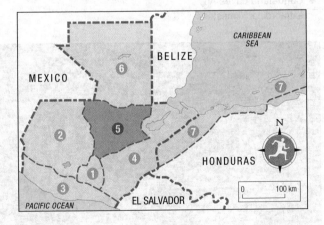

CHAPTER 5 # Highlights

✳ **Quetzal** Search for Guatemala's spectacularly plumed national bird in the cloudforests of the Verapaces. See p.286 & p.294

✳ **Semuc Champey** Bathe in these sublime turquoise pools at the foot of a plunging river valley. See p.295

✳ **Chisec** Explore the magical lakes of Lagunas de Sepalau and the sacred Maya cave of Bombil Pek near this peaceful little town. See p.297

✳ **Candelaria caves** An extraordinary limestone cave system, extending for more than 20km, with some immense chambers to investigate. See p.298

✳ **Laguna Lachúa** A pristine, near-circular lake rimmed by lowland jungle inhabited by jaguar and tapir. See p.300

✳ **Fiestas** Experience spectacular fiestas, with unique dances including the Rabinal Achi and Palo Volador in Baja Verapaz. See p.301

▲ Bombil Pek cave

Cobán and the Verapaces

While essentially a continuation of Guatemala's western highlands, the mountains of Alta (Upper) and Baja (Lower) Verapaz have always been set apart in a number of ways: certainly, the flat-bottomed Salamá valley and the mist-soaked hills around Cobán are physically unlike any of the country's other mountainous areas. **Baja Verapaz**, the more southerly of these two departments, is sparsely populated, a mixture of deep valleys and parched hills with patches of cloudforest coating the highest altitudes. Just two roads cross the department – one connects the fiesta towns of **Salamá**, **Rabinal** and **Cubulco**, the other runs from the Carretera al Atlántico up to Cobán.

Alta Verapaz, the wettest and greenest of Guatemala's highlands, occupies the land to the north. Locals say it rains for thirteen months a year here, alternating between straightforward downpours and the misty drizzle they call the *chipi-chipi*. Deforestation is a serious issue in parts, but most of the area's alpine terrain remains almost permanently moist and vivid with greenery, with almost limitless ecotourism opportunities. The pleasant town of **Cobán** is the departmental capital, and from here roads head north into Petén, west to El Quiché, and east to Lago de Izabal.

Some history and culture

The **history** of the Verapaces is also quite distinct. Long before the Conquest, local Achi Maya had earned themselves a reputation as the most bloodthirsty of all the tribes, said to sacrifice every prisoner they took. Alvarado's Spanish army was unable to make any headway against them, and eventually he gave up trying to control the area, naming it *tierra de guerra*, the "land of war".

The Church, however, couldn't allow so many heathen souls to go to waste. Under the leadership of **Fray Bartolomé de Las Casas**, the so-called "Apostle of the Maya", the Church made a deal with the conquistadors: if Alvarado would agree to keep all armed men out of the area for five years, the priests would bring it under control. In 1537 Las Casas set out into the highlands, befriended the Achi chiefs, and translated devotional hymns after learning the local dialects. By 1538 they had converted large numbers of Maya and persuaded them to move from their scattered hillside homes to the new Spanish-style villages, each with a Catholic church. After five years the famous and invincible Achi were transformed into Spanish subjects, and the king of Spain renamed the province *Verapaz*, "True Peace".

Since the colonial era the Verapaces have remained isolated, their trade bypassing the capital by taking a direct route to the Caribbean along the Río Polochic and out through Lago de Izabal. The area really started to develop with the **coffee boom** at the turn of the twentieth century, when German immigrants flooded into the country to buy and run fincas. By 1914 about half of all Guatemalan coffee was grown on German-owned lands, and Germany bought half of the exported produce.

Around Cobán the new immigrants established an island of European sophistication, the German population reaching around 2000 by the 1930s, with its own schools and clubs (and active Nazi party). A railway was built along the Polochic valley and Alta Verapaz became even more independent. This situation was brought to an end by World War II, when the US insisted that Guatemala do something about the German presence, and the government was forced to expel the landowners.

The area is still dependent on the production of coffee, and Cobán's economy remains heavily influenced by wealthy finca-owning families. Taken as a whole, however, the Verapaces are very much indigenous country: Baja Verapaz retains a small **Achi** Maya outpost around Rabinal, and in Alta Verapaz the Maya population, largely **Poqomchi'** and **Q'eqchi'** speakers, the two languages of

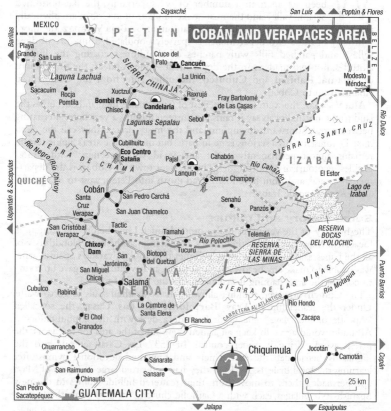

COBÁN AND VERAPACES AREA

Market days in the Verapaces

Monday
Senahú; Tucurú.

Tuesday
Chisec; El Chol; Cubulco; Lanquín; Purulhá; Rabinal; San Cristóbal Verapaz; San Jerónimo; Tres Cruces.

Saturday
Senahú.

Sunday
Chisec; Cubulco; Lanquín; Purulhá; Rabinal; Salamá; San Jerónimo; Santa Cruz Verapaz; Tactic.

the Poqomam group, is predominant. The production of coffee, and more recently **cardamom** for the Middle Eastern market, has cut deep into their land and their way of life, the fincas driving many people off prime territory to marginal plots. Traditional costume is worn less here than in the western highlands, and in its place many indigenous women have adopted a more universal Q'eqchi' costume, using the loose-hanging white *huipil* and machine-made *corte*. Maya men do not wear *traje* in the Verapaces.

Where to go
Tourism is fast becoming a vibrant part of the Verapaz economy, though numbers are still small compared to the western highlands. It's not hard to understand this region's appeal though, as the highlands here are astonishingly beautiful, with their craggy limestone hills, moist, misty atmosphere and boundless fertility. The transport hub of the area is **Cobán**, a fairly attractive mid-sized mountain town with good accommodation and some very civilized coffeehouses and restaurants. In Baja Verapaz, the towns of **Salamá**, **Rabinal** and **Cubulco** are rightly renowned for their fiestas, while **San Jerónimo** has some interesting historic sights.

In isolated patches of cloudforest in northern Baja Verapaz you can occasionally see the quetzal, Guatemala's national bird: the **quetzal sanctuary** is an accessible and popular place to search, though you may have more luck inside the larger adjacent **Reserva Sierra de las Minas**. Northeast of Cobán, the exquisite natural bathing pools of **Semuc Champey** are surrounded by lush tropical forest and fast becoming a key travellers' hangout. A couple of wonderful natural attractions can be found near the town of **Chisec**: the emerald **Lagunas de Sepalau** and the huge cavern of Bombil Pek, a focus for Maya worship. From Chisec it's a short hop to the vast system of **Candelaria caves** and the nearby ruins of **Cancuén**. In the extreme northwest of the region, the astonishingly beautiful lake **Laguna Lachúa**, fringed by rainforest, is well worth the detour it takes to get there.

Baja Verapaz
A dramatic mix of dry hills and fertile valleys, Baja Verapaz is crossed by a skeletal road network. The historic towns of **San Jerónimo**, **Salamá**, **Rabinal** and **Cubulco** have interesting markets as well as being famed for

their fiestas. The other big attractions are the **quetzal sanctuary**, on the western side of the Cobán highway, and the forested mountains, waterfalls and wildlife inside the **Reserva Sierra de las Minas** just to the east.

The main approach to both departments is from the Carretera al Atlántico, where the road to the Verapaz highlands branches off at the **El Rancho** junction. The road climbs steadily upwards, past the excellent, very popular roadside *Villa del Sol* restaurant (at Km88), where a filling meal costs US$3.50. Soon the dusty browns and dry yellows of lower altitudes give way to an explosion of green as dense pine forests and alpine meadows grip the mountains. Some 48km beyond the junction is **La Cumbre de Santa Elena**, where the road for the main towns of Baja Verapaz turns off to the west, and immediately begins to drop towards the floor of the Salamá valley. Surrounded by steep, parched hillsides, with a level flood plain at its base, the valley appears entirely cut off from the outside world.

San Jerónimo

At the valley's eastern end lies the small town of **SAN JERÓNIMO**, 18km from the Cumbre junction. In the Conquest's early days, Dominican priests built a church and convent here and planted vineyards, eventually producing a wine lauded as the finest in Central America. In 1845, after the religious orders were abolished, an Englishman replaced the vines with sugarcane and began brewing an *aguardiente* that became equally famous. These days the area still produces cane, though the cultivation of flowers for export and fish farming have usurped alcohol production in importance.

Thanks to a trio of sights, tranquil San Jerónimo attracts the odd curious visitor. Presiding over the central plaza, the village's seventeenth-century Baroque **church** contains a monumental gilded altar, brought from France, which was crafted from sheets of eighteen-carat gold. Just down the hill from the church, in a wonderful rural setting at the base of the foothills of the Sierra de las Minas, are the remains of the convent complex: the Hacienda de San Jerónimo. Its sugar-mill buildings now form the **Museo Regional del Trapiche** (Mon–Fri 8am–4pm, Sat & Sun 10am–4pm; donation) with displays that explain the history of the hacienda and refining process, while the extensive grassy grounds make an ideal place for a picnic. Also of interest is the colonial **aqueduct**, built in 1679, which once supplied the mill's waterwheels. Many of its 124 original stone arches are still standing on the southern outskirts of the village, about ten-minutes' walk from the plaza – just ask the way to the *acueducto antiguo*.

The excellent colonial-style *Hotel Hacienda Real el Trapiche* (☏7940 2542; ❹), at the entrance to the town, has very attractive rooms, all with good beds, reading lights and fair rates for solo travellers; its restaurant offers great home-cooked food. Running a close second is the *Hotel Posada de Los Frayles* (☏7723 5733; ❹) with similar standards but with the added benefit of a pool. *Los Arcos*, on the plaza, is the pick of the comedores. **Minibuses** connect Salamá and San Jerónimo between 6am and 7.30pm, running every half-hour.

Salamá

Eight kilometres west of San Jerónimo is **SALAMÁ**, capital of the department of Baja Verapaz. The town has a relaxed and prosperous air, and like many of the places out this way, its population is largely ladino. There's not much to do outside of **fiesta time** (Sept 17–21) other than browse the Sunday market, although it's worth checking out the crumbling colonial **bridge**, now used only by pedestrians, on the edge of town, and the old **church**, the gilt of its huge altars darkened by age. The best of the **hotels** is the modern, efficiently run *Hotel Real Legendario*, 8 Avenida 3–57 (☏7940 1751; ❹), with a little café and very clean rooms, all with private bath, comfy beds and cable TV. *Hotel Tezulutlán*, just south of the plaza (☏7940 1643; ❸), is a reasonable colonial-style alternative, though the rooms could be cleaner. For budget digs *Pensión Juárez*, at the end of 5 Calle (☏7940 1114; ❷–❸), is a good bet with plenty of rooms, some with bathroom. For **eating**, try one of the places around the plaza: *El Ganadero* is the best restaurant, while *Deli-Donus* and *Café Central* both score for coffee and snacks. Banrural, opposite the church, has an ATM and will cash dollars and traveller's cheques. Telgua, just east of the plaza, has **internet** access.

To really explore the region contact Eco-Verapaz, 8 Avendia 7–12, Zona 1 (☏7940 0146), who offer good mountain-biking, caving, hiking, horseriding and cultural trips throughout the department. Prices are around US$40 a day for most activities. **Buses** between Guatemala City and Salamá (3hr 15min) run half-hourly from 11 Avenida and 17 Calle, Zona 1, in the capital; many continue on to Rabinal (4hr) and Cubulco (4hr 30min). A steady stream of minibuses runs to San Jerónimo and to the La Cumbre junction, where there are connections with pullman buses running between Cobán and Guatemala City.

Rabinal

To the west of Salamá the road climbs out of the valley over a low pass and through a gap in the hills to **San Miguel Chicaj**, a large traditional village clustered around a colonial church. Beyond here the road climbs again, reaching a pass with magnificent views across the surrounding mountain ranges, which step away into El Quiché.

Less than an hour from Salamá, **RABINAL** is a dusty, isolated farming town where the one-storey adobe and cinderblock houses are dominated by a large colonial church. The proportion of indigenous inhabitants is considerably higher, making both the Sunday market and the fiesta well worth a visit. Founded in 1537 by Bartolomé de Las Casas, Rabinal was the first of the settlements he established in his peaceful conversion of the Achi nation; about 3km northwest, a steep ninety-minute hike away, are the ruins of one of their fortified cities, known locally as **Cerro Cayup**. Nowadays the place is known for its oranges, claimed to be the finest in the country – and they certainly taste like it.

Sights are slim in Rabinal itself, but the town's small **museum**, 4 Avenida and 2 Calle, Zona 3 (Mon–Sat 8.30–5pm), is worth a visit. You'll find exhibits on traditional medicinal practices, cultural history, local crafts including ceramics and weaving, and a room devoted to the impact of the civil war in the region – there were four massacres in 1982 alone in the Río Negro area north of the town. Local people have recently exhumed several of the mass graves that pepper the hillsides around Rabinal and reburied some of the 4400 victims from the municipality, in an effort to give those killed during *la violencia* a more dignified resting-place. In 2004, the Inter-American Court ordered the Guatemalan government to pay US$8 million as compensation to the surviving families of one massacre. Yet despite eight years of legal investigations, only three very junior members of the local PUC (paramilitary conscripts) have been jailed, and the army officers who directed the campaign remain free.

Rabinal's **fiesta**, which runs from January 19 to 24, is renowned for its dances, many of them pre-colonial in origin. The most famous is an extended dance drama known as the "Rabinal Achi" which re-enacts a battle between the Achi and K'iche' tribes and is unique to the town, performed annually on January 23

– it's recently been bestowed UNESCO World Heritage recognition. Others include the *patzca*, a ceremony to call for good harvests, using masks that portray a swelling below the jaw, and wooden sticks engraved with serpents, birds and human heads. **Market days** (Tues and Sun) are fascinating in Rabinal – look for some high-quality local *artesanías*, including carvings made from the *árbol del morro* (calabash tree) and traditional pottery.

The best of Rabinal's several fairly basic **hotels** is the well-run *Posada San Pablo*, 3 Avenida 1–50 (☎7940 0211; ❷), a decent budget place with tidy rooms, some with private bath. If it's full, try the *Hospedaje Caballeros*, 1 Calle 4–02 (❶). For an inexpensive **meal**, count on *Cafetería Mishell del Rosario* on 1 Calle behind the church. The Banrural at 1 Calle and 3 Avenida cashes dollars only. Very regular **buses** connect the town with Salamá (45min). For Guatemala City, there are eight daily via La Cumbre (4hr 20min), and three daily via El Chol and Granados (6hr).

Cubulco

Leaving Rabinal the road heads west, climbing yet another high ridge with fantastic views to the left, into the uninhabited mountain ranges. To the north, in one of the deep river valleys, lies the financially disastrous **Chixoy** hydroelectric plant (see p.287), responsible for producing around fifty percent of both Guatemala's electricity and its national debt.

A further 15km of rough road brings you into the next valley and to **CUBULCO**, an isolated town of Achi Maya and ladinos, surrounded on all sides by steep, forested mountains. Like Salamá and Rabinal, Cubulco is best visited for its fiesta, this being one of the few places where you can still see the **Palo Volador**, a pre-conquest ritual in which men throw themselves from a thirty-metre pole with a rope tied around their legs, spinning down towards the ground as the rope unravels, and hopefully landing on their feet. It's as dangerous as it looks, particularly when you bear in mind that most of the dancers are blind drunk; every few years an inebriated dancer falls from the top of the pole to his death. The fiesta still goes on, though, as riotous as ever, with the main action taking place on July 25. If you're in town at fiesta time be sure to taste the local *chilate* drink, made from corn and spices and served in fruit husks. *Hospedaje Pías* (❶), next to the large farmacia in the centre of town, has some rooms with private bath. Avoid the smelly *Posada Morales* (❶). There are several comedores in the market, but *La Fonda del Viajero* scores highest marks, serving up big portions of Guatemalan food at reasonable prices.

Reserva Sierra de las Minas and Biotopo del Quetzal

Heading for Cobán, and deeper into the highlands, the highway sweeps straight past the turning for Salamá and on around endless tight curves below forested hillsides. The steep slopes on the eastern side of the road form the foothills of the **Sierra de las Minas**, a mighty mountain range that soars to more than 3000m along a slender stretch of land between the Motagua and Polochic valleys. Forming one of Guatemala's largest expanses of **cloudforest**, this misty, thinly populated region harbours abundant wildlife including howler monkeys, white-tailed deer, coyotes and birds including the emerald toucan, hummingbirds and fairly plentiful numbers of quetzals (see box, p.287).

Much of the area has been designated the **Reserva Sierra de las Minas**, which is not easy to **get to** independently. You first need to head for the village of **San Rafael Chilascó**, 12km east of the Guatemala City–Cobán highway via the turn-off at Km145, where you may have to wait a little while for a pick-up or bus. Once in San Rafael, ask for the ecotourism committee (☎5301 8928, ⓦwww.chilasco.net.ms) who will organize accommodation (❶), meals with local families and guides. Good-quality waterproofs and hiking boots are recommended. Trails lead to two spectacular **waterfalls**, El Saltó de Chilascó, which plunges 200m in two drop close to the entrance of the reserve, and the Laguneta falls, which drops an astounding 350m in stages. There are many rare orchids and a liquidambar forest to admire along the way.

Back on the highway north to Cobán, just before the village of Purulhá, the **Biotopo del Quetzal** (daily 7am–4pm; US$3.50) is a much easier place to visit, though Guatemala's national bird is actually most common in the forests south of San Pedro Carchá (see p.294). The nature reserve is designed to protect the habitat of the endangered quetzal and covers a steep area of dense cloud-forest, through which the Río Colorado cascades towards the valley floor, forming waterfalls and natural swimming pools. It's also known as the **Mario Dary Reserve**, in honour of an environmental campaigner who spent years campaigning for a cloudforest sanctuary to protect the quetzal, causing great problems for powerful timber companies in the process. He was murdered in 1988. An ecological foundation, Fundary, has been set up in his name to manage protected areas, including Punta de Manabique on the Caribbean coast.

Visiting the sanctuary
Two paths through the undergrowth from the road complete a circuit that takes you up into the woods above the reserve headquarters (where maps are available for US$0.75). Quetzals are occasionally seen here but they're extremely elusive. The best time of year to visit is just before and just after the nesting season (between March & June), and the best time of day is sunrise. In general, the birds tend to spend the nights up in the high forest and float across the road as dawn breaks, to spend the days in the forest below, and they can be easily identified by their jerky, undulating flight. A good place to look out for them is at one of their favoured feeding trees, the broad-leaved *aguacatillo*, which produces a small avocado-like fruit. Whether or not you see a quetzal, the forest itself, usually damp with *chipi-chipi*, a perpetual mist, is worth a visit: a profusion of lichens, ferns, mosses, bromeliads and orchids spread out beneath a towering canopy of cypress, oak, walnut and pepper trees.

Practicalities
Buses from Cobán and Guatemala City pass the entrance (at Km161) every half-hour.

There are several **places to stay, eat and drink** within a few kilometres of the quetzal sanctuary. Coming from Guatemala City, the first place you reach is the upmarket rural lodge *Hacienda Río Escondido* (☎5208 1407; ❻) at Km144, which has lovely wooden cabañas, some with two bedrooms, and a restaurant with excellent grilled meats. Further north, *Hotel Posada Montaña del Quetzal* at Km156.5 (☎2332 4969 or 6620 0709, ⓦwww.hposadaquetzal.com; ❺–❼) offers attractive stone and timber bungalows with fireplaces and spacious rooms with private bathrooms; many have great forest views and there's a restaurant, bar, swimming pool, walking trails and an orchid garden here. The next place is *Ram Tzul*, Km158.5 (☎5908 4066, ⓔramtzul@internet.net.gt; ❺–❻), where the bizarre glass-fronted restaurant is a blot on the landscape, but there are surprisingly attractive, tasteful rooms to the rear, many with great views of the Verapaz hills. Just 100m past the entrance to the reserve, the simple *Hospedaje Ranchito del Quetzal* (☎2331 3579; ❷–❸) offers basic accommodation either in

The resplendent quetzal

The **quetzal**, Guatemala's national symbol (after which the country's currency and second city are named), has a distinguished past but an uncertain future. The bird's feathers have been sacred from the earliest of times, and in the strange cult of Quetzalcoatl, whose influence once spread throughout Mesoamerica, the bird was incorporated into the plumed serpent, a supremely powerful deity. To the Maya the quetzal was so sacred that killing one was a capital offence, and it is also thought to have been the *nahual*, or spiritual protector, of the Maya chiefs. When Tecún Umán faced Pedro de Alvarado in hand-to-hand combat, his headdress sprouted the long green feathers of the quetzal; and when the conquistadors founded a city adjacent to the battleground they named it Quetzaltenango, "the place of the quetzals".

In modern Guatemala the quetzal's image saturates the country: its image is on the national flag, and citizens honoured by the president are awarded the Order of the Quetzal. The bird is also considered a symbol of freedom, since caged quetzals die from the rigours of confinement. Despite all this, the sweeping tide of deforestation threatens the very existence of the bird, and the **Biotopo del Quetzal** is about the only serious step that has been taken to save it.

There are six species of the bird, but it's the male Resplendent Quetzal (found between southern Mexico and Panama) which is the most exotically coloured. Its head is crowned with a plume of brilliant green, and chest and lower belly are a rich crimson; the unmistakeable iridescent green tail feathers (reaching some 60cm in length) are particularly evident in the mating season. The females, on the other hand, are an unremarkable brownish colour. The birds nest in holes drilled into dead trees, laying one or two eggs at the start of the rainy season, usually in April or May. Quetzals can easily be identified by the strangely jerky way they fly.

very rustic palapa-roofed huts or in a pretty miserable concrete block. You'll find a simple in-house comedor, too, and compensating for the no-frills facilities, quetzals are sometimes seen in the patch of forest around the hotel. Heading on towards Cobán, the Swiss-style *Country Delight Inn* (T5514 0955; ⑤–⑦), Km166.5, offers good rooms with bath and very attractive chalets (that sleep up to six) with fireplaces and full cooking facilities. The inn enjoys a pleasant meadow setting and there's ping pong, a kids' play area and a small pool. Even if you're just passing by, it's well worth sampling some of the inn's hearty, *comida casero* – try the delicious locally reared ham, or home-baked cakes.

Alta Verapaz

Heading north of the quetzal sanctuary the highway crosses into the department of Alta Verapaz, and another 13km takes you beyond the forests and into a luxuriant alpine valley of cattle pastures hemmed in by steep, perpetually green hillsides. Most people speed through this region on their way to Cobán, but there are a few interesting attractions to detain you if you have the time to explore these evergreen hills and their towns' curiosities.

Tactic

The first place of any size is **TACTIC**, a small, mainly Poqomchi'-speaking town adjacent to the main road, which most buses bypass. Tactic has earned its share of fame as the site of an odd attraction, the **pozo vivo** or "living well", sited opposite the northern entrance road at Km184. However, it's certainly not worth going out of your way on the off-chance of a swirl in the mud, as the well remains pretty dried up for most of the year. Far more interesting is the pagan **Chi-ixim** chapel, high above the town up a long flight of steps. This church has a dark-skinned Christ figure that attracts pilgrims from all over the country, but especially on January 15. Dozens of plaques of thanksgiving for miracles ascribed to the black saint of Chi-ixim, who also goes by the name Dios del Maíz ("Lord of Maiz"), adorn the walls. The colonial **church** in the plaza is also worth noting; it boasts an elaborate facade decorated with mermaids and jaguars.

For somewhere **to stay**, the *Hotel Villa Linda*, 4 Calle 6–25 (☎7953 9216; ❸), has clean rooms with private baths. Better still, head for the rustic *Chí'ixím Eco Hotel*, at Km182.5 just off the highway (☎7953 9198; ❹), which has comfortable bungalows with fireplaces and a spotless little dining room. For ranch-style **food**, *Café La Granja*, a little further on at Km187, has a menu of Guatemalan favourites plus sandwiches and salads in a great log-cabin-style setting.

San Cristóbal Verapaz and around

Further towards Cobán, the turn-off for Uspantán peels off to the left at the featureless settlement of **Santa Cruz Verapaz** and then continues west to **SAN CRISTÓBAL VERAPAZ**, an attractive town surrounded by fields of sugarcane and coffee. It's set on the banks of the **Lago de Cristóbal**, a favourite spot for swimming and fishing, although a shoe factory close to the shore has polluted the water. The Poqomchi'-speaking Maya of San Cristóbal are among the last vestiges of one of the smallest and oldest highland tribes. You can find out more about their culture at an interesting little **museum**, located just off the plaza at Calle del Calvario 0–03. The **Museo Katinamit** (Mon–Sat 8am–1pm & 2–5pm, Sun 9am–noon; US$1) hosts exhibits on the maguey plant, which is woven into bags, hammocks and rope; Verapaz flora and fauna; and music – visits to a marimba factory can also be arranged. Handicrafts are for sale too. The museum acts as a base for the Centro Comunitario Educativo Poqomchi' (CECEP; ☎7950 4039, ✉cecep@intelnet.net.gt), which can organize **ethnotourism** trips (from US$9 for a half-day walking tour) of indigenous villages and sights around San Cristóbal, and also offers **Spanish language** classes for US$140 a week, including full board with a local family. The **website** ⓦwww.sancrisav.net has good information about the town and local culture.

San Cristóbal knows how to throw a good **fiesta** – it runs from July 21–26 (the main day is July 25) – and is an excellent, almost tourist-free place to head for **Semana Santa**, when a kilometre-long coloured sawdust carpet is created between the main church in the plaza and the Calvario chapel to the west. As all the hotels in town are pretty grim, you might want to drop by on a day-trip from Cobán.

South of San Cristóbal is the billion-dollar disaster known as the **Chixoy dam** and hydroelectric plant. The dam provides Guatemala with about half its electricity needs but the price of the project has been high. Unchecked deforestation in the area has increased sediment in the river thus reducing the efficiency of the power plant, and the cost of constructing the dam accounts for a sizeable chunk of all Guatemala's considerable foreign-debt payments. Villagers displaced by the huge project are still fighting for compensation from the government more than twenty years after it was completed.

West from San Cristóbal there's 25km of dirt road (that is steadily being paved), then after the bridge over the Río Chixoy a smooth paved highway to **Uspantán**, from where buses run to Santa Cruz del Quiché, via Sacapulas.

Minibuses run about every thirty minutes between Cobán and Uspantán, passing through San Cristóbal until 6pm.

Cobán

The heart of these rain-soaked hills and the capital of the department is **COBÁN**, Guatemala's principal centre for gourmet **coffee** production. Your initial impression of the town may not be that favourable – heavy traffic crawls past the central plaza and the main downtown shopping district is pretty nondescript – but away from here Cobán soon reveals its charms. It's not a large place (the population is around 65,000) and suburbs fuse gently with outlying meadows and pine forests, giving the town the air of an overgrown mountain village.

If the rain sets in, Cobán's atmosphere can become a bit subdued, and in the evenings the air is often damp and cool. The sun does put in an appearance most days, though, and the town certainly makes a useful base for a day or two. Sights include an excellent little Maya archeological museum, an orchid nursery, a coffee farm, and you'll find genteel cafés where you can sample a cup made from the world-renowned Verapaz bean. Outside the town, the spectacular mountains and rivers hold all kinds of exciting **ecotourism** possibilities, many of which can be done as day-trips.

Arrival and information

Transportes Escobar y Monja Blanca, one of Guatemala's best **bus** services, operates half-hourly departures between Guatemala City and its terminal in Cobán at 2 Calle 3–77, Zona 4 (☎7951 1793). The main terminal for **local destinations** is 2km north of the plaza.

Inguat does not have a tourist office here; you'll find the best information at Adrenalina Tours (see "Tours"), *Hostal d'Acuña* and *Casa Luna* (see "Accommodation"). The **website** ⓦ www.cobanav.net is also well worth consulting. For expert guidance and advice about getting to very remote areas of the Verapaces, contact Proyecto Eco-Quetzal (see "Listings").

Like many other Guatemalan towns, Cobán is divided into a number of **zonas**, with the northeast corner of the plaza at 1 Calle and 1 Avenida the dividing point. Zona 1 is to the northwest, Zona 2 to the southwest, Zona 3 to the southeast and Zona 4 to the northeast.

Accommodation

Cobán has a selection of good **hotels**, many with plenty of colonial charm, and some excellent hostel-style places.

Budget

Casa Blanca 1 C 3–25, Zona 1 ☎5931 7862. Currently one of the hottest backpacker places. The dorms (US$5 per head) are quite large, with six and eight beds, and the private rooms with bathroom are only fair value. There is a kitchen for guests, a travel agency and a little comedor. ②–④

Casa Luna 5 Av 2–28, Zona 1 ☎7951 3528. A well-run, traveller-geared place with attractive rooms and dorms (US$6 per bed), reliably hot showers, hammocks to swing in and a grassy courtyard to enjoy. Also home of the Coban Travels tour agency. ②–③

Hostal d'Acuña 4 C 3–17, Zona 2 ☎7951 0482, ⓔ casadeacuna@yahoo.com. Probably the classiest hostel in Central America, this excellent place has great four-bed dorms (US$7 per head) and a couple of small private rooms bordering the lush garden of a colonial house. The location is relaxing and tranquil, a short walk down from the main plaza, and the restaurant is one of the town's finest. Tours are offered, too. ③

Hotel La Paz 6 Av 2–19, Zona 1 ☎7952 1358. No-frills budget hotel run by a slightly gruff but vigilant *señora*. The rooms are fairly featureless,

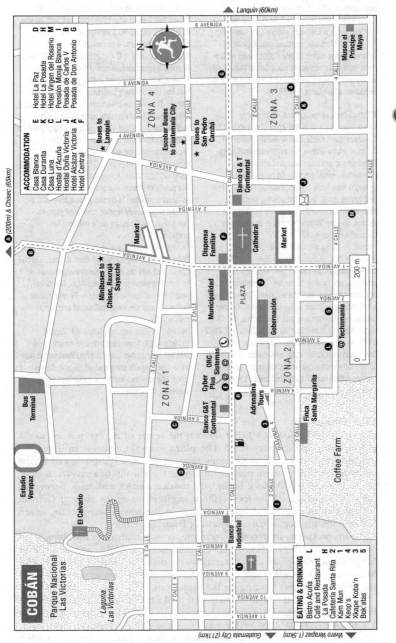

COBÁN

Parque Nacional
Las Victorias

Laguna
Las Victorias

El Calvario

Estadio Verapaz

Bus Terminal

ZONA 1

Banco Industrial

Banco G&T Continental

Cyber ORC Plus Sistemas @ @ @

Adrenalina Tours

DIAGONAL 4

ZONA 2

Finca Santa Margarita

Coffee Farm

Municipalidad

PLAZA

Gobernación

@ Technmania

Market

Cathedral

Dispensa Familiar

ZONA 3

Market

Banco G & T Continental

Buses to San Pedro Carchá

Escobar Buses to Guatemala City

ZONA 4

Buses to Lanquín

Minibuses to ★ Chisec, Raxrujá Sayaxché

Museo el Príncipe Maya

▲ Lanquín (60km)

▲ (200m) & Chisec (65km)

▲ Vivero Verapaz (1.5km) ▲ Guatemala City (211km)

6 AVENIDA
5 AVENIDA
4 AVENIDA
3 AVENIDA
2 AVENIDA
1 AVENIDA

3 CALLE
2 CALLE
1 CALLE
2 CALLE
3 CALLE
4 CALLE
5 CALLE

5 AVENIDA
6 AVENIDA
7 AVENIDA
8 AVENIDA
9 AVENIDA
10 AVENIDA
11 AVENIDA

N

200 m

ACCOMMODATION

Casa Blanca	E	Hotel La Paz	D
Casa Duranta	K	Hotel La Posada	H
Casa Luna	C	Hotel Virgen del Rosario	M
Hostal d'Acuña	L	Pensión Monja Blanca	I
Hostal Doña Victoria	J	Posada de Carlos V	B
Hotel Alcázar Victoria	A	Posada de Don Antonio	G
Hotel Central	F		

EATING & DRINKING

Bistro Acuña	L
Café and Restaurant La Posada	H
Cafetería Santa Rita	2
Kam Mun	1
Keop's	4
Xkape Koba'n	3
Bok'atas	5

but kept clean and tidy – and most have private bath. Safe parking, garden and café. ❸

Hotel Virgen del Rosario 2 Av 4–28, Zona 3 ☏7952 1914. A well-run, secure little hotel with fourteen comfortable, spotless rooms (with or without private bath); all are a little heavy on the floral prints, but represent good value. There's free coffee and drinking water, and the whole place is festooned with plants. ❷–❸

Moderate and luxury

Casa Duranta 3 C 4–46, Zona 3 ☏7951 4188, ⓦwww.casaduranta.com A lovely, converted colonial house where the bedrooms and open-sided dining area are grouped around a wonderful central garden. All rooms have wrought-iron beds and interesting furniture like bed tables made from old sewing machines, though the bathrooms are pretty perfunctory. Rooms do vary in size but not in price; try to book either 7 or 8. ❻

Hostal de Doña Victoria 3 C 2–38, Zona 3 ☏7951 4213, ⓦwww.hotelescoban.com. Refurbished mansion decorated with antiques and artefacts, and oozing character. The stylishly presented bedrooms all have private bath (though avoid the noise-prone streetside rooms). On-site café/bar, restaurant and tour agency, too. ❹–❺

Hotel Alcázar Victoria 1 Av 5–34, Zona 1 ☏7952 1143, ⓦwww.hotelescoban.com. Large, modern hotel, built in colonial style, with plenty of spacious, comfortable rooms, all with good beds, TV and reading lights, set off a covered patio. It's about 750m north of the plaza. ❺

Hotel Central 1 C 1–79, Zona 4 ☏7952 1442. Long-running place with clean, though darkish, rooms that have a little faded style, all with private bathrooms, set round a lovely central courtyard garden. There's also a comedor. ❹

Hotel La Posada 1 C 4–12, Zona 2 ☏7952 1495, ⓦwww.laposadacoban.com. Offering real atmosphere this hotel occupies a 400-year-old colonial building and boasts a beautiful, antique-furnished interior. The very tasteful, comfortable rooms, many with wooden Moorish-style screens (and some with four-poster beds), are set around two leafy courtyards, though traffic noise can be a problem. Excellent restaurant and café. ❼

Pensión Monja Blanca 2 C 6–30, Zona 2 ☏7951 1900 or 7952 0531. Agreeably old-fashioned and has plenty of rooms, many with private bathroom. All accommodation is on the ground level and set around two lovingly tended courtyard gardens. Don't miss the Victorian-style tearoom for breakfast. ❸–❹

Posada de Carlos V 1 Av 3–44, Zona 1 ☏7951 3501, ⓦwww.hotelcarlosvgt.com. It's set in urban Cobán, but this mountain chalet lookalike would be more at home in the Swiss Alps. The twenty pine-trimmed rooms have cable TV and private bathroom and there's a restaurant and ample parking. ❹

Posada de Don Antonio 5 C 1–51, Zona 4 ☏7951 4287. A wonderful double-height lobby sets the tone at this colonial-style hotel which has some fine Spanish tiling and an elegant dining-room. The spacious rooms are excellent value, and breakfast is included. ❺

The Town

Cobán's imperial heyday, when it stood at the centre of its own isolated world, is long gone, and its glory faded. The **plaza**, however, remains an impressive triangle, from which the town drops away on all sides. It's dominated by the **cathedral**, which is worth peering into to see the remains of a massive, ancient, cracked church bell. A block behind, the **market** bustles with trade during the day and is surrounded by food stalls at night. Hints of the days of German control can also be found here and there in the town's architecture, which incorporates the occasional suggestion of Bavarian grandeur.

Cobán's prosperity from coffee (and more recently cardamom and allspice) has built the colonial-style hotels and coffeehouses, nightclubs, and new **Plaza Magdalena** shopping and entertainment mall just west of the centre. Meanwhile, on the other side of town, the crowds that sleep in the market area are migrant labourers heading for the plantations.

For a closer look at Cobán's principal crop, take the guided tour offered by the **Finca Santa Margarita**, a coffee plantation just south of the centre of town at 3 Calle 4–12, Zona 2 (Mon–Fri 8am–12.30pm & 1.30–5pm, Sat 8am–noon; US$2.75). The interesting tour (an English-speaking guide is usually available) covers the history of the finca, founded by the Dieseldorff family in 1888, and examines all the stages of cultivation and production, including a walk through the grounds. You also get a chance to sample different low-, middle- and high-altitude Arabica coffee blends and, of course, purchase some beans.

Several blocks east of here you'll find an excellent assembly of Maya artefacts and carvings inside the small **Museo El Príncipe Maya**, 6 Avenida 4–26, Zona 3 (Mon–Sat 9am–6pm; US$2). The museum has some fine shell necklaces, polychrome bowls, jade earrings and a plethora of clay figurines, including warriors wearing animal masks. Don't miss the eccentric flints, early Classic urn or the main attraction – a stunning panel from a Cancuén altarpiece, embellished with 160 glyphs.

One of Cobán's most intriguing sights is the church of **El Calvario**, which is very popular with indigenous worshippers and a short stroll from the plaza. Head west out of town on 1 Avenida and turn right up 7 Avenida until you reach a steep cobbled path. You'll pass a number of tiny **shrines** on the way up – crosses blackened by candle smoke and decorated with scattered offerings. The faithful stoop to pray at these altars asking for divine help: to cure ills, bring love or wealth or cast misfortune on enemies. There's a commanding view over the town from the whitewashed church itself, which has a distinctly pagan identity, including both Christian and Maya crosses; inside the church hundreds of corn cobs (sacred in indigenous religion) hang from the roof. Next door the **Parque Nacional Las Victorias** (daily 8am–4.30pm; US$0.75) is Cobán's green lung, and a great place to stroll through the pines along attractive pathways; there's a children's playground too.

In the southwest outskirts of town **Vivero Verapaz** (Mon–Sat 9am–noon & 2–5pm, Sun 9am–noon; US$2) is a fascinating orchid nursery; they flourish in Cobán's damp climate. The farm produces some seven hundred indigenous varieties, as well as a handful of hybrids they've created themselves. The plants are nurtured in a wonderfully shaded environment, and a farm worker will show you around and point out the most spectacular buds, which are at their best between November and January. The nursery is about 3km from the plaza: follow

▲ Coffee: Cobán's principal crop

Diagonal 4 and then, at the bottom of the hill, turn left, go across the bridge and follow the main road. A taxi here from the plaza will cost about US$3.

Eating and drinking

Eating in Cobán comes down to a choice between European-style restaurants and very basic, cheap comedores. Look out for the local speciality: *kak-ik*, a terrific turkey soup. You'll find the cheapest food at the market, but as it's closed by dusk, head to the street stalls set up around the plaza. Central Cobán is pretty quiet at night, though you could check out *Xkape Koba'n* for a civilized **drink** or bar-restaurant *Bok'atas*, which gets lively on weekend nights. *Keop's*, 5 Avenida and 3 Calle, is a popular club where DJs play merengue, salsa and reggaeton. The **Plaza Magdalena** mall, 2km west of the plaza, boasts a multiplex cinema with three screens and plenty of fast-food restaurants.

Bistro Acuña 4 C 3–17, Zona 2. An exceptional restaurant in a beautiful colonial garden setting with elegant service, white tablecloths and uplifting classical music. Set breakfast meals (US$4–6) all include tea/coffee and juice, and the bread is home-made. Lunch and dinner (US$10–18) are from an imaginative menu, taking in pasta, grilled meat dishes, seafood and outstanding cakes and desserts. There's a long wine list.
Bok'atas 4 C 3–34, Zona 2. Large, lively and sociable bar-restaurant renowned for its Mediterranean food, including decent paella. Also serves up good margaritas and wine. Closed weekday lunch and Sun.
Café and Restaurant La Posada 1 C 4–12, Zona 2, inside *Hotel La Posada*. Stylish formal dining, serving Guatemalan specialities and international cuisine. There's a long menu and always a daily special, and if the weather permits, you can

eat on a veranda facing the hotel's garden. The more relaxed and inexpensive café (Wed–Mon 1–8.30pm) serves snacks and bagels.
Cafetería Santa Rita 2 C, on the plaza, close to the cathedral. An excellent comedor ideal for filling *comida típica*, including huge breakfasts, and has friendly service.
Kam Mun 1 C 8–12, Zona 2. Large Chinese restaurant with big portions and a solid line-up of economical choices.
Xkape Koba'n Diagonal 4 5–13, Zona 2. A wonderful, stylish café-restaurant in a gorgeous old house where the walls are decorated with *huipiles* and local art. There's a very inventive menu with snacks like *tamales* (US$2) and many local recipes including the famous local *kak-ik* turkey soup (US$7.50), and (a chocolate milk drink flavoured with vanilla, chilli and honey). Service can be slow though.

Listings

Banks and exchange Banco G&T has two branches – 1 C and 4 Av in Zona 1, and 1 C and 2 Av in Zona 3 – both with ATMs.
Car rental Tabarini, 7 Av 2–27, Zona 2 (T 7952 1504, W www.tabarini.com).
Internet Cyber Plus, 1 C 3–23, on north side of plaza, has quick connections, or try Techmania at 4 C 3–18, Zona 2.
Laundry La Providencia, at the western end of the plaza on Diagonal 4 (closed Sun).
Post office 3 C and 2 Av, Zona 3.
Spanish schools Cobán's easy-going atmosphere and relative lack of English-speakers makes it a good place to pick up Spanish. Schools include Oxford Language Center, 4 Av 2–16, Zona 3, Cobán (T 7951 2836, W www.olcenlgish.com), and about 12km from town Eco Cabaña, near San Juan Chamelco (T 7951 5898, E ecocabana@yahoo .com).

Telephones Head to Cyber Plus for cheap calls; see "Internet".
Tours Excursions to Semuc Champey (around US$45), Laguna Lachúa (around US$65) and other destinations, plus shuttle-bus connections are offered by several agencies including Adrenalina Tours, Diagonal 4, 3–36 Zona 2 (T 7951 2200, W www .adrenalinatours.com), Hostal d'Acuña (T 7951 0482) and Aventuras Turísticas, 1 C 3–25 (T 5931 7862). Proyecto Eco-Quetzal, at 2 C 14–36, Zona 1 (T 7952 1047, W www.ecoquetzal.org), is a highly recommended adventure and cultural tourism specialist that enables visitors to get off the beaten track and stay with indigenous villagers in remote areas of the Verapaces. These well-priced ecotourism initiatives include trips to the Chicacnab cloudforest (see p.294), where quetzals are abundant, for US$40 per head; while a two-night stay in the beautiful Río Ik'bolay region (see p.300) costs US$35.

Cobán's mud-bound, open-air bus terminal (also known as Terminal Nuevo or Campo Dos) is 2km north of the plaza. Most local routes are served from here including minibuses running to Chisec (every 20min, last at 6.30pm; 1hr 20min), Salamá (every 20min, last at 6pm; 2hr), Playa Grande (hourly, last at 4pm; 4hr 30min), Fray Bartolomé de Las Casas (every 30min via Chisec, last at 4pm; 3hr plus three daily via Pajal, around 6hr), Sayaxché (eight daily, last at 3.30pm; 4hr) and Uspantán (hourly, last at 5pm; 3hr). Buses also leave from here to Flores (9am and 1.30pm; 5hr), at other times take the first minibus to Saxyaché and another Flores-bound minibus from there.

Minibuses to Lanquín (hourly, last at 5pm; 2hr) and Semuc Champey (5.45am, 7.30am, 8.30am, 11am and noon; 2hr 30min) leave from 3 Calle and 3 Avendia, Zona 4. Heading for San Juan Chamelco (every 30min; 20min) they leave from the Wasen Bridge, Diagonal 15, Zona 7. Buses to Guatemala City (every 30min, last at 5pm; 4hr 30min) leave from the private terminal of Transportes Escobar y Monja Blanca at 2 Calle & 4 Avendia, Zona 4.

You'll also find some very useful "hop-on hop-off" **shuttle bus services** operating out of Cobán. *Hostal d'Acuña* (see "Accommodation") runs two routes: from Cobán to Tikal, with the option of jumping off at places including Chisec, Candelaria, Sayaxché and Flores on the way north; or you could get off at the Biotopo del Quetzal on their other route to Antigua. Adrenalina Tours, Diagonal 4, 3–36 Zona 2 (☏7951 2200, ⓦwww.adrenalinatours.com), runs a daily shuttle bus to Quetzaltenango via Uspantán, Nebaj (if there are passengers), Sayaxché and Huehuetenango. These shuttles may be convenient, but they are more expensive than public transport at US$22 to Flores or Antigua, or US$37 to Quetzaltenango. Shuttles to other destinations including Río Dulce (around US$24) can also be organized.

San Juan Chamelco and around

Seven kilometres southeast of Cobán, **SAN JUAN CHAMELCO** is the most important Q'eqchi' settlement in the area. Some of your fellow bus passengers are likely to be women dressed in traditional costume, wearing beautiful cascades of old coins for earrings. The town's focal point is a large colonial **church**, whose facade is rather unexpectedly decorated with twin Maya versions of the Habsburg double eagle – undoubtedly a result of the historic German presence in the region. The most significant treasure, the church bell, is hidden in the belfry; it was a gift to the Maya leader Juan Matalbatz from no less than the Holy Roman Emperor Charles V.

The large **market** around the church sells anything from local farm produce to blue jeans, but very little in the way of crafts. During the annual **fiesta** procession (July 24) locals dress up in outfits ranging from pre-conquest Maya costumes to representations of local wildlife.

Just 5km from Chamelco is a great **place to stay**, *Don Jerónimo's* (☏5301 3191, ⓦwww.dearbrutus.com/donjeronimo; US$25 per head for full board), a quirky, vegetarian guesthouse-cum-retreat in sublime rolling countryside, run by a friendly American who has been living off the land here for over twenty years. Guest bungalows are rustic but comfortable, and have private bathrooms. There's river tubing and good swimming close by and an impressive library to browse on rainy days. From Chamelco, minibuses heading for the village of Chamíl pass by the lodge; they leave regularly from 0 Calle and 0 Avenida.

Just 500m from *Don Jerónimo's* are the **Grutas de Rey Marcos** (daily 9am–5pm; US$3.50 including guide service, hard hat and boot rental), a series of **caves** discovered in May 1998. The cave system is more than a kilometre long, though the tour only takes you a little way into the complex – you have to wade across an underground river at one stage to see some of the best stalactites and stalagmites, including one that's a dead ringer for the Leaning Tower of Pisa.

Sierra de Caquipec

West of Cobán you pass through the neighbouring town of **San Pedro Carchá**, famous for its silver workshops, then the route climbs southwest up to the dense cloudforests of the **Sierra de Caquipec**, which probably contain the greatest concentration of **quetzals** (see box, p.286) in Central America. There are several hundred in this thinly populated region, which stretches south towards Tucurú, part of which has been declared a habitat sanctuary for Guatemala's national bird. It's possible to visit the Caquipec mountains as part of an excellent low-impact **ecotourism** initiative run by Proyecto Eco-Quetzal (see p.292), staying in the Q'eqchi' Maya village of **Chicacnab**, from where local guides take you into the oak and pine forests where quetzals are abundant, and wild boar, kinkajous and the odd jaguar are also found. Drop by Eco-Quetzal's office or consult their website for more information – living conditions are very basic but it's a highly rewarding experience for visitors.

Lanquín and Semuc Champey

Northeast of Cobán and San Pedro Carchá, a paved road heads off into the lush hills, connecting a string of coffee fincas. After 43km the road reaches the **Pajal** junction (46km from Cobán), where a branch road cuts down deep into a valley to **LANQUÍN** (a further 12km away). This sleepy, modest Q'eqchi' village, where Spanish is very much a second language, shelters beneath towering green hills, whose lower slopes are planted with coffee and cardamom bushes. The village itself is very relaxed and quite attractive, but virtually every visitor in town is here to enjoy the pools of Semuc Champey, a short ride away. There's a Banrural **bank**, which changes US dollars and traveller's cheques (but has no ATM) and **internet** (US$1 per hour) just off the plaza, though connections are erratic.

Accommodation and eating

Places to stay are both in and around the village of Lanquín, and strung out along the road to Semuc. Many are hostel-style places geared at backpackers, for whom this is an almost mandatory stop in Guatemala. There are also basic guesthouses in the village that will do for a night. Of the village **comedores**, two of the best are the bright little *Café Semuc* and the wood cabin *Comedor Shalom*.

Hostal El Portal 100m from Semuc ☎7983 0046. Excellent new community-owned lodge, run by a very helpful team, that enjoys a superb elevated plot with fine views down to the Río Cahabón. The accommodation is very inviting, with well-built screened wood cabañas with hammocks and balcony, five cosy private rooms and an eight-bed dorm (US$4). Bathrooms are very clean and attractive. There's good food, they sell wine and cold beers, and you'll find camping space and great birding too. Tubing and other trips are offered. ❷–❹

Hotel El Recreo 100m south of parque in village ☎7983 0032. Clean place with big, bare but clean screened rooms, some with private bathrooms. Prices are per head so it's not a bad deal for solo travellers. ❸

Posada Illobal 50m south of the parque, ☎7983 0014. The best of the village cheapies, with a nice garden and five plain, clean rooms in an old wooden house. Run by the very friendly owner Ramiro Pop. ❶

Posada Las Marías 1km from Semuc ☎7861 2209, ⓦwww.posadalasmarias.com. A peaceful lodge, just over the road from the Río Cahabón, with good swimming. It's run by young Q'eqchi' Maya, and has comfortable five-bed dorms (US$3 or US$6 with bathroom attached) and five good cabañas. Full restaurant and bar facilities, and caving tours to K'anba, tubing and other trips can be organized. ❷–❸

El Recreo on the entrance road to Lanquín ☎ 7983 0056. This place could try harder. The rooms are in a large, bare wooden building and the pool may or may not be clean. ❺

El Retiro A 10min walk west of Lanquín on road to Cahabón ☎ 7983 0009. A legend in its own brief lifetime, this rustic backpacker HQ enjoys a fine meadow setting on the banks of the Lanquín river. It's very much a gringo scene, with a party vibe most nights, fuelled by lots of drink specials (like double shots for US$1.30). All accommodation is set well apart, with fairly plain palm-leaf-thatched cabañas (some with private bathroom), good dorms (US$5 per head) and also camping space. There's healthy food, including home-made bread, while dinner (US$5.50) is a communal affair. Tons of activities, including caving, rappelling, horse-riding and tubing; shuttle buses can be arranged. Book ahead, as it fills up quickly. ❷–❹

Transport

Connections have improved greatly in recent years, and there are now direct public minibuses running between Cobán and Semuc (five daily 5.45am, 7.30am, 8.30am, 11am & noon; 2hr 30min); the last bus returns from Semuc at 4.30pm. In addition there are hourly minibuses (2hr) connecting Cobán and Lanquín; the last leaves Lanquín at 5pm. For the short hop between Lanquín and Semuc, there's a daily public minibus from the plaza at 9am, which returns at 4pm, plus the above connections. Private shuttle-bus tours run by several hotels in Cobán supplement the above services, charging US$45–65 for a day-trip. A few buses struggle north from the Pajal junction towards Fray Bartolomé de Las Casas, though ongoing road improvements may speed up this route again in the next few years; check with your hotel. Heading east, there are minibuses and buses to Cahabón (roughly hourly; 1hr), from where one daily bus (at 4am; 4hr) and irregular pick-ups head down to El Estor. *Posada Las Marías* operates a shuttle bus to El Estor (Tues and Fri; US$13).

The Lanquín and K'anba caves

Just a couple of kilometres west of Lanquín village, just off the road to Cobán, the **Lanquín caves** are a maze of dripping, bat-infested chambers, stretching for at least 3km underground (daily 8am–5pm; US$4). A walkway has been cut through the first few hundred metres and electric lights have been installed, but it remains dauntingly slippery. It's well worth dropping by the entrance at dusk, when thousands of bats emerge from the mouth of the cave and flutter off into the night. Maya religious rituals are held here (particularly at fiesta time and on Dec 5) when the whole village gathers for candlelit ceremonies.

Just before the entrance to Semuc, the **K'anba cave** system is a lot more fun to explore. Guided spelunking tours (US$5; at 9.30am daily), organized by *Posada Las Marías* (see "Accommodation"); involve scrambling and swimming by candlelight through chambers filled with bats and bizarre rock formations. For the brave (or mad) there are the optional additional thrills of climbing a dodgy rope ladder up the side of a five-metre waterfall or cliff-jumping into a pool in complete darkness. The tour takes about an hour and a half and finishes with some river tubing.

Semuc Champey

The region's prime attraction, however, and one of the most beautiful natural destinations in Guatemala is **Semuc Champey** (US$6; parking US$1), a shallow staircase of sublime turquoise pools suspended on a natural limestone bridge. This idyllic place, 10km south of Lanquín, sits at the base of a towering jungle-clad valley and makes a wonderful spot for a blissful day's wallowing and swimming, though watch out for the odd sharp edge. Just a few years ago very few visitors made it to this remote part of Guatemala, but the secret is now most definitely out, and the pools are very much a key stop on the backpacking trail between Tikal and the western highlands. That said, you can usually find a peaceful spot without too much difficulty.

If you walk a few hundred metres upstream via a slippery path you come to the river source that feeds Semuc: the fast-flowing **Río Cahabón**, the bulk of which plunges into a cavern, cutting under the pools in an aquatic frenzy before emerging again downstream. For a photo-perfect view of the whole scene, you can hike (and climb a little in sections) for thirty minutes up a slippery, vertiginous trail to a *mirador* high above the pools.

Don't leave your belongings unattended as the odd theft has been reported. For bus schedules, see Lanquín.

Cahabón

Beyond Lanquín the road continues to the small town of **CAHABÓN** – which has a few basic pensiones, the best being *Hospedaje Carolina* (❶) – an additional 24km to the east. From here a dirt track spirals around switchbacks to Panzós, cutting high over the mountains then plunging down through spectacular scenery. One daily **bus** (at 4am) makes the four-hour trip to El Estor, while pick-ups ply the route more frequently.

Down the Polochic valley to Panzós

If you're planning to head out towards the Caribbean from Cobán, then the route east along the **Polochic valley** is the one to take – head east from the San Julián junction, shortly after Tactic on the Coban–El Rancho highway. The scruffy towns along the length of this V-shaped valley hold little interest, but you'll witness an immense transformation in scenery as you drop down through the coffee-coated mountains and emerge into lush, tropical lowlands.

The first place at the upper end of the valley is **Tamahú**, 15km below which the town of **Tucurú** marks the point where the valley starts to open out and the river loses its frantic energy. Beyond Tucurú the road plunges abruptly, with cattle pastures starting to take the place of the coffee bushes, and both the villages and the people have a more tropical look about them. After 28km you reach **LA TINTA**, a sprawling town with the clean *Hotel Los Ángeles* (❶–❷) right on the highway, where some rooms have private bath.

Continuing east, it's just 13km to **TELEMÁN**, the largest of the squalid trading centres in this lower section of the valley; here, the agreeable family-run *Hotel de los Ralda* (☎7875 0074; ❷–❸) offers rooms with hot water and fans, while the *Ampakito Comedor* serves the town's best food. From Telemán a side road branches off to the north and climbs high into the fecund hills to the town of **SENAHÚ**, an important coffee centre that sits in a steep-sided bowl. Hikes run from here to the nearby **Cuevas de Seamay**, used by Maya shamen for ceremonies, and a track heads north to Semuc Champey and Lanquín, which is passable in dry season by 4WD. The best pensión is the simple *Edilson* (❶) while the pleasant *Hotel El Recreo Senahú* (☎7983 1637; ❹) is more comfortable; guides can be arranged. Regular buses shuttle between Telemán and Senahú.

Heading on down the Polochic valley you soon reach the large town of **PANZÓS**, which was where the old Verapaz railway ended. In 1978 Panzós made international headlines when 53 protesting campesinos (including women and children) were killed by the army and police, one of the earliest and most brutal massacres of General Lucas García's regime.

North towards Petén

In the northern section of Alta Verapaz, the lush hills drop away steeply onto the plain that marks the frontier with the department of Petén. The terrain is a beguiling mix of dense patches of rainforest, towering tooth-like outcrops of limestone called karsts, and pastureland. Some of the most extensive **cave systems** in Latin America are located here, particularly in the Candelaria region, which is riddled with caverns. One good paved highway runs north from Cobán, passing through Chisec, and then on up to Sayaxché in Petén. Otherwise the road network is rough and ready, though new tracks are running further and further into previously untouched forests up to the Mexican border, and new settlements are being established all the time. Many of the new villages are Q'eqchi' *aldeas*, others have been established by *repatriados*, Guatemalan exiles from highland villages who fled for their lives during the dark days of the civil war, only to return in the 1990s.

Chisec and around

Some 60km north of Cobán, **CHISEC** is a quiet, agreeable little town spread out along the highway that's grown quickly in the last years as land-hungry migrants have moved into the region. It's one of the very few places in Guatemala without a church on its (huge) central plaza – many of its population are former guerrillas and *repatriados* opposed to religious influence. Consult the excellent **websites** ⓦwww.visitchisec.com or www.puertamundomaya.com or drop by *La Huella* (see below) for more information about this fascinating region.

The most popular **place to stay** is *Hotel La Estancia* (☎7979 7748; ❸–❹), about 800m north of the plaza, with three floors of plain but clean rooms with cable TV and either air-conditioning or fan, a good restaurant and small swimming pool for cooling off. Otherwise *Hotel Nopales* (☎5514 0624; ❷) on the plaza is a cheaper, shabbier alternative where the bare rooms have concrete floors. For a **meal** *Cafetería La Huella* on the main road has inexpensive burgers, sandwiches and pupusas, or try the neat, stylish little *El Café*, which serves snacks and cakes; both these places also have **internet** connections. The very clean *Restaurant Bombil Pek* at the southern end of the village is also excellent for filling *comida típica*, if a bit pricier at around US$4 a meal. Banco Agromercantil has an ATM and cashes traveller's cheques. **Microbuses** run from Cobán to Chisec every half-hour (1hr 30min), and to Raxrujá via Candelaria (hourly; 1hr).

Bombil Pek and Lagunas de Sepalau

Chisec makes the perfect base for visiting two remarkable natural attractions, the nearest being the "painted cave" of **Bombil Pek** some 2km north of town. There's a community-run guide office (daily 8am–3.30pm) beside the nearby highway where you pay your entrance fee (US$3.50) and collect a flashlight; they also rent **tubes** (US$3; best July–Oct) for river exploration here. A guide leads you along a delightful forty-minute hike through the *milpa* fields and forest, and down a steep, slippery wooden staircase into the sinkhole and its vast fifty-metre-high main cavern. Many ceramics have been found here, and the cave is still used for Maya religious ceremonies. Your guide will then try to persuade you to squeeze through a tiny hole at the rear to a second, much smaller cave where the faded painted images of two monkeys, possibly representing the hero twins of the Popol Vuh (see box, p.134), adorn the walls.

The three exquisite jade lakes of **Lagunas de Sepalau**, Chisec's other outstanding attraction, are 9km from town along the road that heads west from the *municipalidad*. Pick-ups run sporadically all day from the plaza, and there's a bus at 11am.You'll be dropped off at the Q'eqchi' village of **Sepalau Cataltzul**, where you pay a US$5.50 entrance fee. A local guide will accompany you to the lagoons, 1km further away with a *lancha* for paddling across the water (and lifejackets).The first lake, **Laguna Paraíso**, ringed by untouched dense jungle, is beautiful and peaceful, and makes the perfect spot for a swim. The second, **Atsam'ja**, is much smaller, but the third and largest lake, **Q'ekija**, another kilometre down the track, is the most remarkable of all – a gorgeous blue-green colour, its near-vertical limestone sides backed by towering jungle.You'll almost certainly hear howler monkeys and see kingfishers and perhaps toucans; and there are jaguars in the region, too.

Candelaria caves
The limestone mountains in northern AltaVerapaz are full of caves, of which the most impressive and extensive are those at **Candelaria**, northeast of Chisec. Here the Río Candelaria has formed an astonishingly complex system of caverns and passages, occasionally penetrated by skylights from the surface.Three places on the main Chisec–Raxrujá highway provide access to the Candelaria cave network, which extends for 22km (though if you include all the subsidiary systems it's more like 80km) and includes some truly monumental chambers. **Tubing** trips (both 1hr 30min; US$5) can also be arranged at both the first two communities. Many Cobán travel agents (see p.292) also run trips here.

At **Candelaria Camposanto**, Km309.5, there are two main caves: Entrada de Sol – measuring some 70m in length and 30m in width – and the smaller Murciélago, where you might see some bats, and perhaps hear the roar of the howler monkeys that live nearby.An interpretive trail leads from the highway to the caves, with information panels about the fruits, plants and trees, wildlife and folklore of the region.A little further on at Km315 and 2km south of the highway, a similar community tourism project provides access to the **Mucbilhá** caves where guides will lead you to theVenado Seco (US$4.50) cavern, a return hike of an hour or so.The tubing trip here follows an underground section of the Río Candelaria. There's a good little visitors' **lodge** (❷) by the entrance with bunk beds, camping space and shower facilities.

More spectacular caverns are just a little further to the east at Km316.5. The **Complejo Cultural de Candelaria** (⊛www.cuevasdecandelaria.com) is located in land that was jealously guarded for decades by a Frenchman, though the local community now own the site and provide tours.The largest cave here is the 200-metre-long, 60-metre-wide "Tzul Tacca", where skylight shafts create a spectacular light-show on the rocks and cavern water below. Entrance to the complex, including a two-hour tour and a guide to the first cave system, costs US$3.50 per head.The lovely **hotel** here (☏5861 2203; ❹–❻) has accommodation in a large shared bungalow or very stylish cabins decorated with furniture, art and fabrics, but not all have private bath.You'll find Guatemalan and French cuisine, too, though meals are pricey at upwards of US$15 for lunch or dinner. Note there are some rather picky hotel rules: no outside food is permitted, and all shoes must be left at the entrance gate.

Raxrujá and Fray Bartolomé de Las Casas
RAXRUJÁ is little more than a few streets and some ramshackle buildings straggling round a bridge over the Río Escondido, a tributary of the Pasión, but it does function as a gateway to the extensive ruins of Cancuén and the Candelaria caves, and it offers some decent **accommodation**. First choice is the superb ❧ *Hotel Cancuén* (☏7983 0720; ❸–❹), on the western edge of town, where owner Dr César has constructed a very fine hotel with a

selection of immaculately clean rooms, some with air-conditioning with quality beds, reading lights, terracotta-tiled floors and screened windows. There's a good comedor, internet access (US$1.30 per hr), and caving trips can be organized here. The motel-style *Hotel El Amigo* (℡5872 4136; ❸) has clean, functional tiled rooms with cold-water bathrooms, and some have air-conditioning; the swimming pool is rarely cleaned though. Otherwise *Hotel Gutiérrez* (℡5473 7714; ❷) is a ramshackle but fairly clean place. For **food**, the best of the comedores is *Doña Reyna*. The Banrural here will cash dollars and traveller's cheques.

Microbuses leave every thirty minute south to Chisec (45min), continuing on to Cobán (2hr) and north to Sayaxché (every 30min; 2hr 30min). There are ongoing roadworks on the route south to the Pajal junction (for Lanquín), which is in terrible condition but being slowly upgraded. Irregular buses and pick-ups were taking about five hours to get to Pajal at the time of research, though this should shorten to about three hours when work is completed; check in Raxrujá before you set off this way. The impossibly green alpine Verapaz scenery – a verdant landscape of pine forests and pastureland, tiny adobe-built hamlets and startling jungle-topped karst outcrops – certainly helps compensate for the slow progress on this road.

Sixteen kilometres east of Raxrujá, the featureless town of **Fray Bartolomé de Las Casas** is usually known as "Las Casas" or simply "Fray". You'll find several **hospedajes** here, the best being the *Hotel La Cabaña* (℡7952 0352), but most travellers are in transit. Buses leave here for Cobán (every 30min; 2hr 30min) via Raxrujá, and to Poptún (about every 90min; 4hr 30min), most via Las Conchas (see p.309).

Cancuén

North of Raxrujá is the large Maya site of **Cancuén** (daily 8am–5pm; US$5.50, including Spanish-speaking guide), where a huge Classic-period palace has been unearthed. Cancuén was discovered in 1907, but the sheer size of the ruins had been underestimated, and investigations in 1999 revealed the vast scale of the royal enclave here. The site is enigmatic in many ways: uniquely, Cancuén seems to have lacked the usual religious and defensive structures characteristic of Maya cities and appears to have existed as an essentially secular trading city. The vast amounts of jade, pyrite, obsidian and fine ceramics found recently indicate that this was actually one of the greatest trading centres of the Maya world, with a paved plaza (that may have been a marketplace) covering two square kilometres. Cancuén is thought to have flourished because of its strategic position between the great cities of the lowlands, like Tikal and Calakmul, and the mineral-rich highlands of southern Guatemala.

A trail takes you past the ruined remains of workshops where precious materials including jade were fashioned into jewellery by expert artisans. It continues to a ball court, where there are replicas of some beautifully carved markers; one depicts ruler Taj Chan Ahk passing the staff of the ruling dynasty to his son Kan Maax in 795 AD. Before visiting nobility could enter Cancuén's royal enclave, they'd stop to perform ritual cleansing at a highly unusual ten-metre stone **bathing pool**, then climb a hieroglyphic staircase to the entrance of the elite. The vast, almost ostentatious triple-level **palace** (Structure L7-27) itself has 170 rooms and 11 courtyards. Its sides are adorned with dozens of life-sized stucco figures, and it is Cancuén's most impressive structure. The trail continues past several stricken stelae, and returns through some towering hardwood trees to the modest visitor centre, which has information panels (some with English translations) and a model of the site. Cancuén's very finest carvings lie elsewhere; there's an absolutely stunning altar panel in the Maya museum in Cobán (see p.291).

To **get to** Cancuén, pick-ups and minibuses (approximately hourly) leave Raxrujá for the *aldea* of **La Unión** 12km to the north, where boatmen will take you by *lancha* (reservations ☎5978 1465) for the thirty-minute ride (US$40 return trip for up to sixteen people) along the Río de la Pasión to the site. There is a camping area (US$7 per head) at the ruins with showers and shelters.

Laguna Lachúa and around

West of Raxrujá a poor dirt road snakes across steamy, thinly populated lowlands – the flatness of the landscape broken periodically by soaring forest-topped karst outcrops – to the magical **Parque Nacional Laguna Lachúa** (US$5.50; Ⓦwww.lachua.org), a near-circular lake surrounded by a dense tropical jungle. One of the least-visited national parks in Central America, this is a supremely beautiful, tranquil spot, with pristine azure-blue waters perfect for swimming. About two kilometres in diameter and over 200m deep, Lachúa is thought to be a natural sinkhole in the limestone crust, though its circular shape has led to speculation that it could have been formed by a meteorite impact. The reserve is home to tapir and all the main Central American wild cats, including jaguar, but though these creatures usually prove elusive, you're virtually guaranteed to hear howler monkeys, and armadillos and otters are often seen. There's also an abundance of exotic birdlife (around 300 species have been recorded here), including snail kites and flycatchers, but watch out for mosquitoes.

Lachúa's excellent, recently upgraded **visitors' lodge** (US$7 per head) is a sweltering four-kilometre hike through the forest from the information centre/ticket office/car park on the highway – there's no absolutely no access into the reserve by vehicle. The large wood-and-thatch lodge is divided into very well kept rooms, each with good beds and mosquito nets, or you can camp. You'll have to bring all your own supplies, including drinking water, as there's no restaurant or food store, but you will find a fully equipped kitchen. The rangers are extremely protective of this magnificent national park, and visitors have to carry back all non-biodegradable material. Kayaks can be rented for a dollar an hour. On public holidays the park can quickly fill to its 84-person limit; call ahead on ☎5861 0088 to reserve your place.

About 25km southwest of Lachúa, there's another wonderful natural attraction where the turquoise waters of the broad Río Chixoy are forced through a narrow gap in a limestone plateau known as the **Peyán canyon**. This canyon, just four metres wide in places, is best explored by boat, but you can walk to a viewpoint above it in thirty minutes from the isolated village of **Salacuím**, which is on the road between Cubilhuitz and Playa Grande. Ask around for a boatman in Salacuím or hire a local guide for the walk. There's actually a good *Hospedaje Florentino Prado* (❷) in Salacuím, owned by a Swedish–Guatemalan couple, though it is only open for about half the year, so you may have to push on. For a filling meal, head to *Comedor Korayma*.

Twelve kilometres east of Laguna Lachúa along the road to Chisec is the junction known as San Benito, look out for the excellent roadside *Comedor California*. From here a rough dirt track heads south for 12km to the tiny Q'eqchi' *aldea* of Rocjá Pomtila – the jumping-off point for wonderful boat trips up the **Río Ik'Bolay**. The river journey is extremely scenic, passing banks lined with towering tropical trees, and you're sure to see kingfishers skimming across the water. After 45 minutes a slippery trail climbs up the riverbank, past waterfalls to a *nacimiento* (spring), where you can squat down for a jet-powered

Fiestas

The Verapaces are famous for their fiestas, and in Baja Verapaz especially, you'll see an unusual range of traditional dances. In addition, Cobán hosts the **National Fiesta of Folklore** at the start of August, which is attended by indigenous groups from throughout the country.

January
15 Tactic, large pilgrimage to the town's Chi-ixim chapel
19–24 Rabinal, most important dates are the 23rd (for the Rabinal Achi dance) and the main day, the 24th
22–25 Tamahú, main day 25th

Holy Week
San Cristóbal Verapaz, big religious processions

May
1–4 Santa Cruz Verapaz, includes the dances of Los Chuntos, Vendos and Mamah-Num
4–9 Tucurú, main day 8th

June
9–13 Senahú, main day 13th
10–13 Purulhá, main day 13th
21–24 San Juan Chamelco, main day 24th (includes spectacular costumed processions)
24–29 San Pedro Carchá, main day 29th
25–30 Chisec, main day 29th

July
20–25 Cubulco, includes the Palo Volador on the final day
21–26 San Cristóbal Verapaz, main day 25th

August
July 31–Aug 6 Cobán, followed by the National Fiesta of Folklore
11–16 Tactic, main day 15th
22–28 Lanquín, main day 28th
23–28 Chajal
23–30 Panzós

September
4–8 Cahabón, main day 6th
17–21 Salamá, main day 17th
25–29 San Miguel Chicaj, main day 29th
27–30 San Jerónimo, main day 30th

December
First week Cobán, orchid exhibition held in town's convent (next to the cathedral)
6–8 El Chol, main day 8th

bidet. A community tourism project in Rocjá Pomtila, run with EcoQuetzal in Cobán (see p.292) organizes trips here, but you can also just drop by; ask for village coordinator Javier Ca'al (☏5381 1970). Costs are US$4 entrance, US$25 for the half-day boat trip (for up to six people) and US$10 for a guide; meals are US$2.50, and a bed for the night is US$3.

Getting to the Lachúa region is obviously easiest if you take a tour (see Cobán "Listings"), but it's not that tough under your own steam if you're not in a rush. Staff at Lachúa can help with local transport schedules and information. From Cobán bus terminal, minibuses leave hourly for Playa Grande (4hr 30min) via the turn-off at Cubilhuitz, passing through Salacuím and the three-way junction of San Luís. Pick-ups and buses pass San Luís to the entrance of Lachúa. Coming from Chisec or Raxrujá, get to the Xuctzul junction and it's a four-hour ride in a pick-up or bus to the lake. There are no set times on these last two routes, but more transport in the morning. There's one daily bus (10am) from Cobán's bus terminal to Rocjá Pomtila; it returns at 3.30am.

Playa Grande and into the Ixcán

From Laguna Lachúa it's possible to journey west into northern Huehuetenango, an arduous trip along some of the worst roads in the country, even partly following a river bed in the dry season. The transport hub for this trip and the region is the sprawling, dusty town of **PLAYA GRANDE** (also referred to as Cantabal or Ixcán), a short distance west of the Río Chixoy. This is an authentic frontier settlement of scruffy tin-roofed, cinder-block-built houses, Mexico-bound migrants and a few rough bars. It is, however, the main administrative centre for the Ixcán region and has a few **hotels**, the best options being the good, secure *Hotel España* (T 7755 7645; ❶–❹), which has three classes of room with firm beds, some with private bathroom, and the well-run *Hotel Reina Vasty* (T 5514 6693; ❹), which has very clean air-conditioned rooms. Banrural has an ATM and will change traveller's cheques.

Continuing west of Playa Grande you pass through the **Ixcán** region, which became the scene of bloody fighting in the civil war and is now populated by many *repatriados* who've returned from exile in Mexico. Several daily pick-ups and the odd chicken-bus make the journey from Playa Grande to Barillas, through swampy lowland, parcels of remaining tropical forest and cattle pasture-land. The journey takes a minimum of five hours and sometimes a lot longer (depending on the state of the road), but it's a spectacular route as the growing bulk of the Cuchumatanes rises ever higher on the horizon.

Travel details

Buses and microbuses

Baja Verapaz

Heading for Baja Verapaz from Cobán or Guatemala City, you can also take any bus between the two and get off at **La Cumbre** (de Santa Elena); from here microbuses run to Salamá.

Rabinal to: Guatemala City (8 daily; 4hr 20min or 6hr via El Chal).

Salamá to: Cubulco (hourly; 1hr 30min); Guatemala City (every 30min; 3hr 15min); Rabinal (every 30min; 45min).

Alta Verapaz

For all Cobán transport schedules, see box, p.293.

Cahabón to: El Estor (1 daily; 4hr).

Chisec to: Cobán (every 30min; 1hr 30min); Raxrujá (every 30min; 45min).

Fray Bartolomé de Las Casas to: Cobán, via Chisec (every 30min; 2hr 30min), via Pajal (at least 3 daily; about 5hr); Poptún (every 90min; 4hr 30min).

Lanquín see p.295.

Panzós to: Cobán (6 daily; 6hr).

Raxrujá to: Cobán (every 30min; 2hr); Sayaxché (every 30min; 2hr 30min).

Petén

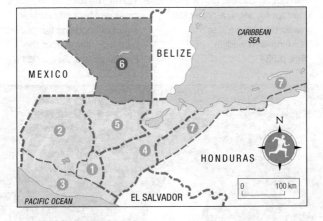

CHAPTER 6

Highlights

✳ **Finca Ixobel** Kick back and enjoy wonderful home cooking at this rural retreat, set in the pine-clad foothills of the Maya Mountains. See p.310

✳ **Flores** Petén's most attractive settlement is a friendly little historic town, with a cosmopolitan choice of restaurants and cafés. See p.311

✳ **Tikal** Explore the spectacular ruins of an ancient Maya metropolis, set in a protected rainforest reserve that's teeming with wildlife. See p.324

✳ **Jungle trekking** Hike through the virtually untouched forests of northern Petén to the remote jungle ruins of El Mirador and Nakbé. See p.337

✳ **Lago de Petexbatún** A beautiful remote lake, fringed by thick rainforest, around whose shores are some fascinating Maya ruins. See p.344

✳ **Yaxhá** The ruins of this once-massive Maya city include a glut of imposing temple pyramids, some from the Preclassic era. See p.351

▲ Jungle trekking to El Mirador

6

Petén

The vast northern department of Petén occupies about a third of Guatemala but contains just over three percent of its population. This huge expanse of tropical rainforest, swamps and savannah forms part of an untamed wilderness that stretches into the Lacandón forest and Calakmul reserve of southern Mexico and across the Maya Mountains to Belize. Totally unlike any other part of the country, large expanses of the Petén remain virtually untouched, with ancient ceiba and mahogany trees that tower 50m above the forest floor. The area is extraordinarily rich in wildlife: some 285 species of bird have been sighted at Tikal alone, including a wide range of hummingbirds, toucans, hawks, falcons, wild turkeys and the motmot (a bird of paradise). Among the mammals are the lumbering tapir, ocelots, jaguars and monkeys, plus thousands of species of plants, reptiles, insects and butterflies.

In the past few decades, however, this privileged isolation has become increasingly under threat. Waves of **settlers** have cleared enormous tracts of jungle, while oil companies and commercial loggers have cut roads deep into the forest. The population of Petén, in 1950 just 15,000, is today estimated at close to 500,000, a number that puts enormous pressure on the remaining forest. Yet despite forty percent of Petén being officially protected as the **Reserva de la Biósfera Maya** (Maya Biosphere Reserve), regulations are widely ignored and ecological activists are subject to routine threats.

Population boom and environmental failure have occurred twice before in the Petén, and most experts concur that these factors precipitated the collapse of both the Preclassic Maya (around 150 AD) and the Classic Maya (around 900 AD). Today the ruins of several hundred ancient Maya sites pepper the region, although many of them still remain completely buried in jungle, and others are known only to locals and looters. In recent years, satellite imagery has uncovered the remains of large cities including El Pajaral and Xulnal, while archeological excavations at other sites, including Cancuén and Wakná have revealed them to be much larger than originally thought. Tikal and El Mirador are among the largest and most spectacular of all **Maya ruins** – Tikal alone has some several thousand buildings – but they represent only a fraction of what was once here.

The **tourism** potential of the department remains largely unexploited and few visitors see anything but the region around Flores and Tikal. But with fast paved highways (one via Sayaxché, the other via Poptún) connecting Petén to the south of the country, road connections are now excellent. A long-term scheme to open up access to the great ruins of the Mirador Basin in the far north exists, perhaps via the construction of a train line, though this controversial proposal is still just at the planning stage.

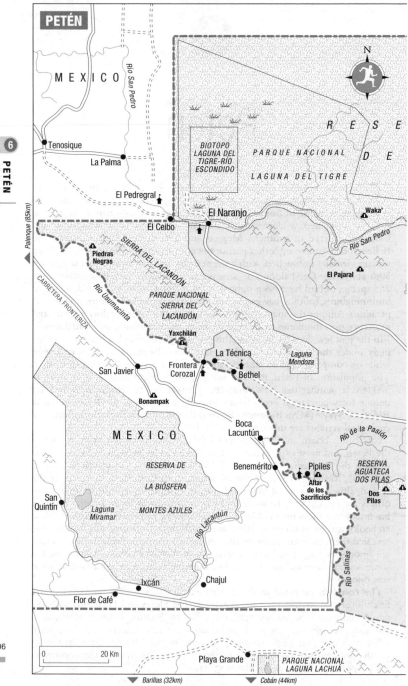

PETÉN

MEXICO

Río San Pedro

Tenosique

La Palma

El Pedregral

BIOTOPO
LAGUNA DEL
TIGRE-RÍO
ESCONDIDO

PARQUE NACIONAL

LAGUNA DEL TIGRE

R E S E
D E

Waka'

El Naranjo

El Ceibo

Río San Pedro

Palenque (85km)

SIERRA DEL LACANDÓN

Piedras
Negras

El Pajaral

CARRETERA FRONTERIZA

Río Usumacinta

PARQUE NACIONAL
SIERRA DEL
LACANDÓN

Yaxchilán

La Técnica

Laguna
Mendoza

San Javier

Frontera
Corozal

Bethel

Bonampak

Boca
Lacuntún

Río de la Pasión

MEXICO

Benemérito

Pipiles

RESERVA
AGUATECA
DOS PILAS

RESERVA DE

Altar
de los
Sacrificios

Dos
Pilas

LA BIÓSFERA

San
Quintín

Laguna
Miramar

MONTES AZULES

Río Lacantún

Río Salinas

Ixcán

Chajul

Flor de Café

0   20 Km

Playa Grande

PARQUE NACIONAL
LAGUNA LACHUÁ

Barillas (32km)   Cobán (44km)

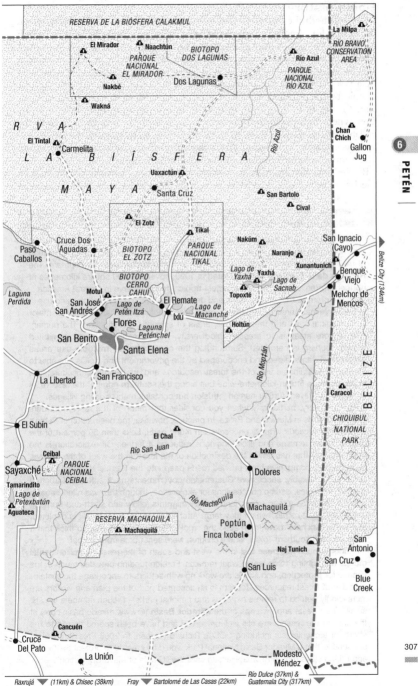

RESERVA DE LA BIÓSFERA CALAKMUL

La Milpa

El Mirador · Naachtún

BIOTOPO
DOS LAGUNAS

RÍO BRAVO
CONSERVATION
AREA

PARQUE
NACIONAL
EL MIRADOR

Río Azul

Nakbé

Dos Lagunas

PARQUE
NACIONAL
RÍO AZUL

Wakná

R V A

El Tintal

Carmelita

Chan
Chich

Gallon
Jug

L A B I Î S F E R A

Río Azul

M A Y A

Uaxactún

Santa Cruz

San Bartolo

Cival

El Zotz

Tikal

BIOTOPO
EL ZOTZ

PARQUE
NACIONAL
TIKAL

Nakúm

San Ignacio
(Cayo)

Cruce Dos
Aguadas

Naranjo

Xunantunich

Paso
Caballos

Lago de
Yaxhá

Yaxhá

Benque
Viejo

BIOTOPO
CERRO
CAHUÍ

Lago de
Sacnab

Laguna
Perdida

Motul

Topoxté

Melchor de
Mencos

San José

Lago de
Petén Itzá

El Remate

Lago de
Macanché

San Andrés

Ixlú

Flores

Holtún

San Benito

Laguna
Peténchel

Santa Elena

Río Mopán

La Libertad

San Francisco

Caracol

B E L I Z E

El Subín

El Chal

Río San Juan

Ixkún

CHIQUIBUL
NATIONAL
PARK

Ceibal

PARQUE
NACIONAL
CEIBAL

Dolores

Sayaxché

Tamarindito

Lago de
Petexbatún

Río Machaquilá

Machaquilá

Aguateca

RESERVA MACHAQUILÁ

Machaquilá

Poptún

Finca Ixobel

San
Antonio

Naj Tunich

San Cruz

San Luis

Blue
Creek

Cancuén

Cruce
Del Pato

La Unión

Modesto
Méndez

Raxrujá ▼ (11km) & Chisec (38km)   Fray ▼ Bartolomé de Las Casas (22km)

Río Dulce (37km) &
Guatemala City (317km) ▼

6

PETÉN

Belize City (134km) ▶

307

Some history

Petén was both the birthplace and heartland of the **Maya civilization**, which flourished for almost two thousand years between 1000 BC and the tenth century AD, by which time Maya culture had reached unparalleled architectural, scientific and artistic achievement (see Contexts, p.421). Great cities rose out of the forest, surrounded by huge areas of raised and irrigated fields and connected by a vast network of causeways to smaller settlements. But forest clearance for temple building caused the fall of the Preclassic Maya in northern Petén just after the time of Christ, and, incredibly, history repeated itself eight centuries later when high population densities and a prolonged drought provoked the collapse of the Classic Maya. At the close of the tenth century, the cities were abandoned, after which some Maya moved north to the Yucatán, where their civilization continued to flourish until the twelfth century.

By the time the **Spanish** arrived the area had been partially recolonized by the Itza, a group of Toltec Maya (originally from the Yucatán) who inhabited

The Reserva de la Biósfera Maya

The idea behind biosphere reserves, conceived in 1974 by UNESCO, was an ambitious attempt to combine the protection of natural areas and the conservation of their genetic diversity with scientific research and sustainable development. The **Reserva de la Biósfera Maya**, created in 1990, covers 16,000 square kilometres of northern Petén: in theory it is the largest tropical forest reserve in Central America.

On the premise that conservation and development can be compatible, land use in the reserve has three designations: **core areas** include the national parks, major archeological sites and the *biotopos*, areas of scientific investigation. The primary role of core areas is to preserve biodiversity; human settlements are prohibited though tourism is permitted. Surrounding the core areas are **multiple-use areas** where inhabitants, aided and encouraged by the government and NGOs, are able to engage in sustainable use of the forest resources and small-scale agriculture. The **buffer zone**, a fifteen-kilometre-wide belt along the southern edge of the reserve, is intended to prevent further human intrusion but contains many existing villages.

Fine in theory, particularly when you consider that much of the reserve borders protected lands in Mexico and Belize. In practice, however, the destruction of Petén's **rainforest** proceeds virtually unchecked in many parts. Less than 50 percent of the original cover remains and illicit logging is reducing it further. Oil exploration is the other industry that has driven the destruction of the forest in the west of the reserve, as petroleum companies have pushed roads deep into the Parque Nacional Laguna del Tigre. Incredibly, successive Guatemalan governments have aided and abetted the oil companies, issuing concessions for exploration, though this was ruled illegal in 2000. As soon as a road exists, land-hungry migrants follow and slash-and-burn the forest and plant *milpas,* which they farm. After a few years the thin soil is depleted, and cattle ranchers move in. In 2003 the smoke from these fires was so thick that it even affected southern Texas, where children were sent home from school.

Although much has been lost in the west and south of the reserve, environmental groups are fighting to conserve what remains. Foreign funding provides much of the finance for protection, and NGOs are working with settlers to encourage the sustainable use of forest resources. Tourism is an accepted part of the plan and visitors are increasingly getting to remote *biotopos* and national parks – though numbers are still small. The forests and swamps of the **Mirador Basin** (@ www.miradorbasin.com) at the core of the reserve are still well-preserved and have been spared thanks to the efforts of archeologists including UCLA's Richard Hansen. In 2008 President Colom announced that a Mirador Basin National Park would be created to protect the forests and ruined cities that form what Hansen calls the "Cradle of Maya Civilization".

the land around Lago de Petén Itzá. The forest proved so impenetrable that it wasn't brought under Spanish control until 1697, more than 150 years after they had conquered the rest of the country, when Tayasal was destroyed. The invaders had little enthusiasm for Petén though, and under their rule it remained a backwater, with little to offer but a steady trickle of chicle – the basic ingredient of chewing gum, which is bled from sapodilla trees. Independence saw no great change, and it wasn't until 1970 that Petén became genuinely accessible by road (and waves of land-hungry settlers arrived). Even today, the network of roads is skeletal, and many routes are impassable in the wet season.

The Petén forests historically provided shelter for some of Guatemala's **guerrilla armies**, which led to many of the settlers being driven across the border into Mexico and becoming refugees. Most of the refugees have returned, though small pockets of tension still exist in the region. Many disputes are over land rights, with Belizean troops evicting Guatemalan campesinos from the disputed border area and mass occupations of privately owned fincas and national-park land by well-organized peasant groups. Drug traffickers have also moved into Petén, flying in cocaine from South America to the region's remote airstrips.

Where to go

The hub of the department is **Lago de Petén Itzá**, home to the delightful lakeside settlement of **Flores**, and its sprawling sister towns of **Santa Elena** and **San Benito**. You'll probably arrive here, if only to head straight out to the ruins of **Tikal**, Petén's prime attraction. From Belize it's more convenient to base yourself at the relaxed village of **El Remate**, halfway between Flores and Tikal. If you plan to reach any of the more distant ruins – **El Mirador**, **Nakbé** or **El Zotz** – then Flores is again a good base for planning an expedition, while the fascinating site of **Yaxhá** is now easily accessible and attracting increasing numbers of visitors. Southwest of here is **Sayaxché**, surrounded by yet more Maya sites such as **Ceibal**, and the ruined cities of the **Lago de Petexbatún** region, including the impressive **Aguateca**. In the southeast of the department the glorious farm **Finca Ixobel**, close to Poptún, makes a fine base for a few days' exploration and socializing.

North to Poptún

Heading north from Río Dulce Town, it's 38km to the dull town of **Modesto Méndez** (known as Cadenas locally) from where a dirt road heads west to the huge, broad waterfalls of **Las Conchas** at the confluence of the rivers Chiyú and Chahal. The large pools here are great for swimming, and there's an isolated backpacker lodge close by, *Oasis Chiyú* (W www.naturetoursguatemala.com; US$30 per day including all meals), with beds in a large, bare wooden house with no electricity; it's owned by a rather self-absorbed American and guests are rare. Minibuses (about every hour) heading west from Cadenas on the road to Fray Bartolomé de Las Casas pass within 4km of the lodge.

Back on the highway to Flores the next place of interest is the scruffy small town of **POPTÚN**, situated at an altitude of 500m. There's no particular reason to stay in the town itself, but there are cybercafés and banks here – Banrural on 5 Calle has an ATM. Virtually everyone stays at *Finca Ixobel* (see below), but the clean, friendly *Hotel Posada de los Castellanos* (T 7927 7222; ❸) on 4 Calle is a good bet in town while the *Villa de los Castellanos* (T 7927 7541; ❹) 6km north

▲ Tree houses at Finca Ixobel

of Poptún on the highway has large, comfortable rustic cabañas with private bathrooms. Speak to Don Placido, who owns both places, about fascinating excursions to the remote Reserva Machaquilá and its ruins.

Minibuses shuttle between Poptún and Flores every thirty minutes until 6.30pm, while a constant stream of buses and minibuses head south to Río Dulce and on to Guatemala City all day and night. Buses also run to Fray Bartolomé de Las Casas (5hr) about every ninety minutes.

Finca Ixobel

About 5km south of Poptún, surrounded by pine forests in the cool foothills of the Maya Mountains, *Finca Ixobel* (☎5410 4037, ⓦwww.fincaixobel.com) is a rural retreat and farm that's also a legendary travellers' meeting point. It was originally run by Americans Mike and Carole DeVine, but on June 8, 1990, Mike was murdered by the army, a crime that prompted the US government to suspend military aid to Guatemala. Five soldiers were convicted of the murder in September 1992, but the soldiers' commanding officer, Captain Hugo Contreras, escaped from jail shortly after his arrest. Carole fought the case for years and remains at the finca.

Finca Ixobel is a supremely beautiful and relaxing place where you can swim in the pond, walk in the forest, dodge the resident "attack" parrots and stuff yourself with delicious (mostly organic and home-grown) food. The finca is run ecologically, utilizing solar power and natural composting. You run a tab for accommodation, food (dinner costs US$3.50–8) and drink, paying when you leave – which can be a rude awakening. Many travellers are quickly seduced by the tranquil nature of the finca and end up staying much longer than planned, some working as cooks or helpers in exchange for board and lodging. There are **hikes** (a three-day jungle-trek hike costs US$30), horseriding trips, tubing, 4WD jungle jaunts, and short excursions to nearby caves. Accommodation is either in attractive bungalows with two beds and a private bathroom (④–⑤), **rooms** (③, with bathroom ④), **dorms** (US$3.75 per bed), tree houses or the campsite (both US$3 per head). You'll also find internet and wi-fi access and a poolside bar. To get to the finca, ask the bus driver to drop you at the gate from where it's a fifteen-minute walk through the pine trees; after dark, take a taxi here from Poptún (US$3).

Around Poptún: the Naj Tunich caves

The limestone hills surrounding Poptún are riddled with **caves** and coated in lush tropical forest. One of the largest caves contains an underground river and waterfall that you can swim through (if you don't mind leaping into a chilly pool in total darkness); walking trips to this cave system are organized by *Finca Ixobel*. The most impressive, however, is the remote **Naj Tunich** or "Stone House", 23km down a rough track from Poptún close to the Belizean border, which has some of the finest cave art of the Maya World, dating back to 100 BC. Due to the fragility of the site, it's not possible to see the original cave paintings, but some fine replicas have been created 400m from the original cave, which you can visit.

Caves were sacred to the ancient Maya, who believed them to be entrances to Xibalbá, the dreaded underworld, and Naj Tunich was one of the most revered sites and a place of pilgrimage. Local artists have re-created some of the extensive hieroglyphic texts, depictions of religious ceremonies and the ball game, as well as the graphic **erotic scenes** thought to be unique to this site.

Tours (around US$130 for up to eight people including lunch) of Naj Tunich are organized by *Finca Ixobel* (see p.310) and *Villa de los Castellanos* (see p.309) using guides from the neighbouring village of La Compuerta.

Dolores and El Chal

North of Poptún, it's 26km to **Dolores**, a dusty, growing town set just east of the highway where many of its inhabitants are originally from the eastern highlands. There's no reason to stop except to take in the town's impressive new archeological museum (Mon–Sat 8.30am–4.30pm; US$3.50), which has modern displays, some intricately carved glyph blocks from Ixtutz and artefacts (including some fine incense-burners) from sites including Ixtuta and Machaquilá. An hour's walk north of town are the Maya ruins of **Ixkún** (8am–5pm; US$3.50), a mid-sized site made up of eight plazas. Fifteen kilometres north of Dolores a road branches northeast at the village of Sabaneta, making a short cut to the **Belize border**. Some Melchor-bound buses use this route, though it's often in bad condition.

A further 30km brings you to the ruins of **El Chal** (daily 8am–5pm; no charge), signed on the west side of the village of the same name, and less than 500m from the road. Call in at the small hut by the entrance to the ruins for a free tour with the guard. The ruins include several plazas and a ball court, and the palace complex, built on a ridge, gives a view of the surrounding country-side. The buildings are largely unrestored – but the remains of a couple of stelae and altars (with clearly visible glyphs and carved features) can be made out.

Flores

Easy-going **FLORES** is a delightfully sedate place with an old-fashioned atmosphere, quite unlike the rest of the region's towns. A cluster of cobbled streets and aging houses built around a twin-domed church, it sits beautifully on a small island in Lago de Petén Itzá, connected to the mainland by a short causeway. The modern emphasis lies across the water in the twin towns of **SANTA ELENA** and **SAN BENITO**, both of which are ugly, chaotic and

▲ Maya murals in Naj Tunich

sprawling places, dusty in the dry season and mud-bound during the rains. Santa Elena, opposite Flores at the other end of the causeway, is strung out between the airport and the market, and takes in several hotels, stores, banks and bus terminals. San Benito, further west, has even less going for it. The three towns are often lumped together under the single name of Flores.

The **lake** is a natural choice for settlement, and its shores were heavily populated in Maya times. The city of **Tayasal**, capital of the Itza, lay on the island that was to become modern Flores. Cortés passed through here in 1525 and left behind a sick horse. In 1618 two Franciscan friars arrived to find the people worshipping a large white idol in the shape of a horse called "Tzimin Chac". Unable to persuade the Maya to renounce their religion they smashed the idol and left the city. Subsequent visitors were less well received: in 1622 a military expedition of twenty men was invited into the city by Canek, chief of the Itza, and they were set upon and sacrificed. The town was eventually destroyed by Martín de Ursúa and an army of 235 in 1697. For the entire colonial period (and indeed up to the 1960s), Flores languished in virtual isolation, having more contact with neighbouring Belize than with the capital.

Today, despite the steady flow of tourists passing through for Tikal, the town retains an enjoyably genteel air, with residents greeting one another courteously as they meet in the streets. Though it has little to detain you in itself – a leisurely thirty-minute stroll around the cobbled streets and lanes is enough to become entirely familiar with the place – Flores does offer enjoyable surroundings and an excellent selection of hotels, restaurants and tour operators.

Arrival

Arriving by bus you'll be dropped off at Santa Elena's large modern Terminal Nuevo on 6 Avenida about 2km south of the causeway (though Línea Dorada buses will continue on to Flores). The **airport** is 3km east of the causeway, a US$3 taxi ride from town. Tuk-tuks are everywhere, charging US$0.75 for a short journey.

Information

There's an **Inguat** booth in Flores (☎5116 3182) close to the causeway, and also in the airport (daily 7am–noon & 3.30–6pm; ☎7926 0533); both have helpful staff, a good supply of leaflets, maps and information in English.

For more detailed maps and specialist information about northern Petén consult **CINCAP** (Centro de Información sobre la Naturaleza, Cultura y Artesanías de Petén) on the north side of Flores's plaza (Mon–Fri 9am–noon & 2–8pm; ☎7926 0718). CINCAP has exhibits on historical and contemporary Petén and you can buy medicinal herbs, collected as part of the effort to promote forest sustainability. This is also the base of the ecologist and

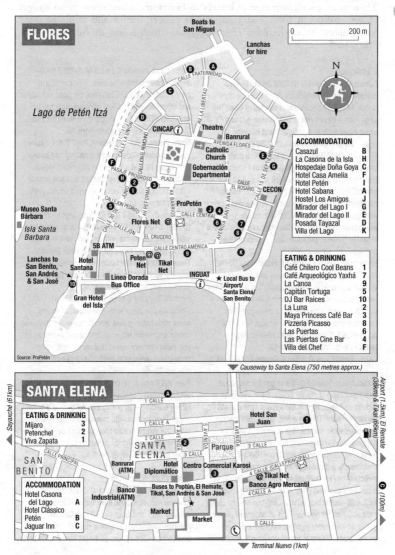

FLORES

Boats to
San Miguel

Lanchas
for hire

0   200 m

N

Lago de Petén Itzá

CALLE FRATERNIDAD

AV. A LIBERTAD

CALLE LA UNIÓN

CALLEJÓN EL PEDACHO

CINCAP ⓘ

Theatre

Banrural

AVENIDA FLORES

Catholic
Church

Gobernación
Departmental

PLAZA

CALLE
EL ROSARIO

CALLE 15 DE SEPTIEMBRE

CECON

PASAJE PROGRESO

AV. REFORMA

CALLEJÓN PEDRITO

AV. BARRIOS

ProPetén

CALLE CENTRAL

AVENIDA SANTA ANA

Flores Net @ ✉

CALLE 30

CALLEJÓN

EL CRUCERO

Museo Santa
Bárbara

Isla Santa
Barbara

Lanchas to
San Benito,
San Andrés
& San José

5B ATM

CALLE CENTRO AMÉRICA

Peten
Net @@

Tikal
Net

INGUAT
ⓘ

★ Local Bus to
Airport/
Santa Elena/
San Benito

Hotel
Santana

Línea Dorada
Bus Office

Gran Hotel
del Isla

ACCOMMODATION

Casazul	B
La Casona de la Isla	H
Hospedaje Doña Goya	C
Hotel Casa Amelia	F
Hotel Petén	I
Hotel Sabana	A
Hostel Los Amigos	J
Mirador del Lago I	G
Mirador del Lago II	E
Posada Tayazal	D
Villa del Lago	K

EATING & DRINKING

Café Chilero Cool Beans	1
Café Arqueológico Yaxhá	7
La Canoa	9
Capitán Tortuga	5
DJ Bar Raices	10
La Luna	2
Maya Princess Café Bar	3
Pizzeria Picasso	8
Las Puertas	6
Las Puertas Cine Bar	4
Villa del Chef	F

Source: ProPetén

▼ Causeway to Santa Elena (750 metres approx.)

SANTA ELENA

Sayaxché (61km)

Airport (1.5km), El Remate
(38km) & Tikal (66km)

1 CALLE

EATING & DRINKING

Mijaro	3
Petenchel	2
Viva Zapata	1

1 CALLE A

2 CALLE

SANTA
ELENA

CALLE PRINCIPAL

SAN
BENITO

ACCOMMODATION

Hotel Casona del Lago	A
Hotel Clássico Petén	B
Jaguar Inn	C

4 AVENIDA

5 AVENIDA

6 AVENIDA

Hotel San
Juan

3 CALLE

Parque

3 CALLE

Banrural
(ATM)

Hotel
Diplomático

Centro Comercial Karosi

CALLE (CALLE PRINCIPAL)

4 CALLE

@ Tikal Net

Banco
Industrial(ATM)

Buses to Poptún, El Remate,
Tikal, San Andrés & San José

Banco Agro Mercantil

4 CALLE A

Market

Market

5 CALLE

ⓒ (100m)

313

▼ Terminal Nuevo (1km)

ecotourism organization Alianza Verde (Ⓦ www.alianzaverde.org), who manage CINCAP.

If you're planning to go on a trip to remote parts of the Reserva de la Biósfera Maya, the tour agencies listed below (see "Listings") are usually the best source of logistical information. You could also check with **ProPetén** on Calle Central (Mon–Fri 8am–5pm; ☎ 7867 5155, Ⓦ www.propeten.org) for current information on route conditions, accommodation and guides; they also run **organized trips** (see p.316) including the Scarlet Macaw trail.

Accommodation

There is an excellent range of **hotels** in Flores, including some good budget places, making it unnecessary to stay in noisier, dirtier and traffic-blighted Santa Elena. Avoid the poor *Hotel San Juan*, which is heavily touted by their pushy staff.

Flores

Casazul C Fraternidad ☎ 7867 5451, Ⓦ www .corpetur.com. Stylishly converted colonial-style house, tastefully decorated in shades of blue. The large rooms have private bath, fridge, a/c and TV, some have walk-in wardrobes and balcony. ⑥

La Casona de la Isla C 30 de Junio ☎ 7867 5153, Ⓦ www.corpetur.com. One of the best mid-range places in Flores, this gorgeous old hotel is very well run and has immaculate rooms (those on the upper floors, particularly 41–43, have the best lake views) with good-quality beds, Alaska-cold a/c, wardrobes and cable TV. Guests have access to a lakeside terrace, pool, Jacuzzi, restaurant/bar and internet. ⑥

Hospedajes Doña Goya 2 C Fraternidad ☎ 7867 5516. Long-running guesthouse with plain but serviceable, spacious rooms (with fan or a/c), some with private bath and balconies with fine views – though some mattresses are a bit saggy. The neighbouring *Doña Goya* 1 is similar, but has a dorm (US$3.75 per bed). Both have rooftop terraces with hammocks. ③–④

Hostel Los Amigos C Central ☎ 7867 5075, Ⓦ www.amigoshostel.com. Sociable backpackers' hostel with a few good-value rooms and a profusion of dorms (US$3–5 per bed) with lockers and fans, though the tropical heat can still be oppressive here. There's a fine, shady, rear garden with hammocks and banana trees that's ideal for hanging out and munching from the (mostly) veggie restaurant menu – filling meals are US$3–5. It's undoubtedly a great base for young travellers, as the switched-on Dutch–Guatemalan owners coordinate trips to Mirador and other ruins – and offer reliable local info, shuttle bus services and bus tickets, cheap calls and internet access – but as dozens of people get up at 4am every night for the Tikal trip, don't expect a deep slumber. No advance reservations. ②

Hotel Casa Amelia C La Unión ☎ 7867 5430, Ⓦ www.hotelcasaamelia.com. This four-storey green-and-white hotel has recently been renovated and offers excellent value, very spacious rooms with cable TV, many with great views of the lake. Single rooms are well priced here. ⑤

Hotel Petén C 30 de Junio ☎ 7867 5203, Ⓦ www .corpetur.com. Modern hotel featuring airy rooms with cable TV and a/c – many have lake views. Small pool, a lakeside restaurant and sun terrace with fabulous sunset vistas. Internet access and kayaks for rent. ⑥

Mirador del Lago I & II C 15 de Septiembre ☎ 7867 5409. A solid choice, this large place has well-furnished rooms with private hot-water bath and fan; you pay more for a lake view. Friendly management, a café-restaurant, internet and laundry. *Number I* is on the lakeshore and *Number II* is across the street. ③–⑤

Posada Tayazal C la Unión ☎ 7867 5151. Efficiently run place with a selection of rooms, some with balcony and private hot-water bath. The rooms and views improve, and prices increase, as you head upstairs. Great rooftop terrace; downstairs, internet access and Skype calls are offered. ②–③

Villa del Lago C 15 de Septiembre ☎ 7867 5181, Ⓦ www.hotelvilladelago.com.gt. Modern three-storey building with a spacious lobby and a great upper-floor terrace with sweeping vistas of the lake. The rooms are comfortable and decent value but the decor is slightly dated; all have a/c and many have great views. Wi-fi. ⑤–⑥

Santa Elena

Hotel Casona del Lago 1 C ☎ 7952 8700, Ⓦ www.corpetur.com. New hotel, painted in powder blue and built in a very attractive colonial-style design, with a decent-sized pool and jacuzzi. The rooms all boast two double beds and a/c and there's a large restaurant, bar, wi-fi and internet. ⑧

Hotel Clásico Petén 4 C & 6 Av ☎7926 1651, ⓦwww.clasicopeten.com. Modern hotel with twenty clean, well-presented and fairly spacious rooms, all with bathroom and a/c. Parking and internet. ④

Jaguar Inn Calzada Rodríguez Macal 8–79 ☎7926 0002, ⓦwww.jaguartikal.com. Eighteen comfortable rooms, all with private bathrooms and TV, plus a choice of a/c or fan, set off a slim plant-filled courtyard. Located about 2km east of the centre but has a restaurant, safe parking and friendly management. ④–⑤

Eating, drinking and entertainment

Flores has plenty of great places to eat, including many restaurants with lake-facing terraces, though prices are a little higher than elsewhere in Guatemala. Santa Elena has a pretty limited selection of comedores, so even if you're staying here you may want to cross the causeway for a little more atmosphere. Be warned: many restaurants serve wild game, often listed on menus as *comida silvestre*, and virtually all this has been taken illegally from reserves – avoid in particular ordering items such as *tepescuintle* (paca, a large relation of the guinea pig), *venado* (deer) and *coche de monte* (peccary, or wild pig).

Nightlife is not Petén's strength, but *Viva Zapata* at 2 Calle and 8 Avenida in Santa Elena is a large, fairly upmarket dancehall/live-music venue/theatre/bar/restaurant all rolled into one. In Flores *Las Puertas* and *Hostel Los Amigos* are good places for a drink while *DJ Bar Raices* has a dancefloor and electronic DJs. Check out *Las Puertas Cine Bar* for movies (nightly at 5pm and 8pm) while *Café Arqueológico Yaxhá* hosts superb lectures (with slides) on Maya archeology.

Flores

Café Arqueológico Yaxhá C 15 de Septiembre ⓦwww.cafeyaxha.com. Offers a fascinating menu that takes in many unusual Maya dishes, including *filete pescado* Tikinchic (US$7), which is served with zucchini and yucca, or chicken in a tamarind sauce. Owner Dieter Richter has visited and worked on many remote Maya sites, and the walls are covered in photos from excavations. Superb jade artefacts are sold here, too.

Café Chilero Cool Beans C 15 de Septiembre. Large café that spills down to the lakeside where there's a lovely, quiet little garden with hammocks. Come here for fresh coffee including espresso and cappuccino, tasty sandwiches (US$2–2.75), nachos, cakes or breakfasts (served all day). Closed Tues.

La Canoa C Centro América. Popular, good-value place serving pasta, great soups, and some vegetarian and Guatemalan food, as well as excellent breakfasts.

Capitán Tortuga C 30 de Junio. Huge place with a vast lakeside terrace covered with a palapa roof. The menu takes in grilled meats, burritos, pizza and pasta at around US$6–10 a main.

La Luna C 30 de Junio. Set in a historic building, this is the classiest place in town, with a relaxed European air and artwork on the walls. Cuisine includes fresh fish, French and Italian classics, vegetarian options like *calebacitas* (stuffed

pumpkins) – and it doesn't serve wild game. About US$15–20 a head. Book ahead at busy times.

Maya Princess Av Reforma. An eclectic menu that includes some Asian-style dishes alongside Guatemalan favourites, for around US$10 a head. Portions are generous.

Pizzeria Picasso C 15 de Septiembre ☎7926 0637. Great pizza served under cooling breezes from the ceiling fans; they also deliver.

Las Puertas signposted from Av Santa Ana. Paint-splattered walls and live music as well as very good pasta, great licuados and healthy break-fasts. Worth it for the atmosphere. Doubles as a bar: try their cocktails.

Villa del Chef C La Unión. A quiet, stylish little restaurant with tables and wicker chairs on a lakeshore terrace. Offers Arab and Middle Eastern dishes like hummus and babaganoush, as well as pizzas and snacks, though service can be slow. Book exchange, too.

Santa Elena

Mijaro two locations: south of the causeway, and on C Principal. Offers good *comida típica* and plenty of meat dishes at local prices, and a daily special.

Restaurant Petenchel 2 C and 4 Av. The menu here concentrates on simple, filling food including steaks and Guatemalan dishes like *ceviche*. It's the nicest place to eat along the main street; most mains are US$4–9.

Listings

Banks In Flores there's an ATM on C 30 de Junio for both MasterCard and Visa. Santa Elena has plenty of banks including two branches of Banrural (both with ATMs) on C Principal. PetenNet (see "Internet") will cash euros, Belizean dollars and Mexican pesos.

Bike & kayak rental *Hotel La Unión*, C La Unión, charges US$8 per day for a mountain bike; kayaks cost US$2.50 per hr.

Car rental Budget, Hertz, Tabarini (with the widest choice; ☎7926 0253, ⊛www.tabarini.com) operate from the airport. Rates (including insurance) start around US$44 a day for a small car, about US$70 for a 4WD.

Doctor The staff at the Centro Médico Maya, 4 Av near 3 C in Santa Elena (☎7926 0180), are helpful and professional, though little or no English is spoken.

Internet Tikal Net, C Centro América, in Flores and C Principal in Santa Elena, and Peten Net, C Centro América, in Flores, all have fairly quick connections and offer photo back-up and discounted international phone calls.

Language schools In Flores, Dos Mundos, C Fraternidad (☎5830 2060, ⊛www .flores-spanish.com), is a new school with a good reputation; a week's tuition and family homestay costs US$165. San Andrés and San José (two attractive villages on the north shore of the lake) also both have good Spanish schools, with rates at around US$175–200 a week. Very few people here speak English so you can progress quite quickly and there are lots of volunteer opportunities. See p.51 for websites and contact information.

Laundry Lavandería Amelia, behind CINCAP in Flores.

Post offices In Flores, Av Barrios; in Santa Elena, on C Principal.

Shopping La Casa de Jade, inside Café Arqueológico Yaxhá (see "Eating") has excellent jewellery inspired by classic Maya designs at fair prices.

Telephones see "Internet".

Travel agents and tour operators Flores is awash with travel agents; most are very mediocre. One highly recommended agency is Martsam Travel, inside *Capitán Tortuga*, C 30 de Junio (☎7867 5093, ⊛www.martsam.com), where the owners speak good English; day-trips to Aguateca, Yaxhá (US$85 per head) and overnight jungle trips to El Zotz (US$225 per head) and many other sites, as well as bespoke tours can be arranged. Mayan Adventure, inside *Café Arqueológico Yaxhá*, C 15 de Septiembre (☎5830 2060, ⊛www.the-mayan-adventure .com), organizes superb trips to Yaxhá and Topoxté (US$49 per head for four people) and overnight trips to Yaxhá–Nakum (US$195 per head). Speak to Matthais at *Hostel Los Amigos* about setting up inexpensive hikes to El Mirador (US$160 per head for four people) or El Zotz. The NGO ProPetén, Calle Central (Mon–Fri 8am–5pm; ☎7867 5155, ⊛www.propeten.org), offers trips to Las Guacamayas, a biological station near the ruins of Waka' (El Perú) where scarlet macaws are common.

Voluntary work The language schools listed above have programmes for volunteers, including helping women's groups, teaching children and doing environmental work. ARCAS (Asociación de Rescate y Conservación de Vida Silvestre), the Wildlife Rescue and Conservation Association (☎7926 0946, ⊛www.arcasguatemala.com), runs an inspiring rescue and rehabilitation programme for animals and birds. To volunteer you need to pay around $100 a week, which covers food, lodging and transportation.

Around Flores

If you have an afternoon or a few days to spare, Lago de Petén Itzá and surrounding hills offer a few interesting diversions. The most obvious excursion is a **trip on the lake**. Boatmen can take you on a circuit that includes a *mirador* and the small Classic-era ruins of Tayasal on the peninsula opposite, as well as the **Petencito zoo** (daily 8am–5pm; US$2.50) near the village of San Miguel, which features a pretty well looked after collection of sluggish local wildlife, pausing for a swim along the way. (Note, though, that the waterslide by the zoo can be dangerous and has caused at least one death.)

You could also visit the new **Museo Santa Bárbara** (8am–noon & 2–5pm; US$1.75) situated on a tiny islet just offshore from *Hotel Santana*, where there's a small collection of Classic-era Maya ceramics. Or drop by **ARCAS**, about 3km east of San Miguel, a rescue and rehabilitation centre for animals formerly kept as pets or confiscated from wildlife traffickers. There's no public access to the rescue area itself, but there is an environmental education centre, botanical trail and bird observation spot here. **Boat trip** prices are set by

Flores transport connections

Flores is very well served by buses and planes from Guatemala City, and there are also buses and flights from Cancún and Belize.

By air

The airlines TAG and Taca (two of their daily flights use an Airbus 319) fly the Guatemala City–Flores route (4 daily; US$210–240 return; 1hr). From Cancún, Taca offers connections (1 daily; US$465 return; 1hr 45min). At the time of research there were no flights between Belize City and Flores, but until 2007 there were four daily services, so connections may resume again. You can also **charter flights** from Flores airport to Dos Lagunas, El Naranjo, Sayaxché, Playa Grande, Puerto Barrios, Río Dulce, Copán (Honduras) and Palenque (Mexico).

By bus

Virtually all buses use Santa Elena's new **Terminal Nuevo bus station** 2km north of the causeway where there's an ATM and a café; Línea Dorada buses continue on to Flores itself. The only exceptions are the hourly services to San Andrés and San José, which leave from the market area, and those operated by San Juan Travel, a company with a very poor record of overcharging tourists.

On the Flores to **Guatemala City** (8–9hr 30min) route you've quite a choice, ranging from inexpensive non-direct chicken buses to nonstop luxury air-conditioned services. Fuente del Norte (℡7926 0666) has 17 daily standard buses (US$14–22), four of which are the more comfortable "Maya de Oro" services. Línea Dorada (℡7926 1788, ⍟www.tikalmayanworld.com) offers three daily luxury buses at 10am, 9.30pm and 10pm (US$20–25). ADN (℡5414 2668, ⍟www.adnautobusesdelnorte.com) have two excellent buses (US$26), which are of a similar standard, and use two drivers, leaving twice daily at 9pm and 11pm. Rapidos del Sur operates two air-conditioned buses daily (US$17) at 10pm and 11pm, with connecting minibuses to Antigua.

For **Cobán** (4hr 30min), via Sayaxché and Chisec, there's a daily shuttle-bus service (US$18; 2pm); book at *Hostel Los Amigos*. You can do it cheaper by taking a microbus to Sayaxché (every 30min; 2hr) and catching a southbound connection there. For **Río Dulce** (3hr) take a Guatemala City–bound bus or a minibus (though these are slower). There are also three daily María Elena buses to **Chiquimula** (US$13) and on to **Esqui-pulas** (US$15) and a Fuente del Norte bus to San Salvador (US$28) at 6am.

Travelling **to Belize**, there are regular microbuses from the terminal for the border at Melchor de Mencos (every 30min; 2hr), plus hourly chicken buses and the odd pullman. Línea Dorada/Mundo Maya operate air-conditioned express services leaving daily at 5am and 7am for Belize City Marine terminal (4hr; US$20) that continue on to the **Mexican border** at Chetumal (another 4hr; US$28) for connections north to Cancún. If you're heading for Mexico via Frontera Corozal or the Río San Pedro, see p.346 and p.348 respectively.

For travel **around Petén**, chicken- and micro-buses leave from Terminal Nuevo, many pausing in the market area to pick up passengers. Services include eight daily buses to Bethel (4hr), a few continuing on to La Técnica (4hr 30min); two daily buses (1pm & 3pm; 3hr) to Carmelita; microbuses to El Naranjo (every 30min; 4hr), Poptún (every 20min; 2hr), Sayaxché (every 15min; 2hr) and El Remate (every 30min; 40min). Half-hourly buses to San Andrés (30min) and San José (40min) leave from the market area.

If you're heading to **Tikal**, virtually all hotels and travel agencies can book you a shuttle bus (US$7 return), which will pick you up at your hotel from 5am onwards.

Inguat (see p.313); it's about US$30 to visit two of the above attractions. You'll find boatmen behind the *Hotel Santana*, in the southwestern corner of Flores. Public boats also run to the village of San Miguel (about every 20min; US$0.25) from *Hotel Sabana*.

Of the numerous **caves** in the hills behind Santa Elena, the most accessible is **Ak'tun Kan** (daily 8am–5pm; US$2) about 2.5km from the causeway, south along 6 Avenida. Otherwise known as *La Cueva de la Serpiente*, the cave is the legendary home of a huge snake. The guard may explain some of the bizarre names given to the various shapes inside, some of which resemble animals and even a marimba.

Skyway Ixpanpajul

At the **Skyway Ixpanpajul**, 10km from Santa Elena, just off the road to Guatemala City (daily; adults US$25 per activity, children US$15; Ⓦwww.ixpanpajul.com), an amazing system of suspension bridges, cable systems and good stone paths connects 3km of forested hilltops in a nine-square-kilometre private jungle reserve. There's a monkey's-eye view of the canopy from a *mirador* with views of virtually the whole of the Petén Itzá basin and the extensive rappel network offers a Tarzan-style jungle encounter. It's best to go in the early morning, after mid-afternoon or even at night, when the wildlife (particularly snakes and kingcacuas) really comes to life; allow a few hours so you can take your time and see the trees and orchids. There's a good self-guided trail leaflet (in Spanish only). Any Poptún-bound microbus will drop you at the entrance.

The attractive **cabañas** (Ⓞ) here sleep up to five, and you can also **camp** for US$5 per head; there are showers and toilets and a café-restaurant. Horseriding (US$15 per hr) and mountain biking (US$8) are offered too.

San Andrés and San José

The quiet villages of **San Andrés** and **San José**, across the lake from Flores are interesting traditional settlements where the pace of life is slow and the

▲ Skyway Ixpanpajul

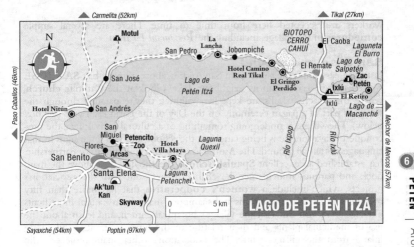

Map labels:
Carmelita (52km) · Tikal (27km)

N

Motul · La Lancha · Jobompiché · BIOTOPO CERRO CAHUÍ · El Caoba · Lagueta El Burro
San Pedro · Hotel Camino Real Tikal · El Remate · Lago de Salpetén
San José · Lago de Petén Itzá · El Gringo Perdido · Zac Petén · Ixlú · El Retiro
Hotel Nitún · San Andrés · Ixlú · Lago de Macanché
Paso Caballos (46km)
San Miguel · Petencito Zoo · Flores · Hotel Villa Maya · Laguna Quexil
San Benito · Arcas · Río Ixpop · Río Ixlú · Melchor de Mencos (57km)
Santa Elena · Laguna Petenchel
Ak'tun Kan · Skyway · 0 — 5 km

LAGO DE PETÉN ITZÁ

Sayaxché (54km) · Poptún (97km)

6

PETÉN | Around Flores

people courteous and friendly. Both places have streets that rise steeply up from the shore, lined with one-storey buildings, some of palmetto sticks and thatch and others hewn in brightly painted concrete. Pigs and chickens wander freely.

In the past, the mainstay of the economy was the arduous and poorly paid collection of **chicle**, the sap of the sapodilla tree, for use in the manufacture of chewing gum. This involves setting up camps in the forest, and working for months at a time in the rainy season when the sap is flowing. Today natural chicle has largely been superseded by artificial substitutes, but there is still a demand for the original product, especially in Japan. Other forest products are also collected, including *xate* (pronounced "shatey"), palm leaves used in floral arrangements and exported to North America and Europe; and *pimienta de jamaica*, or allspice. Harvesters (*pimenteros*) use spurs to climb the trees and collect the spice, they then dry it over a fire. Since the creation of the Reserva de la Biósfera Maya (see p.308), however, efforts have been made to provide villagers with alternative sources of income and **Spanish schools and artesanías projects** have been established in recent years.

Getting to the villages is simple by microbus, which leave about every half-hour from Santa Elena for the forty-minute trip.

San Andrés

Most outsiders in **SAN ANDRÉS** are students at the two **language schools** (see Basics, p.51), and since virtually nobody in the village speaks English, this is an excellent location to immerse yourself in Spanish – though it may be daunting for absolute beginners.

For somewhere to **stay** you'll find the basic but acceptable *Hotel Corina* (❷) on top of the hill as you enter the village, while 3km to the west is the attractive *Hotel Nitún* (☎5201 0759, ⓦwww.nitun.com; ❾, from US$185 including transport from Flores), set above the lakeshore with **accommodation** in stylish thatched stone-and-thatch *casitas*, all with private bathrooms, a restaurant serving superb food (non-guests are welcome for dinner) and a fantastic upper-deck bar-lounge with lake views. The guesthouse is run by Lorena Castillo and Bernie Mittelstaedt, a friendly, knowledgeable couple (both speak perfect English), who also operate Monkey Eco Tours and can organize well-equipped expeditions to remote archeological sites throughout northern Petén. Volunteer workers are accepted here from time to time. There are several simple **comedores** in the village, including the *Restaurant La Troya*.

San José and around

Just 2km east along the shore from San Andrés, above a lovely bay, **SAN JOSÉ** is even more relaxed than its neighbour. Take a look at the Catholic **church**, where three sacred skulls are kept in a cabinet: they're paraded through the streets as part of a pagan ceremony on the Day of the Dead each year (see box below). The village is undergoing something of a cultural revival: Itza, the pre-conquest Maya tongue is being taught in the school, and you'll see signs in that language dotted all around. The Asociación Bio-Itzá, a community partnership, has established an excellent **Spanish school**, the Bio-Itzá, just above the main dock and parque. Students get the chance to help out with the association's projects, which include a **women's cooperative** that has more than fifty members and sells soaps, creams and shampoos made from natural ingredients like aloe vera. You can visit the village's botanical garden, and learn about the use of medicinal plants and their relation to the lunar cycle; it's a kilometre inland from the village centre. The association's other main project is the management of a **forest reserve** north of the village, which is rich in wildlife and contains a thatched visitor shelter and some unexcavated, minor Maya ruins. Volunteer workers are sought: contact the Dos Mundos language school in Flores. There's only one **hotel** in San José, but it's a fine one, *Bahía Taitzá* (☎7928 8125, ⓦwww.taitza.com; ❺), which has a gorgeous lakeside location including a small beach, and eight lovely airy cottages with exposed stone walls and balconies with fine views. Owner Maurico looks after his guests well and the restaurant here (try the pizza from the wood-fired oven) serves food of a high standard. For a more simple meal *El Bungalo*, right by the lakeshore, serves good *comida típica* dishes at fair prices.

Some 4km northwest of San José, down a signed track, are the partly restored ruins of the Classic-period settlement of **Motul** (free). The site, which is historically allied to Tikal, is fairly spread with four plazas, but is little visited.

San José's sacred skulls

San José is famous for its two **fiestas**. The first, to mark the patron saint's day, is held between March 10 and 19 and includes parades and fireworks plus an unusual, comical-looking costumed dance during which a girl (*la chatona*) and a horse skip through the village streets. The second fiesta is distinctly more pagan, with a unique mass, celebrated in the church on All Saints' Day (or Halloween) and a festival that continues on into November 1 – the Day of the Dead. For the evening service, one of three venerated human **skulls** (thought to be the remains of early founders of the village, though some claim they were Spanish missionaries) is removed from its glass case inside the church and positioned on the altar for the ceremony. Afterwards, the skull is carried through the village by black-clad skull bearers, accompanied by children dressed in traditional Itza *traje* and hundreds of devotees, many carrying candles and lanterns. The procession weaves through the streets, stopping at around thirty homes, where prayers are said, chants made and the families ask for blessings. In each home, a corn-based drink called *ixpasá* is consumed and special fiesta food is eaten, part of a ceremony that can take over a day to complete. The exact origin of the event is unclear, but it clearly incorporates a degree of ancestor reverence (or even worship). After all the houses have been visited, the skull is returned to its case in the church, where it remains, and can be seen with the other two skulls, for the rest of the year.

In Plaza B a large stela in front of a looted temple depicts dancing Maya lords. Plaza C is the biggest, with several mounds and courtyards, while Plaza D has the tallest pyramid. It's a tranquil spot, ideal for birdwatching, and probably best visited by bicycle from either of the villages. If you'd rather just chill out for a while by the lake, there are secluded spots east of the village, including a rocky beach with good swimming.

Continuing east from San José along the dirt road that parallels the northern side of the lake towards El Remate, you pass the isolated villages of San Pedro and Jobompiché. Just west of the latter, La Lancha (☎7928 8331, ⓦwww.lalancha.com; ❾, rates depend on room and season) is a small rustic-chic hotel, with ten very stylish rooms, some with marble floors and tribal carvings, others with Guatemalan fabrics and painted wardrobes, are perched on cliffs above Lago de Petén Itzá. The hotel, owned by film director Francis Ford Coppola, enjoys a peaceful location (apart from the local troop of howler monkeys), has a fine pool and gourmet food. Breakfast is included and mountain bikes are free for guests, but beware all the extra taxes added to the standard tariffs.

Two daily buses, plus irregular minibuses, connect Jobompiché with Santa Elena, passing through El Remate (9km to the east) on the way.

El Remate and around

On the eastern shore of Lago de Petén Itzá, 37km from Santa Elena on the road to Tikal, **EL REMATE** offers a tranquil alternative to staying in Flores. Just 2km north of the Ixlú junction, it's a small, friendly village, fast growing in popularity as a convenient base for visiting Tikal as well as several other nearby places, such as the **Biotopo Cerro Cahuí** and the ruins of **Ixlú**. There are several high-quality artisan workshops on the lakeshore (close to the edge of the village, heading south to Ixlú) that sell beautifully carved **wooden handicrafts**; stop by Artesanía Ecológica to see expert carver Rolando Soto at work.

Getting to El Remate is easy: every minibus to Tikal heads through the village, while *colectivo* minibuses from Santa Elena pass through about every thirty minutes or so. Coming from the Belize border, get off at Ixlú – from here you can walk or wait for a ride to El Remate. There's also a daily **shuttle bus** to Cobán (via Chisec), leaving at 8am (4hr 45min); it costs US$26 to travel all the way to Cobán, or you could jump off at points including Candelaria or Chisec on the way. Tickets for this shuttle bus can be bought at *La Casa de Don David*.

Accommodation and eating

El Remate has an excellent range of budget **hotels** and a few more upmarket options, all strung out around the eastern fringes of the lake. In addition, a new upmarket place called *Pirámide Paraíso* is being built next to the *Gringo Perdido*, which should open some time in 2009. You'll find simple comedores in the village centre and most hotels have restaurants. For something a bit more sophisticated, check out the superb Italian-owned ⚔ *Restaurant las Orquideas* (closed Mon), a casual place about 800m along the road to Cerro Cahuí, which serves fine pizza, pasta, *bruchette*, meals such as carpaccio and baked lake fish, as well as wine by the glass; you'll pay around US$8–15 a head.

All these places are listed in the order you approach them from the Ixlú junction.

Casa de Doña Tonita 600m down the road to Cerro Cahuí ☎5701 7114. Five basic wooden rooms and a dorm (US$3). Good, cheap home-cooking is available. ❷

🏃 La Casa de Don David right on the junction ☎7928 8469 or 5306 2190, ⓦwww.lacasadedondavid.com. Defying its location in Guatemala's jungle province, this spotless, efficiently run place offers fifteen spacious rooms, most with a/c and all with private bathroom, dotted around a huge grassy plot that reaches down to the lakeshore. There's a garden palapa shelter with hammocks for chilling, and plenty of *National Geographic* magazines to browse. The American–Guatemalan owners offer great information and filling meals in the open-sided restaurant, change money, arrange trips, and sell bus and shuttle-bus tickets. With meal ⑤–⑥

Casa Mobego 500m down the road to Cerro Cahuí ☏5909 6999. Also known as *Casa Roja*, this slightly scruffy artists' hangout has simple, well-constructed stick-and-thatch cabañas, a dorm (US$5 per bed), camping, inexpensive vegetarian food and kayaks for rent. ②

Ernesto's next to *Dona Tonita*'s ☏5750 8375. Eight attractive, clean, screened cabañas with concrete floors and thatched roofs; half have private bathroom. Comedor. ②–④

El Gringo Perdido on the north shore, 3km from *Don David*'s ☏5804 8639, ⓦwww.hotel elgringoperdido.com. Long-established place in a really tranquil lakeside setting offering relatively simple rooms with bath and nets, small open-fronted cabañas right on the lakeshore, and camping (US$5 per head). Dinner and breakfast are included. ⑥–⑦

Hostal Hermano Pedro down a little lane, 200m before *Don David*'s ☏5719 7394, ⓦwww.hhpedro .com. This efficiently run operation is owned by a friendly local family. All accommodation is in a large well-kept and -swept wooden house that's divided into spacious rooms (some with private bathroom) and a dorm (US$7 a bed). Breakfast and transport can be arranged. ③

Hotel Gardenias just before *Don David*'s ☏5992 3380, ⓦwww.hotelgardenias.com. Right by the junction for Cerro Cahuí, this place doesn't look much but if you pass behind the internet café/ travel agency you'll find big, clean rooms with either two or three beds and private hot-water bathrooms; four have a/c. ③–④

Hotel Sun Breeze opposite *Posada Ixchel* ☏5807 1487. Offering good value, this place has tidy screened rooms that enjoy plenty of natural light; some have lake views and private

bathrooms. The communal facilities are kept very clean. ②–③

La Mansión del Pájaro Serpiente ☏7928 8498. The most comfortable place in the village, this stylish place has good, thatched, two-storey stone cabañas, a suite, and smaller rooms, all with superb lake views. Good food is also available at US$8 per meal, and there's a lovely swimming pool. ⑥–⑦

Mon Ami 800m down road to Cerro Cahuí ☏7928 8413, ⓦwww.hotelmonami.com. Maintaining very high standards and a relaxed atmosphere, this excellent place is owned by Santiago Billy, an amiable Frenchman who's been living in Petén for years. All the delightful, artistically decorated rooms are scattered around a shady plot and include really spacious adobe bungalows with gorgeous hardwood doors, quality beds, and porches with hammocks. The dorm (US$7.50 per bed) here is simply in a class of its own, the best in Guatemala, with beds set well apart and divided by fabrics and wooden screens for privacy. Also home to a superb in-house restaurant with many Gallic dishes and daily specials. Horseriding and tours to Tikal and Yaxhá can be arranged. ③–④

Posada Ixchel 150m before *Don David*'s ☏7928 8475. Simple, friendly place with basic rooms with shared bath or smart tiled rooms with good beds and reading lights in a new block at the rear. ②–③

Sak-Luk high above the lake, reached by a stairway ☏5494 5925. It's looking pretty run down these days, but this chaotic, bohemian place has some intriguing igloo-like, whitewashed stucco huts, a rough dorm (US$3), and offers cheap, tasty food – expect a long wait. Great views though. ②

Westin Camino Real Tikal beyond Cerro Cahuí, 5km from *Don David*'s ☏7926 0207, ⓦwww .caminorealtikal.com.gt. Large luxury hotel in extensive lakeside grounds with excellent views over the water and a private beach, with hammocks for lake views. However the rooms are pretty unimaginative and could do with an update, and the restaurant is pricey and pretty mediocre. A free guided tour of the Biotopo Cerro Cahuí is included. ⑨, US$140 for a double, though discounted packages are also available.

Biotopo Cerro Cahuí

On the north shore of the lake, 3km west of the centre of El Remate, the **Biotopo Cerro Cahuí** (daily 7am–5pm; US$4) is a wildlife conservation area comprising lakeshore, ponds and some of the best examples of undisturbed tropical forest in Petén. The smallest and most accessible of Petén's *biotopos*, it contains a rich diversity of plants and animals, and is especially recommended for birdwatchers. There are two hiking trails, a couple of small ruins and two thatched *miradores* on the hill above the lake; pick up maps and information at the gate where you sign in.

Laguna Macanché and around

From the Ixlú junction it's 7km east to the village of **MACANCHÉ**, on the shore of **Laguna Macanché**, where a signed track leads north for 1.8km to another wonderfully tranquil place to stay, the *Santuario Ecológico El Retiro* (T 5704 1300, W www.retiro-guatemala.com; ③–⑤). Set in forested grounds on the north shore of the lake are private **bungalows** with hot shower and shady porch for US$60 double, as well as spacious **tents** (US$20 per head); you can also **camp** for US$3.50 per head. There's a good restaurant and a dock for swimming – and the crocodiles are not usually seen at this end of the lake. In the base area is a **serpentarium** (guided tours are US$5) with more than twenty species of snake including the deadly fer-de-lance, and a venomous beaded lizard. Volunteer workers are usually welcome; contact owner Miguel for more information.

On top of the hill behind the base area lie the stone remains of ancient **Maya residential complexes** – but far more intriguing are the numbers of *chultunes* found here. A *chultún* is a gourd-shaped hole carved out of the bedrock, with a very narrow entrance on top capped by a circular stone; some have side chambers. Their exact use is still unknown, though suggested functions include storage cavities, a refuge or a place to conduct ceremonial or religious rites.

El Retiro forms part of an extensive private nature reserve and **crocodile sanctuary** that extends along the lake and into two other lagoons beyond. Several **tours** can be organized here. A superb day-trip (US$30 including lunch) involves a forest hike, boat trip across the lake to the gorgeous neighbouring **Laguneta El Burro** (which is surrounded by thick rainforest dotted with Maya ruins) on to another lagoon and huge limestone sinkhole. Crocodile-spotting night tours, including dinner, a hike and boat trip cost US$40.

▲ Laguna Macanché, near Flores

Tikal

Towering above the rain forest, **Tikal** is possibly the most magnificent of all Maya sites. The ruins, 68km from Flores down a smooth paved road, are dominated by five enormous temples, steep-sided limestone pyramids that rise to more than 60m above the forest floor. Around them are literally thousands of other structures, many semi-strangled by giant roots and still hidden beneath mounds of earth.

The site itself is surrounded by the **Parque Nacional Tikal**, a protected area of some 576 square kilometres that is on the edge of the much larger Reserva de la Biósfera Maya. Hundreds of species, including howler and spider monkeys, toucans and parakeets are found here. The sheer scale of the place is overwhelming, and its atmosphere spellbinding. Whether you can spare as little as a morning or as long as a week, it's always worth the trip.

Getting there

The best way to reach the ruins is in one of the **tourist minibuses** (US$7 return) that meet flights at Flores airport and pick up passengers from every hotel in Flores, Santa Elena and El Remate, starting from 4.30am. It's wise to arrive early at Tikal when the air is fresh and heat less intense, but note that it's rare to witness an impressive **sunrise** over the ruins as the appearance of the sun is generally delayed by mist rising from the humid forest.

If you're travelling **from Belize**, change buses at **Ixlú**, the three-way junction at the eastern end of Lago de Petén Itzá, from where there are plenty of passing minibuses (US$3.50 one way) all day long.

Site practicalities

Plane and local bus schedules are designed to make it easy to visit the ruins as a day-trip from Flores or Guatemala City, but if you can spare the time it's well worth staying overnight. You'll need the extra time to do justice to the ruins themselves, but more importantly this allows you to spend dawn and dusk at the site, when the forest canopy bursts into a frenzy of sound and activity. The air fills with the screech of toucans and the roar of howler monkeys, while flocks of parakeets wheel around the temples, and bats launch themselves into the night. With a bit of luck you might even see a grey fox sneak across one of the plazas.

Entrance to the national park (daily 6am–6pm) costs US$22 – if you arrive after 3pm you'll be given a ticket also valid for the following day. For tourist information, Inguat has a desk (6am–4pm) close to the ticket office.

Close to the entrance to the site there's a **post office**, shops and stalls (which sell souvenirs, hats, sun cream, memory cards for cameras, film, batteries and water) and a **visitor centre**, where you'll find a café-restaurant, toilets, luggage storage (US$0.15 per hour) and **licensed guides** (US$48 for up to four people, plus additional US$5 per extra person; 4hr tour). Most guides are excellent and very knowledgeable about Tikal's flora and fauna as well as the ruins. Obviously, if you can get a group together, or join others, it doesn't work out to be that expensive. Three **books** of note are usually available at the visitor centre: William Coe's *Tikal: A Handbook to the Ancient Maya Ruins*, which is a decent guide to the site, though now a little out of date; *The Birds of Tikal*, by Frank Smythe, which is by no means comprehensive but well worth consulting; and Peter D. Harrison's *The Lords of Tikal*, a very comprehensive and readable account of the city's turbulent history.

The **website** Ⓦwww.tikalpark.com has lots of useful information about the site and the reserve.

Accommodation, eating and drinking

There are three **hotels** at the ruins, all of them fairly expensive and not especially good value. Some visitors find that service standards are not very high here – maybe it's the energy-sapping jungle location. Electricity is sporadic (usually 6–9am and 6–10pm), few staff speak much English and credit-card surcharges are routinely hefty. That said, spending a night in the forest so close to the ruins is an unforgettable experience.

First choice is the attractive *Jungle Lodge* (Ⓣ2476 8775, Ⓦwww.junglelodge .guate.com; ⑤–⑧), which offers comfortable bungalows each with two double beds, a few basic rooms with shared bath, and some tents (US$10) with good mattresses; there's also a decent restaurant (US$10 a full meal) and a pool. The *Tikal Inn* (Ⓣ7926 1917, Ⓦwww.tikalinn.com; ⑦–⑧) is a good alternative, offering pleasant thatched bungalows, clean airy rooms and a heat-busting swimming pool. Otherwise the overpriced *Jaguar Inn* (Ⓣ7926 0002, Ⓦwww .jaguartikal.com; ⑦) has 13 bungalows with small verandas and hammocks, a five-bed dorm (US$10 per head), hammocks with nets (US$5), camping (US$3.50 per head), a reasonable restaurant and wi-fi. You can also camp or sling a hammock at Tikal's basic **campsite** (US$4), complete with rudimentary shower-block. Hammocks and mosquito nets (essential in the wet season) are available for rent from the *Comedor Imperio Maya*, opposite the visitor centre. It's illegal to camp or sleep out among the ruins.

Several simple but fairly pricey **comedores** are located at the entrance to the site (the *Comedor Tikal* is fair value with sandwiches for US$2.75 and grilled meats or fish meals for US$7). For a more extensive and expensive menu, head for the decent restaurant at the *Jungle Lodge*. Cold soft-drinks are sold around the ruins by vendors.

The site museums

At the entrance, between the *Jungle Lodge* and *Jaguar Inn* hotels, the one-room **Museo Tikal** (Mon–Fri 9am–5pm, Sat & Sun 9am–4pm; US$1.30) houses some of the artefacts found in the ruins, including ceramics, obsidian eccentric flints, jade jewellery found in Tumba 116 and the magnificent **Stela 31**, which was inaugurated in 445 AD. This limestone monument shows Tikal ruler Siyah Chan K'awil (Stormy Sky) wearing a jaguar-head belt and a jade necklace, flanked by two warriors bearing non-Maya Teotihuacán-style spear throwers and darts as well as shields decorated with the "goggle-eyed" image of the rain god Tlaloc. The stela was cut to mark the completion of the first *katun* under Stormy Sky's rule, but the lengthy glyphic inscriptions on the rear confirm clear alliance with the Mexican metropolis of Teotihuacán.

The museum also has a spectacular reconstruction of the great ruler **Hasaw Chan K'awil's tomb**. One of the richest ever found in the Maya world, the tomb contained 180 worked jade items in the form of bracelets, anklets, necklaces and earplugs, and delicately incised bones, including a famous carving depicting deities paddling a canoe to the underworld. A larger bone, also found at the tomb, shows a poignant image of a bound captive, no doubt awaiting a sacrificial death. The accompanying text explains that this unfortunate individual is from the neighbouring city of Calakmul – the other "superpower" state to the north – a city that Hasaw Chan K'awil defeated in a seminal victory in 695 AD, reversing more than a century of subjugation.

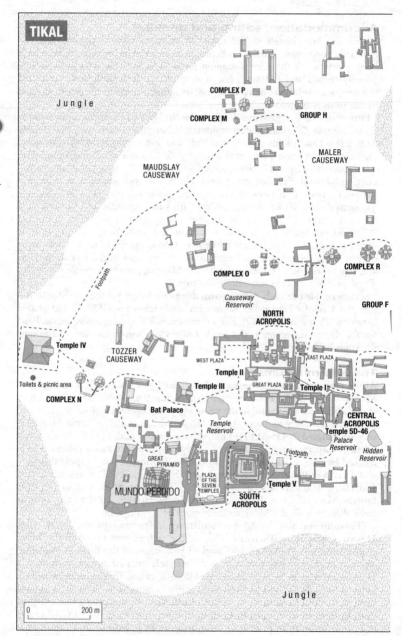

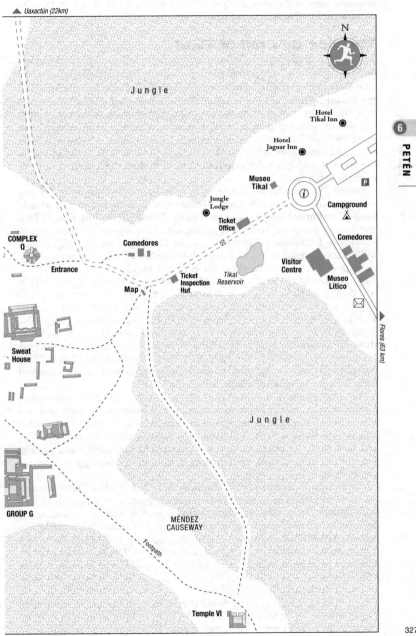

Uaxactún (22km)

N

Jungle

Hotel
Tikal Inn

Hotel
Jaguar Inn

Museo
Tikal

Jungle
Lodge

Ticket
Office

Campground

Comedores

COMPLEX
Q

Comedores

Entrance

Tikal
Reservoir

Visitor
Centre

Ticket
Inspection
Hut

Museo
Lítico

Map

Flores (63 km)

Sweat
House

Jungle

GROUP G

MÉNDEZ
CAUSEWAY

Footpath

Temple VI

The **Museo Lítico** (same hours; US$1.30), inside the visitor centre, holds nineteen more stelae, though they are very poorly labelled and there is no supplementary information in English.

The rise and fall of Tikal

According to recent evidence, the first occupants of Tikal arrived around 900 BC, probably attracted by its position above surrounding seasonal swamps and by the availability of flint for making tools and weapons. For the next four hundred years there's nothing to suggest that it was anything more than a tiny village of thatched huts. By 500 BC, however, the first steps of a modest astronomical stone temple had been constructed, though burials at this time were still relatively simple and ceramics found had been crudely executed. Tikal remained a minor settlement during the latter years of the Middle Preclassic (1000–400 BC), while 50km to the north, towering temples were being built at **Nakbé**, the first city to emerge from the Petén forest.

Around 250 BC, after the collapse of El Mirador, the first significant ceremonial structures emerged. A small pyramid was constructed in the Mundo Perdido, and minor temples were built in the **North Acropolis**, though Tikal was a still a peripheral settlement at this stage. Dominating the entire region, formidable **El Mirador** (see p.338) was the first Maya "superpower", though its Preclassic hegemony was later to be challenged by a distant, and perhaps even more powerful player – **Teotihuacán** in central Mexico.

By the time of Christ, the **Great Plaza** had begun to take shape and Tikal was already established as an important site. For the next two centuries, art and architecture became increasingly ornate and sophisticated as the great pyramid was enlarged to over 30m in height, its sides adorned by huge stucco masks. The styles that were to dominate throughout the Classic period were perfected in these early years, and by 200 AD all the major architectural traits had evolved. It's during this period that **Yax Ehb' Xok** (First Step Shark) established Tikal's first ruling dynasty around 90 AD: a royal lineage recognized by all 33 (known) subsequent kings, until the record fades in 869 AD.

The closing years of the Late Preclassic era (400 BC–250 AD) were marked by the eruption of the Ilopango volcano, which smothered a huge area in a thick layer of volcanic ash, disrupting trade routes. The ensuing years saw the decline and abandonment of El Mirador, presenting an opportunity for Tikal and Uaxactún to emerge as substantial centres of trade, science and religion. Less than a day's walk apart and growing rapidly, the cities engaged in heated competition.

Matters finally came to a head on January 31, 378 AD, when Tikal's warriors overran Uaxactún. The secret of Tikal's success appears to have been its alliance with Teotihuacán and the introduction of new warfare equipment from central Mexico. Inscriptions attest that it was the arrival of a somewhat mysterious warrior, **Siyak K'ak'** (Fire-Born), "from the west" that helped seal the victory. This general is thought to have been dispatched by the Teotihuacán king Spear-thrower Owl, armed with the latest weapon: an *atlatl* (a wooden sling capable of firing arrows). It's probable that the warrior Siyak K'ak' ordered the execution of Tikal ruler Jaguar Paw I, initiating a Mexican-directed takeover, for the next king installed at Tikal, Yax Nuun Ayin I (First Crocodile but also known as Curl Nose), was the son of Spearthrower Owl. First Crocodile married into the Tikal dynasty, and started a new royal lineage, though efforts were made to pay careful reverence to the deposed ruler Jaguar Paw I, and his palace (Structure 5D-46) remained a revered royal residence for the next four centuries.

Tikal from 400–909 AD

The victory over Uaxactún enabled Tikal to dominate central Petén for much of the next five hundred years. During this time it became one of the most elaborate and magnificent of all Maya city-states, monopolizing the crucial lowland trade routes, its influence reaching as far as Copán in Honduras and Yaxchilán on the Usumacinta. The elite immediately launched an extensive rebuilding programme, including a radical remodelling of the North Acropolis and the renovation of most of the city's finest temples. It's clear that Tikal's alliance with Teotihuacán remained an important part of its continuing power: stelae and paintings from the period show that subsequent Tikal rulers adopted central Mexican styles of clothing, pottery and warfare.

Yet as Tikal was expanding and growing in size during the fifth century, a formidable rival Maya "superpower" – **Calakmul**, or the Kingdom of the Snake – was emerging in the jungles to the north. Through an aggressive series of regional alliances, Calakmul steadily encircled Tikal with enemy cities, filling the power vacuum in the Maya heartland that had developed as the influence of Tikal's overstretched backer, Teotihuacán, faded. By the Early Classic period, Calakmul had built up a bloc of vassal states, many previously under the auspices of Tikal, including Naranjo and Waka' (see p.348), and was courting a potentially devastating alliance with **Caracol**, a powerful emerging city to the southeast in modern Belize.

In an apparent attempt to subdue a potential rival, Wak Chan K'awil, or **Double Bird**, the ruler of Tikal, launched an attack (known as an "axe war") on Caracol and its ambitious leader, Yahaw Te ("**Lord Water**"), in 556 AD. Despite capturing and sacrificing a noble from Caracol, Double Bird's strategy was only temporarily successful. In 562 AD, Lord Water (with substantial backing from Calakmul) hit back in a devastating "star war" (a battle timed to an astronomical event like a solstice), which crushed Tikal and almost certainly sacrificed Double Bird. The victors stamped their authority over the humiliated nobles of Tikal, smashing stelae, desecrating tombs and destroying written records. The subsequent 130-year period has long been referred to as Tikal's "**hiatus**", but recent findings at Temple V – which was probably built during this period – have forced Mayanists to re-evaluate the theory. What is clear is that despite the defeat in 562 AD, Tikal was never broken.

Towards the end of the seventh century, Calakmul's position of dominance had begun to weaken, and Tikal gradually started to recover its lost power under the formidable leadership of Hasaw Chan K'awil, or **Heavenly Standard Bearer** (682–723 AD). During his reign the main ceremonial areas, the East Plaza and the North Acropolis, were completely remodelled, reclaimed from the desecration suffered at the hands of Calakmul and Caracol. By 695 AD, Tikal was powerful enough to launch an attack against Calakmul, capturing and executing its king, Yich'aak K'ak' (known as **Fiery Claw** or **Jaguar Paw**) and severely weakening the alliance against Tikal. The following year, Hasaw Chan K'awil repeated his astonishing coup by capturing **Split Earth**, the new king of Calakmul, and Tikal regained its position as the dominant city in the Maya World.

Hasaw Chan K'awil's leadership gave birth to a revitalized and powerful ruling dynasty: in the hundred years following his death five of Tikal's main temples were built, and his son, Yik'in Chan K'awil, or **Divine Sunset Lord** (who ascended the throne in 734 AD), had his father's body entombed in the magnificent **Temple I**. He also constructed Temple VI, remodelled the Central Acropolis and principal city causeways, and defeated Waka' and Naranjo in 743 and 744 AD, breaking the ring of hostile cities that encircled Tikal. Around this time, at the height of the Classic period, Tikal's population had grown to somewhere around 100,000 (some Mayanists argue for much more) spread across a central area covering about thirty square kilometres. Its authority also extended to include a series of vassal states, among them Naranjo, Waka', Uaxactún and many more minor settlements – a domain of perhaps 500,000 subjects. During this time we know the city was called **Mutul** (or Yax Mutul), a name that could be "Great Green Bundle" or a reference to a knot of hair on Tikal's emblem glyph. (Early explorer Morely coined what's surely the most appropriate name for the site – "Place Where the Gods Speak".)

By the beginning of the ninth century, severe signs of crisis emerged across the entire Maya region – probably sparked by a period of climate change, including a catastrophic drought. Population levels at Tikal plummeted, as people fled the area. Tikal's last recorded monument is inscribed on Stela 24, completed in 869 AD. What brought about Tikal's final **downfall** remains a mystery, but what is certain is that at about 900 AD almost the entire lowland Maya civilization collapsed, and Tikal was effectively abandoned by the end of the tenth century. Afterwards, the site was used from time to time by other groups, who worshipped here and repositioned many of the stelae, but it was never occupied again.

Rediscovery

After its mysterious decline little is known of Tikal until 1695 when a lost priest, Father Avendaño, stumbled upon a "variety of old buildings". The colonial powers were distinctly unimpressed by Petén and for the next 150 years the ruins were left to the jungle. In 1848 they were rediscovered by a government expedition led by Modesto Méndez. Later in the nineteenth century, a Swiss scientist visited the site and removed the beautifully carved wooden lintels from the tops of Temples I and IV – they are in a museum in Basel – and in 1881 the English archeologist Maudslay took the first photographs of the ruins, showing the main temples cloaked in tropical vegetation.

Until 1951 the site could only be reached on horseback – with considerable difficulty – and although there was a steady trickle of visitors the ruins remained mostly choked in jungle. The gargantuan project to excavate and restore the site started in 1956 and involved teams from the University of Pennsylvania in the US and Guatemala's Institute of Anthropology. Much of the major work was completed by 1984, but thousands of minor buildings remain buried by roots, shoots and rubble. There's little doubt that an incredible amount is waiting to be found – as recently as 1996 a workman unearthed a stela (Stela 40, dating from 468 AD) while mowing the grass on the Great Plaza. And in 2003 inscriptions discovered at Temple V have provided convincing evidence that Tikal may not have suffered a Classic-era hiatus at all.

The ruins

The sheer scale of the ruins at Tikal can at first seem daunting. The **central area**, with its five main temples, forms by far the most impressive section; if you start to explore beyond this, you can ramble seemingly forever in the maze of smaller, **unrestored structures** and complexes. Compared with the scale and magnificence of the main area, they're not that impressive, but armed with a good **map** (the best is in Coe's guide to the ruins, available in the visitor centre), it can be exciting to search for some of the rarely visited outlying sections. Don't even think about exploring the more distant structures without a map; every year at least one tourist gets lost in the jungle.

From the entrance to the Great Plaza

Walking into the ruins, a path bears to the right from the site **map** towards the prosaically named **Complex Q** and **Complex R**, two of the seven sets of twin pyramids. Commissioned by Yax Ain II, also known as **Chitam**, one of Tikal's last-known rulers, they were built to mark the passing of a *katun* (twenty 360-day years). Twinned pyramids are an architectural feature found only in the Tikal region, with several at the city itself, and a few others found at sites nearby (including Nakúm, Yaxhá and Ixlú). At Complex Q (inaugurated in 771 AD), the first set you come to, only one of the pyramids has been restored, with the stelae and altars re-erected in front of it. Ceremonies are held here by Maya shamen on auspicious days in the Maya calendar. On the north side is a copy of **Stela 22** (the original is in the Museo Lítico), its glyphs recording the ascension to the throne of Chitam II, who is portrayed in full regalia complete with an enormous sweeping headdress and jaguar-skin kilt, holding the staff of authority.

Following the path as it bears around to the left after the twin temples of **Complex R** (built in 790 AD), you approach the back of Temple I through the **East Plaza**. On the left side, behind a small ball-court, is a broad platform supporting a series of small buildings known as the **marketplace**, and in the southeast corner of the plaza stands an imposing temple, beneath which were found the remains of several severed heads, the victims of human sacrifice. Behind the marketplace, the **Sweat House** probably functioned as a kind of sauna (similar to those used by highland Maya today). Priests and rulers would have taken a sweat bath in order to cleanse themselves before conducting religious rituals.

From here, a few short steps bring you to the **Great Plaza**, the heart of the ancient city. Surrounded by four massive structures, this was the focus of ceremonial and religious activity at Tikal for around a thousand years. The earliest part is the North Acropolis; the two great temple-pyramids (which disrupted the city's original north–south axis) weren't built until the eighth century. The plaza covers an area of one and a half acres, and beneath today's grass lie four layers of paving, the oldest of which dates from about 150 BC and the most recent from 700 AD. Climbing Temple I has been prohibited for several years, but there are terrific views from Temple II. The symmetry of the two temples perfectly reflects the Maya's preoccupation with astronomy – during an **equinox** Temple I's shadow "kisses" the base of Temple II, and later in the day Temple II reciprocates the gesture.

Temple I, towering 44m above the plaza, is the hallmark of Tikal – it's also known as the Jaguar Temple because of the jaguar carved in its door lintel, though this is now in a museum in Basel. The temple was built as a burial monument to contain the magnificent **tomb of Hasaw Chan K'awil**, one of Tikal's greatest rulers, who ascended the throne in 682 AD (see p.329) and defeated the archenemy state of Calakmul. It was constructed shortly after his death in 721 AD, under the direction of his son and successor, Yik'in Chan K'awil. Within the tomb at the temple's core, his remains were found facing north, surrounded by an assortment of jade, pearls, seashells and stingray spines, which were a traditional symbol of human sacrifice. There were also some magnificent bone ornaments, perhaps spoils of victory over Calakmul, depicting a journey to the underworld made in a canoe rowed by mythical animal figures. A reconstruction of the tomb (Tumba 116) is on show in the Museo Tikal.

Architecturally, Temple I was radically different from anything that had been constructed in the Maya region up to that point – an unequivocal statement of confidence no doubt designed to reassert Tikal's position as a dominant power.

Comprising a series of nine ascending platforms, the style emphasizes the vertical dimensions of the temple and draws the eye to the roof comb. To create this soaring effect, hundreds of tons of flint and rubble were poured on top of the completed tomb and the temple was built around this, with a staircase of thick plastered blocks running up the front. The monument is topped by a three-room building and a hollow roof-comb originally painted in cream, red and possibly green. On the front of the comb it's just possible to make out a seated figure and a stylized serpent.

Standing opposite, like a squatter version of Temple I, is **Temple II**, also known as the Temple of the Masks for the two grotesque masks, now heavily eroded, that flank the central stairway. The temples were arranged to form a twin pyramid alignment, and their construction marked a seminal change to the ceremonial core of the city. Not only was the sheer size of these new temples a powerful statement, but their position purposely deflected attention away from the adjacent North Acropolis, rising above the monuments where Tikal's elite had been buried for at least five hundred years. Temple II dates from the beginning of the eighth century, and was almost certainly built to honour Hasaw Chan K'awil's wife, Lady Twelve Macaw. The structure now stands 38m high, although with its roof comb intact it would have equalled Temple I. It's an easy climb up a wooden staircase to the upper level of the structure, where the echo is fantastically clear and crisp; and the view, almost level with the forest canopy, is incredible, with the great plaza spread out below.

The North Acropolis

Occupying the whole north side of the plaza, the **North Acropolis** is one of the most complex structures in the entire Maya World. In traditional Maya style it was built and rebuilt on top of itself, and beneath the twelve temples that can be seen today are the remains of about a hundred other structures. As early as 100 BC the Maya had constructed elaborate temples and tombs here; in around 250 AD the entire thing was torn down and rebuilt as a platform and four vaulted temples, each of which was rebuilt twice during Early Classic times. Archeologists have removed some of the surface to reveal these earlier structures, including two four-metre-high Preclassic stone **masks**, which can be glimpsed under thatched protective roofs; one depicts a hook-nosed god with earplugs wearing a crown-like headdress. Originally these great masks, which adorn many Maya Preclassic temple staircases, would have been finished with a stucco coating of limestone and painted in scarlet and green.

Two lines of **stelae**, carved with images of Tikal's elite, with circular altars at their bases, stand in front of the North Acropolis. These rulers were certainly obsessive in their recording of the city's dynastic sequence, linking it with great historical moments and reaching as far back into the past as possible. Many of the stelae bear the marks of ritual defacement, perpetrated by invaders from Caracol during the Classic era, acts carried out by conquerors as rites of humiliation.

The Central Acropolis

On the other side of the plaza, the **Central Acropolis** is a maze of 45 tiny interconnecting rooms and stairways built around six smallish courtyards. The buildings here are thought to have been palaces, law courts and administrative centres. **Structure 5D-46**, a partly ruined rectangular building with short frontal and rear stone staircases, is particularly intriguing. Dating from around 360 AD, it was the residential home of Chak Tok Ich'aak I (Great Jaguar Paw), and functioned as a royal residence for at least four hundred years, its importance deemed so hallowed that no ruler carried out any significant structural alterations after the fourth century AD. Take a look, too, at the large two-storey building in Court 2 known as **Maler's Palace**, named after the archeologist Teobert Maler who made it his home during expeditions in 1895 and 1904. Behind the acropolis is the palace reservoir, one of at least twelve clay-lined pools that were fed by a series of channels with rainwater from all over the city.

From the West Plaza to Temple IV
Behind Temple II is the **West Plaza**, dominated by a large Late Classic palace on the north side, and scattered with various altars and stelae. From here the **Tozzer Causeway** – one of the raised routes that connected the main parts of the city – leads west to the unrestored **Temple III** (60m), covered in jungle vegetation and inaccessible to visitors. A fragment of Stela 24, found at the base of the temple, dates it at June 24, 810 AD, which marked the end of a *katun*. It was customary to construct twin temples to mark this auspicious event, but by this time it's clear that the Classic Maya were in severe difficulties across the region and just raising the manpower necessary to build Temple III would have been quite an achievement. Many Mayanists believe Temple III is a burial monument to Dark Sun, the last of Tikal's great rulers, and that it is he depicted as a portly figure wearing a magnificent jaguar costume on the badly eroded lintels that crown the temple's summit. Around the back of the building is a huge palace complex, of which only the **Bat Palace**, characterized by broad staircases, has been restored. Further down the causeway, on the left-hand side, is **Complex N**, another set of Late Classic twin pyramids. In the northern enclosure of the complex, the superbly carved **Stela 16** shows a flamboyantly dressed Hasaw Chan K'awil, who was buried beneath Temple I, depicted with a huge plumed headdress. **Altar 5** at its base bears a sculpted scene of Hasaw presiding over a sacrificial skull and bones with a lord from Maasal, formerly a vassal state of Calakmul, a clear indicator that Tikal had successfully expanded into the orbit of its bitter rival by 711 AD, when the altar was completed. The accompanying text mentions the death of Hasaw's wife, Lady Twelve Macaw.

At the end of the Tozzer Causeway, **Temple IV** is the tallest of all the Tikal structures at 64.6m (212ft). Built in 741 AD by Yik'in Chan K'awil (Hasaw's son), it is thought by many archeologists to be his burial monument. Ongoing excavations, including the burrowing of five tunnels into the heart of the structure, have failed to find his tomb as yet, though an early pyramid (over which Temple IV was constructed) has been discovered. Temple IV is most famous for the stunning, carved **wooden lintels**, embellished with images of the victorious king and a riot of glyphs that once adorned its summit. Nowadays you'll have to travel to Switzerland to see them – though you can see an excellent replica of Lintel 3 in Guatemala City's archeological museum.

Twin stairways – one for the ascent, the other for the descent – provide access to the uppermost level of this unrestored temple. Slow and exhausting as the climb is, the finest views of the whole site await. All around you the forest canopy stretches out to the horizon, over the ruins of Naranjo towards the Maya Mountains of Belize, interrupted only by the great roof-combs of the other temples. Given the vistas, it's not surprising that the sunrise tribe gather here in great numbers, and though the humidity and mist usually shroud the visuals somewhat, the dawn jungle-chorus rarely fails to disappoint.

From Temple IV the **Maudslay Causeway** leads to **Group H**, which includes two more twin-pyramid structures, and from here the **Maler Causeway** takes you back down to the East Plaza, past yet another set.

The Mundo Perdido and the Plaza of the Seven Temples

The other main buildings in the centre of Tikal are to the southeast of Temple IV. The first of these, occupying the **Mundo Perdido**, or Lost World, form another magical and very distinct section of the site with its own atmosphere and architecture. Little is known about the ruins in this part of the city. The main feature is the **Great Pyramid**, a 32-metre-high structure whose surface hides four earlier versions, the first an astronomical temple from 500 BC. Very faint remains of sixteen masks, four on each side of the pyramid, can still be made out. At the time of research it was not possible to climb the structure, but if access resumes its summit offers sweeping views towards Temple IV and the Great Plaza and makes an excellent base to watch the visual dramatics at sunrise. Just east of here, the **Plaza of the Seven Temples** forms part of a complex dating back to before Christ. Archeological digs and restoration work are ongoing here. There's an unusual triple ball-court on the north side of this plaza, and its eastern flank is formed by the unexcavated South Acropolis.

Temple V, Temple VI and beyond

A short trail from the southern part of the Plaza of the Seven Temples leads to the rear of the 58-metre-high **Temple V**, whose commanding, flared facade has now been fully restored. Recent evidence suggests that this monument, the construction of which took fifty years, was started around 600 AD by the ruler Animal Skull (which would make it the original of Tikal's six great temples) though very little about Temple V is currently known. A vertiginous wooden staircase (closed when it's been raining heavily) attached to the side of the temple rises to a very slender upper level, just beneath the roof comb, from where you get a stomach-churning perspective of the temples of the Great Plaza and an ocean of jungle beyond.

Finally, there's **Temple VI**, also known as the Temple of the Inscriptions, reached along the Méndez Causeway from the Central Acropolis. The temple (only rediscovered in 1957), about 1km from the plaza, is another of Yik'in Chan K'awil's constructions, completed in 766 AD. It's a medium-sized temple, famous for its twelve-metre roof comb, on the back of which is a huge hieroglyphic text, only just visible these days. More than 180 glyphs chart the history of the city from a founding date in 1139 BC (which is quite close to the first archeological evidence of settlement). Temple VI is another candidate as the burial place of Yik'in Chan K'awil, Tikal's most prodigious monument-builder, along with Temple IV.

Outside the main area are countless, smaller, **unrestored structures**. Compared with the scale and magnificence of what you've seen already they're not that impressive, but armed with a good map (the best is in Coe's guide to the ruins), it can be exciting to explore some of the rarely visited outlying sections. Tikal is certain to exhaust you before you exhaust it.

Uaxactún and around

Twenty-three kilometres north of Tikal, the adobe and clapboard houses that comprise the friendly village of **UAXACTÚN** are spread out on both sides of an airstrip, as are the ruins of the same name. With a couple of places to stay, a few comedores and daily bus connections from Flores, the village is an ideal jumping-off point for the remote northern ruins of **El Zotz, Naachtún and Río Azul**. Substantially smaller than Tikal, the site (known as Sia'an K'aan in

Maya times) rose to prominence in the Late Preclassic era when it grew to become a major player. Uaxactún developed an intense rivalry with Tikal, which peaked in January 16, 378 AD, when Tikal's warriors conquered Uaxactún armed with the latest high-tech weaponry of the day – spear-throwing slings from Mexico. Uaxactún never recovered from this epochal defeat, and for the remainder of the Classic period was reduced to little more than a provincial backwater.

Uaxactún **ruins** (officially US$7.50, but often no fee is collected) are not that extensive, and may be a little disappointing after the grandeur of Tikal, but you'll probably have the site to yourself. Village children will offer to guide you around; their charm is irresistible – as are the dolls made from corn husks decorated with beads and dried flowers you'll be implored to buy – though their archeological knowledge is limited. A tip of a quetzal or two is fine.

The most interesting buildings are in **Group E**, east of the airstrip, where three low, reconstructed temples – Temples E-1, E-II and E-III – built side by side, are arranged to function as an observatory. Viewed from the top of a fourth temple, the sun rises behind the north temple (E-I) on the longest day of the year and behind the southern one (E-III) on the shortest day. It's an architectural pattern that was first discovered here but has since been found at a number of other sites. This point of observation is above the famous **E-VII sub**, a buried Preclassic temple that was once thought to date back to 2000 BC, though a much later date is now accepted. The pyramid has simple staircases on all sides, the steps flanked by pairs of elaborate **stucco masks** of jaguar and serpent heads. It's clear that this was a sacred monument, a platform for blood-letting and sacrifice, for the jaguar signifies the Jaguar God of the underworld, one of the most powerful deities; the serpent is the fabled "vision serpent".

On the other side of the airstrip are **Groups A and B**, a series of larger temples and residential compounds, some of them reconstructed, spread out across the high ground. In amongst the structures are some impressive stelae, each sheltered by a small thatched roof, but most lying poignantly broken and supine.

Practicalities

Two daily **buses** (at 1pm & 3pm; 2hr 15min) from Flores pass through Tikal en route for Uaxactún; alternatively, you could take a tour from Flores (see p.316). **Staying overnight** you have two options. The welcoming *Campamento Ecológico El Chiclero* (☎7783 3917, ✉campamentoelchiclero@gmail.com; ❸) offers simple rooms with decent mattresses and nets, camping and hammock space (both US$3.50); bathrooms are shared but kept clean. Owner Antonio Baldizón also organizes 4WD trips (in the dry season Feb–May) to Río Azul and Naachtún. His wife Neria prepares excellent food – large-portioned meals cost US$6.50. Otherwise *Aldana's* (❷) run by Bárbara Aldana is friendly but very basic, with wooden rooms and camping (US$2 per head). For a cheap **meal**, head to *Comedor Uaxactún* on the north side of the airstrip.

In the grounds of *El Chiclero*, there's a small but interesting **museum** (free), with an astonishing collection of intact vases, plates and other ceramics crammed onto its wooden shelves. Many of the vessels are decorated with glyphs and animal figures, and some have a hole drilled in the centre to ceremonially "kill" the power they contain. Other items include a beautiful necklace and flint axe-heads, polished to a glass-like gleam.

El Zotz and Río Azul

Lost in a sea of jungle around Tikal are several other substantial **ruins** – unrestored and for the most part uncleared but with their own unique atmosphere. The bulk of the temples lies beneath mounds of earth, their sides coated in vegetation, and only the tallest roof-combs are still visible. A dirt road (actually an old Maya causeway or sacbé) heads north to Río Azul, and rough tracks head southwest to El Zotz and east to San Bartolo. So if you're in search of adventure and want to see a virtually untouched Maya ruin, these sites are perfect.

El Zotz

Twenty-five kilometres west of Uaxactún, along a jeep track that's usually passable in the dry season (by 4WD), **El Zotz** is a large Maya site set in its own *biotopo* next to the Tikal national park. To **get there** speak to the owners of *El Chiclero* in Uaxactún or the tour operators in Flores (see p.316), who can arrange pack horses, camping gear, food and a guide. Three-day trips involving a hike to El Zotz, a day at the ruins and then a hike to Tikal are highly recommended, costing from US$245 per head (minimum two people).

Totally unrestored, El Zotz has been systematically looted, although there are guards on duty all year now and there's also a CECON biological station close to the ruins. The three main temples are smothered in soil and vegetation, but using the workers' scaffold you can climb to the top of the tallest structure, the **devil's pyramid**, which is spectacular. The roof combs of the Tikal temples, 23km west of here, can be glimpsed on clear days. *Zotz* means "bat" in Maya and each evening at dusk you'll see tens, perhaps even hundreds of thousands of **bats** of several species emerge from a cave near the campsite. It's especially impressive in the moonlight, the beating wings sounding like a river flowing over rapids – one of the most remarkable natural sights in Petén. Keep an eye out, too, for bat falcons, swooping with talons outstretched in search of their prey.

Río Azul

The remote site of **Río Azul**, almost on the tripartite border where Guatemala, Belize and Mexico meet, was only rediscovered in 1962. Its name was Sak Há Witznal ("Clear Water Mountain") in Maya times, a reference to the river that passed close to the site. Although almost totally unrestored, the core of the site resembles Tikal in many ways, though it is smaller. The tallest temple (A-III) stands some 47m above the forest floor, poking its head out above the treetops and giving magnificent views across the jungle.

Investigations suggest that the site dates back to 900 BC and was an important city until the Middle Classic era. Río Azul prospered as both a trading centre between the Caribbean (where cacao was abundant) and wider Maya World and also as an important agricultural centre (extensive irrigation channels have been unearthed here). The site's history is deeply intertwined with Tikal and Calakmul, the two superpowers of the era. It's likely that Tikal's ruler Stormy Sky installed one of his sons here as king, but by the sixth century Río Azul's position on the fringes of Tikal's domain had become alarmingly precarious, and Calakmul's Tuun K'ab' Hix (Stone Hand Jaguar) overran the city in 530 AD. After this defeat, Río Azul was virtually abandoned, before being occupied again in Late Classic times, only to be sacked again in 830 AD by marauding Puuc Maya from the Yucatán.

Several incredible **tombs** have been unearthed here, lined with white plaster and painted with vivid red glyphs. Tomb 1 is thought to have contained the remains of Stormy Sky's son, while nearby tombs 19 and 23 contained bodies of warriors dressed in clothing typical of the ancient city of Teotihuacán in central Mexico, further supporting the theory that Tikal derived much of its power from an alliance with that mighty city. Many of these finds, including a richly decorated jar with a curved handle, which turns to open the vessel, are displayed in the archeology museum in Guatemala City (see p.81).

Extensive **looting** occurred after the site's discovery, with a gang of up to eighty men plundering the tombs, and unique treasures (including some incredible green jade masks and pendants) found their way onto the international market. Tombs were stripped bare, and some of the finest murals in the Maya world hacked from walls – though Tomb 1 escaped the worst of the damage. Today there are two resident guards, who may collect the official US$7.50 entrance fee and will accompany you throughout your visit. The tallest temples are now becoming unsafe to climb, so always heed the advice of the guards. For more information on the site, see *Río Azul: An Ancient Maya City*, by Richard Adams (University of Oklahoma).

Getting there

The **road** that connects Tikal and Uaxactún continues for an additional 95km north to Río Azul. This route is only passable in the dry season, and can be covered by 4WDs in as little as five hours, depending on the conditions. **Walking** or on **horseback** it's four days each way – three at a push. Trips can be arranged through *El Chiclero* in Uaxactún or through ProPetén or a number of travel agents in Flores (see p.316).

The Mirador Basin

The remains of the first great cities of the Maya are still engulfed by the most extensive forests in the Maya region, an area known as the Mirador Basin, tight against the Mexican border in the extreme north of the country. Intensive archeological excavations have only been ongoing for about a decade, but the discoveries here have already led to a complete rethink about the origins of the Maya, and it's now clear that this remote region was once the cradle of the Maya civilization. The main focus of interest has been the giant site of **El Mirador**, the first Maya "superpower", which is famous for its colossal triadic temple complexes. But neighbouring **Nakbé**, the first city to emerge (around 800 BC), **Wakná** (which was only discovered in 1998) and the massive ruins of **El Tintal** (which could be as big as Tikal) are just three of the myriad other cities that once thrived in this now remotest of regions.

The conditions are very difficult – marshy mosquito-plagued terrain that becomes so saturated that excavations can only be attempted for five months of the year. However, undoubtedly the greatest challenge facing the archeologists and Guatemalan authorities is to save the ruins from the constant threat of encroaching settlers, loggers, drug smugglers, cattle ranchers and tomb looters. Because of this lack of security, environmentalists and Mayanists are lobbying hard to get the entire Mirador region – 2169 square kilometres of jungle stretching from the Mexican border as far south as El Zotz – declared the **Mirador Basin National Park**. President Colom announced in his 2008 inaugural speech that the creation of a national park here was a priority, and that it should be linked with the neighbouring Calakmul reserve in Mexico to form a bi-national protected area. An application is also registered with UNESCO to get Mirador declared a World Heritage Site.

Immediate and effective protection is essential. Successive Guatemalan governments have dithered while the neighbouring reserves like Laguna del Tigre have gone up in smoke. Forty armed rangers patrol the Mirador area, otherwise, according to archeologist **Dr Richard Hansen** (who has led the excavations here for decades) "we'd lose the whole city". Hansen sees strictly managed ecotourism, including the construction of a jungle lodge and narrow-gauge railway, as the way to preserve the forest and the 26 known Maya sites of the Mirador Basin. But his vision is not universally shared. Many settlers on the fringes, and inside the reserve, see little future in ecotourism and are lobbying for timber and farming concessions to be allowed. Occasionally these land-hungry campesinos torch a ranger station, and villagers at Dos Aguadas have even been granted a concession to farm inside the Maya Biosphere Reserve. So the choice seems to be fewer trees or more tourists.

Currently only around three thousand people make it to Mirador each year, and archeologists outnumber visitors at any one time. Numbers are tiny because of the effort or expense required to **get to** the ruins (see below), which either involves days of hard hiking through dense jungle and swamps or a brief visit as part of a helicopter tour.

El Mirador

El Mirador is perhaps the most exotic and mysterious Maya site of all. Encircled by the Petén and Campeche jungles, this massive city surpasses Tikal's scale although we are only now beginning to piece together its history. We're not even certain of its name – *el mirador* means "the lookout" in Spanish – but it could have been **Ox Te Tun** (The Birthplace of the Gods). Until the 1980s, it was assumed Mirador was a large city from the Classic era that flourished at the same time as Tikal, Copán and Palenque. As excavations have intensified this theory has been totally overthrown, and we now know that Mirador was a Preclassic capital of unprecedented scale, and its fall around 150 AD was just the first of two catastrophic collapses suffered by the Maya civilization.

The ruins are surrounded by some of the densest tropical forests in the Americas, and you're sure to encounter some spectacular **wildlife**, including the resident troops of howler and spider monkeys, toucans and perhaps even a scarlet macaw. Wild-cat numbers in the proposed Mirador Basin National Park

▲ El Mirador

that surrounds the ruins are some of the healthiest in Latin America, with an estimated four hundred jaguar, as well as ocelot, *jaguarundi* and puma.

Some history

The latest research indicates that it was the boggy nature of the Mirador Basin that drew the first settlers here, the richness of its *bajo* mud allowing the early Maya to found villages based on crop cultivation. By 1000 BC (though some ceramic evidence suggests as far back as 1480 BC) these settlements were established and thriving at Mirador. The site chosen for the city itself was a commanding one, on an outcrop of karstic (limestone) hills at an altitude of 250m, with swamps providing protection to the east.

By the Middle Preclassic, ceremonial structures were being built, including early temples at Los Monos, El Tigre and the Central Acropolis (generations later all these structures would be built over and enlarged to a much grander scale). For centuries Mirador flourished, peaking between 350 BC and 100 AD, when it was unquestionably the largest city in Central America, home to over one hundred thousand Maya, its empire controlling hundreds of thousands more in the Basin region.

Mirador became a great trading centre as jade and obsidian were brought from the highlands; granite, shells and coral beads imported from the Caribbean and salt carried in from the Yucatán. The city grew to dominate the entire region, and by the time of Christ it must have been something to behold, its emblematic triadic temples painted scarlet with cinnabar and soaring high above the forest canopy, with a web of stone causeways connecting the great capital to dozens of other cities in its empire.

The exact reasons for Mirador's downfall are unclear, but it's probable that a millennia of temple- and empire-building, intensive agriculture and especially forest-burning (to create lime for the thick plaster that covered every building) dried out the swamps and provoked **environmental collapse**. Other great cities including Teotihuacán in central Mexico and Tikal were beginning to flex their muscles by the second century AD, perhaps necessitating the building of the twenty-metre-high defensive walls that ring the sacred precinct.

All the great cities of the Basin were abruptly abandoned in the late Pre-Classic era around 150 AD, but it now seems the rulers may have upped sticks and shifted 50km to the north to found a second superstate, for recently found inscriptions strongly link the ruling Kaan dynasty of Calakmul to Mirador. Presently Mayanists are only able to piece together fragments of the history of these empire builders, however, for their story has never been told.

The site

The **ruins** (US$8) of El Mirador are still covered in dense jungle, and though many buildings have been stabilized, only a few buildings have been partially reconstructed. In many ways you're experiencing the city the way the great nineteenth-century explorers like Maudslay would have seen Tikal, so you'll have to exercise your imagination to get a vision of its sheer scale and grandeur. But as the archeological project here is the largest in the Americas – home to around forty archeologists, dozens of students and around three hundred workers each season – exciting new discoveries are being unearthed all the time.

The centre of the site covers some sixteen square kilometres, stretching between two massive pyramid groups facing each other across the forest on an east–west axis. Mirador's **ceremonial core**, sometimes called the West Group, is thought to have been largely the preserve of the elite and high priests and contains hundreds of temple structures and buildings, reservoirs and aqueducts, all ringed by a defensive wall, and probably guarded by gateways. On the western edge of this sacred precinct is the mighty **Tigre Complex**, made up of a huge single pyramid base, and an upper platform with three temples. This triadic temple design, peaking at 55m, is characteristic of El Mirador's architecture (and a model that's replicated at all of the area's Preclassic sites). Tigre's temple base measures 125m by 135m, which is enough to cover around three football fields. Giant stucco **jaguar masks** have been uncovered here, their teeth and claws painted red. A staircase has been cut into the side of the Tigre pyramid, and this temple's summit is a favoured spot for sunset (as it's only a 15min walk back to the campsite from here).

In front of the Tigre Complex is El Mirador's sacred hub: the **Central Acropolis**, a long, narrow plaza, where sacrificial ceremonies would have been performed. Burial chambers unearthed in this central section had been painted with ferric oxide to prevent corrosion and contained the bodies of priests and noblemen, surrounded by the obsidian lancets and stingray spines used to pierce the penis, ears and tongue in ritual bloodletting ceremonies (see Contexts, pp.426–427). The spilling of blood was seen by the Maya as a method of summoning and sustaining the gods, and was clearly common at all the great ceremonial centres.

South of the Tigre Complex, the **Monos Complex** is another triadic structure (rising to 42m) and plaza, named after the local howler monkeys that roar long into the night and after heavy rainfall. To the north, the **León Pyramid** and the **Cascabel Complex** mark the northern boundaries of the sacred precinct.

Heading away to the east, it's about 1.5km from the Central Acropolis along the Puleston Causeway, past a couple of reservoirs, to the East Group, which rises in tiers from the forest floor. The cluster of monumental buildings here all sit on a vast stone base platform that measures 600m by 330m. The trail ascends to a second platform, where you encounter the Pava temple group, winding below the jungle-clad Pava pyramid and then climbing up to a third level and then up the flanks of the iconic **Danta Pyramid** itself. Vegetation is steadily being cut from the front of this vast structure, but it's planned to just expose the facade of the pyramid and leave the jungle intact to the rear and sides. A sturdy new wooden staircase leads to the summit of this 2000-year-old temple, which is 72m above the base platform (and 79m above the forest floor), making it the tallest pre-Columbian structure in the Americas. From the top, high above the jungle canopy, the hills in the distance are the forest-covered pyramids of other great Maya cities and you should be able to make out the temple tops of Nakbé to the south. On very clear days it's even possible to catch a glimpse of Structure 2 at Calakmul in Mexico, way to the north, a city almost certainly founded by Maya from El Mirador.

The area **around El Mirador** is riddled with other residential suburbs and smaller Maya sites – you'll pass through about a dozen small ruins if you arrive on foot from Carmelita. Raised **causeways**, ancient trading routes called *sakbe'ob* – some up to 40m wide and 4m in height – connect many of these smaller sites to El Mirador. One trail leads south to **La Muerte**, 2km away, where several temples have been restored and some fine tombs and glyphic carvings (now protected by a new polycarbonate protective roof) uncovered.

Nakbé, El Tintal and Wakná

About 12km to the southeast of El Mirador down one of the main *sakbé*, **Nakbé** was the first substantial city to emerge in the Maya region (though it's quite possible that earlier sites have yet to be rediscovered). Ruins of the earliest buildings are from around 1000 BC, the community growing to become a city of many thousands by 400 BC, and one of the key centres of Maya culture, calendrics, religion and writing.

Today the site (free), which has been partially cleared, is virtually unvisited by anyone except archeologists, *xateros* (palm-leaf gatherers) and *chicleros* (rubber tappers). Excavation work by Richard Hansen and his UCLA team has revealed that the city had a ceremonial core of **temples**, separated into two groups via a kilometre-long limestone causeway – much like El Mirador. At the eastern end, the temples rise from a platform to peak at 35m, and there are the remains of the earliest ballcourt ever found in the Maya world, dating back to around 450 BC. Nakbé's tallest building is in the western group, where Structure I reaches 45m; from its summit, La Danta in El Mirador is visible. Archeologists have also found evidence of skilful stucco work – a huge **mask** (measuring 5m by 8m) was found on the side of one of the temples here, though it has since been covered in earth for protection. Resident guards will show you **chultunes** (storage chambers cut into the limestone bedrock) that you can lower yourself down into – though watch out for snakes and spiders. Nakbé probably has hundreds of outlying structures, including residential complexes grouped around plazas, though doubtless many more exciting discoveries will follow.

El Tintal, another massive Preclassic site south of El Mirador, was also connected by a broad causeway to its giant neighbour, and the ruins, though severely looted, make an ideal campsite on the route to Mirador basin. The unrestored temples here are from a slightly later era, but also arranged in a triadic formation with a central staircase flanked by elaborate stucco masks – some of the earliest examples of Maya sculptural art. Climb to the top of the largest pyramid, which ascends 50m, for spectacular views over towards El Mirador in the distance.

There are dozens of other sites in the Mirador Basin that have barely been touched, including many very early Preclassic settlements. The large site of **Wakná**, or "house of six", was only rediscovered in 1998, after careful analysis of satellite photographs detected temple-like mounds in the jungle. Dr Hansen, accompanied by *chicleros*, led a team to the region and confirmed that the mounds were indeed the remains of a city, later established to be Preclassic in origin. Unfortunately, they weren't the first people to discover the site – a trench cut into one of the temples confirmed that looters had already been active here, and had raided a tomb. Tour operators (see Flores "Listings"), include Wakná and Nakbé on seven-day trek itineraries to El Mirador.

Meanwhile, recent investigations at extremely remote **Naachtún**, about 25km east of El Mirador and just a kilometre south of the Mexican border, have revealed it to be a very substantial site that flourished in the Late Classic period. More than forty stelae have been unearthed, and the architecture at the site (perilously located between the two giants of Tikal and Calakmul) reflects styles found in both cities – around its main plaza the temples show strong Tikal influence, while its royal palaces draw on Calakmul design traditions.

Getting to the Mirador Basin

Getting to El Mirador is a substantial undertaking by land, involving a rough 77-kilometre bus journey from Santa Elena to the chicle- and *xate*-gathering centre of **Carmelita**, followed by two days of hard jungle hiking – you'll need a horse or mule to carry your food and equipment. The journey, impossibly muddy in the rainy season, is best attempted from mid-January to July (Feb to April is the driest period). The trip offers an exceptional chance to see virtually untouched forest and perhaps some of the creatures that inhabit it – you're nearly guaranteed to see howler and spider monkeys, bats (including vampires), toucans, pizotes and deer, and plenty of bugs, spiders and quite possibly a scorpion or snake.

Tours are best arranged in Flores (those run by *Hostel Los Amigos* usually offer the cheapest rates) or directly with the Turismo Cooperativa in Carmelita (T 5800 0293 or 7861 0366; Spanish only). Either way you'll need guides, pack horses, food, water and camping gear. The more people you can gather together to go on the trip, the cheaper the price is: a group of four people pay about US$215 per head for a five-day trek. Consult the highly informative website W www.mostlymaya.com for more information about organizing the hike, what to take and what to expect. Essentials are bug repellent, plasters for blisters, energy snacks and some supplies for the guards, who spend forty days at a time in the forest, largely subsisting on beans and tortillas.

If you'd rather organize a trip well in advance, contact Maya Expeditions (see Guatemala City "Listings"), who run excellent tours to the main sites in the Mirador Basin region led by prominent archeologists. Or if you'd rather skip the mud and jungle completely, **helicopter trips** organized by Tikal/Mirador Park (T 2367 2837, W www.tikalpark.com) offer the perfect alternative. Day-trips cost around US$380 per head, while the recommended "heli-mule" tours allow you far more time to explore the ruins; these involve one journey by helicopter from Flores and jungle hike either to/from Carmelita.

One daily **bus** (at 1pm) plus pick-ups make the three-hour journey from Santa Elena to the village of Carmelita, where there's a new Mirador visitor centre where you can research the trip and contact local guides. *Campamento Nakbé* (●), 1.5km before Carmelita, offers basic but clean **accommodation**, with large thatched shelters with mosquito nets, camping space and hammocks. For a good feed, visit *Comedor Pepe Toño*, in the centre of the village, run by Brenda Zapata, who is a mine of information about the area.

Sayaxché and around

Southwest of Flores on a lazy bend in the Río de la Pasión, **SAYAXCHÉ** is a fairly rough-and-ready frontier settlement that's a convenient base for exploring the forests of southern Petén and its huge collection of archeological remains. Situated at the junction of road and river, Sayaxché is a market town and supply centre for a vast surrounding area that is being steadily cleared and colonized. The complex network of rivers and swamps that cuts through the jungle here has been an important trade route since Maya times. Several ruins can be found in the area: upstream is **Ceibal**, a compact but beautiful site in a wonderful jungle setting, while to the south is **Lago de Petexbatún**, a stunning lakeside setting for the Maya sites of **Aguateca** and Punta de Chimino, and the trailhead for the substantial ruins of **Dos Pilas** and smaller Tamarindito. A visit to this region offers great opportunities to explore the Petén forest and watch the wildlife, including howler and spider monkeys, crocodiles, iguanas and superb birdlife.

Sayaxché practicalities

Getting to Sayaxché from Flores is very straightforward, with minibuses (every 15min) and four daily buses plying the smooth 62-kilometre road from Santa Elena to the river bank opposite Sayaxché. A ferry (US$0.20 per head) takes you over the Río de la Pasión. Of the **places to stay** in Sayaxché, *Hotel Guayacán* (T 7928 6111; ●) on the riverside has clean, functional rooms with tiled floors and private bath, some with air-conditioning, and a restaurant terrace with river views; filling meals are US$5–7. *Posada Segura* (T7928 6162; ❷–❸), 250m to the right of the dock, is cheaper and has good rates for solo travellers; you pay more for a private bathroom here. Close by is the very good, new *Hotel Del Río* (T7928 6138; ❸–❹) with very spacious, immaculately clean rooms (some with a/c), a comfortable sitting area and a very friendly host family. For a bite **to eat** *Restaurant Yaxkín* (closes 8pm) has huge portions of very Guatemalan-style *comida típica*, or a kilometre west of town *Oasis* (closed Sun) is a remarkably civilized air-conditioned place that has an espresso machine and serves snacks like hot dogs.

There are plenty of **boatmen** eager to take you up- or downriver, though prices are quoted in dollars – you'll have to be patient and bargain hard to get a good deal. Try Viajes Don Pedro (T7928 6109), which offer **tours** of the area from their office on the riverfront. The very helpful Julián Mariona, who owns *Posada El Caribe* (see p.344), can also arrange **trips** to the nearby ruins and fishing expeditions (both around US$55 a day). Banrural has an **ATM** (accepting all cards) and you'll find several internet places in town.

Moving on from Sayaxché, there are microbuses to Raxrujá (every 30min; 2hr 30min), Flores (every 15min; 2hr), and a few buses direct to Cobán.

Ceibal (Seibal)

The compact site of **Ceibal** (sometimes spelt "Seibal"), which you can reach by land or river, is the most accessible Maya ruin near Sayaxché. By **boat** it's US$60–70 for a round-trip journey, including two hours at the ruins; the hour-long boat trip is followed by a short walk through towering rainforest. **By road** Ceibal is just 17km from Sayaxché. Any transport heading south out of town towards Cruce del Pato passes the entrance road to the site, from where it's an eight-kilometre walk through the jungle to the ruins. A taxi from Sayaxché, including an hour at the ruins, should cost about US$25.

Surrounded by forest and shaded by huge ceiba trees, **the ruins** of Ceibal (daily 7.30am–5pm; US$8) are partially cleared and restored, and beautifully landscaped into a mixture of open plazas and untamed jungle. During the Classic period, Ceibal was a relatively minor site, but it grew rapidly between 830 and 910 AD, possibly after falling under the control of Putun colonists from what is now Mexico. In this period it grew to become one of the largest southern lowland sites, with an estimated population of around ten thousand. Outside influence is clearly visible in some of the carving here: speech scrolls, straight noses, waist-length hair and serpent motifs are all decidedly non-Maya. The architecture also differs from other Classic Maya sites, including the round platforms that are usually associated with the Quetzalcoatl cult.

Ceibal has four main clusters of buildings, all connected by flagstone causeways (*calzadas*) that cut through the forest, and two ball-courts. Although most of the largest temples (Structure 10 rises to 28m) lie buried under mounds, Ceibal does have some outstanding **carving**, superbly preserved due to the use of hard stone. Of the 57 **stelae** – some of which weigh more than four tonnes – found here, the most impressive are in the large Plaza Central (where the surrounding temples are unrestored and still jungle-clad) and in the neighbouring Plaza Sur. The latter plaza's low central temple, **Structure A-3**, has four fine stelae set around its cardinal points and another (Stela 21) in the room at the top of the temple – all were commissioned in 849 AD to commemorate the Maya year 10.1.0.0.0. Fragments of stucco found on Structure A-3 suggest that its doorways and roof were originally decorated with ornate **friezes**, carved with both low relief and free-standing fully rounded figures, and painted in brilliant shades of red, blue, green, pink, black and yellow. East of the plaza along Calzada I, the crudely carved but unusual monkey-faced Stela 2 is particularly striking, beyond which, straight ahead down the path, lies Stela 14, another impressive sculpture.

If you turn right here along Calzada II and walk for a few minutes, you'll reach the only other restored part, the highly unusual **Structure 79**, a massive circular stone platform superbly set in a clearing in the forest. The exact purpose of this platform, whose foundations date from the Late Preclassic period, is unclear, but it was certainly used for religious ceremonies (a niche where copal resin was burned has been found) and possibly also functioned as an observation deck for astronomy. In front of Structure 79's stairway, a huge, roughly carved **altar**, measuring more than 2m in diameter and bearing the face of a jaguar, is supported by two crouching humanoid figures.

Lago de Petexbatún

A similar distance to the south of Sayaxché, **Lago de Petexbatún** is a spectacular expanse of water ringed by dense forest and containing plentiful supplies of snook, bass, alligator and freshwater turtle. The shores of the lake abound with birdlife and howler monkeys, and there are a number of Maya ruins – the most impressive of which is the partially restored Aguateca, suggesting the lake was an important trading centre for the Maya.

As it's not that feasible to get around the lake independently, it's probably best explored as part of a **tour**. Most tour operators in Flores can organize excursions to Aguateca (these usually include Ceibal as well), though the ideal way to explore this beautiful region is to arrange a boat and guide locally (ask at *Posada El Caribe* or *Chiminos*; see below) to take you on a two- or three-day trip around the lake. There are plenty of options – touring the lake on foot, by boat or on horseback, exploring the jungle, fishing or bathing in the natural warm springs on the lakeshore.

You'll find three **hotels** in the lake area. It's a 45-minute speedboat trip from Sayaxché to the northern tip of Lago de Petexbatún, where you'll find the very friendly *Posada El Caribe* (☎7928 6114, ✉posadacaribe@peten.net; ❻, full board). Run by the Mariona family, it has clean and comfortable screened cabins and good food. Don Julián, the owner, has lived in this part of the Petén all his life and is highly recommended for lake and ruin tours to Aguateca and Dos Pilas; he can arrange horses, 4WD and boat transport, though he speaks very limited English. South of here on the western shore of the lake, *Petexbatún Lodge* (☎7926 0501; ❸–❺) enjoys great lake views but few guests. Continuing south of here, ⚑ *Chiminos Island Lodge* (☎2335 3506, ⓦwww.chiminosisland.com; from US$95 per head including all meals) just has to be Guatemala's ultimate jungle retreat, with six huge, commodious thatch-roofed bungalows, all set well apart from each other, with stylish bathrooms and furnishings and wonderful private viewing decks above the lake. Bungalow "2 Norte" is the most attractive, with bungalow "1 Norte" second choice. There are some minor ruins in the patch of jungle around the hotel, which is also home to howler monkeys and amazing birdlife. The hotel also has docks for sunbathing and swimming, cooking that's of a very high standard, and attentive and helpful staff.

Aguateca and Punta de Chiminos

Aguateca, perched on a high outcrop at the southern tip of the lake, is the furthest away from Sayaxché but the most easily reached Petexbatún site, as a boat can get you to within twenty-minutes' walk of the ruins. This intriguing

Maya architecture

Maya architecture spans thousands of years, and in grandeur and design rivals the great cities of antiquity. Maya cities were characterized by a ceremonial core of imposing buildings grouped around a paved plaza. These sacred centres were the realm of rulers, priests and the elite, and they contained the principle religious and administrative structures and usually a palace or two. All the main structures were typically built from limestone blocks, which were then covered in thick layers of stucco and painted in vivid colours – red usually predominated with carved reliefs and detailing picked out in green, blue and yellow.

Tikal temple complex ▲

Maya temple at Tikal ▼

Temples and pyramids

The first Maya pyramids were simple low structures built on top of burial mounds, but by 750 BC far more impressive temples were rising at Nakbé (see p.340). During this era, the Preclassic temple construction followed a **triadic** format of a huge base topped by three small stepped temples. This architectural design reached its zenith at El Mirador (see p.338), where a 78m-high temple group was constructed about 1 AD. Virtually all of these early pyramids were adorned with huge stucco masks (some up to 5m high) of stylized serpents or jaguar heads.

The Maya were obsessed with **time**, and many temple complexes were orientated to match calendrical and astronomical events; on auspicious days the Maya would perform ceremonies to mark the occasion. At Uaxactún (see p.334) temples were constructed in perfect alignment so priests could view the sun rise over adjacent temples on solstice days. Tricks of light were also popular: at Chichén Itzá in Mexico the Castillo temple was built so that a tail-like shadow would connect to a carved serpent head during each equinox.

A Maya temple rises in platforms like a wedding cake, and by the Classic era upright stone **roofcombs** were being added to the summits of these structures; at Tikal, Temples I and II have magnificent crests (see p.324). Cities in the Usumacinta region (see p.370) such as Yaxchilán and Palenque favoured a honeycomb design, but all roofcombs were highly decorated with painted stucco reliefs.

In many cities, temples were built over earlier ceremonial buildings;

Coatimundi at Tikal ▼

archeologists have uncovered the remains of several early structures below Tikal's North Acropolis. Copán has the best examples of this practice, and here it's possible to enter a tunnel that burrows into the heart of Temple 16 to view the spectacular facade of the much earlier Rosalila Temple (see p.364).

Many but not all Maya temples were burial monuments to rulers. Temple I at Tikal was constructed to honour the great leader Hasaw Chan K'awil, and his tomb revealed some magnificent jade ornaments.

▲ Temple replica at Copán

▼ Carved stela at Quiriguá

Stelae and altars

Stelae are upright stone slabs, most 3–4m in height, but those at Quiriguá (see p.247) are as large as 8m. Most were erected to commemorate an important event – a victory in battle or the accession of a monarch. Virtually all were carved by master sculptors, the front of the stela usually bearing a full-length portrait of a ruler in full regalia with glyphs detailing a historic occasion and date. These stelae are today impressive examples of Maya art.

At Copán, stela-carving reached a high art form by 700 AD, with all four sides of the stone monument carved in intricate detail, the front and rear in deep relief and side panels covered in glyphs reciting the achievements of ruler Eighteen Rabbit.

Circular **altars** were often commissioned to accompany a stela. These were also elaborately carved, often with images of bound captives, a custom which has lead Mayanists to assume that they may have been used for performing the sacrifices and offerings of dynastic ritual.

Maya ball court ▲

Carved stone at Copán ▼

View from El Mirador ▼

Tikal ▼

Ball courts

Pitz – the Maya **ball game** – was much more than a sport; it represented a battle between the forces of life and death. Though the exact rules are unclear, it's known that the game was between two players (or two teams) who competed on a court by striking a heavy rubber ball with their elbows and hips. Results were sometimes associated with divine judgement and they may have been used to settle conflicts – with the losers being decapitated.

All courts were a similar shape, consisting of a narrow paved playing area flanked by sloping walls, and were usually open-ended. However, they varied greatly in size: most were only 15m or 20m long and around 5m across but the great court of Chichén Itzá measured nearly 100m by 30m. Many courts had stone rings, which the players would attempt to pass the ball through; on others beautifully carved circular stone markers delineated areas of play. Ball courts were a central feature of Maya life, and aside from the ball game were also used for cultural events and rituals. Significant ball courts can be found in Tikal, Copán, Iximché, Mixco Viejo and Zaculeu.

Stucco

All temples were covered in thick layers of lime **stucco**. As the Preclassic Maya got more and more extravagant with stucco (which could only be produced by burning crushed limestone using freshly cut green timber, blazing at a temperature high enough to create lime plaster), they lavished thicker and thicker layers of stucco on their temples, and the forest environment collapsed, killed off by conspicuous consumption.

site (US$7), split in two by a natural chasm, was only rediscovered in 1957 and has undergone recent restoration work. The atmosphere is magical, surrounded by dense tropical forest and with superb views of the lake from two *miradores*. Throughout the Late Classic period, Aguateca was closely aligned with (or controlled by) nearby Dos Pilas, the dominant city in the southern Petén, and reached its peak in the eighth century, when the latter was developing an aggressive policy of expansion. Indeed, Aguateca may have been a twin capital of an ambitious Petexbatún state. Military successes, including a conclusive victory over Ceibal in 735 AD, were celebrated at both sites with remarkably similar stelae – Aguateca's Stela 3 shows Dos Pilas ruler Master Sun Jaguar in full battle regalia, including a Teotihuacán-style face mask. After 761 AD, however, Dos Pilas began to lose control of its empire and the members of the elite moved their headquarters to Aguateca, attracted by its strong defensive position. But despite the construction of 5km of walls around the citadel and its agricultural land, their enemies soon caught up with them, and sometime after 790 AD Aguateca itself was overrun.

The resident guards will provide you with stout walking sticks – essential as the slippery paths here can be treacherous – before escorting you around the site's steep trails. The tour, which takes a little more than an hour, takes in part of the site's palisade defences, temples and palaces (including the residence of Aguateca's last ruler, Tante K'inich) and a barracks. The carving at Aguateca is superbly executed and includes images of hummingbirds, pineapples and pelicans. Its plazas are dotted with stelae, including one on the Plaza Principal depicting Tante K'inich lording it over a ruler from Ceibal, who is shown cowering at his feet, and another that has been shattered by looters who hoped to sell the fragments. Aguateca is also the site of the Maya World's only known **bridge**, which crosses a narrow gash in the hillside, but it's not that impressive in itself. The *Posada El Caribe* and *Chiminos* hotels (see p.344) run trips to all the sites in the area or you can book a tour in Flores (see p.316), where prices start at around US$135 for a two-day tour. There's a visitor centre close to the entrance, where Aguateca's guards are based. The guards always welcome company, and if you want to **stay** they'll find some space for you to sling a hammock or pitch a tent. If you do stay, you'll need to bring a mosquito net and food.

About four kilometres to the north, jutting out from the west shore of the lake, is a club-shaped peninsula known as **Punta de Chiminos**. This site was the final refuge of the last of the Petexbatún Maya in the Late Classic era, as the region descended into warfare and chaos at the beginning of the ninth century. Here they constructed some formidable defences across the narrow stem of the peninsula, including three rock-hewn trenches and 9m ramparts, which created a man-made citadel. The point is now the spectacular location for the lovely *Chiminos Island Lodge* (see p.344), though there's very little to see there today.

Dos Pilas and around

Some 12km west of the northern tip of Lago de Petexbatún, still buried in the jungle, is another virtually unreconstructed site, **Dos Pilas**, which has one of the most fascinating and best-documented histories of any Maya city. **Dos Pilas** was established around 640 AD by a renegade group from Tikal who fled the great city during the dark ages that followed its defeat by Calakmul. The leader of this breakaway tribe, a lord named B'alaj Chan K'awil (Lightning Sky), was clearly a brazen individual. It's thought that even though he claimed membership of the Tikal royal line he swore a treacherous allegiance with

Calakmul in 648 AD in an attempt to launch a rival dynasty at Tikal. Dos Pilas clashed with Tikal several times in the years afterwards, as Tikal sought to humble the upstart Dos Pilas ruler. Though B'alaj Chan K'awil ultimately failed in his bid to claim the Tikal lineage, he did repel Tikal in 679 AD, a victory which he celebrated by commissioning several new stelae and launching a substantial reconstruction of the plaza.

Dos Pilas continued to throw its weight around for another century, provoking a series of battles with neighbouring cities, defeating Ceibal in 735 AD and capturing lords from Yaxchilán and Motul. Monuments including three hieroglyphic stairways were built, though by the latter half of the eighth century the region was becoming so unstable (probably due to attacks by Putun Maya from Mexico) that the rulers fled Dos Pilas in 761 AD and soon after the site was completely abandoned.

Sadly, the **remains of the city** are less than spectacular, as many temples were partly dismantled during the chaos of the late eighth century. Nevertheless, there's some superb carving to admire, including several wonderful stelae and four small **hieroglyphic stairways**, now protected by thatched shelters grouped around the grassy plaza. On the south side of the plaza are the ruins of a palace, while on the east side a rich tomb was discovered under Temple L-51, probably belonging to the ruler Itzamnaaj K'awiil. Encircling the remains of this ceremonial core, it's still possible to make out the remains of the fortifications, a double defensive wall and stockade that the final occupiers erected.

Getting to Dos Pilas is by no means straightforward or cheap. It's best to try and organize transport in Sayaxché or Flores. Either way you'll have to travel from Sayaxché, and then via a 45-minute speedboat trip to the *Posada El Caribe* (see p.344) followed by a further 12km on foot or horseback to the ruins. The hike takes you past the small site of **Arroyo de Piedra**, where you'll find a plaza and two fairly well-preserved stelae, and the ruins of **Tamarindito** where another hieroglyphic stairway has been found.

Routes to Mexico

Heading west to Mexico from Petén is fairly straightforward and highly scenic in places, passing remote ruins and patches of dense rainforest. Though the Mexican state of Chiapas has been relatively calm for several years, tensions do remain between government and Zapatista-aligned campesinos, and you can expect army security checks every hour or so as you get around. That said, travel is perfectly safe in the region, and the armed forces courteous and polite.

The most popular route by far involves crossing the Río Usumacinta into Chiapas at **Frontera Corozal**, from either **Bethel**, or a little upstream at **La Técnica** on the Guatemalan bank of the river. This trip enables you to pass the first-class ruins of **Yaxchilán** and Bonampak on the way. Alternatively, it's possible to head northwest **from Flores** to El Naranjo by bus, then along the Río San Pedro to La Palma in Mexico, though there's no regular boat schedule on this route.

From Bethel to Frontera Corozal

The cheapest and most straightforward route to Mexico is via **BETHEL**, on the Río Usumacinta, where there's a Guatemalan **migración** post. Minibuses and daily buses (roughly hourly, 5am–3pm; 4hr) leave Santa Elena's Terminal Nuevo for Bethel. At Bethel it's relatively easy to find a shared *lancha* heading downstream (around US$7 per head; 30min) to Frontera Corozal. Alternatively, it's cheaper and usually possible to get off the bus, obtain your exit stamp in Bethel and continue on the same bus for a further 12km to the tiny settlement of **La Técnica**, where you can cross the Usumacinta (US$1) to Corozal on the opposite bank. La Técnica lacks accommodation or other facilities. Some agencies in Flores (see p.316) offer cross-border tickets direct to Palenque using this route (about US$30 per head), though there have been reports of Mexican drivers demanding additional payments on tickets issued by dodgy San Juan Travel in Santa Elena.

Bethel itself is a pleasant village with wide grassy streets, plenty of trees to provide shade and a couple of comedores. The tall, tree-covered mounds that comprise the **Bethel ruins**, unknown to archeologists until 1995, are 1.5km from the village. Though not that extensive, they occupy an imposing stretch of the Usumacinta, and the settlement must have played a key role in controlling trade along the river. A twenty-minute trail leads from the ruins up to a *mirador*, where you'll find the remains of a pyramid, probably a ceremonial centre, that's some 75m above the plaza floor.

Bethel has an excellent, community-run **place to stay**, the *Posada Maya* (⊕7861 1799 or 7861 1800), that offers comfortable wood-and-thatch cabins (❸), camping and hammock space (❷) and good food.

Getting to Yaxchilán

Boat trips to Yaxchilán can be arranged in Bethel, but it's far more convenient and cheaper to cross the Usumacinata to tranquil **Frontera Corozal** in Mexico where there's a regular service. It's usually easy to hook up with other people or a tour group to share the costs of hiring the boat, a good idea as it's quite steep at around US$85 return for four people or US$110 for up to eight. It's a lovely 45-minute run downstream to the ruins; the banks of the Usumacinta are still covered in thick jungle, particularly on the Guatemalan side and there's plenty of birdlife. Corozal has two good **places to stay**: the attractive, comfortable riverside *Escudo Jaguar* (⊕55 3290 0993; ❹–❺) and *Nueva Alianza* (⊕55 5339 0995; ❸) with good budget rooms in a large partitioned wooden structure – both serve meals. Be sure to drop by the little **museum**, which has some superb stelae. The village is 18km east of the main Palenque–Comitán highway; *colectivo* taxis (US$2.50per head) and minibuses shuttle between the two. From the highway there are regular minibuses to Palenque (roughly hourly, last around 4pm; 2hr 45min).

Piedras Negras

Sixty kilometres downstream from Yaxchilán, the Maya ruins of **Piedras Negras** loom high over the Guatemalan bank of the river. It's one of the most extensive sites in Guatemala, but it's also one of the least accessible and least visited. The city was called Yokib' ("the entrance") in Maya times; the Spanish name of Piedras Negras refers to the black stones lining the riverbank here. Founded about 300 AD, an unrelenting rivalry developed between the city and Yaxchilán for dominance over Usumacinta trade routes, contested by bloody battles and strategic pacts with Calakmul and Tikal. Like its adversary, Piedras Negras is best known for the extraordinary quality of its **carvings**, considered by many to be the very finest to emerge from the Maya World. Several of the best of these are on display in the Museo Nacional de Arqueología in Guatemala City, including a royal throne, some exquisitely carved stelae and panels. The most important of these panels, discovered in June 2000, has an unusually long hieroglyphic text that has allowed Mayanists to compile an excellent record of the city's Late

Classic history under the ruler Itzamk'anahk K'in Ajaw (626–686 AD). However, there's still plenty to experience on site.

Upon arrival, the most immediately impressive monument is a large rock jutting over the river bank with a carving of a seated male figure presenting a bundle to a female figure. This was once surrounded by glyphs, now badly eroded and best seen at night with a torch held at a low angle. Continuing up the hill, across plazas and over the ruins of buildings you get some idea of the city's size. Several buildings are comparatively well preserved, particularly the **sweat baths**, used for ritual purification; the most imposing of all is the **acropolis**, a huge palace complex of rooms, passages and courtyards towering 100m above the river bank. A **megalithic stairway** at one time led down to the river, doubtless a humbling sight to visitors (and captives) before the forest invaded the city. Another intriguing sight is a huge double-headed turtle glyph carved on a rock overhanging a small valley. This is a reference to the end of a *katun*; inside the main glyph is a giant representation of the day sign Ahau (also signifies Lord), recalling the myth of the birth of the maize god. During research carried out at Piedras Negras in the 1930s, artist and epigrapher Tatiana Proskouriakoff noticed that dates carved on monuments corresponded approximately to a human life span, indicating that the glyphs might refer to events in one person's lifetime, possibly the rulers of the city. Refuted for decades by the archeological establishment, the theory was later proved correct.

Traditionally, the presence of FAR guerrillas in the region protected the ruins from systematic looting. Today *narcotraficantes* (cocaine smugglers) are highly active in this region and the site's future is precarious.

Getting to Piedras Negras is not straightforward. The perfect way to arrive is by boat along the Usumacinta, following the ancient Maya trade route, though this involves booking an expensive tour (Maya Expeditions are highly recommended, see Guatemala City "Listings"; or speak to the owners of the *Posada Maya* in Bethel). The least expensive and most accessible route is from Mexico: Willy Fonseca, owner of the *Restaurante Vallescondido* (T01 91634 80721) at Km 61 on the Palenque–Comitán road, runs very well organized day-trips by 4WD and boat for US$500, which works out at US$100 per head if there are five of you (the maximum number).

El Naranjo and the San Pedro river route

This route is very seldom used by travellers, but it is a pretty straightforward way to get from Flores to Mexico via the San Pedro river. It's not a particularly scenic route – it winds through a remote, deforested area, but connections are fairly dependable if you get an early start. Buses (every 30min from 6am; 3hr 15min) run from Santa Elena along a paved road to **EL NARANJO**, a rough place consisting of little more than an army base. There's a **migración** here (be sure to get your exit stamp), stores (offering poor exchange rates), comedores and very basic hotels. Regular boats (roughly hourly until 3pm; US$6; 45min) leave for El Ceibo in Mexico, where there's Mexican immigration. Regular buses then leave for Tenosique (1hr 15min) from where there are microbuses to Palenque (every 30min; 1hr 45min).

Waka' (El Perú) and the Ruta Guacamaya

To the east of El Naranjo, in the upper reaches of the Río San Pedro, is Waka' (also called El Perú), a seldom-visited and largely unreconstructed archeological site buried in some of the wildest rainforest in Petén. Waka' ("stood up place") gets its name from its position on a 130-metre-high escarpment towering above a tributary of the Río San Pedro. The city grew to become an important middle-ranking Petén settlement in the Late Classic period, controlling important overland and water routes. Despite being the nearest place of any size west of Tikal, it sided with the other great "superpower" – distant Calakmul – in the power politics of the time. Around 650 AD, Yuknoom the Great of Calakmul attended the accession of Waka' ruler K'inich B'alam ("Great Sun Jaguar") here – the same leader later married a Calakmul princess. Waka' continued to remain under the Calakmul overlordship in the early eighth century, but would later pay for this affiliation when a resurgent Tikal overran the city in 743 AD, after which no monuments were carved here for 47 years.

Most of the site's temple mounds are still coated in vegetation, but Waka' is perhaps most famous for its many well-preserved **stelae** and the recent discovery of a fascinating **royal tomb** of a female ruler dating from around 620 AD. This queen was clearly a formidable and highly revered figure as she was buried in a battle helmet with stingray spines (for ritual bloodletting) placed near her pelvis – burial customs usually only bestowed on male rulers. An archeologist may be available to show you around, but if not the guards here welcome visitors and can act as guides, particularly if you bring along a little spare food.

Tours to Waka', best arranged in Flores (see p.316), are often dubbed **La Ruta Guacamaya** or "Scarlet Macaw Trail." These exciting two- or three-night trips are by 4WD pick-up and boat along rivers and through primary forest, camping at the ruins; prices start at US$210 per head. Close to the site, at the confluence of the San Pedro and Sacluc, there's a biological station at which rangers monitor forests that contain the largest concentrations of scarlet macaws in northern Central America. You've also an excellent chance of observing spider and howler monkeys, crocodiles, river turtles and the Petén turkey, and may even see a tapir on the banks of the Sacluc river. The best time to see scarlet macaws is between February and June when they nest in hollows of larger trees, but there are a plethora of other exotic birds in the Waka' region at all times of year.

Yaxhá to the Belize border

East of the Ixlú junction, a paved but potholed road runs 65km to the Belize border, passing a turn-off for gorgeous Laguna Macanché (see p.323). Thirty kilometres from Ixlú there's a sign on the right for the ruins of **Holtún**, a twenty-minute walk from the road. A substantial site first settled around 850 BC it has tall, unrestored temples adorned with masks, several stelae and altars, and the twinned temples of Pyramid X and Structure 7. On the roadside, look out for the sign put up by Borman Peréz, who sells good-value wood and ceramic art from his house. He can guide you to the site and offers a couple of budget **rooms** (❷) and space for camping; he also rents bikes and horses to visit Yaxhá.

Continuing east along the road to Belize, it's about a kilometre to the junction for **Yaxhá**, a huge Maya city on the fringes of two beautiful lakes: lagunas Yaxhá and Sacnab. The lakes are encircled by the dense jungle, swamps, savannah and wetlands of the **Monumento Natural Yaxhá–Nakúm–Naranjo**, whose 37,000 hectares contain mahogany, ceiba, *ramón* and sapodilla

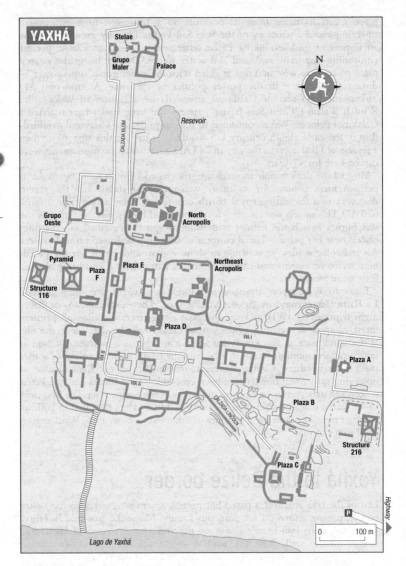

YAXHÁ

Stelae

Grupo Maler

Palace

N

Reservoir

CALZADA BLOM

Grupo Oeste

North Acropolis

Pyramid

Plaza E

Northeast Acropolis

Plaza F

Structure 116

Plaza D

VIA I

Plaza A

VIA B

VIA A

CALZADA LINCOLN

Plaza B

Structure 216

Plaza C

Highway

P

0   100 m

Lago de Yaxhá

hardwood trees. Fauna found here include jaguar and margay cats, two species of crocodile, three species of turtle and dozens of other reptiles as well as prolific birdlife – spoonbills, the giant jabiru stork, eagles and vultures. It's one of the very few places in Guatemala where tapir are known to be breeding. The Postclassic ruins of **Topoxté** are also accessible from Yaxhá, and a third large site, **Nakúm**, is about 18km to the north. Many Flores-based tour operators offer trips to the Yaxhá area; the two-day tours run by Mayan Adventure (see p.316) cost US\$195 (minimum four people) are highly recommended, and include Nakúm.

Yaxhá

Yaxhá (daily 8am–5pm; US$10.75), covering several square kilometres of a limestone ridge overlooking Laguna Yaxhá, is a highly compelling and rewarding Maya site to visit. This was the location for the *Survivor Guatemala* TV show. Its name means "green-blue water", a reference to the wonderful turquoise hue of the lake just below. Of all Guatemala's ruins, only Tikal and El Mirador (and possibly El Tintal) can trump the sheer scale and impact of this site, which has forty stelae, numerous altars, soaring temple pyramids and two ball courts. The dense jungle and lack of crowds only add to the special atmosphere of the place, and the wildlife is prolific (particularly howler monkeys and toucans).

Relatively little is known about the history of Yaxhá, partly due to a relative lack of inscriptions and also because substantial archeological excavations have only recently begun. North of Plaza D the ruins are mostly Preclassic, while the bulk of the large structures in the south of the city date from the Classic era. The sheer size of the city indicates that Yaxhá was undoubtedly an important force in the central Maya region during this era, its influence perhaps only contained by the proximity of the "superstate" Tikal, with which it shares several archeological similarities and close ties. For much of the Classic period, Yaxhá seemed locked in rivalry with the city of Naranjo, about 20km to the northeast, dominating its smaller neighbour for much of this time but suffering a heavy defeat in 799 AD when ruler Itzammnaaj K'awill of Naranjo defeated K'iinch Lakamtuun of Yaxhá.

Restoration work is ongoing at Yaxhá, but most of the buildings have yet to be cleared and many are still choked in thick forest. The ruins are spread out over nine plazas, with around five hundred structures having been mapped so far. From the entrance head north towards Plaza F, and climb the staircase up the large **pyramid** here to get an overview of the ruins, its temple tops and Lago de Yaxhá far below. Continuing north from here up Calzada Blom, it's about 750m to the imposing **Grupo Maler** complex (named after the great early twentieth-century Austrian explorer Teobert Maler), where restoration is virtually complete. Here a pair of temples face each other across a grassy plaza in an arrangement that follows the twin-temple alignment tradition established at Tikal. Several weathered stelae stand in front of the ruins of the palace structure as well as the broken remains of a huge circular altar, possibly destroyed by invaders from Naranjo. Heading south back along Calzada Blom you come to the **Acropolis Norte**, where restoration is also nearing completion, its central plaza surrounded by temples on three sides. The rectangular structure with unusual curved edges on the northern side of this plaza reaches around 22m in height.

South from the Acropolis Norte you follow a grassy avenue-like trail, its sides overshadowed by soaring unrestored temples to Plaza D, then east up Vía 1 to Plaza B, an open area bordered by low walls. Steps lead up from here to Plaza A, from where you can scramble up a bank on its south side towards Yaxhá's tallest and most impressive pyramid, the fully restored **Structure 216**. This imposing, classic Maya temple rises in tiers to a height of more than 30m and has a broad central staircase. There are spectacular vistas over the forest and lakes from its summit – particularly at sunset.

Practicalities

The main Flores–Belize road passes 11km south of the clearly signposted turn-off for Yaxhá. If you're not on a tour, then it's possible to hitch from the main

Fiestas

Petén may not offer Guatemala's finest fiestas, but those there are abound with typical ladino energy, featuring fireworks and heavy drinking. In some of the smaller villages, you'll also see traditional dances and hear the sounds of the marimba – transported here from the highlands along with many of the inhabitants of Petén.

January
12–15 Flores, the final day is the most dramatic

March
10–19 San José, a small fiesta with parades, fireworks and dances

April
April 27–May 1 Poptún, held in honour of San Pedro Martír de Merona

May
1–9 San Benito, sure to be wild and very drunken
15–22 Melchor de Mencos, main day 22nd
23–31 Dolores, main day 28th

June
16 Sayaxché, held in honour of San Antonio de Padua

July
18–26 Santa Ana

August
16–25 San Luís, main day 25th

October
1–4 San Francisco
31 San José, a fascinating pagan fiesta (see box, p.320) starting at 8pm with a mass in the church and continuing all night when a human skull is paraded through the town's streets

November
21–30 San Andrés, main day 30th

December
9–12 La Libertad

road as there is regular traffic to and from the village of La Máquina, 2km before the lakes.

If you want to **stay** near Yaxhá, the wonderful, solar-powered *Campamento El Sombrero* (☎7861 1687, ⒲www.ecosombrero.com; ❹–❾), on the south side of the lake, has nine good, thatched wooden cabañas (some with private bathroom), a **campsite**, restaurant, and superb library, and the Italian owner can arrange boat trips on the lagunas and horseriding. A trail from the hotel leads through the forest to other minor Maya ruins, past *chultunes* and ancient quarries. There's another *campamento* on the far side of the lake, below Yaxhá, where you can pitch a tent or sling a hammock beneath a thatched shelter for free.

Topoxté and Nakúm

Topoxté, a much smaller site on an island close to the west shore of Lago de Yaxhá, is best reached by boat from *El Sombrero* (see below). There's a four-kilometre trail to a spot opposite the island, but you still have to get over to it (and large crocodiles inhabit the lake). Though it's only a small site, this is a highly unusual ruin as it was occupied as late as 1450 AD, making it the most substantial Postclassic settlement yet found. The restored temples here have upright walls, columns, flat stone roofs and balustraded steps, there are several plazas and the site is riddled with *chultunes*. Seventeen skulls of sacrificed children were found here in one tomb.

The substantial **ruins of Nakúm**, which have been the subject of extensive investigation in the last few years, are 18km north of Lago de Yaxhá. This site now has the second largest number of restored buildings in Guatemala, after Tikal. It's thought that Nakúm was a trading post in the Tikal empire, funnelling goods to and from the Caribbean coast, a role for which it was ideally situated at the headwaters of the Río Holmul. Settlers first arrived in the Middle Preclassic, but Nakúm rose to prominence in the Late Classic and prospered well into the Terminal Classic period; new buildings were being constructed here as the cities across the rest of the Maya World were collapsing. The city was abandoned around 950 AD.

Nakúm's ceremonial centre is split between northern and southern sections, which are connected by a causeway. The southern section has been impressively restored, its acropolis containing a huge **palace** (Structure D) of 44 rooms and myriad interior patios. There are several other imposing temple buildings here, some with fine roof combs, while Structure A has an impressive triadic-style upper level. Access from Yaxhá is along a rough track, but it is passable for most of the year in a 4WD (though it still takes at least an hr to drive). Two-day horseback tours can be organized by *El Sombrero*; Flores tour operators also run trips here.

Melchor de Mencos and the border

The nondescript but bustling border-town of **MELCHOR DE MENCOS** boasts little of interest for the visitor (though there are a few stelae in the parque). Despite the differences between Guatemala and Belize, border formalities are fairly straightforward; you'll probably be asked for a small (illegal) departure tax on leaving Guatemala. **Moneychangers** will pester you on either side of the border – most give a fair rate, and you may choose to use their services as the **bank** just beyond the immigration building does not give cash advances or change dollars. Next to immigration, by the river bank, is the very pleasant *Río Mopán Lodge* (T 7926 5196, W www.tikaltravel.com; ④–⑦), which has a small pool and comfortable rooms with balconies. Great trips to remote Maya sites are offered here; you can also safely change money.

For details of microbuses and buses between Santa Elena and Melchor, see p.317. From the border **to Tikal** taxi drivers charge around US$15 per head for a shared ride (they leave when they have four people), or you can do it independently by catching a bus or minibus to Ixlú and getting another from there.

On the Belize side of the border, buses leave **for Belize City** every thirty minutes or so (3hr), usually right from the frontier. If there's no bus waiting, you may have to take a shared taxi to Benque Viejo or to San Ignacio (US$3 per head; 20min) and catch a connection there.

Travel details

For more detailed information about travel from Flores and Santa Elena, see box, p.317.

Buses

Poptún to: Fray Bartolomé de Las Casas (every 90min; 5hr).
Sayaxché to: Cobán (2 daily; 4hr); Flores (every 15min; 2hr); Raxrujá (every 30min; 2hr 30min).

Boats

Bethel to: Frontera Corozal (30min), leave when full.
El Naranjo to: Mexico, see p.348.

La Técnica to: Frontera Corozal (5min), leave when full.
Sayaxché to: Benemérito, Mexico. A trading boat leaves about every other day (8–24hr).

Flights

Flores to: Cancún (daily; 1hr 45min); Guatemala City (4 daily; 50min–1hr).

7

Into Honduras: Copán and the Bay Islands

CHAPTER 7

Highlights

✳ **Copán Ruinas** Combining a delightfully relaxed ambience with a cosmopolitan array of restaurants, bars and boutique hotels, this is a gorgeous little highland town. See p.359

✳ **Copán** Examine the exquisite carvings and temples at the archeological site dubbed the "Athens of the Maya World". See p.363

✳ **Utila** A travellers' mecca, this island is famed for its budget-priced scuba schools and reggae-powered party scene. See p.375

✳ **Whale shark** Search for the world's largest fish, a year-round resident in the seas around Utila. See p.380

✳ **Roatán's West End** The region's finest beach-reef resort, with a selection of great seafood restaurants and old-school Caribbean charm. See p.383

✳ **Guanaja's coral reefs** The plunging reef walls, coral canyons and sea mounts around Guanaja make for world-class scuba diving. See p.386

▲ Copán altar

Into Honduras: Copán and the Bay Islands

Across the border in **Honduras**, about five hours by road from Guatemala City, are the ruins of **Copán**, one of the most magnificent of all Maya sites. While its compact scale is not initially as impressive as Tikal or Mexico's Chichén Itzá, it boasts an astonishing number of decorative carvings, stelae and altars, including a towering hieroglyphic stairway. Throw in a wonderful site museum and the delightful and friendly village of Copán Ruinas, where most people stay, and it's easy to appreciate Copán's appeal. Within easy striking distance of Copán, the **Bay Islands** (Islas de la Bahía) of Utila, Roatán and Guanaja have a completely different but equally alluring appeal: palm-fringed white-sand beaches, balmy Caribbean waters and near-pristine coral reefs perfect for snorkelling and scuba diving. Culturally distinct from the rest of Honduras, the inhabitants are the descendants of Cayman Islanders, buccaneers and shipwrecked African slaves, and most still speak a melodic, archaic-sounding English. For the visitor, **Utila** and **Roatán** offer a tremendous opportunity to visit affordable, friendly and accessible islands with none of the tourist overkill or high prices that can taint other Caribbean destinations, while the less accessible **Guanaja** has some legendary dive sites.

Getting to Honduras is pretty straightforward from Guatemala. If you're heading to Copán, there are excellent transport links from Antigua and Guatemala City by direct daily shuttle and luxury buses (see p.112 & p.88), or you can also travel via Chiquimula (see p.271), a longer but cheaper route. From Copán you can get to the Bay Islands the same day. The other main overland crossing between Guatemala and Honduras links the Caribbean ports of Puerto Barrios and Puerto Cortés (see p.372). Note that the **country code** for Honduras is 504 and there are no area codes.

Copán and around

Delightfully located in a sweeping highland valley, the city-state of **Copán** was the southernmost centre of the Maya civilization. It's easy to understand what attracted the Maya to the site, which lies on the fertile banks of the Río Copán

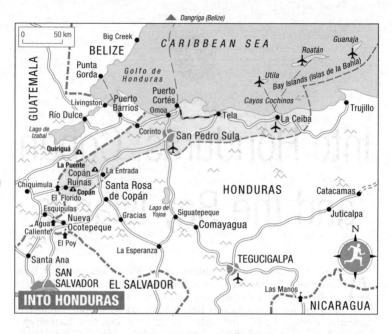

at a pleasingly temperate altitude of 600m. Today the countryside around Copán is equally appealing and fecund, with green rolling hills of pastureland and tobacco and coffee farms interspersed with patches of pine forest. Though the archeological site is the main attraction, there's plenty more to explore in the surrounding area, with hot springs, a butterfly park and bird reserve close by. A short walk west of the ruins, easy-going **Copán Ruinas** is not much more than an overgrown village, but it makes a great base, with attractive hotels, good cafés and restaurants, and fast onward transport connections with Guatemala and the rest of Honduras.

Getting to Copán

Speedy, direct **shuttle buses** (US$17 one way) leave Antigua daily at 4am, pausing to pick up passengers in Guatemala City an hour later on demand, and getting to Copán by about 10am; they return to Guatemala at 5.30am and noon from Copán. These shuttle buses are operated by several companies in Antigua (see p.112) and Copán including Base Camp, inside *Café Via Via* (☎651 4695, ⓦ www.basecamphonduras.com). Two daily luxury air-conditioned pullman buses (at 5.15am & 9am; US$35 one way) also cover the Guatemala City–Copán route, operated by Hedman Alas, based at 2 Avenida 8–73, Zona 10 (☎2362 5072), in Guatemala City.

Alternatively, you could save a little cash by travelling via the Guatemalan town of **Chiquimula**, which is regularly served by Rutas Orientales buses from Guatemala City and local buses from Puerto Barrios. From Chiquimula, minibuses leave every thirty minutes (7am–6pm; 1hr 30min) for the border at **El Florido**, some via the town of Jocotán. Border formalities are straightforward, though they can be slow – and you'll almost certainly be asked for unofficial US$2–3 taxes to cross here. Virtually all Western nationalities do not need to pay to enter Honduras as the country is part of the CA–4 open-border agreement (for more on this, see "Red tape and visas" in the Basics section of this book).

The Banrural **bank** (daily 8am–5pm), at the border just inside Guatemala, changes traveller's cheques and cashes dollars, or you can deal with the ever-present moneychangers at the border post who handle dollars, lempiras and quetzals at pretty fair rates.

From El Florido, minibuses leave when full (about every 30min until 7pm; US$1.50) to the town of Copán Ruinas, taking around twenty minutes. If you plan to **drive** inside Honduras, note that you need permission from your Guatemalan rental-car company.

For **transport schedules** from Copan, see box, p.364.

Copán Ruinas: the town

Two kilometres northwest of the archeological site of Copán lies the small town of **COPÁN RUINAS**, a charming place of steep, cobbled streets and red-tiled roofs set among the lush scenery of Honduras's western highlands. Despite a fast-increasing number of visitors, income from whom now forms the mainstay of the town's economy, it has managed to remain a largely unspoilt and genuinely friendly place. Many travellers are seduced by Copán's delightfully relaxed atmosphere, clean air and rural setting, and end up spending longer here than planned, studying Spanish, eating and drinking well, or exploring the region's other minor sites, hot springs and beautiful countryside.

Arrival and information

Almost everything of interest is within a few blocks of Copán's Parque Central. **Street names** are being introduced though few locals use them. For transport information, see "Getting to Copán" above and the "Moving on" box on p.364. Tuk-tuks (also called "mototaxis") are plentiful in Copán, and will whisk you around the village or to the ruins for around US$0.50 per head a journey.

For local information, check out the **tourist office** (daily 8am–7pm; ☎651 4394, ⓔinfo@copanhonduras.org) just off the Parque Central, or the two excellent local **websites**, ⓦwww.copanruinas.com and ⓦwww.copanhonduras .org. The **post office** is just off the parque behind the museum.

Accommodation

Many of the town's older **hotels** have undergone refits to attract the ever-expanding organized-tour market, while plenty of stylish new mid-range places have opened in the last few years. Budget options tend to fill up quickly so book ahead, if arriving late in the day.

Budget

Hotel Los Gémelos a block east of parque ☎651 4077. Friendly, venerable backpackers' stronghold with basic but clean rooms with fans (all shared bath), set off a slim central garden. Has reliable hot water and fills up rapidly. ❷

Iguana Azul next to the *Casa de Café B&B* (and under the same ownership) ☎651 4620, ⓦwww.iguanaazulcopan.com. Very attractive budget base that has three private doubles and two good dorms, all with shared bath and decent mattresses. Amenities include private lockers, free drinking water, a pretty little garden and laundry facilities. Dorm US$5; doubles ❸

Manzana Verde c/Macanudo ☎651 4652. Youth-hostel-style place run by the *Vía Vía* team with a good vibe, three large dorms (US$4 per bed), lockers, kitchen and laundry facilities, a lounge with TV, and an information-rich notice board. ❷

Vía Vía two blocks west of parque ☎651 4652, ⓦwww.viaviacafe.com. Simple, smallish but spotless rooms with en-suite bathrooms and a six-bed dorm (US$5 per bed) at the rear of a popular travellers' café. It can be a bit noisy here at night, but it's decent value. ❸

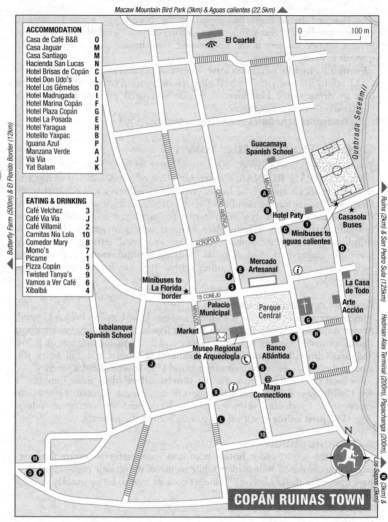

Macaw Mountain Bird Park (3km) & Aguas calientes (22.5km) ▲

ACCOMMODATION
Casa de Café B&B	O
Casa Jaguar	M
Casa Santiago	M
Hacienda San Lucas	N
Hotel Brisas de Copán	C
Hotel Don Udo's	L
Hotel Los Gémelos	D
Hotel Madrugada	I
Hotel Marina Copán	F
Hotel Plaza Copán	G
Hotel La Posada	E
Hotel Yaragua	H
Hotelito Yaxpac	B
Iguana Azul	P
Manzana Verde	A
Via Via	J
Yat Balam	K

EATING & DRINKING
Café Velchez	3
Café Via Via	J
Café Villamil	2
Carnitas Nia Lola	10
Comedor Mary	8
Momo's	7
Picame	1
Pizza Copán	5
Twisted Tanya's	9
Vamos a Ver Café	6
Xibalbá	4

El Cuartel

Guacamaya Spanish School

Hotel Paty
Casasola Buses
Minibuses to aguas calientes

Mercado Artesanal

La Casa de Todo

Arte Acción

Minibuses to La Florida border

Palacio Municipal

Parque Central

Ixbalanque Spanish School

Market

Museo Regional de Arqueología

Banco Atlántida

Maya Connections

COPÁN RUINAS TOWN

N

Butterfly Farm (500m) & El Florido Border (12km) ◄

Ruins (2km) & San Pedro Sula (125km) ►
Hedman Alas Terminal (200m), Papachanga (200m), ►
Los Sapos (3km) ►

Moderate and expensive

Casa de Café B&B at the southwest edge of town, overlooking the Río Copán valley ☎651 4620, ⓦwww.casadecafecopan.com. A charming place owned by an American–Honduran couple, with ten comfortable and airy rooms, all simply yet elegantly presented with wood panelling, desks and private bathrooms with steaming hot water. There's also a fabulous garden where you could lie in a hammock and enjoy the views all day, and a pavilion for massages (US$25). A substantial breakfast is included, and there's free coffee or ice tea all day. ⑥

Casas Jaguar and Santiago ☎651 4620, ⓦwww.casajaguarcopan.com and ⓦwww.casadedonsantiagocopan.com. These two gorgeous private houses have a lovely Mediterranean feel, with stylish furnishings, high ceilings, TV, DVD player and full kitchen facilities. Both enjoy a quiet location and are ideal for families or small groups. ⑦–⑨

Hacienda San Lucas 5km south of parque ☎651 4106, ⓦwww.haciendasanlucas .com. Wonderful, converted adobe-walled, solar-powered farmhouse in the hills south of town, with startling views over the valley. It's an ideal place to relax, with plenty of space (the grounds include the Los Sapos archeological site and a zipline network; see p.370) and plenty of colonial style. All rooms are spacious and chic, with hand-crafted cedar-wood beds and local textile decorations. Gourmet food is served (a five-course dinner is US$20) and horseriding can be arranged. ❽

Hotel Brisas de Copán one block north of parque ☎651 4118. Modern, clean rooms on several levels, all with reading lights and hot-water bathrooms. There's a sun terrace with a great view and parking. ❹

Hotel Don Udo's c/Mirador ☎651 4533, ⓦwww.donudos.com. Classy new Dutch–Honduran-owned hotel with sixteen comfortable rooms and suites, most with a/c, set around a garden courtyard. Facilities here include a sauna/jacuzzi, sun deck with valley views and a well-regarded restaurant. ❺–❾

Hotel Madrugada southeast of parque ☎651 4092. This decidedly creaky old hotel has a magnificent aspect over Copán valley and a broad communal balcony with chairs and hammocks that makes the most of the views. The rooms are a little tired, and would really benefit from some regular maintenance, but have a certain charm and are kept clean. It's managed by a lovely lady, Celestina Smith. ❹

Hotel Marina Copán c/Centro América ☎651 4070, ⓦwww.hotelmarinacopan.com. The most luxurious accommodation in town. The stylish rooms, all with a/c and TV, are well presented and spacious, plus there's a small pool, a sauna, a gym and bar on site. ❽

Hotel Plaza Copán east side of parque ☎651 4508, ⓦwww.plazacopanhotel.com. Twenty-one slightly pricey rooms, some overlooking the square and all with a/c and cable TV. The hotel also features a pleasant courtyard with a fountain and a small kidney-shaped pool, as well as a restaurant. ❻

Hotel La Posada c/Centro América ☎651 4059, ⓦwww.laposadacopan.com. Rooms here are good value, with TV and bathroom, set off covered walkways with plenty of greenery around. It's a few steps off the plaza. ❺

Hotel Yaragua half a block east of parque ☎651 4050, ⓦwww.yaragua.com. Pleasant hotel with twenty four smallish but comfortable, good-value rooms, set around a little courtyard, with good-quality double beds and cable TV. ❹

Hotelito Yaxpac c/ Macanudo ☎651 4025. Run by a friendly family, the *Yaxpac* features four simple and clean rooms, all with private bath and two with little balconies. ❸

Yat Balam ☎651 4338, ⓦwww.yatbalam.com. An excellent new place, the closest thing to a boutique hotel in town, with four superb rooms (two have a lounge area and balcony). The design theme combines exposed stone and wood beams with soothing creams. All have fridges, TV and beautiful bed linen. It's above a few gift shops and a café. ❼

The Town

Half a day is enough to take in virtually all the town's attractions. The **Parque Central** – lined with banks, municipal structures and an attractive, white-washed Baroque-style church – was designed and built by visiting archeologists Tatiana Proskouriakoff and Gustav Stromsvik. Unfortunately, the simple elegance of the original layout, which followed classical Spanish lines, has been somewhat spoilt by grandiose remodelling initiatives. It does remain a popular place to kill time, however, its benches filled with cowboy-booted farmhands and camera-touting visitors.

On the west side of the parque and somewhat eclipsed by the sculpture museum at the site itself is the **Museo Regional de Arqueología** (daily 9am–5pm; US$3). Inside are some impressive Maya carvings collected from the Copán region, including the glyph-covered Altars T and U; Stela B, depicting the ruler Waxaklajuun Ub'aah K'awiil (Eighteen Rabbit); and some remarkable and intricately detailed flints – ornamental oddities with seven interlocking heads carved from obsidian. There are also two remarkable **tombs**. The first contains the remains of a female shaman, complete with jade jewellery and the skulls of a puma, deer and two human sacrificial victims. The other (10J-45), discovered in 1999 during road-building work, was created for an Early Classic–period ruler of Copán during the sixth century and comprises a vaulted burial chamber where the as yet unidentified ruler was buried with numerous ceramics and two large, carved jade pectoral pieces.

Five blocks north of the parque, **El Cuartel** (Tues–Sun 9am–5pm; free) is an interactive children's learning centre with exhibits about the Maya civilization and a play area. It's located in a renovated army fort and has great views over the town.

Copán's outskirts

About 3km north of the plaza, the **Macaw Mountain Bird Park and Nature Reserve** (daily 9am–5pm; $10; ⓦwww.macawmountain.com) has abundant parrots, parakeets, toucans, six species of macaw, grey hawks, and a great horned owl and makes a wonderful half-day excursion. Most of the birds have been previously kept as pets and donated to the centre, and breeding programmes have been started for very rare species such as the Buffon macaw and the yellow-lored amazon. There are walk-through aviaries and nature trails that wind through a lovely old-growth forest of cedar, mahogany, fig and zapote trees, interspersed with elevated viewing decks. You'll also find a coffee-roasting house and an excellent café-restaurant (meals are US$4–12) serving gourmet coffee from the Copán region, as well as an information centre explaining the relationship between the Maya and birds, and a wonderful natural pool for swimming.

On the other side of town, a twenty-minute walk from the plaza along the road to Guatemala, stands the **Enchanted Wings Butterfly House and Nature Centre** (daily 8am–5pm; $6; ⓦwww.copannaturecenter.com), owned by an American enthusiast and his Honduran wife. Butterflies to look out for include the speckled brown "giant owl" and the scarlet-and-yellow "helicopter", two of the hardier species. Butterflies hatch in the morning hours, so it's best to time your visit accordingly. There's also a display of more than two hundred orchids, around a third of Honduras's native species, with the periods of February to April and July to August being the best time to see them flowering.

Eating and drinking

Copán has some superb places to eat and drink. Standards are usually very high, with generous portions and good service, although virtually all restaurants stop serving at 10pm. The most popular place for a drink is *Café Vía Vía*, which pretty much has the backpacker market covered, followed by *Carnitas Nia Lola* and *Xibalbá*. As for **nightlife**, *Café Viá Vía* is undoubtedly the liveliest place in town with a salsa night on Wednesday (with a teacher present to help you learn those steps), live guitar music on Friday, electronic DJs on Saturday and movies on Sunday.

Café Velchez c/Centro América. Upmarket European-style café, serving good but fairly pricey coffees (including espresso), juices and licuados, alcoholic drinks (wine by the glass), cakes and light meals.

Café Vía Vía two blocks west of parque. The most happening place in town, this huge, hip Belgian-owned bar-restaurant has modish lighting, a garden terrace at the rear and a real vibe on busy nights. Offers an array of sandwiches (using home-made bread), good breakfasts, omelettes, set meals, salads like *ensalada griega* and plenty of veggie options. Also home to Big Foot Tours.

Café Villamil c/Acrópolis. Upmarket new café-restaurant, occupying a triple-level, beautifully constructed colonial-style building. Espresso and cappuccino, crêpes and omelettes, and some of the richest cakes in town.

Carnitas Nia Lola two blocks south of parque. This highly atmospheric and enjoyable restaurant-bar looks like an alpine lodge with quirky decor including an excess of car license plates on the walls. Serves quite pricey but large portions of delicious grilled and barbecued meats, plus some vegetarian dishes. It's equally frequented as a drinking venue, with an early-evening happy hour and a good mix of locals and visitors.

Comedor Mary c/Mirador. Spotting a gap in the market, this simple, popular and welcoming place offers filling, unpretentious Central American cuisine for around US$3–5 a head. Tuck into pupusas; and grilled meat dishes in the attractive interior or side patio.

La Casa de Todo ⓦwww.lacadadetodo .com. Simply superb café, with a lovely garden setting where you can spend hours enjoying the flavoursome, healthy food, lush licuados and coffee. Breakfasts include granola and fruit and pancakes, for lunch there are home-made soups and sandwiches with gouda cheese or mozzarella and pesto; mains include oriental chicken. The premises also include Copán's best gift shop, an internet café, and laundry.

Momo's one block south of parque. Known for its huge, well-priced meat dishes, this atmospheric, log restaurant has an open-air barbecue where the food is cooked in front of you.

Picame c/Acrópolis. Casual, enjoyable Dutch-owned place with gingham tablecloths that's renowned for its spit-roast chicken but also good for an inexpensive breakfast, burrito or baguette.

Pizza Copán opposite Hondutel. Popular with locals and tourists alike who come to indulge in decent pizza and pasta. Be sure to check out the original stone sculptures.

Twisted Tanya's a block south and a block west of parque ⓦwww.twistedtanya.com. The nearest thing Copán has to gourmet dining, this large, stylish English/Bay Islander-owned restaurant has an ambitious menu that includes red snapper with cream caper sauce and roast beef with horseradish and sherry gravy. A three-course meal is US$18, plus there's a daily backpacker menu (4–6pm) for US$6.

Vamos a Ver Café one block south of parque. Busy garden café that offers affordable and delicious home-made soups, sandwiches and snacks.

Xibalbá southeast corner of the parque. Opening daily at 6.30am, this intimate place functions as a café by day, offering very substantial breakfasts (the Full Monty is an ideal kick-start) and as a sociable bar in the evening.

Listings

Banks Banco Atlántida and two other banks are on the parque, all have ATMs and will change traveller's cheques and cash dollars.

Book exchange La Casa de Todo has a good selection.

Internet Maya Connections, just south of the plaza, and La Casa de Todo (daily 8am–8pm). Rates are around US$1.25 an hr.

Language schools Copán is an excellent place to study, with two Spanish schools to choose between, though it's a more expensive learning centre than Guatemala – four hours of classes plus full family-based accommodation and meals costs US$210–225 a week. Guacamaya (☎651 4360, ⓦwww.guacamaya.com), two blocks north of the plaza, is the older of the two schools and more expensive, though Ixbalanque (☎651 4432, ⓦwww.ixbalanque.com), southwest of the plaza, is also worth considering.

Laundry La Casa de Todo (see above) charges around US$1.50 for a normal load.

Shopping La Casa de Todo, a block west of the parque, has a wonderful selection of handicrafts and souvenirs, or try Arte Acción, just over the road.

Tour operators Base Camp, inside Café Vía Vía (☎651 4695, ⓦwww.basecamphonduras.com) has an excellent range of hikes, including full-day walks to Maya Chortí villages (US$35), motorbike tours (US$35–45) and trips throughout Honduras. Yaragua Tours (☎651 4147, ⓦwww.yaragua .com), half a block east of the plaza, offers trips to the hot springs (US$30 per head), El Rubí waterfall (US$20), a spectacular local cave, the Cueva el Boquerón (US$40), horseriding (US$20 for 3hr) and river tubing (US$15). Robert Gallardo at the butterfly farm (see p.362) runs top-class birdwatching tours from around US$40 for a half-day.

Copán ruins

COPÁN RUINS lie 2km east of town, a pleasant fifteen-minute walk along a raised footpath that runs parallel to the highway. Entrance to the site (daily 8am–4pm; US$15 including the Las Sepulturas ruins, though access to the archeological tunnels costs an extortionate US$15 extra) is through the **visitor centre** on the left-hand side of the car park, where a small exhibition explains Copán's place in the Maya World. Inside the visitor centre there's a ticket office and a desk where you can hire a registered site **guide** (US$25 for up to ten people; 2hr) – an excellent investment if you really want to get the most out of Copán. On the other side of the car park is a **cafeteria**, serving drinks and reasonable meals, and a small souvenir shop.

Opposite the visitor centre is the terrific **Museum of Mayan Sculpture** (daily 8am–3.45pm; US$7), arguably the finest in the entire Maya region, with a tremendous collection of stelae, altars, panels and well-labelled explanations in English. You enter through a dramatic entrance doorway, resembling the jaws of a serpent, and pass through a tunnel (signifying the passage into *Xibalbá*, or the underworld). Dominating the museum is a full-scale, flamboyantly painted replica of the magnificent **Rosalila Temple**, built by Moon Jaguar in 571 and discovered intact under Temple 16. A vast crimson-and-jade-coloured mask of the Sun God, depicted with wings outstretched, forms the main facade of the temple. Other ground-floor exhibits concentrate on aspects of Maya beliefs and cosmology, while the upper floor houses many of the finest original sculptures from the Copán valley, comprehensively displaying the skill of the Maya craftsmen.

From the museum it's a 200m walk east to the **warden's gate**, the entrance to the site proper, where your ticket will be checked and where there are usually several squabbling **scarlet macaws** to greet your arrival – these are tame and sleep in cages by the gate at night.

A brief history of Copán

Archeologists believe that settlers began moving into the Río Copán valley around 1400 BC, taking advantage of the area's rich agricultural potential, although construction of the city is not thought to have begun until around 100 AD.

Once the most important **city-state** on the southern fringes of the Maya World, Copán was geographically isolated from the main Maya region, except the city of **Quiriguá**, 64km away to the north. However, despite the distances involved, relations were maintained with other Maya cities, particularly Tikal and Palenque.

Copán remained a small, isolated settlement until the arrival in 426 AD of an outsider, **Yax K'uk Mo'** (Great Sun First Quetzal Macaw), a warrior-shaman

Moving on from Copán

To reach other destinations **within Honduras**, including the Bay Islands, you'll have to travel on to the large industrial city of San Pedro Sula, from where there are regular flights to the Bay Islands, or press on to the coastal city of La Ceiba, which has daily boat connections to Roatán and Utila and several daily flights to all three islands. Four daily Hedman Alas air-conditioned luxury buses (℡651 4106, ⓦwww.hedmanalas .com) to San Pedro Sula (US$13.50–16.50; 3hr) leave Copán from a private terminal 500m south of the plaza; there's an extra service on Sundays and Mondays. Casasola and Gama buses offer less-expensive bus services to San Pedro Sula (6 daily; US$6) leaving from stops opposite the football pitch.

For Guatemala, direct shuttle buses operated by Base Camp Tours (see p.363) to Antigua (US$17; 6hr) run twice daily at 5.30am and noon; they travel via Guatemala City, if there are passengers. Hedman Alas run luxury air-conditioned bus services to Guatemala City (US$35–45; 5hr) daily at 1.30pm and 5.30pm; onward shuttle connections to Antigua for US$6 per head are offered.

If you want to explore Guatemala's eastern highlands or Caribbean region, it's cheapest to take a minibus (US$1.50) to the border at El Florido, then a local bus (every 30min, the last at 6.30pm; US$1.25) to Chiquimula from where there are regular buses to destinations including Puerto Barrios.

who established the basic layout of the city and founded a royal dynasty that lasted for four hundred years. It's unclear whether he was from Teotihuacán, the Mesoamerican superpower, or Tikal (which was under strong Teotihuacán influence at the time), but Yax K'uk Mo' became the object of an intense cult of veneration, first established by his son **Popol Hol** and continued by subsequent members of the dynasty over fifteen generations.

Little is known about the next seven kings who followed Popol Hol, but in 553 AD, the **golden era** of Copán began with the accession to the throne of **Moon Jaguar**, who constructed the magnificent Rosalila Temple, now buried beneath Temple 16. The city thrived through the reigns of **Smoke Serpent** (578–628 AD), **Smoke Jaguar** (628–695 AD) and **Eighteen Rabbit** (695–738 AD), as the great fertility of the Copán region was exploited and wealth amassed from control of the jade trade along the Río Motagua. These resources and periods of stable government allowed for unprecedented political and social growth, as the population boomed to about 28,000 by 760 AD, the highest urban density in the entire Maya region.

Ambitious rebuilding continued throughout this era, using local andesite, a fine-grained, even-textured volcanic rock that was easily quarried and particularly suited to detailed carving, as well as the substantial local limestone beds, which were ideal for stucco production. The highly artistic carved-relief style for which Copán is famous reached a pinnacle during the reign of Eighteen Rabbit – whose image is depicted on many of the site's magnificent stelae and who also oversaw the construction of the Great Plaza, the final version of the ball court and Temple 22 in the East Court.

Following the audacious capture and decapitation of Eighteen Rabbit by Quiriguá's Cauac Sky, construction at Copán came to a complete halt for seventeen years, possibly indicating a period of subjugation by its former vassal state. The royal dynasty subsequently managed to regroup, however, flourishing gloriously, albeit briefly, once more. **Smoke Shell** (749–763 AD) completed the **Hieroglyphic Stairway**, one of the most impressive of all Maya constructions, in an effort designed to symbolize this revival. Optimism continued during the early years of the reign of **Yax Pasaj** (763–820 AD), Smoke Shell's son, who commissioned **Altar Q**, which illustrates the entire dynasty from its beginning, and completed the final version of **Temple 16**, which towers over the site, about 776 AD. Towards the end of his rule, however, the rot set in: skeletal remains indicate that the decline was provoked by inadequate food resources created by population pressure, resulting in subsequent environmental collapse. The seventeenth and final ruler, **Ukit Took'**, assumed the throne in 822 AD, but his reign proved miserably inauspicious. Poignantly, the only monument to his reign, Altar L, was never completed, as if the sculptor had downed his tools and walked out on the job.

The site was known to the Spanish, although they took little interest in it. A court official, Don Diego de Palacios, in a letter written in March 1576, mentions city ruins "constructed with such skill that it seems that they could never have been made by people as coarse as the inhabitants of this province". Not until the nineteenth century and the publication of *Incidents of Travel in Central America, Chiapas and Yucatán* by **John Lloyd Stephens** and **Frederick Catherwood** did Copán become known to the wider world. Stephens, the then acting US ambassador, succeeded in buying the ruins in 1839 and, accompanied by Catherwood, a British architect and artist, spent several weeks clearing the site and mapping the buildings. Stephens' plans to float Copán's monuments down the Río Copán and on to the US were never realized, but

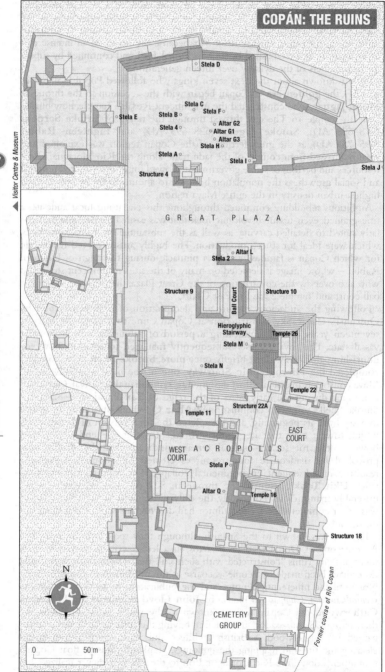

▲ Visitor Centre & Museum

COPÁN: THE RUINS

Stela D

Stela C
Stela B   Stela F
Stela E   Altar G2
Stela 4   Altar G1
                 Altar G3
Stela A   Stela H
                Stela I   Stela J
Structure 4

GREAT PLAZA

Altar L
Stela 2
Structure 9   Ball Court   Structure 10

Hieroglyphic
Stairway   Temple 26
Stela M
Stela N

Temple 22

Temple 11   Structure 22A
                              EAST
                              COURT
         WEST A C R O P O L I S
         COURT
              Stela P

Altar Q   Temple 16

Structure 18

N

CEMETERY
GROUP

Former course of Rio Copan

0   50 m

the instant success of the book and the interest it sparked in Mesoamerican culture ensured that Copán became a magnet for explorers.

British archeologist **Alfred Maudsley** began a full-scale mapping, excavation and reconstruction of the site in 1891. A second major investigation was begun in 1935 by the Carnegie Institution in Washington, during which the Río Copán was diverted to prevent it carving into the site. Since 1977, the Instituto Hondureño de Antropología e Historia has been running a series of projects with the help of archeologists from around the world. Copán is now perhaps the best understood of all Maya cities, and a series of **tunnelling projects** beneath the Acropolis has unearthed remarkable discoveries including, in 1989, the Rosalila Temple, which is now open to the public. In 1993 the Papagayo Temple, built by Popol Hol and dedicated to his father Yax K'uk Mo', was uncovered, and in 1998 further burrowing revealed the tomb of the founder himself.

The Great Plaza
Straight ahead through the avenue of trees lies the **Great Plaza**, a large rectangular arena strewn with the magnificently carved and exceptionally well preserved stelae that are Copán's outstanding features. Initially, however, the visual impact of this grassy expanse may seem a little underwhelming: the first structure you see is **Stucture 4**, a modestly sized pyramid-temple, while the stepped buildings bordering the northern end of the plaza are low and unremarkable. This part of the Great Plaza was once a public place, the stepped sides bordered by a densely populated residential area. The grandest buildings are confined to the monumental temples that border the southern section of the plaza, rising to form the Acropolis, the domain of the ruling and religious elite.

Dotted all around are Copán's famed **stelae** and altars, made from local andesite. Most of the stelae represent **Eighteen Rabbit**, Copán's "King of the Arts" (stelae A, B, C, D, F, H and 4). **Stela A**, dating from 731 AD, has incredibly deep carving, although the faces are now eroded; its sides include a total of 52 glyphs, translating into a famous inscription that includes the emblem glyphs of the four great cities of Copán, Palenque, Tikal and Calakmul – a text designed to show that Eighteen Rabbit saw his city as a pivotal power in the Maya World. **Stela B** depicts a slightly oriental-looking Eighteen Rabbit wearing a turban-like headdress intertwined with twin macaws; his hands support a bar motif, a symbol designed to show the ruler holding up the sky. **Stela C** (730 AD) is one of the earliest stones to have faces on both sides and, like many of the central stelae, has an altar at its base, carved in the shape of a turtle. Two rulers are represented here: facing the turtle (a symbol of longevity) is Eighteen Rabbit's father, Smoke Jaguar, who lived well into his eighties; on the other side is Eighteen Rabbit himself. **Stela H**, perhaps the most impressively executed of all the sculptures, shows Eighteen Rabbit wearing the latticed skirt of the Maize God, his wrists weighed down with jewellery, while his face is crowned with a stunning headdress.

The Ball Court and Hieroglyphic Stairway
South of Structure 4, towards the Acropolis, is the I-shaped **Ball Court**, one of the largest and most elaborate of the Classic period and one of the few Maya courts still to have a paved floor. It was completed in 738 AD, just four months before Eighteen Rabbit's demise at the hands of Quiriguá; two previous versions lie beneath it. Like its predecessors, the court was dedicated to the great macaw deity, and both sloping sides of the court are lined with three sculpted **macaw heads**. The rooms that line the sides of the court, overlooking the

playing area, were probably used by priests and members of the elite as they watched the game.

Pressed up against the Ball Court and protected by a vast canvas cover is the famed **Hieroglyphic Stairway**, perhaps Copán's most astonishing monument. The stairway, which takes up the entire western face of the Temple 26 pyramid, is made up of some 72 stone steps; every block is carved to form part of the glyphic sequence – around 2200 glyph blocks in all. It forms the longest-known Maya hieroglyphic text, but, unfortunately, attempted reconstruction by early archeologists left the sequence so jumbled that a complete interpretation is still some way off. What is known is that the stairway was initiated to record the dynastic history of the city: some of the lower steps were first put in place by Eighteen Rabbit in 710 AD, while Smoke Shell rearranged and completed most of the sequences in 755 AD as part of his efforts to reassert the city's dignity and strength. At the base of the stairway, the badly weathered **Stela M** depicts Smoke Shell and records a solar eclipse in 756 AD.

Adjacent to the Hierogylphic Stairway, and towering over the extreme southern end of the plaza, are the vertiginous steps of **Temple 11** (also known as the Temple of the Inscriptions). The temple was constructed by Smoke Shell, who is thought to be buried beneath it, though no tomb has yet been found. At its base is another classic piece of Copán carving, **Stela N** (761 AD), representing Smoke Shell, with portraits on the two main faces of the stela and glyphs down the sides. The depth of the relief has protected the nooks and crannies, some of which still bear traces of paint – originally the carvings and buildings would have been painted in a whole range of bright colours, but for some reason only the red has survived.

The Acropolis

From the southwestern corner of the plaza, a trail runs past some original drainage ducts beyond which stone steps climb steeply up the side of Temple 11 to a soaring cluster of temples, dubbed the **Acropolis**. This lofty inner sanctum was the preserve of royalty, nobles and priests; it was the political and ceremonial core where religious rituals were enacted, sacrifices performed and rulers entombed. The whole structure grew in size over four hundred years, the temples growing higher and higher as new structures were built over the remains of earlier buildings. A warren of excavated tunnels, some open to the public, bores through the vast bulk of the Acropolis to the Rosalila Temple and several tombs. From the summit of Temple 11, beside a giant ceiba tree (a tree held sacred by the Maya), there's a panoramic view of the site below, over the Ball Court and Great Plaza to the green hills beyond.

A few metres east of Temple 11 are the **Mat House** (Structure 22A), a governmental building distinguished by its interlocking weave-like patterns, and **Temple 22**, which boasts some superbly intricate stonework around the door frames. Constructed by Eighteen Rabbit, Temple 22 functioned as a "sacred mountain" where the elite performed religious blood-letting ceremonies. Above the door is the carving of a double-headed snake, its heads resting on two figures, which are in turn supported by skulls. The decoration here is unique in the southern Maya region – only Yucatán sites such as Kabáh and Chicanna have carvings of comparable quality.

The East Court

Below Temple 22 are the stepped sides of the **East Court**, a graceful plaza that also bears elaborate carvings, including life-sized jaguar heads with hollow eyes that would have once held pieces of jade or polished obsidian. In the middle of the western staircase, flanked by the jaguars, is a rectangular Venus mask, carved in superb deep relief. Rising over the court and dominating the Acropolis is the tallest structure in Copán, **Temple 16**, a 30m pyramid completed by the city's sixteenth ruler, Yax Pasaj, in 776 AD. To construct the temple Yax Pasaj had to build on top of the **Rosalila Temple**, though it was built with extraordinary care so as not to destroy the earlier temple. The temple served as a centre for worship during the reign of Smoke Serpent, or Butz' Chan (578–628 AD), Copán's eleventh ruler, a period that marked the apogee of the city's political, social and artistic growth – so the discovery of the Rosalila was a very exciting find. You can now view the brilliant original facade of the buried temple by entering through a short **tunnel** – an unforgettable, if costly (US$15), experience. The admission price does at least include access to two further tunnels, which extend below the East Plaza past some early cosmological stucco carvings – including a huge macaw mask – more buried temple facades and crypts including the Galindo tomb.

At the southern end of the East Court, **Structure 18** is a small square building with four carved panels in which Yax Pasaj was buried in 821 AD. The diminutive scale of the structure reveals how quickly decline set in, with the militaristic nature of the panels symptomatic of the troubled times. The tomb was empty when excavated by archeologists and is thought to have been looted on a number of occasions. From Structure 18 there's a terrific view of the valley, over the Río Copán, which eroded the eastern buildings of the Acropolis over the centuries until its path was diverted by early archeologists. South of Structure 18, the **Cemetery Group** was once thought to have been a burial site, though it's now known to have been a residential complex and home of the ruling elite. To date, however, little work has been done on this part of the ruins.

The West Court

The second plaza of the Acropolis, the **West Court**, is confined by the south side of Temple 11, which has eight small doorways, and Temple 16. **Altar Q**, at the base of Temple 16, is the court's most famous feature and an astonishing example of ancestral symbolism. Carved in 776 AD, it celebrates Yax Pasaj's accession to the throne on July 2, 763 AD. The top of the altar is carved with six hieroglyphic blocks, while the sides are decorated with sixteen cross-legged figures, all seated on cushions, who represent previous rulers of Copán. All are pointing towards a portrait of Yax Pasaj which shows him receiving a ceremonial staff from the city's first ruler Yax K'uk Mo', thereby endorsing Yax Pasaj's right to rule. Behind the altar is a small crypt, discovered to contain the remains of a macaw and fifteen big cats, sacrificed in honour of his ancestors when the altar was inaugurated.

Las Sepulturas

Two kilometres east of the ruins along a stone pathway is the much smaller site of **Las Sepulturas** (daily 8am–4pm; entrance with the same ticket as for Copán), the focus of much archeological interest in recent years because of the information it provides on daily domestic life in Maya times. Eighteen of the forty-odd residential compounds at the site have been excavated, comprising one hundred buildings that would have been inhabited by the elite. Smaller compounds on the edge of the site are thought to have housed young princes, as well as concubines and servants. It was customary to bury the nobility close to their residences, and more than 250 tombs have been excavated around the compounds – given the number of women found in the tombs it seems likely that the local Maya practised polygamy. One of the most interesting finds – the tomb of a priest or shaman, dating from around 450 AD – is on display in the museum in Copán Ruinas town.

Around Copán

The **Hacienda San Lucas** (see p.360) is a lovely rural hotel about 8km south of town, within whose grounds are a couple of interesting attractions. A wonderful sixteen-stage **zipline** (US$35) network has been set up here, with wires commencing in the hills and plunging across the Copán valley, offering a stunning view of the town, then down across the Río Copán and ending up beside the ruins of the Acropolis. Also here are the ruins of **Los Sapos** (US$1.50), dating from the same era as Copán, a small site whose name derives from a rock carved in the shape of a toad. It's thought to have been a place where Maya women came to bear children, though unfortunately time and weather have eroded much of the carving. You can walk here in around an hour or so from Copán – cross the river after the Hedman Alas bus terminal, bear left and follow the signs, or take a tuk-tuk (US$3).

Pick-ups leave Copán regularly throughout the day for the peaceful town of **Santa Rita**, 9km to the northeast. At the river bridge, just before entering the town, a path leads up to **El Rubí**, a pretty double-waterfall on the Río Copán, about 2km away. Organized tours (see p.363) here from Copán are US$20 per head. Around 22km north of Copán are some (very) **hot springs** (US$1.50), set in lush highland scenery dotted with coffee fincas and patches of pine forest. Once there you can either wallow around in man-made pools or head to the source via a short trail where cool river water and near boiling-hot spring waters combine. On the other side of the river, **Luna Jaguar** (daily 8am–5pm; Ⓦwww.lunajaguar.com; US$10) is a new day-spa set in forested grounds where a stone path connects thirteen different treatment stations (US$30 each) that include natural steam baths, masseurs and a hot spring–fed jacuzzi. It's undoubtedly a lovely natural environment, even if the experience is a little bit themed, and pricey. You can get here on the reasonably frequent buses (45min), which leave from *Hotel Paty* in Copán, though it's easier to join one of the trips offered by Copán's tour operators.

A kilometre or so further north is the *agroturismo* centre at **Finca El Cisne** (Ⓣ651 4695, Ⓦwww.fincaelcisne.com), a working finca involved in the production of cardamom, coffee and cattle. Tours involving you in the daily running of the centre as well as providing information on farming and agricultural practices in the region are well organized and can be arranged through Base Camp tours (see p.363) in Copán, who charge US$59 for a day-trip that includes horseriding.

From Copán to the coast

Excellent road transport links connect Copán to the large and unappealing city of **San Pedro Sula**, where you'll have to change buses for the slightly more attractive coastal town of **La Ceiba**. If you leave Copán early enough, it's possible to make it to the Bay of Islands in a day, catching a flight in San Pedro or a ferry or flight from La Ceiba.

San Pedro Sula

Though it's Honduras's second city and the country's driving economic force, **SAN PEDRO SULA** is uninspiring as well as uncomfortably hot and humid for most of the year. This is a place for business rather than sightseeing, so if you can, press on to La Ceiba or catch a flight from here to the Bay Islands – the city has a modern bus terminal and an international airport. **Taxis** are plentiful and pretty cheap: expect to pay around US$3 per journey in the central area, or around US$12 to the airport 12km southeast of town.

If you do **stay**, all the following places have air-conditioning: *Tamarindo's Hostel*, 9 C NO 1015 (☎557 0123, ⊛www.tamarindohostel.com; dorm beds US$12), is a decent backpacker lodge; for more comfort *Dos Molinos*, 21 Avenida & 14 Calle (☎510 0335; ❺), is a great B&B; while *Hotel Ejecutivo*, at 10 Avenida, 2 Calle SO (☎552 4289, ⊛www.hotel-ejecutivo.com; ❼), has large and comfortable rooms. **Moving on** from San Pedro Sula, several companies operate frequent buses for **La Ceiba** (21 daily; 3hr–3hr 30min), the gateway city to the Bay Islands; all leave from San Pedro's new bus terminal, Gran Central Metropolitana, about 4km from the centre. Hedman Alas (⊛www.hedmanalas.com) run the most luxurious and reliable services. If you'd rather get to the Bay Islands as quickly as possible, **flights** in Honduras are quite reasonably priced. Three airlines – Taca/Isleña (☎668 3333, ⊛www.flyislena.com), Sosa (☎668 3223) and Atlantic Air (☎668 7309, ⊛www.atlanticairlinesint.com) – connect San Pedro with Utila (3 daily; US$98), Roatán (8 daily; US$110) and Guanaja (2 daily; US$125); all flights are via La Ceiba.

La Ceiba

Some 190km east along the coast from San Pedro Sula, steamy **LA CEIBA** is one of the more approachable Honduran cities. Though it lacks sights and its beaches are not the cleanest, the city has a cosmopolitan mix of inhabitants, including a large Garífuna community (see p.258), and a bustling atmosphere. However, it's the night that's really celebrated in La Ceiba – the city is unquestionably the **party capital** of the country, with a vibrant dancehall scene and a legendary May carnival.

All Catisa-Tupsa buses arrive at the **bus terminal**, 2km west of the Parque Central. Hedman Alas buses use a private terminal a five-minute walk south of the Megaplaza mall, which is about 1.5km south from the parque. Local buses and shared taxis run very frequently to the centre from all terminals. La Ceiba's **airport** is 9km south of town; a taxi to the centre costs US$7. Of Ceiba's **hotels** the best budget bet is the recommended *Banana Republic Guesthouse*, Avenida Morazón (☎440 1282; ❷–❸), a five-minute walk from the vast Megaplaza mall. It has private rooms and dorms (US$5 per bed), helpful staff, laundry, internet connections and a garden with hammocks. Otherwise the landmark *Gran Hotel Paris*, on the Parque Central (☎443 2391, ⊛www.granhotelparis.com; ❻), has an excellent location and large, comfortable rooms (all with a/c, phone & TV), plus a pool, bar and restaurant. If you want to sample La Ceiba's club scene, the action is concentrated in the string of bars and dance venues along the seafront.

Moving on from La Ceiba, ferries run twice daily to Utila, at 9.30am and 4.30pm (US$17 one way; 1hr), and Roatán, at 9.30am and 4pm (US$22 one way; 1hr 15min). Ferries leave from the Muralla de Cabotaje municipal dock, about 5km to the east of the city; there's no bus service, so you'll need to take a taxi (US$6 from the centre; US$12 from the airport). **Flying** to the islands is also uncomplicated, with about twelve flights daily to Roatán (30min; US$39), four daily to Utila (20min; US$33) and four daily to Guanaja (40min; US$39). Availability is rarely a problem, and you can usually buy your tickets on the spot at the airport, though it's best to book ahead in the peak holiday seasons (Christmas, Easter and Aug). The domestic airlines Taca/Isleña (☎443 0179) and Sosa (☎443 2519) have offices on the Parque Central in La Ceiba, while

Atlantic Airlines (☎440 2343) has an office on Avenida La República; all have desks at the airport, too.

Overland from Guatemala to Puerto Cortés

Although the beach and village of **Omoa** has a laid-back appeal and the faded resort of **Tela** some terrific nature reserves close by, few people linger long on Honduras's north coast, such is the appeal of the Bay Islands. Travelling overland this way you'll have to negotiate the sprawling, unattractive cities of Puerto Cortés and San Pedro Sula.

Minibuses leaving Puerto Barrios in Guatemala take an hour to reach the border crossing with Honduras, just past the huge Arizona bridge over the Río Motagua. Immigration is generally straightforward for travellers, with US$1–2 entry and exit charges being levied by the border officials. (However, drivers with foreign plates entering Honduras here have reported customs officials demanding that the necessary permit, and fee of around US$120, are processed in Puerto Cortés). Minibuses leave when full for the scruffy town of **Corinto**, a couple of kilometres or so away. Buses leave Corinto every sixty minutes for Puerto Cortés (1hr 30min; the last at 3.30pm).

Omoa

Fifty kilometres from Corinto there's a turn-off for the sleepy, slightly ramshackle little fishing village of **Omoa**, 2km from the highway down a side road, which draws a steady trickle of travellers. Omoa is most famous for the monumental remains of a colonial **fort** (Mon–Fri 8am–4pm, Sat & Sun 9am–5pm; US$2) that stands in mute witness to the region's colourful history. Although the Spanish began construction of the fort in 1759, it was never fully completed. Omoa's narrow beach is lined with fishing boats and offers stunning views west across the curve of the bay to the Sierra de Omoa peaks in the distance. It can get busy with day-trippers at weekends, however. For a **room**, *Roli's Place* (☎658 9082; ❷) is a reasonable budget base with private rooms as well as camping (US$3 per head), hammocks (US$3 per head) and dorms (US$4 per head); they also have kayaks and bikes, a kitchen and laundry facilities – and a lot of hotel rules. Otherwise *Hotel Tatiana* (☎658 9182; ❹) is a decent-value option with en-suite rooms. The best places for meals are the *champas* along the seafront, which serve fresh seafood at very reasonable prices, or the great new deli-restaurant *Punto Italia* for pizza and pasta. Buses leave from the highway every thirty minutes for Puerto Cortés.

Puerto Cortés

Honduras's main port, **PUERTO CORTÉS**, 19km from Omoa, is a run-down town where the unstinting heat and dilapidated wooden buildings merely add to the rough-and-ready feel of the place. You'll hopefully pass through only to change buses en route to San Pedro Sula. Three companies run **buses** between Puerto Cortés and San Pedro Sula, including the reliable Citul, who run the hour-long trip every thirty minutes between 6am and 6pm from their terminal a block north of the main plaza at 4 Avenida and 4 Calle. Travelling in the other direction, there are hourly buses to Corinto (8am–4pm; 1hr 30min) and half-hourly connections to Omoa (40min).

The Bay Islands

Strung along the southern fringes of the world's second-largest barrier reef, the **Bay Islands** (Islas de la Bahía) are Honduras's major tourist attraction. With their clear, calm waters and abundant marine life, the islands are the ideal destination for inexpensive diving, sailing and fishing, while less active types can sling a hammock on one of the many palm-fringed, sandy beaches and snooze in the shade, watching the magnificent sunsets that paint the broad skies with colours as vibrant as the coral below.

Composed of three main islands and some 65 smaller cayes, this sweeping 125km island chain lies on the Bonacca Ridge, an underwater extension of the Sierra de Omoa mountain range that disappears into the sea near Puerto Cortés on the coast. **Utila**, the island closest to the mainland, attracts budget travellers from all over the world, while **Roatán** is the largest and most developed. **Guanaja**, to the east, is a more upmarket and exclusive resort destination. All three islands offer superb diving and snorkelling.

Even old hands get excited about **diving** the waters around the Bay Islands, where lizard fish and toadfish dart by, scarcely distinguishable from the coral; eagle rays glide through the water like huge birds flying through the air; parrot fish chomp steadily away at the coral; and barracuda and harmless nurse sharks circle the waters, checking you out from a distance. In addition the **whale shark**, the world's largest fish (it can reach up to 14m in length), is a resident of the Cayman Trench, which plummets to profound depths just north of the islands. It's most frequently spotted close to Utilan waters between March and June and in October and November when dive boats run trips to look for it, but can be encountered year-round.

The best **time to visit** the islands is from March to September, when the water visibility is good and the weather is clear and sunny. The rains start in October, while late November and December are usually very wet, with squally showers continuing until late February. Daytime temperatures range between 25°C and 29°C year-round, though the heat is rarely oppressive, thanks to almost constant east–southeast trade winds. Mosquitoes and sandflies are endemic on all the islands, and at their worst when the wind dies down; lavish coatings of baby oil help to keep the latter away.

Some history

The Bay Islands' history of conquest, pirate raids and constant immigration has resulted in a society that's unique in Honduras. The islands' original inhabitants are thought to have been the **Pech**, described by Columbus on his fourth voyage in 1502 as being a "robust people who adore idols and live mostly from a certain white grain from which they make fine bread and the most perfect beer". Post-conquest, the indigenous population declined rapidly as a result of enslavement and forced labour. The islands' strategic location as a provisioning point for the Europe-bound Spanish fleets ensured that they soon became the targets for **pirates**, initially Dutch and French, and subsequently English. The Spanish decision to evacuate the islands in 1650 left the way open for bands of pirates, including Henry Morgan, to move in and set up bases in Guanaja and Port Royal in Roatán. For nearly a century, the islands served as a stronghold from which buccaneers launched sporadic attacks on Spanish ships and against the mainland settlements.

British forces occupied the Bay Islands in 1742, and then contested control of Port Royal in Roatán (the main settlement at that time) with the Spanish for the next forty years. But in 1782 the Spanish left Roatán, and the island was

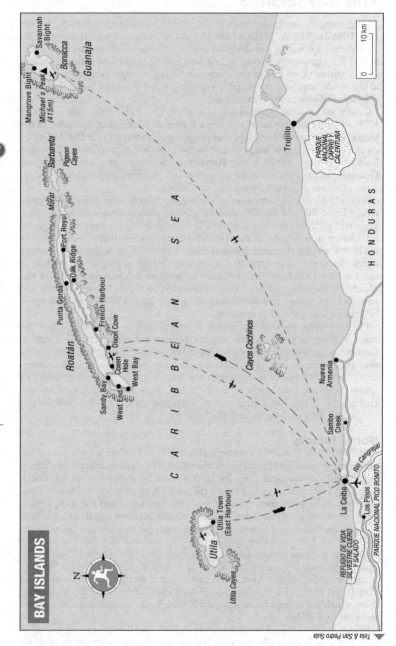

BAY ISLANDS

N

CARIBBEAN SEA

Savannah Bight
Mangrove Bight
Michael's Peak (415m)
Bonacca
Guanaja

Barbareta
Pigeon Caves
Morat
Port Royal
Oak Ridge
Punta Gorda
French Harbour
Dixon Cove
Coxen Hole
West Bay
Sandy Bay
West End
Roatán

Utila
Utila Town (East Harbour)
Utila Cayes

Cayos Cochinos

Trujillo

PARQUE NACIONAL CAPIRO Y CALENTURA

HONDURAS

Nueva Armenia

Sambo Creek

La Ceiba

Los Pinos

Río Cangrejal

REFUGIO DE VIDA SILVESTRE CUERO Y SALADO

PARQUE NACIONAL PICO BONITO

0   10 km

deserted until the arrival of the **Garífuna** in 1797. Forcibly expelled from the British-controlled island of St Vincent following a rebellion, most of the three-thousand-strong group were persuaded by the Spanish to settle in Trujillo on the mainland, leaving a small settlement at Punta Gorda on the island's north coast. Further waves of settlers came after the abolition of slavery in 1830, when white **Cayman Islanders** and freed **slaves** arrived first on Utila, later moving on to Roatán and Guanaja. These new inhabitants fished and built up a very successful fruit industry – until a hurricane levelled the plantations in 1877.

Honduras acquired rights to the islands following independence in 1821, yet many – not least the islanders themselves – still considered the territory to be British. In 1852 Britain declared the islands a Crown Colony, breaking the terms of the 1850 Clayton–Bulwer Treaty, an agreement not to exercise dominion over any part of Central America. Forced to back down under US pressure, Britain finally conceded sovereignty to Honduras in the Wyke–Cruz Treaty of 1859.

Today the islands retain their cultural separation from the mainland, although with both Spanish-speaking Hondurans and expats settling in growing numbers, the island's ethnic make-up continues to change. A unique form of **Creole English** is still spoken on the street, but due to the increasing number of mainlanders migrating here, Spanish – always the official language – is becoming almost as common. This government-encouraged migration has sparked tensions between English-speaking locals and the Latino newcomers, especially in Roatán, where many islanders feel they are being swamped by land-hungry outsiders with whom they have little in common. The huge growth in **tourism** since the early 1990s, a trend that shows no signs of abating, has also been controversial, with growing concerns about the environmental impact of the industry and the question of who exactly benefits most from the boom.

For full details of **getting to the islands** from the rest of Honduras, see p.371 and p.388. There are also several **international flights** to Roatán: Continental operates four weekly flights from Houston and one weekly flight from Newark; Delta has two weekly flights from Atlanta; Taca flies here from Houston, Miami and San Salvador; and Atlantic connects Belize City with the island.

Utila

Smallest of the three main Bay Islands, **UTILA** is a key destination for budget travellers, and one of the cheapest places in the world to **learn to dive** – and even if you don't want to don tanks, the superb waters around the island offer great swimming and snorkelling. Utila is still the cheapest of the Bay Islands, with a cost of living only slightly higher than that on the mainland, although prices are gradually rising. Though the island is now largely dependent on tourism, it stills retains a good deal of old-fashioned charm. The well-swept streets are lined with wonderful old wooden Caribbean-style houses, built on stilts, with shuttered windows and sunny verandas, their gardens bursting with bougainvillea. Life is laid-back and people are generally friendly, but watch out for the odd dancehall brawl. As elsewhere, respect local customs in dress and don't walk around in your bathing suit. Note also that drinking from glass bottles on the street is prohibited.

Arrival and information

All **boats** dock in the centre of **Utila Town** (also known as East Harbour), a large, curved harbour that's the island's only settlement and home to the vast majority of its 3000-strong population. The island's principal road, about a forty-minute walk end to end, runs along the seafront from The Point in the east to Blue Bayou in the west. The airstrip is 4km north of Utila Town, at the end of the island's other main street, Cola de Mico Road, which heads inland from the dock.

Wherever you arrive, you'll be met by representatives from the **dive schools** laden with maps and information on special offers. Many schools offer free accommodation during their courses, but it's worth checking out the various options before signing up. For more objective information, the Utila branch of the Bay Islands' Conservation Association (BICA) has a **visitor and information office** on the main street, 100m east of the dock (Mon–Fri 9am–noon & 2–5pm; ☎425 3260). Consult the excellent community **website** ⓌWww .aboututila.com for more information and news about the island or the Utila *East Wind* newspaper (Ⓦwww.utilaeastwind.com).

Accommodation

Utila has about 30 **guesthouses and hotels**, and a profusion of rooms for rent; there's always somewhere available, even at Christmas and Easter. Most of the dive schools have links with a hostel, so that enrolling on a scuba course gets you a few free or discounted nights' accommodation. Most places are within walking distance of the dock. Be sure that your room has adequate security as there are regular burglaries of backpackers' rooms.

East of the dock

Cooper's Inn a 5min walk from the dock ☎425 3184, Ⓦwww.coopersinn.com. This well-run place has a choice of accommodation, most with lagoon views, including eight good budget rooms with fans, doubles with a/c and some small apartments with kitchenettes. Good deals for longer stays are available. ❷–❹

Rubi's Inn a 2min walk from the dock ☎425 3240, ©rubisinn@yahoo.com. Owned by a charming local couple this place has twelve airy rooms, each with two double beds and fridge, and those on the upper level have great sea views. The Honeymoon Suite has a/c and a balcony. Pleasant gardens with shade and hammocks, and a guests' kitchen. ❹

Sharkey's Reef Hotel behind *Sharkey's Reef Restaurant*, near the old airstrip ☎425 3212. Set in a peaceful garden, the five large rooms (each with two double beds) and two apartments here all have a/c, private bathrooms and cable TV, and some have kitchens. There's also a terrace with great views over the lagoon. ❺–❻

Utopia Dive Village 2km east of the dock ☎3344 9387, Ⓦwww.utopiadivevillage.com. Stunning new beachfront dive-resort where the accommodation is finished to a very high standard, with polished wooden floors, Balinese furnishings, a/c, and modish bathrooms. Wave-front bar, restaurant with a healthy menu, and the lounge room has a book/DVD library and pool table; a pool is planned. Dive/hotel packages offer the best value. ❾

Cola de Mico Road

Bavaria Hotel behind the *Mango Inn* ☎425 3809, ©petrawhitefield3@hotmail.com. Well-constructed,

German-owned place with six pleasant, good-value rooms, all with fans and private bathroom. ❸

Jade Seahorse next to *Tony's Place* ☎425 3270, Ⓦwww.jadeseahorse.com. Unquestionably the most eccentric place to stay on the island. Owned by an American artist and designed in his own unique fantasy-meets-Gaudí style, the highly quirky rooms are modern and well equipped with a/c, two double beds, minibar and tiled bathroom. ❼

Mango Inn a 5min walk up the road from the dock ☎425 3335, Ⓦwww .mango-inn.com. A beautiful, well-run place, timber-built in Caribbean style and set in a garden shaded by fruit trees with a lovely pool. The range of rooms stretches from thatched, a/c bungalows and cabins to pleasant dorms with shared bath. Also on offer: a book exchange, laundry service, and the lively *Mango Café* (see "Eating"). Rates drop considerably if diving with the affiliated Utila Dive Centre; a number of packages are available. Dorms US$3 first night, then US$10 (or free if enrolling on a course), rooms ❻, bungalows and cabins. ❽–❾

Tony's Place opposite *Mango Inn* ☎425 3376. Simple, inexpensive rooms (with fan) and the shared bathrooms are kept pretty clean. The talkative owner is friendly and informative. ❷

West of the dock

Deep Blue Resort just across the lagoon west of Blue Bayou ☎425 3211, Ⓦwww.deepblueutila .com. Very attractive small-scale dive-resort with ten spacious rooms, all with two double beds, a/c and fridges, stylish wooden furniture and balconies with commanding ocean views. Faces a private white-sand beach and has a bar and restaurant with good home-cooking. **❾**

Seaside Inn opposite Ecomarine-Gunter's Dive Shop ☎ 425 3150, ✉ hotelseaside@yahoo.com. Popular place with comfortable en-suite rooms, all with two double beds and some with a/c, three dormitories (US$5 per bed), plus two apartments

available for monthly rent. Kitchen, wi-fi and internet access available. **❸–❺**

Tropical Hotel behind Rose's supermarket ☎ 425 3568. Backpackers' stronghold offering 18 small, functional rooms with fans and a communal kitchen. **❷**

Diving

Most visitors come to Utila specifically for the **diving**, attracted by the low prices, clear warm water (temperatures fluctuate between 25–28°C), and abundant marine life. Common sightings include turtles, parrot fish, trumpet fish, spotted eagle rays and yellow stingrays, porcupine fish and tarpon. As it's the north coast of Utila that offers the best diving, make sure your dive school regularly goes to that side of the island. The reef walls are near vertical on this side, where the best sites include Blackish Point, Duppy Waters and The Maze. On the east side of Utila the seamount of Black Hills offers prolific sealife, but on the south coast the sea bottom is much shallower and the reef in poorer condition. Many of the schools with larger, more powerful boats head to the dive sites of the north coast via seamounts where currents converge and **whale sharks** (see box, p.380) are frequently seen. The good schools will be happy to spend time talking to you about the merits of the various sites.

Rather than signing up with the first dive-school representative who approaches you, it's worth spending a morning walking around checking out all the schools. **Price** is not really a consideration, with the dozen or more dive shops all setting a uniform rate (US$259) for Open Water, Advanced and Rescue Diver PADI courses. Divemaster (US$750) and various levels of Instructor courses are also on offer, as are fun dives at US$250 for a package of ten. **Safety** is a more pertinent issue: for peace of mind, you should make sure that you understand – and get along with – the instructors, many of whom speak a number of languages. Before signing up, also check that classes have no more than six people, that the equipment is well maintained and that all boats have working oxygen and a first-aid kit. Anyone with asthma or ear problems should not be allowed to dive. Diving **insurance** sold by BICA is a compulsory extra at US$3 per day and helps fund the island's decompression chamber and medical treatment in the event of an emergency.

Recommended schools include the Utila Dive Centre (☎ 425 3326, ⊛ www.utiladivecentre.com), about 300m east of the dock; its sister school, Cross Creek (☎ 425 3397, ⊛ www.crosscreekutila.com), about 200m east of the dock; Alton's (☎ 425 3704, ⊛ www.altonsdiveshop.com), 350m east of the dock; Deep Blue Divers (☎ 425 3211, ⊛ www.deepblueutila.com) just west of the dock; and Ecomarine-Gunter's Dive Shop (☎ 425 3350, ⊛ www.ecomarineutila.com), about 400m west of the dock. Many of the dive shops also rent out **snorkelling** equipment for around US$5 a day, free for divers.

It's important to bear in mind that the coral reef dies when it is touched. BICA has installed buoys at each of the sites to prevent boats anchoring on the reef, and all the reputable schools will use these.

Around Utila

The best swimming near town is at the attractive little bay known locally as **Chepe's Beach**, a fifteen-minute walk west of the centre, where the sands are gently shelving. The beach has a couple of bar-restaurants, hammocks slung in the shade of coconut trees, and locals gather here at weekends to barbecue and play Latin, country, and reggae music. Five minutes further on, the **Blue Bayou** bay has excellent snorkelling (US$1.50 charge to use the area), particularly just before sundown when barracuda, turtles and eagle rays are often seen. There's also a rickety wooden pier here where you can sunbathe in peace away from the sandflies.

East of town, **Airport Beach**, at the end of the old dirt airstrip past the Point, also offers good snorkelling just offshore (though access is more difficult), as does the little reef beyond the lighthouse. The path from the end of the airstrip up the east coast of the island leads to a couple of small coves – the second is good for swimming and sunbathing. Five minutes beyond the coves, you'll come to the **Ironshores**, a mile-long stretch of low volcanic cliffs with lava tunnels cutting down to the water.

A kilometre inland from Utila Town, down a well-signposted route from Cola de Mico Road is the **Iguana Research Station** (Mon, Wed & Fri 2–5pm; ⓦ www.utila-iguana.de; US$2.50), where an environmental charity is trying to breed the rare Utila iguana, known locally as the "swamper". Found nowhere else in the world, the swamper is under threat from poachers (locals have traditionally eaten them) and habitat loss. You can see the swamper up close in the centre's enclosures, along with the two other kinds of iguana found in Utila; there's also information here about the island's environment.

Another pleasant diversion is the five-kilometre walk or cycle along Cola de Mico Road up to the northern tip of the island to **Pumpkin Hill and beach**, passing the site of the airport. The 82-metre hill, the eroded crest of an extinct volcano, provides good views over the island and across to the mainland and the dark bulk of the Pico Bonito mountains. Down on the beach, lava rocks cascade into the sea, forming underwater caves – there's good snorkelling here when the water is calm.

The cayes

Utila Cayes – eleven tiny outcrops strung along the southwestern edge of the island – were designated a wildlife refuge in 1992. **Pigeon Caye** (also known as Suc Suc Caye) and **Jewel Caye**, connected by a narrow causeway, are both inhabited by descendants of the original settlers from the Cayman Islands, and the pace of life here is even slower than that on Utila. Small launches regularly shuttle between Suc Suc and Utila (US$2), or can be hired with a skipper for a day's snorkelling, if you have your own equipment. *Vicky's Rooms* on Suc Suc (❷) offers basic accommodation, and a couple of reasonable restaurants and a good fish market complete the scene.

Water Caye, a blissful stretch of white sand, coconut palms, pellucid water and a small coral reef, is even more idyllic, given its absence of sandflies. You can **camp** here, but you'll need to bring all your own food, fuel and water; a caretaker turns up every day to collect the US$1.50 fee for use of the island, and hammocks can be rented for an extra US$1. Water Caye is also the venue for occasional **full-moon parties** as well as a spectacular annual two-day rave held in July or August each year, with international house and techno DJs, organized by Sunjam (see ⓦ www.sunjamutila.com for information). **Transport** to the caye is organized during such events; at other times, dive boats will often drop you off on their way to the north coast for a small fee, or you can ask the owner of the *Bundu Café* (see "Eating") in Utila Town.

Eating

Fish, crab and lobster are obviously staples on the islands, along with the usual rice and beans. With the tourists, however, have also come European and

American foods – pasta, pizza, burgers, pancakes and granola. Since most things have to be brought in by boat, **prices** are higher than on the mainland: main courses start at about US$4.50, and beers cost at least US$1.25. For eating on the cheap, head for the evening stalls on the road by the dock, which do a thriving trade in *baleadas*. Note that many restaurants stop serving at around 10pm.

Bundu Café on the main street, east of the dock. One of the most happening places in town, this barn-like café-restaurant serves a wide range of food and always has a lively vibe. Breakfast options include home-made granola and crêpes, for lunch there are good sandwiches, bagels and baguettes while the dinner menu takes in Mexican food, pasta and barbecued chicken. Wine, cocktails and live music some nights.

Camila's Bakery a 5min walk east of the dock. The finest pastries, cakes and bread in town, run by a longtime Danish resident.

Indian Wok at the *Tranquila* bar east of the dock. Offers a Pan-Asian menu of tandoori chicken, curries, satay, Thai food and stir-fry dishes. Open Sun–Thurs, dinner only.

Island Café a 2min walk west of the dock. A well-run, locally owned restaurant with excellent fish and seafood at moderate prices and friendly service.

Mango Café *Mango Inn*. Very flavoursome well-presented European cooking, with good salads and seafood and pizzas (baked in a wood-fired oven) that are definitely the best on the island. Also offers espresso coffee and delicious fresh fruit smoothies.

Munchie's a 1min walk west of the dock. Wonderful breakfasts and licuados, and offers an interesting lunch and dinner menu including some island specialities. Check out the Iguana Garden at the rear, a steep wall inhabited by a group of spiny-tailed iguanas.

La Piccola just west of the dock. Authentic Italian restaurant boasting a wide selection of fresh pasta, salads and daily specials; mains start at around US$7. Also has a good wine list. Closed Mon & Tues.

RJs at The Point beside the bridge. Popular with dive crews and students, with a gregarious atmosphere and excellent meat and fish barbecues. Get there early if you want a table, as it fills up quickly. Open Wed, Fri & Sun only.

Nightlife

Despite its tiny population, Utila is a fearsomely hedonistic party island, except on Saturday night as most islanders are Seventh-Day Adventists. One of the hottest places in town is the *Coco Loco Bar*, just west of the dock, which has tables on a pier above the sea and draws a lively bunch of party heads with its extended happy hour and regular house, techno and reggae parties. *Tranquila*, just next door, is equally popular though the music policy can be banal, while the *Bundu Café*, east of the dock, can get lively and occasionally has live music. On Cola de Mico Road, you simply have to see the amazingly eccentric *Treetonic* bar inside the *Jade Seahorse* hotel, while *Turkimango* is another lively seafront place. The *Bar in the Bush*, on Cola de Mico Road, is Utila's liveliest dancehall; the hip-grinding action is hottest on Wednesdays and Fridays.

Listings

Banks BGA bank just east of the dock has an ATM. If it's out of cash, cash advances can be arranged here or at the neighbouring Banco Atlántida. Henderson's store, just west of the dock, will change cash and traveller's cheques outside bank hours.

Bicycles Can be rented for around US$5 a day from Delco, just west of the dock.

Book exchange The *Bundu Café*, on the main street, east of the dock.

Doctor The Community Medical Clinic is 2min west of the dock (Mon–Fri 9am–noon).

Horseriding Red Ridge Stable, on the road to the airport (T 3390 4812), offers horseback tours of the island.

Immigration office At the port building (Mon–Fri 9am–noon & 2–4.30pm).

Internet access 2min west of the dock, Utila Phone Company (daily 8am–8pm) has internet access for US$2.25 an hour, plus discounted international calls.

Post office In the large building at the main dock (Mon–Fri 9am–noon & 2–4.30pm, Sat 9–11.30am).

Utila's waters are graced year-round with the presence of the world's biggest fish, the **whale shark**. Yet despite its size – the shark grows to an estimated 14m in length and can tip the scales at around 15 tonnes – little is known about this creature. Its scientific name (*rhincodon typhus*) wasn't even determined until 1984, and their reproductive cycle – females are live bearers of around 300 fully developed 50cm shark pups – was only verified in 1996. Largely solitary, pelagic (oceanic) fish, whale sharks are found in all tropical seas, though so little is known about their numbers that the World Conservation Union consider their status to be "indeterminate" and the International Union for Conservation of Nature and Natural Resources classify them as "vulnerable" because of their size and late maturity. Whale sharks have a gentle nature, and are not known to have any natural enemies except man (their meat is eaten in some Asian countries, including Taiwan where they are known as "tofu fish" because of the taste of the flesh) and killer whales, though juveniles are targeted by large oceanic predators such as blue sharks and marlin.

It's known that the whale sharks of the western Caribbean travel between Cozumel in Mexico and Honduras, timing their arrival at feeding spots to coincide with incoming tides, which create rich upcurrents. Plankton and microscopic crustaceans form whale sharks' main diet, but they also ingest some sardine-sized fish and, occasionally, small tuna, and are known to dive as deep as 1000m in search of food. The sharks have also been recorded circling around coral reefs (including Gladden Spit in Belize) for hours awaiting full-moon snapper-egg spawns. It's highly likely that whale sharks move across substantial distances in the western hemisphere, as it's known that they migrate thousands of kilometres across the Indian and Pacific oceans.

In Utila whale sharks are most frequently spotted in open waters two or three kilometres north of Pumpkin Hill, where currents converge around underwater seamounts, creating an upswell of plankton, krill and baitfish on which the whale sharks feed. Although they're occasionally encountered in the seas off the other Bay Islands, Utila is one of the very few places in the world (alongside the Maldives) where the sharks are found year-round. The **best times of year** to see whale sharks are between February and May and between September and early November. When the sea is too rough, dive boats don't set out to look for them, and afternoon searches are very rare at any time of year because of choppy water.

When conditions are right, dive boats seek out whale sharks in a favourable region between Utila Town and the dive sites of the north coast of the island, with the

Spanish school Central American Spanish School, east of the dock (ⓦ www.ca-spanish .com), charges US$150 per week for 20 hr of tuition.

Telephones See "Internet" above.
Travel agents Morgan's Travel (ⓣ 425 3161) at the dock can help you with ferry and flight tickets.

Roatán

Some 50km from La Ceiba, **ROATÁN** is the largest of the Bay Islands, a curving ridged hump almost 50km long and 5km across at its widest point. It still draws backpackers, but the island is increasingly geared to higher-spending tourists, including cruise-ship passengers. Many of the dozen or so luxury resorts attract divers on all-in packages, though there are some fine guesthouses and smaller hotels too. The rich reefs do offer superb **diving**, but Roatán's hills also offer some great hiking and horseriding, while stretches of idyllic sands provide the chance to do nothing except laze on a beach. **Coxen Hole** is the island's commercial centre, while **West End** is the most lively resort.

captain first scanning the horizon for seabirds, particularly diving terns (which also feed on baitfish). Next, all eyes look out for "**boils**" created by the frenzied feeding of bonito (black-fin tuna), which also prey on krill and baitfish. Whale sharks glide around just below the surface, hoovering up mouthfuls of plankton-rich seawater. Often the shark surfaces to feed in a vertical position – an unforgettable sight as the great fish steadies itself upright (a little like a performing seal), exposing its white underbelly, vast mouth agape and sucking in seawater, which it filters through a gill-raker and then expels via five pairs of huge gill slits. The captain then gives a signal and everyone aboard jumps into the ocean for a glimpse of the shark – though they rarely hang around for more than a minute or two under these circumstances. Whale sharks are not considered dangerous to humans, but snorkellers are not permitted to attempt to touch the behemoths.

The sharks themselves are quite astonishing to behold. They have a broad, flat head, and the upper side of their body is usually a steely grey-blue colour and covered in white spots and square checkerboard-style markings. By photographing the intricate patterns of lines and spots directly behind the sharks' gill slits, individuals can be recognized. A database of Utila sightings is being compiled as part of a study of the island's sharks; see ⓦ www.utilawhalesharkresearch.com for more information.

Research findings show that whale sharks average between six and nine metres – though local fishermen talk about an eighteen-metre barnacle-encrusted specimen they've nicknamed Old Tom. The sheer concentration of them in Utilan waters suggests that the seas north of the island could perhaps be a breeding ground. With Utila now established as a whale shark hotbed, dive operators have agreed upon "whale shark **encounter guidelines**" designed to ensure that boats do not encroach too closely on the feeding sharks, with a maximum of eight snorkellers officially permitted in the water with the shark at one time.

Visitors are welcome to drop by Utila's **Whale Shark & Oceanic Research Center,** a three-minute walk west of the dock (Mon–Sat 9am–5pm; ⓣ425 3760), on the grounds of the *Utila Lodge*. There you can learn more about this giant fish and sign up for shark-spotting trips (US$40 per head). A weekly whale-shark presentation is held here, and T-shirts, DVDs and merchandise are sold. Volunteers are also needed to conduct monitoring and identification; contact the centre for more information.

Arrival, information and getting around

Regular **flights** from La Ceiba (and the US) land at the airport, on the road to French Harbour, 3km from Coxen Hole. A taxi to West End from here costs an extortionate US$12, or you could walk to the road and wait for one of the public minibuses that head to Coxen Hole every twenty minutes or so (US$0.75) and change there. There's an information desk, a hotel reservation desk, car rental agencies and a bank at the airport. **Ferries** to the island dock in a new terminal at Dixon Cove near Brick Bay, which is not served by public transport; a taxi to West End costs US$15.

A paved road runs west–east along the island, connecting the major communities. **Minibuses** leave regularly from Thickett Road in Coxen Hole heading west to Sandy Bay and West End (every 20min until 6pm; US$1) and east to Brick Bay, French Harbour, Oak Ridge and Punta Gorda (every 20min; US$1–2.25) If you really want to explore, you'll need to rent a **car**: several agencies at the airport can sort you out, including Caribbean Rent-a-Car (ⓣ445 6950, ⓦwww.caribbeanroatan.com), who rent out small cars from US$33 a day, excluding insurance. For **information** about the island and its

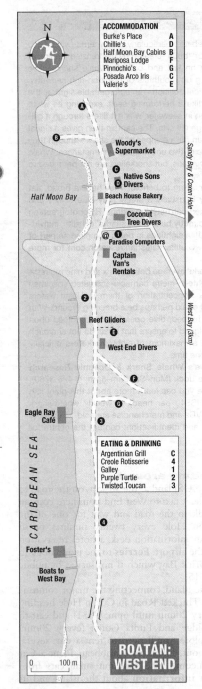

ACCOMMODATION

Burke's Place	A
Chillie's	D
Half Moon Bay Cabins	B
Mariposa Lodge	F
Pinnochio's	G
Posada Arco Iris	C
Valerie's	E

Woody's
Supermarket

Native Sons
Divers

Half Moon Bay

Beach House Bakery

Coconut
Tree Divers

@ Paradise Computers

Captain
Van's
Rentals

Reef Gliders

West End Divers

Eagle Ray
Café

Sandy Bay & Coxen Hole

West Bay (3km)

EATING & DRINKING

Argentinian Grill	C
Creole Rotisserie	4
Galley	1
Purple Turtle	2
Twisted Toucan	3

C A R I B B E A N   S E A

Foster's

Boats to
West Bay

**ROATÁN:
WEST END**

0   100 m

events, consult the excellent monthy magazine *Bay Islands Voice* or its **website**, Ⓦ www.bayislandsvoice .com; alternatively, try Ⓦ www .roatanisland.net.

Coxen Hole

COXEN HOLE is dusty and run-down, and most visitors avoid the place now that there are banks elsewhere. All the town's practical facilities and most shops are on a 100m stretch of **Main Street**, near where the buses stop. You'll find the headquarters of BICA (Mon–Fri 9am–noon & 2–5pm) here, if you want to learn more about Roatán's reefs, flora and fauna, as well as Banco Atlántida, which has an ATM and changes traveller's cheques and dollars. The **migración** and **post office** are both near the small square on Main Street. HB Warren is the largest **supermarket** on the island, while a small and not too impressive general market can be found just behind Main Street.

There's no reason to stay in town, but there are some restaurants and comedores dishing out cheap eats, while *Qué Tal Café* (Mon–Fri 9am–4pm) on the exit road towards Sandy Bay, serves European-style breakfasts, deli-style sandwiches and cappuccinos. Next door, Librería Casi Todo sells used **books**.

Sandy Bay

Midway between Coxen Hole and West End, **SANDY BAY** is an unassuming community with a couple of interesting attractions. The **Institute for Marine Sciences** (Mon, Tues, Thurs–Sun 9am–5pm; US$3), based at *Antony's Key Resort* (see below), has exhibitions on the marine life and geology of the islands and a museum with useful information on local history and archeology. The institute also puts on bottle-nosed **dolphin shows** (weekdays 10am & 4.30pm, Sat & Sun 10am, 1pm & 4pm; US$5), and offers the chance to dive or snorkel with the dolphins (US$112 & US$84 respectively; must be booked in advance on ☎445 1327). Across the road from the institute, several short nature trails weave through the jungle at the **Carambola Botanical Gardens** (daily 7am–5pm; US$5), a riot of flowers, lush ferns and tropical trees. A twenty-minute walk from the gardens up Monte Carambola, the **Iguana Wall** is a section of cliff that's a breeding ground for iguanas and parrots. From the top of the mountain you can see across to Utila on clear days.

The Sandy Bay area has several places **to stay**, all of which are clearly signposted, including the pleasant *Tri R Resort* (☎445 1623; ❺), with large air-conditioned rooms with private bath and a good restaurant; and several dive resorts, the best of which is PADI five-star *Anthony's Key Resort* (☎445 1003, ⓦ www.anthonyskey.com; weekly packages from US$559). *Anthony's* is one of the smartest places on the island, with 56 gorgeous cabins set among the trees and on a small caye. Popular places **to eat** include *Rick's American Café* (closed Wed) set on the hillside above the road and serving giant US-style burgers and ribs.

West End

With its calm waters and incredible white beaches, **WEST END**, 14km from Coxen Hole, makes the most of its ideal setting, gearing itself mainly towards independent travellers on all budgets, with a good selection of attractive accommodation. Set in the southwest corner of the island, round a shallow bay, the village has retained a laid-back charm, and the gathering pace of tourist development has done little to dent the locals' friendliness.

The paved road from Coxen Hole finishes at the northern end of the village, not far from **Half Moon Bay**, a beautifully sheltered sandy beach ringed with hotels. Turning to the south at the end of the paved road from Coxen Hole, a sandy track runs alongside the water's edge through the heart of West End, passing a merry bunch of guesthouses, bars and restaurants set between patches of coconut palms. You can rent **cars** from Roatán Rentals, at the north of West

▲ Sandy Beach, Roatán

End, or Sandy Bay Rent-a-Car close by; Captain Van's rent out bicycles (US$11), and overpriced mopeds (from US$46) and motorbikes (from US$50). For **internet access** head to Paradise Computers (daily 8am–9.30pm) near the junction for Coxen Hole.

Accommodation

Most of the **accommodation** in West End and Half Moon Bay is charmingly individualistic, though pricey by Central American standards. Discounts are available during low season (April–July & Sept to mid-Dec), particularly for longer stays.

Chillie's Half Moon Bay ☎445 4003, ⓦwww.nativesonsroatan.com/chillies.htm. A great choice for budget travellers, this deservedly popular place has dorm beds (US$8) and private rooms (some with private bath) plus a guests' kitchen in an attractive wooden house. Camping (US$6) available. It's right on the beach and also home to Native Sons Divers. ❸–❹

Half Moon Bay Cabins Half Moon Bay ☎445 1075. Fourteen secluded, simply furnished cabins scattered around wooded grounds close to the water's edge; all have fan or a/c. There's also an expensive restaurant. Kayaks and snorkel gear are free for guests. ❼–❽

Mariposa Lodge up a side street ☎445 4460, ⓦwww.mariposa-lodge.com. Occupying a lovely old Caribbean building, this quiet lodge has two apartments – complete with sundecks, kitchen and cable TV – plus some spacious private rooms. Massages ($35) can be arranged. ❻

Pinocchio's up a side road ☎445 1481, ⓔpinocchio69@bigfoot.com. A small, personable hotel, occupying a wooden building set on a small hill above the village. Rooms are clean and airy, if a little basic, though all have hot-water bath and ceiling fans. There's a good restaurant here, too. ❺

Posada Arco Iris Half Moon Bay ☎445 4264, ⓦwww.roatanposada.com. A small, well-run lodge just off the beach with excellent, stylishly presented and spacious rooms, studios and apartments, all with fridge and hammocks, and some with a/c. ❺–❼

Valerie's about 100m along West End, then up a signposted dirt track ⓦwww.roatanonline.com /valeries. Venerable love-it-or-hate-it bohemian hostel set up with a profusion of quirky accommodation, including two trailer-style rooms, two apartments, a small house, a flat with hot tub and a large dorm (US$5 per head); guests can also use the kitchen. ❷–❸

Eating and drinking

There's a more than adequate range of **places to eat** in West End, with fish, seafood and pasta featuring heavily on many menus, though prices are well above mainland Honduran rates. **Drinking** can also drain your pocket fast, so it's best to seek out the half-price happy hours. The *Purple Turtle* and *Twisted Toucan*, halfway along the seafront, are two of the liveliest bars, except on Fridays, when everyone heads to *Foster's* for the weekly reggae jump-up.

Argentinian Grill Half Moon Bay. Argentinean-run restaurant with authentic *churrascos*, grilled meat and seafood at mid-range prices; expect to pay around US$12–20 a head. Portions are huge, the service efficient and there's an extensive wine list including Malbec and Sauvignon Blanc wines from South America.

Creole Rotisserie close to the junction. Humble place offering very flavoursome spit-roasted chicken, plus a few other options at budget prices. **Galley** beside Paradise Computers. Relaxed, laid-back place that's good for breakfast and has some very tasty, well-priced lunch specials; the pasta is excellent at around US$4 a plate.

West Bay

Two kilometres southwest of West End, towards the extreme western tip of Roatán, is the stunning white-sand beach of **WEST BAY**, fringed by coconut palms and washed by crystal-clear waters. The beach's tranquillity has been mildly disrupted by a rash of cabaña and hotel construction, but provided you avoid the sandflies by sunbathing on the jetties, it's still a sublime place to relax and enjoy the Caribbean. There's decent **snorkelling** at the southern end of the beach too, though the once pristine reef has suffered in recent years from increasing river run-off and the close attentions of unsupervised day-trippers.

From West End, it's a pleasant forty five-minute stroll south along the beach and over a few rock outcrops; alternatively, take one of the small **launches** that leave *Foster's* regularly – the last one returns around 7pm (9pm in high season). A paved road also runs here: from West End, head up the road to Coxen Hole and take the first turning on the right. If you want **to stay**, the *Bananarama* (ⓣ992 9679, ⓦwww.bananaramadive.com; ⑦–⑨) has overpriced but cute and comfortable wood cabins with mosquito nets and suites, while the very well run ⚐ *West Bay Lodge* (ⓣ445 5069, ⓦwww.westbaylodge.com; ⑧–⑨ including breakfast) behind the beach offers lovely, stylishly presented wooden bungalows, some with kitchens for a little more. Both *Bananarama* and the *Island Pearl* hotel on West Bay have good in-house **dive schools**.

Eastern Roatán

Leaving Coxen Hole, the paved road runs northeast past the small secluded cove of Brick Bay and the ferry terminal at Dixon Cove to **FRENCH HARBOUR**, a busy fishing port and the island's second largest town. Less run-down than Coxen Hole, it's an enjoyable place to visit for a meal, though the hotels here are not great value. *El Faro* (ⓣ455 5214; ⑥) is a reasonable place; it's above the renowned, if pricey, *Gio's* harbourfront restaurant where there's a great outdoor deck and the speciality is king crab. Also on the waterfront *Casa Romeo* (ⓣ455 5854, ⓦwww.casaromeo.com; ⑦) is a modern hotel with comfortable air-conditioned rooms and a fine restaurant with fresh pasta and plenty of seafood. Should you have time, stop by the **Iguana Reserve** (daily 8am–4pm; US$5), home to more than 2800 specimens of four species; all the proceeds of the entry fee go towards the care of the reptiles; it's just west of town.

From French Harbour the road cuts inland along a central ridge to give superb views of both the north and south coasts of the island. After about 14km it reaches **OAK RIDGE**, an attractive fishing port with wooden houses strung along its harbour. There are some nice unspoiled beaches to the east of town, accessible by launches from the main dock. About 5km from Oak Ridge on the northern coast of the island is the village of **PUNTA GORDA**, the oldest Garífuna community in Honduras. The best time to visit is for the anniversary of the founding of the settlement (April 6–12), when Garífuna from all over the country attend the celebrations. At other times it's a quiet and slightly dilapidated little port with no historical buildings. Sadly, the new "cultural centre" Yübu (Tues–Fri 10am–3pm; ⓦwww.garifunaexperience.com; US$5) is a disappointing tourist trap geared at cruise-ship passengers. Punta Gorda does have a few inexpensive comedors. From the end of the paved road at Punta Gorda you can continue driving along the dirt track which runs east along the island, passing the turn-off for the secluded **Paya Beach** after around 1.5km, where there's a good, small hotel, the *Paya Beach Resort* (ⓣ924 2220, ⓦwww.payabay .com; ⓞ US$1175 for a week package including full board, diving and meals), which is beautifully situated above two sandy bays; scuba diving is organized in conjunction with a neighbouring dive school. A further 5km or so along is **Camp Bay Beach**, an idyllic, almost undeveloped stretch of white sand and coconut palms. The road ends at the village of **PORT ROYAL**, on the southern edge of the island, where the faint remains of a fort built by the English can be seen on a caye offshore. The village lies in the **Port Royal Park and Wildlife Reserve**, the largest refuge on the island, set up in 1978 in an attempt to protect endangered species such as the yellow-napped Amazon parrot, as well as the watershed for eastern Roatán.

The eastern tip of Roatán is made up of mangrove swamps, with the small island of **Morat** just offshore. Beyond is **Barbareta Caye**, which has retained much of its virgin forest cover. The reef around Barbareta and the nearby Pigeon Cayes offers excellent snorkelling; launches can be hired to reach these islands from Oak Ridge for around US$75 for a return trip.

Guanaja

The easternmost Bay Island, **GUANAJA**, was the most beautiful, densely forested and undeveloped of them all until Hurricane Mitch laid siege to it for more than two days during October 1998, lashing the land with winds of up to 300kph. Reforestation projects have been implemented, but the landscape will take decades to recover. The island is some 25km long and up to 4km wide, and is divided by a narrow canal – the only way to get around is by water-taxi, which adds to the cost of living. Most of Guanaja's 12,000 inhabitants live in **Bonacca** (also know as Guanaja Town), a crowded settlement that sits on a small caye a few hundred metres offshore. It's here that you'll find the island's shops, as well as the bulk of the reasonably priced accommodation. The only other settlements of any substance are **Savannah Bight** (on the east coast) and **Mangrove Bight** (on the north coast).

Arrival and information

Guanaja **airstrip** is about 2km east of Bonacca. There are no roads, aside from a couple of dirt tracks, and the main form of transport is in small launches. **Boats** from the main dock in Bonacca meet all flights and rides can be hitched on private boats to Mangrove Bight for a nominal fee. There's a twice-weekly **ferry** (US$30; 2hr) to/from the mainland, leaving Trujillo (Tues 3pm & Sat 9am) and returning from Guanaja (Wed 9am & Sun 3pm), plus daily flights from La Ceiba.

Virtually all the houses in Bonacca are built on stilts – vestiges of early settlement by the Cayman Islanders – the buildings clinging to wooden causeways over the canals, many of which have now been filled in. The main causeway, running for about 500m east–west along the caye, with a maze of small passages branching off it, is where you'll find all the shops, businesses and a couple of banks, though no ATMs – expect a long wait to cash traveller's cheques or organize a cash advance.

Accommodation

Most hotels in Guanaja are all-inclusive luxury **dive resorts** offering weekly packages. You'll also find a small number of mid-range **hotels** in Bonacca – though none are particularly good value for money.

Bonacca

Hotel Miller halfway along the main causeway ☎ 453 4327. Family-run hotel with tidy rooms, all with hot water, a/c and cable TV. ❹

Hotel Nights Inn at the extreme western end of the causeway ☎ 453 4465. Clean, comfortable and fairly spacious rooms, all with cable TV and a/c. ❺

The rest of the island

Dunbar Rock ☎ 453 4506. Unusual modern hotel with six rooms and a bar-restaurant. built on a small rocky island. All the rooms have spectacular sea views, there's great snorkelling, and diving can be organized. Obviously it is very isolated! ❽

Island House on the north side of the island ☎ 991 0913, ⓦ www.bosislandhouse.com. Pleasant Caribbean-style accommodation, and owned by a friendly local dive instructor, this place is close to several expanses of beautiful beach and a quick swim from the reef wall. Dive/ non-dive all-inclusive, full-board packages are US$500–650 per week.

West Peak Inn ⓦ www.westpeakinn.com. Enjoys a great beach location and has stylish wooden cabins. The lovely palapa-roofed restaurant serves healthy cuisine including plenty of fresh seafood. Great kayak trips and scuba diving can be organized. ❾

Around the island

Guanaja's Caribbean pine forests were flattened by Mitch but are now regrowing, and there's still some decent **hiking** across the island. A wonderful trail leads from Mangrove Bight up to **Michael's Peak** (415m), the highest point of the entire Bay Islands, and down to Sandy Bay on the south coast, affording stunning views of Guanaja, Bonacca and the surrounding reef. Fit walkers can do the trail in a day, or you can camp at the summit, provided you bring your own provisions.

Some of the island's finest white-sand **beaches** lie around the rocky headland of **Michael's Rock**, near the *Island House Resort* on the north coast, with good snorkelling close to the shore. **Diving** is excellent all around the main island, but particularly off the small cayes to the east, and at **Black Rocks**, off the northern tip of the main island, where there's an underwater coral canyon. The **Mestizo Dive Site** was opened in 2002 to mark the 500th anniversary of Columbus's visit, with sunken statues of the explorer and national hero Lempira on a reef surrounded by genuine Spanish colonial artefacts, including a cannon.

To get to these sites you'll have to contact one of the hotel-based dive schools. The *Island House Resort* usually has the best rates at around US$80 for two dives including equipment. **Fishing** and **snorkelling** can be arranged with local boatmen. In many areas the reef is close enough to swim to if you have your own snorkel gear.

Eating and drinking

There are several **restaurants** in Bonacca, though none are particularly cheap. In the centre of Bonacca itself, try *Pirate's Den* for fresh seafood with daily lunch specials and Friday barbecues. For Mexican food head to *Mexi-Treats*, while *Best Stop*, next to the basketball court, is good for snacks, cakes and sticky buns, as well as a variety of fast food. The funkiest **bar** in town is *Nit's Bar*, just east of the main dock, where the clapboard walls shake to classic reggae sounds.

Travel details

Buses

Copán Ruinas Town see "Moving on from Copan", p.364.
Corinto to: Puerto Cortés (hourly; 1hr 30min).
El Florido border to: Chiquimula (every 30min; 1hr 30min); Copán Ruinas Town (every 30min; 20min).
Puerto Cortés to: Corinto (hourly; 1hr 30min); San Pedro Sula (every 30min; 1hr).
San Pedro Sula to: La Ceiba (21 daily; 3hr 30min); Puerto Cortés (every 30min; 1hr).

Shuttle buses

Antigua to: Copán (1 daily at 4am; 6hr).
Copán to: Antigua (2 daily at 5.30am & noon; 6hr).

Boats

La Ceiba to: Roatán (2 daily at 9.30am & 4.30pm; 1hr 15min); Utila (2 daily at 9.30am & 4pm; 1hr).
Roatán to: La Ceiba (2 daily at 7am & 2pm).
Utila to: La Ceiba (2 daily at 6.20am & 2pm).

Flights

See p.375 for international flight details.
La Ceiba to: Guanaja (4 daily; 40min); Roatán (12 daily; 30min); Utila (4 daily; 20min).

Contexts

Contexts

History

L ittle is known about the area that is now called Guatemala in the days before the advent of Maya civilization, and even the early origins of the Maya remain fairly mysterious. Today, the Maya region is one of the world's hottest archeological areas, and recent excavations have fostered a greater understanding of the region's history but also ripped apart many previously accepted theories. Although the historical picture is becoming much clearer, many issues are still subject to furious academic polemic.

Prehistory

Opinions differ as to when the first people arrived in the Americas, but the most widely accepted theory is that **Stone Age hunter-gatherers** crossed the Bering land bridge from Siberia to Alaska in several waves beginning 25,000 years ago. Travelling along an ice-free corridor (and possibly in small boats along the coastline) they migrated south into Central America. The first recognizable culture, known as **Clovis**, had emerged by 11,000 BC, and stone tools, including spearpoints, blades and scrapers, dating from 9000 BC have been found in the Guatemalan highlands.

In **Mesoamerica**, an area defined as stretching from north-central Mexico through Central America to Panama, the first settled pattern of development took place around 8000 BC, as a warming climate forced the hunter-gatherers to adapt to a different way of life. The glaciers were in retreat and the big game, upon which the hunters depended, became scarce due to the warmer, drier climate (and possibly over-hunting). This period, in which the hunters turned to more intensive use of plant foods, is known as the Archaic period and lasted until about 2000 BC. During this time the food vital to the subsequent development of agriculture, such as corn, beans, peppers, squash and probably maize, were domesticated.

The early Maya

After 2000 BC we move into the **Preclassic** era, a name used by archeologists to describe the earliest developments in the history of the **Maya**. During the **Early Preclassic** (2000–1000 BC), the Maya settled in villages throughout the region, as the foragers became farmers and began making pottery. By 1100 BC, the **Olmec**, often called Mesoamerica's "mother culture", were constructing pyramid-like ceremonial platforms and carving colossal stone heads at San Lorenzo, just to the northwest of the Maya region. Their artistic, polytheistic religious (and almost certainly political) influence spread throughout Maya lands, and Olmec-style carvings have been found at numerous sites along Guatemala's Pacific coast, in El Salvador and at Copán, in Honduras. The Olmec also developed an early writing system and a calendar known as the "Long Count", later adopted by the Maya.

The population increased substantially across the Maya region during the **Middle Preclassic** period (1000–400 BC). In northern Petén, **Nakbé** had, by

750 BC, grown to become perhaps the first Maya city, complete with imposing temples and stucco sculptures – evidence that the Maya had progressed far beyond a simple peasant society. By 500 BC other settlements – including El Mirador and Cival – were building their first ceremonial structures and astronomical observatories. It is thought that a common language was spoken throughout the Maya lands, and that a universal belief system, practised from a very early date, may have provided the stimulus and social cohesion to build bigger towns and religious temples. Materials including obsidian and jade from the Guatemalan highlands and granite and salt from Belize were widely traded. Pottery, including red and orange jars and dishes of the Mamon style, has been found at a number of settlements, indicating increasing pan-Maya communication. At the same time, food surpluses and rising prosperity levels gradually enabled some inhabitants to eschew farming duties and become seers, priests and astronomers.

Greater advances in architecture were achieved in the **Late Preclassic** (400 BC–250 AD) as other cities prospered in northern Petén, and the Mirador Basin (see p.337) became the focus of Maya civilization. At the start of this era, Nakbé was the dominant city – its ceremonial core rebuilt to include a soaring cluster of temples and its plazas studded with carved stelae. But the focus quickly shifted to **El Mirador**, 12km to the north, which expanded to become a massive city, spread over twenty square kilometres, with a population of around 100,000. Taking advantage of the swampland that surrounded their city, Mirador's inhabitants fertilized vast fields of crops using rich muck from nearby marshes and seasonal lakes. Almost nothing is known about the power politics of these times, but the sheer size of El Mirador indicates that the city must have acquired "superstate" status by around 100 BC. Positioned at the heart of a vast trading network, the city was surrounded by hundreds of other smaller settlements like Tintal and Xulnal, all connected by a web of stone causeways. The La Danta temple complex at Mirador was constructed to a height of 78m – the highest building ever to have been built by a pre-Columbian culture in the Americas – a feat that took an estimated 15 million days of labour. El Mirador's only serious rival during the Late Classic era was located several hundred kilometres to the south, on the site of the modern capital of Guatemala City. **Kaminaljuyú** had established a formidable commercial empire based on the supply of obsidian and jade, and held sway over a string of settlements along the Pacific coast, including Takalik Abaj. It's clear that the southern Maya area was much more influenced by Olmec advances at this time. From 1 AD pyramids and temple platforms were emerging at Tikal, Uaxactún and many other sites in Petén, in what amounted to an explosion of Maya culture. The famous Maya corbelled arch was developed in this period, and architectural styles became more ambitious. (The corbelled arch was not a true arch, with a keystone, but consisted of two sides, each with stones overlapping until they eventually met, and thus could only span a relatively narrow gap.) A stratified **Maya society** was also becoming established, the nascent states led by rulers and shamanic priests who presided over religious ceremonies dictated by astronomical and calendrical events. There were specialist craftsmen, architects, scribes and artists capable of creating the exquisite murals of San Bartolo (which were only rediscovered in 2002). Intensive agriculture was also practised using irrigation from vast reservoirs via extensive canal networks.

But towards the end of the Late Preclassic period, during the second and third centuries AD, environmental disasters, and possibly protracted warfare, plagued the region. El Mirador and all its satellite cities collapsed by 150 AD, after a long dry climatic period and the severe over-exploitation of the forest

Maya archeological periods

The names given to **Maya archeological periods** are confusing, not least because when the time periods were established in the mid-twentieth century very little was known about the formative years of Maya civilization. Recent findings have pushed back the dates when the earliest breakthroughs were made and it's only in the past fifteen years that remote cities like El Mirador and Nakbé have begun to be substantially excavated, revealing that the Preclassic period was far more advanced than previously thought.

The archeological periods vary according to the source. This guide follows those used in the *Chronicle of the Maya Kings and Queens* by Simon Martin and Nikolai Grube (see "Books", p.454).

Pre–2000 BC	Archaic
2000 BC–1000 BC	Early Preclassic
1000 BC–400 BC	Middle Preclassic
400 BC–250 AD	Late Preclassic
250 AD–600 AD	Early Classic
600 AD–800 AD	Late Classic
800 AD–909 AD	Terminal Classic
909 AD–1200 AD	Early Postclassic
1200 AD–Spanish Conquest	Late Postclassic

environment which severely cut agricultural production. In the southern region, the eruption of the **Ilopango volcano** in central El Salvador smothered a vast area in ash, probably provoking mass migration from cities as far away as Kaminaljuyú, which was virtually abandoned around 250 AD. Temple building and stelae carving ceased. Pacific trade routes between the southern Maya region and Mexico were disrupted, and much of the trade was re-routed to the north, bringing prosperity (but also Central Mexican influence) to the cities of central Petén, including Tikal.

The Classic Maya

The development that separates the Late Preclassic from the **Classic period** (250–909 AD) is the introduction of the Long Count calendar and a recognizably Maya form of writing. This occurred by the end of the third century AD and marks the beginning of the greatest phase of Maya achievement.

During the Classic period all the cities we now know as ruined or restored sites were built, almost always over earlier structures. Elaborately carved **stelae**, bearing dates and emblem glyphs, were erected at regular intervals. These tell of actual rulers and of historical events in their lives – battles, marriages, dynastic succession and so on. Developments in the Maya area during the Early Classic period were still heavily influenced by a giant power to the north – **Teotihuacán**, which dominated Central Mexico and boasted a population of over 150,000. Its **armed merchants**, called *pochteca*, spread the authority of Teotihuacán as far as Petén, the Yucatán and Copán. It's unlikely that Teotihuacán launched an outright military invasion of Maya territory, but the city's influence was strong enough to precipitate fundamental changes in the region. In 378 AD, an armed merchant called Siyak K'ak ushered in a takeover of Tikal, establishing a new dynasty, while at

Copán, Yax K'uk Mo' (who was almost certainly from Teotihuacán) founded that city's royal lineage in 426 AD. These Mexicans also brought alternative religious beliefs, and new styles of ceramics, art and architecture – Kaminaljuyú was rebuilt in Teotihuacán style, and Tikal and Copán temples and stelae from the era depict Central Mexican gods.

Yet while Tikal was positioning itself within the Teotihuacán sphere of influence and dominating the Petén region, an increasingly precocious rival Maya state was emerging to the north in Campeche: **Calakmul**, "the kingdom of the snake". From the fifth century, these two states grew to eclipse all other cities in the Maya World, establishing dominion over huge swathes of the region. Each controlling sophisticated trade networks, they jostled for supremacy, a struggle which eventually erupted into open warfare once Teotihuacán influence faded in the sixth century. Calakmul formed an alliance with **Caracol** (today located in Belize) and defeated Tikal in 562 AD – detailed carvings depict elaborately costumed lords trampling on bound captives. This victory caused a hiatus in Tikal's empire building during which there was little new construction at the city or in the smaller centres under its patronage.

The prosperity and grandeur of the **Late Classic** period (600–800 AD) reached across the Maya lands: from Bonampak and Palenque in the west, to Labná, Sayil, Calakmul and Uxmal in the north, Altun Ha in the east, and Copán and Quiriguá in the south, as well as hundreds of smaller centres. Bound together by a coherent religion and culture, Maya architecture, astronomy and art reached degrees of sophistication unequalled by any other pre-Columbian society. Trade prospered and populations grew – by 750 AD it's estimated that the region's people numbered around ten million. Many Maya states were larger than contemporary western European cities, then in their "Dark Ages". Masterpieces of painted pottery and carved jade (their most precious material) were created, often to be used as funerary offerings. Shell, bone and, occasionally, marble were also exquisitely carved; temples were painted in brilliant colours, inside and out. Most of the pigments faded long ago, but vestiges remain, enabling experts to reconstruct vivid images of the appearance of the ancient cities.

In the power politics of the era, Tikal avenged its bitter defeat by overrunning Calakmul in 695 AD and reasserting its influence over its former vassal states of Río Azul and Waka' (El Perú). In a furious epoch of monument building, five of the great temples that define the ceremonial heart of the city were finished between 670 and 810 AD. Elsewhere across Maya lands, cities including Piedras Negras, Yaxhá, Yaxchilán and Dos Pilas flourished as never before, giving rise to more and more imposing temples and palaces, and unparalleled artistic achievements.

The Maya in decline

The glory days were not to last very long, however. By 750 AD political and social changes were beginning to be felt; alliances and trade links broke down, wars increased and stelae recording periods of time were carved less frequently. After 800 AD we move into a period known as the **Terminal Classic** during which the great cities gradually became depopulated, and new construction virtually ceased in the central area after about 830 AD. Bonampak was abandoned before its famous murals could be completed, while many of the great sites along the Usumacinta river (now part of the border between Guatemala and Mexico) were occupied by militaristic outsiders.

The reason for the decline of the Maya is not (and may never be) known, though it was probably a result of several factors. It's known that Maya lands were already under severe pressure from deforestation by the late ninth century, when the region was struck by a terrible **drought**. An incredibly high population density put great strains on food production, possibly exhausting the fertility of the soil, and epidemics may have combined to cause the abandonment of city life. Some Mayanists speculate that there may have been a peasant revolt caused by mass hunger and the demands of an unproductive elite. Whatever the causes, strife and disorder appear to have spread throughout Mesoamerica by the end of the Classic period. In the Maya heartland, virtually all the key cities were abandoned, and those few that remained were reduced to a fairly primitive state. Some survived on the periphery, however, particularly in northern Belize, with Lamanai and other cities remaining inhabited throughout the **Postclassic** period (909 AD to the Spanish conquest). The settlements in the Yucatán peninsula also struggled on, and though the region escaped the worst of the depopulation, it was conquered by the militaristic **Toltecs** from central Mexico in 987 AD, creating a hybrid of Classic Maya culture.

With the decline of Maya civilization in the Petén lowlands undoubtedly came an influx of population into Belize, Yucatán and the Guatemalan highlands to the south. These areas, formerly marginal regions of relatively little development, now contained the last vestiges of Maya culture, and it's at this time that the Guatemala highland area began to take on some of the tribal characteristics still in evidence today. By the end of the Classic period there were small settlements throughout the highlands, usually built on open valley floors and supporting large populations sustained by terraced farming and irrigation. Little was to change in this basic village structure for several hundred years.

Pre-conquest: the highland tribes

Towards the end of the thirteenth century, however, the great cities of the Yucatán, such as Chichén Itzá and Uxmal, which had been under the control of **Toltec Maya** from the gulf coast of Mexico, were also abandoned. At around the same time, Toltec–Maya invaded the central Guatemalan highlands. Their numbers were probably small but their impact was profound, and following their arrival life in the highlands was radically altered.

What once had been a relatively settled, peaceful and religious society became, under the influence of the Toltecs, fundamentally secular, aggressive and militaristic. The Toltec invaders were ruthlessly well organized and in no time at all they established themselves as a ruling elite, founding a series of competing empires. The greatest of these were the **K'iche'**, who dominated the central area and established their capital, **K'umarkaaj** (later known as Utatlán), to the west of the modern town of Santa Cruz del Quiché. Next in line were the **Kaqchikel**, who were originally based around the modern town of Chichicastenango, but moved their capital to **Iximché** to the south. On the southern shores of Lago de Atitlán, the **Tz'utujil** had their capital on the lower slopes of the San Pedro volcano. To the west the **Mam** occupied the area around the modern town of Huehuetenango, with their capital at **Zaculeu**, while the northern slopes of the Cuchumatanes were home to a collection of smaller groups such as the **Chuj**, the **Q'anjob'al**, and further to the east the **Awakateko** and the **Ixil**. The eastern highlands, around the modern city of Cobán, were home to the notoriously fierce **Achi** nation, with the **Q'eqchi'** to their north, while around the modern site of Guatemala City the land was controlled by the **Poqomam**, with their capital at **Mixco Viejo**. Finally, along the Pacific coast, the **Pipil**, a tribe that had also migrated from the north, occupied the lowlands.

The sheer numbers of these tribes give an impression of the extent to which the area was fragmented, and it's these same divisions, now surviving on the basis of language alone, that still shape the highlands today (see map, p.430).

The Toltec rulers probably controlled only the dominant tribes – the K'iche', Mam and Kaqchikel – while their lesser neighbours were still made up entirely of people indigenous to the area. Arriving in the latter part of the thirteenth century, the Toltecs must have terrorized the local K'iche'–Kaqchikel highlanders and gradually established themselves in a new, rigidly hierarchical society. They brought with them many northern traditions – elements of a Nahua-based language, new gods and an array of military skills – and fused these with local ideas. Many of the rulers' names are similar to those used in the Toltec heartland to the north, and they claimed to trace their ancestry to Quetzalcoatl, a mythical ruling dynasty from the Toltec city of Tula. Shortly after the Spanish conquest, the K'iche' wrote an account of their history, the Popol Vuh, in which they lay claim to a Toltec pedigree, as do the Kaqchikel in their account, *The Annals of the Kaqchikel*.

The Toltec invaders were not content with overpowering just a tribe or two, so under the direction of their new rulers the K'iche' began to expand their empire – between 1400 and 1475 they brought the Kaqchikel, the Mam and several other tribes under their control. At the height of their power, around a million highlanders bowed to the word of the K'iche' king. But in 1475 the man who had masterminded their expansion, the great K'iche' ruler **Quicab**, died, and the empire lost much of its authority. The Kaqchikel were the first to break from the fold, anticipating the death of Quicab and moving south to a new and fortified capital, Iximché, in around 1470. Shortly afterwards the other tribes managed to escape the grip of K'iche' control and assert their independence. For the next fifty years or so the tribes were in a state of almost perpetual conflict, fighting for access to the inadequate supplies of farmland. The archeological remains from this era give evidence of this instability; gone are the valley-floor centres of pre-Toltec times, and in their place are fortified hilltop sites, surrounded by ravines and man-made ditches.

When the Spanish arrived, the highlands were in crisis. The population had grown so fast that it had outstripped the food supply, forcing the tribes to fight for any available land in order to increase their agricultural capacity. With a growing sense of urgency both the K'iche' and the Kaqchikel had begun to encroach on the lowlands of the Pacific coast. The situation could hardly have been more favourable to the Spanish, who fostered this intertribal friction, playing one group off against another.

The Spanish conquest

While the tribes of highland Guatemala were fighting it out amongst themselves, their northern neighbours, in what is now Mexico, were confronting a formidable new enemy. In 1521, the Spanish conquistadors had captured the Aztec capital at Tenochtitlán and were starting to cast their net further afield. Amidst the horrors of the Conquest there was one man whose ambition, cunning and cruelty stood out above the rest – **Pedro de Alvarado**.

In 1523, conquistador leader Hernán Cortés dispatched Alvarado to Guatemala, entreating him to use the minimum of force "and to preach matters concerning our Holy Faith". His army included 120 horsemen, 173 horses, 300 soldiers and 200 Mexican warriors, largely Tlaxcalans who had allied themselves with Cortés in the conquest of Mexico. Marching south they entered Guatemala along the Pacific coast, where they met with the first wave of resistance, a small army of K'iche' warriors. These were no match for the Spaniards, who cut through their ranks with ease. From here Alvarado turned north, taking his troops up into the highlands and through a narrow mountain pass to the Quetzaltenango valley, where they came upon the deserted city of **Xelajú**, a K'iche' outpost.

Warned of the impending arrival of the Spanish, the K'iche' had struggled to build an alliance with the other tribes, but old rivalries proved too strong and the **K'iche'** army stood alone. Three days later, on a nearby plain, they met the Spaniards in open warfare. Alvarado claimed the invaders were confronted by some 30,000 K'iche' warriors (though this figure is almost certainly an exaggeration) led by their leader **Tecún Umán** in a headdress of quetzal feathers. Despite the huge disparity in numbers, slingshot and foot soldiers were no match for cavalry and gunpowder, and the Spaniards were once again able to triumph, and burnt the K'iche' capital to the ground. Having dealt with the K'iche', Alvarado turned his attention to the other tribal groups. The **Kaqchikel**, recognizing the military superiority of the Spanish, decided to form some kind of alliance with them. As a result, the Spaniards established their first headquarters, in 1523, alongside the Kaqchikel capital of **Iximché**. From here they ranged far and wide, overpowering the countless smaller tribes. Travelling west, Alvarado's army defeated the **Tz'utujil** on the shores of Lago de Atitlán, aided by Kaqchikel warriors who arrived on the scene in some three hundred canoes. In 1524, Alvarado sent his brother Gonzalo on an expedition against the **Mam**, who were conquered after a month-long siege during which they holed up in their fortified capital, **Zaculeu**. The next year, Alvarado himself set out to take on the **Poqomam** at their capital, **Mixco Viejo**, where he came up against an army of some three thousand warriors. Once again they proved no match for the well-disciplined Spanish ranks.

Despite this string of relatively easy victories, it wasn't until well into the 1530s that Alvarado managed to assert control over the more remote parts of the highlands. Moving into the Cuchumatanes his forces were beaten back by the **Uspanteko** and met fierce opposition in the **Ixil** region. And while Alvarado's soldiers were struggling to contain resistance in these isolated mountainous areas, problems also arose at the very heart of the campaign. In 1526, the Kaqchikel revolted against the Spanish, abandoning their capital and moving into the mountains, from where they waged a guerrilla war against their former partners. The Spanish were forced to abandon their base at Iximché, and moved instead to a site near the modern town of Antigua.

Here, on St Cecilia's Day, November 22, 1527, they established their first permanent capital, the city of **Santiago de los Caballeros**. For ten years indigenous labourers toiled in the construction of the new city, neatly sited at the base of the Agua volcano, building a cathedral, a town hall, and a palace for Alvarado. Meanwhile, one particularly thorny problem for the Spanish was presented by the **Achi** and **Q'eqchi'** Maya, who occupied what are now the Verapaz highlands. Despite all his efforts, Alvarado was unable to conquer either of these tribes, who fought fiercely against the invading armies. In the end he gave up on trying to control the area, naming it Tierra de Guerra. The situation was eventually resolved by the Church. In 1537, **Fray Bartolomé de Las**

Casas, the "protector of the Indians", travelled into the region in a bid to persuade the locals to accept both Christianity and Spanish authority. Within three years the priests had succeeded where Alvarado's armies had failed, and the last of the highland tribes was brought under colonial control in 1540. Thus did the area earn its name of Verapaz, "true peace".

Alvarado himself grew tired of the Conquest, disappointed by the lack of plunder, and his reputation for brutality began to spread. He was forced to return to Spain to face charges of treason, but returned a free man with a young wife at his side. Life in the New World soon sent his bride to an early grave, however, and Alvarado set out once again, in search of the great wealth that had eluded him in Guatemala. First he travelled south to Peru, where it's said that Francisco Pizarro, conqueror of the Inca nation, paid him to leave South America. He then returned to Spain once again, where he married **Beatriz de la Cueva**, his first wife's sister, and the two of them made their way back to Guatemala, where he dropped off his new bride before setting sail for the Spice Islands. Along the way he stopped in Mexico, to put down an uprising, and was crushed to death beneath a rolling horse.

From 1524 until his death in 1541, Alvarado had ruled Guatemala as a personal fiefdom, desperately seeking adventure and wealth, and enslaving and abusing the local population. By the time of his death all the Maya tribes had been overcome (except for tiny numbers of Itza), although local uprisings had already started to take place.

Colonial rule

The early years of colonial rule were marked by a turmoil of uprisings and political wrangling. When Alvarado's wife Beatriz de la Cueva heard of his death, she plunged the capital into a period of prolonged mourning. She had the entire palace painted black, inside and out, and ordered the city authorities to appoint her as the new governor. Meanwhile, the area was swept by a series of storms, and on the night of September 10, 1541, it was shaken by a massive earthquake. The sides of the Agua volcano shuddered, undermining the walls of the cone and releasing its contents. A great wall of mud and water swept down the side of the peak, burying the city of Santiago and most of its inhabitants.

The surviving colonial authorities moved up the valley to a new site, where a second **Santiago de los Caballeros** was founded in the following year. This new city served as the administrative headquarters of the **Audiencia de Guatemala**, which was made up of six provinces: Costa Rica, Nicaragua, San Salvador, Honduras, Guatemala and Chiapas (now part of Mexico). With Alvarado out of the way, the authorities began to build a new society, recreating the splendours of the homeland with a superb array of arts and architecture. By the mid-eighteenth century its population approached 80,000. Here colonial society was at its most developed, rigidly structured along racial lines with pure-blood Spaniards at the top, indigenous slaves at the bottom, and a host of carefully defined racial strata in between. The city was regularly shaken by scandal, intrigue and earthquakes, and it was eventually destroyed in 1773 by the last of these, after which the capital was moved to its modern site: Guatemala City.

Perhaps the greatest power in colonial Central America was the **Church**. The first religious order to reach Guatemala was the Franciscans, who arrived with Alvarado himself, and by 1532 the Mercedarians and Dominicans had followed suit, with the Jesuits arriving shortly after. **Francisco Marroquín**, the country's first bishop, rewarded these early arrivals with huge concessions, including land and indigenous people, which later enabled them to earn tax-free fortunes from sugar, wheat and indigo. In later years a whole range of other orders arrived in Santiago, and religious rivalry became an important shaping force in the colony. Through its wealth and power, the Church fostered the splendour of the colonial capital while ruthlessly exploiting the native people and their land. In Santiago alone there were some eighty churches, and alongside these were schools, convents, hospitals, hermitages, craft centres and colleges. The religious orders became the main benefactors of the arts, amassing a wealth of tapestry, jewels, sculpture and painting, and staging concerts, fiestas and endless religious processions. Religious persecution was at its worst between 1572 and 1580, when the office of the **Inquisition** sought out those who had failed to receive the faith and dealt with them harshly.

By the eighteenth century the power of the Church had started to get out of control, and the Spanish kings began to impose taxes on the religious orders and to limit their power and freedom. The conflict between Church and State came to a head in 1767, when Carlos III banished the Jesuits from the Spanish colonies.

The Spanish must have been disappointed with their conquest of Central America as it offered little in the way of plunder except meagre amounts of silver around Huehuetenango. In Central America the **colonial economy** was based on agriculture. The coastal area produced cacao, tobacco, cotton and, most valuable of all, indigo; the highlands were grazed with sheep and goats; and cattle were raised on coastal ranches. In the lowlands of Petén and the jungles of the lower Motagua valley, the mosquitoes and forests remained unchallenged, although here and there certain aspects of the forest were developed: chicle, the raw material of chewing gum, was bled from the sapodilla trees, as was sarsaparilla, used to treat syphilis.

At the heart of the colonial economy was the system of *repartamientos*, whereby the ruling classes were granted the right to extract labour from the indigenous population. It was this that established the system whereby the Maya population was transported to work in the plantations, a pattern – though no longer legally enforced – that remains a tremendous burden today.

Meanwhile, in the capital it was graft and corruption that controlled the movement of money, with titles and appointments sold to the highest bidder. All of the colony's wealth was funnelled through the city, and it was only here that the monetary economy really developed.

The impact of the Conquest was perhaps the greatest in the highlands, where the **Maya population** had their lives totally restructured. The first stage in this process was the *reducción*, whereby scattered native communities were combined into new Spanish-style towns and villages. Between 1543 and 1600 some seven hundred new settlements were created, each based around a Catholic church. Ostensibly, the purpose of this was to enable the Church to work on its newfound converts, but it also had the effect of pooling the available labour and making its exploitation (and the demand of tribute) that much easier. Maya **social structures** were also profoundly altered by post-conquest changes. The great central authorities that had previously dominated were now eradicated, replaced by local structures based in the new villages. *Caciques* (local chiefs) and *alcaldes* (mayors) now held the bulk of local power, which was bestowed on them by the Church. In the distant corners of the highlands, however, priests were few and far between, only visiting the villages from time to time. Those that they left in charge developed not only their own power structures but also their own religion, mixing the new with the old. By the start of the nineteenth century, the Maya population had largely recovered from the initial impact of the Conquest, and in many places these local structures became increasingly important. In each village *cofradías* (brotherhood groups) were entrusted with the care of saints, while *principales* (village elders) held the bulk of traditional authority, a situation that still persists today. Throughout the highlands, village uprisings became increasingly commonplace as the new indigenous culture became stronger and stronger.

Even more serious for the indigenous population than any social changes were the **diseases** that arrived with the conquistadors. Waves of plague, typhoid and fever swept through a population without any natural resistance to them. In the worst-hit areas the native population was cut by some ninety percent, and in many parts of the country their numbers were halved.

Two centuries of colonial rule totally reshaped the structure of Guatemalan society, giving it new cities, a new religion, a transformed economy and a racist hierarchy. Nevertheless, the impact of colonial rule was perhaps less marked than in many other parts of Latin America. Only two sizeable cities had emerged and the outlying areas had received little attention from the colonial authorities. And although the indigenous population had been ruthlessly exploited and suffered enormous losses at the hands of foreign weapons and imported diseases, its culture was never eradicated. It simply absorbed the symbols and ideas of the new Spanish ideology, creating a dynamic synthesis that is neither Maya nor Catholic.

Independence

The apartheid-style nature of colonial rule had given birth to deep dissatisfaction amongst many groups in Central America. Spain's policy was to keep wealth and power in the hands of those born in Spain (*chapetones*), a policy that left growing numbers of Creoles (including those of Spanish blood born in Guatemala) and *mestizos* (of mixed blood) resentful and hungry for power and change. (For the majority of the indigenous people, both power and wealth were way beyond their reach.) As the Spanish departed, Guatemalan politics was dominated by a struggle between **conservatives**, who sided with the Church and the Crown, and **liberals**, who advocated a secular and more egalitarian state. One result of the split was that independence was not a clean break, but was declared several times.

The spark, as throughout Spanish America, was Napoleon's invasion of Spain and the abdication of King Fernando VII. In the chaos that followed, a liberal constitution was imposed on Spain in 1812 and a mood of reform swept through the colonies. At the time, Central America was under the control of **Brigadier Don Gabino Gainza**, the last of the Captains General. His one concern was to maintain the status quo, in which he was strongly backed by the wealthy landowners and the Church hierarchy. Bowing to demands for independence, but still hoping to preserve the power structure, Gainza signed a formal **Act of Independence** on September 15, 1821, enshrining the authority of the Church and seeking to preserve the old order under new leadership. Augustín de Iturbide, the short-lived emperor of newly independent Mexico, promptly sent troops to annex Guatemala to the Mexican empire, a union which was to last less than a year.

Through a second Declaration of Independence, in 1823, Guatemala joined the Central American states in a loose **federation**, adopting a constitution modelled on that of the United States, abolishing slavery and advocating liberal reforms. These moves were bitterly opposed by the Church and conservatives throughout Central America, and provoked several inter-federation (and internal) conflicts. But in 1830 the political left of Salvador, Honduras and Guatemala united under the leadership of **Francisco Morazán**, a Honduran general, under whom **Mariano Gálvez** became the chief of state in Guatemala: religious orders were abolished, the death penalty done away with, and trial by jury, a general school system, civil marriage and the progressive Lívingston law code were all instituted.

This liberal era lasted until 1838 when the ailing Central American Federation was dissolved and the reforming Guatemalan administration overthrown by a revolt from the mountains. Throughout the turmoil of independence and brief years of the federation, life in the highlands remained harsh, with the indigenous population still bearing the burdens imposed on them by two centuries of colonial rule. Seething with discontent, the Maya were united behind an illiterate but charismatic leader, the 23-year-old **Rafael Carrera**, under whose command they marched on Guatemala City. Independence was declared in 1839, with Carrera installed first as a *caudillo* (strongman), and later as president.

Carrera respected no authority other than that of the Church, and his immediate reforms swept aside the changes instituted by the liberal government. The religious orders were restored to their former position and traditional Spanish titles were reinstated. Under Carrera, Guatemala fought a succession of conflicts against liberals in other parts of Central America, and eventually established itself as an independent republic in 1847. Carrera's greatest internal challenge came from the state of **Los Altos**, which included much of the western highlands and proclaimed itself an independent republic. It was a short-lived threat, however, and the would-be state was soon brought back into the republic.

When Carrera died, at the age of fifty in 1865, Guatemala was an impoverished nation (the export of indigo and cochinel had plummeted after the invention of artificial dyes), while its transport network was backward at best. Little was to change under his successor, **Vicente Cerna**, another conservative, who ruled until 1871, but during this period liberal opposition was again gathering momentum, and 1867 saw the first **liberal uprising**, led by **Serpio Cruz**. His bid for power was unsuccessful, but it inspired two young liberals, Justo Rufino Barrios and Francisco Cruz, to follow suit. In the next few years, they mounted several other unsuccessful revolts, and in 1870 Serpio Cruz was captured and hanged.

Rufino Barrios and the coffee boom

The year 1871 marked a major turning-point in Guatemalan politics, for in that year rebels Rufino Barrios and Miguel García Granados entered Guatemala from Mexico with an army of just 45 men. The **liberal revolution** set in motion was an astounding success, the army growing by the day as it approached the capital, which was finally taken on June 30, 1871. Granados took the helm of the new liberal administration but held the presidency for just a few years, surrounding himself with aging comrades and offering only very limited reforms.

Meanwhile, out in the district of Los Altos, **Rufino Barrios**, now a local military commander, was infuriated by the lack of action. In 1872 he marched his troops to the capital and installed them in the San José barracks, demanding immediate elections. These were granted and he won with ease. Barrios was a charismatic leader with tyrannical tendencies (monuments throughout the country testify to his sense of his own importance) who regarded himself as a great reformer. His most immediate acts were classic liberal gestures: the restructuring of the education system and an attack on the Church. The University of San Carlos was secularized and modernized, while clerics were forbidden to wear the cloth and public religious processions were banned. The Church was outraged and excommunicated Barrios, which prompted him to expel the archbishop in retaliation. Barrios' liberal perspective was undoubtedly instilled with a deep arrogance, and he would tolerate no political opposition, developing an effective network of secret police and ensuring that the army became an essential part of his political power base.

Barrios also set about reforming agriculture, and he presided over a boom period, largely as a result of the cultivation and export of **coffee**. To foster this expansion Barrios extended the railway network, established a national bank, and developed the ports of Champerico, San José and Iztapa. Between 1870 and 1900 the volume of foreign trade increased twenty times.

All this had an enormous impact on Guatemalan **society**. Many of the new plantations were owned and run by German immigrants, and the majority of the coffee eventually found its way to Europe. The newcomers soon formed a powerful elite and, although most of the Germans were later forced out of Guatemala (during World War II), their influence can still be felt, directly in the Verapaz highlands, and more subtly in the continuing presence of an extremely powerful political clique. The new liberal perspective maintained that foreign ideas were superior to indigenous ones, and while European immigrants were welcomed with open arms, the Maya population was still regarded as hopelessly inferior.

Indigenous society was also deeply affected by the needs of the coffee boom, as Barrios instituted a system of **forced labour**. By 1876 up to one quarter of the male Maya population could be dispatched to work on the coffee fincas, often under appalling conditions, while in the highlands landowners continued to employ a system of debt peonage.

As a result of the coffee boom, many Maya lost not only their freedom but also their land, as huge amounts of the country were seized. In many areas the villagers rose up in defiance, with significant **revolts** throughout the western highlands continuing into the twentieth century. Five hundred armed men faced the authorities in Momostenango, only to find their village overrun by troops and their homes burnt to the ground. These land seizures forced the Maya to become dependent on seasonal labour.

Jorge Ubico and the banana empire

Rufino Barrios, who was eventually killed in 1885 while fighting to re-establish a unified Central America, was succeeded by a string of short-lived but likeminded presidents. The next to hold power for any time was **Manuel Estrada Cabrera**, a stern authoritarian who restricted union organization and supported the interests of big business. He ruled from 1898 until he was overthrown in 1920, by which time he was on the verge of insanity.

Meanwhile, a new and exceptionally powerful player was becoming involved in the country's affairs – the **United Fruit Company**, which would assert its influence over much of Central America until the 1960s. The company, which got its start in Costa Rica, moved into Guatemala in 1901, when it bought a small tract of land on which to grow bananas. Three years later, it was awarded a contract to complete the railway from Guatemala City to Puerto Barrios, and in 1912 ownership of the Pacific railway network also fell to the company, giving it a virtual transport monopoly. Large-scale banana cultivation really took off, and by 1934 United Fruit controlled a massive amount of land, exporting around 3.5 million bunches of bananas annually and reaping vast profits. In 1941 some 25,000 Guatemalans were employed in the banana industry.

The influence of the United Fruit Company was so pervasive that it earned itself the nickname *El Pulpo*, "the octopus". Control of the transport network brought with it control of the coffee trade: during the 1930s it cost as much to ship coffee from Guatemala to New Orleans as it did from Río de Janeiro to New Orleans.

Against this background the power of the Guatemalan government was severely limited, with the influence of the United States increasing alongside that of the United Fruit Company. Indigenous farmers began to express their anger at the United Fruit Company monopoly, while the company demanded the renewal of long-standing contracts, squeezing Lázaro Chacón (president 1926–30) from both sides.

The way became clear for **Jorge Ubico**, a charismatic leader with a reputation for efficiency, who was well connected with the ruling and land-owning elite. As president, however, he inherited financial disaster. Guatemala had been badly hit by the Depression, but Ubico fought hard to expand the export market for Guatemalan produce, managing to sign trade agreements that exempted coffee and bananas from import duties in the United States. Within Guatemala, Ubico steadfastly supported the United Fruit Company and the interests of US business. This relationship was of such importance that by 1940 ninety percent of all Guatemalan exports were being sold to the United States and in the run-up to World War II, Ubico was forced to bow to US pressure and expel German landowners from the country.

Internally, Ubico embarked on a radical programme of reform, including a sweeping drive against corruption and a massive road-building effort. But the system of debt peonage continued as a new **vagrancy law** compelled all landless peasants to work 150 days a year for the state or landowners. Not surprisingly, sporadic local protests and revolts against landowners continued in the late 1930s and early 1940s.

Internal security was another obsession that was to dominate Ubico's years in office, as he became increasingly paranoid. He maintained that he was a reincarnation of Napoleon and operated a network of informers whom he regularly used to unleash waves of repression. But while Ubico tightened his grip on every aspect of government, the rumblings of opposition grew louder. In 1944 discontent erupted in student violence, and Ubico was finally forced to resign after fourteen years of tyrannical rule.

Ten years of "spiritual socialism"

The overthrow of Jorge Ubico released a wave of opposition, with students, professionals and young military officers all demanding democracy and freedom. It was a mood that was to transform Guatemalan politics, one so extreme a contrast to previous transitions in power that the handover was dubbed **the 1944 revolution**.

A joint military and civilian junta took control in the interim period before elections, and in March 1945 a new constitution was instituted, extending suffrage to include all adults and prohibiting the president from standing for a second term. In the elections **Juan José Arévalo**, a teacher, won the presidency with 85 percent of the vote. His political doctrine was dubbed "**spiritual socialism**", and he immediately set about implementing much-needed structural reforms. Under a new budget, a third of the government's income was allocated to social welfare, to be spent on the construction of schools and hospitals, a programme of immunization, and a far-reaching literacy campaign. The vagrancy laws were abolished, a national development agency was founded, and in 1947 a labour code was adopted, granting workers the right to strike and union representation.

Some former coffee farms were turned into cooperatives, while new laws protected tenant farmers from eviction. Technical assistance and credit were also made available to peasant farmers.

In Arévalo's final years the pace of reform slackened somewhat as he concentrated on evading various attempts to overthrow him. Despite his popularity, Arévalo was still wary of the traditional elite: Church leaders, old-school army officers and wealthy landowners all resented the new wave of legislation, and repeated coup attempts were made.

Elections were scheduled for 1950, and during the run-up the two main candidates were both colonels: **Francisco Arana** and **Jácobo Arbenz**. In 1949, Arana, who was favoured by the right, was assassinated. Suspicion fell on Arbenz, who was backed by the peasant organizations and unions, but there was no hard proof. Arana was replaced by **Brigadier Miguel Ydígoras**, an army officer from the Ubico years.

Arbenz won the election with ease, taking 65 percent of the vote, and declared that he would transform the country into an independent capitalist nation and raise the standard of living. But the process of overthrowing feudal society and ending economic dependency led to direct confrontation with the American corporations that still dominated the economy.

Arbenz enlisted the support of the masses, encouraging the participation of peasants in the programme of agrarian reform and inciting the militancy of students and unions. He also attempted to break the great American-owned railway, power and port monopolies and sought to reclaim unpaid taxes from them. Internally, these measures aroused a mood of national pride, but they were strongly resented by the US companies whose empires were under attack.

The situation became even more serious with the **law of agrarian reform** passed in July 1952, which stated that idle and state-owned land would be distributed to the landless, at a fraction of its market value. The new laws outraged landowners, despite the fact that they were given the right to appeal. Between 1953 and 1954 around 8840 square kilometres were redistributed to the benefit of some 100,000 peasant families – the first time since the arrival of the Spanish that the government had responded to the needs of the indigenous population. The landowner most seriously affected by the reforms was the United Fruit Company, which lost about half of its property.

As the pace of reform gathered, Arbenz began to take an increasingly radical stance. In 1951, the Communist Party was granted legal status, and in the next election four party members were elected to the legislature, which was staunchly anti-American.

In the United States the press repeatedly accused the new Guatemalan government of being a communist beachhead in Central America, and the US government attempted to intervene on behalf of the United Fruit Company. Tellingly, Allen Dulles, the new director of the CIA, also happened to be a member of the fruit-company's board.

In 1953, President Dwight Eisenhower approved plans to overthrow the government and the CIA set up a small military invasion of Guatemala to

Che Guevara in Guatemala

Ernesto "Che" Guevara arrived in Guatemala on New Year's Eve 1953, broke and with no place to stay. He had graduated as a doctor in his native Argentina five months previously, and immediately left to explore Latin America – hitching rides, sleeping rough and cadging meals along the way.

The future *comandante* spent eight months in Guatemala City, living in Zona 1, the historic heart of the capital, in a number of cheap hospedajes. Most of his days were spent in a fruitless search for work as a doctor, surviving on the generosity of the people he met and scratching a meagre income from a series of casual jobs: teaching a few Spanish classes, doing some translation work, and peddling encyclopedias and images of the Black Christ of Esquipulas in the capital's streets.

But Guevara had not just come to Guatemala to look for work. In the early 1950s, Guatemala City was a mecca for political idealists, communists and budding revolutionaries from Latin America, all attracted to the country by reformist president Arbenz and his party's doctrine of "spiritual socialism". In a letter to his aunt, Guevara wrote of his travels through the region, and avowed his intentions to challenge American hegemony:

Along the way, I had the opportunity to pass through the dominions of the United Fruit ... I have sworn before a picture of the old and mourned comrade Stalin that I won't rest until I see these capitalist octopuses annihilated. In Guatemala I will perfect myself and achieve what I need to be an authentic revolutionary.

One of the first people he met in Guatemala was Hildea Gadea, a well-connected young Peruvian who later became his first wife. Gadea, an exiled member of Peru's ARPA rebels, introduced Che to a number of other young political activists, including Rolando Morán, who was to become the leader of the Guatemalan EGP guerrillas (see p.142). Guevara formed his political consciousness in Guatemala City, his beliefs shaped by hours spent reading Marx, Trotsky and Mao, an instinctive hatred of US imperialism, and marathon theological debates. Of the city's myriad Latino leftist groups, the Cubans most impressed Che, for they alone had actually launched an armed uprising against a dictatorship (the failed Moncada assault after Batista had cancelled the 1952 Cuban elections). Guevara met Ñico López, the Cuban who would later introduce him to Fidel and Raúl Castro, and with whom he would later regroup in Mexico, set sail for Cuba in 1956 and initiate the revolution.

Guevara remained in Guatemala City throughout the attacks on the capital in June 1954. The young radical wrote to his family denouncing the indecisiveness of the Arbenz government and its inability to organize local militias to defend the country. He swore allegiance to the Soviet Union, and joined the Communist Party while holed up in the Argentine embassy, awaiting deportation after Arbenz had been deposed.

Many of the young Guatemala-based comrades later reassembled in Mexico City where they digested the downfall of Arbenz. Perhaps the biggest lesson Guevara learned was that rather than attempt to negotiate with Washington, it was essential to combat American interference with armed resistance. He was convinced that Guatemala had been betrayed "inside and out", and argued that future revolutionaries must be prepared to establish their internal authority by force and eliminate enemies using repression and firing squads if necessary – "Victory will be conquered with blood and fire, there can be no pardon for the traitors."

depose Arbenz. A ragtag army of exiles and mercenaries was put together in Honduras, and on June 18, 1954, Guatemala City was bombed with leaflets demanding the resignation of Arbenz. The Guatemalan president failed to obtain the support of the army, and on the night of June 18, Guatemala was strafed with machine-gun fire while the invading army, described by Arbenz as "a heterogeneous Fruit Company expeditionary force", was getting closer to the city by the hour.

On June 27, Arbenz declared that he was relinquishing the presidency to **Colonel Carlos Enrique Díaz**, the army chief of staff. And on July 3, John Peurifoy, the US ambassador to Guatemala, flew the new government to Guatemala aboard a US Air Force plane. Guatemala's attempt to escape the clutches of outside intervention and bring about social change had been brought to an abrupt end.

Counter-revolution and military rule

Following the overthrow of Arbenz, the army – backed by US aid – rose to fill the power vacuum; it would dominate politics for the next thirty years, propelling the country into a spiral of violence and economic decline.

In 1954 the US ambassador persuaded a provisional government to accept **Carlos Castillo** as the new president, and Castillo wasted no time sweeping away the progressive legislation of the previous ten years. The constitution of 1945 was replaced by a more restrictive version; illiterates were disenfranchised; left-wing parties were outlawed; and large numbers of unionists and reformers were simply executed. The regime lifted the restrictions that had been placed on foreign investment and returned all the land that had been confiscated to its previous owners, a measure which badly affected the indigenous population. A referendum was rigged to provide a supportive response to Castillo's rule, but his government had only limited backing from the armed forces, and coup rumblings persisted until finally he was shot by his own bodyguard in 1957.

The assassination was followed by several months of political turmoil, out of which **Miguel Ydígoras** (a former candidate) emerged as the next president. His disastrous five-year rule was marked by corruption, incompetence, outrageous patronage and economic decline caused by a fall in coffee prices; the formation of the Central American Common Market during his tenure did help to boost light industry, however. Ydígoras was eventually overthrown when Arévalo threatened to return to Guatemala and contest the 1963 elections, which he might well have won. The possibility of another socialist government sent shock waves through the establishment in both Guatemala and the United States, and President John F. Kennedy gave the go-ahead for another coup. In 1963 the army once more took control, under the leadership of **Enrique Peralta**.

Peralta was president for just three years, during which he fiddled with the constitution and took his time in restoring the electoral process. Meanwhile, the authoritarian nature of his government came up against the first wave of armed resistance. Two failed coupsters from 1960, Turcios Lima and Marco Yon Sosa, both army officers, took to the highlands of Verapaz and Izabal and waged a **guerrilla war** against the state. A second organization, FAR, emerged later that year, and the Guatemalan Labour Party (PGT) formed a shaky alliance with the guerrillas, attempting to represent their grievances in the political arena.

Peralta finally lost control in the 1966 elections, which were won by **Julio Méndez** of the centre-left Partido Revolucionario. Before taking office, however, Méndez was forced to sign a pact with the military, obliging him to give them a totally free hand in all affairs of national security. Then, after Méndez's offer of amnesty to the guerrillas was rejected, a ruthless counterinsurgency campaign swung into action using US military advisors, aerial bombardment and napalm. By the end of the decade, the guerrilla movement had been virtually eradicated in the east and its activities, greatly reduced, shifted to Guatemala City, where the US ambassador was assassinated by FAR rebels in 1968.

Meanwhile, Méndez declared his government to be "the third government of the revolution", aligning it with the socialist administrations of Arévalo and Arbenz. But despite the support from the left his hands were tied by the influence of the army. Political violence became commonplace as **death squads**, backed by the military, operated with impunity, killing anyone they deemed subversive to the state.

Economic decline and political violence

Extreme political violence, economic crises and electoral fraud dominated Guatemala's history between 1970 and the early 1990s. At the heart of the crisis was the injustice and inequality of Guatemalan society: although the country remained fairly prosperous, the benefits of its success never reached the poor, who were denied access to land, education or healthcare.

The 1970 elections confirmed the power of the military and the far right (represented by the MLN and PID). **Colonel Carlos Arana**, who had directed the counterinsurgency campaign in the east, was elected president, though only a small percentage of the population was enfranchised.

Once in power he set about eradicating armed opposition, declaring that "If it is necessary to turn the country into a cemetery in order to pacify it, I will not hesitate to do so." The reign of terror, conducted by both the armed forces and the "death squads", reached unprecedented levels, as around 15,000 political killings occurred during the first three years of Arana's rule.

Presidential elections followed in 1974, which were tainted by manipulation and fraud, resulting in the declaration of the right's candidate, **Kjell Laugerud**, as the winner. Laugerud offered limited reforms, allowing greater tolerance towards unions and the cooperative movement, but the army continued to consolidate its authority, spreading its influence across a wider range of business and commercial interests.

All of this was interrupted by a massive **earthquake** on February 4, 1976. The quake left around 23,000 dead, 77,000 injured and a million homeless. The poor, their homes built from makeshift materials on unstable ground, suffered the most, and subsistence farmers were caught out just as they were about to plant their corn.

In the wake of the earthquake, during the process of reconstruction, powerful new forces emerged to challenge the status quo. A revived trade-union organization resurfaced, while a new guerrilla organization, the Guerrilla Army of the Poor (EGP), emerged in the Ixil area. Army operations became increasingly ferocious. In 1977, US President Jimmy Carter suspended all military aid to Guatemala because of the country's appalling human-rights record.

In the following year, Guatemala's elections were once again dominated by the army, which engineered a victory for **Brigadier General Fernando Lucas García**. Lucas García promised to bring the situation under control, and unleashed a fresh wave of violence. All opposition considered subversive was met with severe repression. Conditions throughout the country deteriorated rapidly, and the economy was badly affected by a fall in commodity prices, while several guerrilla armies developed strongholds in the highlands.

As chaos threatened, the army resorted to extreme measures, and within a month there was a major massacre in **Panzós**. In Guatemala City the situation became so dangerous that political parties were driven underground. Two leading members of the Social Democrats, who were expected to win the next election, lost their lives in 1979. Once they were out of the way, the regime turned on the Christian Democrats, killing more than a hundred of their members and forcing the party's leader, Vinicio Cerezo, into hiding.

The **army** became increasingly powerful and the death toll rose steadily. In rural areas the war against the guerrillas was reaching new heights as army casualties rose to 250 a month, and the demand for conscripts grew rapidly. The four main guerrilla groups had an estimated 6000 combatants and some 250,000 unarmed collaborators. Under the Lucas García administration the horrors of **repression** were at their most intense. The victims included students, journalists, academics, politicians, priests, lawyers, teachers, unionists, and above all peasant farmers, massacred in their hundreds. Accurate figures are impossible to calculate but it's estimated that around 35,000 Guatemalans were killed during the four years of the Lucas García regime.

But while high-ranking officers became more and more involved in big business and political wrangling, the officers in the field began to feel deserted. Here there was growing discontent as a result of repeated military failures, inefficiency and a shortage of supplies, despite increased military aid and weaponry from Israel.

Ríos Montt

The 1982 elections were also manipulated by the far right, who ensured a victory for **Ángel Aníbal**. However, on March 23 a group of young military officers led a successful coup, which installed **General Efraín Ríos Montt** (who had been denied the post in 1974) as the head of a three-member junta.

Ríos Montt was an evangelical Christian, a member of the Iglesia del Verbo, and throughout his rule Sunday-night television was dominated by marathon presidential sermons. He immediately declared his determination to defeat the guerrillas, restore law and order, and eradicate corruption. Government officials were issued with identity cards inscribed with the words "I do not steal. I do not lie." A state of siege was declared.

Initially, repression dropped in the cities as corrupt police officers were forced to resign, but in the highlands the war intensified. An **amnesty** was offered, which only a few rebels accepted, and the army set about destroying the guerrillas' infrastructure by undermining their support base.

Montt called his military campaign, "*frijoles y fusiles*" (beans and guns). Villagers were provided with rations and forcibly organized into **civil defence patrols** (PACs), armed with ancient rifles, and ordered to patrol the countryside. Those who refused were denounced as "subversives" and carted off to re-education camps or army-base torture chambers. Campesinos were forced to take sides, caught between the attraction of guerrilla propaganda and the extreme brutality of the armed forces.

Ríos Montt's iron-fist policy was as successful as it was murderous as soldiers swept through the mountains committing massacre after massacre, wiping villages off the map that were deemed to have collaborated with the enemy and leaving nothing but scorched earth. Ten of thousands of campesinos fled to safety in Mexico. The guerrillas, their network of support virtually eradicated, were driven into remote corners, and occasionally responded with desperate measures, including the ambush and slaughter of PAC members and villagers. The massacre carried out at the village of Txacal Tze in the Ixil region on June 13, 1982, by EGP guerrillas left an estimated 125 dead.

Meanwhile, the "state of siege" became a "state of alarm", under which special tribunals were given the power to try and execute suspects. By the middle of 1983, Ríos Montt faced growing pressure from all sides, particularly the Catholic Church, which was outraged by the murders of dozens of its priests.

In August 1983, Ríos Montt was pushed aside by yet another military coup. **General Mejía Víctores** became president, and although the death squads and disappearances remained a fixture, moves towards democratic elections were implemented. Battles continued in the mountains, but some rehabilitation began as internal refugees were grouped in "model villages". Scarcely any money was made available for rebuilding the devastated communities however, and it was often widows and orphans who were left to construct their own homes. In the Ixil Triangle alone the war had displaced 60,000 people (72 percent of the population), and nine model villages were built to replace 49 that had been destroyed. Nationwide more than 600 villages had been destroyed and around 180,000 had lost their lives.

In 1985 presidential elections were held, the first free vote in Guatemala for thirty years.

Cerezo and the return to democratic rule

The elections were won by **Vinicio Cerezo**, a Christian Democrat not associated with the traditional ruling elite. His election victory was the result of a sweeping wave of popular support, and in the run-up to the election he offered a programme of reform that he claimed would rid the country of repression.

Once in office, however, Cerezo knew that his room for manoeuvre was severely limited. He argued that the army still held 75 percent of power, and declared "I'm a politician not a magician. Why promise what I cannot deliver?" Throughout his six-year rule Cerezo offered a **non-confrontational approach**, seeking above all else to avoid upsetting the powerful alliance of business interests, landowners and generals. To protect himself, he courted the support of a group of sympathetic officers, and with their aid survived several coup attempts. Political killings dropped in the late 1980s, but the civil war continued in remote parts of the highlands and death squads linked to rogue elements in the military operated in the capital.

The country's leading **human-rights organization**, the Mutual Support Group (GAM), hoped that civilian rule would present them with a chance to investigate the fate of the "disappeared" and bring the perpetrators of violence to trial. Cerezo, however, chose to forget the past, and ongoing abuses went largely uninvestigated and unpunished. GAM's leaders, meanwhile, became targeted by hit men.

Nevertheless, a measure of civilian rule created a general thaw in the political climate, fostering the growth of numerous pressure groups and sparking fresh demands for reform. Real change, however, never materialized. Despite the fact that at least 65 percent of the population still lived below the official poverty line, little was done to meet their needs in terms of education, health, employment, land or tax reform. Acknowledging that his greatest achievement had been to survive, Cerezo organized the country's first civilian transfer of power in decades, in 1990.

The Serrano and Carpio administrations

The **1990 elections** were dogged by controversy. Ex-military dictator Ríos Montt was banned from standing as a candidate, but **Jorge Serrano**, a former minister in his government, won (albeit with the support of less than a quarter of the people). An engineer and evangelical with a centre-right economic position, Serrano proved both uninterested and incapable of effecting any real reform or bringing an end to the civil war. The level of human-rights abuse remained high, death-squad activity continued, the economy remained weak and the army was still a powerful force, using intimidation and murder to stamp out opposition. Economic activity was still controlled by a tiny elite, and some 85 percent of the population lived in poverty.

Nevertheless, Guatemala's dispossessed and poor continued to clamour for change. Maya peasants became increasingly organized and influential, rejecting the presence of the army and the system of civil patrols. Matters were brought into sharp focus in 1992 when **Rigoberta Menchú** was awarded the Nobel Peace Prize for her campaigning work on behalf of Guatemala's indigenous population. In spite of the efforts of the Serrano administration, the country's civil war still rumbled on and three main guerrilla groups, united as the **URNG**, continued to confront the army.

Small groups of refugees began to return from exile in Mexico and start civil communities, though an estimated 45,000 still remained. The territorial dispute with **Belize** was officially resolved when the two countries established full diplomatic relations in 1991; but the decision to recognize Belize as an independent country provoked hostility with ultra-nationalists and the Guatemalan military.

By early 1993, Serrano's reputation had plummeted following a series of **scandals** involving corruption and his business ventures, some of which had suspected links with Colombian drug cartels. In May 1993, Serrano pronounced a self-coup, though within days massive demonstrations and the suspension of US aid forced him out. Further public protests then blocked an army-backed appointee, and finally **Ramiro Carpio**, the country's human-rights ombudsman, was declared the new president. He reshuffled the senior military command, but rejected calls for revenge, declaring that stability was the main goal. Public frustration quickly grew as the new government failed to address fundamental issues, such as crime, land ownership, tax and constitutional reform. Some progress was made in peace negotiations with the URNG guerrilla leadership, however, and the Indigenous Rights Act, passed in 1995, allowed greater constitutional freedom for Guatemala's *indígenas*.

Arzú and the peace accords

Álvaro Arzú of the centre-right PAN party, a former mayor of Guatemala City, was elected president in 1996 with a commitment to private-sector-led growth and the free market. He quickly adopted a relatively progressive stance, shaking up the armed forces' power structure and moving quickly to bring an end to the 36-year civil war by meeting the URNG guerrilla leaders. The **Peace Accords**, signed on December 29, 1996, concluded almost a decade of talks and terminated a conflict that had claimed 200,000 lives. A commitment to investigate wartime human-rights violations through a Truth Commission overseen by MINUGUA (the UN mission to Guatemala) was agreed. However progress on development issues was slow, and a constitutional amendment to allow greater Maya rights was rejected by the electorate.

There were token cuts in military numbers, but the army's influence and position remained unchallenged throughout his term. Army officers implicated in orchestrating massacres successfully avoided prosecution – Arzú simply dared not touch them. Then in April 1998, two days after publishing a long-awaited human-rights investigation into wartime slaughters (see p.437) that blamed the military for ninety per cent of the deaths, **Bishop Juan Geradi** was bludgeoned to death in his own garage. The murder stunned the nation, one newspaper declaring "This wasn't supposed to happen. Not any more."

The acute fragility of the nascent Guatemalan democracy was revealed – most immediately suspecting that a vengeful military was responsible for Geradi's assassination. Despite international and domestic outrage – hundreds of thousands attended a silent protest in the capital days after the killing – the Arzú government proved incapable of reigning in the real perpetrators of the murder. The investigation descended to near-farcical levels at times (a priest's dog was implicated at one stage) as terrified judges, prosecutors and key witnesses fled abroad following death threats. As Arzú departed the presidential palace in December 1999, Geradi's murderers remained at large and the investigation unsolved.

There was also an alarming upsurge in the crime rate. A new police force, the PNC, quickly gained a reputation as bad as its predecessor for endemic corruption and ineffectualness. But crime and the Geradi case aside, Arzú left office with his reputation as a skilled administrator who got things done intact. Huge infrastructure projects, including a massive upgrading of Guatemala's highways, were completed efficiently and to budget. Arzú was re-elected mayor of Guatemala City for a third term in 2007, with a mandate to modernize the capital's transport system.

President Portillo

Former lawyer and professor **Alfonso Portillo** won Guatemala's 1999 presidential elections with a promise to implement the Peace Accords and tackle crime and gangs. In the grossest of ironies, Portillo confessed to killing two men in Mexico in 1982, declaring, "A man who defends his life will defend the lives of his people." He claimed he had acted in self-defence. But perhaps the most decisive factor in his victory was the support of his political mentor, former general and founder of the right-wing FRG party, Ríos Montt. Throughout Portillo's disastrous term of office Montt was widely perceived to be really in control, pulling all the strings behind the scenes.

Portillo immediately set about attempting to solve the **Geradi case** as three senior military personnel were charged with murder within weeks of his inauguration. Credibly, the military suspects (an intelligence chief and two members of the elite presidential guard) and a priest (who was found guilty of acting as an accomplice) were brought to trial, and found guilty of plotting Geradi's murder in June 2001. Despite intense pressure on the prosecution, and a bomb exploding outside the home of one judge on the first day of the trial, justice prevailed.

The Geradi case aside, Portillo lurched from crisis to crisis, and after four years of catastrophic presidency he departed office leaving Guatemala virtually bankrupt. The stench of **corruption** pervaded his entire term as a series of scandals were unearthed and public coffers were emptied. Little or no progress was made on the terms of the Peace Accords, which included improving indigenous rights, health and education, and increasing income from tax collection.

Crime levels soared during his term. Human-rights workers, journalists and environmentalists who dared to challenge powerful political interests were threatened and killed, while gangs terrorized the city suburbs. Seventy of the country's most notorious criminals – murderers, rapists, kidnappers and gang leaders – blasted their way out of jail in 2001 and Portillo even dispatched his own family to Canada after a kidnap threat.

Meanwhile, the **economy** continued to falter, as traditional exports (principally coffee, sugar and bananas) slumped, and low commodity prices affected profitability. On the other hand, the cocaine trade boomed, as Guatemala became a key transit country. Behind this boom were shadowy **organized crime cartels** – locally known as *poderes ocultos* ("hidden powers") – thought to be headed up by retired generals and including a network of corrupt officials. The US decertified Guatemala as a partner country in their so-called "war against drugs" in 2002.

With Guatemala seemingly teetering on the brink, Ríos Montt stood as the FRG candidate for the 2003 elections, but fell at the first hurdle, polling less than 20 percent of the vote. Most Guatemalans heaved a collective sigh of relief as the enigma of the Montt legend, which had cast a shadow over Guatemala for more than twenty years, at last seemed extinguished.

Óscar Berger

Inaugurated as president in January 2004, Óscar Berger declared that the country was nearly broke and that his goal would be to govern in an austere, cost-conscious manner. Many key positions in his government were filled by members of the Guatemalan elite but he also made several progressive appointments including Rigoberta Menchú (see p.439) as a goodwill ambassador with a brief to implement the Peace Accords.

Significantly, Berger curbed the power of the **armed forces** by slashing military spending: cutting army numbers from 27,000 to 15,500 and closing thirteen military bases. But at the same time Berger ordered the army to patrol *zonas rojas*, poor barrios of Guatemala City, in an effort to combat the intimidation, extortion and violence wreaked on the capital by its notorious gangs, a militarization of society that conflicted with Peace Accords recommendations.

Unsurprisingly, given his links to big business and the country's oligarchy, Berger was an enthusiastic supporter of **CAFTA** (the US–Central American Free Trade Agreement). This accord proved highly contentious, leading to big demonstrations as opponents reasoned that heavily subsidized US agricultural exports would mean ruin for small-scale Central American farmers.

The other key issue in the countryside, the seemingly intractable issue of **agrarian reform**, proved even more combustible. Berger immediately began evicting thousands of landless peasants from the fincas they were squatting, a course of action that provoked protests in twenty of the country's 22 departments in July 2004. Eleven campesinos died at Finca Nuevo Linda near Retalhuleu as 2000 police violently ejected 3000 squatters. Campesino and human-rights leaders charged Berger with pandering to his privileged support base, the landowning elite.

These protests served to confirm the desperately poor living standards affecting most Guatemalans, particularly in rural and indigenous areas. In 2006 the UN estimated that over 30 percent of the population lived on less than US$2 a day.

As Berger's term neared its end, the key issue for the 2007 election campaign (as in 2003) was crime. With street gangs effectively in control of dozens of poor barrios, a murder rate ten times that in the US, and drug mafias with military links operating with virtual impunity Guatemala had, in the words of the Dutch ambassador, become "a paradise for organized crime". Few in the media, electorate or politics disagreed, and the question was who would best deal with the issue. Social democrat Álvaro Colom advocated "combating violence with intelligence", while his opponent in the presidential run-off Otto Pérez (an ex-chief of military intelligence, who was implicated in the Geradi murder) called for a "*mano dura*" or iron-fist approach. Colom got the nod by 52.8 percent of the vote to Pérez's 47.2 percent.

Guatemala today

President **Álvaro Colom** was elected on a progressive mandate promising social change and investment, but headed a political coalition of disparate political interests. Colom, a worthy if slightly uninspiring personality from the centre-left is a former textile businessman who has also studied Maya religion. His charismatic deputy, Rafael Espada, a heart surgeon who combined working in a leading Houston hospital with charitable medical work in Guatemala before entering politics, is a more flamboyant man, fond of motorbikes.

Colom's challenge is how to go about tackling the most pressing issues facing the nation – crime and violence, poverty, land issues, indigenous rights and the environment – without upsetting elements of his coalition, which includes representatives from big business and the oligarchy.

Over fifty percent of Guatemalans (and more than seventy per cent of the Maya) live below the poverty line. Income retribution remains woefully skewed, with taxation accounting for less than ten percent of GDP, the lowest in the western hemisphere. Tax reform is urgently needed to fund social programmes, but Colom will have to take on powerful business interests adept at protecting their wealth. Guatemala also has little industry of its own, except for a booming foreign-owned *maquiladora* textile-factory sector where garments are assembled in tax-exempt zones for export to the US and Korea.

As far as developing nations go, Guatemala has returned pretty modest **economic figures**, averaging 2–3 percent GDP growth per year since the mid-1990s, a little behind most of Latin America, and trailing India, China and most of Southeast Asia by some distance. The country's poor education system (30 percent of adults are illiterate) is a serious handicap, while social instability and crime levels also impact upon international competitiveness and inward investment. Lawlessness also hampers the potential of the nation's **tourism industry**. Though tourist arrivals have accelerated and exceed 1.5 million visitors per year, these numbers are quite modest given Guatemala's unique cultural and natural diversity, low cost of living, and location just a couple of hours' flight from the southern USA.

Environmental policy is another critical arena. Berger pursued an aggressive free-trade approach that encouraged inward investment while antagonizing many rural communities. Mining concessions were granted which permitted corporations access to indigenous land, none more controversial than the open-pit gold mine at Sipacapa in San Marcos, which was bitterly opposed locally. Vast tracts of the Petén jungle have disappeared in smoke as settlers, loggers and cattle ranchers have overrun protected reserves including Laguna del Tigre. Some of these invaders have links to drug mafias who clear airstrips in the forest to facilitate the transit of cocaine. In 2008 Colom moved to protect the Mirador Basin (see p.337), home of some of the densest remaining forests and dozens of Maya ruins including El Mirador, with a view to creating a new national park. But with settlers established in several other reserves it will take firm political resolve to evict the squatters and confront the very powerful, and heavily-armed, cocaine cartels.

Perhaps Colom's biggest challenge will be to establish a functioning **justice system**. In 2007, there were 6100 murders in Guatemala – the vast majority connected to gangs or drugs – of which about 100 made it to court. The impact of gang culture has spread like a cancer throughout the nation: women are targeted with extreme violence (see p.437), and extortion affects everyone from market vendors to bus drivers who enter gang territory (twelve were killed in a two-day period in 2008).

CICIG, the UN-backed International Commission against Impunity in Guatemala, requires strong political backing to restore faith in the police and judiciary, which are riddled by corruption and widely thought to be not only involved, but often to be instrumental, in some crimes. In 2008 rioters torched a police station in Sololá. In Guatemala, barely a week passes without a lynching, as mobs take violent action against suspected criminals. The commission is also tasked with identifying the illegal security groups thought to be responsible for organized crime, death squads, and their possible links to the state.

Much will depend on the determination of government to address the security question, for long-term prosperity, stability, the economy and social development are all heavily dependent upon the issue.

Chronology of the Maya

c.20,000–10,000 BC ▶ **Paleo-Indian culture (also called Lithic or Early Hunter periods)**. Waves of hunter-gatherers from Asia cross the Bering land bridge (and possibly also use a maritime route) to the American continent.

c.10,000 BC ▶ **Clovis culture**. Worked-stone projectile points – first identified at Clovis, New Mexico – used to hunt large herbivores, including mammoths, found at many sites in North and Central America.

c.6000–2000 BC ▶ **Archaic (Proto-Maya) period**. General warming of the climate following the retreat of northern ice sheets. The Pacific littoral region in Guatemala is the most intensely inhabited area of the Maya World, though there are well-established villages and trade routes throughout the region. Villagers farm maize and beans, catch fish and make pottery. Clay figures discovered from this period may be the first religious artefacts. A Proto-Maya language is thought to have been spoken.

August 13, 3114 BC ▶ The mythical starting date of the Maya Calendar (13.0.0.0.0. 4 Ahau 8 Kumk'u) marks the beginning of the current "Great Cycle", the creation of the present world; the cycle is due to end on December 21, 2012.

2000 BC–250 AD ▶ **Preclassic (or Formative) period**. The **Olmec** culture, the first emergent civilization of Mesoamerica, brings an early calendar and new gods. Trade in jade, salt and cacao increases between villages in Guatemala, and the first Maya great cities, Nakbé and El Mirador, emerge towards the end of the period.

1700 BC ▶ Olmec civilization emerges on Gulf coast of Mexico, just outside the Maya region.

1400 BC ▶ First settlement in Copán valley.

c.1000 BC ▶ Earliest confirmed settlement at Nakbé and Cival.

1000–400 BC ▶ **Middle Preclassic period**. Relatively sophisticated building construction at Nakbé in northern Petén. Many of the earliest foundations of the central region's sites established. Olmec, then Iztapa cultures, dominate the Pacific coast.

750 BC ▶ Temple complexes are constructed at Nakbé, possibly the very first Maya "city". Maya culture eclipses Olmec influence in Petén.

500 BC ▶ First evidence of ceremonial buildings at **Tikal**. Pyramid and astrological observatory built at Cival.

400 BC–250 AD ▶ **Late Preclassic**. Early development of the foundations of Maya civilization: calendar, writing, architectural design and sophisticated artistic style. Monumental temple cities emerge. Causeways (*sacbés*) are built and trade links flourish.

300 BC ▶ Nakbé temples rebuilt to 45-metre height, and colossal stucco masks constructed. Massive building projects commence at **El Mirador** and Stela 2 carved at Cival. Early Maya glyph writing at San Bartolo.

200 BC ▶ **Miraflores culture** thrives on Pacific coast and Guatemalan highlands, centred at **Kaminaljuyú**; elaborate stelae carved. First ceremonial structures built at **Tikal** and **Uaxactún**.

150 BC ▶ **El Mirador** enters its greatest era as seventy-metre-high temples are built, their soaring stone staircases framed by giant masks.

100 BC ▶ Murals of the Maya creation myth painted at San Bartolo.

36 BC ▶ First known Long Count date, corresponding to December 7, 36 BC, inscribed on Stela 2 at **Chiapa de Corzo**, Chiapas.

c.1 AD ▶ Major pyramids, platforms and giant stucco masks constructed at Uaxactún, Tikal and Cerros, but the region is dominated by El Mirador with a population that peaks at around 100,000. Emergence of **Teotihuacán** in Mexico.

36 AD ▶ Stela 1 carved at **El Baúl** on Pacific coast using Long Count date.

90 AD ▶ Tikal dynasty starts.

c.150 AD ▶ **El Mirador** and other cities in the Mirador Basin abandoned, probably due to environmental collapse; Yax Ehb' Xok establishes the first ruling dynasty at Tikal.

199 AD ▶ Earliest recorded use of Long Count date in central region.

250 AD ▶ **Kaminaljuyú** all but abandoned.

250–600 AD ▶ **Early Classic period**. Maya region and much of Mexico influenced, or even dominated by, the great metropolis of Teotihuacán, north of modern-day Mexico City, until around 450 AD. Calakmul later emerges as the regional superpower, challenging and defeating Tikal. Dated inscriptions emerge in the lowlands. Elaborate carved stelae erected throughout central region after 435 AD. Extensive trade network along Caribbean coast between Yucatán and Honduras.

292 AD ▶ Stela 29 carved at **Tikal**, with Long Count calendar date.

c.359 AD ▶ Yoaat B'alam I (Progenitor Jaguar) becomes first king of **Yaxchilán**.

378 AD ▶ Siyak K'ak' (Lord Fire-Born), probably from **Teotihuacán**, ejects (and almost certainly kills) **Tikal**'s ruler Chak Tok Ich'aak (Great Jaguar Paw I) and defeats **Uaxactún**.

400 AD ▶ Guatemalan highlands under strong Teotihuacán influence; **Kaminaljuyú** rebuilt in its style.

426 AD ▶ Yax K'uk Mo' (Great Sun First Quetzal Macaw), probably from Teotihuacán, founds dynasty at **Copán**.

435 AD ▶ Completion of Baktun 8 (9.0.0.0.0). Population of **Copán** rises and building work accelerates.

534–593 AD ▶ **Middle Classic hiatus**: dearth of stelae carving and building throughout region previously under Tikal control.

556 AD ▶ Wak Chan K'awil (Double Bird) of **Tikal** (537–562 AD) enacts an "axe war" against **Caracol**.

562 AD ▶ Yajaw Te' K'inich II (Lord Water) of **Caracol** retaliates in concert with Sky Witness of **Calakmul** and overruns Tikal. Calakmul becomes regional superpower.

c.600 AD ▶ Population density in core Maya region reaches an estimated 965 people per square kilometre.

600–800 AD ▶ **Late Classic period**. Golden age of the Maya, as civilization reaches intellectual and artistic peak and numerous powerful city-states emerge in central region, though the mighty superpowers of **Calakmul** and a re-emergent **Tikal** dominate. Monumental construction of temples, plazas, pyramids and palaces. Puuc, Río Bec and Chenes cities all flourish in northern area; spectacular construction throughout the Maya World.

611 AD ▶ Scroll Serpent of **Calakmul** attacks Palenque and destroys the city centre.

615 AD ▶ K'inich Hanaab Pakal (Great Sun Shield) begins 68-year reign at **Palenque**.

628 AD ▶ Smoke Imix's (Ruler 12) 67-year reign begins at **Copán**.

645 AD ▶ B'alaj Chan K'awil (Lightening Sky) founds city of **Dos Pilas**.

c.650 AD ▶ Latest evidence suggests Tikal's **Temple V** completed around this date.

657 AD ▶ Yuknoom the Great of **Calakmul** attacks Tikal, whose ruler Nuun Ujol Chaak (Shield Skull) takes refuge in Palenque.

659 AD ▶ Nuun Ujol Chaak of **Tikal** wins battle against Yaxchilán, probably launched from his exile.

672 AD ▶ Nuun Ujol Chaak of **Tikal** returns from exile and launches a "star war" against **Dos Pilas**. B'alaj Chan K'awil takes refuge (probably in Calakmul). In 677 AD he returns to Dos Pilas, and in 679 AD successfully repels Tikal.

682 AD ▶ Hasaw Chan K'awil (Heavenly Standard Bearer) begins 52-year reign at **Tikal** and achieves its resurgence in a series of successful military campaigns against Calakmul and vast construction projects. Lightening Sky of **Dos Pilas** sends his daughter Lady Six Sky to **Naranjo** to re-establish the royal house there. Itzamnaaj B'alam II (Shield Jaguar) begins reign at **Yaxchilán**.

693 AD ▶ K'ak Tilaw Chan Chaak (Smoking Squirrel), new ruler of **Naranjo**, retaliates against **Caracol** by repeatedly attacking its allies, Ucanal (693 AD and 698 AD), Yaxhá (710 AD) and Sacnab (711 AD).

695 AD ▶ Smoke Imix of Copán dies; succeeded by Waxaklajuun Ub'aah K'awil (Eighteen Rabbit). Hasaw Chan K'awil of **Tikal** captures Yich'aak K'ak (Fiery Claw) of **Calakmul**, breaking its power in the central Petén.

c.700 AD ▶ **Yaxchilán** dominates the Usumacinta region. Population of Caracol estimated at more than 100,000.

734 AD ▶ Hasaw Chan K'awil of **Tikal** dies; succeeded by his son, Yik'in Chan K'awil (Divine Sunset Lord). He organizes Tikal's attacks on **Waka'** (743 AD) and **Naranjo** (in 744 AD). These are the last recorded "star war events" in Petén.

735 AD ▶ Ruler 3 of **Dos Pilas** captures Yich'aak B'alam (Jaguar Claw) of **Ceibal**, and reduces Ceibal to subjugation for the next sixty years.

738 AD ▶ **Copán's** Waxaklajuun Ub'aah K'awil killed by Cauac Sky of **Quiriguá**, a subordinate city. No monuments are built at Copán for seventeen years.

c.750 AD ▶ Population peaks in central region, total Maya numbers estimated to be around ten million.

790 AD ▶ **Bonampak** murals painted, but site abandoned shortly afterwards. **Dos Pilas** overrun. End of the *katun* celebrated across the Maya World with carved stelae.

800–909 AD ▶ **Terminal Classic period**. Overpopulation and intense agricultural cultivation in region, and an epochal drought, leads to environ-mental collapse. **Ceibal** flourishes briefly in isolation. Most main cities almost abandoned by 900 AD except in the northern area (Mexico) and in Belize, where trade continues along the rivers and coast.

808 AD ▶ Skull Mahk'ina III of **Yaxchilán** captures Ruler 7 of **Piedras Negras**' ending Classic Maya culture in the upper Usumacinta region.

810 AD ▶ Dark Sun builds Temple III, the last of **Tikal**'s temple pyramids. Last dated inscription at **Quiriguá**.

830 AD ▶ Completion of Baktun 9.

849 AD ▶ **Ceibal** erects five stelae to commemorate the *katun* (10.1.0.0.0).

c.860 AD ▶ Population of central region down to a third of previous level.

869 AD ▶ Last recorded date at **Tikal**.

c.900 AD ▶ **Uxmal** and **Chichén Itzá** abandoned.

909 AD ▶ Erection of the last stela in Maya region at **Toniná** (to commemorate the *katun* ending 10.4.0.0.0.0).

909–c.1530 AD ▶ Postclassic period.

909–1200 AD ▶ **Early Postclassic period**. Maya collapse sees cities abandoned throughout the region. The **Toltec** from Central Mexico invade Yucatán, bringing a new religious cult and architectural styles such as the *Chacmool*. Itza influence replaces Toltec.

1200 AD ▶ **Chichén Itzá** reoccupied by Toltec; new construction begins. Itza driven from Campeche coast.

c.1250 AD ▶ Toltec enter Guatemala. **Utatlán** founded.

c.1450 AD ▶ Itza establish **Tayasal** (also called Noh Petén) on Lago de Petén Itzá.

1450 AD ▶ K'iche' state dominates warring highlands.

1470 AD ▶ Kaqchikel throw off K'iche' control and found their capital at **Iximché**.

1500 AD ▶ Continual conflict in Guatemalan highlands between the main tribal groups.

1519 AD ▶ **Cortés** lands in Cozumel.

1521 AD ▶ Aztec capital of **Tenochtitlán** falls to Spanish under Cortés.

Chronology of Guatemala

1523 ▶ Alvarado arrives in Guatemala. Establishes capital at Tecpán next to Iximché in 1524.

1523–40 ▶ **Spanish conquest** of Guatemala proceeds: first Spanish capital founded 1527.

1541 ▶ Alvarado dies; new capital founded at **Antigua**.

17th c. ▶ **Colonial rule** is gradually established throughout the country. Antigua is the capital of the whole of Central America, and the power of the Church grows.

1697 ▶ Conquest of the Itza at Tayasal on Lago de Petén Itzá: the last of the independent Maya.

1773 ▶ Earthquake destroys Antigua.

1776 ▶ Guatemala City becomes capital.

18th c. ▶ Colonial Guatemala remains a backwater, with no great riches for the Spanish.

1821 ▶ Mexico and Central America gain **independence** from Spain; Guatemala annexed by Mexico, then joins Central American Federation.

1847 ▶ Guatemala becomes a republic, independent of Central America, under **Rafael Carrera**.

1850 ▶ Guatemala and Britain continue to squabble over Belize.

1862 ▶ Belize becomes part of the British Empire.

1867 ▶ First **liberal uprising** under Serpio Cruz.

1871 ▶ Liberal revolution; Justo **Rufino Barrios** becomes president. Start of coffee boom.

1906 ▶ Railway to Pacific coast completed.

1930 ▶ **Jorge Ubico** president – banana boom and height of **United Fruit Company** power.

1944–54 ▶ "Spiritual Socialism"presidencies of **Arévalo** and **Arbenz**; ended by CIA-backed military coup.

1954 ▶ **Carlos Castillo** president: the start of **military rule** and a series of military-backed dictators.

1960s ▶ First **guerrilla** actions, rapidly followed by repressive clampdowns and rise of **death squads** under **Colonel Carlos Arana**.

1968 ▶ US ambassador John Gordon Mein killed by FAR guerrillas in Guatemala City; Guatemalan writer Miguel Ángel Asturias wins Nobel Prize for Literature.

1970 ▶ **Colonel Carlos Arana** president.

1974 ▶ Electoral fraud wins presidency for **Kjell Laugerud**.

1976 ▶ **Earthquake** leaves 23,000 dead, a million homeless.

1978 ▶ **Lucas García** president; thousands die through repression. US bans arms sales to Guatemala. Intense fighting in the highlands between army and guerrillas.

1982 ▶ **Efraín Ríos Montt** seizes presidency. Army begins scorched-earth campaign in the highlands. Belize becomes independent.

1986 ▶ **Vinicio Cerezo** elected: return to civilian rule though power of military remains great.

1990 ▶ **Jorge Serrano** elected with less than 25 percent of vote.

1991 ▶ Guatemala recognizes Belizean independence. Peace talks between guerrillas and government.

1992 ▶ **Rigoberta Menchú** wins Nobel Peace Prize.

1993 ▶ Serrano ousted by generals; **Ramiro Carpio** appointed.

1996 ▶ **Álvaro Arzú** and the PAN elected. **Peace Accords** signed.

1998 ▶ **Hurricane Mitch** devastates much of Central America and kills hundreds in Guatemala; Bishop Juan Geradi assassinated.

2000 ▶ FRG's **Alfonso Portillo** sworn in as president, backed by Ríos Montt.

2001 ▶ Growing instability and disillusion with Portillo: crime wave and riots against VAT tax increases.

2003 ▶ Lawlessness continues. US decertifies Guatemala as "war on drugs" partner as cocaine-smuggling gangs' influence proliferates. Ríos Montt and FRG defeated in elections.

2004 ▶ **Óscar Berger** inaugurated as president. Armed forces numbers are slashed. Portillo flees to Mexico.

2005 ▶ CAFTA trade agreement approved by Guatemalan Congress. Land evictions continue in countryside.

2008 ▶ **Álvaro Colom**'s presidential term begins.

The Maya achievement

For some three thousand years before the arrival of the Spanish, Maya civilization dominated Mesoamerica, leaving behind some of the most impressive architecture in the entire continent. The scale and grandeur of some Maya cities, such as El Mirador around 100 BC rivalled their European contemporaries, and the artistry and splendour of Maya civilization at the height of the Classic era arguably eclipsed that in the Old World. Maya culture was complex and sophisticated, fostering the highest standards of engineering, astronomy, stone carving and mathematics, as well as an intricate writing system.

To appreciate all this you have to see for yourself the remains of the great centres. Despite centuries of neglect, abuse and encroaching jungle, they are still astounding – the biggest temple-pyramids tower up to 70m above the forest floor, well above the jungle canopy. Stone monuments, however, leave much of the story untold, and there is still a great deal that we have to learn about Maya civilization. What follows is the briefest of introductions to the subject, hopefully just enough to whet your appetite for the immense volumes that have been written on it; some of these are listed in "Books", on pp.449–456.

The Maya society

By the Early Classic period, the Maya cities had become organized into a hierarchy of power, with cities such as Tikal and Calakmul dominating vast areas and controlling the smaller sites through a complex structure of **alliances**. The cities jostled for power and influence, occasionally erupting into open warfare, which was also partly fuelled by the need for sacrificial victims. The distance between the larger sites averaged around 30km, and between these were myriad smaller settlements consisting of religious centres and residential groups. The structure of the alliances can be traced through the use of **emblem glyphs**. Only the glyphs of the main centres are used in isolation, while the names of smaller sites are used in conjunction with those of their larger patrons. Of all the myriad Classic cities, the dominant ones were clearly Tikal and Calakmul, with Palenque, Copán, Caracol, Naranjo, Piedras Negras, Yaxhá and Yaxchilán accepting secondary status until the early eighth century when the hierarchy began to dismantle. Cancuén, Dos Pilas and Quiriguá were other key cities, each lording it over, and probably extracting tribute from, many more minor settlements. Trade, marriages and warfare between the large centres were commonplace as the cities were bound up in an endless round of competition and conflict.

By the Late Classic period, population densities across a broad swathe of territory in the central area were as high as 965 people per square kilometre – an extraordinarily high figure, equivalent to densities in rural China or Java today – and as many as ten million people lived in the wider Maya region. It's thought there were strict divisions between the classes, with perhaps eighty percent being preoccupied with intensive cultivation to feed these vast numbers. The peasant farmers, who were at the bottom of the social scale, also provided the labour necessary to construct the monumental temples that decorate the

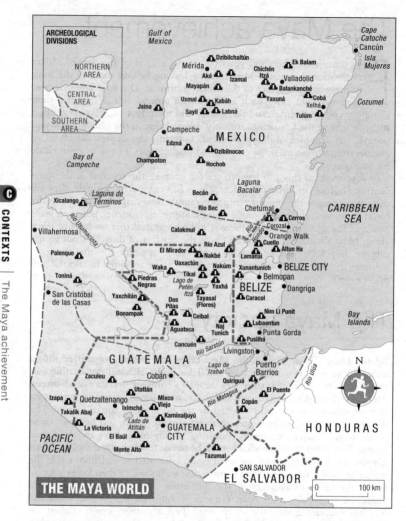

THE MAYA WORLD

ARCHEOLOGICAL DIVISIONS

NORTHERN AREA

CENTRAL AREA

SOUTHERN AREA

Gulf of Mexico

Cape Catoche
Cancún
Isla Mujeres

Dzibilchaltún
Mérida
Aké   Izamal   Chichén Itzá   Ek Balam
Mayapán   Valladolid
Balankanché
Uxmal   Kabáh   Yaxuná   Cobá
Jaina   Sayil   Labná   Xelhá
Tulúm

Cozumel

Campeche
MEXICO
Edzná
Champoton   Dzibilnocac
Hochob

Bay of Campeche

Laguna Bacalar

Becán
Laguna de Términos
Xicalango   Río Bec   Chetumal
CARIBBEAN SEA
Cerros
Corozal
Villahermosa   Calakmul   Orange Walk
Cuello   Altun Ha
Palenque   Río Azul   Lamanai
El Mirador   Nakbé
Toniná   Waka   Uaxactún   Nakúm   Xunantunich   **BELIZE CITY**
Piedras   Tikal   Belmopan
San Cristóbal   Negras   *Lago de*   Yaxhá   **BELIZE**
de las Casas   Yaxchilán   *Petén Itzá*   Tayasal   Dangriga
Dos   (Flores)
Bonampak   Pilas   Ceibal   Caracol
Naj   Nim Li Punit
Aguateca   Tunich   Lubaantun   *Bay Islands*
Cancuén   Pusilhá   Punta Gorda
Río Sarstún   Lívingston

GUATEMALA   *Lago de*   Puerto
Zaculeu   Cobán   *Izabal*   Barrios
Utatlán   Quiriguá
Izapa   Quetzaltenango   Mixco   El Puente
Iximché   Viejo   *Río Motagua*   Copán
Takalik Abaj   Kaminaljuyú
La Victoria   *Lado de*   **GUATEMALA**   **HONDURAS**
El Baúl   *Atitlán*   **CITY**
Monte Alto
Tazumal

PACIFIC OCEAN

N

Río Ulúa

SAN SALVADOR
EL SALVADOR

0   100 km

centre of every city (the Maya did not have the wheel) as well as perform regular "military service" duties. Even in the suburbs where the peasants lived, there are complexes of religious structures with simple, small-scale temples where ceremonies took place.

Although the remains of the great Maya sites are a testament to the scale and sophistication of Maya civilization, they offer little insight into daily life in Maya times. To reconstruct the lives of the ordinary Maya, archeologists have turned to the smaller residential groups that surround the main sites, littered with the remains of household utensils, pottery, bones and farming tools. These groups are made up of simple structures made of poles and wattle-and-daub, each of which was home to a single family. The groups as a whole probably housed an extended family, who would have farmed and hunted together and may well have specialized in some trade or craft. The people living in these groups were commoners, their lives largely dependent on agriculture. Maize, beans, cacao, squash, chillies and fruit trees were cultivated in raised and irrigated fields, while wild fruits were harvested from the surrounding forest. It's not certain whether the land was privately or communally owned.

Until the 1960s, Mayanists had long shared the view that the ordinary Maya were ruled by a scholarly astronomer-priest elite, who were preoccupied with religious devotion and the study of calendrics and the stars. They were thought to be men of reason, with no time for the barbarity of war and conquest, and were often likened to the ancient Greeks. However, this early utopian vision could not have been further from the truth: the decipherment of Maya glyphs has shown that the Maya rulers were primarily concerned with the glories of battle and conquest and the preservation of their royal bloodlines; human sacrifice and bloodletting rituals were also a pivotal part of elite Maya society. The rulers considered themselves to be god–humans and thought that the line of royal accession could only be achieved by sacred validation in the form of human **bloodletting** (see box, p.426).

There were two **elite classes**: *ahau* and *cahal*, who between them probably made up two or three percent of the population. The *ahau* title was reserved exclusively for the ruler and extremely close blood relatives – the top echelon of Maya society; membership could only be inherited. One step down was the *cahal* class, most of whom would have shared bloodlines with the *ahau*. The *cahal* were mainly governors of subsidiary settlements that were under the control of the dominant city-state, and their status was always subordinate to the *ahau*. Although *cahal* lords commissioned their own stelae, the inscriptions always declared loyalty to the regional ruler.

The rulers lived close to the ceremonial centre of the Maya city, in imposing palaces, though the rooms were limited in size because the Maya never mastered the use of the arch. Palaces doubled as administrative centres and were used for official receptions for visiting dignitaries, with strategically positioned thrones where the ruler would preside over religious ceremonies.

The "**middle class**" of Maya society consisted of a professional class (*ah na: ab*) of architects, senior scribes (*ah tz'ib*), sculptors, bureaucrats and master artisans, some of whom were also titled, and probably young princes and important court performers. Priests and shamen can also be included in this middle class though, surprisingly, no title for the priesthood has yet been recognized. It's possible that not giving the priests a title may have been a method used by a fearful ruler to limit their influence. Through their knowledge of calendrics and supernatural prophecies, the priests were relied upon to divine the appropriate time to plant and harvest crops.

There's no doubt that **women** played an influential role in Maya society, and in the Late Classic period there were even some women rulers – Lady Ahpo Katun at Piedras Negras, Lady Ahpo-Hel at Palenque and a Lady Six Sky at Naranjo. Women also presided at court and were given prestigious titles – Lady Cahal of Bonampak, for example. More frequently, however, as in Europe, dynasties were allied and enhanced by the marriage of royal women between cities. One of the best-documented strategic marriages occurred after the great southern city of Copán had suffered the humiliation of having its leader captured and sacrificed by upstart local rival Quiriguá in 738 AD – a royal marriage was arranged with a noblewoman from Palenque more than 500km away.

Maya **agriculture** adapted to the needs of the developing society, adopting intensive and sophisticated methods from as early as 400 BC when farmers at

El Mirador used vast quantities of swamp mud to fertilize their crops. Some land was terraced, drained or irrigated in order to improve its productivity and ensure that fields didn't have to lie fallow for long periods, and the capture of water became crucial to the success of a site.

The large lowland cities, which are today hemmed in by forest, were once surrounded by open fields, canals and residential compounds, although slash-and-burn was probably practised in marginal and outlying areas. Agriculture became a necessary absorption, with the ordinary Maya trading at least some of their food in markets, although all households still had a kitchen garden where they grew herbs and fruit.

Maize has always been the basis of the Maya **diet**, in ancient times as much as it is today. Once harvested it was made into *saka*, a cornmeal gruel that was eaten with chilli as the first meal of the day. During the day labourers ate a mixture of corn dough and water, and we know that *tamales* were also a popular speciality. The main meal, eaten in the evenings, would have been similarly maize-based, although it may well have included meat and vegetables. As a supplement to this simple diet, deer, peccary, wild turkey, duck, pigeon and quail were all hunted with bows and arrows or blowguns. The Maya also made use of dogs, both for hunting and the dinner table. Fish were also eaten, and the remains of fishhooks and nets have been found at some sites, while there is evidence that those living on the coast traded dried fish and salt far inland. The forest provided firewood as well as food, and cotton was cultivated to be dyed with natural colours and then spun into cloth.

The Maya calendar

One of the cornerstones of Maya thinking was an obsession with **time**. For both practical and mystical reasons the Maya developed a highly sophisticated understanding of arithmetic, calendrics and astronomy, all of which they believed gave them the power to understand and predict events. All great occasions were interpreted on the basis of the Maya calendar, and it was this precise understanding of time that gave the ruling elite its authority. The majority of the carvings, on temples and stelae, record the exact date at which rulers were born, ascended to power, and died.

The basis of all Maya **calculation** was the vigesimal counting system, which used multiples of twenty. All figures were written using a combination of three symbols – a shell to denote zero, a dot for one and a bar for five – which you can still see on many stelae. When calculating calendrical systems, the Maya used a slightly different notation known as the head-variant system, in which each number from one to twenty was represented by a deity, whose head was used to represent the number.

When it comes to the Maya **calendar** things start to get a little more complicated, as the Maya used a number of different counting systems, depending on the reason the date was being calculated. The basic unit of the Maya calendar was the day, or *kin*, followed by the *uinal*, a group of twenty days roughly equivalent to our month; but at the next level things start to get even more complex as the Maya marked the passing of time in three distinct ways. The **260-day almanac** (16 *uinals*) was used to calculate the timing of ceremonial events. Each day was associated with a particular deity that had strong influence over those born on that particular day. This calendar wasn't divided into months but had 260 distinct day-names – a system still in use among some Kaqchikel and Mam Maya who name their children according to its structure and celebrate fiestas according to its dictates. A second calendar, the so-called **"vague year"** or *haab*, was made up of eighteen *uinals* and five *kins*, a total of 365 days, making it a close approximation of the solar year. These two calendars weren't used in isolation but operated in parallel so that once every 52 years the new day of the solar year coincided with the same day in the 260-day almanac, a meeting that was regarded as very powerful and marked the start of a new era.

Finally, the Maya had another system for marking the passing of history, which is used on dedicatory monuments. The system, known as the **Long Count**, is based on the great cycle of thirteen *baktuns* (a period of 5128 years). The current period dates from August 13, 3114 BC, and is destined to come to an end on December 10, 2012. The dates in this system simply record the number of days that have elapsed since the start of the current great cycle, a task that calls for ten different numbers – recording the equivalent of years, decades, centuries, and so on. In later years, the Maya sculptors obviously tired of this exhaustive process and opted instead for the Short Count, an abbreviated version.

Astronomy

Alongside their fascination with time, the Maya were obsessed with the sky and devoted much time and energy to unravelling its patterns. Observatories were being constructed as early as 500 BC and many of the large sites such as Copán, Uaxactún and Chichén Itzá have temples carefully aligned with solar and lunar sequences.

The Maya showed a great understanding of **astronomy**, and with their 365-day "vague year" they were just a quarter of a day out in their calculations of the solar year. At Copán, towards the end of the seventh century AD, Maya astronomers had calculated the lunar cycle at 29.53020 days, not too far off our current estimate of 29.53059. In the Dresden Codex (a copy of which can be found in Guatemala City's Popol Vuh museum), their calculations extend to the 405 lunations over a period of 11,960 days, as part of a pattern that set out to predict eclipses. At the same time, they had calculated with astonishing accuracy the movements of Venus, Mars, and perhaps Mercury. Venus was of particular importance to the Maya as they linked its presence with success in war; several stelae record the appearance of Venus prompting the decision to strike at an enemy – an attack known as a **"star war"**.

Maya time: the units

1 *kin* = 24 hours
20 *kins* = 1 *uinal*, or 20 days
18 *uinals* = 1 *tun*, or 360 days
20 *tuns* = 1 *katun*, or 7200 days
20 *katuns* = 1 *baktun*, or 144,000 days
20 *baktuns* = 1 *pictun*, or 2,880,000 days
20 *pictuns* = 1 *calabtun*, or 57,600,000 days
20 *calabtuns* = 1 *kinchiltun*, or 1,152,000,000 days
20 *kinchiltuns* = 1 *alautun*, or 23,040,000,000 days

Religion

Maya cosmology is far from straightforward as at every stage an idea is balanced by its opposite and each part of the universe is made up of many layers. To the ancient Maya (and many indigenous people today) this is the third version of the earth, the previous two having been destroyed by deluges. The current version is a flat surface, with four corners, each associated with a certain colour: white for north, red for east, yellow for south and black for west, with green at the centre. Above the earth, the sky is supported by four trees, each a different colour and species – these are also sometimes depicted as gods, known as *Bacabs*. At its centre, the sky is supported by a ceiba tree. Above the sky is a heaven of thirteen layers, each of which has its own god, with the very top

Ritual bloodletting and the Maya

Ritual bloodletting was a fundamental part of Maya religious life, practised by all strata of society. It took many forms, from cursory self-inflicted blood offerings to elaborate ceremonies involving the mass sacrifice of captive kings and enemy warriors. The Maya modelled their lives according to a vision of the cosmos, and within this arena, human actions could affect the future, auspiciously or otherwise. Pivotal to this vision was the concept that blood-spilling helped repay man's debt to the gods, who had endowed the gift of life.

The K'iche' Maya creation story, the **Popol Vuh**, tells of the creation, destruction and re-creation of previous imperfect worlds before their own was made. Earlier races had been conceived and then destroyed for failing to praise their creators. The Maya people were made by mixing ground maize, the region's food staple, with the sacrificial blood of the gods. Consumed by the omnipresent fear that the world could again be destroyed, the Maya sought to appease the gods and ensure continued prosperity through bloodletting.

First practised by the **Olmec**, Mesoamerica's "mother culture", more than 3000 years ago, bloodletting continued until the arrival of the conquistadors. Among the early Maya, ritual blood offerings were primarily concerned with renewal and agricultural fertility, closely linked to creation mythology. Later, in the Classic period, with increasing social complexity and proven agricultural reliability, bloodletting may have become more related to the shifting concerns of the day, including warfare and political alliances. The practice later grew to apocalyptic degrees of carnage among the **Aztecs**, horrifying the Spanish, whose chronicler Diego Duran describes the sacrifice of 80,000 victims at the rededication of the Templo Mayor in their capital.

As well as direct representations of the sacrificial act, the Maya developed a symbolic iconography of bloodletting, so that the smallest motif, such as three knotted bands or smoke scrolls, could express blood sacrifice. Maya bloodletting iconography had its roots in Olmec art, including the elaborate vision-quest serpent, depicted in the eighth-century Yaxchilán lintels, which grew from the corpus of Olmec serpentine motifs. Through their wealth and control of resources, the Maya nobility recorded their actions by using non-perishable artistic mediums – the fact that depictions of bloodletting were chosen for preservation on **stone**, a costly and laborious medium, confirms its religious, social and political significance.

A common bloodletting ritual may have consisted of cutting earlobes, cheeks, thighs or other fleshy parts of the body and collecting the blood to burn, or sprinkling it directly on a shrine or idol. Undertaken for numerous reasons – to bless a journey, the planting of crops, or the passing of a family member – these rites may have been layer overseen by an owl. Other attested models of the world include that of a turtle (the land) floating on the sea. However, it's the underworld, *Xibalbá*, the "Place of Fright", which was of greatest importance to the ancient Maya (and many traditionalists today), as it is in this direction that they pass after death, on their way to the place of rest. The nine layers of hell are guarded by the "Lords of the Night", and deep caves are thought to connect with the underworld.

The ancient Maya also recognized an incredible array of gods, though today this concept of a pantheon is much less common. Every divinity had four manifestations based upon colour and direction, and many also had counterparts in the underworld and consorts of the opposite sex. In addition, the Maya also had an extensive array of patron deities, each associated with a particular trade or particular class, while every activity from suicide to sex had its deity.

performed individually or by an entire community, accompanied by prayers, the sacrifice of animals and the burning of copal incense.

Elite bloodletting rituals often took place at important or auspicious occasions: during accession ceremonies, at the birth of an heir, to mark the passing of a calendar round, in times of war, drought or disease, and to ensure regeneration and prosperity. Bloodletting also served as a rite of passage, or the individual quest for a prophetic vision and communication with the gods, providing access to the spiritual world.

There seem to have been two main **auto-sacrificial rituals** practised by the Maya elite. These were not undertaken lightly and carried severe physical and psychological repercussions. As part of a larger ceremony, the actual act of letting blood may have been preceded by days of preparation, meditation, fasting, sexual abstinence and bodily purification with sweat baths. A male rite was to draw blood by pricking the penis with either a stingray spine, obsidian lancet or flint knife. The second rite – piercing the tongue – was probably performed by both sexes, although it's most famously illustrated by Lady Xoc in the **Yaxchilán lintels** (now housed in the British Museum). The blood offering was then soaked into bark paper and collected in ceremonial bowls to be burnt as a presentation and petition to the gods.

The Maya also practiced bloodletting in the form of **captive sacrifice**, a highly ceremonial affair in which prolonged death and torture were features – gruesomely depicted in the Bonampak murals. Prisoners then either faced death by decapitation, or by having their hearts removed. Hearts were then burnt as an offering to the gods, while decapitated heads might be displayed on a skull-rack.

Maya **warfare** often reflected the need for ritual bloodletting, as warriors frequently sought to capture alive rulers of rival cities, who would then be imprisoned and sacrificed at a later date. The soaring temples of the city centre served as ceremonial theatres for elaborate religious rituals, allowing victories to be proclaimed to the entire community. Sacrificial victims would have been especially important to mark the accession of a new ruler, the bloodletting adding legitimacy to the king and affirming his power.

Blood offerings were integral to ancient Amerindian life, a tradition passed from the Olmec to the Maya and then on to the Aztec. Bloodletting developed from culture to culture through material and ideological exchange but always retained its central elements – links to the supernatural, mythical origins, and a vital connection with the continued prosperity of mankind and mother earth.

Simone Clifford-Jaeger

Religious ritual

The combined complexity of the Maya pantheon and calendar gave every day a particular significance, and the ancient Maya were bound up in a demanding **cycle of religious ritual**. The main purpose of ritual was the procurement of success by appealing to the right god at the right time and in the right way. As every event, from planting to childbirth, was associated with a particular divinity, all of the main events in daily life demanded some kind of religious ritual. For the most important of these, the Maya staged elaborate ceremonies.

Although each ceremony had its own format, a certain pattern bound them all. The correct day was carefully chosen by priestly divination, and for several days beforehand the participants fasted and remained abstinent. The main ceremony was dominated by the expulsion of all evil spirits, the burning of incense before the idols, a sacrifice (either animal or human), and **bloodletting** (see box, pp.426–427).

In divination rituals, used to foretell the pattern of future events or account for the cause of past events, the elite used various **drugs** to achieve altered states of consciousness. Perhaps the most obvious of these was alcohol, either made from fermented maize or a combination of honey and the bark of the balanche tree. Wild tobacco, which is considerably stronger than the modern domesticated version, was also smoked. The Maya also used a range of hallucinogenic mushrooms, all of which were appropriately named, but none more so than the *xibalbaj obox*, "underworld mushroom", and the *k'aizalah obox*, "lost judgement mushroom".

Indigenous Guatemala

A vital indigenous culture is perhaps Guatemala's most unique feature. Although the Maya people may appear quiet and humble, their costumes, fiestas and markets are a riot of colour, creativity and celebration. Most Maya people remain extremely attached to local traditions and values, and regard themselves as *indígenas* first and Guatemalans second.

The indigenous Maya, the vast majority of whom live in the western highlands, make up about half of Guatemala's population, although it's extremely hard to define exactly who is Maya. For the sake of the national census, people who consider themselves indigenous are classed as such, regardless of their parentage. And when it comes to defining the Maya as a group, culture is more important than pedigree, as the Maya define themselves through their relationships with their land, gods, villages and families. Holding aloof from the melting pot of modern Guatemalan society, Maya people adhere instead to their traditional *costumbres*, codes of practice that govern every aspect of life.

As a result, the only way to define Maya culture is by describing its main traits, acknowledging that all indigenous Guatemalans will accept some of these attributes, and accepting that many are neither *indígena* nor ladino, but combine elements of both.

Indigenous culture

When the Spanish set about conquering the Maya tribes of Guatemala they altered every aspect of life for the indigenous people, uprooting their social structures and reshaping their communities. Before the Conquest the bulk of the population had lived scattered in the hills, paying tribute to a tribal elite, and surviving through subsistence farming and hunting. Under Spanish rule they were moved into new **villages** known as *reducciones*, where their homes were clustered around a church. Horizons shrank rapidly as allegiances became localized and the village hierarchies that still dominate the highlands today replaced existing tribal structures.

For almost five hundred years the Maya population has suffered repeated abuse, as the elite has exploited indigenous land and labour, regarding the Maya as an expendable commodity. But within their own communities indigenous Guatemalans were left pretty much to themselves and developed an astoundingly introspective culture that is continually adapting to new threats, reshaping itself for the future. **Village life** has been insulated from the outside world until very recently and in remote areas few women speak much Spanish; 28 native languages and dialects (see map, p.430) are still spoken. Today's indigenous culture is a complex synthesis which includes elements of Maya, Spanish and modern American cultures.

The majority of the indigenous population still live by **subsistence agriculture**, their homes either spread across the hills or gathered in small villages.

Throughout this guide we have used the terms "Maya" or "*indígenas*" to refer to those Guatemalans of Maya origin. You may also hear them called *Indio* (or Indian), though in Guatemala this term has racially pejorative connotations.

Farmers tend their *milpas*, growing beans, chillies, maize and squash – the staple diet for thousands of years. To the Maya, land is sacred and the need to own and farm it is central to their culture, despite the fact that few can survive by farming alone. Some cash crops are also grown – including broccoli, snow peas, fruit and coffee – much of it for export.

Many Maya migrate to the coast for several months a year, where they often work in appalling conditions on plantations to supplement their income. However, huge numbers are now choosing to head north to the US to work illegally instead, their overseas **remittances** now forming a crucial part of the local economy in virtually every mountain village. Traditional crafts (like rope-making, pottery and textile production) remain important in some areas while cut-flower production for the export market is increasingly profitable. **Tourism** dollars also make a financial impact here and there, particularly around Lago de Atitlán, but also in the Ixil, Todos Santos and Quetzaltenango areas, too.

Family life tends to bow to tradition, with large families very much a part of the indigenous culture. Marriage customs vary from place to place but in general

the groom is expected to pay the bride's parents, and the couple may well live with their in-laws. Authority within the village is usually given to men, although women are increasingly involved in decision making. Customs are slowly changing, but generally men spend most of the day tending the *milpas* and vegetable plots, while women are based in the family home, looking after the children, cooking and weaving. However, Maya women are by no means confined to the house and frequently travel to distant markets to sell excess fruit, vegetables and textiles and to buy, or barter for, thread and supplies. In some places particularly noted for their weavings, such as Nebaj or Chajul, whole families decamp to Antigua or Panajachel for three or four days to sell their crafts to tourists.

Indigenous religion

Every aspect of Maya life – from the birth of a child to the planting of corn – is loaded with religious significance, based on a complicated **fusion of the Maya pantheon and Catholic religion**. Christ and the saints have taken their place alongside *Dios Mundo*, the God of the World, and *Hurakan*, the Heart of Heaven. The two religions have merged to form a hybrid, in which the outward forms of Catholicism are used to worship the ancient pantheon, a compromise that was probably fostered by Spanish priests. The symbol of the cross, for example, was well known to the Maya, as used to signify the four winds of heaven, the four directions, and everlasting life. Today many of the deities have both Maya and Hispanic names, and are usually associated with a particular saint. All the deities remain subordinate to a mighty and remote supreme being, and Christ takes a place in the upper echelons of the hierarchy.

For the Maya, **God** is everywhere, bound up in the seasons, the mountains, the crops, the soil, the air and the sky. Prayer and offerings mark every important event, with disasters often attributed to divine intervention. Even more numerous than the gods, **spirits** are found in every imaginable object, binding together the universe. Each individual is born with a *nahaul*, or spiritual counterpart, in the animal world, and his or her destiny is bound up with that particular animal. The spirits of dead ancestors are also ever-present and have to be looked after by each successive generation.

Traditionally, a community's religious hierarchy organizes its worship. All office-holders are male, and throughout their lives they progress through the system, moving from post to post. The various posts are grouped into *cofradías*, ritual brother-hoods, each of which is responsible for a particular saint. Throughout the year the saint is kept in the home of an elder member, and on the appointed date, in the midst of a fiesta, it's paraded through the streets, to spend the next year somewhere else. The elder responsible for the saint will have to pay for much of the fiesta, including costumes, alcohol and assorted offerings, but it's a responsibility, or cargo, that's considered a great honour. In the traditional village hierarchy, it's these duties that give the elders, known as *principales*, a prominent role in village life and it's through these duties that they exercise their authority, such as the organization of the annual **fiesta**. (In some villages, such as Chichicastenango and Sololá, a *municipalidad indígena*, or indigenous council, operates alongside the *cofradías*, and is similarly hierarchical. As men work their way up through the system they may well alternate between the civil and religious hierarchies.) The *cofradías* don't necessarily confine themselves to the traditional list of saints, and have been known to foster "evil" saints, such as San Simón or **Maximón**, a drinking, smoking ladino figure, sometimes referred to as Judas or Pedro de Alvarado.

On a more superstitious level, native priests (*costumbristas*, or *aj'itz* in K'iche' and Kaqchikel areas) communicate with the gods and spirits to cater to people's personal religious needs. This is usually done on behalf of an individual client who's in search of a blessing, and often takes place at shrines and caves in the mountains, with offerings of copal, a type of incense, and alcohol. The *costumbristas* also make extensive use of old Maya sites, and small burnt patches of grass litter many of the ruins in the highlands. Indigenous priests are also credited with the ability to cast spells, predict the future and communicate with the dead.

Evangelism in Guatemala

One of the greatest surprises awaiting first-time travellers in Guatemala is the number of evangelical churches in the country, with fundamentalist, Pentecostal or neo-Pentecostal services taking place in most towns and villages. Although early Protestant missions came to Guatemala as far back as 1882, the impact of US-based churches remained marginal and largely unnoticed until the 1950s, when **state repression** and the subsequent **guerrilla war** began to weaken the power of the Catholic Church. Up until this time, more than 95 percent of the population was officially Catholic, though the rural Maya had their own hybrid forms of worship that mixed Catholic ceremony with pagan rite.

While the hierarchy of the Catholic Church remained fervently anti-Communist and closely aligned with the economic, political and military elite, during the early 1960s many rural Catholic priests became heavily influenced by liberation theology, supporting peasant leagues and development projects, and some even joined the guerrillas. Subsequently, the ruling class of generals, politicians and big landowners began to consider the Catholic Church as being riddled with Communist sympathizers, and targeted perceived troublemakers accordingly. By the early 1980s, so many priests had been murdered by the state-sponsored death squads that the Catholic Church pulled out of the entire department of El Quiché in protest. In contrast, many evangelical missionaries preached the importance of an army victory over the guerrillas and, with their pro-business, anti-Communist rhetoric, attracted many converts anxious to avoid suspicion and survive. In addition, the early evangelicals had made it a priority to learn the native Maya languages, and had the Bible translated into K'iche', Mam, Kaqchikel and other tongues.

However, it was the devastating **1976 earthquake** that really sparked the march of US evangelism in Guatemala. Church-backed disaster-relief programmes brought in millions of dollars of medicine, food and toys to those prepared to convert, and shattered villages were rebuilt with new schools and health centres. In the eyes of the impoverished rural villagers, Protestantism became linked with prosperity, and lively evangelical church services, where dancing, music and singing were the norm, quickly gained huge popularity.

The movement received another boost in 1982, when **General Efrían Ríos Montt** seized power in a military coup to become Guatemala's first evangelical leader. The population was treated to Montt's maniacal, marathon Sunday sermons, and a new flood of mission teams entered the country from the southern United States. For many Guatemalans, Ríos Montt represented the best and worst of evangelism: he was frenzied and fanatical, yet also fostered a reputation for strictness and probity (despite the terrible human-rights violations under his brief tenure). Ríos Montt was ousted after just seventeen months in power, though he was to dominate Guatemalan politics through the 1990s as leader of the FRG party, and ran for president himself in 2003, only to be soundly defeated.

Guatemala is today the least Catholic country in Latin America, with around sixty percent of the population looking to the Vatican for guidance and about forty percent supporting the evangelicals.

For specific medical problems, the Maya appeal to *zahorines* who practise traditional medicine with a combination of invocation and herbs, and are closely associated with indigenous religious traditions.

Until the 1950s, when Catholic **missionaries** became active in the highlands, many indigenous Guatemalans had no idea that there was a gulf between their own religion and orthodox Catholicism. At first, the missionaries drew most of their support from the younger generation, many of whom were frustrated by the rigidity of the village hierarchy. Gradually, this eroded the authority of the traditional religious system, undermining the *cofradías*, disapproving of traditional fiestas, and scorning the work of the native priests. As a part of this, the reforming movement Catholic Action, which combines the drive for orthodoxy with an involvement in social issues, has also had a profound impact.

After the 1976 earthquake, waves of Protestant missionaries, known as *evangélicos*, arrived in Guatemala, and their presence has also accelerated the decline of traditional religion (see box, p.432). In the 1980s their numbers were greatly boosted by the influence of Ríos Montt, at a time when the Catholic Church was suffering severe repression. These days there are at least three hundred different sects, backed by a huge injection of money from the US, and offering all sorts of incentives to fresh converts. But indigenous religion is no stranger to oppression, and despite the efforts of outsiders the *costumbristas* and *cofradías* are still in business, and fiestas remain drunken and vaguely pagan. Indeed, since the end of the civil war there has been an upsurge in interest in Maya religious practice – the current president of Guatemala, Álvaro Colom, has studied Maya spiritualism.

Markets and fiestas

At the heart of the indigenous economy is the **weekly market**, which remains central to life in the highlands and provides one of the best opportunities to see Maya life at close quarters. The majority of the indigenous population still lives by subsistence farming but spares a day or two a week to gather together in the nearest village and trade surplus produce. The market is as much a social occasion as an economic one and people come to talk, eat, drink, gossip and have a good time. In some places the action starts the night before with marimba music and heavy drinking.

On market day itself the village is filled by a steady flow of people, arriving by pick-up or bus, on foot, or by donkey. In no time at all trading gets under way, and the plaza is soon buzzing with activity and humming with conversation, although raised voices are a rarity, with deals struck after protracted, but always polite, negotiations. The scale and atmosphere of markets varies from place to place. The country's largest is in **San Francisco el Alto**, on Fridays, and draws traders from throughout the country. Other renowned ones are the vegetable market of **Almolonga** and **Sololá**'s huge Tuesday and Friday affairs, but almost every village has its day. **Chichicastenango**'s vast Thursday and Sunday markets are probably Guatemala's most famous, and remain important gatherings for highlanders, though the tourist-orientated souvenir stalls are mushrooming here. But perhaps the most enjoyable of Guatemala's markets are well away from the Carretera Interamericana, in tiny, isolated hamlets. Up high in the folds of the mountains, in places like lonely Chajul or isolated Santa Eulalia, the pleasure is simply soaking up the scene, as traders and villagers barter and banter in the hushed clicks of the local dialect and near-whispers, in the unhurried commercial ritual that so defines Maya highland life.

Once a year every village, however small, indulges in an orgy of celebration in honour of its patron saint – you'll find a list of them at the end of each chapter. These **fiestas** are a great swirl of dance, music, religion, endless firecrackers, eating and outrageous drinking, and express the vitality of indigenous culture. Everyone tries to return to their home town at fiesta time, with emigrants journeying from Guatemala City (and even the US) to join in the celebrations. Religious processions are given due importance, as the image of the local patron saint is paraded through the streets, accompanied by the elders of the *cofradía*, who dress in full regalia. The larger fiestas also involve funfairs and week-long markets. Traditional music is played with marimbas, drums and flutes; professional bands also may be hired, blasting out popular tunes through crackling PA systems.

Dance, too, is very much a part of fiestas, and incorporates routines and ideas that date from ancient Maya times. Dance costumes are incredibly elaborate, covered in mirrors and sequins, and have to be rented for the occasion. Despite the cost, which is high by highland standards, the dancers see their role both as an obligation – to tradition and the community – and an honour. Most of the dances form an extension of dramatic tradition through which local history was retold in dance dramas. The Dance of the Conquistadors is one of the most popular, modelled on the Dance of the Moors and introduced by the Spanish as a re-enactment of the Conquest, although in some cases it's been instilled with a significance that can never have been intended by the invaders. The dancers often see no connection with the Conquest, but dance instead to release the spirits of the dead, a function perhaps closer to Maya religion than Catholicism. The Palo Volador, a dramatic spectacle in which men swing perilously to the ground from a twenty-metre pole, certainly dates from the pre-Columbian era (these days you'll only see it in Cubulco, Chichicastenango and Joyabaj), as does the *Dance of the Deer*, while the Dance of the Bullfight and the Dance of the Volcano relate incidents from the Conquest itself. Most of the dances do have steps to them, but the dancers are usually blind drunk and sway around as best they can in time to the music, sometimes tumbling over each other or even passing out – so don't expect to see anything too dainty.

The Maya today

The Maya were the main victims of the decades-long civil war, which not only killed 160,000 highlanders and left a million homeless, but also attacked the very foundation of indigenous culture in Guatemala. The military viewed the Maya as inherently subversive, and communities were set against each other as men were conscripted into PAC paramilitary patrols and pressured to betray anyone showing signs of dissidence against the state.

But under civilian rule, a **Maya cultural revival** has steadily matured, as Guatemala's indigenous people have pursued the freedom of organization, protest and participation denied them for centuries. Hundreds of schools have been founded to educate Maya children in their own tongues, increasing numbers of indigenous writers and journalists have emerged, more and more Maya books and magazines are being published, and *indígena* radio stations have been set up. The shifting mood has even influenced youth culture, with Maya shamanic courses becoming popular and ladino university students asserting their mixed-race identity and proclaiming a Maya heritage. Yet despite these changes Guatemala remains a seismically divided country. Racism is endemic and most Maya, still subject to institutionalized discrimination, live in poverty (over 70 percent, according to the government's own figures).

Human rights in Guatemala

Since the arrival of the Spanish, Guatemalan history has been character-ized by political repression and economic exploitation, involving the denial of the most basic human rights. A horrific catalogue of events stretches across the past five hundred years, but reached levels as barbaric as any previously seen in the late 1970s and the early 1980s when the civil war was at its peak. Some progress has been made in recent years to improve the human-rights situation, but campaigners who speak out routinely face intimidation, violence and death if they dare to upset the country's shadowy hidden powers. In 2007 the nation even made *Foreign Policy* magazine's list of "Failed States" as the government did not "provide domestic security or basic public services to its citizens".

A brief history

When conquistador **Pedro de Alvarado** arrived in the region in 1523, he introduced the notion of race-based exploitation that has dominated Guatemala to the present day. Once the initial conquest was over the majority of survivors were systematically herded into villages, deprived of their land, and forced to work in the new plantations. Revolts against colonial and ladino rule were common throughout the eighteenth and nineteenth centuries, but these tended to flare up in specific towns rather than amount to nationwide rebellions. All were met with severe repression. The demands of the coffee industry put fresh strains on the indigenous population, as their land and labour were once again exploited for the benefit of foreign investors and the ruling elite.

The most significant human-rights developments came during the govern-ments of **Arévalo** and **Arbenz** (1945–55), which for the first time sought to address the needs of the indigenous population. Local organizations such as unions and cooperatives were free to operate, suffrage was extended to include all adults, health and schooling were expanded, and land was redistributed to the dispossessed. For the first time in the country's history the issues of inequality and injustice were seriously addressed. However, in 1954 the government was overthrown by a CIA-backed coup, which cleared the stage for military rule and ushered in the modern era of repression.

After 1954 the army dominated the government, operating in alliance with the landowning elite and foreign business interests to consolidate their power. Large-scale repression of leftists followed in the mid-1960s, which was countered by a **guerrilla** movement in the east.. The army was unable to strike directly at its enemy and opted instead to eradicate their support in the community: between 1966 and 1977 some 10,000 noncombatants were killed. **Death squads** became a permanent feature of Guatemalan politics during military rule – assassinating unionists, left-wing politicians and students.

By 1975 the guerrilla movement was once again on the rise, as were peasant organizations like the Committee for Campesino Unity (CUC), cooperatives and unions, many inspired by the move towards **liberation theology**, under which the Catholic Church began to campaign on social issues. By 1979 three **guerrilla movements** were well established, operating across the country from Petén to the Pacific coast. **General Lucas García** unleashed an era of unprecedented mass repression against politicians, labour leaders, priests and leftists in the cities, while in the countryside the war against the guerrillas also reached a new intensity, as selective killings were replaced by outright massacres. Once again the army found itself pitched against an elusive enemy and resorted to indiscriminate killings in a bid to undermine peasant support for the guerrillas. It's estimated that perhaps 35,000 died during the first four years of the Lucas administration, the vast majority killed either by the security forces or by death squads.

Under the next military leader, **General Efrían Ríos Montt**, the state's tactics changed as the government ordered PAC paramilitary groups to patrol the countryside. The level of violence increased as the army began to make big gains in the fight against the rebels. Amnesty International charge Montt with operating a genocidal campaign in the department of Quiché, where the slaughter was worst.

Ríos Montt was replaced by **Mejía Víctores** in August 1983, and there followed a drop in the level of rural repression, and the process of reconstruction began. Guerrilla forces fell to around 1500, and although military campaigns continued, "model villages" were now being built to replace those that had been destroyed. Important grassroots **human-rights organizations** began to spring up in this period, including the Mutual Support Group (GAM), comprising families of the disappeared, and the National Commission of Guatemalan Widows (CONAVIGUA), a very significant and largely indigenous group. Though the members of these groups faced routine intimidation and frequent death threats, they marked the emergence of a new period of Maya political activism.

Towards the end of 1985 the country faced its first free elections in thirty years.

Civilian rule and the Peace Accords

A marked decrease in the quantity of human-rights violations followed the election of civilian president **Vinicio Cerezo** in 1986, although things quickly started to deteriorate once again and abductions, killings and intimidation remained widespread. No one accused Cerezo of involvement in the murders; however, members of the security forces apparently carried them out, and so it was a measure of his inability to control them.

Although the early 1990s saw limited progress in improving the human-rights situation, the government was forced to tackle several high-profile cases, including the murder of street children and the assassinations of US citizen Michael Devine and anthropologist Myrna Mack Chang, and for the first time members of the armed forces were convicted of human-rights violations. A number of defiant local groups continued to denounce these abuses, particularly GAM, many of whose members and leaders were kidnapped and murdered. The government's Human Rights Commission received more than one thousand complaints of human-rights violations and acted on none of them.

Meanwhile, out **in the highlands**, the people of Santiago Atitlán expelled the army from their village, after troops shot and killed thirteen people (see p.162), and a number of other villages called for army bases to be closed. The confidence of the Maya population was further boosted in 1992, when the

Nobel Peace Prize was awarded to **Rigoberta Menchú**, briefly focusing world attention on the plight of Guatemala's indigenous population. The Indigenous Rights Accords of 1995 sought to tackle outstanding issues relating to the Maya, including education and the promotion of indigenous languages, but only limited progress has been made on these issues to date.

One of the most crucial strands of the **Peace Accords of December 1996** was the establishment of a Truth Commission, overseen by MINUGUA (the UN mission to Guatemala), to investigate human-rights abuses committed during the civil war. Though the commission lacked legal teeth, military forces (including the army, civil patrols, police and death squads) were held culpable for 93 percent of the killings. A parallel investigation, REMHI, established by the Catholic Church, also concluded that the military and civil patrols were accountable for 91 percent of the killings, while the guerrillas and unknown assailants were responsible for the remainder.

Two days after the report was presented, **Bishop Juan Geradi**, who was in charge of the REMHI project, was found beaten to death at his home in Guatemala City. The assassination of one of Guatemala's most prominent human-rights campaigners outraged the nation, bringing thousands onto the streets in protest. Eventually three elite military chiefs and a priest were found guilty but the weakness of the nation's justice system was all too clear. A climate of fear persists and those who dare to challenge the interests of the elite, hidden powers and criminal gangs face intimidation and violence.

The situation today

Amnesty International's 2007 report on Guatemala concentrated on the high rates of violent crime in society and the continuing culture of impunity that shielded the perpetrators of these attacks.

The most perturbing issue remains the number of women murdered in Guatemala, many dying the most gruesome of deaths for apparently motiveless reasons, a sadistic phenomenon known as **femicide**. At least 580 women died in 2007, with many of the victims' bodies showing evidence of torture, mutilation and rape in the moments before death. These deaths were related to gang violence and territorial disputes, most killed in street gang initiation rituals. For years the police unit dedicated to investigating these killings was woefully under-resourced, but in 2007 the UN Commission against Impunity in Guatemala (CICIG) promised to devote far greater resources to targeting the gangs and bringing the murderers to justice. Historically, one of the obstacles to successful prosecutions has been inadequate legislation, including the lack of an effective law against rape. Progress was made when Congress approved a new law dealing with femicide and violence against women in April 2008 after intense lobbying from women's groups and human-rights organizations, with life sentences for gender-based crimes and long sentences for physical and psychological abuse.

Another pressing human-rights issue is the plight of the several thousand **street children**, most of whom live in the capital and are frequently subject to violent attack by vigilantes, security guards and policemen. Large numbers of children scratch a living on the city's streets through petty crime and begging. Using meticulous documentation and dogged perseverance, charities including Casa Alianza have pursued the perpetrators through the courts and scored a number of successes, including the payment of US$500,000 in June

For more information on human rights in Guatemala contact either the Guatemalan Human Rights Commission – USA (@www.ghrc-usa.org), Amnesty International (@www.amnesty.org) or Human Rights Watch (@www.hrw.org). These organizations all publish regular bulletins and reports on the current situation in the country.

2001 to the families of five children who had been tortured and murdered by two policemen.

Campaigning against violent crime or corruption, or challenging the authority of Guatemala's organized crime networks, is dangerous work. Every year there are hundred of attacks on campaigning journalists and human-rights leaders and organizations focusing on economic, social and cultural rights. Death threats are common and families of activists are also targeted. In September 2008 Yuri Melini, director of CALAS (the Centre for Environmental, Social and Legal Action), was shot by masked men, and 2-year-old Yira Argueta López, daughter of a REMHI project leader investigating civil war deaths, was strangled to death in Chimaltenango in January 2005. Few in Guatemala doubt that these attacks are carried out by *poderes ocultos*, or "hidden powers", mafia-like crime structures fearless of retribution.

"Clandestine and **illegal armed groups** still operate with impunity in Guatemala," Amnesty says. "These groups have been linked to organized crime and are thought to have infiltrated the police, army and some state institutions." According to GAM, the human-rights group, "These structures are made up of those who violated human rights in the recent past and today seek the manner to enrich themselves and prevent the investigation of their crimes."

Land reform, another critical issue, has never been tackled in Guatemala. Though the hard statistics are difficult to pin down, it's generally accepted that seventy percent of the country's agricultural land is owned by just three percent of the population. The squatting of fincas by landless campesinos has proliferated in recent years, and today Guatemala has dozens of potentially incendiary disputes. President Berger ramped up the eviction rate during his term, including a notorious incident at Finca Nuevo Linda, where roughly two thousand police took on some three thousand peasant squatters, resulting in eleven deaths and hundreds of injured. Berger reacted by applying the full might of the law against these landless peasants in actions that placated his natural constituency, the landowning elite or, as MINUGUA put it, "with an undue deference by the government to the demands of landowners".

The state's efforts to deal with the perpetrators of **civil war crimes** – and safeguard the security of the victims' families who are pressing for investigation – has also been woeful, contrary to the demands of the Peace Accords. Guatemalan human-rights groups attempted to prosecute ex-military leaders through the international and national courts, and Spain issued an international arrest warrant for Efraín Ríos Montt (and other generals) in 2007, though Montt evaded this when he was elected to Congress, which granted him immunity. However other organizations have successfully obtained compensation from the Guatemalan government through the Inter-American justice system for the families of victims of violence (including a US$8 million payout to the families of one massacre). It has been essential to organize international accompaniment for the communities who have presented the legal actions, in order to prevent reprisals against them.

Rigoberta Menchú and the Nobel Peace Prize

ive hundred years after Columbus reached the Americas the Nobel committee awarded their Peace Prize to Rigoberta Menchú Tum, a 33-year-old K'iche' Maya woman who had campaigned tirelessly for peace in Guatemala and for the advancement of indigenous people across the world. In their official statement, the Nobel Institute described Menchú as "a vivid symbol of peace and reconciliation across ethnic, cultural and social dividing lines".

Within Guatemala, however, the honour provoked controversy. Few doubted that Menchú had firm connections and deep sympathies with Guatemala's guerrillas, although after she was awarded the prize she distanced herself from the armed struggle. Nevertheless, many people argued that her support for armed uprising made her an inappropriate winner of a peace prize. Others feared that the prize would be interpreted as a vindication of the guerrillas and only serve to perpetuate the civil war.

The first volume of Menchú's autobiography, I, Rigoberta Menchú, shows her to be essentially a pacifist and suggests that her unspoken support for the guerrillas was very much a last resort. "For us, killing is something monstrous. And that's why we feel so angered by all the repression … Even though the tortures and kidnappings had done our people a lot of harm, we shouldn't lose faith in change. This is when I began working in a peasant organization and went on to another stage of my life. There are other things, other ways."

Menchú's story is undeniably tragic, and her account offers a harrowing look into the darkest years of Guatemalan history and the plight of the nation's indigenous people. However, the accuracy of sizeable parts of her life story, as recounted in her autobiography, were later challenged in Rigoberta Menchú and the Story of All Poor Guatemalans, an iconoclastic biography published in 1998 by David Stoll. Stoll concluded that substantial sections of the Menchú legend had been fabricated or greatly exaggerated, and that she had "drastically revised the pre-war experience of her village to suit the needs of the revolutionary organization she had joined".

In I, Rigoberta Menchú, Menchú describes how the barbaric cruelty of the Guatemalan civil war affected her family, who were political activists, and how they were branded guerrilla sympathizers by the military. Menchú recounts the fight to protect the family farm from greedy ladinos, her family's days working in the plantations of the Pacific coast, and her lack of formal schooling. The deaths of her brother, mother and father at the hands of the armed forces are agonizingly retold. Expanding to cover the wider picture in Guatemala, Menchú condemns the massive disparities between the country's ladino and Maya, and rich and poor. The biography has gone on to sell more than 500,000 copies, while Menchú has been invited to speak at events and conferences all over the world. Campaigning for the rights of the Guatemalan Maya and other oppressed minorities from exile in Mexico, she frequently travelled to the United Nations in Geneva and New York to press her case. This period of the Nobel laureate's life is narrated in Crossing Borders, the second volume of her autobiography, and an altogether less traumatic and controversial read.

Rigoberta Menchú returned to Guatemala in 1994 as an iconic but refractory figure; in the global arena, however, her reputation was unblemished until the publication of David Stoll's biography. Stoll's book provided compelling evidence that Menchú's family's land dispute was an internecine family feud rather than a racially charged indigenous-ladino altercation; that she never had toiled in the fields of Pacific-coast plantations and had been educated at two private convent schools. He alleged a guerrilla past and questioned the accuracy of her account about the deaths of two of her brothers.

After the biography's publication an international furore ensued, with allegations from *The New York Times* that she had received "a Nobel prize for lying". Menchú evaded responding directly to Stoll's charges, though admitted that she had received some formal education at a convent school in Chiantla. She later sought to distance herself somewhat from *I, Rigoberta Menchú*, and inferred the input of her editor and translator – Arturo Taracena, a guerrilla attaché – had distorted her testimony. Geir Lundestad, director of the Nobel Institute, has expressed support for Menchú, declaring that the decision to give Menchú the award was because of her work on behalf of indigenous people, and not because of her family history.

As the dust settled, a roster of academics lined up to support Menchú's reputation, questioning Stoll's motives and defending the value of her *testimonio* – which, they reasoned, was recounting the civil-war experiences of indigenous Guatemalans as a whole – and followed a tradition of Maya testimonial writing that dated back to the time of the Conquest. No one disputed that her mother, father and brothers died at the hands of the military (with another 200,000 Guatemalans) whose extreme brutality has been documented in exhaustive reports compiled by the UN and Catholic Church. Her success bringing global attention to the terrible suffering inflicted on (and continuing repression of) Guatemala's Maya is incontestable, and her work on behalf of the world's indigenous peoples has been unrelenting and highly effective. The two sides of the debate are set out in *The Rigoberta Menchú Controversy* published in 2001, a collection of articles edited by Arturo Arias.

Today, Menchú is admired by most Guatemalan Maya and the political left, mistrusted by most of the Guatemalan oligarchy, and tends to be despised by the military and those on the right. She was a goodwill ambassador for the Peace Accords in the Berger government, and through her foundation, campaigned for human and indigenous rights in Guatemala, and beyond. Declaring "that there's no peace without justice" she has fought to end the impunity of the armed forces for their civil-war atrocities and filed genocide charges in the international courts against the former military rulers. Spain issued an arrest warrant for Ríos Montt in 2007, though he evaded extradition.

Menchú formed the political party Encuentro por Guatemala and contested the 2007 presidential election, though she only polled 3 percent of the vote. She's also campaigned on healthcare issues, with the aim of providing low-cost generic medicines to all. For more information on the Rigoberta Menchú Foundation, consult the website @www.frmt.org (in Spanish).

Landscape and wildlife

G uatemala embraces an astonishingly diverse collection of environments, ranging from the permanently moist rainforests and mangroves of the Caribbean coast to the exposed *altiplano* highlands, where the ground can be hard with frost. Its wildlife is correspondingly varied; undisturbed forests provide a home to both temperate species from the north and tropical ones from the south, as well as a number of indigenous species found nowhere else in the world.

The Pacific coast

Guatemala's **Pacific coastline** is marked by a thin strip of black volcanic sand, pounded by the surf. There are no natural harbours and boats have to take their chances in the breakers or launch from one of the piers (though Puerto Quetzal takes large, ocean-going ships). The sea itself provides a rich natural harvest of shrimp, tuna, snapper and mackerel, most of which go for export. The coastal waters are also ideal for sport-fishing. A couple of kilometres offshore, dorado, which grow to around forty pounds, are plentiful, while farther out marlin, sailfish, wahoo and skipjack ply the waters.

The **beach** itself rises from the water to form a large sandbank, dotted with palm trees, behind which the land drops off into low-lying mangrove swamps and canals. In the east, from San José to the border, the **Chiquimulilla Canal** runs behind the beach for around 100km. For most of the way it's no more than a narrow strip of water, but here and there it fans out into swamps, creating a maze of waterways that are an ideal breeding ground for young fish, waterfowl and a range of small mammals. The sandy shoreline is an ideal nesting site for three species of **sea turtle**, including the giant leatherback (see box, p.254), which periodically emerge from the water, drag themselves up the beach and deposit a clutch of eggs before hauling their weight back into the water. At Monterrico, east of San José, a nature reserve protects a small section of the coastline for the benefit of the turtles, and with luck you might see one here. The **Reserva Monterrico–Hawaii** is in fact the best place to see wildlife on the Pacific coast, as it includes a superb mangrove swamp, which you can easily explore by boat.

The **mangroves** are mixed in with water lilies, bulrushes and tropical hardwoods, amongst which you'll see **herons, kingfishers** and an array of **ducks** including **muscovies** and **white whistling ducks**. In the area around Monterrico, flocks of **wood stork** are common, and you might also see the **white ibis** or the occasional **great jabiru**, a massive stork that nests in the area. With real perseverance and a bit of luck you might also catch a glimpse of a **racoon, anteater** or **opossum**. You'll also be able to see **alligators** and **iguanas**, if not in the wild then at the reserve headquarters where they are kept in a breeding programme. Other birds you might see almost anywhere along the coast include **plover, coot** and **tern**, and a number of winter migrants including **white** and **brown pelican**.

Between the shore and the foothills of the highlands, the **coastal plain** is an intensely fertile and heavily farmed area, where the volcanic and alluvial soils are ideal for sugarcane, cotton, palm oil, banana and rubber plantations and cattle ranches. In recent years soya and sorghum, which require less labour, have been added to this list. Guatemala's coastal **agribusiness** is high cost and high yield: the soils are treated chemically and the crops regularly sprayed with a cocktail of pesticides, herbicides and fertilizers. There's little land that remains untouched by the hand of commercial agriculture so it's hard to imagine what this must once have looked like, but it was almost certainly very similar to Petén, a mixture of savannah and rainforest supporting a rich array of wildlife. These days it's only the swamps, steep hillsides and towering hedges that give any hint of its former glory, although beautiful flocks of white **snowy** and **cattle egret** feed alongside the beef cattle.

Finally, one particularly interesting lowland species is the **oropendola**, a large oriole which builds a long woven nest hanging from trees and telephone wires. They tend to nest in colonies and a single tree might support fifty nests. You'll probably notice the nests more than the birds, which thrive throughout Guatemala and neighbouring countries.

The Boca Costa

Approaching the highlands, the coastal plain starts to slope up towards a string of volcanic cones, and this section of well-drained hillside is known as the **Boca Costa**. The volcanic soils, high rainfall and good drainage combine to make it ideal for growing **coffee**, and it's here that some of Guatemala's best beans are produced, with rows of olive-green bushes ranked beneath shady trees.

Where the land is unsuitable for coffee, lush tropical forest still grows, clinging to the hills. As you head up into the highlands, through deeply cleft valleys, you pass through some of this superb forest, dripping with moss-covered vines, bromeliads and orchids. Close to the most active volcanoes, in areas where farming has not disturbed the environment, are some incredibly rich ecosystems. Around Volcán Santiaguito near Quetzaltenango, more than 120 species of bird have been sighted here, including some real rarities such as **solitary eagle**, **quetzal** and **highland guan**. The **azure-rumped tanager**, **maroon-chested ground dove** and **Pacific parakeet** are endemic to this region. The Guatemala Birding Resource Center (Ⓦwww.xelapages.com/gbrc), a specialist tour operator, runs excellent trips to the Boca Costa region.

The highlands

The highlands proper begin with a chain of **volcanoes**. There are 37 peaks in all, the main backbone ranged in a direct line that runs parallel with the Pacific coastline from the southwestern border with Mexico into El Salvador. (In the eastern highlands, away from the main chain, there's another sprinkling of older, less-spectacular weathered cones.) The highest of the main peaks is **Tajumulco** (4220m), near the Mexican border, while three highly active cones – **Fuego**, **Pacaya** and **Santiaguito** – all belch sulphurous fumes, volcanic ash and the occasional fountain of molten rock. Beneath the surface their subterranean fires heat the bedrock, and in several places hot spring water emerges, offering the luxury of a warm, mineral-rich bath (for the best of these see Fuentes Georginas, p.184, and the *Las Cumbres* hotel, p.185).

On the southern side of the central highlands, volcanic peaks surround two large lakes, Lago de Amatitlán and Lago de Atitlán, both of which are set in superb countryside. South of Guatemala City, **Lago de Amatitlán** has suffered years of environmental mismanagement, and its waters are heavily contaminated and blackened by pollution. The lake remains a popular picnic spot for the capital's not-so-rich. Farther west, **Lago de Atitlán** is still spectacularly beautiful, with crystal blue water, but increasing tourist development and a population explosion threaten to damage its delicate ecological balance. Atitlán's ecosystem was upset as far back as 1958, when **black bass** were introduced in a bid to create sport-fishing. The bass is a greedy, rapacious fish and in no time at all its presence had reshaped the food chain. Smaller fish became increasingly rare, as did crabs, frogs, insects and small mammals. The **Atitlán grebe**, a small, flightless water bird unique to the lake, was worst hit. Young grebes were gobbled up by the hungry bass, and by 1965 just eighty of them survived. By 1984, falling water levels caused by the 1976 earthquake, combined with tourist development of the lakeshore, cut their numbers by a further thirty. Today the bird is extinct.

On the northern side of the volcanic ridge are the **central valleys** of the highlands, a complex mixture of sweeping bowls, steep-sided valleys, open plateaux and jagged peaks. This central area is home to the vast majority of Guatemala's population, and all the available land is intensely farmed, with hillsides carved into workable terraces and portioned up into a patchwork of small fields. Here the land is farmed by campesinos using techniques that predate the arrival of the Spanish. The *milpa* is the mainstay of Maya farming practices: a field is cleared, usually by slash and burn, and planted with maize as the main crop, with beans, chillies and squash grown as well. Traditionally, the land is rotated between *milpa* and pasture, and also left fallow for a while, but in some areas it's now under constant pressure, the fertility of the soil is virtually exhausted and only with the assistance of fertilizer can it still produce a worth-while crop. The pressure on land is immense and each generation is forced to farm more marginal territory, planting on steep hillsides where exposed soil is soon washed into the valley below.

Some areas remain off limits to farmers, however, and substantial tracts of the highlands are still **forested**. In the cool valleys of the central highlands, pine trees dominate, intermixed with oak, cedar and fir. To the south, on the volcanic slopes and in the warmth of deep-cut valleys, lush subtropical forest thrives in a world kept permanently moist – similar in many ways to the forest of Verapaz, where constant rain fosters the growth of cloudforest.

Heading on to the north, the land rises to form several **mountain ranges**. The largest of these are the Cuchumatanes, a massive chain of granite peaks that reach a height of 3837m above the town of Huehuetenango. Further to the east there are several smaller ranges such as the Sierra de Chuacús, the Sierra de las Minas and the Sierra de Chamá. The high peaks support stunted trees and open grassland, used for grazing sheep and cattle, but are too cold for maize and most other crops.

Birdlife is plentiful throughout the highlands; you'll see a variety of **hummingbirds**, flocks of screeching **parakeets**, **swifts**, **egrets** and the ever-present **vultures**. Slightly less commonplace are the **quails** and **wood partridges**, **white-tailed pigeons**, and several species of dove including the **little Inca** and the **white-winged dove**. Last but by no means least is the **quetzal**, which has been revered since Maya times. The male quetzal has fantastic green tail-feathers which snake behind it through the air as it flies: these have always been prized by hunters and even today the bird is very rare indeed. Near

Cobán is the **Biotopo del Quetzal**, a protected area of cloudforest in the department of Baja Verapaz where quetzals breed, but you'll have a better chance of spotting Guatemala's national bird in the more remote mountains of the **Sierra de Caquipec** to the northeast.

The highlands also support a number of small **mammals**, including foxes and small cats, although your chances of seeing these are very slim.

The rainforests of Petén

Northeast of the highlands the land drops away into the **rainforests** of Petén, a large chunk of which remains undisturbed, although recent oil finds and a huge influx of cattle ranchers, timber merchants and migrant settlers have cut a swathe through virgin jungle in the past thirty years. The forest of Petén extends across the Mexican border, where it merges with the Lacandón and Campeche rainforests, and into Belize, where it skirts around the lower slopes of the Maya Mountains, reaching to the Caribbean coast.

Today around forty percent of Petén is still covered by **primary forest**, with a canopy that towers between 30 and 50m above the forest floor, made up of hundreds of species of tree, including ceiba, mahogany, aguacate, ebony and sapodilla. The combination of a year-round growing season, plenty of moisture and millions of years of evolution have produced an environment that supports literally thousands of species of plants and trees. While temperate forests tend to be dominated by a single species – fir, oak or beech, say – it's diversity that characterizes the tropical forest. Each species is specifically adapted to fit into a particular ecological niche, where it receives a precise amount of light and moisture.

This biological storehouse has yielded some astonishing **discoveries**. Steroid hormones, such as cortisone, and diosgenin, the active ingredient in birth-control pills, were developed from wild yams found in these forests; and the highly potent anesthetic tetrodoxin is derived from a species of Central American frog.

Despite its size and diversity the forest is surprisingly **fragile**. It forms a closed system in which nutrients are continuously recycled and decaying plant matter fuels new growth. The forest floor is a spongy mass of roots, fungi, mosses, bacteria and microorganisms, in which nutrients are stored, broken down with the assistance of insects and chemical decay, and gradually released to the waiting roots and fresh seedlings. The thick canopy prevents much light reaching the forest floor, ensuring that the soil remains damp but warm, a hotbed of chemical activity. The death of a large tree prompts a flurry of growth as new light reaches the forest floor, and in no time at all a young tree rises to fill the gap. But once the trees are removed the soil is highly vulnerable, deprived of its main source of fertility. Exposed to the harsh tropical sun and direct rainfall, an area of cleared forest soon becomes prone to flooding and drought. Recently cleared land will contain enough nutrients for four or five years of good growth, but soon afterwards its usefulness declines rapidly and within twenty years it will be almost completely barren. If the trees are stripped from a large area, soil erosion will silt the rivers and parched soils will disrupt local rainfall patterns.

Settlement needn't mean the end of the rainforest. In the past this area supported a huge population of Maya, who probably numbered as many as ten million during the Late Classic era. (Some archeologists, however, argue that during Maya occupation Petén was a mixture of savannah and grassland, and that relatively recent climatic changes have enabled it to evolve into rainforest.) Only one small group of Maya, the Lacandones, still farm the forest using traditional methods. They allow the existing trees to point them in the right direction, avoiding areas that support mahogany, as they tend to be too wet, and searching out ceiba and ramon trees, which thrive in rich, well-drained soils. In April a patch of forest is burnt down and then, to prevent soil erosion, planted with fast-growing trees such as banana and papaya, and with root crops to fix the soil. A few weeks later they plant their main crops: maize and a selection of others, from garlic to sweet potatoes. Every inch of the soil is covered in growth, a method that mimics the forest and thereby protects the soil. The same land is cultivated for three or four years and then allowed to return to its wild state – although they continue to harvest from the fruit-bearing plants – and in due course return to the same area. The whole process is in perfect harmony with the forest, extracting only what it can afford to lose and ensuring that it remains fertile. Sadly, the traditional farming methods of the Lacandones are now very rarely practiced. New settlers burn the forest and plant grass for cattle pasture, and vast areas of former jungle now have very little biodiversity or fertility.

In its undisturbed state the rainforest is still superbly beautiful and is home to an incredible range of wildlife. Amongst the birds, the spectacular scarlet, blue and emerald-green **ocellated turkey**, found only in Petén, is perhaps the most famous. But the forest is also home to three species of **toucan**, **motmot** (a type of bird of paradise), several species of **parrot** including **Aztec** and **green parakeets**, and the endangered **scarlet macaw**, which is said to live to at least fifty. As in the highlands, **hummingbirds**, **buzzards** and **hawks** are all common. A surprising number of these can be seen fairly easily in the **Parque Nacional Tikal**, particularly if you hang around until sunset.

Although **mammals** are widespread, they are almost always elusive, and your best chance of seeing them is at the bigger reserves and archeological sites, where they may have lost some of their fear of humans. At many forest sites you'll almost certainly see **monkeys**, including the acrobatically agile **spider** and the highly social **howlers**, which emit a chilling, deep-throated roar. The largest land animal in Guatemala is the **tapir** (dante), weighing up to 300kg, and usually found near water. Tapirs are endangered and you're not likely to see one without a guide. Two species of **peccary** (wild pig), the collared and the white-lipped, wander the forest floors in large groups, seeking out roots and palm nuts. The smaller herbivores include the **paca** (also known as the tepescuintle and agouti), a rodent about the size of a piglet, which is hunted everywhere for food. You'll often see **coati** (locally known as *pizotes*), inquisitive and intelligent members of the raccoon family, foraging in the leaf litter around archeological sites with their long snouts, often in family groups of several dozen. Coatis and small **grey foxes** are frequently seen at Tikal, and in many places you can see **opossums** and **armadillos**.

Five species of wild **cat** are found in the region, though most are now rare outside the protected areas. **Jaguars** (called *tigres* in Guatemala) formerly ranged over the whole of the country, but today the densest population is found in the northern Petén, though they are very rarely seen. **Pumas** live in remote forest areas; less rare but still uncommon are the much smaller **ocelot** and the **margay**, which is about the size of a large domestic cat. The **jaguarundi** is the smallest and commonest of the wild cats, and as it hunts during the day you might spot one on a trail.

Take a trip along almost any river in Petén and you've a good chance of seeing **green iguanas**, **mud turtles** or **Central American river turtles** sunning themselves on logs. **Egrets** and **kingfishers** fish from overhanging branches, while large rivers such as Río de la Pasión and lakes, including Lago de Petexbatún, are also rich, packed with **snook**, **tarpon** and **mullet**.

Crocodiles are becoming increasingly common in Petén, after previously being hunted almost to extinction, and are now frequently spotted at Lago de Yaxhá and Laguna Perdida. They are not dangerous to humans unless they are very large – at least 3m long – but heed the warnings of locals if they advise against swimming in particular lagoons.

Although there are at least fifty species of **snake** in the region, only a few are venomous and you're unlikely to see any snakes at all. The **boa constrictor** is one of the most common and also is the largest, growing up to 4m, though it poses no threat to humans. Others you might see are **coral snakes** (which are venomous) and **false coral snakes** (which are not); in theory they're easily distinguished by noting the arrangement of adjacent colours in the stripes, but it's best to admire all snakes from a distance unless you're an expert.

At night in the forest, you'll hear the characteristic chorus of frog mating calls, and you'll also frequently find the **red-eyed tree frog** – a beautiful pale-green creature about the size of the top joint of your thumb – in your shower in any rustic cabin. Less appealing perhaps are the giant **marine toads**, the largest toad in the Americas, weighing in at up to 1kg and growing to more than 20cm. Like most frogs and toads, the marine toad has toxic glands, and its toxin has hallucinogenic properties – an effect put to use in ceremonies by the ancient Maya, who licked the toad's glands and interpreted the resultant visions.

The Caribbean coast and the Bay Islands

Much of Guatemala's small **Caribbean coastline** is protected as part of the Biotopo Punta del Manabique, a rich wetland habitat, while just inland there are several additional, ecologically diverse reserves around the Río Dulce and Lago de Izabal. This region offers some of the country's finest birdwatching territory, with more than three hundred species spotted inside the Reserva Bocas del Polochic alone. Though there are tiny coral outcrops in Guatemalan waters, there's much more to see around the exceptional reefs of the **Bay Islands**, where the three main islands all have excellent scuba-diving schools.

Immediately inland from the Guatemalan coast, the **littoral forest** is characterized by salt-tolerant plants, often with tough, waxy leaves which help conserve water. Species include red and white **gumbo limbo**, **black poisonwood**, **zericote**, **palmetto** and, of course, the **coconut**, which typifies Caribbean beaches, though it's not actually a native. The littoral forest supports a very high density of fauna, especially **migrating birds**, owing to the succession of fruits and seeds yet, due to its location, it's also facing increased development pressure.

Much of the shoreline around Punta del Manabique and Lívingston is still largely covered with **mangroves**, which play an important economic role, not merely as nurseries for commercial fish species but also for their stabilization of the shoreline and their ability to absorb the force of gales and hurricanes. The dominant species of the coastal fringe is the **red mangrove**, although in due course it undermines its own environment by consolidating the sea bed until it becomes more suitable for the less salt-tolerant black and white mangroves. The basis of the shoreline food chain is the nutrient-rich mud, held in place by the mangroves, whose roots are home to **oysters** and **sponges**. In the shallows, "meadows" of **seagrass beds** provide nurseries for many fish and invertebrates, and pasture for conch and turtles. The extensive root system of seagrasses also protects beaches from erosion by holding the fragments of sand and coral together.

The coastal zone is home to sparse numbers of the **West Indian manatee**, which can reach 4m in length and weigh up to 450kg. These placid and shy creatures move between freshwater lagoons and the open sea. They were once hunted for their meat but are now protected, and the Biotopo Chocón Machacas has been established in the Golfete region of the Río Dulce as a manatee sanctuary. Despite this measure, the manatee remains very rare in Guatemala, and you've a much better chance of spotting one in Belize, where their habitat is much less depleted.

In the **Bay Islands**, the **coral reefs** are some of the best preserved in the Caribbean, forming an astoundingly beautiful world where fish and coral come in every imaginable colour. The corals look like a brilliant underwater forest, but in fact each coral is composed of colonies of individual **polyps**, feeding off plankton wafting past in the current. There are basically two types of coral: the hard, calcareous, reef-building corals, such as **lettuce coral**, **brain coral** and **elkhorn coral** (known scientifically as the **hydrocorals**; 74 species), and the soft corals such as **sea fans** and **feather plumes** (the ococorals; 36 species). On the reefs you'll find the **chalice sponge**, which is a garish pink, the appropriately named **fire coral**, the delicate **feather-star crinoid** and the **apartment sponge**, a tall thin tube with lots of small holes in it.

Incredibly, the extensive reefs surrounding the Bay Islands survived the ten-metre waves of **Hurricane Mitch** in 1998 almost intact. Even in Guanaja, which took a direct hit (Mitch pounded the island for more than two days), the coral remains in generally excellent condition, though fish numbers have declined a little because of overfishing around the reefs, despite the island's marine-reserve status. The Bay Islands' reef environment is characterized by between 500m and a kilometre or so of shallow **fringing reef**, interspersed with sandy patches, which extends from the shoreline – this area is no deeper than 12m. This fringing reef then reaches a **reef crest**, where the waves break, from where the coral plummets almost vertically off the northern coasts of Roatán, Utila and Guanaja. These steep drop-offs form dramatic **reef walls**, spectacular topographic features for which the Bay Islands are particularly renowned. The reef walls form the edge of the **continental shelf**, which plunges down to a depth of 3000m within a few kilometres north of the islands, forming a vast underwater canyon called the Cayman Trench.

It's the Bay Islands' position between these shallow and deep-water habitats that makes for such exciting scuba-diving. When cruising the reef walls on the northern coasts of the islands, it's possible to observe the abundant coral life while keeping an eye on the big blue, and perhaps spot **pelagic sealife** like tarpon or manta rays swept close to the shore. The southern coasts of all the islands are a little different: here the reef has a shallower profile with coral outcrops interspersed with channels and small cayes, and pelagic species are less common.

The seas around the Bay Islands are rich with all the main marine species found in the Caribbean. You're pretty much guaranteed to see a wide variety of reef life including **angel-** and **parrotfish**, **tiger groupers**, **trumpet fish** and small striped **sergeant-majors**, while **seahorses** and **hawksbill turtles** are also frequently spotted. **Yellow stingrays** and **spotted eagle rays** are usually

Conservation organizations

Alianza Verde (Green Alliance, Ⓦ www.greendeal.org). Based in CINCAP, Flores (see p.313), this is a consortium of ecotourism operators and conservation organizations, working closely with Guatemala's National Protected Areas Commission (CONAP) and ProPetén (see p.314), focusing primarily on sustainable development in the Maya Biosphere Reserve. It's developed the "Green Deal", a code of practice and certification for ecotourism businesses.

Arcas (Ⓦ www.arcasguatemala.com). Conservation group that provides a refuge for wild animals in Petén (see p.316) and also runs a sea turtle project in the Monterrico–Hawaii area (see p.237).

Centre for Conservation Studies (CECON). A department of Guatemala's University of San Carlos, with head offices at the Botanical Gardens of Guatemala City (see p.79). CECON manages and conducts scientific research in all seven of the nation's *biotopos*. These are often the best-protected areas within reserves, such as Cerro Cahuí in Petén, Monterrico on the Pacific coast and the Biotopo del Quetzal in Baja Verapaz.

Defensores de la Naturaleza (Ⓦ www.defensores.org.gt). Ecological group that combines conservation with sustainable tourism in the Sierra de las Minas and the Bocas del Polochic reserves (see p.284 & p.267). It also manages the vast Sierra de Lacandón national park in Petén.

Fundary (Ⓦ www.guate.net/fundarymanabique). Working with communities in Punta de Manabique (see p.254) to establish sustainable tourism. Spanish-speaking volunteers, preferably with a background in biology or ecotourism, are sometimes needed to patrol turtle nesting beaches or undertake manatee and dolphin observation.

ProPetén (Ⓦ www.propeten.org). Petén's largest NGO works on numerous conservation and resource-management projects in the Maya Biosphere Reserve including Las Guacamayas, a biological station near Waka' (El Perú) ruins. Volunteers are needed.

Proyecto Eco-Quetzal (Ⓦ www.ecoquetzal.org). Long-established NGO (see p.292), with a successful record in protecting the forests around Cobán by offering economic alternatives to indigenous people, including excellent ecotourism projects where visitors stay with Q'eqchi' Maya villagers.

Whale Shark & Oceanic Research Center (Ⓦ www.wsorc.com). Utila-based project monitoring whale-shark behaviour and migration patterns. Volunteers are sought.

a little more elusive, while **reef sharks** (the harmless nurse-shark is the most common species) are only occasionally encountered. Keep an eye out for **conger** and **moray eels**, **spiny lobster** and the giant **king crab** hiding in holes and crevices in the reef wall, while solitary **great barracuda** can often be seen hunting on the reef crest at dawn and dusk.

The world's largest fish, the plankton-feeding **whale shark**, is resident to the waters around Utila. The fish, which can grow to 14m, also visits the coasts around Roatán and Guanaja in October and November to gorge on snapper and grouper eggs (see box, pp.380–381). Dolphins are sometimes seen just offshore as well – mostly the **Atlantic bottle-nosed dolphin**, though farther out large schools of smaller **spotted dolphin** sometimes follow ocean-going ships.

Books

Guatemala has never inspired a great deal of writing until the past few decades, when the civil war and political turmoil has spawned plenty of nonfiction. In recent years, there has also been a boom in titles about contemporary and ancient Maya culture. Yax Te' Books (ⓦwww .yaxtebooks.com) produce a fascinating collection of titles, concentrating on indigenous Maya culture, literature and language.

Books that we especially recommend are marked with a symbol (⚹).

Travel

Stephen Connoly Benz *Guatemalan Journey*. Concentrates on the complexities of Guatemalan society and the impact of US culture and evangelism, with informative accounts of life in the capital and the textile-factory businesses.

Peter Canby *Heart of the Sky – Travels Among the Maya*. The author treads a familiar path through the Maya World, encountering an interesting collection of expats, Mayanists, priests, Guatemala City's idle rich and a female shaman. An accessible and informative account.

Anthony Daniels *Sweet Waist of America*. A delight to read. Daniels takes a refreshingly even-handed approach to Guatemala and comes up with a fascinating cocktail of people and politics, discarding the stereotypes that litter most books on Central America.

Thomas Gage *Travels in the New World*. Unusual account of a Dominican friar's travels through Mexico and Central America between 1635 and 1637, including some intriguing insights into colonial life as well as some great attacks on the greed and pomposity of the Catholic Church abroad.

⚹ **Aldous Huxley** *Beyond the Mexique Bay*. Huxley's travels in 1934 took him from Belize through Guatemala to Mexico, swept on by his fascination for

history and religion, and sprouting bizarre theories on the basis of everything he saw. There are some terrific descriptions of Maya sites and indigenous culture, with superb one-liners summing up people and places.

Patrick Marnham *So Far from God*. A saddened and vaguely right-wing account of Marnham's travels through the Americas from the US to Panama (missing out Belize). Dotted with amusing anecdotes and interesting observations, the book was researched in 1984, and its description of Guatemala is dominated by the reign of terror.

Jonathan Evan Maslow *Bird of Life, Bird of Death*. Maslow sets out in search of the quetzal, using the bird's uncertain future as a metaphor for wartime Guatemala in a work that merges travel and political comment.

Peter Moore *The Full Montezuma*. Puerile backpacking yarn about an Australian's misadventures with the "girl next door" around Mexico and Central America. About as lucid as a muddy puddle.

Christopher Shaw *Sacred Monkey River: A Canoe Trip with the Gods*. Engaging account of the author's canoe journey along the Usumacinta River that divides Mexico and Guatemala. Nicely crafted prose is enlivened with convincing analysis of ancient Maya cosmology and culture, and the contemporary political and environmental issues affecting the region.

🏃 **John Lloyd Stephens** *Incidents of Travel in Central America, Chiapas, and Yucatán.* Stephens was a classic nineteenth-century explorer. Acting as US ambassador to Central America, he indulged his own enthusiasm for archeology; while the republics fought it out among themselves, he was wading through the jungle stumbling across ancient cities. His journals, told in a restrained Victorian style punctuated with sudden waves of enthusiasm, make great reading. Some editions include fantastic illustrations by Catherwood of the ruins overgrown with tropical rainforest.

🏃 **Ronald Wright** *Time Among the Maya.* A vivid and sympathetic account of travels from Belize through Guatemala, Chiapas and Yucatán, meeting the Maya of today and exploring their obsession with time. The book's twin points of interest are the ancient Maya and the civil-war violence. An encyclopedic bibliography offers ideas for exploration in depth, and the author's knowledge is evident in the superb historical insight he imparts through the book. Certainly one of the best travel books on the area.

Fiction, autobiography and poetry

🏃 **Miguel Ángel Asturias** *Hombres de Maíz.* Guatemala's most famous author, Asturias is deeply indebted to Guatemalan history and culture in his work. "Men of Maize" is generally regarded as his masterpiece, classically Latin American in its magic-realist style, and bound up in the complexity of indigenous culture. His other works include *El Señor Presidente*, a grotesque portrayal of social chaos and dictatorial rule, based on Asturias's own experience; *El Papa Verde*, which explores the murky world of the United Fruit Company; and *Weekend in Guatemala*, describing the downfall of the Arbenz government. Asturias won the Nobel Prize for Literature before his death in 1974.

Jane Bowles used the same visit for *A Guatemalan Idyll* and other tales republished in *Everything is Nice: Collected Stories of Jane Bowles.*

Paul Bowles *Up Above the World.* Bowles is at his chilling, understated best in this novel based on experiences of Guatemala in the late 1930s.

🏃 **Francisco Goldman** *The Long Night of White Chickens.* Drawing on the stylistic complexity of Latin American fiction, this novel tells the tale of a young Guatemalan orphan who flees to the US and works as a maid. When she finally returns home to her politically turbulent nation, she is murdered. It's an interesting and ambitious story, though its chaotic timeline gives the book a Byzantine intricacy that make it a dense and laborious read at times. Goldman's third novel, *A Divine Husband* (Atlantic), set in the nineteenth century, adopts a similar prose, following the adventures of a charismatic half-Maya girl and her many suitors in New York and Central America.

Gaspar Pedro Gonzáles *A Mayan Life.* Absorbing story about the personal and cultural conflicts facing a Q'anjob'al Maya in the Cuchumatanes mountains as he seeks a higher education.

Norman Lewis *The Volcano Above Us.* Vaguely historical novel published in 1957 that pulls together all the main elements of Guatemala's history. The image that it summons is one of depressing drudgery and eternal conflict, set against a background of repression and racism. In the light of what's happened it has a certain prophetic quality, and remains gripping despite its miserable conclusions.

Kathy Reichs *Grave Secrets*. In this compelling thriller, forensic scientist Tempe Brennon flies to Guatemala to investigate the mass graves of civil-war victims, but is then persuaded to look into the disappearances of four wealthy girls from the capital. Her efforts are thwarted by violence, judicial inadequacies and corruption.

History, politics and human rights

Tom Barry *Guatemala – A Country Guide*. A concise account of the political, social and economic situation in Guatemala, with a mild left-wing stance. Published in 1990.

William V. Davidson *Historical Geography of the Bay Islands, Honduras*. An interesting study of how waves of settlers, from pirates to Hondurans from the mainland, have shaped the culture of the islands. Useful for pieces of interesting background information.

Edward F. Fisher and R. McKenna Brown (eds) *Maya Cultural Activism in Guatemala*. Effectual summary of the indigenous movement in Guatemala, with strong chapters on clothing and identity, and the revival of interest in Maya language and hieroglyphic writing.

Francisco Goldman *The Art of Political Murder*. Investigative journalism at its very best, this is a meticulously researched and passionately told account of the Geradi murder case, and represents the culmination of seven years of reporting. Goldman weaves absorbing profiles of the characters – assassins, military intelligence officers, street kids and Church figures – into the tale to pull off a riveting whodunit.

Greg Grandin *The Blood of Guatemala – A History of Race and Nation*. Terrific study of Quetzaltenango's elite class of K'iche' Maya and their impact on the region and nation. Covers the period between the mid-eighteenth century and the fall of the Arbenz government in 1954.

Jim Handy *Gift of the Devil*. Superb history of Guatemala: concise and readable with a sharp focus on the Maya population and the brief period of socialist government. Though written in the mid-1980s, the book nevertheless manages to offer a convincing perspective on the modern Guatemalan state. By no means objective, Handy sets out to expose the development of oppression and point the finger at the oppressors.

George Lovell *A Beauty That Hurts: Life and Death in Guatemala*. A good contemporary analysis enlivened by interviews with exiles and community leaders. The book reviews the historical context that has shaped twenty-first-century Guatemala.

Víctor Montejo *Testimony: Death of a Guatemalan Village*. Yet another horrifying account of murder and destruction. In this case it's the personal testimony of a school teacher, describing the arrival of the army in a small highland village and the killing that follows.

Víctor Perera *Unfinished Conquest*. Superb, extremely readable account of the civil-war tragedy, plus comprehensive attention to the deep inequalities that affect the late author's native country. The book's strength comes from the extensive interviews with both ordinary and influential Guatemalans and incisive analysis of recent history. A great introduction to the subject.

REMHI *Guatemala: Never Again.* Abridged translation of the seminal report published by the Catholic Church of Guatemala into the civil-war atrocities. The investigation contains an excellent historical background to the conflict, harrowing personal testimonies, incisive analysis of military and guerrilla strategies, and a chapter devoted to preventing a recurrence.

Victoria Sanford *Buried Secrets: Truth and Human Rights in Guatemala.* A powerful, exhaustively researched investigative study of *la violencia* is based on more than four hundred interviews with massacre survivors, the military and guerrilla forces.

Jennifer Schirmer *The Guatemalan Military Project: A Violence Called Democracy.* Offers an insider's view of the ideology and mentality of the Guatemalan armed forces, based on numerous interviews with senior officers, six ex-defence ministers and three former heads of state.

Stephen Schlesinger and Stephen Kinzer *Bitter Fruit: The Untold Story of the American Coup in Guatemala.* This book traces the US connection in the 1954 coup, delving into the murky water of United Fruit Company politics and showing that the invading army received its orders from the White House.

Jean-Marie Simon *Eternal Spring – Eternal Tyranny.* Highly authoritative photojournalistic study of Guatemala's civil-war period, with crisp text and evocative imagery.

Daniel Wilkinson *Silence on the Mountain: Stories of Betrayal and Forgetting in Guatemala.* Part historical narrative, part personal travelogue and part public testimony, Wilkinson's book gives a voice to those who suffered most during Guatemala's civil war.

Central American politics

Tom Barry *Central America Inside Out.* Well-informed background reading on the entire region, though a little dated.

Peter Dale-Scott and Jonathan Marshall *Cocaine Politics: Drugs, Armies and the CIA in Central America.* Polemical but well-researched exposé of CIA involvement in cocaine trafficking and political oppression in Central America in the 1980s. Reveals the truth behind the Iran–Contra scandal and gives the lie to the rhetoric of the war on drugs.

James Dunkerley *Power in the Isthmus.* Detailed account of Central American politics offering a good

summary of the situation, albeit in a rather turgid academic style. His later book, *The Pacification of Central America* (Verso Editions), published in 1994, is a similarly well-compiled account with plenty of supporting statistics, covering the period up to the beginning of the peace process.

Walter Lafeber *Inevitable Revolutions: The United States in Central America.* A highly critical analysis of US involvement in Central America, from the 1823 Monroe Doctrine through the United Fruit Company years to the Reagan era.

Susan C. Stonch (ed) *Endangered Peoples of Latin America.* Assesses the problems facing the minorities of the region, including a chapter about the English-speaking Bay Islanders.

William Weinberg *War on the Land: Ecology and Politics in Central America*. The author tells a story of inter-twining conflicts and causes between conservation (and to a small extent ecotourism), land rights and politics in Central America.

Ralph Lee Woodward Jr *Central America: A Nation Divided*. Despite its daft title, a good general summary of the Central American situation that's written in an accessible style. The latest edition covers the aftermath of the peace treaties and the neoliberal economics of the late 1990s.

Indigenous culture

Robert Carmack *Quichean Civilization*. Thorough study of K'iche' history and highland society, drawing on archeological evidence and accounts of the Conquest.

Krystyna Deuss *Shamans, Witches, and Maya Priests: Native Religion & Ritual in Highland Guatemala*. A unique and fascinating study of Maya customs in the remote Cuchuma-tanes – in villages where the Maya calendar is still in use – based on decades of research and beautifully illustrated with photographs.

Ann Hecht *Textiles from Guatemala*. Slim volume documenting the richness of Guatemala's textile weaving traditions.

Grant D. Jones *The Conquest of the Maya Kingdom*. A massive academic tome that's also a fascinating history of the Itza Maya and a gripping tale of how the Spanish entered and finally defeated the last independent Maya kingdom, at Tayasal, site of present-day Flores.

🏃 **Rigoberta Menchú**
I, Rigoberta Menchú – An Indian Woman in Guatemala and *Crossing Borders*. Momentous story of one of Latin America's most remarkable women, Nobel Peace Prize–winner Rigoberta Menchú. The first volume is a horrific account of family life in the Maya highlands, recording how Menchú's family were targeted,

terrorized and murdered by the military. The book also reveals much concerning K'iche' Maya cultural traditions and the enormous gulf between the ladino and indigenous societies in Guatemala. The second volume is more optimistic, documenting Menchú's life in exile in Mexico, her work at the United Nations fighting for indigenous people and her return to Guatemala. Although Menchú's courage and determination are undeniable, some, including author David Stoll (see p.454), have criticized the accuracy of parts of her story.

Hans Namuth *Los Todos Santeros*. Splendid book of black-and-white photographs taken in the village of Todos Santos Cuchumatán, to the north of Huehuetenango. The book was inspired by the work of anthro-pologist Maud Oakes (see below).

Maud Oakes *Beyond the Windy Place: The Two Crosses of Todos Santos*. An anthropologist who spent many years in the Mam-speaking village of Todos Santos. Oakes' studies of life in the village were published in the 1940s and 1950s and still make fascinating reading.

🏃 **The Popol Vuh** The great K'iche' creation epic, written shortly after the Conquest, is an amazing swirl of mythological characters and their wanderings through the K'iche' highlands, tracing the tribe's ancestry. There are several versions on offer though many of them are half-hearted, including only a few lines from the original. The best is translated by Dennis Tedlock.

🏃 **James D. Sexton** (ed) *Son of Tecún Umán*; *Campesino*; and *Ignacio*. Three excellent autobiographical accounts written by a Tz'utujil Maya from Lago de Atitlán. The books give an impression of life inside a modern Maya village, bound up in poverty, local politics and a mixture of Catholicism and superstition, and manage to avoid the stereotyping that usually characterizes descriptions of the indigenous population. Sexton's *Mayan Folktales: Folklore from Lake Atitlán, Guatemala* and *Heart of Heaven, Heart of Earth and other Maya Folktales*

unveil a world of wonderfully imaginative fables that underpin a society's strict moral codes and notions of justice and fate.

David Stoll *Rigoberta Menchú and the Story of All Poor Guatemalans*. Iconoclastic biography that delivers a formidable broadside against considerable pieces of the Menchú legend, though some academics have criticized Stoll's literal interpretation of Maya testimonial traditions.

Philip Werne *The Maya of Guatemala*. A short study of repression and the Maya of Guatemala. The latest edition (published in 1994) is now a little out of date but still interesting.

Archeology

🏃 **Michael D. Coe** *The Maya*. Now in its seventh edition, this clear and comprehensive introduction to Maya archeology is one of the best on offer. Coe has also written several more weighty, academic volumes. His *Breaking the Maya Code* owes much to the fact that Coe was at many of the most important meetings leading to the breakthrough of glyph-reading. *The Art of the Maya Scribe*, written with Justin Kerr, developer of "rollout" photography – a technique enabling the viewer to see the whole surface of a cylindrical vessel – is a wonderfully illustrated history of Maya writing which also takes the reader on a journey through the Maya universe and mythology via the astonishingly skilful calligraphy of the Maya artists themselves.

🏃 **David Drew** *The Lost Chronicles of the Maya Kings*. Superbly readable and engaging, Drew draws on a wealth of material to deliver an excellent account of ancient Maya political history. The alliances and

rivalries between the main cities are skilfully unravelled, and there's a particularly revealing analysis of Late Classic Maya power-politics. This is currently one of the most up-to-date references to consult.

William L. Fash *Scribes, Warriors and Kings*. The definitive study of the ruins of Copán, including the complete historical background, superb maps, and lavish drawings and photographs.

Peter D. Harrison *The Lords of Tikal*. Outstanding study of the Petén metropolis that includes recent hieroglyphic readings and a tremendous amount of detail about the city's monuments and artefacts and the rulers who commissioned them, Temple V excepted.

🏃 **Simon Martin and Nikolai Grube** *Chronicle of the Maya Kings and Queens*. Published to universal acclaim, this groundbreaking work (now in its second edition) is based on exhaustive new epigraphic studies, and the re-reading of previously translated glyphic texts. It also includes the historical records of several key Maya cities – including Tikal, Naranjo and Dos Pilas – complete with biographies of 152 kings and 4 queens, full dynastic sequences and all the key battles. As Michael D. Coe, author of *The Maya*, says: "There's nothing else like this book. It supersedes everything else ever written on Maya history".

Mary Miller and Simon Martin *Courtly Art of the Ancient Maya.* Sumptuously illustrated with images of jade, stucco, stonework and pottery artistry, this book also explains the rituals and customs that defined daily life in the royal courts.

John Montgomery *Tikal: An Illustrated History of the Ancient Maya Capital.* An instructive history of the site that's packed with information about the Maya, including a thorough chronology.

Linda Schele and David Freidel (et al). The authors, in the forefront of "new archeology", have been personally responsible for decoding many Maya glyphs. *A Forest of Kings: The Untold Story of the Ancient Maya*, in conjunction with *The Blood of Kings* by Linda Schele and Mary Miller, shows that, far from being governed by peaceful astronomer-priests, the ancient Maya were ruled by hereditary kings, lived in populous, aggressive city-states, and engaged in a continual entanglement of alliances and war. *The Maya*

Cosmos by Schele, Freidel and Joy Parker, is perhaps more difficult to read, but it also examines Maya ritual and religion in a unique and far-reaching way. *The Code of Kings*, written in collaboration with Peter Matthews and lavishly illustrated, examines the significance of the monuments at selected Maya sites and is a classic of epigraphic interpretation.

Peter Schmidt, Mercedes de la Garza and Enrique Nalda (eds) *Maya Civilization.* Monumental collaborative effort, with sections written by many prominent Mayanists, lusciously presented with more than six hundred colour images of some breathtaking Maya art. The scholarly text is also impressive, with contributions on the importance of Calakmul to the classic Maya history and detailed essays on the highlands of Guatemala, Maya cosmology and codices.

Robert Sharer *The Ancient Maya.* The classic, comprehensive account of Maya civilization, now in its sixth edition, yet as authoritative as ever. Required reading for archeology students, it provides a fascinating reference for the non-expert, as does his *Daily Life in Maya Civilization.*

J. Eric S. Thompson *The Rise and Fall of the Maya Civilization.* A major authority on the ancient Maya during his lifetime, Thompson produced many academic studies, of which this is one of the more accessible.

Wildlife and the environment

Les Betelsky *Belize and Northern Guatemala.* Other specialist wildlife guides may cover the subject in more detail, but this is a reasonably comprehensive and well-organized single-volume guide to the mammals, birds, reptiles, amphibians and marine life of the region.

Louise H. Emmons *Neotropical Rainforest Mammals.* Supported by François Feer's colour illustrations, this highly informative book is written by experts for non-scientists. Local and scientific names are given, along with plenty of interesting snippets.

Steve Howe and Sophie Webb *The Birds of Mexico and Northern Central America*. A tremendous work, this is the definitive book on the region's birds. Essential for all serious birders.

🏃 Thor Janson *In the Land of Green Lightning*. Exquisite photographic collection, concentrating on the diverse wildlife and environment of the Maya region. Includes some astounding images of an exploding Volcán Pacaya.

Frank B. Smythe *The Birds of Tikal*. This near-comprehensive book is fairly widely available in Guatemala, and can be bought in Tikal.

Guides

Elizabeth Bell *Antigua Guatemala: The City and Its Heritage*. The best guide to Antigua, written by a long-term resident and prominent historian. It's available from several shops in Antigua, as is the author's *Lent and Easter Week in Antigua*.

William Coe *Tikal: A Handbook to the Ancient Maya Ruins*. A detailed account of the site, usually available at the ruins, though it does not include the latest findings. The map of the main area is essential for in-depth exploration.

Sharon Collins *Diving and Snorkeling Roatán and Honduras' Bay Islands*. Covers many of the main dive sites in Utila and Roatán, though the Guanaja content is sketchy.

🏃 Joyce Kelly *Archaeological Guide to Northern Central America*.

Detailed and practical guide to dozens of sites with excellent photographs and accurate maps. This volume covers 38 Maya sites and 25 museums in Guatemala, Belize, Honduras and El Salvador, and though now a little outdated, it still makes an indispensable companion.

Barbara Balchin de Koose *Antigua for You*. A very comprehensive account of Antigua's colonial architectural wonders, but doesn't offer much else.

Lily de Jongh Osborne *Four Keys to Guatemala*. One of the best guides to Guatemala ever written, including a short piece on every aspect of the country's history and culture. Osborne also wrote a good book on indigenous arts and crafts in Guatemala. Both books are now out of print.

Cookbooks

Catalina B. Figueroa *Cocina Guatemalteca: Arte, Sabor y Colorido*. Features a comprehensive range of national dishes and regional specialities, and is available in many bookshops in Antigua.

Copeland Marks *False Tongues and Sunday Bread: A Guatemalan and Maya Cookbook*. If you've travelled widely in Guatemala and suffered an endless onslaught of beans and tortillas, it may be a surprise to find that the country has an established culinary tradition. Marks' book includes many fine Guatemalan recipes like chicken with *mole* sauce as well as the staples like black beans.

Language

Language

Spanish

Guatemala takes in a bewildering collection of languages, but fortunately for the traveller, Spanish will get you by in all but the most remote areas. Some middle-class Guatemalans speak English, but it's essential to learn at least a few Spanish phrases or you're in for a frustrating time.

The **Spanish** spoken in Guatemala has a strong Latin American flavour to it, and if you're used to the dainty intonation of Madrid then this may come as something of a surprise. If you're new to Spanish it's a lot easier to pick up than the Castilian version. Everywhere you'll find people willing to make an effort to understand you, eager to speak to passing gringos.

The rules of **pronunciation** are pretty straightforward and, once you get to know them, strictly observed. Unless there's an accent, words ending in d, l, r and z are **stressed** on the last syllable, all others on the second last. All **vowels** are pure and short.

A somewhere between the A sound of back and that of father.

E as in get.

I as in police.

O as in hot.

U as in rule.

C is soft before E and I, hard otherwise: *cerca* is pronounced serka.

G works the same way, a guttural H sound (like the ch in loch) before E or I, a hard G elsewhere – *gigante* becomes higante.

H is always silent.

J is the same sound as a guttural G: *jamón* is pronounced hamON.

LL sounds like an English Y: *tortilla* is pronounced torteeya.

N is as in English unless it has a tilde (accent) over it, when it becomes NY: *mañana* sounds like manyana.

QU is pronounced like an English K.

R is rolled, RR doubly so.

V sounds more like B, *vino* becoming beano.

X is slightly softer than in English – sometimes almost SH – *Xela* is pronounced shela.

Z is the same as a soft C, so *cerveza* becomes servesa.

Below is a list of a few essential words and phrases, though if you're travelling for any length of time a **dictionary** or **phrase book** is obviously a worthwhile investment. Any good Spanish phrase book or dictionary should see you through in Guatemala, but specific Latin American ones are the most useful. The *University of Chicago Dictionary of Latin-American Spanish* is a good all-rounder, while *Mexican Spanish: A Rough Guide Phrasebook* has a menu reader, rundown of colloquialisms and a number of cultural tips are relevant to many Latin American countries, including Guatemala. If you're using a dictionary, remember that in Spanish, CH, LL and Ñ count as separate letters and are listed after the Cs, Ls and Ns respectively. If you really want to get to grips with Guatemalan slang, swear words and expressions, look out for *¿Qué Onda Vos?* by Juan Carlos Martínez López and Mark Brazaitis, which includes a superb round-up of *guatemaltequismos*. It's available from several bookshops and the La Unión language school in Antigua (see p.50).

Maya languages

After years of state-backed *castellanización* programmes when Spanish was the only language of tuition and Maya schoolchildren were left virtual classroom spectators, a network of Maya schools has now been established, with hundreds alone in Q'eqchi' areas of Guatemala. A strong indigenous cultural movement has now developed in the country, intent on preserving the dozens of different Maya languages still spoken (for a comprehensive map, see p.430). Because the Maya birthrate is much higher than the ladino, there is now every chance that the main languages like K'iche', Kaqchikel and Mam will survive, though the fate of the more isolated tongues is far from secure.

If you're planning an extended stay in a remote indigenous region to do development work, it's extremely helpful to learn a little of the local language first. There are a number of language schools (see p.50) where you can **study a Maya language** and pick up the essentials. Cleveland State University's K'inal Winik Cultural Center (Ⓦwww.csuohio.edu/kinalwinik) is devoted to Maya linguistics and culture and publishers of Yax Te' Books, who have several titles on indigenous Guatemalan languages and literature. The Yax Te' Foundation (Ⓦwww.yaxte.org), devoted to promoting and supporting Maya culture and language, has some excellent study material and dictionaries.

Maya words do not easily translate into Spanish (or English) so you may see the same place spelt in different ways: *K'umarkaaj* can be spelt *K'umarcaah* or even *Gumarcaj*. Nearly all Maya words are pronounced stressing the final syllable, which is often accented: Atitlán is A-tit-LAN, Wakná is wak-NA.

C is always hard like a K, unlike Spanish.	a word – Uaxactún is pronounced wash-ak-TOON.
J is a guttural H, as in Spanish.	
U like a W at the beginning of a word and like an OO in the middle or at the end of	X sounds like SH – *Ixcún* is pronounced ish-KOON.

Spanish words and phrases

Basics

Yes, No	Sí, No	Open, Closed	Abierto/a, Cerrado/a
Please, Thank you	Por favor, Gracias	With, Without	Con, Sin
Where?, When?	¿Dónde?, ¿Cuándo?	Good, Bad	Buen(o)/a, Mal(o)/a
What?, How much?	¿Qué?, ¿Cuánto?	Big, Small	Gran(de), Pequeño/a
Here, There	Aquí, Allí	More, Less	Más, Menos
This, That	Este, Eso	Today, Tomorrow	Hoy, Mañana
Now, Later	Ahora, Más tarde	Yesterday	Ayer

Greetings and responses

Hello, Goodbye	Hola, Adiós	Sorry	Lo siento/discúlpeme
Good morning	Buenos días	Excuse me	Con permiso/perdón
Good afternoon/night	Buenas tardes/noches	How are you?	¿Cómo está (usted)?
See you later	Hasta luego	I (don't) understand	(No) Entiendo

Could you speak more slowly?	¿Podría hablar más lento?	American	americano (a)
Not at all/You're welcome	De nada	Australian	australiano(a)
		British	británico(a)
Do you speak English?	¿Habla (usted) inglés?	Canadian	canadiense
		Dutch	holandés(a)
I don't speak Spanish	No hablo español	Irish	irlandés(a)
What (did you say)?	¿Mande?	New Zealander	neocelandés(a)
My name is …	Me llamo …	Scottish	escosés(a)
What's your name?	¿Cómo se llama usted?	South African	sudafricano(a)
		Welsh	galés(a)
I am English	Soy inglés(a)		

Needs – hotels and transport

I want	Quiero	Is there a hotel nearby?	¿Hay un hotel aquí cerca?
I'd like	Quisiera		
Do you know …?	¿Sabe …?	How do I get to …?	¿Por dónde se va a …?
I don't know	No sé	Left, right, straight on	Izquierda, derecha, derecho
There is (is there)?	(¿)Hay(?)		
Give me … (one like that)	Deme … (uno así)	Where is …?	¿Dónde está …?
		… the bus station	… el terminal de camionetas
Do you have …?	¿Tiene …?	… the nearest bank	… el banco más cercano
… the time	… la hora		
… a room	… un cuarto	… the post office	… el correo/la oficina de correos
… with two beds/ double bed	… con dos camas/ cama matrimonial		
		… the toilet	… el baño/sanitario
It's for one person (two people)	Es para una persona (dos personas)	Where does the bus to … leave from?	¿De dónde sale la camioneta para …?
… for one night one week)	… para una noche (una semana)	I'd like a (return) ticket to …	Quisiera un boleto (de ida y vuelta) para …
It's fine, how much is it?	¿Está bien, cuánto es?		
It's too expensive	Es demasiado caro	What time does it leave (arrive in …)?	¿A qué hora sale (llega en …)?
Don't you have anything cheaper?	¿No tiene algo más barato?	What is there to eat?	¿Qué hay para comer?
Can one …?	¿Se puede …?	What's that?	¿Qué es eso?
… camp (near) here?	¿… acampar aquí (cerca)?	What's this called in Spanish?	¿Cómo se llama este en español?

Numbers and days

0	cero	7	siete
1	un/uno/una	8	ocho
2	dos	9	nueve
3	tres	10	diez
4	cuatro	11	once
5	cinco	12	doce
6	seis	13	trece

14	catorce	2000	dos mil
15	quince	1,000,000	un millión
16	dieciséis	first	primero/a
20	veinte	second	segundo/a
21	veintiuno	third	tercero/a
22	veintidós	fourth	cuarto/a
30	treinta	fifth	quinto/a
31	treinta y uno	sixth	sexto/a
40	cuarenta	seventh	séptimo/a
50	cincuenta	eighth	octavo/a
60	sesenta	ninth	noveno/a
70	setenta	tenth	décimo/a
80	ochenta		
90	noventa	Monday	lunes
100	cien	Tuesday	martes
101	ciento uno	Wednesday	miércoles
200	doscientos	Thursday	jueves
201	doscientos uno	Friday	viernes
500	quinientos	Saturday	sábado
1000	mil	Sunday	domingo

Menu reader

Basics

Azúcar	Sugar	Pescado	Fish
Carne	Meat	Pimienta	Pepper
Ensalada	Salad	Queso	Cheese
Huevos	Eggs	Sal	Salt
Mantequilla	Butter	Salsa	Sauce
Pan	Bread	Verduras/Legumbres	Vegetables

Soups (sopas) and starters

Sopa	Soup	Caldo	Broth (usually with meat)
de arroz	with rice		
de fideos	with noodles	Ceviche	Raw fish salad, marinated in lime juice
de lentejas	Lentil		
de verduras	Vegetable	Entremeses	Hors d'oeuvres
Consome	Consomme		

Meat (carne) and poultry (aves)

Alambre	Kebab	Carne (de res)	Beef
Bistec	Steak	Carnitas	Stewed chunks of meat
Cabrito	Kid goat	Cerdo	Pork

Chorizo	Sausage	Milanesa	Breaded escalope
Chuleta	Chop	Pato	Duck
Codorniz	Quail	Pavo/Guajalote	Turkey
Conejo	Rabbit	Pechuga	Breast
Cordero	Lamb	Pierna	Leg
Costilla	Rib	Pollo	Chicken
Guisado	Stew	Salchicha	Hot dog or salami
Higado	Liver	Ternera	Veal
Lengua	Tongue	Venado	Venison

Specialities

Chile relleno	Stuffed pepper	Taco	Rolled and stuffed tortilla
Chuchitos	Stuffed maize dumplings	Tamale	Boiled and stuffed maize pudding
Enchilada	Flat, crisp tortilla piled with salad or meat	Tapado	Fish stew with plantain and vegetables, served on Caribbean coast
Mosh	Porridge		
Pan de banana	Banana bread		
Pan de coco	Coconut bread		
Quesadilla	Toasted or fried tortillas with cheese		

L

LANGUAGE | Menu reader

Vegetables (legumbres, verduras)

Aguacate	Avocado	Lechuga	Lettuce
Ajo	Garlic	Pacaya	Bitter-tasting local vegetable
Casava/Yuca	Potato-like root vegetable	Papas	Potatoes
Cebolla	Onion	Pepino	Cucumber
Col	Cabbage	Plátanos	Plantain
Elote	Corn on the cob	Tomate	Tomato
Frijoles	Beans	Zanahoria	Carrot
Hongos	Mushrooms		

Fruit (frutas)

Banana	Banana	Melocotón	Peach
Ciruelas	Greengages	Melón	Melon
Coco	Coconut	Naranja	Orange
Frambuesas	Raspberries	Papaya	Papaya
Fresas	Strawberries	Piña	Pineapple
Guanabana	Pear-like cactus fruit	Pitahaya	Sweet, purple fruit
Guayaba	Guava	Sandía	Watermelon
Higos	Figs	Toronja	Grapefruit
Jocote	Small, plum-like fruit	Tuna	Cactus fruit
Limon	Lime	Uvas	Grapes
Mamey	Pink, sweet, full of pips	Zapote	Sweet, pink-fleshed fruit
Mango	Mango		

Eggs (huevos)

a la Mexicana	Scrambled with mild tomato, onion and chilli sauce	**Rancheros**	Cheese-fried and smothered in hot chilli sauce
con Jamón	with ham	**Revueltos**	Scrambled
con Tocino	with bacon	**Tibios**	Lightly boiled
Fritos	Fried		
Motuleños	Fried, served on a tortilla with ham, cheese and sauce		

Common terms

a la Parilla	Grilled	**Empanado/a**	Breaded
al Horno	Baked	**Picante**	Hot and spicy
al Mojo de ajo	Fried in garlic and butter	**Recado**	A sauce for meat made from garlic, tomato and spices
Asado/a	Roast		

Sweets (postres)

Crepas	Pancakes	**Pie de queso**	Cheesecake
Ensalada de Frutas	Fruit salad	**Plátanos al Horno**	Baked plantains
Flan	Crème caramel	**Plátanos en Mole**	Plantains in chocolate sauce
Helado	Ice cream		

Glossary of frequently used terms

Aguardiente Raw alcohol made from sugarcane.

Aguas Bottled fizzy drinks such as Coca-Cola or Pepsi.

Alcalde Mayor.

Aldea Small settlement.

Altiplano The highlands of western Guatemala.

Atol Drink usually made from maize dough, cooked with water, salt, sugar and milk. Can also be made from rice.

Ayuntamiento Town hall.

Baleada Stuffed tortilla street-snack (Honduras only).

Barranca Steep-sided ravine.

Barrio Residential district.

Biotopo Protected area of ecological interest, usually with limited tourist access.

Boca Costa Western volcanic slopes of the Guatemalan highlands, prime coffee-growing country.

Brujo Maya shaman.

CAFTA Central American Free Trade Agreement.

CALDH Centre for Legal Action on Human Rights. Pressure group campaigning for justice on behalf of the victims of the civil-war violence.

Calvario Church, often with pagan religious traditions, always located on the western outskirts of a town; also known as the house of the ancestors.

Camioneta Second-class, or "chicken", bus. In other parts of Latin America the same word means a small truck or van.

Campesino Peasant farmer.

Cantina Local hard-drinking bar.

Casita Hut, small house.

Cayuco Canoe.

Chapín Nickname for a citizen of Guatemala.

Chicle Sapodilla tree sap from which chewing gum is made.

Chuj Maya steam sauna.

Classic Period during which ancient Maya civilization was at its height, usually given as 250–909 AD.

Codex Maya manuscript made from the bark of the fig tree and written in hieroglyphs. Most were destroyed by the Spanish, but a copy of the Dresden Codex can be found in the Popol Vuh museum in Guatemala City (see p.79).

Cofradía Religious brotherhood dedicated to the protection of a particular saint. These groups form the basis of religious and civil hierarchy in traditional highland society and combine Catholic and pagan practices.

Comedor Basic Guatemalan restaurant, usually with just one or two things on the menu, and always the cheapest place to eat.

Comida típica Literally "typical food", this indicates a menu of regular Guatemalan-style dishes, nothing fancy but always filling and inexpensive.

Conavigua National Coordination of Guatemalan Widows. Influential, mainly indigenous, pressure group.

Copal Pine-resin incense burned at religious ceremonies.

Corriente Another name for a second-class bus.

Corte Traditional Guatemalan skirt.

Costumbres Guatemalan word for traditional customs of the highland Maya, usually of religious and cultural significance. The word often refers to traditions that owe more to paganism than to Catholicism; practitioners are called **costumbristas**.

Creole Guatemalan of mixed Afro-Caribbean descent.

Cuadra Street block.

CUC Committee of Peasant Unity.

Cusha Home-brewed liquor.

Don/Doña Sir/Madam. A term of respect mostly used to address a professional person or employer.

Efectivo Cash.

EGP (Ejército Guerrillero de los Pobres) (Guerrilla Army of the Poor). A Guatemalan guerrilla group that operated in the Ixil Triangle and Ixcán areas.

Evangélico Christian evangelist or fundamentalist, often missionaries. Name given to numerous Protestant sects seeking converts in Central America.

FAR (Fuerzas Armadas Rebeldes) (Rebel Armed Forces). Guatemalan guerrilla group that was mainly active in Petén.

Finca Plantation-style farm.

FRG (Frente Republicano Guatemalteco) (Guatemalan Republican Front). Right-wing political party of Ríos Montt and Alfonso Portillo.

GAM (Mutual Support Group). Pressure group campaigning for justice for the families of the "disappeared".

GANA Right-wing political coalition currently in power.

Garífuna Black Carib with a unique language and strong African heritage living in Livingston and villages along the Caribbean coast between Belize and Nicaragua. See p.258.

Gringo/gringa Any white-skinned foreigner, not necessarily a term of abuse.

Hospedaje Another name for a small, basic hotel.

Huipil Woman's traditional blouse, usually woven or embroidered.

Indígena Indigenous person of Maya descent.

Indio Racially abusive term to describe someone of Maya descent. The word **indito** is equally offensive.

Inguat Guatemalan tourist board.

I.V.A. Guatemalan sales tax of twelve percent.

Ixil Highland tribe grouped around the three towns of the Ixil Triangle – Nebaj, Chajul and San Juan Cotzal.

Kaqchikel (Also spelt "Cakchiquel"). Indigenous highland tribe occupying an area between Guatemala City and Lake Atitlán.

K'iche' (Also spelt "Quiché"). Largest of the highland Maya tribes, centred on the town of Santa Cruz del Quiché.

Ladino A vague term – at its most specific defining someone of mixed Spanish and Maya blood, but more commonly used to describe a person of "Western" culture, or one who dresses in "Western" style, be they pure Maya or of mixed blood.

Legua The distance walked in an hour, used extensively in the highlands.

Leng Slang for **centavo**.

Mam Maya tribe occupying the west of the western highlands, the area around Huehuetenango.

Mariachi Mexican musical style popular in Guatemala.

Marimba Xylophone-like instrument used in traditional Guatemalan music.

Maya General term for the large tribal group who inhabited Guatemala, southern Mexico, Belize, western Honduras and a slice of El Salvador since the earliest times, and still do.

Mestizo Person of mixed native and Spanish blood, more commonly used in Mexico.

Metate Flat stone for grinding maize into flour.

Milpa Maize field, usually cleared by slash and burn.

Minugua United Nations mission, in Guatemala to oversee the peace process.

MLN (Movimiento de Liberación Nacional) (National Liberation Movement). Right-wing political party in Guatemala.

Natural Another term for an indigenous person.

PAC Village civil-defence patrols, set up by Ríos Montt in the 1980s. They were responsible for many massacres, and still form a powerful pressure group today.

Palapa Thatched palm-leaf hut.

Parque Town's central plaza; or a park.

Pensión Simple hotel.

Pila Washhouse; sink for washing clothes.

Pipil Indigenous tribal group that occupied much of the Guatemalan Pacific coast at the time of the Conquest. Only their art survives, around the town of Santa Lucía Cotzumalguapa.

Pisto Slang for cash.

Pullman Fast and comfortable bus, usually an old Greyhound.

Punta rock The music of the Garífuna.

Q'eqchi' (Also spelt "Kekchi"). Maya tribal group based around Cobán, the Verapaz highlands, Lake Izabal and the Petén.

Remhi The Catholic Church's Truth Commission, set up to investigate the civil-war atrocities.

Repatriados Guatemalan refugees from the civil war, who have now returned to their country.

Sierra Mountain range.

Tecún Umán Last king of the K'iche' tribe, defeated in battle by Alvarado.

Telgua National telecom company.

Tienda Shop.

Típica Clothes woven from multicoloured textiles, usually geared towards the Western customer.

Traje Traditional Maya costume.

Tzute Headcloth or scarf worn as a part of traditional Maya costume.

Tz'utujil Indigenous tribal group occupying the land to the south of Lake Atitlán.

URNG (Unidad Revolucionaria Nacional Guatemalteca) (Guatemalan National Revolutionary Unity). Umbrella organization of the four former guerrilla groups, now disbanded.

USAC (Universidad de San Carlos) University of San Carlos. Guatemala's national university, formerly a hotbed of political activism.

La Violencia Term often used to describe the bloodiest civil-war years; literally "the violence".

Xate Decorative palm leaves harvested in Petén for export to the US, to be used in flower arrangements.

Xela Another name for the city of Quetzaltenango.

Maya architectural terms

Altar Elaborately carved altars, often of a cylindrical design, were grouped round the fringes of the main plaza. Used to record historical events, they could have also functioned as sacrificial stones. See also zoomorphs.

Ball court Narrow, stone-flagged rectangular court with banked sides where the Maya ball game was played. The courts symbolized a stage between the real and supernatural worlds and for the ball players it could be a game of life and death: losers were sometimes sacrificed.

Chultún Underground storage chamber.

Corbel arch "False arch" where each stone slightly overlaps the one below. A relatively primitive technique which severely limits the width of doorways and interiors.

Glyph Element in Maya writing, roughly the equivalent of a letter or phrase; used to record historical events. Some glyphs are phonetic, while others represent an entire description or concept as in Chinese characters. Dominant Classic and Postclassic sites had unique emblem glyphs; some like Copán and Tikal used several.

Lintel Top block of stone or wood above a doorway or window, often carved to record important events and dates. Those from Yaxchilán are especially well executed.

Palace Maya palaces occupied prominent locations near the ceremonial heart of the city, usually resting on low platforms, and almost certainly housed the royal elite. There are particularly striking palaces at Tikal and Cancuén.

Postclassic Period between the decline of Maya civilization and the arrival of the Spanish, 909–1530 AD.

Preclassic Archeological era preceding the blooming of Maya civilization, usually given as 2000 BC–250 AD.

Putún Style dominant at Ceibal in central Petén, exhibiting strong Mexican characteristics.

Roof comb Decorative top crest on stone temples, possibly intended to enhance verticality. Originally painted in arresting colours and often framed by giant stucco figures.

Sacbé Paved Maya road or raised causeway near the centre of Maya cities. Probably designed for ceremonial processions and to save rulers from sloshing through the lowland marshes. Sacbés were also trade routes and there are hundreds of kilometres still evident in northern Petén today.

Stela Freestanding, often exquisitely carved, stone monument. Decorating major Maya sites, stelae fulfilled a sacred and political role commemorating historical events.

467

Among the largest and most impressive are the ones at Quiriguá and Copán.

Temple Monumental stone structure of pivotal religious significance built in the ceremonial heart of a city, usually with a pyramid-shaped base and topped with a narrow room or two used for secretive ceremonies and bloody sacrifices. Those at Tikal and El Mirador reach more than 60m.

Toltec Style of the central Mexican tribal group who invaded parts of the Maya region.

Zoomorph Spectacular stone altar intricately carved with animal images and glyphs; there are wonderful examples at Quiriguá.

Small print and
Index

A Rough Guide to Rough Guides

Published in 1982, the first Rough Guide – to Greece – was a student scheme that became a publishing phenomenon. Mark Ellingham, a recent graduate in English from Bristol University, had been travelling in Greece the previous summer and couldn't find the right guidebook. With a small group of friends he wrote his own guide, combining a highly contemporary, journalistic style with a thoroughly practical approach to travellers' needs.

The immediate success of the book spawned a series that rapidly covered dozens of destinations. And, in addition to impecunious backpackers, Rough Guides soon acquired a much broader and older readership that relished the guides' wit and inquisitiveness as much as their enthusiastic, critical approach and value-for-money ethos.

These days, Rough Guides include recommendations from shoestring to luxury and cover more than 200 destinations around the globe, including almost every country in the Americas and Europe, more than half of Africa and most of Asia and Australasia. Our ever-growing team of authors and photographers is spread all over the world, particularly in Europe, the USA and Australia.

In the early 1990s, Rough Guides branched out of travel, with the publication of Rough Guides to World Music, Classical Music and the Internet. All three have become benchmark titles in their fields, spearheading the publication of a wide range of books under the Rough Guide name.

Including the travel series, Rough Guides now number more than 350 titles, covering: phrasebooks, waterproof maps, music guides from Opera to Heavy Metal, reference works as diverse as Conspiracy Theories and Shakespeare, and popular culture books from iPods to Poker. Rough Guides also produce a series of more than 120 World Music CDs in partnership with World Music Network.

Visit www.roughguides.com to see our latest publications.

Rough Guide travel images are available for commercial licensing at www.roughguidespictures.com

Rough Guide credits

Text editor: Melissa Graham, Mani Ramaswamy
Layout: Sachin Tanwar
Cartography: Rajesh Chhibber
Picture editor: Nicole Newman
Production: Rebecca Short
Proofreader: Diane Margolis
Cover design: Chloë Roberts,
Photographer: Tim Draper
Editorial: **London** Ruth Blackmore, Andy Turner, Keith Drew, Edward Aves, Alice Park, Lucy White, Jo Kirby, James Smart, Natasha Foges, Róisín Cameron, Emma Traynor, James Rice, Emma Gibbs, Kathryn Lane, Christina Valhouli, Monica Woods, Mani Ramaswamy, Alison Roberts, Harry Wilson, Joe Staines, Peter Buckley, Matthew Milton, Tracy Hopkins, Ruth Tidball; **New York** Andrew Rosenberg, Steven Horak, AnneLise Sorensen, Ella Steim, Anna Owens, Sean Mahoney, Paula Neudorf; **Delhi** Madhavi Singh, Karen D'Souza, Lubna Shaheen
Design & Pictures: **London** Scott Stickland, Dan May, Diana Jarvis, Mark Thomas, Sarah Cummins, Emily Taylor; **Delhi** Umesh Aggarwal, Ajay Verma, Jessica Subramanian, Ankur Guha, Pradeep Thapliyal, Anita Singh, Nikhil Agarwal
Production: Vicky Baldwin

Cartography: **London** Maxine Repath, Ed Wright, Katie Lloyd-Jones; **Delhi** Ashutosh Bharti, Rajesh Mishra, Animesh Pathak, Jasbir Sandhu, Karobi Gogoi, Alakananda Roy, Swati Handoo, Deshpal Dabas
Online: **London** George Atwell, Faye Hellon, Jeanette Angell, Fergus Day, Justine Bright, Clare Bryson, Áine Fearon, Adrian Low, Ezgi Celebi, Amber Bloomfield; **Delhi** Amit Verma, Rahul Kumar, Narender Kumar, Ravi Yadav, Debojit Borah, Rakesh Kumar, Ganesh Sharma, Shisir Basumatari
Marketing & Publicity: **London** Liz Statham, Niki Hanmer, Louise Maher, Jess Carter, Vanessa Godden, Vivienne Watton, Anna Paynton, Rachel Sprackett, Libby Jellie, Laura Vipond; **New York** Geoff Colquitt, Nancy Lambert, Katy Ball; **Delhi** Ragini Govind
Manager India: Punita Singh
Reference Director: Andrew Lockett
Operations Manager: Helen Phillips
PA to Publishing Director: Nicola Henderson
Publishing Director: Martin Dunford
Commercial Manager: Gino Magnotta
Managing Director: John Duhigg

Publishing information

This fourth edition published March 2009 by
Rough Guides Ltd,
80 Strand, London WC2R 0RL
345 Hudson St, 4th Floor,
New York, NY 10014, USA
14 Local Shopping Centre, Panchsheel Park,
New Delhi 110017, India
Distributed by the Penguin Group
Penguin Books Ltd,
80 Strand, London WC2R 0RL
Penguin Group (USA)
375 Hudson Street, NY 10014, USA
Penguin Group (Australia)
250 Camberwell Road, Camberwell,
Victoria 3124, Australia
Penguin Group (Canada)
195 Harry Walker Parkway N, Newmarket, ON,
L3Y 7B3 Canada
Penguin Group (NZ)
67 Apollo Drive, Mairangi Bay, Auckland 1310,
New Zealand

Cover concept by Peter Dyer.
Typeset in Bembo and Helvetica to an original design by Henry Iles.
Printed in China
© Iain Stewart 2009

480pp includes index
A catalogue record for this book is available from the British Library.
ISBN: 978-1-84836-017-4

Help us update

We've gone to a lot of effort to ensure that the fourth edition of **The Rough Guide to Guatemala** is accurate and up to date. However, things change – places get "discovered", opening hours are notoriously fickle, restaurants and rooms raise prices or lower standards. If you feel we've got it wrong or left something out, we'd like to know, and if you can remember the address, the price, the hours, the phone number, so much the better.

Please send your comments with the subject line **"Rough Guide to Guatemala Update"** to ®mail@roughguides.com. We'll credit all contributions and send a copy of the next edition (or any other Rough Guide if you prefer) for the very best emails.

Have your questions answered and tell others about your trip at
®community.roughguides.com

Acknowledgements

Thanks above all to my family in Brighton – Fiona, Louis and Monty – and also Betty, Aubs, Susan, Jan, Simone and David for helping out. I couldn't manage without you and all your support. In Guatemala a special mention to Migdalia de Barrillas and my mate Marlon Luz of *Inguat* and my very close friends Lorena and Jose in Guatemala City. At my second home on the lake a big *hola* to all the *Iguana* team, Philippa Myers, Ana, Wendy, Roberta, Mark and Stephanie. Also thanks to John of *Café No Sé* fame, Don David and Tom in Xela. And my gratitude to all the Rough Guides team, particularly my editors. Finally I'd like to dedicate this book to the late Peter Eltringham – one hell of an author and a mate – we'll never see your like again Pete.

Readers' letters

Thanks to all the readers who have taken the time to write in with comments and suggestions (and apologies if we've inadvertently omitted or misspelt anyone's name):

Thanks to everyone who's got in touch, including Philippe Samama for the detailed letter, Nancy Frane & Rebeca Nye, Chris Sowerbutts, Doris Guzman, David Bryden, Reuxtreme, Nirma Macz, Guen Gifford, Stig Björkas, Myrna Oudega, Orla Keating, Guillaume Furminger, Pats Clark, Stacey Holeman, Sonia Zamborsky, Kaff Christinna Merrild, Sandy J Jensen, Fred Lubin, J J Fleury, Francine Haenni, Sijmen, C Goran, Pam Harris, Usherle, serious Steve, J Wortis, Liliana Queme, Lyman and Rony Spa.

Photo credits

All photos © Rough Guides except the following:

Things not to miss
04 Villagers racing on horseback, Todos Santos Cuchumatán © Daniel LeClair/Corbis
05 Believers honouring a statue of Maximón © Tom Campbell/Jupiter
07 Whale shark and snorkeller © Tom Salyer/ Jupiter
13 Pacaya volcano © Ron Levy/DRR.net
16 Quetzal © Todd Gustafson/DRR.net
17 Yaxhá © Danita Delimont/Alamy

21 Leatherback turtle © Ellen McKnight/fotoLibra
23 Semana Santa, Antigua © Tom Campbell/ Jupiter
25 Scuba diving © Dennis Sabo/iStock
30 Tobacco fields in the eastern highlands © Ken Welsh/photolibrary

Black and whites
p.383 Sandy Beach, Roatan © Devon Stephens/ iStock

Selected images from our guidebooks are available for licensing from:
ROUGHGUIDESPICTURES.COM

Index

Map entries are in colour

R

S

T